DESIGNING A QUALITY LIGHTING ENVIRONMENT

DESIGNING A QUALITY

LIGHTING ENVIRONMENT

SUSAN M. WINCHIP

Illinois State University

FAIRCHILD PUBLICATIONS, INC. ▪ NEW YORK

Executive Editor:	Olga T. Kontzias
Development Editor:	Sylvia Weber/Joseph Miranda
Production Editor:	Elizabeth Marotta
Art Director:	Adam B. Bohannon
Production Manager:	Ginger Hillman
Associate Development Editor:	Suzette Lam
Copy Editor:	Roberta Mantus
Illustrations by:	Timothy Bayley
Photo researcher:	Susan Day
Cover Design:	Adam B. Bohannon
Cover Art:	© Corbis
Text Design:	Carla Bolte

Library of Congress Catalog Card Number: 2005930305

ISBN: 1-56367-317-7

GST R 133004424

Printed in China

CH04, TP04

BRIEF CONTENTS

EXTENDED CONTENTS

PREFACE

Designing a Quality Lighting Environment evolved from a response to searching for a comprehensive textbook on quality lighting from a design perspective. Many books written from an engineering perspective contain a great deal of technical and quantitative detail, but without enough content about the understanding and application of quality lighting to an environment. There are numerous examples of "coffee-table" books filled with beautiful photographs, but these books lack the technical details that a designer or architect needs to create a functional and aesthetically pleasing environment. These books also lack the comprehensive, integrative approach that helps students to understand lighting within the context of the design process.

In teaching a lighting course at the university level, I have used several books, references, and articles to cover the essential content adequately. Not only is this approach expensive for the students, but extrapolating information from a variety of sources also inhibits the continuity of concepts and integration of subject matter that can be accomplished from one textbook.

Designing a Quality Lighting Environment is written for college students who are studying lighting in their quest to be interior designers, architects, or lighting designers. In addition, practicing professionals, including interior designers, architects, builders, contractors, and lighting industry specialists, can use this text as a reference. The textbook is a comprehensive approach to quality lighting with a primary focus on the design process. Specifically, the textbook has an integrative approach to lighting that not only includes the basics of lighting systems, but also demonstrates how lighting is interrelated with the design process, human factors, sustainability, global issues, design fundamentals, regulations, business practices, and professional values.

Many of the topics and suggestions provided in the text reflect the results of research studies. The exercises and pedagogical suggestions in the accompanying Instructor's Guide are written to reinforce the

content of the textbook and help to develop critical skills for a practicing professional, such as programming, schematic design, concept development, design development, preparation of contract documents, drafting, writing, listening, critiquing, sketching, teamwork, presenting, rendering, model building, and learning how to think visually and volumetrically.

The text can be used in a variety of courses and formats. The amount of content usually cannot be covered in one course. Thus, the book can serve as the primary textbook in introductory and advanced lighting courses, and it can be used as a supplement for other courses, such as commercial and residential studio courses. Students should be encouraged to keep their books after an initial lighting course, and then use the text as a reference when they are required to develop lighting plans in other courses and in their future professional practices. The interdisciplinary nature of the content makes the book an excellent choice for reinforcing content throughout the curriculum. For example, in non-lighting courses, this textbook could be used as a reference when discussing topics such as sustainable design, energy standards, codes, wayfinding systems, or the phases of the design process.

Organization of the Textbook

This comprehensive textbook is organized sequentially to develop the expertise and skills required to design quality lighting environments. It is divided into three units. Unit I explores basic concepts and elements of a quality lighting environment, including components of lighting systems, daylight integration, directional effects of illumination, energy considerations, environmental factors related to lighting, and human factors. This content serves as the foundation for exploring specific applications in Unit II. The purpose of Unit II is to learn how the principles of quality lighting covered in Unit I are manifest in specific applications. These applications include safety, security, illumination of visual art, light art, interior architecture, inspirational mediums, residential interiors, and commercial interiors. Unit III serves as the culminating experience of the textbook, explaining the lighting design process

within the context of the content of Units I and II. Unit III covers project management, comprehensive programming, schematic design, design development, contract documents, and contract administration.

About the Title

The words selected for the title of this book address the aforementioned needs and represent the essence of the content.

Designing

The first word in the title, *Designing,* reflects the book's emphasis on the conviction that lighting should be designed. Many buildings have lighting plans that were developed according to traditional solutions for a specific space or activity. For example, offices and classrooms generally have rows of fluorescent fixtures, regardless of how the space is utilized or the amount of daylight it receives. This "one solution fits all" approach does not reflect an outcome from the design process. It fails to create an environment that is designed for the needs of the users of the space and the specific characteristics of the interior.

Focusing on design and the design process, this book provides the content an interior designer needs to design lighting within the context of other important elements of an interior, including addressing the needs of the users of the space and the built environment. To facilitate the gathering of data regarding the users of the space and attributes of existing interiors, several guides are provided in Unit III that can be customized for each client. Guides in Chapter 21 can be used for conducting field observations and for interviewing or surveying people. In Chapter 22 there is a form that can be used to evaluate lighting options by cross-referencing lighting criteria. Forms are also provided to assist in planning projects and writing lighting system schedules. Chapter 23 has a detailed chart that can be useful in writing lighting specifications.

Because lighting should be viewed as an interdependent component of an environment, the book integrates lighting with other constructs that affect the design, such as human factors; design elements; codes;

energy policies; business practices; and the health, safety, and welfare of people. Many of the illustrations in the book use architecture and the visual arts to explain a concept or lighting effect. This integrative approach helps students understand lighting and reinforces material that is studied in other courses. Explaining lighting within a variety of contexts can also enable diverse learners to better understand the material.

Rather than dictating lighting solutions for spaces or activities, the book provides the information, considerations, and applications that should be analyzed when designing a quality lighting environment. For example, in Chapters 20 and 21, the focus is not on prescribed lighting solutions for a bathroom or an office, but instead is on a variety of design factors that have had an impact on the quality of lighting in these spaces, such as the ages of the users, activities, design elements, anthropometric data, dimensions of furniture, and human behavior. The intent of the book is to teach students how to think critically and creatively as interior designers. Students must learn how to gather the information and resources needed to design a lighting environment. This requires knowledge of lighting systems, interrelated concepts, means to acquire resources and facts, and ways to engage successfully in the design process for the satisfaction of the client and/or users of the space.

The numerous hand-drawn line illustrations beautifully present lighting concepts and techniques and provide instructional value and an appreciation of creativity associated with sketching techniques. The inclusion of nontraditional topics and novel approaches to conventional material also emphasizes creativity. Standardized lighting plans have tended to stifle creative lighting solutions. Improvements in the technologies of lamps, luminaires, and controls provide the impetus to designing new and creative lighting environments that are site-specific. This transformative process requires a fresh examination of lighting systems and environmental conditions and inspiration from a variety of sources.

Creativity should be inspired for not only aesthetic purposes, but also for solutions that affect the life, safety, and welfare of people. Interior designers must use their creativity to design site-specific lighting

plans that can help make buildings safe and secure while conserving energy and natural resources. Therefore, in an attempt to provide the spark for creative thinking, this textbook progresses beyond the traditional content of lighting books by including material that aims to reframe perspectives regarding illumination.

Quality Lighting

The words *Quality Lighting* in the title were specifically selected to shift the attention away from an exclusive focus on the quantity of light in a space. Throughout the text, the principles of quality lighting are applied to the fundamentals of lighting, elements of lighting systems, case studies, and presentations of lighting solutions.

What is quality lighting? Quality lighting environments allow users to function in a space, feel safe, and appreciate the aesthetic components of the interior simultaneously. Environments with quality lighting are specifically designed for the client, users, architectural features, site, and location. These environments reflect a skillful application of the principles of design by integrating lighting into the entire composition. Lighting is no longer an afterthought. Quality lighting includes the art of balancing and integrating general, task, accent, and decorative lighting in every space. Designing quality lighting environments results in reduced energy costs and a conservation of natural resources.

Environment

The last word in the title, *Environment,* represents the book's focus on the importance of designing lighting within the context of the surroundings, conditions, and influences. The emphasis is on the environment rather than solely on the examination of a space, room, or interior. Studying the lighting environment prompts a holistic examination of the factors that can influence lighting and the effects of illumination on people, spaces, interior architecture, and materials. This systemic approach is especially important when studying lighting from a global perspective. A focus on the environment addresses global energy consumption patterns, energy management, and sustainable practice.

Pedagogical Features

Every chapter in the textbook has pedagogical features that are designed to assist teaching and enhance learning. To help explain concepts and techniques, every chapter has hand-drawn line illustrations and numerous full-color illustrations. Each chapter begins with a list of objectives, which can be used as an assessment tool at the beginning and end of a lesson. The list of the key terms, summary, references, and exercises in every chapter are designed to reinforce the content and develop important professional skills.

The appendices are very important to learning the content of the book and can be an excellent reference for practicing professionals. The charts in the appendices include anthropometric data, shapes of lamps, spectral power distribution curves, candlepower distribution graphs, beam spread tables, and lighting/drafting abbreviations. The appendices also include a substantial list of contact information for lighting manufacturers, distributors, suppliers, professional organizations, government agencies, and trade associations; an extensive bibliography; and a glossary related to the key terms listed in each chapter.

The Instructor's Guide that accompanies this text offers additional activities and assignments designed to enhance teaching and learning. It explains in full detail the pedagogical approach of the text and elaborates on the comprehensive nature of the content embodied in the title *Designing a Quality Lighting Environment*.

ACKNOWLEDGMENTS

An author is only one individual in the process of publishing a textbook. I am very grateful to all the other individuals who dedicated their best work and time to this endeavor. My first note of appreciation is extended to Olga Kontzias, executive editor, Fairchild Books. This book would not exist if it weren't for Olga's enthusiasm for publishing a lighting textbook and her willingness to sign me as the author. I constantly marveled at her level of professionalism and her unparalleled sense of design. I am also extremely grateful to Olga for assigning a fantastic staff to work with me throughout the publishing process. Joseph Miranda, acquisition editor, expressed great support by discussing with me topics and conceptual ideas.

I would also like to thank the peer-reviewers selected by Fairchild Books, whose thoughtfully provided suggestions helped to improve the original proposal and manuscript: Dee Ginthner, University of Minnesota; Cheryl Gulley, Watkins College of Art and Design; Paulette Hebert, University of Louisiana at Lafayette; Robert Meden, Marymount University; Susan Ray-Degges, North Dakota State University; and Suzanne Scott, University of Wisconsin. Sincere appreciation is offered to Roberta Mantus, copyeditor, who fastidiously prepared the manuscript for publication.

A deep appreciation is extended to Sylvia Weber, development editor, and Elizabeth Marotta, production editor. Sylvia's impeccable editorial skills and considerable knowledge of conceptualization helped tremendously in improving the quality of the book. Liz's optimism, organizational skills, and meticulous attention to detail contributed to a smooth and enjoyable production process. Liz was extraordinarily proficient at organizing the illustration program by coordinating the manuscript with the photos, which were researched by Susan Day, and Timothy Bayley's line illustrations. I am very grateful for the expertise and time Susan dedicated to the project. The extensive time she spent researching the ideal photograph contributes a great deal to the quality of the textbook.

Timothy Bayley's extraordinary hand-drawn line illustrations are not only important for a quality presentation, but their creativity, details, and eloquent style help to communicate the essence of the book. I am enormously grateful to my dear friend, Tim, for our years of friendship and the beautiful drawings he painstakingly drew with exceptional skill.

Writing a textbook within a prescribed timeline requires a great amount of discipline and an unwavering commitment to time and work. As a result, family and friends are impacted by the experience. I am incredibly appreciative to my family and friends for their patience, understanding, and support. I love them all dearly. Our wonderful friends, Dave and Joan Falcone, and Alan and Barbara Nourie, shared our vacation in South Carolina with my book writing. Our dearest friend, Roger Laramee, conceded many evening hours and weekends to time spent on illustrations. My daughter Amy and her friend also shared our Florida vacation with my writing. My three children, Kristi, Kyle, and Amy, have always been loving, patient, and understanding when they had to share our time together with my work. Most of all I want to express my sincerest gratitude to my incredible husband, Galen, whom I love very much. He unselfishly supported my work and provided endless encouragement. Without his love and devotion this book could not have been written.

DESIGNING A QUALITY LIGHTING ENVIRONMENT

PRINCIPLES OF LIGHTING

Introduction to Lighting

OBJECTIVES

- Describe the development of lighting from prehistoric times until the 1930s.
- Identify the key characteristics of light and some of the effects light has on the human response.
- Analyze the basic parts of the eye and the vision process.
- Comprehend and assess the importance of quality lighting.
- Describe the roles and responsibilities of a lighting designer.

LIGHT, one of the essential elements of life, exists in natural and electrical forms. Designers must consider both these sources when they plan a quality lighting environment. To understand natural and electrical light, it is important to review historical developments of light sources and how civilizations invented technologies to produce light. Electric light, the form to which we are accustomed, has been in existence for approximately 100 years. This is an extremely short period of time compared to the thousands of years of civilization. Advancements in lighting will continue to transform our lives and society.

As a form of energy, light travels through space and affects every living organism. Light sources and the physiological process of vision affect what we see. Inadequate and poor lighting environments negatively affect vision, the ability to perform tasks, and psychological responses. To design functional and aesthetic interiors requires a focus on quality lighting. The principles of quality lighting should be applied to the fundamentals of illumination, elements of lighting systems, and specific interior applications.

History of Lighting

The history of lighting begins with an examination of the earliest civilizations and how they planned their activities around the availability of a natural source. **Natural light** includes direct light from sunlight, the moon, and stars. **Indirect natural light** results from reflections from clouds, structures, and the landscape. When people relied primarily on natural light, most activities occurred during the daylight hours. The Greeks were very sophisticated in understanding how to plan outdoor theatrical dramas and amphitheatres during the daylight hours (see Figure 1.1). A Greek drama was written and staged to coincide with the angle and quantity of sunlight available for the stage at different times of the day (Rosenthal and Wertenbaker, 1972). The

Natural light
Illumination from sunlight, the moon, and stars.

Indirect natural light
Illumination derived from reflections from clouds, the moon, and stars.

FIGURE 1.1 An outdoor Greek amphitheatre was oriented and designed to take advantage of the available daylight.

FIGURE 1.2 The design of this Roman interior courtyard maximizes the amount of daylight that enters the interior and provides shelter from the hot sun.

Romans designed their residential dwellings with interior courtyards to maximize the amount of daylight that would enter the interiors (see Figure 1.2). An **oculus**, a round opening in the ceiling, was designed at the top of domes to maximize direct and indirect sunlight entering the interior (see Figure 1.3).

Oculus
An opening in a dome of an architectural structure.

FIGURE 1.3 The oculus in the dome of the Pantheon, in Rome, Italy, maximizes direct and indirect sunlight entering the interior.

When civilizations had depended upon natural light only, activities essentially ended at sunset except during a full moon. People frequently would wait for a full moon to conduct an activity that required light during the evening hours; for example, long trips or visits to neighbors.

Early Developments of Light Sources

Fire is the most primitive source of artificial light. The ability to create and control fire allowed civilizations to have interior lighting. Some people today still have only fire for lighting. The use of fire to illuminate an interior began at least during the time when paintings were drawn on the caves in the grotto of Lascaux in France dated to the Perigordian period 15,000–13,000 B.C. To illuminate interiors, primitive civilizations used fire burning on the ground or in handheld torches. It is assumed that when people prepared food, they discovered that the fat of animals burned intensely. These observations appear to have led to the development of the **oil lamp**. Thus, the original fuel for oil lamps was derived from the fat and oils of fish, whales, and land animals. The oils from olives and nuts were also used to fuel oil lamps. Wicks were generally made from fibrous plants. Original oil lamps were made from shells, shaped stones, and glazed and unglazed clay (see Figure 1.4). In 2700 B.C. Egyptians and Persians made oil

Oil lamp
Luminaires that use an oil substance and a wick to produce light.

FIGURE 1.4 Original oil lamps were made from various materials and an assortment of shapes.

lamps from copper and bronze. A bronze oil lamp was discovered in the excavations of Pompeii, Italy, and various clay oil lamps were also found in the excavations. The design of oil lamps was not improved until the end of the eighteenth century. The efficiency and light output of oil lamps was greatly improved when the wick was widened and when a mechanism that adjusted the height of the wick was added. Today oil lamps burn paraffin or kerosene.

Rushlights were used to illuminate interiors of the residences of common people. Dipping the ends of a rush, a tall grasslike plant, into melted fat created these light sources. Rushlights did not produce very much light and eventually were replaced when the candle was introduced.

Rushlight
Luminaires made from a tall grasslike plant that utilizes melted fat to create illumination.

Candles

Candles are another example of a primitive light source. Candles were extensively developed at the beginning of the Christian era. The most expensive candles were made from beeswax and were often found in churches and in the homes of the nobility. King Louis XIV of France (1774–1792) used 25,000 candles for one evening at Versailles. This occurred at a time when the common people would only have 5 to 10 candles per year. The most common and least expensive candles were made of tarrow, a dense animal fat. These candles burned quickly, produced a great deal of smoke, and were very smelly. To maximize the light output from a candle, a shiny material that reflected the light was often positioned next to the flame. **Snuffers** were hired by the wealthy to maintain candles. An efficient snuffer was able to cut off the burnt piece of the wick while maintaining the flame. This was especially critical in interiors that required constant illumination. For example, quality snuffers were needed to sustain lighting during an indoor theater performance.

Snuffer
Originally an individual who maintained burning candles by cutting off the burnt piece of the wick. Subsequently, the term has come to be used for the tool that is used to extinguish candle flames.

Gas Lamps

Burning gas for illumination purposes greatly advanced the development of light sources. Developed during the Industrial Revolution (late nineteenth and early twentieth centuries), fixtures for interiors generally consisted of a metal pipe and an open flame. One **gas lamp** produced the same amount of light emitted from several candles. Thus, gas lamps greatly improved people's ability to perform tasks indoors at night. Because they provided continuous and intense illumination, gas lamps were used extensively as street lamps. In the early 1800s, London was well known for having gas lamps throughout the city. The Eiffel Tower was originally illuminated with gas lamps. Gas lamps finally enabled people to engage in activities after sunset on a regular basis. All these original light sources were hazardous, smelly, and difficult to maintain; burned considerable black smoke; and deposited soot on surfaces. It became easier to use these light sources with the invention of the match in 1827 and paraffin in 1860. None of these earlier forms of lighting have been eliminated from use in today's interiors; but they are no longer the main sources of illumination.

Electrical Lighting

To provide a historical perspective of electrical lighting, this section focuses on initial developments of the primary sources including incandescent, halogen, fluorescent, and high-intensity discharge lamps. Commonly referred to as a light bulb, a **lamp** is the term for a source that produces optical radiation. Advanced and current technologies are covered in Chapters 3 and 4. Electricity is the most important invention for developing an efficient and effective artificial light source. Thousands of years ago the Greeks studied static electricity, but serious technological developments did not occur until the work of Dufay in the 1700s and Benjamin Franklin in 1746. In the earliest years of development, the primary use for electricity was lighting. The ability to use electrical energy to produce visible light was successful in the early 1800s. Sir Humphrey Davy, an English chemist, experimented with **arc lamps**. Using a battery of 2000 cells to heat sticks of charcoal created this light source. The flame was in the shape of an arc, thus the reason for the name "arc lamp." Arc lamps were not satisfactory because they were hard to install and were a fire hazard. In addition they emitted an extremely bright light. Therefore, arc lamps were not used in interiors, and were primarily used in street lamps and lighthouses.

Mass produced electrical light was not available until the invention of the **incandescent carbon-filament lamp** in the late 1870s. Many scientists worked on the filament lamp, but the best-known inventors were Thomas Edison from the United States and Joseph Swan from Great Britain. A major hurdle in the development of electrical light sources was identifying the ideal material for the lamp's filament. Edison experimented with various materials, including platinum, human hair, and bamboo. Threads hanging from a button on Edison's jacket inspired the successful carbonized solution. To produce light in an incandescent lamp, an electrical current heats a carbonized filament. In 1880 Edison installed about 100 incandescent lamps in his laboratory in Menlo Park, New Jersey. People from around the world traveled to Menlo Park to see one of the world's greatest achievements. Edison's exhibits were featured in Paris and London in 1881, followed by an extensive display at the 1893 World's Columbian Exposition in Chicago. Originally people feared electricity and thought the incandescent lamp would cause eye injury. As a consequence shades and reflectors were designed to accommodate the new lamp, even though initial lamps emitted a very low level of illumination.

Early electric lights competed with the prolific use of gas illumination. Homes, businesses, and communities had invested in the costs associated with gas illumination, including distribution systems, installations, and fixtures. People were accustomed to the operation and maintenance of gas lamps. However, gas lamps did not emit high levels of illumination. Attitudes toward electrical sources changed with the development of the tungsten-filament lamp in 1910 by William Coolidge. This new technology produced a high illumination level that far exceeded the light emitted from gas lamps. Eventually, people became interested in eliminating dirty gas lamps and replacing the light source with the bright and clean incandescent lamp.

To ensure success of electrical lights, Edison designed a complete electrical system, and he developed a lamp design that could be mass produced easily. The electrical system had to produce electricity and distribute the energy to communities, businesses, and homes. Edison's

Incandescent carbon-filament lamp
A light source that uses an electrical current to heat the conductive material until incandescence is produced.

Electric-discharge lamp
An electrical light source that produces illumination without filaments and operates on low or high pressure. An electric current passes through a vapor or gas.

Neon lamp
A special application of cold-cathode lamps produced by a craftsperson who bends the heated glass into the various shapes of the design. A transformer with a high-voltage source is directed to the electrodes.

Fluorescent lamp
An electric-discharge light source that generally uses electrodes, phosphors, low-pressure mercury, and other gases for illumination.

High-intensity discharge (HID) lamp
Electric-discharge lamp that includes mercury vapor, metal halide, and high-pressure sodium.

Mercury lamp
A high-intensity discharge electrical light source that uses radiation from mercury vapor for illumination.

Metal halide (MH) lamp
A high-intensity discharge lamp that utilizes chemical compounds of metal halides and possibly metallic vapors such as mercury.

electrical lighting system resembled the technology that was used to distribute gaslight. Eventually, electrical lines determined the layout of cities. Edison's focus on the mass production of lamps enabled people to purchase the light source. Initially, only wealthy people could install electricity in their homes. As electrical production increased and improved, the technology became available for the masses. As a supplement to daylight, electrical lights eventually transformed the design of buildings and the lives of people forever.

The incandescent lamp was an incredible technological invention. However, the lamp did not have a long life and consumed high levels of electricity. In the early twentieth century scientists and engineers focused on developing lamps that would be more efficient than the incandescent lamp. As a result of these research efforts, **electric-discharge lamps** were developed. Electric-discharge lamps produce light by running an electrical current through a gas, or vapor, under pressure. Electrical-discharge lamps include neon, fluorescent, mercury, metal halide, and sodium. A **neon lamp** is produced by a craftsperson who bends the heated glass into the various shapes of the design. A **fluorescent lamp** generally uses electrodes, phosphors, low-pressure mercury, and other gases for illumination.

Mercury, metal halide, and high-pressure sodium are high-intensity discharge (HID) lamps. **High-intensity discharge** (HID) **lamps** are electric-discharge lamps, which have a light-producing arc that is stabilized by the temperature of the bulb (IESNA, 2000). A **mercury lamp** uses radiation from mercury vapor for illumination. **A metal halide (MH) lamp** utilizes chemical compounds of metal halides and possibly metallic vapors such as mercury. A **high-pressure sodium (HPS) lamp** uses sodium vapor for illumination.

Peter Cooper Hewitt patented the first mercury lamp in 1901. At this time, the lamp was two to three times more efficient than the incandescent lamp. The mercury lamp was efficient, but it produced an unpleasant blue-green color. Georges Claude invented neon tubes in 1910, but the gas produced a red light. Phosphors used in neon lamps prompted researchers to experiment with coating the tubes of lamps. In the late 1920s and early 1930s, French and German scientists experimented with fluorescent lamp coatings. Friedrich Meyer, Hans

Spanner, and Edmund Germer patented the first fluorescent lamp in 1927. By the late 1930s, researchers at General Electric and Westinghouse developed the fluorescent lamp and featured the new technology at the 1939 New York World's Fair and the Golden Gate Exposition in San Francisco.

The need for efficient electrical lights during World War II promoted mass production and use of fluorescent lamps. The first fluorescent lamps were coated with halophosphate and were very efficient. The fluorescent lamp had better color rendering properties than the mercury lamp, but the color was cool and basically unappealing.

The twentieth century introduced several modern electric sources including the **tungsten-halogen lamp**. In the early 1950s Alton Foote was employed by General Electric to improve heat lamps. As a result of his experiments, he determined that quartz could endure high levels of heat. Eventually chemists identified iodine as an element that could redeposit tungsten on a lamp's filament. This process greatly improved the efficiency of filament lamps. As a result, the tungsten-halogen lamp was introduced to the public at the 1964 New York World's Fair.

Another kind of lamp that was launched at the 1964 New York World's Fair was the metal-halide lamp. Metal halide resulted from efforts to improve the blue-green color emitted by mercury lamps. In the 1950s researchers determined that halogen could reduce the evaporation of electrodes. Experiments with electrical discharge and the chemistry of metal halides resulted in a successful metal-halide lamp in 1962. The lamp was more efficient than mercury lamps and emitted an appealing white light.

In a collaborative effort with scientists in England, the Netherlands, and Germany, experiments with low-pressure sodium lamps were conducted in the early 1930s. This kind of lamp was efficient, but it emitted a strange yellow color. The corrosive nature of sodium led to the development of better glass. In the 1950s researchers at General Electric explored the possibilities of using ceramic tubes for sodium lamps. As a result of this research and experimenting with various chemicals and sealing techniques, the high-pressure sodium lamp was introduced in 1962. The strong yellow color emitted by high-pressure sodium lamps has restricted their use to applications that demand high

High-pressure sodium (HPS) lamp
A high-intensity discharge electrical light source that uses sodium vapor for illumination.

Tungsten-halogen lamp
An incandescent lamp that contains halogen.

efficiency but where color is inconsequential, such as for warehouses, streets, highways, and bridges.

In 1974, the color rendering properties of fluorescent lamps saw significant improvements with the development of triphosphors made from rare-earth phosphors. This discovery was a tremendous advancement for a lamp that was widely used throughout the world. The next step in fluorescent-lamp research focused on a lamp that did not need a **ballast**; a control device used with electric-discharge lamps, which starts a lamp and controls the electrical current during operation. Eventually, this research led to the unexpected development of the **Compact fluorescent lamp (CFL)**. CFLs are very efficient and can be used in traditional incandescent fixtures. When first introduced in 1979, they were very expensive to purchase. In due course, production costs were reduced, and the price for CFLs became more reasonable.

Since the 1980s scientists and engineers have focused on improving incandescent, halogen, fluorescent, and high-intensity discharge lamps. The continuous improvement objectives are to produce lamps that are more efficient, last a long time, exhibit precision control, render colors accurately, and are available in a variety of shapes and sizes. In addition, a tremendous research effort is being conducted on developing light-emitting diodes. As a semi-conductor device **light-emitting diodes (LEDs)** have a chemical chip embedded in a plastic capsule. The light is focused or scattered by using lenses or diffusers. LED lights exhibit extraordinary potential as a major light source in the future.

What Is Light?

Technically **light** is a form of energy that is part of the electromagnetic spectrum visible to the human eye. The spectrum also includes cosmic rays, microwaves, gamma rays, radar, radio waves, ultraviolet, and X-rays. Based upon Isaac Newton's (1642–1727) prism experiments, the human eye is able to see light in the red (700–650 nanometers) to violet (440–390 nanometers) wavelengths. One billion nanometers equal one meter (10^{-9}m). Light travels at a speed of 186,000 miles per second or 300,000 kilometers per second. The unit for measuring the quantity of light emitted by a light source is a **lumen (lm)**. The light level or **illuminance** that falls on a surface can also be measured in **footcandles** or **lux** (see Chapter 7). A footcandle (fc) is a unit of illuminance equal to the amount of light that falls on a surface in a 1-foot radius of the source. Lux (lx) is the international system of units (SI) unit of illuminance.

Light and Emotive Responses

Light is a remarkable element that can be exciting, mysterious, magical, or terrifying. Paris, "the City of Lights," evokes excitement. Fireworks, used in Chinese New Year's celebrations as early as the ninth century, are an excellent example of how lights can create a festive atmosphere. Lights are often used to inspire people during sorrowful times. To memorialize the victims of the 1995 Oklahoma City bombing, the Butler Design Partnership firm designed clear chairs, one for each victim, that are illuminated during the evening. More recently, to honor the victims of the attack on the World Trade Center in New York City on September 11, 2001, the city had lighting designers project two vertical beams of light where the towers had stood (see Figure 1.5). The life of President John F. Kennedy is honored in a memorial with a cenotaph, a monument, designed by the architect Philip Johnson. The words "John Fitzgerald Kennedy" are engraved in gold on black granite in the center of the sculpture (Figure 1.6). These are the only words on the sculpture and are illuminated only by the reflections of the surrounding white walls. The words are dark during the evening hours, thus representing the loss of a leader.

While these lighting examples demonstrate inspirational uses, light also can be

FIGURE 1.5   To honor victims of the World Trade Center in New York City on September 11, 2001, two vertical beams of light were projected from the location of the structures.

Illuminance
The total amount of light on a surface; measured in lux (lx) or footcandle (fc).

Footcandle
Amount of light that falls on a surface in a 1-foot radius of the source.

Lux (lx)
The international system of units (SI) unit of illuminance.

FIGURE 1.6 To honor the life of President John F. Kennedy, the architect Philip Johnson designed a memorial with a cenotaph, an open tomb.

very frightening, as with lightning or a severe fire. For example, lightning is often used in movies and on the stage to create a fearful setting. A raging fire can create panic in people and animals. Flashing red lights on fire trucks or ambulances cause apprehensive feelings of being in a crisis or a life-threatening situation.

To design quality lighting environments, an interior designer must understand the power and effect of light on people within the context of the setting. This requires an understanding of the purpose of the space and characteristics of the users. For example, low levels of illumination are appropriate for a romantic restaurant, but they would be very wrong for a workplace. Flashing lights can promote excitement in a nightclub, but they would be very annoying in a museum. An important element in addressing the needs of the users of the space focuses on the variability of the vision process. Quality lighting must support the basic functions of vision. This requires an understanding of what happens when light enters the eye and the conditions that alter the vision process.

Vision and Lighting

The vision process starts when light enters the pupil, the aperture of the iris, of the eye (Figure 1.7). The lens adjusts the perception of light for near and far vision, and the cornea focuses light on the retina of the eye by refraction. This function is known as **accommodation**. The retina is the inner lining of the eye that is light-sensitive, and the fovea of the retina is where light is focused. Rods and cones are detector cells located at the back of the retina. Rods are activated primarily at lower illuminance levels and are important in night vision. Cones are activated with bright light, color, and detail. The fovea does not contain any rods. The cones and rods convert light energy into nerve impulses. The optic nerve sends impulses from the retina to the brain for interpretation. Through this entire process brightness and color are adjusted and images are compared to experiences in memory.

Adaptation occurs when the eye alters itself to the amount of brightness that is entering the pupil. Similar to the optics of a camera, the pupil in bright light constricts; it expands in dark settings. The adaptation process can take some time. Consider what happens when you enter a dark movie theater on a bright sunny day. Eyes require more time to adjust from bright to dark than from dark to light. To assist the adaptation that occurs in the vision process, designers should consider a lighting system that provides a transition in light levels. For low-level illuminated interiors used during daylight times, a transitional system

Accommodation
A function of the eye that enables one to see objects at varying distances.

Adaptation
A function of the eye that alters itself to the amount of brightness entering the pupil.

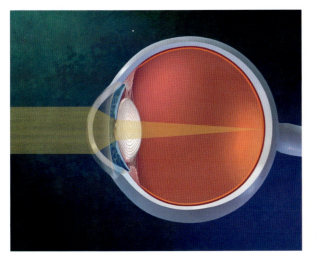

FIGURE 1.7 Cross section of the eye.

should begin with higher light levels as one enters the space. The light levels should increasingly be lowered as one travels through the interior. If possible, the amount of time it requires to enter the space until an individual is in the darkest space should be equal to the amount of time it takes for adaptation to occur in the vision process. Seating should be provided for individuals, such as the elderly, who require more time than younger people for the adaptation process. During evening hours, to reduce the contrast in lighting from the outside to the indoors, the lighting levels should be decreased in the entry area and be respectively reduced as one progresses through the interior.

The **eye's field of vision** is also an important consideration in designing quality lighting environments. The horizontal direction is the most natural movement for seeing objects. The field of vision includes a central and a peripheral area. The central field of vision for the eye is approximately 2 degrees above and 2 degrees below the direct line of sight (Figure 1.8). **Visual acuity**, the ability of the eye to see detail and color, is best in this small range. The peripheral area is the horizontal area to the sides of the central field of vision and the vertical areas above and below the central field of vision. Brightness and motion, such as flashing lights, are best seen in peripheral vision. Designers should consider the eye's field of vision when they plan the lighting for detailed visual tasks or when specifying bright or flashing lighting systems. For example, when planning the lighting for a work surface, a designer should position the light source to illuminate the work area in the central field of vision. Flashing emergency light fixtures are best located in areas that are within the peripheral field of vision. Since the location of the eye's field of vision changes when a person moves from a sitting to a standing position, a designer might have to specify several light sources to accommodate all the lighting needs.

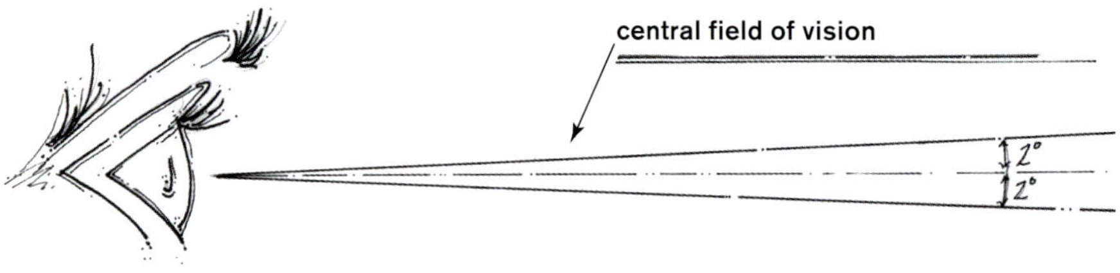

Eye's field of vision
The central and peripheral areas that are visible to the eye.

Visual acuity
The ability of the eye to see details.

FIGURE 1.8 The central field of vision for the eye is approximately 2 degrees above and below the direct line of sight.

central field of vision

2°
2°

The eye's aging process affects visual acuity, color identification, the adaptation process, peripheral vision, depth perception, and tolerance for glare. As one ages the lens of the eye yellows and **presbyopia**, the decrease in the eye's ability to adjust the shape of the lens, occurs. As a result, when designing spaces for the elderly, designers must specify higher illumination levels, especially in areas where detailed tasks are performed and where there are stairs. (Chapter 13 provides additional information regarding aging vision.)

Presbyopia
A decrease in the eye's ability to change the shape of the lens. This affects an individual's ability to focus on near or distant objects.

Quality Lighting

Quality lighting is a relatively new concept. The invention of electricity and the light bulb in the 1800s prompted engineers to develop new and better lamps and lighting systems. From that time, the focus has been primarily on the quantity of light needed in a space. Because we can measure lighting, it is fairly easy to have an adequate amount of lighting in a space. Now that scientists and engineers have developed systems that produce a large quantity of light, it is necessary for designers to focus on quality lighting. The subjective nature of quality lighting means that it is complicated and difficult to accomplish. The new *IESNA Lighting Handbook,* 9th edition, focuses on the importance of quality lighting and on the quantity of lighting.

Definition

What is quality lighting? **Quality lighting** allows users to simultaneously function comfortably in a space, feel safe, and appreciate the aesthetic components of the interior. Achieving a quality lighting environment requires complete control over the lighting system. Environments with quality lighting are specifically designed for the client, users, architectural features, site, and location. These environments reflect a skillful application of the principles of design by integrating and layering light into the entire composition. **Layered lighting** includes natural light and multiple electrical light sources. With the focus on quality, lighting is no longer an afterthought that is added to a design plan. Quality lighting includes the art of balancing and integrating

Quality lighting
A layered illumination plan that reduces energy costs, conserves natural resources, allows users of the space to function comfortably, feel safe, and appreciate the aesthetic components of the environment.

Layered lighting
An illumination plan that includes natural light and multiple electrical light sources.

daylight and general, task, accent, and decorative lighting. Designing quality lighting environments results in reduced energy costs and conservation of natural resources. Throughout this text, the principles of quality lighting are applied to the fundamentals of lighting, elements of lighting systems, case studies, and presentations of lighting solutions. The goal of every chapter is to build the knowledge and skills designers need to create quality lighting environments.

Lighting Designers

Since the extensive development of electrical light sources is a relatively new field, professionals are currently formulating the tasks and responsibilities of a lighting designer. A **lighting designer** is a professional who plans, specifies, and oversees the implementation of the natural and electrical illumination for residential and commercial interiors. A lighting designer specifies the light sources, controls, and layout requirements. Critical to the success of this profession is the concept of working collaboratively with all the individuals involved with architecture and interiors, including architects, interior designers, contractors, electricians, plumbers, and suppliers. This cooperation is especially important to the development of quality lighting environments. Quality lighting environments start with collaboration at the conceptual phase of the design process and continue through to postoccupancy interviews. Unit III discusses in detail the process a designer should follow in creating quality lighting environments.

Designers must be able to make detailed observations, and they must be good at problem solving. To understand the effects of lighting and its impact on users, a designer must intensely observe and study existing lighting applications and how people react to them. Identifying successful or problematic lighting installations can teach a designer a great deal that can be applied to planning other interiors. Every lighting plan is a result of problem solving. As with observation, problem solving is a developed skill that designers must practice extensively to be effective. The problem-solving process includes gathering all the information involved with a project. Data collection includes recording existing lighting applications, conducting interviews, distrib-

Lighting designer
A professional who plans, specifies, and oversees the implementation of the natural and electrical illumination for residential and commercial interiors.

uting surveys, and observing how users are functioning in the space. Specific skills related to problem solving for quality lighting are explored in Chapters 21 and 22.

Many of today's experienced lighting designers received their training in another field such as architecture, interior design, engineering, or theatrical lighting. Lighting designers tend to specialize in either commercial or residential interiors. The National Council on Qualifications for the Lighting Professions (NCQLP) was established to create a certification program for the lighting industry. Designers who meet the certification requirements are able to use LC (Light ing Certified) after their name. The International Association of Lighting Designers (IALD) serves as the professional organization for lighting designers. Many lighting designers in the United States are also members of the Illuminating Engineering Society of North America (IESNA). IESNA develops many of the standards of illumination used throughout the industry.

The content of this textbook is intended to assist individuals who elect to become professional lighting designers and other professionals who want to ensure that the lighting of interiors enhances the environment. This requires a comprehensive approach to the lighting field and life-long learning. This textbook should serve as a foundation for professionals interested in designing a quality lighting environment, but follow-up must be conducted by reading current journals, product literature, and by attending professional conferences.

SUMMARY

- Natural light includes direct and indirect light from sunlight, the moon, stars, clouds, structures, and the landscape.
- Until the invention of electricity, light sources included fire, oil lamps, rushlights, candles, and gas lamps.
- Mass produced electrical light was not available until the invention of the incandescent carbon-filament lamp in the late 1870s by Thomas Edison from the United States and Joseph Swan from Great Britain.

- Light is a form of energy that is part of the electromagnetic spectrum visible to the human eye. Light has the ability to elicit significant emotional responses from people.

- The vision process starts when light enters the pupil. The lens adjusts the light for near and far vision, and the cornea focuses light on the retina by refraction. Rods and cones are detector cells located at the back of the retina. Rods are activated primarily in lower illuminance levels, and cones are activated with bright light, color, and detail. The optic nerve sends impulses from the retina to the brain for interpretation.

- Because light/dark adaptation occurs in the vision process, designers should consider a lighting system that provides a transition in light levels.

- The eye's field of vision includes a central and peripheral area.

- The aging of the eye affects visual acuity, color identification, the adaptation process, peripheral vision, depth perception, and tolerance for glare.

- Quality lighting environments allow users to simultaneously function in a space, feel safe, and appreciate the aesthetic components of the interior. These environments reflect a skillful application of the principles of design by integrating and layering lighting into the entire composition.

- A lighting designer is a professional who plans, specifies, and oversees the implementation of the natural and electrical illumination for residential and commercial interiors. Observation and problem solving are two essential skills for a lighting designer.

Key Terms

accommodation	electric-discharge lamp
adaptation	eye's field of vision
arc lamp	fluorescent lamp
ballast	footcandle (fc)
Compact fluorescent lamp (CFL)	gas lamp

High-intensity discharge (HID) lamp	lux (lx)
High-pressure sodium (HPS) lamp	mercury lamp
	Metal halide (MH) lamp
illuminance	natural light
incandescent carbon-filament lamp	neon lamp
	oculus
	oil lamp
indirect natural light	presbyopia
lamp	quality lighting
layered lighting	rushlight
light	snuffer
lighting designer	tungsten-halogen lamp
Light-emitting diodes (LEDs)	visual acuity
lumen (lm)	

Exercises

1. Research various fixtures that have been designed for illumination, including oil lamps, candle holders, and gas lamps. Identify the advantages and disadvantages of these fixtures. Record how these fixtures influenced the design of contemporary light fixtures.

2. Examine a large white object outdoors at different times of the day, under various weather conditions, and in different locations. Record your observations of the color of the object, time of the day, weather conditions, and surrounding landscape. Describe how the object color changed according to the various conditions, including the effect of reflective light.

3. Identify several experiences you have had with changes in lighting such as when you enter a movie theater on a bright, sunny day. Describe what occurs in the vision process as you experience these changes.

4. Developing observational and problem-solving skills are critical to the success as a designer. Identify five public spaces you can observe during various times of the day and on different days of the

week. Write a report that could include sketches and photographs responding to the items listed below:

   a. Determine whether the space meets all the criteria for a quality lighting environment.

   b. Given the users and elements of the space, identify special needs for vision.

   c. Determine the human response elicited from the space and identify the lighting techniques that contribute to the response.

   d. Compare and contrast how the space would work with nonelectrical light fixtures.

5. Using the Internet, identify five lighting design firms. For each firm record the major projects, the number of employees, requirements for employment, and location.

REFERENCES

Alton, J. (1995). *Painting with Light.* Berkeley, CA: University of California Press.

Benya, J., Heschong, L., McGowan, T., Miller, N., and Rubinstein, F. (2001). *Advanced Lighting Guidelines.* White Salmon, WA: New Buildings Institute.

Bourne, J., and Brett, V. (1991). *Lighting in the Domestic Interior.* London: Sotheby's.

Bowers, B. (1998). *Lengthening the Day: A History of Lighting Technology.* Oxford: Oxford University Press.

Bowmaker, J.K., and Dartnall, H.J. (1980). Visual pigments of rods and cones in human retina. *Journal of Physiology, 298,* 501–511.

Boyce, P.R. (1981). *Human Factors in Lighting,* New York: Macmillan.

Boylan, B.R. (1987). *The Lighting Primer.* Ames, IA: Iowa State University Press.

Coaton, J.R., and Marsden, A.M. (1997). *Lamps and Lighting,* 4th ed. London: Arnold.

Egan, M.D. (1983). *Concepts in Architectural Lighting.* New York: McGraw-Hill.

General Electric (1989). *Lighting Application Bulletin.* Cleveland, OH: General Electric.

Gordon, G. (2003). *Interior Lighting for Designers,* 4th ed. New York: John Wiley & Sons.

Gordan, G., and Nuckolls, J.L. (1995). *Interior Lighting for Designers.* New York: John Wiley & Sons.

Gregory, R.I. (1979). *Eye and Brain: The Psychology of Seeing,* 3rd ed. New York: McGraw-Hill.

Greif, M. (1986). *The Lighting Book.* Pittstown, NJ: The Main Street Press.

Harvey, E.N. (1957). *A History of Luminescence from the Earliest of Times until 1900.* Philadelphia: America Philosophical Society.

Hill, H., and Bruce, V. (1996). The effects of lighting on the perception of facial surfaces. *Journal of Experimental Psychology: Human Perception and Performance, 22*(4), 986–1004.

Hunter, R.S. (1975). *The Measurement of Appearance.* New York: John Wiley & Sons.

Illuminating Engineering Society of North America (IESNA) (2000). *IESNA Lighting Handbook,* 9th ed. New York: Illuminating Engineering Society of North America.

Illuminating Engineering Society of North America (IESNA). (1998). Lighting for the aged and partially sighted committee. *Recommended Practice for Lighting and the Visual Environment for Senior Living,* RP-28-98. New York: Illuminating Engineering Society of North America.

Kaufman, J. E. (ed.) (1984). *IES Lighting Handbook Reference Volume 1984.* New York: Illuminating Engineering Society.

Lam, W.C. (1977). *Perception and Lighting as Formgivers for Architecture.* New York: McGraw-Hill.

Lawrence Berkeley National Laboratory. 1997. *Lighting Source Book.* Berkeley, CA: Lawrence Berkeley National Laboratory.

Lewis, A.L. (1998). Equating light sources for visual performance at low luminances. *Journal of the Illuminating Engineering Society, 27(1), 80.*

Loe, D.L., Mansfield, J.F., & Rowlands, E. (1994). Appearance of lit environment and its relevance in lighting design: Environmental study. *Lighting Research & Technology, 26(3),* 119–133.

Loe, D.L., and Rowlands, E. (1996). The art and science of lighting: A strategy for lighting design. *Lighting Research & Technology, 28(4),* 153–164.

Lynes, J.A. (1978). *Developments in Lighting—1.* London: Applied Science Publishers Ltd.

Moore, F. (1985). *Concepts and Practice of Architectural Daylighting.* New York: Van Nostrand Reinhold Company.

Phillips, D. (2000). *Lighting Modern Buildings.* Oxford: Architectural Press.

Rosenthal, J., and Wertenbaker, L. (1972). *The Magic of Light.* Boston: Little, Brown and Company.

Veitch, J. (July 9–11, 2000). Lighting guidelines from lighting quality research. *CIBSE/ILE Lighting 2000 Conference.* New York, United Kingdom.

Veitch, J., and Newsham, G. (August, 1996). Experts' quantitative and qualitative assessment of lighting quality. *Proceedings of the 1996 Annual IESNA Conference.* Cleveland, OH. Available at: http://fox.nrc.ca/irc/fulltext/nrcc39874.html.

Watson, L. (1977). *Lighting Design Handbook.* New York: McGraw-Hill.

Weale, R.A. (1961). Retinal illumination of age. *Illuminating Engineering Society (London),* 26(2), 95–100.

Wright, G.A., and Rea, M. S. (1984). Age, a human factor in lighting. *Proceedings of the 1984 International Conference on Occupational Ergonomics.* D.A. Attwood and C. McCann (Eds.). Rexdale, Ontario, Canada: Human Factors Association of Canada.

CHAPTER 2

Lighting Environments

OBJECTIVES

- Describe how to accomplish layered lighting by integrating natural light with multiple electrical sources.

- Identify the advantages and disadvantages of using daylight as a lighting source.

- Describe the factors and conditions that affect the quantity and quality of daylight in an interior.

- Describe general, task, accent, and decorative lighting techniques.

- Identify fixtures that are used for general, task, accent, and decorative lighting.

- Develop a fundamental understanding of the factors that affect quality in general, task, and accent lighting.

CREATING a quality lighting environment requires a comprehensive plan that is based upon natural light and multiple electrical sources. Designers often use the term layered lighting to describe this practice. This concept is introduced early in the text because it so important to successful quality lighting. Knowledge of this practice should be applied to all the topics covered throughout the rest of the book. Think about layered lighting on a daily basis as you observe the lighting in public and private spaces. This habit will help you develop the observation and problem-solving skills that are addressed in Chapter 1.

In order to understand how designers accomplish layered lighting, we must first examine daylight and the importance of integrating it with electrical systems. Integrating and controlling daylight involve an understanding of solar geometry, distribution of daylight into spaces, glazing technologies, and energy considerations. **Solar geometry** is the movement of the earth around the sun.

Lighting requirements in a space can be described as belonging to one of three main categories: general, task, and accent. The first is **general**, or **ambient lighting**, which provides overall illumination in a space, including lighting that allows people to safely walk through a space. The second is **task lighting**, which is the lighting that is specified for each task that is performed in a space. The third is **accent lighting**, which is used to create interest and magic in a space, as well as to highlight special features such as architectural details, artwork, plant foliage, or decorative accessories. **Decorative lighting** includes light sources that provide illumination and are also artistic pieces. For a quality lighting environment, it is critical to include daylight and to specify lighting for general, task, and accent lighting in every space in an interior. This layered lighting approach will assist the designer in creating lighting that is available for the purpose of the space and the needs of its users. Decorative lighting is an optional source that could be used as a focal point in select locations.

Daylight Integration and Control of Daylight

Daylight is not only essential to life but it is also critical to the psychological and biological well-being of people. From an architectural perspective, daylight enters an interior through **apertures** that include windows and skylights. Everyone appreciates windows in the majority of interior spaces. Offices that have windows, especially spaces with windows in the corners, are usually associated with status. Daylight is generally perceived as constant and is considered the standard for determining "true" colors. To determine an object's accurate color, people will often take the item outdoors or examine it near a window. Restaurants with a beautiful view of a city skyline, water, or golf course have prime seating close to these windows. Unfortunately with the invention of electrical light sources and air conditioning, many contemporary buildings do not effectively integrate daylight into spaces. Many buildings have spaces with no windows or skylights. The value and importance of integrating daylight into interiors is vital to quality environments. This practice includes **harvesting daylight**, which is the expression that describes capturing daylight for the purpose of illuminating interiors.

The key to a quality lighting environment is distinguishing between sunlight and daylight. **Sunlight** is considered light that enters a space directly from the sun. This type of light is generally not good lighting for an interior. Direct sunlight can produce glare and excessive heat, and it can fade materials. **Daylight** or *skylight* is the term that describes the desirable natural light in a space. Daylight results in a perceived even distribution of light that avoids the glare and ill effects of direct sunlight. A designer should always focus on ways to integrate daylight into an interior while avoiding the glare of sunlight.

Advantages and Disadvantages of Natural Light

Planning quality daylight for an interior requires examining the advantages and disadvantages of the source. Advantages to integrating daylight into interiors include energy savings resulting from a reduction in electrical lights and passive solar energy penetration in the winter. Another advantage to daylight is the even distribution of light that appears to reveal the "true" colors of objects and surfaces. Daylight enhances visual acuity thereby providing better light for reading and writing. Advantages to integrating daylight into interiors also include benefits associated with windows, such as providing a view and ventilation.

Daylight also has positive psychological and physiological effects on people by reducing stress, satisfying circadian rhythms, and encouraging positive attitudes. A **circadian rhythm** is the biological function that coordinates sleeping and awake times through hormones and metabolic processes. Research in hospitals, schools, and retail stores indicate that daylight has positive effects on human performance (Heschong, 1997; Heschong, 1999; Littlefair, 1996). Littlefair reported on the positive effects of using light shelves to maximize

Harvesting daylight
Term that describes capturing daylight for the purpose of illuminating interiors.

Sunlight
Light from the sun that enters a space directly.

Daylight (skylight)
Desirable natural light in a space.

Circadian rhythm
A biological function that coordinates sleeping and awake times through hormones and metabolic processes.

daylight in the patient rooms of hospitals. The Heschong Group (1999) found that students in classrooms with significant daylight had 7 to 18 percent higher scores than students working in classrooms with little or no daylight. It also found that retail stores that had skylights reported 40 percent higher sales. (Human factors related to lighting are examined in detail in Chapter 13.)

Disadvantages of natural light often are a result of the direct sun penetrating a space. The ultraviolet rays of the sun can fade fabrics and artwork. The fabric's fiber and weave determine how easily the material will be damaged. Natural fibers such as silk, cotton, or linen are more susceptible to damage than acrylics or polyesters. Tight weaves, shiny fabrics, and thick fibers are more resistant to damage from the sun. If direct sunlight cannot be avoided, a designer can specify a fabric that is more impervious to deterioration than others. Infrared rays of the sun cause some woods to crack and peel. Disadvantages associated with windows include glare, noise penetration, cleaning maintenance, lack of privacy, and heat gain in the summer. In addition, the beautiful views enjoyed during the day can become "black holes" at night. Windows at night resemble mirrors by reflecting distracting images into the room. This problem can be resolved with appropriate window treatments and by reducing the contrast, such as adding exterior lighting to the landscaping. The key to resolving problems associated with sunlight is first an awareness that these negative consequences exist and then planning solutions that address the concerns. (Effective solutions are discussed later in this chapter and in Chapters 6, 10, and 12.) Many solutions include installing appropriate devices that help to control sunlight and layering light whereby daylight penetration is integrated with electrical systems.

History of Designs that Accommodate Sunlight

Integrating daylight into spaces is essentially the foundation and basis for the field of lighting design. As discussed in Chapter 1, prior to the invention of electricity, a major source of illumination was sunlight. For most of human history, civilizations had to creatively design structures that responded to the variability of the sun. Based upon climate and orientation, buildings were designed to allow light penetration while dealing with the weather and geographic characteristics of the location. For example, in the hot climate of the African desert, the Egyptians designed structures that had clerestory windows. These windows allowed light to penetrate an entire space, provided privacy, and had an opening for heat to escape. The atrium designed in ancient Roman residences included overhangs that simultaneously allowed daylight penetration and prevented direct sunlight from entering rooms.

In colder climates, the focus was on large spans of glass on the south side of a structure; this provided warmth of the sun in the winter. Early residences in Britain, Holland, and the Scandinavian countries often had these characteristics. Early churches were designed with clerestories to provide illumination to the center of the church. Buildings constructed in the 1800s and early 1900s still had to provide for sunlight and ventilation. The U shapes of the Hilton Hotel in Chicago and the Woolworth building in New York illustrate a design that provides windows in every space (see Figure 2.1). Large department stores used to have many windows for this purpose as well as to assist for color identification.

FIGURE 2.1 The U shapes of the Hilton Hotel in Chicago allows for sunlight and ventilation in all of the spaces.

Solar Geometry and the Variability of Sunlight

Solar geometry
The movement of the earth around the sun.

Modeling
Emphasizing the three-dimensions of a piece or surface through light, shade, and shadows.

Designing buildings that maximize penetration of daylight requires a great deal of analysis and planning. This process begins with an understanding of solar geometry and the variability of sunlight. **Solar geometry** examines the movement of the earth around the sun. Sunlight changes daily, by the hour, by the season, with the weather, and with geographical location. Colors, shadows, forms, and shapes vary during the day according to the sun's position. The oblique shafts of light produced by midmorning and late afternoon sun create long and soft shadows. The harsh shadows produced by sunlight at noon emphasize the three dimensions of objects; this **modeling** is best achieved with side lighting rather than lighting from a ceiling (see Figure 2.2).

As illustrated in Figure 2.3, the path of the sun is dramatically different in the summer and winter. In the northern hemisphere during the summer, the sun rises in the northeast and sets in the northwest. In contrast, the path of the winter sun is lower; it rises in the southeast and sets in the southwest. On October 21 and March 21 the sun's path is identical. The directional qualities of the sun are determined by the earth's latitude. A more northerly sunrise and sunset will occur with

FIGURE 2.2 Colors, shadows, forms, and shapes vary during the day according to the sun's position. Harsh shadows produced by sunlight at noon emphasize the shape of an object.

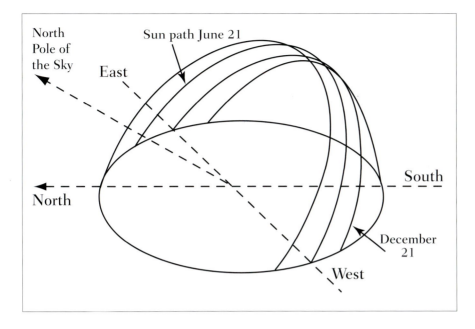

North
Pole of
the Sky

North

East

Sun path June 21

South

December
21

West

FIGURE 2.3 The path
of the sun is different in the
summer and winter.

greater latitudes. To determine the sun's path in a specific location, one can contact the American Society of Heating, Refrigeration, and Air-Conditioning (ASHRAE). To maximize quality daylight at the point at which a space is entered, a designer utilizes this solar geometry to specify the size, shape, and location of windows. Ideally window and shielding units should be positioned to allow the maximum amount of sunlight into a space during the winter months and the minimum amount during the hot summer. Shielding devices can include roof overhangs, louvers, and deciduous trees. A very sophisticated shielding device was designed for the Arab Institute in Paris. The south side of the building is a glass wall (Figure 2.4) covered with photoelectrical control units. The metallic structure of the control units is aesthetically pleasing, and the photosensor mechanism allows the lenses to change according to the daylight light levels. Functioning like a camera lens, on a cloudy day the aperture opens very wide to allow the maximum amount of daylight into the building. On a sunny day the lenses close to prevent a great deal of heat and sunlight penetration. This design helps to reduce energy costs, and the variability of daylight creates an ever-changing artistic composition on the south wall of the Institute.

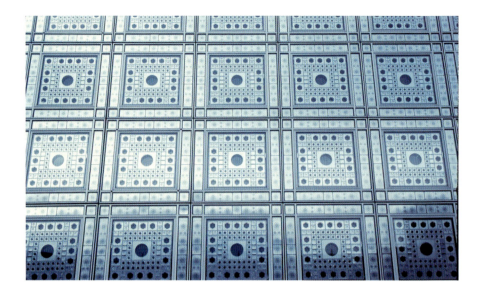

FIGURE 2.4 The south side of the Arab Institute in Paris is a glass wall covered with photoelectrical control units. The photosensor mechanism allows the lenses to change according to the daylight light levels.

In addition to the geometry of the solar system there are several other factors that influence the level and quality of daylight entering a space. These include clouds, weather, atmospheric pollution, orientation, landscaping, and surrounding structures. The amount and type of clouds affect the characteristics of daylight. Atmospheric pollution tends to create a hazy lighting condition, especially at sunset. Overcast days generally provide a uniform level of intensity that lacks the dynamic qualities of bright sunlight. Cloudy days reduce contrast and shadows. The U.S. Weather Bureau provides the number of overcast days per year by geographical location. A designer needs this information in planning the integration of daylight with electrical systems. For example, if a building is located in an area that experiences a high number of overcast days, it may be necessary to have extra large windows and an adequate number of electrical sources in order to have enough illumination.

Integrating Daylight into the Lighting Design

Successfully integrating daylight into a lighting design requires a plan that provides the flexibility of having electrical sources in areas away from windows and lights that dim or turn off in areas close to windows (see Figure 2.5). If people turn lights on in the morning, they generally

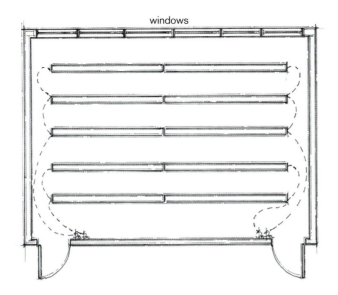
windows

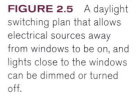
FIGURE 2.5 A daylight switching plan that allows electrical sources away from windows to be on, and lights close to the windows can be dimmed or turned off.

will leave them on during the rest of the day. To save electricity and maximize the benefits of daylight, a designer can specify an electrical plan that has multiple switching plans and photoelectric control units. The brightness of a window can make it appear that the surrounding wall area is dark. Thus, to assist the eye in the adaptation process, people will often turn on lights even on a sunny day. To reduce the perceived need for additional light, the wall area around a window should be a light color, and, if possible, a skylight or other source originating from the ceiling should illuminate the wall.

The site orientation of a structure affects the type of daylight that enters the windows. Light entering on the south side of a building has significant variation in intensity and color. The southern exposure can fade and deteriorate fabrics, carpeting, and wall coverings. Northern light generally has a constant intensity and even spectrographic characteristics. Because of these color-rendering properties, artists prefer to paint in rooms located on the north side of a building.

Reflected light from surfaces can affect the quantity of daylight in a space. For example, the landscaping and surrounding structures affect the quality and quantity of daylight entering a building. Trees and tall shrubs close to the windows help to diffuse the sunlight. The color of the ground next to a window also affects the quality of light inside. Grass, dirt, or dark-colored rocks will reduce the amount of daylight that enters the window. A white material, such as limestone, will maximize the quantity of light reflected into the space. A building close to a window can reflect light into the interior. As with the choice of ground materials, if the building next door is faced in a dark-colored material, there will be less light reflected into the space than if the surface is white or a light color.

Currently, in response to energy conservation and sustainable buildings, many manufacturers are developing more effective daylight-integration products. Initiatives focus on products that maximize the benefits of daylight, while eliminating glare and reducing electrical energy consumption. Lighting control systems are key to effective and efficient daylight integration (see Chapter 10). Major advancements in the technologies associated with lighting controls allow centralized dimming, switching, sunlight diffusion, and energy management. As one of the most progressive technologies in the field of lighting, it is imperative for an interior designer to stay current with new products and installation techniques.

The Influences of Windows and Skylights

Effective daylight integration requires an understanding of how the design of openings and the size, shape, and location of windows affect the quantity and quality of daylight in an interior. The design of a window opening affects the quantity of light entering a room (Figure 2.6a). Flush openings, the most common design for windows, are not designed to reflect light into a space. Deep openings (see Figure 2.6b) will cause more light to be reflected into a space. A light shelf and splayed or rounded jambs also reflect more light into an interior (see Figure 2.6c). The design and height of the ceiling also affects the amount of light in a space. Tall ceilings and chamfered ceilings will result in a greater amount of light in an interior. Surfaces designed to reflect light into a space should have a matte finish and be painted white or a light color. Ceilings and the wall directly across from windows will provide the maximum amount of light reflection into a room. It is more difficult to obtain significant amounts of reflected illumination from the side walls and floor.

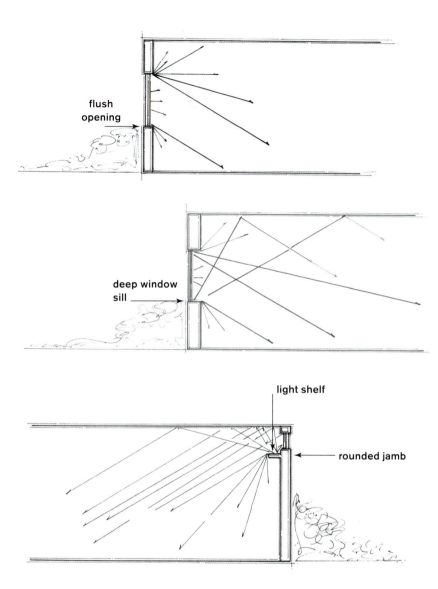

FIGURE 2.6a The design of a window opening affects the quantity of light entering a room. This flush opening does not maximize the amount of light that can enter the room.

FIGURE 2.6b Deep openings cause more light to be reflected in the space.

FIGURE 2.6c A light shelf and splayed or rounded jambs also reflect more light into the interior.

Even a small patch of sunlight can cause positive psychological reactions and provide visual interest to a space. In general, larger openings will allow more daylight into a space. To maximize the amount of daylight in a space, window openings should be approximately one-fourth the area of the floor. For example, if the floor area is 120 square feet, there should be approximately 30 square feet of space planned for windows. Most windows have a horizontal or vertical shape. Both shapes will allow an approximate equal amount of daylight into a space if they are the same size. However, windows in a horizontal design are generally preferred in order to maximize a view and to accommodate the eye's natural direction of movement. An interior with long vertical windows could maximize reflected daylight into the space by using a light-colored floor surface.

To maximize the amount of daylight in a space, the windows should be placed high on a wall. Light entering a window close to a ceiling will reflect off of the ceiling and possibly the adjacent walls and then into the room (Figure 2.7a). Windows on two walls in a space can effectively balance the amount of daylight in that space. Daylight penetration through bilateral openings could be accomplished with windows, skylights, or window wells (see Figure 2.7b). To allow daylight and ventilation into adjacent areas, such as another room or hallways, transoms can be installed.

Window placement influences the arrangement of furniture, technology, and equipment in a space. In planning an interior, a designer must consider when the space will be used, the purpose of the space, and how to accommodate the adaptation function of the eye. To reduce glare on tasks, work surfaces should be positioned perpendicular

FIGURE 2.7a Light entering this clerestory window reflects off of the ceiling, adjacent walls, and then enters the room.

FIGURE 2.7b Daylight penetration through bilateral openings helps to increase the amount of daylight in the center of the room.

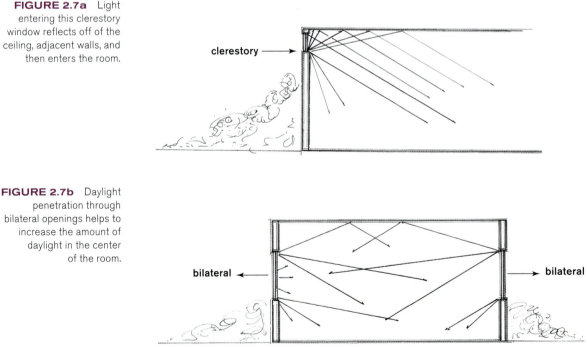

to the window opening. If possible, windows should be on the left side of people while they are seated at a desk or workstation. This helps to prevent shadows on a task that can occur with right-handed individuals, who represent the majority of people. When an interior designer is specifying a custom layout for a left-handed person, the light source should be located to the right of the work surface. Equipment and technology such as computer monitors or televisions should be positioned to avoid the direct rays of sunlight. To determine if glare is a problem from a window or light fixture, place a mirror on the viewing screen. If a light fixture or window is visible in the mirror, then the user will experience glare from the source.

Generally, the amount of daylight provided in a specific location in a room is dependent upon the amount of sky one observes while standing or sitting in the area. For example, in Figure 2.8, people sitting in the chairs close to the windows are able to see a great deal of sky. Thus, the amount of daylight in this area would be significant. People sitting on the sofa in this space are not able to see the sky at all. Thus the amount of daylight in this area would be minimal. By knowing this information, a designer might want to explore installing a unit that would admit daylight to the area around the sofa or include sufficient electrical sources.

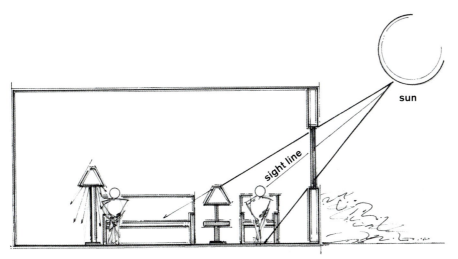

FIGURE 2.8 The individual sitting close to the window is able to view a significant amount of daylight because of the amount of sky that is visible. The other individual is not able to see the sky, therefore a luminaire is added to supplement lighting needs.

Skylights provide an excellent source of daylight by illuminating a large area of a room. They also provide excellent ways of illuminating spaces away from windows, such as hallways. They are an especially good light source for geographic areas that experience a high number of overcast days. Skylights are available in a variety of shapes, materials, and installation methods. Skylights installed in a deep light well will allow a significant amount of illumination in a space (Figure 2.9a). Light wells can be installed to allow daylight penetration to the center of multistory buildings. The V-shaped lens on a skylight will also distribute a great amount of light into a space (Figure 2.9b). The sawtooth design of skylights, a series of openings in the ceiling, distributes the light over a larger area of a room. A roof monitor distributes daylight from the center of the space (Figure 2.9c). As with a window, a clear glass skylight will admit direct sunlight that can cause glare and deteriorate fabrics and wood. A shielding device might have to be installed to help control the ill effects of direct sunlight.

Glazing systems, glass coatings, window treatments, roof overhangs, and awnings are some ways of controlling direct sunlight. Double or triple glazing on windows can reduce the amount of heat gain through a window and help to reduce noise from entering a room. Coatings applied to tint glass allow solar energy to penetrate through a window and can reduce glare. Glass coatings distort the colors of interiors, buildings, and landscaping outside the window. A variety of fixed and movable devices are available to control direct sunlight. Roof overhangs and awnings are fixed units used to control sunlight.

Draperies, shades, shutters, and horizontal and vertical blinds are examples of movable window treatments. These can be operated by hand or electrically. Centralized lighting control systems integrate energy conservation techniques and window treatment controls (see Chapter 10). A great deal of research has been conducted on the materials used for shades. New advancements in the composition of fabrics have created shades that can redirect heat to the outdoors during the summer, reduce glare, and minimize fading and damage from ultraviolet rays. In addition, shades are available in a range of options that include materials that provide total darkness, or minimal translucence. There are also shades that can filter daylight while maximizing a view.

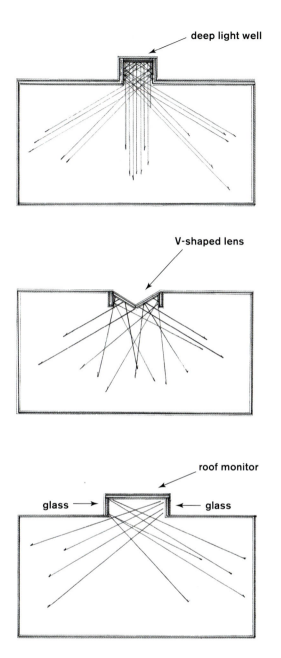

deep light well

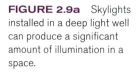

FIGURE 2.9a Skylights installed in a deep light well can produce a significant amount of illumination in a space.

V-shaped lens

FIGURE 2.9b The V-shaped lens on a skylight can distribute a great amount of light into a room.

roof monitor

glass → ← glass

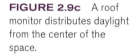

FIGURE 2.9c A roof monitor distributes daylight from the center of the space.

All the factors and characteristics identified in this section affect the amount of daylight in an environment. To estimate the quantity of daylight in a space, an interior designer can calculate the **Daylight factor (DF)**. DF is the ratio of the amount of daylight in specific areas in a room to the light outdoors. Performing the calculations is beyond the

Daylight factor (DF)
The ratio between the amount of daylight in specific areas in a room and the light outdoors.

scope of this textbook. However, software packages are available that calculate the DFs for a variety of climates. These programs can assist a designer in planning the number of windows that should be in a room and the number of electrical sources. For example, in a climate that has a great number of overcast days, a designer would specify more windows, skylights, and supplemental electrical sources than in an area that has a great number of sunny days.

Specification of Lighting by Category

The integration and control of daylight can be applied to each category of lighting technique, including general, task, and accent. This requires that layered lighting be combined with multiple light sources. Identifying light sources for each purpose provides the users of the space with the flexibility of selecting and adjusting the lighting for the specific activity. An important element in achieving a flexible light plan is to have multiple switching and dimming controls. The light fixture in and illumination level of each category of lighting technique should reinforce the overall theme of an interior.

In the early days of specifying electrical light sources, a typical practice was to mount a light fixture in the center of a ceiling. Many times this fixture served as the source for the general, task, and accent lighting needs of the space. However, a single source cannot serve all the illumination needs of an interior. It is critical for a designer to plan during the initial design-concept phase an approach to each category of lighting technique. Specifying the general, task, and accent lighting for an interior accommodates the needs of the users and creates a pleasing environment by having a variety of lighting effects.

General Lighting

As discussed earlier in this chapter, general lighting is sometimes referred to as ambient lighting, a category of lighting technique designed to provide uniform lighting to a space. Often light fixtures for general lighting are hidden from view and are designed as an indirect type of illumination. General lighting is the background lighting that allows people to walk safely through a space. This lighting helps to reduce sharp contrasts between light sources and enables people to perceive the overall shape and size of a space. General lighting also establishes the mood or character of an interior.

The design of a general lighting plan should be based upon the purpose of the space and the needs of its users. General lighting is the source that establishes the overall impression of a space and is determined by the light level, light source, and fixtures. For example, the general lighting in a high-end restaurant or retail store will usually be dimmer than they are in a fast-food restaurant or a discount store. High-end spaces usually have a flexible lighting system that includes electrical fixtures that present an expensive image. Designers of low-end or discount settings plan systems that economize on electrical usage, maintenance, and fixtures.

In spaces with many windows or skylights, daylight can be the source for general lighting on sunny days. The space should be designed to provide general lighting by electrical sources during the evening or on a dark, cloudy day. A variety of light fixtures and structural lighting systems are available to provide the indirect lighting required for general illumination. (Lighting systems and styles of fixtures are discussed in Chapters 9 and 11, respectively.) Any light fixture that provides indirect light could be used for general lighting. To have an adequate level of illumination, the space must have several indirect fixtures in various locations, or it must be supplemented with light that is integrated into walls, ceilings, or furniture.

Structural lighting systems include cornice, cove, and wall bracket. A **cornice** is located on vertical surfaces and directs the light downward. A **cove** is close to the ceiling and directs the light upward. A **wall bracket** is located on a wall and directs the light upward and downward. Ceiling-mounted lighting systems include a wallslot, recessed luminaries, and surface-mounted fixtures. A **wallslot** is integrated into the ceiling system and distributes light down onto vertical surfaces. A **luminaire** is an element of a lighting system, which includes the light source, housing elements, ballasts, transformers, controls, a mounting mechanism, and a connection to electrical power. Recessed luminaires include a **downlight** or **high-hat**, which are fixtures mounted above the ceiling and direct the light downward. Examples of surface-mounted

Cornice lighting
Illumination technique that may be mounted on a wall, or above a window; the light is directed down.

Cove lighting
Illumination technique that is mounted on a wall or ceiling; the light is directed up toward the ceiling.

Wall bracket lighting
Illumination technique that is mounted on a wall and in which the light is directed up and down.

Wallslot
A structural lighting system that is integrated in the ceiling and distributes light down on vertical surfaces.

Luminaire
An element of a lighting system, which includes the light source, housing elements, ballasts, transformers, controls, a mounting mechanism, and a connection to electrical power.

Downlight luminaire
Recessed ceiling-mounted luminaire. Also referred to as high-hat luminaire.

High-hat luminaire
Recessed ceiling-mounted luminaire. Also referred to as downlight.

luminaries include track lighting, pendants, and any other type of luminaire that is installed on a ceiling.

To employ daylight and electrical sources effectively requires that light be reflected from surfaces in the space, including from walls, the ceiling, and the floor. The highest level of illumination will be achieved when surfaces have a matt finish and are white or a light color. In smaller rooms, walls can provide a high level of reflection. In larger rooms reflection from surfaces is derived primarily from the ceiling and floor. Surfaces and reflections also affect the amount of light in an environment (see Chapter 6). To achieve an adequate balance of light in a space, the general lighting should be approximately one-third the illumination level of the task lighting. Wall partitions can affect the amount of general lighting that illuminates specific areas.

Task Lighting

Task lighting is another category of lighting technique which is used commercial and residential environments. The purpose of this technique is to provide quality lighting for specific activities and tasks. Task lighting is a direct form of lighting that enables users to see the critical details of an activity. A quality lighting environment requires the appropriate balance of general lighting and task lighting. The illumination level of task lighting should be approximately three times the level of general lighting. This ratio ensures an illumination level that allows the eye to shift from the task to the surrounding area and vice versa with a minimum amount of adaptation.

Some task lighting requires special consideration. For example, it is critical that lighting be excellent for activities that require precision such as surgery. The more time that is spent engaged in an activity, the more important it is to specify appropriate task lighting. Special considerations for quality task lighting are also necessary for individuals with sight deficiencies, including the elderly.

In planning task lighting, it is important to specify a lighting system that provides flexibility and control for the users of the space. Adjustable luminaries and dimmers can accomplish this objective. This customizes the lighting for the specific needs of a user at a particular time and can save energy by localizing the high-illumination levels where they are required. Often an illumination level for a space is specified for the entire area regardless of the specific needs of the users. This results in a waste of electricity for individuals who either do not need a high level of illumination or who are absent from the space. In a large, open, office space customized task lighting enables a user to have flexibility and control, providing the appropriate illumination level at the brightness required for the duration of an activity.

Planning quality task lighting requires a careful examination of potential problems and development of successful solutions. Task lighting can become a problem because the illumination levels needed for many activities can be very high. Consequently problems can occur with visual acuity and eye adaptation. An individual can have difficulty with visual acuity if the light source is creating glare, veiling reflections, or shadows. Glare and **veiling reflections** occur when the light source is reflected on the task. For example, computer monitors can reflect fixtures mounted on a ceiling, or light can cause glare on shiny surfaces such as glossy magazines. Often the solution to these problems is to change the direction of the light source or moving the task. Locating a light source to the sides of a task rather than in front of a task will generally eliminate reflected glare. (These directional effects of lighting are covered in detail in Chapter 6.)

Problems with eye adaptation occur if there is a severe contrast of illumination levels between the task and its surrounding area. It is especially difficult to have the proper illumination ratios in tasks that require high levels of illumination, such as using black thread to sew black fabric or reading very small type. Close work fatigues the eye by creating strain. Generally, the more light on the task, the less strain on the eye. To reduce strain on eyes, a designer should consider factors in addition to increasing the illumination level. One possibility would be to increase the contrast or size of a task. For example, extremes of black and white enable the greatest amount of visibility. This is the reason why most books are printed with black type on white paper. To improve visibility, a designer might also change the color of a work surface or change the position of a piece of furniture. Designers can use computer analysis tools to predict visibility patterns and illumination levels in an environment. (Computer software designed for this analysis are covered in Chapter 7.)

Veiling reflections
Reduction in light contrast on a task as a result of reflected images on a surface.

In planning task lighting, a designer must first identify the activities that occur in a space and then determine which characteristics of those tasks need to receive special lighting treatment. National codes and standards have been established for task illumination levels for commercial and residential spaces. Excellent sources for this information include the *National Handbook of the Illuminating Engineering Society of North America* (IESNA) and the *CIBSE Code for Interior Lighting* in the United Kingdom. The illuminance recommendations are averages, not minimum requirements. Therefore, it is important to avoid over lighting an area while providing adequate illumination for special populations, especially the aging eye. For example, higher illumination levels should be specified for long-term care facilities for the elderly.

Numerous worker-productivity studies have been conducted to determine appropriate levels of illumination and effective fixture design and placement for different jobs. Research results indicate that worker productivity in offices and factories improves with quality lighting. The age of a lamp and the amount of dirt accumulated affect illumination levels. Light output decreases with age and dust or dirt. (Detailed information regarding maintenance factors and productivity studies can be found in Chapters 12 and 13, respectively.)

In addition to illumination levels for a task, a designer must consider the design and placement of the luminaries. Luminaries for task lighting include portable fixtures; pendants, recessed, track, and structural lighting. Some office furniture has task lighting built into it. This lighting includes task-ambient sources whereby direct light is positioned for tasks and indirect light sources provide the general or ambient light surrounding the workstation. Task-ambient furniture systems can be an effective way to illuminate a large, open, office space that accommodates users with a variety of needs.

Task lighting can also be provided by daylight. Daylight is excellent for helping people to discern critical details and make color distinctions. The ability to distinguish details also enhances reading and writing. Therefore, daylight can be very effective in interiors such as schools, offices, and libraries. Supplemental electrical sources have to be planned, however, to meet the needs of the users on dark days and in the evenings.

Accent and Decorative Lighting

Accent lighting is another layer of illumination in a quality lighting environment. Some of the illumination from accent lighting can contribute to the interior's general lighting. The purpose of accent or *highlight lighting* is to bring attention to an object or element in a space. Accent lighting creates drama, variety, interest, and excitement in an interior. The form and style of accent lighting should be designed to contribute to the room's atmosphere and theme. Designers often study stage lighting and photography to learn special accent techniques (see Chapter 18).

In planning accent lighting, it is important for the designer to identify what should be highlighted and the characteristics of the surrounding areas. Designers use accent lighting to emphasize artwork, sculptures, water, fabrics, architectural details, textures, forms, and plants. The location and aiming angle must be positioned to avoid direct glare to the eyes of users. To avoid problems with viewing, the preferred angle to a wall is 30 degrees (see Figure 2.10). Exterior views, especially in the evening, can also be excellent focal points of an interior. Trees, shrubs, water, sculptures, and exterior architectural elements are excellent selections for accent lighting.

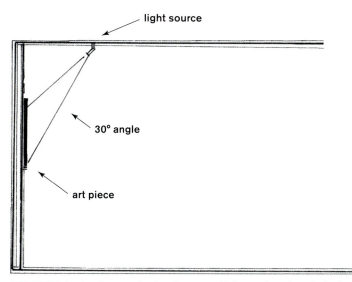

FIGURE 2.10 To accent artwork on a wall, the preferred angle to the wall is 30°.

Creating contrast and specifying the best angle to position a light are key to successful accent lighting. To attract the eye to an object or area requires contrast. In creating contrast, the characteristics of the surrounding area of the accented object are important. A white object surrounded by white walls will blend into the space (see Figure 2.11a). An illumination level that is the same for the surrounding area and the accent item will not effectively emphasize the item (see Figure 2.11b). Contrasts in illumination levels enhance the accent item and distinguishes it from the surrounding area (see Figure 2.11c).

FIGURE 2.11a
In creating contrast the characteristics of the surrounding area of the accented object are important. The white walls surrounding the white object on the pedestal affect the visibility of the sculpture.

FIGURE 2.11b
An illumination level that is the same for both the surrounding area and the accent item will not effectively emphasize merchandise. A lack of contrast in illumination levels also reduces an emphasis on the details of the clothing.

FIGURE 2.11c
Contrasts in illumination levels enhance the merchandise.

The drama and emphasis of extreme light and shadow is often illustrated in the *chiaroscuro* technique in paintings. This technique emphasizes patterns of light, shade, and shadows.

One approach to achieving contrast is to illuminate the object to be accented with a greater amount of light than its surrounding area. Since the eye is attracted to light, the users of the space will focus their attention on the areas of the room with the highest illumination levels. Generally, to achieve an illumination level that creates enough contrast to accent an object requires a minimum ratio of 5 to 1 between the accent and general lighting. Ratios lower than this will generally not provide enough contrast to be considered accent lighting. Extreme drama can be accomplished with a 10 to 1 ratio, but the ratio should not exceed 20 to 1. Differentials higher than this create a setting that seriously hinders the adaptation function of the eye. Specifying effective contrast ratios is difficult in spaces that have many accented areas or objects. For example, a retailer might want to emphasize several displays that are close to one another in the store. The close proximity of the displays may result in a setting that eliminates the contrast required to bring attention to the items (Figure 2.12). In addition to varying the illumination levels, a designer might have to contrast other

FIGURE 2.12
Several highlighted displays located next to each other can result in a lack of emphasis.

elements in the space such as employing complementary colors and varying textures, forms, shapes, and lines. Motion is also an excellent technique for attracting the eye, especially peripheral vision.

Direction and angle of a source are also key considerations to accent lighting. The perceived shapes, of three-dimensional objects can be affected if the direction and angle of light are not well planned (see Figure 2.13). Plant foliage can provide interesting patterns and shadows on walls and ceilings if a light source is placed close to a plant. In fact, revealing textures and form of an object often requires that the light source be close to the object (see Figure 2.14). This technique is referred to as **grazing**. In contrast, **backlighting** will create a silhouette of an object (Figure 2.15). A specific direction and angle of light can also create dramatic shadows that the designer wants to emphasize. Accent lighting is especially effective in modeling, which enhances the shape and form of three-dimensional objects.

Accent lighting allows a designer to be very creative in highlighting areas or objects. Frequently it can be more interesting and effective if a designer selects a specific point of emphasis on an accent piece. For example, instead of providing a uniform distribution of light to a paint-

Grazing
A lighting technique whereby the light source is placed close to a surface or object to highlight interesting textures and produce dramatic shadows.

Backlighting
Illumination that is directly behind an object. Also referred to as silhouetting.

FIGURE 2.13 The direction and angle of illumination can affect the perceived shapes of three-dimensional objects.

FIGURE 2.14 By positioning the light source close to an object, this grazing technique reveals textures and form.

FIGURE 2.15 Backlighting is used to create silhouettes of the objects on the top shelf.

ing or architectural detail, it might be far more dramatic to illuminate only portions of a painting or only one interesting detail of a column on a fireplace. Highlighting flower petals that fell from a bouquet sitting on a table rather than the entire arrangement is another creative approach to accent lighting. Spotlighting the specific element and having the appropriate contrast illuminating levels can focus the emphasis on the focal point. The best approach to accenting a sculpture or objet d'art is to have two light sources aimed at the piece from two different angles.

Shadows play an important role in accent lighting. A strong spotlight used in accent lighting can create some undesirable shadows on a surface. For example, a spotlight on a painting could create a shadow from the frame on the artwork. Thus, it is critical to position the spotlight at the proper mounting location and aiming angle. From a positive perspective, shadows can be planned to be the unique focal point of an area or object. This occurs with the shadows of foliage on a ceiling and on walls (see Figure 2.16). The shadow of a unique form could also be the accented element. Shadows of architectural details of an interior enhance the sculptural elements and three-dimensional aspect of a façade. The location and aiming angle are critical to ensuring that a

FIGURE 2.16   The proper location of a luminaire can create interesting shadows on walls and ceilings.

façade is viewed as having three dimensions rather than two dimensions. Depending upon the intensity of a light source, distance from the object, and the aiming angle, shadow lines can be hard or soft. From a design perspective a hard shadow line will project an image that is dramatic and harsh. A soft shadow line does not attract the eye easily and promotes a subdued theme.

Light fixtures used for accent lighting include **uplights, recessed spots, spotlight projectors** with optical control, and wall brackets. Depending upon their location in a space, luminaries for accent lighting can be a decorative element of an interior or hidden from view. Some furniture is designed with accent lighting hidden from direct view. Curio cabinets, breakfronts, and cabinets often have accent lighting to enhance crystal, china, and objets d'art. As with general lighting, it is often intriguing to hide the light source when specifying accent lighting. Viewing an object or area that is enhanced with illumination without seeing the source adds mystery and drama to a setting (see Figure 2.17). Since accent lighting is often a small, bright light

Uplight
Luminaire that directs the light up: generally a portable luminaire.

Recessed spots
Luminaires mounted in a ceiling or furniture piece; they have a lamp that distributes the light in a concentrated area.

Spotlight projector
A device that allows a designer to select a very precise area to be illuminated.

FIGURE 2.17 Viewing only the effects of light can add mystery and excitement to a room.

source, unexpected glare can create a safety concern. Through narrow slits or various small openings, daylight could be a bright source that accents an object or area in a space. The variability of daylight will affect the quality of the accent.

Decorative lighting is designed to be a focal point in a space. It can be a fixture that is designed to be an ornamental element of the interior, or it can be a specialty architectural lighting solution. Chandeliers, Tiffany glass shades, neon tubes, lasers, holograms, holiday lights, wall sconces, and some fiber optics are examples of decorative lighting. Daylight can be a source of decorative lighting when it illuminates a stained glass window. To appreciate the stained glass window in the evening, exterior lighting should be included in the lighting plan. Decorative lighting can also be an art form (see Chapter 16). Candles and flames in a fireplace are decorative sources that add warmth and enhance the appearance of people and objects in an environment. Whenever possible, candles should be considered an important element of the layered lighting in a space.

The purpose of a decorative fixture should remain ornamental. For example, most chandeliers are designed to be only decorative. However, quite frequently a chandelier in a dining room functions as the source for general, task, and decorative lighting. As a result the illumination level has to be very high to meet all three needs. The high illumination level could discourage people from viewing the chandelier, which negates the purpose of having it as a decorative fixture. This is especially problematic if the chandelier has exposed **flame-shaped lamps**. Decorative lighting serves an important role in reinforcing the theme and style of the space. These sources should supplement the lighting specified for general, task, and accent purposes.

Flame-shaped lamp
Decorative, small lamp that is in the shape of a flame. The bulb is clear or frosted glass.

SUMMARY

■ It is essential to distinguish between sunlight and daylight. Direct sunlight can produce glare, excessive heat, and fading of materials. Daylight is the term that describes the desirable natural light in a space.

- Advantages to integrating daylight into interiors include energy savings resulting from a reduction in electrical lights and passive solar energy penetration in the winter. Another advantage to daylight is the even distribution of light that appears to reveal the true colors of objects and surfaces. Daylight enhances visual acuity, thereby providing better light for reading and writing.

- Advantages to integrating daylight into interiors also include benefits associated with windows, such as providing a view and ventilation.

- Disadvantages associated with windows include glare, noise penetration, cleaning maintenance, lack of privacy, and heat gain in the summer.

- Designing buildings that maximize penetration of daylight begins with an understanding of solar geometry and the variability of sunlight.

- Factors that influence the level and quality of daylight entering a space include clouds, weather, atmospheric pollution, orientation, landscaping, and surrounding structures.

- Effective daylight integration requires an understanding of how the size, shape, and location of windows affect the quantity and quality of daylight in an interior.

- To estimate the quantity of daylight in a space, a designer can calculate the daylight factor (DF).

- Daylight integration and control can be applied to each category of lighting technique, including general, task, and accent.

- General or ambient lighting is a category of lighting technique designed to provide uniform lighting to a space.

- Task lighting is a direct form of lighting that enables users to see the critical details of an activity.

- The purpose of accent or highlight lighting is to bring attention to an object or element in a space. Creating contrast and determining the direction and angle of a source are key considerations in accent lighting.

- Decorative lighting is designed to be an ornamental element of an interior.

Key Terms

accent lighting	harvesting daylight
ambient lighting	high-hat luminaire
aperture	luminaire
backlighting	modeling
circadian rhythm	recessed spots
cornice lighting	solar geometry
cove lighting	spotlight projector
daylight (skylight)	sunlight
Daylight factor (DF)	task lighting
decorative lighting	uplight
downlight luminaire	veiling reflections
flame-shaped lamp	wall bracket lighting
general lighting	wallslot
grazing	

Exercises

1. Photograph a building at various times of the day and under several different weather conditions. Compose a reflective essay that describes how the appearance of the building changes according to the various conditions.

2. Purchase a clamp light fixture and a variety of lamps at a hardware store. At a minimum, select clear and frosted lamps that have the same wattage. Select a variety of three-dimensional objects that have various textures and forms. In a dark room illuminate the object from a variety of angles and distances. Record all angles and distances and how the differences effect the object and the shadows. Compose a reflective essay that describes how the appearance of the object and shadows changed according to the lamp, aiming angle, and distance. The clamp light will be used for future exercises in the text.

3. Select photographs of five residential interiors and five nonresidential interiors. Identify the electrical fixtures in the space, and deter-

mine which category (general, task, accent) of lighting, each fixture is being used for. If a fixture does not exist for a category of lighting, provide a suggestion for a fixture that would be effective for the specific lighting technique. The identification and analysis should be submitted in written form. Photographs must be included.

4. Design a decorative fixture for one of the following interiors:

    a. Waiting area of a pediatric ward of a hospital.

    b. Hotel lobby at Walt Disney World.

    c. Lobby of a performing arts center in London.

5. The purpose of this project is to develop an understanding of how to integrate daylight with general, task, and accent lighting. As a designer you have been commissioned to create a layered lighting plan for an elementary school in a warm climate and a discount retail store located in a cold climate. You are to submit to the clients a written document that may include sketches and photographs that includes the following information:

    a. Critical spaces for integrating daylight.

    b. Recommendations for windows and skylights.

    c. For each space in the interior, identify what the needs are for general, task, and accent lighting.

    d. Suggestions for fixtures for general, task, and accent lighting.

    e. Recommendations for locations of general, task, and accent lighting.

REFERENCES

Allphin, W. (1963). Sight lines to desk tasks in schools and offices. *Illuminating Engineering, 58(4)*, 244–249.

Ander, G. (1997). *Daylighting Performance & Design.* New York: John Wiley & Sons.

BSI (1992). *Code of Practice for Daylighting.* British Standard BS 8206 Part 2.

Benya, J., Heschong, L., McGowan, T., Miller, N., and Rubinstein, F. (2001). *Advanced Lighting Guidelines.* White Salmon, WA: New Buildings Institute.

Bierman, A., and Conway, K. (2000). Characterizing daylight photosensor systems performance to help overcome market barriers. *Journal of the Illuminating Engineering Society, 29(1)*, 101–115.

Bowers, B. (1998). *Lengthening the Day: A History of Lighting Technology.* Oxford: Oxford University Press.

CIBSE (1987). *Window Design.* CIBSE Applications Manual.

Coaton, J.R., and Marsden, A.M. (1997). *Lamps and lighting* (4th ed.). London: Arnold.

Davis, R.G. (1987). Closing the gap: Research, design, and the psychological aspects of lighting. *Lighting Design Applications, 17(5),* 14–15; 52.

Egan, M.D. (1983). *Concepts in Architectural Lighting.* New York: McGraw-Hill.

Eklund, N., Boyce, P., and Simpson, S. (2000). Lighting and sustained performance. *Journal of the Illuminating Engineering Society, 29(1),* 116.

Flynn, J.E., Segil, A.W., and Steffy, G.R. (1988). *Architectural Interior Systems: Lighting, Acoustics, Air Conditioning* (2nd ed.). New York: Van Nostrand Reinhold.

Flynn, J.E. and Spencer, T.J. (1977). The effects of light source color on user impression and satisfaction. *Journal of the Illuminating Engineering Society, (4),* 167–179.

General Electric (1989). *Lighting Application Bulletin.* Cleveland, OH: General Electric.

Gordan, G., and Nuckolls, J. L. (1995). *Interior Lighting for Designers.* New York: John Wiley & Sons.

Henderson, S.T. (1977). *Daylight and Its Spectrum* (2nd ed.). Bristol, England: Adam Hilger.

Heschong Mahone Group (HMG) (1999, August). *Skylighting and Retail Sales, and Daylighting in Schools.* For Pacific Gas & Electric. URL: http://www.pge.com.pec/daylight.

Heschong Mahone Group (HMG) (1997, May). *The Lighting Efficiency Technology Report, vol. I: California Lighting Baseline.* For the California Energy Commission.

Illuminating Engineering Society of North America (IESNA) (2000). *IESNA Lighting Handbook* (9th ed.). New York: Illuminating Engineering Society of North America.

International Dark-Sky Association (IDA) (1996). Information sheets 10 and 20. URL: http://www.ida.org.

Jennings, J.F., Rubinstein, R., and DiBartolomeo, D.R. (2000). Comparisons of control options in private offices in an advanced lighting controls test bed. *Journal of the Illuminating Engineering Society, 29(29),* 39–60.

Kaufman, J.E. (ed.) (1984). *IES Lighting Handbook Reference Volume 1984.* New York: Illuminating Engineering Society.

Lawrence Berkeley National Laboratory (1997). *Lighting Source Book.* Berkeley, CA: Lawrence Berkeley National Laboratory.

Lewis, A.L. (1998). Equating light sources for visual performance at low luminances. *Journal of the Illuminating Engineering Society, 27(1),* 80.

Lighting Design Lab (1998). *Daylight Models* (video). Seattle, WA: Lighting Design Lab.

Littlefair, P.J. (1996). *Designing with Innovative Daylighting.* London: CRC, Garston.

Littlefair, P.J. (1991). *Site Layout Planning for Daylight and Sunlight: A Guide to Good Practice.* BRE Report BR 209.

Maniccia, D., Rutledge, D., Rea, M., and Morrow, W. (1999). Occupant use of manual lighting control in private offices. *Journal of the Illuminating Engineering Society, 28(2),* 42–56.

Moore, F. (1985). *Concepts and Practice of Architectural Daylighting.* New York: Van Nostrand Reinhold.

Phillips, D. (2000). *Lighting Modern Buildings.* Oxford: Architectural Press.

Rea, M.S., and Ouellette, M.J. (1991). Relative visual performance: A basis for application. *Lighting Research Technology, 23(3),* 135–144.

Rea, M.S., Ouellette, M.J., and Kennedy, M.E. (1985). Lighting and task parameters affecting posture, performance, and subjective ratings. *Journal of Illuminating Engineering Society, 15(1),* 231–238.

Rowlands, E., Loe, D.L., McIntosh, R.55M., and Mansfield, K. P. (1985). Lighting adequacy and quality in office interiors by consideration of subjective assessment and physical measurement. *CIE Journal, 4(1),* 23–27.

U.K. Department of the Environment (1998, March). Desktop guide to daylighting for architects. *Good Practice Guide 245*. Harwell, Oxfordshire, England: ETSU.

Van den Beld, G.J., Begemann, S. H.A., and Tenner, A.D. (1997). Comparison of preferred lighting levels for two different lighting systems in north-oriented offices. *Light and Engineering, 5(3):*, 48–52.

Veitch, J., and Newsham, G. (2000). Exercised control, lighting choices, and energy use: An office simulation experiment. *Journal of Environmental Psychology, 20(3)*, 219–237.

Veitch, J., and Newsham, G. (1999, June). Preferred luminous conditions in open-plan offices: implications for lighting quality recommendations. *CIE Proceedings.* CIE Pub no. 133, vol. 1, part 2: 4–6.

Veitch, J., and Newsham, G. (1998). Lighting quality and energy-efficiency effects on task performance, mood, health, satisfaction, and comfort. *Journal of the Illuminating Engineering Society, 27(1)*, 107.

CHAPTER 3

Lighting Systems: Electrical Sources

OBJECTIVES

■ Identify and describe several characteristics of electrical light sources.

■ Identify the primary functional components of incandescent-filament, halogen, fluorescent, and high-intensity discharge lamps.

■ Understand the operating principles of incandescent-filament, halogen, fluorescent, and high-intensity discharge lamps.

■ Describe the various types of lamps that are available for incandescent-filament, halogen, fluorescent, and high-intensity discharge lamps.

■ Determine applications for incandescent-filament, halogen, fluorescent, and high-intensity discharge lamps.

■ Compare and contrast the advantages and disadvantages of incandescent-filament, halogen, fluorescent, and high-intensity discharge lamps.

INTEGRATING daylight with electrical lights is extensively examined in Chapter 2. This chapter covers characteristics of electrical sources that are utilized in interiors, including incandescent-filament, halogen (tungsten-halogen), fluorescent, and high-intensity discharge (HID). Electrical sources are used to complement daylight and to provide general, task, accent, and decorative lighting in an environment.

An electrical lighting system is composed of the electrical power, light source, luminaire, controls, maintenance, and service. All these elements affect the quantity and quality of illumination in an interior. In reviewing electrical sources, it is critical to remember that a total understanding of quality lighting systems cannot occur until all the elements have been studied. Upon completing Unit I of this book, the reader will be able to apply an understanding of quality lighting systems to the design applications explored in Unit II.

Characteristics of Electrical Light Sources

An understanding of electrical light sources begins with an examination of the general characteristics of lamps. Having a working knowledge of electrical light sources requires a review of a lamp's light output, efficacy, lamp life, color, maintenance factors, and cost. A lamp's **light output** is measured in lumens. A footcandle is the amount of light that falls on a surface in a one-foot radius from the source (see Figure 3.1). This measurement is a lamp's lumen per square foot. It is appropriate for designers to review the guidelines established by IESNA regarding the amount of light necessary to adequately perform a specific task. The **candlepower** measurement, a lamp's **candela** (**cd**), describes the intensity of a light source in a specific direction. **Watts** (**W**) is a measure of an electrical circuit's ability to do work, such as producing light and waste heat. Therefore, a 20-watt lamp consumes 20 watts of electricity.

The **lumens per watt** (**lpW**) consumed are used to determine the energy efficiency of a lamp. The term for this is **efficacy**. The more lumens produced by a lamp per watt, the more efficient the lamp is and the more energy is saved. Typical lamp efficacies are provided in Table 3.1. **Lamp life** is a calculation derived from a record of how long it takes for approximately 50 percent of 100 lamps to burn out.

Chromaticity and the color-rendering index are used to specify lamps and color. The **chromaticity** or the **color temperature** of a light source indicates the degree of red or blue of a light source. Chromatic-

---

Light output
The amount of illumination produced by a lamp; measured in lumens.

Candlepower
The measurement for the intensity of a light source in candelas.

Candela (cd)
The SI unit of measurement of luminous intensity. One candela represents the luminous intensity from a source focused in a specific direction on a solid angle called the steradian.

Watts (W)
A measure of an electrical circuit's ability to do work, such as producing light and waste heat.

Lumens per watt (lpW)
A rating that describes the amount of electricity consumed for a given amount of illumination.

Efficacy
A rating that is based upon the lumens per Watt consumed; this reflects the energy efficiency of a lamp.

Lamp life
The operational time of a lamp expressed in hours.

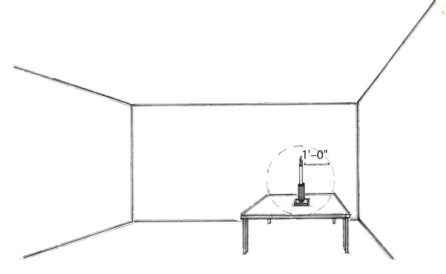

FIGURE 3.1 A footcandle is the amount of light that falls on a surface in a one-foot radius from the source.

ity of a light source is measured by kelvins (K). On the kelvin scale a warmer apparent color of a light source will have a lower number. For example, the warm color of light emitted from a candle is 2000K, and the color appearance of cool daylight is 5000K. A neutral color temperature is 3500K. Lamps that provide a warm and cool appearance are 3000K and 4100K, respectively. The **color-rendering index (CRI)**

TABLE 3.1
Typical Lamp Efficacies

Lamps	Efficacies
Incandescent	10–40 lpW
Halogen incandescent	20–45 lpW
Fluorescent	35–105 lpW
Mercury	50–60 lpW
Metal halide	60–120 lpW
High-pressure sodium	60–140 lpW

Adapted from: GE Lighting Lamp Products Catalog, 2004.

measures how good a light source makes objects appear. The index range is from 0–100. The higher the CRI number, the better the color rendering ability of the lamp. (Color is examined extensively in Chapter 5.)

Maintenance factors include replacement considerations based upon lamp life and reduced light output. Costs include the initial cost of the lamp, installation, energy requirements, and replacement considerations. The location of a lamp and the high cost of labor are factors to be considered when planning the replacement of lamps. (Chapter 12 includes an examination of maintenance considerations for lighting systems.)

A lamp's size, wattage, shape, lpW, candelas, life, color temperature, and CRI are provided in a lamp manufacturer's catalog. Figure 3.2 is a lamp manufacturer's chart for a halogen lamp. A designer should always refer to such charts when selecting and specifying lamps. For the most current information the designer should refer to the manufacturer's Web site. Figure 3.2 also explains how a designer uses the information in a specific application.

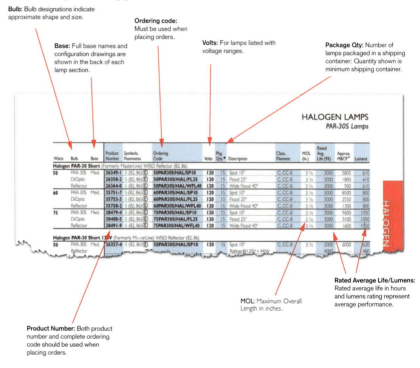

The $ symbol indicates lamps with high energy efficiency, which reduces electricity costs.

FIGURE 3.2 A lamp manufacturer's chart for halogen lamps.

Incandescent and Halogen Lamps

The incandescent lamp is the oldest electrical light source and provides the greatest amount of flexibility for designers. This kind of lamp can provide directional or nondirectional illumination. The variability of the lamp's size and shape allows it to be used in a wide range of luminaires. Other advantages include easy dimming, quick on, good performance with frequent starts, optical control, and low initial cost. The incandescent lamp provides excellent color rendition and chromaticity. The incandescent lamp is used for general, task, accent, and decorative applications. Disadvantages to the incandescent lamp include a low efficacy rating, generation of heat, and a relatively short life. For energy conservation purposes an interior designer should limit the use of incandescent lamps.

Incandescent Lamps

The history of lighting covered in Chapter 1 includes the origins of the incandescent lamp. Because of the simultaneous work conducted by Edison in the United States and Swan in England, 1879 is the year credited with the start of the lamp. Figure 3.3 illustrates a drawing of the basic components of an incandescent lamp. An electrical current heats the tungsten filament until **incandescence** is reached at which point an incandescent lamp is lit (Benya, Heschong, McGowan, Miller, and Rubinstein, 2001; Coaton and Marsden, 1997; IESNA, 2000). Tungsten is usually the conductive material used for this purpose because it has a high melting point and a low evaporation point. The tungsten filament is made in three basic shapes and in a variety of widths and lengths. Shapes of the filament include straight, coil, and coiled coil. The longest filaments will be coiled. The wider and longer the filament, the greater the amount of illumination that will be emitted from the lamp. Eventually the heat causes the filament to become so thin that it breaks, and the lamp is no longer functional. A three-way lamp (50, 100, 150 watts) has two filaments. One filament will accommodate the lowest wattage (50), and the second filament produces the next highest wattage (100). The two filaments operating together produce the highest illumination wattage level (150).

Incandescence
Light is produced by having an electric current heat the tungsten filament of an incandescent lamp.

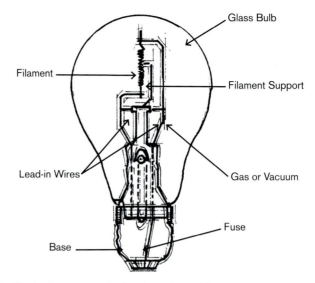

Glass Bulb

Filament

Filament Support

Lead-in Wires

Gas or Vacuum

Fuse

Base

FIGURE 3.3 The basic components of an incandescent lamp.

Heating the tungsten filament causes fragments of tungsten to be deposited on the glass of the bulb. Eventually the tungsten accumulation will cause the bulb to burn out. Inert gases have been added to bulbs to reduce the oxidization of the tungsten filament. A standard incandescent lamp has argon with some nitrogen to prevent arcing. Adding krypton is expensive, but it reduces the wattage per lumen rating and extends the life of an incandescent lamp. Halogen, either iodine or bromine gas, improves the performance of an incandescent lamp by redistributing the oxidizing tungsten on the filament rather than allowing it to accumulate on the glass (Benya, Heschong, McGowan, Miller, and Rubinstein, 2001; Coaton and Marsden, 1997; IESNA, 2000). These halogen (tungsten-halogen) lamps are available in line (120 volts) and low (generally 12 volts) voltage. Low-voltage lamps can produce more light output per watt.

The efficacy of the incandescent lamp is affected by the amount of heat produced by the lamp. Generally only 10–15 percent of the energy consumed to illuminate an incandescent lamp produces light. While 85–90 percent of the energy consumed produces heat. This can be observed by someone feeling the heat produced by an incandescent lamp after it has been on for a period of time. Dimming will reduce the amount of light and heat generated by the lamp. Heat generated from the lamps not only affects the life of a lamp, but it can damage artwork, fabrics, and other precious materials. In commercial environments the heat can seriously affect the loads on air-conditioning systems. The operating volts of a system will also affect the life of an incandescent lamp. For example, if a 120-volt lamp is operated at 125 volts, the lamp life will be shortened by 40 percent. In contrast a lower voltage will increase the life of an incandescent lamp. Incandescent lamps are designed to operate in either a horizontal or a vertical position. Changing the specified position will affect the life of the lamp.

Incandescent lamps are available in a variety of sizes, wattages, shapes, and colors. Sizes of incandescent lamps range from very small holiday lights to extremely large exterior search lamps. A variety of sizes corresponds to a wide range of wattages that is available. A small, night-light lamp is generally 4 watts, and large theater lamps can be as high as 10,000 watts. Incandescent lamps have been manufactured in a variety of shapes; however, there are standard shapes that are used throughout the industry (see Appendix). Codes developed by the American National Standards Institute (ANSI) include a letter that designates the shape of the lamp followed by a number that describes the diameter of the lamp in ⅛ inches. For example, in reviewing a lamp manufacturer's catalog, a designer will find an A19 listed in the incandescent lamp section. The A is the code for an "arbitrary" shape, and the lamp is 2⅜ (¹⁹⁄₈) inches wide at its widest point.

The bulbs of incandescent lamps are blown-soda lime (soft) glass and are available in clear, frosted, soft-white, crown-silvered, and colors; they are also available with protective coatings. Clear lamps can produce glare and harsh shadows. Frosted lamps are made by etching an acid on the glass. Soft-white lamps are coated with silica to produce a milky white color. Frosted and soft-white lamps soften and diffuse the illumination. Crown-silvered lamps have a coating that covers the top half of the bulb. This coating directs all the light in one direction. Thus designers use this lamp when they want all the lumens to illuminate a specific area and the luminaire does not have a reflector. Bulbs of incandescent lamps can be coated with any color of the rainbow; however, the most common colors are red, blue, yellow, and green. The base of the incandescent lamp is usually made from aluminum or brass and is available in a variety of sizes and shapes (see Appendix). For special purposes lamps are available with a protective coating applied to the bulb. This coating holds the glass if the bulb breaks. These are especially useful in food service areas and luminaires placed in spaces frequented by children. A rough-service incandescent lamp is used for a unit that has a great deal of vibration, such as a garage door opener.

To improve the efficacy and directional qualities of the incandescent lamp, engineers developed the reflector (R) lamp. The cone shape of the lamp and the vaporized silver or aluminum coating create a complete optical control system. The R lamp replaced the standard incandescent lamp in tracks, recessed downlights, and accent luminaires. However, guidelines developed by the U.S. Energy Policy Act (EPACT) in 1992 imposed limitations on lamp energy consumption. To comply with the standards, some of the incandescent R and PAR (parabolic aluminized reflector) lamps are no longer manufactured. This includes the incandescent R30, R40, and PAR38 lamps. Frequently, the incandescent R lamp is replaced by a halogen PAR lamp. Energy policies and their implications to designers are covered in Chapter 12. The reflector BR shape was designed to provide an even distribution beam of light.

The PAR lamp has a borosilicate, heat-resistant, pressed prismatic glass that enables the lamp to be used outdoors. The prismatic glass produces exceptional optical control. The cool-beam PAR lamp was designed to reduce the amount of heat distributed at the front of the lamp. Cool-beam PAR lamps are often used in applications that can be adversely affected by heat, such as illuminating a salad bar.

Lamps with optical control systems are available in a variety of beam spreads ranging from **"spot"** (**SP**) to **"flood"** (**FL**). Codes for descriptors of incandescent lamps are shown in Table 3.2. Lamps that are designed with a spot beam provide a very focused area of light. The size of the area illuminated is dependent upon the type of spot utilized. The traditional spot will illuminate a small area. An area will become more focused by using a narrow spot (NSP) or a very narrow spot (VNSP). Some lamp manufacturers add a specific degree of beam to the code. For example, a SP10 represents a spot lamp with a 10-degree

Spot (SP)
A narrow beam spread.

Flood (FL)
A wide beam spread.

TABLE 3.2

Selected Codes for Descriptors of Lamps

Lamp Code	Description
A/*	Arbitrary
AR/	Aluminum Reflector
B/	Flame (smooth)
C/	Cone Shape
CA/	Candle
CMH/	Ceramic Metal Halide
ED/	Ellipsoidal Dimpled
F/	Flame (irregular)
**/FL	Flood
G/	Globe shape
GT/	Globe-Tubular
/H	Halogen
/HIR	Halogen Infrared Reflecting
/HO	High Output
MR/	Multifaceted Mirror Reflector
/MWFL	Medium Wide Flood
P/	Pear shape
PAR/	Parabolic Aluminized Reflector
PS/	Pear-Straight neck
R/	Reflector
/SP	Spot
S/	Straight side
T/	Tubular
TB/	Teflon Bulb
/VHO	Very High Output
/VWFL	Very Wide Flood
/WFL	Wide Flood

*Letters before / represent a lamp shape
**Letters after / represent a descriptor of a lamp

beam spread. Flood lamps are designed to illuminate a large area. A traditional flood illuminates the smallest area. A wide flood (WFL), a medium wide flood (MWFL), and a very wide flood (VWFL) lamp illuminate larger areas. Figure 3.4 illustrates the candela distribution from a light source.

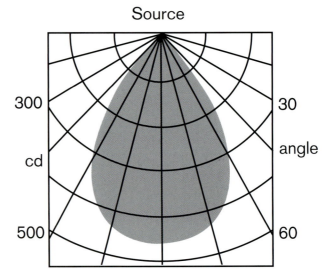

FIGURE 3.4 Candela distribution from a light source.

Halogen Lamps

As a member of the incandescent family, the halogen lamp has the same positive qualities as incandescent lamps; however, the **halogen regenerative cycle** produces a lamp that is much improved by having the evaporated tungsten redeposit on the filament. The halogen gas and the compact size of the tube cause tungsten to be reapplied to the filament. This halogen regenerative cycle significantly reduces the amount of black sediment that accumulates on the incandescent filament. As a result its lamp life is longer than the incandescent lamp, and it is approximately 20–30 percent more efficient. The halogen lamp will emit more luminance using the same amount of electricity. Lumen maintenance is also improved because of the reduction or elimination of the bulb blackening.

Creating the halogen regenerative cycle requires a very high temperature. Thus, the halogen lamp has a hot wire in a small space. Accommodating the gas pressures and enclosing the hot filament requires a heat-resistant glass, which is usually quartz. For fire safety and in case of breakage, the halogen lamp must have a plastic shield or protective glass. Some lamps are manufactured with a shield, which is required on all luminaires that are designed for halogen lamps. The halogen

PAR lamp has a shield built into the lamp. Shields are useful for avoiding the bright light that is generated from the intense heat and the ultraviolet rays that can penetrate quartz glass. This intense heat also produces a whiter light than the standard incandescent lamp. For luminaires that are using halogen and are dimmed for most of their operating time, it is necessary to periodically illuminate the lamps at full power in order to activate the halogen regenerative cycle.

The halogen lamp produces a very focused, bright, white light to far distances. The lamp is compact and has a long life. Compared to the incandescent lamp, the halogen lamp has a higher color temperature and efficacy rating. For these reasons the halogen lamp is used frequently to illuminate artwork, jewelry, and displays.

The halogen lamp is available in the T shape (single- and double-ended), which is often used in display cases, and a modified shape (TB/H/19), which is similar to the A-shaped incandescent lamp. The reflector shapes include the multifaceted reflector (MR), aluminum reflector (AR), and PAR lamps. The MR lamp has a very small halogen tube that is surrounded by multiple faceted mirror surfaces. Because of the superior optical control and small size (MR 16, MR11, and MR8) of the low-voltage MR lamp, it is an excellent choice for accent lighting. The AR lamp also has a small halogen tube and reflector surfaces. Some AR lamps have a cap over the filament that helps to deflect glare. The optical control systems in the AR and PAR lamps prevent spill light and can provide precise spotlighting from long distances. The halogen PAR lamp has replaced the incandescent PAR lamp and is most effective for accent lighting and general illumination in large areas, such as lobbies.

To increase the efficacy of the halogen lamp, the halogen infrared reflecting (HIR) was developed. With a coating on the glass this lamp converts the infrared rays into visible light that results in an improvement in the lpW rating. To improve quality and the quantity of light, General Electric recently announced a new halogen lamp that adds a silver coating to the IR film. Compared to the HIR PAR38, the additional silver coating on the "Optimum" PAR38 results in a lamp that is more efficient and has a longer life. There is also a slight increase in energy savings.

An increase in the size of the filament wire of the incandescent lamp created low-voltage lamps. Halogen and HIR lamps are available for line voltage and low-voltage systems. Line voltage in the United States is between 110 and 220 volts. A low-voltage application is between 6 and 75 volts. For a low-voltage application a transformer is most often used to step down the electrical current. For luminaires with multiple fixtures, it is important to not exceed the maximum wattage permitted by a transformer. To accommodate high wattages, luminaires may require more than one transformer. The low-voltage halogen lamp has excellent qualities including precise beam control, good resistance to vibration, high efficacy, high lumen output, and an extremely compact size. For more information regarding the principles of electricity, refer to Chapter 8.

Fluorescent Lamps

The fluorescent lamp is one of the discharge lamps. Discharge lamps do not have the filaments that exist in incandescent lamps and operate on low or high pressure. Discharge lamps are made from glass, use mercury or sodium, and require a ballast to start the lamp and control the electrical current. The majority of these lamps have electrodes and maintain a fairly consistent color.

Characteristics of Fluorescent Lamps

Fluorescent lamps were developed in 1938 and were used extensively after World War II in commercial and industrial settings. By the 1970s fluorescents were used to produce approximately 80 percent of the world's illumination needs. Today, fluorescent lamps are used extensively because they are energy-efficient, have a high lumen output, have a long life, radiate less heat than incandescent lamps, have a moderate initial cost and low operating cost, and have a variety of color options. Fluorescent lamps use up to 80 percent less energy and can last up to 18 times longer than incandescent lamps. Some fluorescent lamps are rated to last up to 20,000 hours. To accommodate various luminaires and structural installations, fluorescent lamps are available in a variety of shapes, sizes, and wattages. Fluorescent lamps produce a diffused light that is often effective for general illumination and numerous task applications.

As shown in Figure 3.5 the fluorescent lamp operates by having an electrical current pass through hot tungsten cathodes at either end of a long tubular shape (Benya, Heschong, McGowan, Miller, and Rubinstein, 2001; Coaton and Marsden, 1997; IESNA, 2000). This shape is necessary in order for the electrical discharge to occur. The glass tube is filled with low-pressure mercury vapor gas and other inert gases including argon, neon, and krypton. The cathodes emit electrons that excite the mercury gas. The vaporized mercury produces radiant energy that is primarily invisible ultraviolet rays. The phosphorous coating on the inside of the glass tube reradiates the ultraviolet rays into the visible spectrum. As visible light is produced, the phosphor coating fluoresces. Since this glow occurs at a very low temperature, fluorescent lamps require very little electricity. The phosphorous coating determines the color of the light produced. Initial fluorescent lamps were manufactured with a halophosphate that limited the range of colors. Most of these lamps produced the very cool light that is even now often associated with fluorescent lamps. Cool white and warm white lamps are produced by adding a single coating of halophosphate.

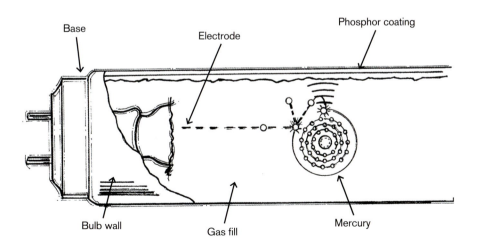

FIGURE 3.5 A fluorescent lamp operates by having an electrical current pass through hot tungsten cathodes at either end of a long, tubular shape.

The development of triphosphors made from rare-earth phosphors improved the color properties and efficacy ratings of fluorescent lamps. Lamps can be coated with only triphosphors, or triphosphors can be applied over a layer of halophosphate. Triphosphors are applied in a thin or thick coat. The thicker coat produces a better color. The RE-70 fluorescent lamp has a thin coat of conventional phosphors and triphosphors. RE is the nomenclature for "rare earth," and the 7 represents the CRI range between 70 and 79. The RE-80 has a thick coat of triphosphors that results in a CRI range between 80 and 89. There is also a RE-90 fluorescent lamp that has an excellent CRI rating in the 90s. Some nomenclatures include the temperature in kelvins. For example, for a RE-730 the 7 represents the CRI range between 70 and 79 and the 30 is the temperature of 3000–3099 kelvins. These nomenclatures help a designer to know immediately the color properties of a fluorescent lamp (see Chapter 5 for more color temperature information).

Fluorescent lamps can operate only in a system that includes a ballast. The ballast starts the lamp and then regulates the flow of electrical current to it. The operating life of a ballast is approximately three times that of a fluorescent lamp. Ballasts are available in magnetic and electronic versions. The electronic ballast is generally preferred because it is more energy-efficient, it is quieter, and it weighs less than the magnetic ballast. However, the initial cost of electronic ballasts is higher than the cost of magnetic ballasts.

Fluorescent lamps are available in three lamp-ballast circuits, including preheat, instant start, and rapid start. The preheat system operates by heating the cathodes electrically at the start of the illumination and is used for lower-wattage lamps. To start the luminaire, the button must be held down for a short period of time. The instant start lamp functions without a starter and has a high open-circuit voltage that slightly reduces the life of the lamp. The rapid start operates by continuously heating the cathodes and is the most common system used today. The rapid start can illuminate lamps at high wattages and has a longer life than the other two lamp-ballast circuits. Dimming can be done only with a rapid start system

Fluorescent lamps are available in a variety of sizes, shapes, and wattages, but the most common lamps are the straight tubes—T12,

T8, and T5 (see Appendix). For energy conservation purposes, the T12 should no longer be specified. These designations are derived from the industry's nomenclature for fluorescent lamps. For example, a F40T8/835 is the nomenclature for a fluorescent (F) lamp, with 40 watts (40), a tubular shape (T) that is ⅝ inches in diameter (8) with a CRI rating in the 80s (8) and with a chromaticity of 3500K (35). Some of the nomenclature can vary among lamp manufacturers. A designer must refer to the manufacturer's key to ascertain the nomenclature for that company. The primary shapes of fluorescent lamps are the straight tubular, U shape, and circle. Bending a straight tube makes the U shape and the circle. To comply with the 1992 U.S. Energy Policy Act (EPACT), standard 40-watt fluorescent lamps are no longer produced.

Advancements in Fluorescent Lamps

For many years the T12 was the fluorescent lamp most frequently specified by designers and architects. The high cost of the desirable triphosphors coatings led to the development of lamps in smaller diameters. The T8 has become the most successful because of its improved efficiency, enhanced color, and small 1-inch diameter. In addition, the lamps are physically interchangeable with the popular T12 lamps. However, the T8 and T12 use different ballasts. The T8's lpW is approximately 25 percent better than the T12's. As the T8 lamp becomes increasingly popular, it will eventually eliminate T12 lamps. The smaller T5 lamp is only slightly more efficient than the T8 and poses retrofit problems. The T5 lamp is available only in metric sizes and its mini-bipin bases can be installed only in luminaires that are designed for the lamp. Because of improvements in the operating characteristics and cost, the very small ¼-inch (6 mm) diameter T2 lamp is starting to become more popular. A note of caution: the electrodes are close to the surface of fluorescent lamps with small diameters; as a result the lamp at the ends can be hot to the touch. In addition, the small diameter can appear to be a bright source of light.

HO and VHO indicate that the lamp produces a high output and very high output of illumination, respectively. The high output from these lamps indicates that a high level of illumination is emitted relative to the length of the lamp. This can result in glare. In addition, because of the high amount of electricity required to operate HO and VHO lamps, they are generally considered to be a rather expensive fluorescent lamp.

There are disadvantages to fluorescent lamps: they need a ballast; they flicker; they are intended for indoor use only; they consume time before reaching the maximum lumen output; they are sensitive to ambient temperatures; and dimming is difficult and expensive. Fluorescent lamps have shape and size limitations resulting from the operating requirements of the lamp and the need for a ballast. Designers must be cautioned about a mismatch that can occur with lamps and ballasts. Moreover, variations between lamp manufacturers result in lamps and ballasts that may not be interchangeable. Continuously turning a fixture on and off is detrimental to the life and performance of the lamp. The diffused light quality associated with the fluorescent lamp eliminates shadows and highlighting. In settings that use only fluorescent lamps, the environment can appear to be very monotonous.

As an energy efficient alternative to the incandescent carbon-filament lamp, the compact fluorescent lamp (CFL) or the energy saving light bulb has become a very popular choice. One or two of the linear fluorescent tubes is folded to create the CFL. Some of the CFLs have a screw base that replicates the base of an incandescent lamp. CFLs are available in twin, triple, and quadruple tubes. To maximize the light output and reduce the size of the lamp, manufacturers have developed the spiral-shaped CFL. The ballast for the lamp is either a separate control gear (see Figure 3.6a) or is built into the unit (see Figure 3.6b). These lamps produce a high lumen output and can have up to 75 percent energy savings compared to the incandescent lamp. Some local building codes require the commercial use of CFLs because of the energy savings factor. Some CFLs are not designed to be dimmed; thus they should never be used in a luminaire that has a dimming control. Some CFLs have almagen added to the lamp, which improves the performance of the lamp and allows the lamp to be used in a variety of temperatures. There are fluorescent lamps that are considered in the "special" category. These are discussed in Chapter 4.

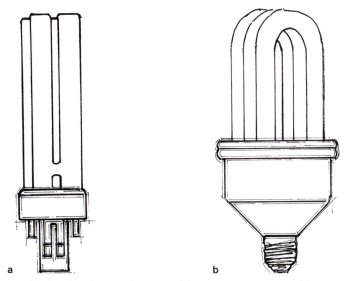

FIGURE 3.6 A ballast for a lamp can be either a (a) separate control gear or (b) built into the unit.

High-intensity Discharge Lamps

The three basic types of high-intensity discharge (HID) lamps are mercury (MV), metal halide (MH), and high-pressure sodium (HPS) (see Figure 3.7a–c). The technology for MV lamps started in 1901; how-

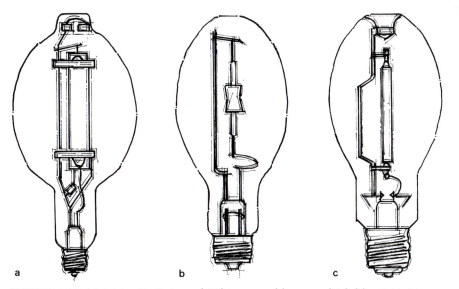

FIGURE 3.7 High-intensity discharge (HID) lamps are (a) mercury (MV), (b) metal halide (MH), and (c) high-pressure sodium (HPS).

ever, these lamps were not utilized on a regular basis until the 1930s. The primary use of MV lamps has been for street lighting. The development of MH and HPS lamps started in the 1960s. The performance of MH and HPS lamps has far exceeded MV lamps. As a result MV lamps are becoming extinct. For this reason this textbook focuses primarily on MH and HPS lamps.

Characteristics of HID Lamps

HID lamps operate in a manner that is fairly similar to the fluorescent lamp. As with a fluorescent lamp, illumination from HID lamps begins with an arc between 2 electrodes, operate in a gas-filled cylindrical tube, require ballasts, and create radiant energy from gases and metal vapors. HID lamps do not use phosphors for the purpose of generating light in the visible range (Benya, Heschong, McGowan, Miller, and Rubinstein, 2001; Coaton and Marsden, 1997; IESNA, 2000). The names of the HID lamps indicate the primary gas that is used. The primary gas for MV lamps is mercury, HPS lamps utilize sodium, and MH lamps use chemical compounds of metal halides and possibly metallic vapors such as mercury (Benya, Heschong, McGowan, Miller, and Rubinstein, 2001; Coaton and Marsden, 1997; IESNA, 2000). Mercury gas produces a greenish-blue color, and sodium emits a golden-orange glow. The gases and compounds used in MH lamps produce a color that is closest to true white. HID lamps operate under high-pressure, and the electrodes are close together. One electrode serves as the starting unit for MV and MH lamps. HPS lamps do not have starting electrodes. The electrical arc discharge that occurs in the arc tube of HID lamps creates such a high temperature that a great amount of visible radiant energy is generated. The efficacy ratings are best at the higher wattages.

HID ballasts are made for specific lamp types and wattages. Thus, it is not possible to interchange different lamps or wattages. Electronic ballasts are the best choice for HID lamps because they are more efficient than magnetic ballasts and can best control voltages. Precise control of voltage results in longer life and a more consistent color over the life of the lamp. To dim HID lamps requires a ballast designed for dimming. Dimming does affect the color rendition and efficacy of HID lamps. Most HID lamps are enclosed in a glass bulb, but some are available with no outer jacket. To protect occupants against lamp ruptures or high exposure from ultraviolet rays, lamps without an outer jacket must be installed in lamps that have a cover glass.

The primary shapes for HID lamps include the A, B, BT, E, ED, T, and the directional PAR and R (see Appendix). The nomenclature for HID lamps start with a letter that represents the type of HID. The letter for MV is "H," which stands for the Greek word for mercury. The letter for MH and HPS are "M" and "S" or "LU," respectively. Following the letter for the lamp is generally the wattage. Manufacturers adopt variations of the nomenclature that may signify any special characteristics of the lamp. MH lamps are specifically designed to operate in a universal, vertical, or horizontal position. The universal position MH lamp can operate in a vertical or horizontal position. Lamp performance will be adversely affected if a lamp is installed in a different position from that which is specified. HPS lamps can operate in a horizontal or vertical position.

HID lamps have been excellent choices for applications that require high efficacy, long life, high lpW performance, operation in a wide range of ambient temperatures, and positive long-term economics. MH lamps have a high efficacy, good color rendition, long life, good lumen maintenance, and a wide spectrum of colors and wattages. MH lamps are available in the shape of the arbitrary incandescent lamp and have warm and cool color renditions. Because of its excellent optical control and ability to be operated in a variety of temperatures, the MH lamp has many indoor and outdoor applications. MH lamps can be used for general, task, accent, and decorative lighting.

The HPS lamp has an extremely high lpW rating, exceptionally long service, and excellent long-term economics. HPS lamps can last 40,000 hours, but over-wattage can shorten the life of the lamps. Lamp life ratings are based upon ten hours per start. Compared to other HID lamps, MH lamps are the most adversely affected by frequent starts. As with the fluorescent lamp, HID lamps are designed to operate over long periods of time. Seasoning, an initial operating time for new lamps, is required to reach full operating capacity.

Low-pressure sodium (LPS) lamp
An electrical-discharge light source that uses sodium vapor at partial pressure.

An older lamp that also utilizes sodium gas is the **low-pressure sodium (LPS)**. LPS lamps are not technically considered a discharge lamp and are not often specified by designers. The lamp is very energy-efficient, but it has a monochromatic yellowish-brown color that greatly distorts surrounding colors. It is used only outdoors in applications where good color rendition is not necessary such as in tunnels or near telescopes.

Disadvantages and Advancements in HID Lamps

Disadvantages of HID lamps include the required start-up time, color shifts during the life of the lamp, variations in color between the same lamps, strict ballast requirements, and the fact that they are not easily dimmable. Start-up times for HID lamps are between two and ten minutes. The **restrike** time can be several minutes because the lamp must cool down before starting again. This is especially problematic in applications where safety and security are critical issues. Good restrike time is necessary with a power interruption or insufficient voltage in the system. Some instant restrike HID lamps are available but only at high wattages, and they must be used with special luminaires and ballasts. In applications that require illumination at all times, a designer should specify an additional luminaire that would illuminate the space during the restrike time or specify an HID lamp that has an auxiliary unit built into it that lights up when the lamp shuts down. Because of the warm-up and restrike characteristics of HID lamps, it is not advisable to use these lamps on units that have motion detectors.

Restrike
Result of a lamp having to start again because of a power interruption or reduction in voltage.

To improve consistency between lamps and over the life of HID lamps, **relamping** operations should include changing all the lamps at the same time. This should occur even if some of the lamps are still operating. Relamping is also an important maintenance consideration that is discussed in Chapter 12. Tremendous color rendition improvements have been made with MH lamps; however, HPS renders colors poorly. The orange and gold color of HPS lamps has led to their use

Relamping
Replacing lamps that have burned out or are operating at less than an acceptable performance level.

outdoors or in warehouse applications where color rendition is not necessary. HPS lamps will look the best when they are used on buildings that have a material color toward the warm spectrum such as red brick.

The technology of MH and HPS lamps is continually improving. The compact MH lamp is available in lower wattages, making the lamp an ideal solution for display and track systems. The "Pulse Start" and the "Ceramic" MH lamps (CMH) have improved the standard MH lamp. These lamps have an external high-voltage circuit, thus eliminating the need for a starting electrode. To withstand high temperatures and corrosive vapors, the tube of the CMH lamp is made from polycrystalline alumina rather than quartz. The newest CMH lamps have improved efficacy, lumen maintenance, color rendition, and lamp life. The CMH lamp has the most superior performance characteristics, including better color consistency over the life of the lamp. CMH lamps are available in CRI ratings 80-94 and 3000K and 4200K. The CMH lamp is still not available with an instant-on function. The new 20-watt CMH PAR lamp is designed for accent lighting applications. The color rendering properties of HPS lamps have been improved by the development of the "improved color" and "white" HPS lamps. However, efficacy is reduced with these new lamps.

Comparative Performance Evaluation

Quality lighting environments require the selection of the best lamp for the purpose of the space, users, economics, and maintenance. To assist in an overall understanding of the most common lamps, Table 3.3 illustrates the characteristics of incandescent, fluorescent, metal halide, and high-pressure sodium lamps. The table includes wattage, life hours, lumens (initial and mean), CRI rating, color temperature in kelvins, and beam spread if applicable. Lamp life for fluorescent and HID lamps is based upon three and ten hours of burning per start, respectively.

TABLE 3.3

Characteristics of Incandescent, Fluorescent, Metal Halide, and High-pressure Sodium Lamps

Lamps	Rated Watts	Life Hours	Light Output (lumens) (initial/mean)	CRI	CCT (K)	Beam Angle
Incandescent						
A19–Soft White	40	1,000	490/NA	97–100	2500–2800	N/A
A19–Standard	40	1,000	505/NA	97–100	2500–2800	N/A
A19–Inside frost	50	1,000	490/NA	97–100	2500–2800	N/A
Halogen/HIR						
TB19 Frost	50	2,000	710/NA	97–100	2800	N/A
MR11	20	3,500	N/A	97–100	2900	SP15/NFL30
MR16	20	5,000	N/A	97–100	2900	NSP/15/FL40
PAR20/H	50	2,500	570/NA	97–100	2800	SP10/FL25
PAR30/H	50	3,000	630/NA	97–100	2800	SP10/FL25
PAR30/HIR	50	4,000	825/NA	97–100	2810	SP9/FL25
PAR38/H	50	2,000	600/NA	97–100	2750	SP10/FL25
PAR38/HIR	50	3,000	800/NA	97–100	2810	SP9/FL25
Fluorescent						
T5/830	49	20,000	4900/4606	85	3000	N/A
T5/841	49	20,000	4900/4606	85	4100	N/A
T8/730 U-shaped	32	20,000	2700/2565	78	3000	N/A
48"T8/730	32	20,000	2800/2660	78	3000	N/A
48"T8/830	32	20,000	2950/2800	86	3000	N/A
48"T8/741	32	20,000	2800/2660	78	4100	N/A
48"T8/841	32	20,000	2950/2800	86	4100	N/A
CFL–SPIRAL	20	8,000	1200/965	82	2700	N/A
CFL–BIAX	20	15,000	1200/960	82	2700	N/A
Metal Halide PAR38	70	12,000	5500/3500	70	3200	N/A
CMH PAR38	70	10,000	4800/NA	82	3000	SP15/FL25
Metal Halide PAR 38	100	15,000	9000/6200	70	3200	N/A
CMH PAR38	100	10,000	6500/NA	81	3000	SP15/FL25
High-pressure Sodium						
HPS	70	24,000+	6400/5450	22	1900	N/A
HPS DELUXE	70	10,000	3800/3040	65	2200	N/A

SUMMARY

- An understanding of electrical light sources and their advantages and disadvantages requires a review of a lamp's light output, efficacy, lamp life, color, maintenance factors, and cost.

- An incandescent lamp operates by having an electrical current heat the tungsten filament until incandescence is reached. A standard incandescent lamp uses argon with some nitrogen to prevent arcing.

- Halogen, either iodine or bromine gas, improves the performance of an incandescent lamp by redistributing the oxidizing tungsten on the filament rather allowing it to accumulate on the glass. These lamps are halogen and are available in line and low voltage.

- To improve the efficacy and directional qualities of the incandescent lamp, engineers developed the reflector (R) lamp. Improvements with the design of the reflector lamp evolved to the multifaceted reflector (MR), aluminum reflector (AR), and parabolic aluminized reflector (PAR) lamps.

- The fluorescent lamp is a discharge lamp. Discharge lamps do not have the filaments that exist in incandescent lamps and operate on low or high-pressure. Discharge lamps are made from glass, use mercury or sodium, and require a ballast to start the lamp and control the electrical current.

- Fluorescent lamps are available in three lamp-ballast circuits including preheat, instant start, and rapid start. Fluorescent lamps are available in a variety of sizes, shapes, and wattages, but the most common lamps are the straight tubes of the T12, T8, and T5.

- Compact fluorescent lamps (CFL) produce a high lumen output and can achieve up to 75 percent energy savings compared to the incandescent lamp.

- The three basic types of high-intensity discharge (HID) lamps are mercury vapor (MV), metal halide (MH), and high-pressure sodium (HPS)

- HID lamps have been excellent choices for applications that require high efficacy, long life, high lpW performance, operation in a wide range of ambient temperatures, and positive long-term economics.

■ HID lamps operate in a manner that is fairly similar to the fluorescent lamp. As with a fluorescent lamp, illumination from HID lamps begins with an arc between two electrodes. They operate in a gas-filled cylindrical tube, require ballasts, and create radiant energy from gases and metal vapors.

Key Terms

candela (cd)	lamp life
candlepower	light output
chromaticity	low-pressure sodium (LPS)
color rendering index (CRI)	lamps
color temperature	lumens per watt (lpW)
efficacy	relamping
flood (FL)	restrike
halogen regenerative cycle	spot (SP)
incandescence	watts (W)

Exercises

1. Review the HID and fluorescent lamp charts published by a lamp manufacturer. Write a summary report of the type of information that is available about each lamp. Be sure to include information that is only provided for specific lamps.

2. Select two types of lamps from the following categories: incandescent, fluorescent, and HID. Locate the lamps in the catalogs of three different lamp manufacturers. In a summary essay compare and contrast the performance of the lamps.

3. Write a summary paper that describes the operating functions and materials of incandescent, fluorescent, metal halide, and high-pressure sodium lamps.

4. In an essay provide examples of how incandescent, fluorescent, metal halide, and high-pressure sodium lamps could be used for general, task, and accent lighting. This discussion should also include how daylight can be successfully integrated with these electrical light sources.

5. Developing observation and problem-solving skills is critical to the success of a designer. Find installations of incandescent, fluorescent, and HID lamps in residential or commercial interiors. For each installation respond to the items listed below.

a. Identify the purpose of the space.

b. Identify the purpose of the lighting, including an identification of general, task, and accent lighting.

c. Describe the luminaire.

d. Describe the effect of each light source in each space.

e. Describe the effect of the light source on colors.

f. Evaluate the appropriateness of the illumination level.

g. Based upon the definition of quality lighting environments described in Chapter 1, evaluate the overall quality of lighting in each space.

h. Based upon your observations and reflections, provide recommendations for improving the lighting environment.

REFERENCES

Benya, J., Heschong, L., McGowan, T., Miller, N., and Rubinstein, F. (2001). *Advanced Lighting Guidelines*. White Salmon, WA: New Buildings Institute.

Bleeker, N., and Veenstra, W. (August, 1990). The performance of four-foot fluorescent lamps as a function of ambient temperature on 60Hz and high frequency ballasts. *Proceedings of the 1990 Annual IESNA Conference*. Baltimore, MD.

Borg, N. (March, 1993). The ABCs of UV. *IAEEL Newsletter*.

Boyce, P.N., Elkund, N., and Simpson, S. (2000). Individual lighting control: Task performance, mood and illuminance. *Journal of the Illuminating Engineering Society*, 29(1), 131–142.

Boylan, B.R. (1987). *The Lighting Primer*. Ames, IA: Iowa State University Press.

Carriere, L., and Rea, M. (1988). Economics of switching fluorescent lamps. *IEEE Transactions on Industry Applications*, 24(3), 370–379.

Coaton, J.R., and Marsden, A.M. (1997). *Lamps and lighting*, (4th ed.). London: Arnold.

Ducker Research. (August, 1999). Lighting quality-key customer values and decision process. Report to the Light Right Research Consortium.

Egan, M.D. (1983). *Concepts in Architectural Lighting.* New York: McGraw-Hill.

Elenbass, W. (1971). *Fluorescent Lamps, Philips Technical Library* (2nd ed.). London: Macmillan.

General Electric (1989). *Lighting Application Bulletin.* Cleveland, OH: General Electric.

Gifford, R. (1993). Scientific evidence for claim about full-spectrum lamps: Past and future. *IRC internal report no. 659.*

Gordon, G. (2003). *Interior Lighting for Designers,* 4th ed. New York: John Wiley & Sons.

Gordan, G., and Nuckolls, J.L. (1995). *Interior Lighting for Designers.* New York: John Wiley & Sons.

Greif, M. (1986). *The Lighting Book.* Pittstown, NJ: The Main Street Press.

Hunter, R.S. (1975). *The Measurement of Appearance.* New York: John Wiley & Sons.

Illuminating Engineering Society of North America (IESNA). (2000). *IESNA Lighting Handbook* (9th ed.). New York: Illuminating Engineering Society of North America.

Jennings, J.F., Rubinstein, R., and DiBartolomeo, D.R. (2000). Comparisons of control options in private offices in an advanced lighting controls test bed. *Journal of the Illuminating Engineering Society,* 29(29), 39–60.

Ji, Y., Davis, R., and Chen, W. (1999). An investigation of the effect of operating cycles on the life of compact fluorescent lamps. *Journal of the Illuminating Engineering Society,* 28(2), 57–62.

Kaufman, J.E. (ed.) (1984). *IES Lighting Handbook Reference Volume 1984.* New York: Illuminating Engineering Society.

Lawrence Berkeley National Laboratory. (1997). *Lighting Source Book.* Berkeley, CA: Lawrence Berkeley National Laboratory.

Lewis, A.L. (1998). Equating light sources for visual performance at low luminances. *Journal of the Illuminating Engineering Society,* 27(1), 80.

Maniccia, D., Von Neida, B., and Tweed, A. (2000). Analysis of the energy and cost savings potential of occupancy sensors for commercial lighting systems. *Proceedings of the 2000 Annual Conference of the Illuminating Engineering Society of North America.*

Maniccia, D., Rutledge, D., Rea, M., and Morrow, W. (1999). Occupant use of manual lighting control in private offices. *Journal of the Illuminating Engineering Society,* 28(2), 42–56.

Mistrick, R., Chen, C., Bierman, B., and Felts, D. (2000). A comparison of photosensor-controlled electronic dimming systems. *Proceedings of the 2000 Annual Conference of the Illuminating Engineering Society,* 29(1), 66–80.

National Lighting Product Information Program (NLPIP). (March, 1998). Specifier reports: Photosensors.

Navvab, M. (2000). A comparison of visual performance under high and low color temperature fluorescent lamps. *Proceedings of the 2000 Annual Conference of the Illuminating Engineering Society of North America.* Washington, DC.

Phillips, D. (2000). *Lighting Modern Buildings.* Oxford: Architectural Press.

Phillips Lighting. (1994). Fluorescent lamps: *Correspondence Course, Lesson 9.* Netherlands: Philips Lighting BV.

Portland Energy Conservation, I. (1992). *Building Commissioning Guidelines* (2nd ed.). Bonneville Power Administration.

Runquist, R.A., McDougall, T.G., and Benya, J. (1996). *Lighting Controls: Patterns for Design.* Prepared by R.A. Rundquist Associates for the Electric Power Research Institute and the Empire State Electrical Energy Research Corporation.

Southern California Edison. (1999). Energy Design Resources Case Studies: REMO and Timberland. Available from: http://www.energydesignresources.com.

Steffy, G.R. (2002). *Architectural Lighting Design* (2nd ed.) New York: Van Nostrand Reinhold.

Waymouth, J.F. (1971). *Electric Discharge Lamps.* Cambridge, MA: MIT Press.

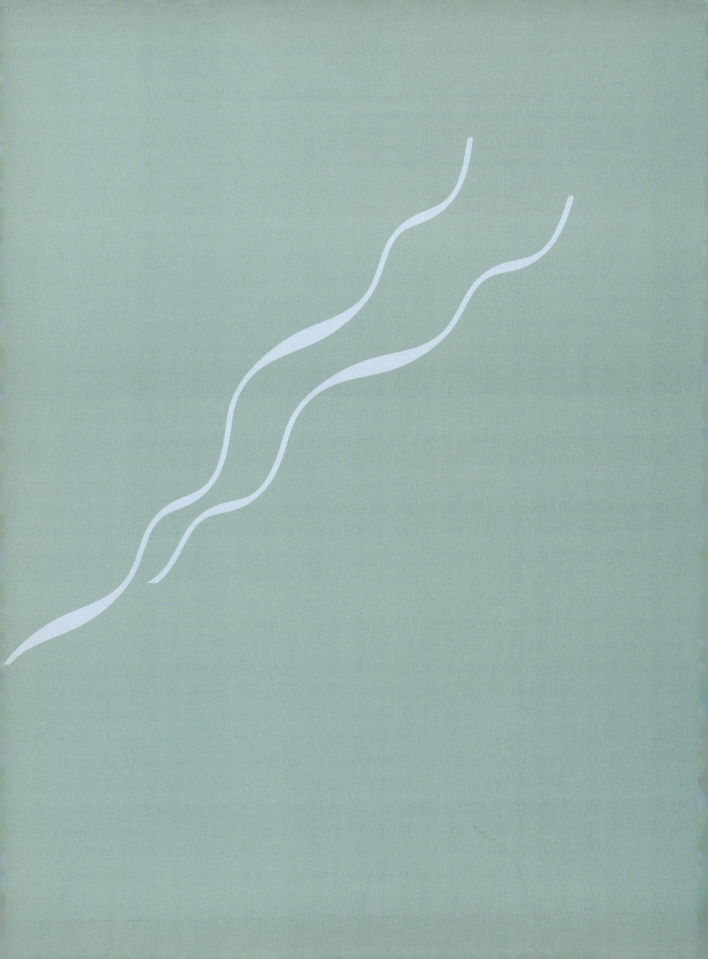

CHAPTER 4

Lighting Systems: Lamps for Special Applications

OBJECTIVES

■ Identify and describe characteristics of fiber optics, neon, electrodeless, and electroluminescent lamps.

■ Identify the primary functional components and operating principles of fiber optics, neon, electrodeless, and electroluminescent lamps.

■ Determine applications for fiber optics, neon, electrodeless, and electroluminescent lamps.

ELEMENTS of a quality lighting system are covered in Chapter 3. It includes discussion about the operating functions and characteristics of incandescent, tungsten-halogen, fluorescent, and high-intensity discharge lamps. These lamps are the most common electrical light sources specified by designers. However, an examination of electrical light sources would not be complete without a discussion of specialty lamps.

Specialty lamps are electrical light sources that designers can use in a quality layered lighting plan that includes general, task, and accent illumination. Some specialty lamps are in their infancy of product development and identification of appropriate applications. Lamp manufacturers are conducting research to expand the efficient and effective use of these lamps.

Remote Source Illumination Systems: Fiber Optic Lighting

Fiber optic lighting is one of the newest forms of electrical light sources and can be used for general, task, accent, and decorative applications. Fiber optics is a light source that utilizes a remote source for illumination. Light is transmitted through a bundle of optical fibers.

Characteristics of Fiber Optic Lighting

Since the late 1700s scientists and engineers have been experimenting with optical technology. However, it wasn't until 1930 that the potential of fiber optics was realized. In Germany, Heinrich Lamm demonstrated the first successful image transmission through optical fibers. After this breakthrough numerous other researchers explored the various possibilities of using optical fibers, including telecommunications and optical communication. In 1970, at the Corning Glass Works, Robert Maurer worked with other researchers to design and manufacture the first optical fibers. As a result of this technological advancement, in the late 1970s manufacturers started to produce industrial fiber optic illumination products. Currently fiber optic lighting is used in a variety of applications, including architectural, custom, landscape, and signage.

Fiber optics' light source is housed in a box called the **illuminator**, and the directional lamp is usually metal halide or tungsten-halogen (see Figure 4.1). Metal halide lamps are used for applications that require long lamp life. Some systems are starting to use LEDs as the light source. The optical fibers are bundled together at the "port" or the opening in the side of the illuminator. The fibers are made from glass or plastic, and hundreds of optical fibers can be used in the system. Glass is the preferred material because it transmits excellent color, transmits light well, lasts long, requires minimum maintenance, and

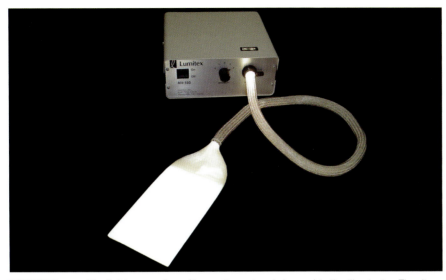

FIGURE 4.1 The light source for a fiber optic system is housed in the illuminator. The directional lamp, located in the illuminator, is usually metal halide or tungsten-halogen.

bends easily. Light produced from fiber optics is a result of internal reflection; light is visible at the end of the fibers, **end-emitting** (see Figure 4.2a), or the sides of the entire length of the fibers, **side-emitting** (see Figure 4.2b).

End-emitting fiber optic systems produce directional illumination and are made from glass. End fittings are available in a variety of

End-emitting fiber optic lighting system
Light illuminates through the cylindrical optical fibers and is visible at the end of the fibers.

Side-emitting fiber optic lighting system
Light illuminates through the cylindrical optical fibers and is visible along the sides of the fibers.

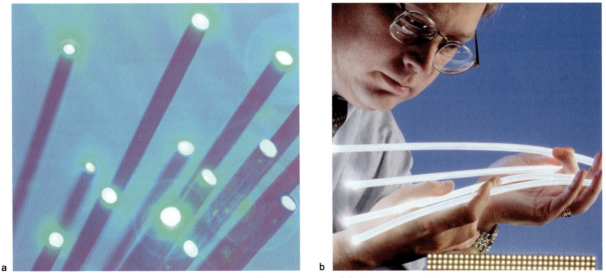

FIGURE 4.2 In fiber optic systems, light is visible by (a) end-emitting or (b) side-emitting cables.

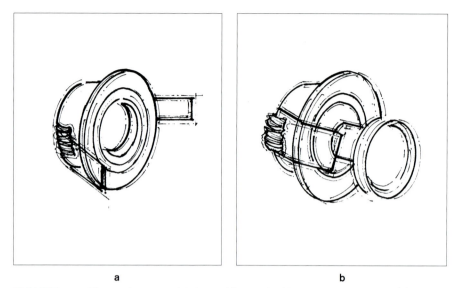

a   b

FIGURE 4.3 The most common interior end fittings for fiber optic systems are a (a) fixed or (b) adjustable downlight.

finishes and styles. The most common interior end fittings are fixed or adjustable downlights (see Figure 4.3a and b). The fittings are small, approximately 2 inches in diameter. Crystal end fittings produce sparkle and are only 1-inch in diameter. Side-emitting systems are made from glass or plastic and produce an even distribution of illumination over the length of the fibers. The longest optical fibers are made from plastic and can be 100 feet long. A variety of special effects are available that are housed in the illuminator. Wheels can be installed to provide color changes or twinkling. The twinkling wheel provides a touch of animation to the light. Fiber optic systems can also be dimmed.

Advantages of Fiber Optic Lighting

There are many advantages to using fiber optic lighting, including safety, ease of maintenance, low transmission of heat to objects being illuminated, and very small amounts of the infrared (IR) and ultraviolet (UV) wavelengths. Since the light source in fiber optic systems is located in the illuminator, the fibers only transmit light and do not have an electrical current. This allows a designer to install the illuminator at a remote location. This makes it possible for fibers to be placed in wet spaces, such as swimming pools, ponds, saunas, spas, steam rooms, and showers.

Fiber optic lighting is easy to maintain because there are few lamps to replace and the illuminator can be mounted in a location that is easily accessible. Few lamps also result in energy savings. Because of the intense heat produced by some lamps, fans should be installed in the illuminator. Installing the lamp at a remote site eliminates the detrimental effects of heat and IR and UV rays. Thus, fiber optic lighting is an excellent choice for heat-sensitive products, artwork, and decorative objects, especially fragile museum artifacts.

There are many design options with fiber optic lighting. The tiny point of light emitted from fiber optics can be quite decorative, presents a high-tech look, and attracts attention without glare (see Figure 4.4). Designers use end-emitting systems in display cases to highlight jewelry

FIGURE 4.4 Tiny points of light emitted from fiber optics can present a spectacular look.

and crystal. Cabinetmakers install fiber optic lighting in a variety of furniture pieces including curio cabinets, breakfronts, bookcases, and entertainment units. Fiber optic lighting is also very effective for illuminating steps and pavers.

Cold-cathode and Neon Lamps

Cold-cathode and neon lamps are customized designs that can be costly to purchase. As specialty lamps, cold-cathode systems have limited applications and require the expertise of individuals with experience in designing and installing the lighting. Most cold-cathode lighting is for decorative purposes.

Cold-cathode Lamps

> **Cold-cathode lamps**
> A discharge light source similar to a neon lamp.

Cold-cathode lamps were developed in the early 1900s and served as a technological foundation for all fluorescent lamps. In comparison to the functional operation of fluorescent lamps, the cathodes in cold-cathode lamps are not preheated. To start the lamps, cold-cathode systems must have a high-voltage transformer. This results in a noisy system that can be complicated to install. The diameter, length, configuration, and color of the tubes are custom designed. This contributes to the high cost of such systems and can produce some inconsistencies in quality.

Cold-cathode lamps can be used for signage and for installations that require a continuous line of color, such as cove lighting or wallslot applications. In addition, the long life of cold-cathode lamps can be useful in installations that are hard to reach for relamping. Cold-cathode lamps are available in numerous colors and are frequently used in applications that require bright colors.

Neon Lamps

Neon is a special application of cold-cathode lamps. Georges Claude in Paris invented neon lamps in 1910. Neon lamps resulted from experiments Claude was conducting to find a lamp that would last longer than the popular incandescent lamp and that did not corrode. The techniques that Claude developed in 1910 are still used today to produce neon lamps. Unlike other lamps, machines do not make neon lamps. A master glass-bending craftsperson creates the shapes and forms of neon lamps by hand. This is becoming a lost art because current masters are retiring and there are few apprenticeship programs.

The process begins with a drawing on asbestos of the neon design. The craftsperson bends the heated glass tube into various shapes and designs. An electrode is placed at each end of the glass (Figure 4.5). Air is partially removed and is replaced with an inert gas that is mixed with a small amount of mercury. Neon and argon are the most common inert gases utilized in the glass tubes. A transformer with a high-voltage source is directed to the electrodes. This causes the gases to ionize and produce a bright, uniform light. The small diameter of the tube creates a concentrated source of illumination. As a result, the light appears to be bright, but, in reality, lamps with larger diameters emit higher levels of illumination. The color produced is dependent upon the color of the glass, gases, and phosphors that might be coated on the inside of the tubes. A combination of these elements can produce over 150 colors. Neon gas produces a red-orange color, and argon with mercury creates a bright blue.

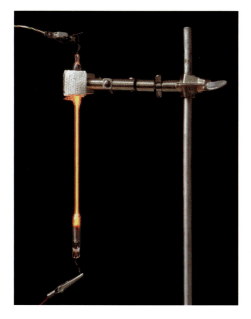

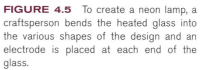

FIGURE 4.5 To create a neon lamp, a craftsperson bends the heated glass into the various shapes of the design and an electrode is placed at each end of the glass.

FIGURE 4.6 Neon lights are used at Chicago O'Hare airport to outline interior architectural details.

The advantages to neon lamps include low heat, a wide assortment of colors, low maintenance, and an extremely long life. Neon lamps can last for over 30 years of daily use. They require no warm-up period and use very little electricity. Neon can be used indoors and outdoors under a variety of weather conditions and in various temperatures. The most common use of neon lamps is advertising. Signage has changed over the years to reflect the prevailing style. Neon has the ability to provoke a great deal of excitement in large areas. This is evidenced by the neon advertising in New York City in Times Square, Las Vegas, downtown Tokyo, and Piccadilly Circus in London. Neon lamps are often used in retail and hospitality applications. Neon lamps are designed to emphasize silhouettes and can appear to be animated. Some designers are using neon to outline interior architectural details and as an emphasis in transitional areas (see Figure 4.6). Neon is also used in art as is discussed in Chapter 16.

Electrodeless lamp
An electrical light source that uses an electromagnetic (EM) field to excite gases within a tube rather than cathodes. The EM field is produced by a microwave or induction discharge.

Electrodeless Lamps

Advances in the field of electronics have led to the development of **electrodeless lamps**. These lamps, introduced in the 1990s, use an electromagnetic (EM) field to excite gases within a tube rather than cathodes. The EM field is produced by a microwave or induction discharge. Microwave-discharge lamps utilize microwaves to excite the gases that emit the light. Inductive-discharge lamps are also referred to as induction lamps. The operation of an induction lamp is similar to that of a fluorescent lamp. Radio-frequency energy supplies power to an induction coil and causes the mercury in the tube to be charged (Benya, Heschong, McGowan, Miller, and Rubinstein, 2001; Coaton and Marsden, 1997; IESNA, 2000). This results in ultraviolet energy that excites the phosphor coating on the inside of the linear tube so that light is emitted. The rare-earth phosphors used in induction lamps results in good color rendition.

Most lamps eventually fail because of the deterioration of their cathodes. Therefore, eliminating cathodes enhances lamp life and reduces depreciation. An electrodeless lamp produces light immediately and is not affected by the number of times a luminaire is turned on and off. Electrodeless lamps have high efficacy ratings and are available in shapes that are similar to those of an arbitrary incandescent lamp. A reflector design is available for flood lighting applications. Some electrodeless lamps are designed for very long-burning applications and high-illumination requirements in locations that are hard to reach. The primary commercial applications have been roadways, signage, and landscaping. The famous clock tower Big Ben, in London, is illuminated with induction lamps.

Electroluminescent Lamps

In 1907 Henry Joseph Round discovered the phenomenon of electroluminescence. **Electroluminescent lamps** operate through an interaction between an electrical field and a phosphor (Benya, Heschong, McGowan, Miller, and Rubinstein, 2001; Coaton and Marsden, 1997; IESNA, 2000). Electroluminescent lamps include light-emitting diodes (LEDs) and lamps used for instrument panels and liquid crystal displays. These lamps are lightweight, have long life, require high-voltage drivers, and use very little electricity. Some lamps have operated for over 10 years.

Electroluminescent lamp
An electrical light source that operates through an interaction between an electrical field and a phosphor.

Characteristics of LEDs

LED is the first solid-state electronic light source for lighting, and the technology has improved dramatically since the mid-1990s. Currently, a tremendous amount of research is being conducted to create LED light that is viable for interior lighting. This light is expected to be available by 2010. The first LEDs started with the invention of the semiconductor *gallium arsenide* in the 1950s. The red light was invisible until the development of gallium phosphide in the 1960s. At that time LEDs were used for indicator lights and alphanumeric displays. Typical applications included stereos, digital watches, phones, and calculators. Further experiments with gallium produced more colors and brighter lights. A significant breakthrough with LED technology occurred with the invention of blue lights in the 1990s. This development was especially important to the production of white LEDs and a brighter light source.

As a semiconductor device, LEDs have a chemical chip embedded in a plastic capsule (see Figure 4.7). A volt from a direct current energizes the chip and light is visible. A transformer is needed to operate the lamps with a direct current. The light is focused or scattered by using lenses or diffusers. The lamp life of LEDs is determined by the mean time between failures (MTBF).

FIGURE 4.7 LEDs have a chemical chip embedded in a plastic capsule.

The chemicals contained in the chip determine the color of the light. The first colors were red, green, and amber. As mentioned above, the development of blue in the 1990s enabled lamp manufacturers to produce white. This ability has significantly improved the application of LEDs for general illumination. One method used to produce the color white is through color mixing by combining red, green, and blue LEDs in one unit. This approach is not very successful because white is altered as the individual LEDs depreciate. The preferred way to create a white light is to use an LED with phosphors that absorb blue and hence produce a white color. The white produced is a "cool" white that is generally undesirable for interior applications. Scientists and engineers are working to develop phosphors that will produce a warmer white that can emit a high level of illumination.

LEDs are available in stand-alone or networked applications. Solar LEDs are also available. Many stand-alone applications are similar to the shape and configuration of incandescent, halogen, fluorescent, and neon lamps. For example, LEDs have been installed in a unit that allows a drop-in replacement for a halogen flood or accent light. A tube system that resembles the tube systems in neon lamps provides colored illumination throughout the element. To produce illumination, colored LEDs are positioned at each end of the tube. Continuous light strips illuminated by LEDs are designed for architectural banding applications, such as cove or wallslots. LED retrofit systems can replace low wattage fluorescent lamps in portable luminaires. In the future, industrial engineers are likely to design systems that are unique to the characteristics of LEDs.

Networked arrangements include several luminaires and one controller. LEDs that are digitally controlled provide the flexibility to specify colors, brightness, and special effects, such as twinkling or synchronization with music. These systems are especially effective for specialty architectural lighting and in retail stores, restaurants, and nightclubs. Software and hardware LED systems allow a user to manage, design, and control large-scale installations. For example, LED systems are available that use a series of tiles, or panels, to create scenes. Each tile is edged with red, blue, and green LEDs. These three colors allow the user to create every possible color. Computer graphics programs can be used to create images. A programmable controller creates synchronous color that changes LED light in each tile. This same technology is also available for tube lighting systems.

Advantages and Disadvantages of LEDs

As an illumination source in its infancy stage, LEDs have advantages and significant disadvantages. LED lamps are durable and small, have a long life, use minimal electrical power, have a directional source, and do not emit UV or IR radiation. The efficacy is better than that for incandescent lamps. In addition, LEDs do not have glass or filaments that can break. The lack of electrodes contributes to the life of the LED lamp. Disadvantages to LED lamps include unappealing white colors, low levels of illumination, and cost per lumens. LED products also differ among manufacturers and can be affected by drive current and temperature.

As a new illumination technology LEDs have not been used in a lot of interior applications. LEDs are primarily used for signage, display backlights, automobiles, and pedestrian signals. Interior applications have focused on settings that need decorative lighting in various colors, such as bars, restaurants, or retail stores (see Figure 4.8). As LEDs improve, especially the color rendition properties, and increases in

FIGURE 4.8 Interior applications using LEDs focus on settings that desire decorative lighting in various colors.

levels of illumination, designers will use LEDs for a variety of general, task, and accent applications. The LED light is a significant emerging technology, and designers should be alert to new developments.

A lamp with light emitting polymer (LEP) is a developing low voltage technology involving organic semiconducting materials. A primary advantage to LEP technology is ultrathin illumination at low voltages. More LEP research is required before this lamp can be used for general illumination.

SUMMARY

- Fiber optic lighting is an electrical source that utilizes a remote source for illumination. The light source is housed in a box called the illuminator, and the directional lamp is usually metal halide or tungsten-halogen. The fibers are made from glass or plastic, and hundreds of optical fibers can be used in the system.
- Fiber optics illumination is visible at the end of the fibers, end-emitting, or the sides of the entire length of the fibers, side-emitting.
- There are many advantages to using fiber optic lighting, including safety, ease of maintenance, low transmission of heat to objects being illuminated, and very small amounts of the infrared (IR) and ultraviolet (UV) wavelengths.
- Neon is a special application of cold-cathode lamps and was invented by Georges Claude in 1910.
- Neon lamps are produced by a craftsperson who bends heated glass into the various shapes of the design. An electrode is placed at each end of the glass, and inert gases fill the glass tubes. A transformer with a high-voltage source is directed to the electrodes.
- The neon lamp color produced is dependent upon the color of the glass, gases, and phosphors that might be coated on the inside of the tubes. A combination of these elements can produce over 150 colors. Neon gas produces a red-orange color, and argon with mercury creates a bright blue.
- Electrodeless lamps use an electromagnetic (EM) field to excite the gases within a tube rather than cathodes. The EM field is produced by a microwave or induction discharge. The operation of an

induction lamp is similar to the operation of a fluorescent lamp. The rare-earth phosphors used in induction lamps result in good color rendition.

- Electroluminescent lamps operate through an interaction between an electrical field and a phosphor.
- As a semiconductor device LEDs have a chemical chip embedded in a plastic capsule. A volt from a direct current energizes the chip, and light is visible. A transformer is needed to operate the lamps with a direct current. The light is focused or scattered by using lenses or diffusers.

Key Terms

cold-cathode lamp	fiber optic lighting
electrodeless lamp	illuminator
electroluminescent lamp	side-emitting fiber optic
end-emitting fiber optic lighting system	lighting system

Exercises

1. Identify several commercial and residential applications for end-emitting and side-emitting fiber optics systems. Write an essay that identifies the applications and discusses the advantages and disadvantages to using the two major types of fiber optic lighting.

2. As a designer for a firm that specializes in retail design, design a signage that includes neon lamps for three different stores. The summary report with sketches should also include the size, color, location, and purpose of the neon signage.

3. Walk in an area that has traffic lights and pedestrian signals. Examine the fixtures to determine if LEDs are used. Determine how far away (in blocks) a pedestrian can see the lights. Write a summary report that includes the visible distances for the LEDs, the colors used, and any problems with the system. This summary should include the visible distances for each color that is used in the LED system.

4. In an essay provide the following information: (a) examples of how fiber optics, neon lamps, and LEDs could be used for general, task, accent, and decorative lighting; and (b) how the specialty lamps compare to incandescent, fluorescent, metal halide, and high-pressure sodium lamps.

5. Identify a local retail store, restaurant, museum, and fitness center. Write a report, including sketches and photographs, that responds to the following items:

   a. Identify two applications for a fiber optics system and describe why fiber optics would be an appropriate choice.

   b. Specify a fiber optic manufacturer. Based upon the manufacturer's literature, specify
      1) Lamps
      2) Type of fiber optic system (side-emitting or end-emitting)
      3) Color, if applicable
      4) Fittings for end-emitting systems, including size and finish
      5) Special features

   c. Determine the location of the illuminator and the fiber optics.

   d. Provide recommendations for maintenance.

REFERENCES

Benya, J., Heschong, L., McGowan, T., Miller, N., and Rubinstein, F. (2001). *Advanced Lighting Guidelines*. White Salmon, WA: New Buildings Institute.

Coaton, J.R., and Marsden, A. M. (1997). *Lamps and Lighting* (4th ed.). London: Arnold.

Illuminating Engineering Society of North America (IESNA). (2000). *IESNA Lighting Handbook* (9th ed.). New York: Illuminating Engineering Society of North America.

Kay, G.N. (1999). *Fiber Optics in Architectural Lighting*. New York: McGraw-Hill.

Narendran, A.N., Bullough, J.D., Maliyagoda, N., and Bierman, A. (July/August, 2000). What is useful life for white light LEDs? *Proceedings of the 2000 Annual Conference of the Illuminating Engineering Society of North America*. Washington, DC.

Stern, R. (1988). *The New Light There Be Neon*. New York: Harry N. Abrams, Inc., Publishers.

Webb, M. (1984). *The Magic of Neon*. Salt Lake City, UT: Gibbs M. Smith, Inc.

CHAPTER 5

Color

- Summarize the basic concepts associated with color, including physics and color theory.

- Explain how chromaticity and the color rendering index can be used to specify lamps and color.

- Describe the effects of vision and perceptions on the selection of colors.

- Explain how a light source affects the colors of objects.

- Describe how the perceived color of objects is determined by multiple factors.

COLOR was identified in chapter 2 as an important element in integrating and controlling daylight and electrical lights. Generally, people perceive daylight to reveal an object's "true" color. However, weather conditions, reflections, and the time of the day can affect color. Changes in color resulting from a light source greatly affect the work of an interior designer. This is especially challenging with electrical light sources. Chapter 3 introduced two ratings, CRI and CCT, to assist designers in selecting electrical light sources that enhance colors. This chapter expands on these topics and explores the important relationship between quality lighting and color.

Basic Concepts

Specifying a lighting system that will enhance the desired color scheme of an environment requires a basic understanding of the physics and theory of color. Knowing these basic concepts provides the foundation for understanding the technical and aesthetic attributes associated with specifying light and colors.

Physics of Color

The eye can detect over five million colors. All these colors are affected by numerous factors, but, most important, the perceived color is influenced by its light source. Color cannot be seen without light. To prove this to yourself, walk through a room at dusk and attempt to identify and distinguish colors. You will notice that you can see objects but that it is nearly impossible to discern the colors of these objects and surfaces. Once the lights are turned on, the colors become visible. To create quality lighting in an environment, a designer must have a thorough understanding of color and how light sources affect perceptions of color.

Scientist Isaac Newton demonstrated that a beam of white or natural light could be dispersed through a prism into a spectrum of colors (Figure 5.1). This spectrum, or rainbow, of colors is composed of different wavelengths of color. The longest wavelength is red, followed by orange, yellow, green, blue, and violet. In general, the measure in nanometers of each color is as follows (Egan, 1983):

Red	700–650 nanometers
Orange	640–590 nanometers
Yellow	580–550 nanometers
Green	530–490 nanometers
Blue	480–450 nanometers
Violet	440–390 nanometers

The absorption and reflectance properties of a light source and an object determine the color we see. An object appears red because it absorbs the other colors in the spectrum, and red is reflected to the eye

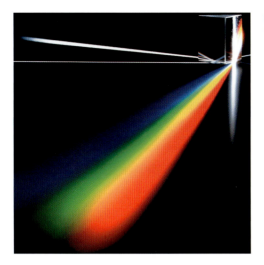

FIGURE 5.1 Light dispersed through a prism into a spectrum of colors.

(Figure 5.2). An object appears to be blue because all the other colors in the spectrum are absorbed and blue is reflected. An object is white when all the colors in the spectrum are reflected. An object is black when all the colors in the spectrum are absorbed.

The wavelengths of daylight vary according to the time of the day, sky conditions, time of the year, and geographic location. Daylight at sunset appears to be redder than it does at noon, because the light will have more red and yellow wavelengths than blue or green ones. Northern daylight has more blue and green wavelengths than does southern

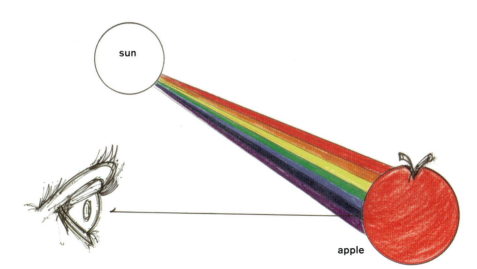

sun

apple

FIGURE 5.2 This object is red, due to the absorption of the other colors in the spectrum, and red is reflected to the eye.

daylight; this results in a cooler appearance. Impressionist artists extensively studied how colors and objects changed appearance with the conditions of light and atmosphere. For example, Claude Monet painted the western façade of Rouen Cathedral at many different times of the day and under a variety of weather conditions (Figures 5.3a and b). From 1890–1891, Monet created 35 paintings of stacks of grain in various atmospheric effects, including snow.

These facts are important when a lighting designer selects a light source. If a light source does not have a balanced spectrum of colors, the color of the object being illuminated will be altered. For example, some 4100K fluorescent lamps have few wavelengths at the warm end of the spectrum, such as reds and oranges. When a red object is placed under some 4100K fluorescent lamps, the red color appears subdued. This occurs because the uneven distribution of wavelengths produced by the lamp does not allow much of the red to be reflected to the eye. From an application perspective, a designer might select a red

FIGURE 5.3a Effect of noon sunlight on the façade of Rouen Cathedral as painted by Claude Monet.

FIGURE 5.3b Effect of a cloudy day on the façade of Rouen Cathedral as painted by Claude Monet.

upholstery fabric for an office chair at a fabric manufacturer's showroom. The showroom lighting could have lamps that have a good balanced spectrum of colors, thus revealing vibrant red upholstery fabrics. If the office lamps enhance cool colors, the designer's intent to have an office chair upholstered in a vibrant red will fail. In this lighting environment, the fabric will appear to be a dull red.

Color Theory

Properties of color are its hue, value, and intensity. **Hue** is the color itself. Blue is a hue. Hues at the red end of the spectrum are considered warm colors and are associated with warm elements in nature, such as fire or the sun. These colors appear to advance and tend to physiologically increase heart rate and blood pressure.

Hues at the violet and blue end of the spectrum are viewed as cool colors. Cool elements of nature are associated with these colors, including water and a green forest. Cool hues tend to recede and promote a calm and serene setting. In order for colors to remain the desired red, or blue, the designer must select a lamp that will enhance a color that is in either the warm or the cool spectrum. For example, in a restaurant that is predominantly designed in red hues, a combination of incandescent lamps and 3000K fluorescents with a minimum 80 CRI could enhance the color scheme.

Hues vary depending upon changes in their value and intensity. The **value** affects the lightness and darkness of a color. Adding either white or black changes the value of a color. Navy blue has a dark value, or shade, of the blue hue. Light blue has a light value, or tint, of the blue hue.

The **intensity** is the strength or purity of the color. Colors as they appear on a **color wheel** (Figure 5.4) are at full intensity. Adding the color's complement decreases a color's intensity. The **complement** of a color is the color directly across from another on the color wheel. Thus, the complement of blue is orange. To reduce the intensity of blue, one would mix it with orange.

Developed by A.H. Munsell in 1898, the **Munsell Color System** is the most commonly accepted color theory in the United States utilized

Hue
The name of a color.

Value
The lightness or darkness of a color.

Intensity
The strength or purity of a color.

Color wheel
Circular arrangement of colors in a fixed order.

Complement
The color directly opposite a color on the color wheel.

Munsell Color System
A method for classifying colors using a letter and number designation that identifies a particular hue with a given value and intensity.

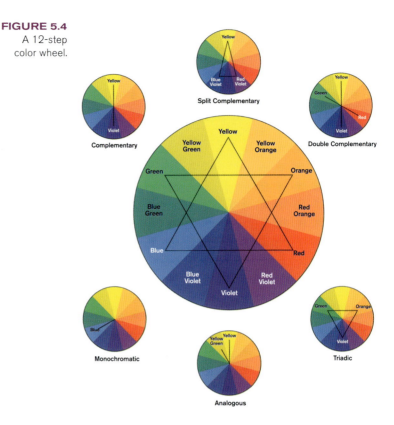

FIGURE 5.4
A 12-step color wheel.

in the field of lighting (Figure 5.5). There are other color systems, such as the Natural Color System (NCS) and the Oswald Color System. The Munsell system has a letter and number designation to identify a particular hue with a given value and intensity. Hues have a number and letter. Pure red is a 5R and red-purple is 5RP. Values of a color are identified on the system's vertical axis. On this scale white is on the top with a designation of 10, and black is on the bottom with a designation of 0. There are equally spaced shades of gray between these two neutral colors. The value designation is the first number identified after the hue's number/letter.

The intensity of a color is represented on the horizontal axis of the Munsell system. The intensity scale utilizes a 0 to represent a neutral gray, and the scale extends to 16 at full strength. The intensity designation is the last number in the Munsell code. Thus, a 5R 4/6 is pure red, with a value of 4, and an intensity of 6. As a widely accepted designation, the Munsell system helps designers to communicate to others not in the same location exactly which color they are specifying.

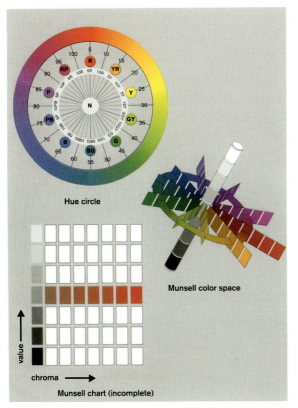

FIGURE 5.5 The hues, values, and intensity on a Munsell Color System.

Hue circle

Munsell color space

value

chroma

Munsell chart (incomplete)

Lamps and Color

In specifying a quality lighting system, a designer selects lamps that will enhance the colors in the environment. To assist designers with the lamp selection process, lamp manufacturers provide data about lamp color specifications, such as chromaticity ratings and the color-rendering index.

Chromaticity

The chromaticity, or the color temperature, of a light source helps to create the atmosphere of a space and often reflects the quality of the interior. The color temperature indicates the degree of red or blue of a light source. Chromaticity is measured by kelvins (K); this information is provided by lamp manufacturers. As mentioned in Chapter 3, on a Kelvin scale, the warmer the apparent color of a light source, the lower the number of kelvins will be. A higher number on the scale represents a cooler or bluer color. For example, the warm color of light emitted from a candle is approximately 2000K, and the color of cool daylight is 5000K. A neutral color falls at about 3500K. Lamps that provide a warm and cool appearance are 3000K and 4100K, respectively. One way to understand the scale is to think about a hard material, such as steel, being heated. One of the first colors the steel will turn is red, followed by yellow, then white, and finally blue-white. Generally, an interior that has a warm glow will have a relatively low chromaticity rating (3000K). In contrast, an interior that appears to be cool and bright will have a relatively high chromaticity rating (4100K). To comply with state energy codes, the most common chromaticity ratings for fluorescent sources are 3000K, 3500K, and 4100K. These lamps are available with CRIs in the 70s and 80s; some manufacturers produce lamps in the 90s.

In an attempt to measure color, an international organization for color, CIE (International Commission on Illumination), developed a diagram with colors ranging from red to violet, plotted on x and y axes (Figure 5.6). The diagram represents **correlated color temperature (CCT)**. The mathematics of the colors form the triangular-shaped

Correlated color temperature (CCT)
A color temperature in kelvins determined by the x and y location on a color diagram (developed by the International Commission on Illumination).

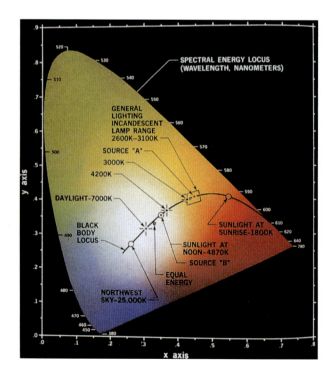

FIGURE 5.6 CIE Chromaticity diagram for natural and artificial light sources.

diagram. The wavelengths of colors in nanometers are identified around the perimeter of the color triangle. All colors in the spectrum blend in the center to become white.

The x and y coordinates on the diagram help designers to locate a color. In the center of the triangle is the "black body locus." This black curved line demonstrates the progression in color temperature in kelvins (K). As illustrated in Figure 5.6, one of the circles on the black body locus represents sunlight at noon with 4870K. The warm color appearance of a lamp is shown to have a 3000K. In practice, designers can use the CIE chromaticity diagram to quickly determine how a specific lamp compares to sunlight, or the cool northwest sky. For example, 3000K lamps are located on the black curved line midway between sunlight at sunrise and sunlight at noon. This location on the curved black line indicates that these lamps tend to enhance warm colors. Another lamp is located in the blue-green colored area, thus indicating that this lamp tends to enhance cool colors. This diagram also provides a designer with the ability to easily compare the chromaticity ratings of various lamps.

Color Rendering Index

A designer must know the color temperature and rendering ratings of lamps in order to specify those that are appropriate. The color rendering index (CRI) measures how good a light source makes objects appear. Manufacturers of lamps also provide this measurement. The CRI number represents how well a light source is able to show the true color of objects. The index range is from 0–100. The higher the CRI number, the better the color rendering ability of a lamp. The number is based upon an average of how eight colors appear in comparison to a standard test lamp. Thus, a source may be very good on most of the hues but not as good for other hues. Incandescent lamps have a CRI of 95–100 because the standard test lamp is close to incandescent.

When color is important, select a lamp with a CRI in the 80s or higher. A CRI in the 90s should be specified in settings where color appearance is very important. Compared to lamps with a CRI in the 70s, the cost of lamps with a CRI in the 80s or higher is greater because of additional rare earth phosphors used and a slightly lower efficacy rating. To determine the colors of objects and surfaces, an interior designer should always examine the samples under the lamps and/or any daylight in the space.

To integrate a lamp's color temperature and rendering ability, General Electric developed a chart that demonstrates the relationship between chromaticity in kelvins and the CRI (Figure 5.7). As shown in Figure 5.7, a warm (3000K) fluorescent lamp has approximately the same chromaticity as a different fluorescent lamp. However, the color rendering ability for each lamp is approximately 80 and 50, respectively. Thus, because the chromaticity is similar, both lamps will appear to be a cool light source, but the differences in CRI result in better color rendering with the lamp with an 80 CRI. A designer selecting lamps for the high-end retail store could first select lamps with a low chromaticity rating, and then select the lamp within this grouping with the highest CRI.

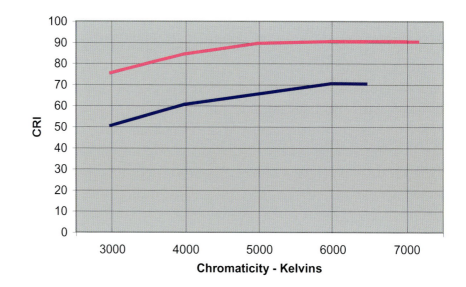

Lamp Chromaticity and CRI Comparison

FIGURE 5.7 The CRI and chromaticity of artificial light sources.

Vision and Color Perceptions

How colors are perceived in an environment is determined by numerous factors, including individuals' vision and perception. In specifying a quality lighting environment, a designer must understand the color of light produced by a lamp and numerous variables that affect an object's color.

Visual Perception

The brain, the eyes, and the age of the individual are physiological factors that affect color perception. As addressed in Chapter 1, the brain and eyes work together to enable us to see objects and color. As the corneas of the eye yellow with age, the ability to distinguish colors decreases, especially those in the blue spectrum. Generally, a 10-year-old child will see colors better than a 90-year-old adult. As a result of the unique characteristics of eyes and the brain, everyone sees colors differently.

Another visual characteristic that affects the apparent color of an object is a phenomenon termed **simultaneous contrast**. This occurs when a color appears different based upon its surrounding color. For example, a color will appear to be intensified when placed next to its complementary color on a color wheel or the neutral colors of black or white. A light blue circle surrounded by a medium blue appears to be duller than when the light blue circle is surrounded by black.

To create even more complications in specifying colors, everyone has subjective perceptions of color based upon psychology, cultural meanings, and life experiences. Psychologically, red is usually considered a color associated with danger, excitement, and warmth. Blues and greens tend to have a calming effect on people. The symbolic meaning of colors can vary with cultures. Generally, in Western cultures white is associated with life, purity, and hope. This is why brides have traditionally worn white wedding gowns. Hospitals have typically used white to represent a sterile environment. However, to resolve problems associated with simultaneous contrast, hospitals now use a bluish-green color in operating rooms to relax the eye and create a balance for the surgeons' visual systems. In other cultures

Simultaneous contrast
A phenomenon that occurs when a color appears to change as a result of surrounding colors.

white is associated with death. The color green has an association with ecology, including the development of "green design" products.

Color constancy is a phenomenon based upon experiences (Smith and Bertolone, 1986). Experience has taught us that bananas are yellow. If a light source makes a banana look violet, an individual will know that the light source is not accurate and will adapt to the situation. If a hot-pink neon light reflects on someone's face, color constancy informs us that the face is not hot pink. Light sources that create unusual colors, such as violet or hot pink, should not be used in color-critical environments, such as health-care facilities, food display areas in restaurants, art museums, and most retail stores.

Furthermore, color selection is complicated by the inconsistency of the names of many colors, as well as an individual's interpretation of the color. For example, if several individuals were asked to identify moss green from the group of colors, most likely each person would select a different color. Moreover, an individual might have a negative association with the color or name moss green.

Color constancy
Expectations people have about the color of common objects.

Light Source Color

The color of light produced by a lamp determines the apparent color of objects, the atmosphere of the space, and the quality of the interior. Manufacturers have developed a variety of lamps that have different CRI and CCT measurements. Spectral-power distribution curves provide a profile of color characteristics of lamps correlated with radiant power (see Appendix). For example, the chart in the appendix illustrates the distribution of a 4100K fluorescent. The lamp has high "spikes" in the green and blue spectrum. The radiant power axis emitted by the 4100K fluorescent is the highest at the green and blue wavelengths. Generally, using this lamp in an interior with warm colors results in a distortion of colors. In contrast, the incandescent spectral power distribution diagram (see Appendix) illustrates a smooth and continuous distribution of wavelengths. This results in a good rendition for all colors. Therefore, designers will often specify incandescent lamps for display and accent lighting in interiors that require good color rendition, such as a high-end clothing store or a fine restaurant.

To reduce color distortion, a designer should specify a lamp that has continuous spectra.

Differences in spectral-power distributions help to explain why colors can look different under various light sources. **Metamerism** occurs when two samples match each other under one light source, but do not match under a different light source. This phenomenon can present problems when a designer selects colors in a design studio, and the colors no longer match when the product is installed for the client. To help solve this problem, it is important for designers to view the color samples either in the space in which the light source will be installed or under two vastly different light sources, such as incandescent and daylight. In practice, to select a fabric for a living room, a designer should examine fabrics in the client's living room at different times of the day. Fabrics will look different during the day and at night depending upon the electrical light sources.

Other factors that determine how a light source affects color are the level of illumination and the age of the lamp. The spectral-power distribution diagrams illustrate the color spectrums for new lamps at full intensity. Generally, when a lamp is dimmed, the warm end of the spectrum is enhanced. When the lamp life is significantly reduced, generally the intensity of all colors will be reduced.

Unfortunately, there is generally a loss of efficiency with lamps that have good color rendition. For example, incandescent lamps have excellent color rendering properties (95–100 CRI); however, they consume high amounts of electricity and are short-lived. In contrast, a cool (4100K) fluorescent lamp may have a poorer color rendering rating (70 CRI), but consumes low levels of electricity and has a long lamp life. This information helps a designer select the appropriate lamp for the situation. If the client wants colors to be true and is not concerned about the cost of the lamps and maintenance, then an incandescent lamp may be the best solution providing it meets the energy code. This often occurs with residential clients and owners of high-end businesses. In contrast, a designer could specify a fluorescent lamp for a client who is not concerned about the apparent color of objects and wants to reduce the cost of lighting. Fast-food restaurants and discount retailers are examples. In specifying lamps for these

Metamerism
A phenomenon in which two samples appear to be the same color under one light source, but do not match under another light source.

interiors, intermediate (3500K) color temperatures are effective choices. In complying with EPACT by using more energy-efficient lighting systems, CFLs and metal halide lamps with CRIs in the 80s are also good solutions.

In an attempt to balance a lamp's color rendering properties and efficiency, lamp manufacturers have engaged in a great deal of research and product development. The development of triphosphors made from rare-earth phosphors improved the color properties and efficacy ratings of fluorescent lamps. Lamps can be coated with only triphosphors or triphosphors can be applied over a layer of halophosphate. Triphosphors are applied in a thin or thick coat. The thicker coat produces a better color.

Table 5.1 summarizes color properties of common lamps produced by three major manufacturers. According to the chart, a 4100K fluorescent lamp with a CRI in the 80s has an initial and mean lumen of 2860 and 2710, respectively. It should be noted that for each of the major CCT ratings (3000K, 3500K, 4100K), fluorescent lamps are available in two CRI ratings (70s and 80s). Table 5.1 also provides some lamp suggestions for specific applications. For example, according to the chart, a 5000K fluorescent lamp is excellent for checking the color of textiles during the printing process and other situations that evaluate the quality of color.

Object Color

The perceived color of an object or surface is determined by numerous factors, including the object, texture of the object, surrounding background, lamp, luminaire, eyes, color constancy, brain, size of the room, light direction, intensity of the lamp, and distance of the light fixture from an object. A change in any one of these factors will change the perceived color of an object. (Intensity and directional effects of lighting are further discussed in Chapter 6.) Figures 5.8 a and b illustrate the perceived changes in object colors under different light sources. Figure 5.8a is illuminated with an incandescent lamp. All the colors, textures, and complexions are enhanced with this light source. Cool colors are enhanced with the cool (4100K) fluorescent lamp illustrated

TABLE 5.1

Lamp Color Specifications and Suggested Applications

Lamps			CRI (approx.)	CCT (K) (approx.)	Suggested Applications
Incandescent			97–100	2500–2800K	Residential, special applications, such as niches, historic fixtures, sconces, night-lights, pendants
Halogen			97–100	2800–3000K	Residential, hospitality, gallery, retail (high-end)
Fluorescent F32T8's					
General Electric Initial/Mean Lumen	*Osram Sylvania*	*Phillips*			
SPX50/ECO 2715/2580	850/ECO	TL850/ALTO	5000K	80s	Color-critical areas in galleries, printing, jewelry displays, medical examinations
SP50/ECO 2665/2530	750/ECO	TL750/ALTO	5000K	70s	Galleries, printing, jewelry displays, medical examinations
SPX41/ECO 2860/2710	841/ECO	TL841/ALTO	4100K	80s	Color-critical areas in offices, retail (discount), and hospitality, florists, classrooms, conference rooms
SP41/ECO 2715/2580	741/ECO	TL741/ALTO	4100K	70s	Offices, retail (discount), and hospitality, florists, classrooms, conference rooms
SPX35/ECO 2860/2710	835/ECO	TL835/ALTO	3500K	80s	Color-critical areas in offices, reception areas, retail, hospitality, hospital, residential
SP35/ECO 2715/2580	735/ECO	TL735/ALTO	3500K	70s	Offices, reception areas, retail, hospitality, hospital
SPX30/ECO 2860/2710	830/ECO	TL830/ALTO	3000K	80s	Color-critical areas in offices, retail (high-end); and hospitality, libraries, hospital, residential
SP30/ECO 2715/2580	730/ECO	TL730/ALTO	3000K	70s	Offices, retail (high-end), and hospitality, Libraries, hospital, residential
Ceramic Metal Halide Initial/Mean Lumen					
General Electric Initial/Lumen	*Osram Sylvania*	*Phillips*	3000K–4200K	80–93	
CMH70/PAR38 4800/NA	MCP70PAR18	CDM70/PAR38	3000K	80s	Offices, retail, hospitality, hospital
CMH150/T6 13000/11000	MC150T6	CDM150/T6	4000K–4200K	90s	Offices, retail, hospitality, hospital
High Pressure Sodium Initial/Mean Lumen			1900K–2100K	22	
LU250/D 28000/27000	LU250/D	C250S50/D	2100K	22	Efficiency critical: industrial, outdoors
LU250/DX 22500/20700	N/A	C250S50/C	2200K	65	Industrial, outdoors

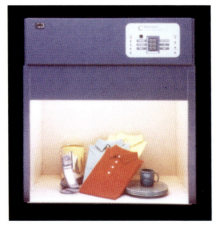

FIGURE 5.8a Colors and objects illuminated by an incandescent lamp.

FIGURE 5.8b Colors and objects illuminated by a cool fluorescent lamp.

in Figure 5.8b. Warm colors and complexions are subdued with this lamp.

Colors have various reflectance properties that are designated in percentages (Table 5.2). Colors that are light in value have higher reflectance properties and can reflect more light. For example, the reflectance of white is 82 percent and a dark gray is 14 percent. Manufacturers often include the reflectance percentage on paint-chip samples, acoustical tiles, and nonresidential carpet. The Color Marketing Group has developed the "Color Key Program" that includes the light reflectance values of 800 colors. A heavy surface texture, such as carpet or a brick wall, will alter reflectance properties. It is very difficult to match values to the Munsell scale and predict the reflectance. The most effective techniques are measuring the reflectance or obtaining reflectance data from manufacturers.

The size of a room can alter perceived color. For example, an intense color applied to the walls in a small room will amplify the color. The color of a small red bathroom will appear to be more intense than the same red paint on the walls of a large living room. The texture of an object can also alter perceived color. For example, an object that has a smooth high gloss will generally appear to have a more intense color than an object with a thick texture. This occurs because light tends to

TABLE 5.2

Relationship between Munsell Value and Luminous Reflectance Factor

Munsell Value	Luminous Reflectance Factor (percent)
10.0	100.0
9.5	87.8
9.0	76.7
8.5	66.7
8.0	57.6
7.5	49.4
7.0	42.0
6.5	35.3
6.0	29.3
5.5	24.0
5.0	19.3
4.5	15.2
4.0	11.7
3.5	8.8
3.0	6.4
2.5	4.5
2.0	3.0
1.5	2.0
1.0	1.2
0	0

Source: Reprinted from the *IESNA Lighting Handbook* (9th ed.), pp. 4–12, with permission from the Illuminating Engineering Society of North America.

reflect off shiny objects and be absorbed by heavily textured objects. In practice, a designer might have to increase the wattage to illuminate a heavily textured object. To illuminate a shiny object, a designer might decrease the wattage or alter the angle of a light source.

Figure 5.9a illustrates an interior before elements that affect lighting are altered. The list below describes how changing elements alters the perceived color of an object in a setting:

- Increasing the distance between the light fixture and the sofa causes the color of the sofa to be less intense (Figure 5.9b).

FIGURE 5.9a An interior before changes occur that can affect colors.

- The red sofa becomes less intense when the light source has been changed from an incandescent to a compact fluorescent lamp (Figure 5.9c).
- All the colors in the interior become less intense when viewed by a person who is 80 years old (Figure 5.9d).
- All the colors are subdued when the size of the room is increased (Figure 5.9e).
- The sofa color becomes uneven when the light direction is changed from above the sofa to directly next to the sofa (Figure 5.9f).
- Changing the inside finish of the light fixture from white to black alters perceived colors of the interior (Figure 5.9g).
- Changing the fabric texture of pillows from a smooth one to a deep velvet alters the apparent colors of the pillows (Figure 5.9h).

In specifying lighting, a designer should determine the purpose of the space and who will be using it. For example, in a grocery produce

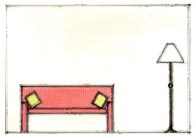

FIGURE 5.9b Interior colors changed by increasing the distance between the light source and the sofa.

FIGURE 5.9c Interior colors altered by changing the light source.

Compact fluorescent lamp (CFL)

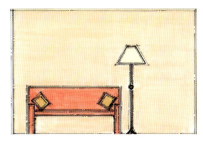

FIGURE 5.9d Interior colors altered as viewed by an elderly individual.

FIGURE 5.9e Interior colors altered by changing the size of the room.

FIGURE 5.9f Interior colors altered by changing the direction of the light source.

FIGURE 5.9g Interior colors altered by changing the color of the interior lining of the luminaire.

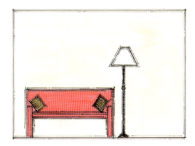

FIGURE 5.9h Colors altered by changing textures on the pillows.

department it is important that fruits and vegetables be displayed in vibrant, true colors. Therefore, a designer should consider all the factors that affect perceived color and specify a lighting plan that enhances the appearance of fruits and vegetables. In contrast, quality color rendition is not as critical in the nails and screws section of a hardware store. In this environment, it might be more important to have a lighting system that is efficient and economical.

Chapter 5 introduces some of the basic elements of color that an interior designer considers when specifying a quality lighting environment. Lamp manufacturers provide a great deal of information that assists in the process of specifying a lighting system that meets the needs of the project and users of the space. Chapter 6 further explores the topic of color by reviewing the directional effects of lighting on colors in an interior.

SUMMARY

- Absorption and reflectance properties of a light source and object determine the color that we see.
- The wavelengths of daylight vary according to the time of the day, sky conditions, time of the year, and geographic location.
- Properties of color are its hue, value, and intensity.
- Chromaticity ratings and the color rendering index are two methods for providing data about lamp color.
- Chromaticity, or the color temperature of a light source, helps to create the atmosphere of a space and often reflects the quality of the interior. The color temperature indicates the degree of red or blue of a light source. Chromaticity of a light source is measured by kelvins (K) and is provided by lamp manufacturers.
- The warmer the apparent color of a light source, the lower the number on the kelvin scale will be. For example, the warm color of light emitted from a candle is 2000K, and the color appearance of cool daylight is 5000K.
- The color rendering index (CRI) measures how well a light source makes objects appear. The index range is from 0–100. The higher the CRI number, the better the color rendering ability of the lamp.
- To comply with state energy codes, the most common fluorescent sources are 3000K, 3500K, and 4100K. These lamps are available with CRIs in the 70s and 80s; some manufacturers produce lamps in the 90s.
- The brain, the eyes, and the age of the individual are physiological factors that affect color perception.

- People have subjective perceptions of color based upon psychology, cultural background, and life experiences.
- The color of light produced by a lamp determines the perceived colors of objects, the atmosphere of the space, and the quality of the interior.
- The perceived color of an object or surface will be determined by numerous factors, including the object, texture of the object, surrounding background, lamp, light fixture, eyes, color constancy, brain, size of the room, light direction, intensity of the lamp, and distance of the light fixture from an object.

Key Terms

color constancy	intensity
color wheel	metamerism
complement	Munsell Color System
correlated color temperature (CCT)	simultaneous contrast
hue	value

Exercises

1. Cut four 2 inch by 2 inch pieces of paper in a medium blue color. Cut one 8 inch by 8 inch square from each of the following colors: white, black, dark blue, and orange. Glue each of the small pieces in the center of each of the bigger pieces. Mount these to a foam core board. Identify how the apparent color of the small squares is altered by the surrounding color.

2. In groups of three to four individuals, select four fabrics with warm and cool colors in a variety of textures and four wall coverings with warm and cool colors. Take the material samples to a variety of commercial settings, including a grocery store, retail stores, a residence, and a library. Examine the fabrics and wall coverings under the various light sources. For each of the settings, record the type of light source and each group member's subjective reactions to the appearance of the colors.

3. Draw a CRI and chromaticity graph similar to General Electric's chart illustrated in Figure 5.7. Using the data in Table 5.1, identify and locate on the graph three lamps each with chromaticity ratings in the ranges of 3000, 4000, and 5000.

4. As an interior designer you have been commissioned to design a lighting environment for a high-end retail store in Dallas, Texas. In planning the project, determine the information listed below and present in a written report:

   a. Identify the characteristics of the users that could affect vision and perception of the space.

   b. Select the colors that will be used throughout the store.

   c. Identify the lamps that could be selected for the store, and include chromaticity and color rendering indexes. Provide a rationale for your selection of the lamps.

   d. Identify other factors that should be considered in determining the perceived colors of clothing, accessories, furnishings, interior materials, and surfaces in the retail store.

REFERENCES

Albers, J. (1963). *Interaction of Color*. New Haven: Yale University Press.

Birren, F. (1969). *Light, Color and Environment*. New York: Van Nostrand Reinhold.

Boylan, B.R. (1987). *The Lighting Primer*. Ames, IA: Iowa State University Press.

Coaton, J.R., and Mawrsden, A. M. (1997). *Lamps and Lighting* (4th ed.). New York: John Wiley & Sons.

Egan, M.D. (1983). *Concepts in Architectural Lighting*. New York: McGraw-Hill.

Flynn, J.E. and Spencer, T. J. (1977). The effects of light source color on user impression and satisfaction. *Journal of the Illuminating Engineering Society*, (4), 167–179.

General Electric (1989). *Lighting Application Bulletin*. Cleveland, OH: General Electric.

Gordon, G. (2003). *Interior Lighting for Designers* (4th ed.). New York: John Wiley & Sons.

Gordan, G., and Nuckolls, J. L. (1995). *Interior Lighting for Designers*. New York: John Wiley & Sons.

Gregory, R.I. (1979). *Eye and Brain: The Psychology of Seeing* (3rd ed.). New York: McGraw-Hill.

Halse, A.O. (1968). *The Use of Color in Interiors*. New York: McGraw-Hill.

Halstead, M.B. (1997). Colour. In J. R. Coaton and A. M. Marsden (eds.), *Lamps and Lighting*. New York: John Wiley & Sons.

Henderson, S.T. (1977). *Daylight and Its Spectrum* (2nd ed.). Bristol, England: Adam Hilger.

Hunt, R.W.G. (1991). *Measuring Colour*, (2nd ed.). Chichester, England: Ellis Horwood.

Hunter, R.S. (1975). *The Measurement of Appearance*. New York: John Wiley & Sons.

Itten, J. (1961). *The Art of Color*. New York: Van Nostrand Reinhold.

Kaufman, J.E. (ed.) (1984). *IES Lighting Handbook Reference Volume 1984*. New York: Illuminating Engineering Society.

Lam, W.C. (1977). *Perception and Lighting as Formgivers for Architecture*. New York: McGraw-Hill.

Phillips, D. (2000). *Lighting Modern Buildings*. Oxford: Architectural Press.

Smith F.K., and Bertolone, F. J. (1986). *The Principles and Practices of Lighting Design: Bringing Interiors to Light*. New York: Whitney Library of Design.

Steffy, G.R. (2002). *Architectural Lighting Design*, (2nd ed.). New York: Van Nostrand Reinhold.

Varley, H. (1980). *Color*. Los Angeles: Knapp.

Watson, L. (1977). *Lighting Design Handbook*. New York: Mc-Graw Hill.

Wright, W.D. (1971). *The Measurement of Colour*, (4th ed.). London: Adam Hilger.

Wyszecki, G. and Stiles, W. S. (1967). *Color Science*. New York: John Wiley & Sons.

CHAPTER 6

Directional Effects of Lighting

OBJECTIVES

- Identify the elements of an environment that contribute to brightness and glare.

- Provide design solutions that maximize the positive attributes of brightness and that control glare.

- Determine appropriate illuminance levels for the seeing zones of an interior.

- Describe the reflectance properties of colors and materials.

- Apply the principles of reflectance and optical control to an environment.

- Describe the positive and negative effects of light, shade, and shadow in an environment.

- Apply effective patterns of light, shade, and shadows to objects and an interior.

DESIGNING a quality lighting environment requires an understanding of how the intensity and direction of a light source affects an object's appearance, the architectural features, the ability to perform a task, and the quantity of illumination. In layered lighting plans, an interior designer must coordinate the intensity and directional effects from all the light sources. A lighting plan must be developed so that it is in harmony with the physical attributes of furniture, objects, walls, floors, window treatments, and interior architecture. Colors, textures, shape, forms, and size are affected by the intensity and directional qualities of light sources. Concurrently, the elements of design can affect the quantity and direction of light.

Brightness and Glare

To have a quality lighting environment, an interior designer must develop a plan that maximizes the positive attributes of brightness and that controls glare.

Brightness

Brightness is a subjective concept that has positive and negative connotations. The bright lights we see during the Christmas holidays are exciting and contribute to the gaiety of festivities. In contrast, the bright lights of an automobile's high beams directed toward a driver on a dark highway are distracting and dangerous. Ideally, an interior designer plans an environment that results in only positive reactions to brightness.

Brightness
An effect from a light source at a high illuminance level that can be perceived as either positive or distracting.

Technically, **brightness** is the result of the interaction between an illumination level and reflectance. An interior designer can measure the quantity of light in a space that results from the reflectance of objects and surfaces. (Measuring illumination is reviewed in Chapter 7.) However, the quantity of illuminance and reflectance are only two factors that affect brightness. Illumination levels can be significantly increased although they may not appear to be brighter. For example, even though footcandle levels are very high on a cloudy day, people perceive the day as gloomy. Furthermore, an increase in illumination levels does not necessarily improve the quality of lighting. For example, changing the direction of a light source, rather than increasing the quantity of lighting, can often improve a dark work area. Successfully dealing with brightness requires an interior designer to consider all the factors that affect this phenomenon, including subjective responses, the context of the situation, personal vision attributes, light sources, directional qualities, simultaneous contrast, and characteristics of elements of the design.

Brightness is generally a subjective reaction to an environment and is dependent upon individuals' expectations and comparative contexts as well as the physical condition of their eyes. In analyzing the perceived brightness of an environment, an interior designer must anticipate expectations of a setting within the variability of different times of the day and year. Through accumulated experiences, people have expectations for illumination levels and perceived brightness. For example, people generally expect light levels to be lower in the evening than during the day. Lighting levels are also expected to be higher during the summer months than in the winter. Expectations of brightness are also affected by activities within a comparative context. For example, a lighting plan for an office may not appear to be too bright, whereas the same illumination level in a romantic restaurant would most likely be perceived as too bright.

Perceived brightness is also affected by the physical condition of eyes. Elderly people might not consider a light source as bright because corneas become yellow with age and this condition affects their vision. On the other hand, a younger individual might perceive the same environment as very bright. The eye has the ability to adjust to an enormous range of illumination levels; however, the adaptation function of vision affects perceived brightness. For example, if an individual moves from a very dark space to a lighter area, the lighter area may appear very bright until the eye adapts to the higher illumination level.

Light sources and their directional qualities are factors that affect the perceived brightness of an environment. The design of a luminaire and the type of lamp used affect the perceived brightness of electrical sources. A luminaire that provides direct illumination can be perceived as being bright; indirect light sources generally provide softer lighting (Figure 6.1a and b). Exposed lamps, especially those with clear glass, can appear to be bright. The perceived brightness of a light source also depends upon the location of the luminaire in relation to users. A luminaire may appear to be bright only when one looks directly at the exposed lamps. Thus, the perceived brightness can be altered by moving the location of the task or changing the direction of the light source.

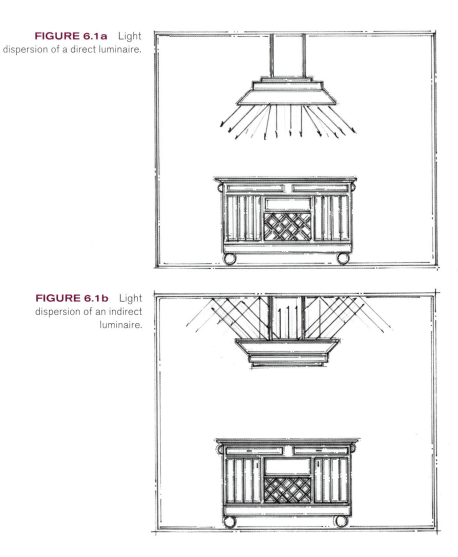

FIGURE 6.1a Light dispersion of a direct luminaire.

FIGURE 6.1b Light dispersion of an indirect luminaire.

The perceived brightness of a setting is affected by simultaneous contrast. This occurs when a color appears to be more or less intense based upon the surrounding colors. For example, gray will appear to be darker when it is surrounded by white; gray appears lighter when it is surrounded by black. In a lighting environment, an object will appear to be brighter when the area surrounding the light source is dark, and dimmer with a lighter background. For example, high-beam lights on an automobile appear to be bright at night, but are not perceived as bright during the day.

The color, texture, and finish of objects also affect the perceived brightness of an interior. White and light colors will appear to be brighter than will black and dark colors. Smooth and shiny textures will be perceived as brighter than rough and matte finishes. For example, a room painted white in a high-gloss finish will appear to be brighter than a room paneled in a dark, rough wood.

Glare

When a natural or electrical light source appears to be excessively bright, the descriptor changes to the term **glare**. As with perceived brightness, there are a variety of factors that affect glare. Glare can easily occur in illumination settings that require contrast for effective visibility and attention. For example, retail displays designed to attract attention to a product will often have a higher illumination level on the product than on the surrounding area. Also when the contrast is too great between the two areas, glare can occur. When the eye has to adjust to contrasting light levels, there is a loss in visual acuity and one can experience eye fatigue and strain. Because of contrast and high illumination levels, glare can often occur with activities that require task lighting; for example, if there is concentrated light on a task and the rest of the room is in darkness, or when bright, concentrated light sources are located above and in front of where the task is performed (Figure 6.2). Direct and indirect glare occurs as a result of the intensity

Glare
A distracting high illuminance level that can cause discomfort or be disabling.

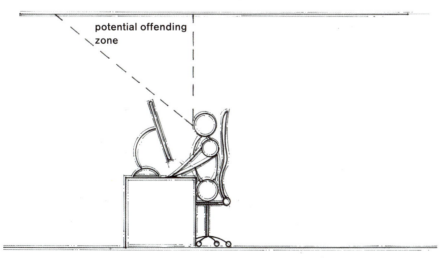

FIGURE 6.2 Luminaire locations that can cause glare to the user of the desk.

and direction of a light source. Discomfort glare and disability glare are terms that describe the severity of the glare that occurs while someone is trying to perform a task or view an object.

Direct glare occurs when a light source is at a high illumination level and is usually unshielded. It also often occurs on a bright sunny day if there is no window treatment. Any lamp that is exposed and illuminated at a high level can cause direct glare. Generally, any unshielded lamp greater than 25 watts can cause glare. A flame-shaped lamp in a chandelier can cause glare at a high illumination level, but the same lamp appears to glitter or sparkle at lower light levels. (For more information regarding types of luminaires, refer to Chapter 9.) Direct glare can also be the result of extreme contrasts in illumination levels between rooms. For instance, glare can occur from luminaires in a space while the adjoining areas are dark. This can occur in a residential interior when the living room and dining room are located next to each other, and one of these rooms is in darkness. To help reduce glare, all spaces adjoining a room should have some illumination.

Indirect glare occurs from light that is reflected from surfaces or objects. It is important to examine how an individual can be affected by the reflections from indirect light sources. For example, on a sunny day one can experience indirect glare from the sunlight reflected off light-colored surfaces or materials such as snow, concrete, or sand. Indoors, indirect glare can be the result of a light source being reflected from a light color or a shiny surface. Glass, mirrors, and high-gloss surfaces, such as a highly polished wood or ink on a printed page, can cause indirect glare when the light source is directed toward these specular materials. Often an indirect light source can cause glare on visual display terminal (VDT) screens. As discussed in Chapter 2, indirect light that is reflected from a surface of a task is termed "veiling reflections."

Discomfort glare and disability glare are terms that describe the degree of disturbance caused by a bright light source. **Discomfort glare** occurs when a natural or electrical light source causes glare that is uncomfortable, but still allows an individual to see objects and perform tasks. Discomfort glare can be especially annoying when an individual is exposed to the glare for a long time. **Disability glare** arises when the

Direct glare
A distracting high illuminance level that is frequently caused by viewing a bare light source.

Indirect glare
A distracting high illuminance level that is caused by a light source reflecting off a surface or object.

Discomfort glare
A distracting high illuminance level that makes it difficult to see.

Disability glare
A distracting high illuminance level that prevents one from seeing.

glare from a light source is so severe that the individual is unable to see. This can happen when an individual is unable to see objects under a windowsill on a sunny day. Disability glare can also occur when one is walking toward windows in a dark hallway, and it is extremely difficult to see the faces of people walking toward you (Figure 6.3). Disability glare can also occur when an individual is unable to read text on a glossy magazine page because of the reflection of the light on the surface. The high gloss of oil paints can cause disability glare on artwork. Some interior designers rely upon disability glare to discourage users from looking at undesirable elements in an interior, such as mechanical systems in an exposed ceiling.

Glare must be controlled in a quality lighting environment, and there are many approaches for an interior designer to consider depending upon the specific elements of an interior and the users of the space. Glare is easier to control when using more luminaires with lower wattages than fewer luminaires at high wattages. Locating luminaires out of the field of vision can control glare. This requires an examination of the direction of a light source and all locations where people are sitting, standing, or walking. Unshielded downlights can be

FIGURE 6.3 Disability glare in this hallway is the result of a bright light source.

problematic because they are permanent installations and because of the direct angle of the beam of light. For example, glare can result in a restaurant lighting plan that utilizes downlights above the tables. The original lighting plan might have the downlights located directly in the center of the tables, thereby avoiding glare for the patrons. However, tables in restaurants are frequently moved to accommodate various groups of people or during floor cleaning. As a result of the tables being moved, the downlights are no longer centered and might cause glare by being positioned directly over the faces of people. The glare is disturbing, and the mottling effect on faces can be very unflattering. Shielding lamps with a material, such as a fabric shade, coves, valances, baffles, louvers, or lenses, can reduce glare. (These terms are discussed more thoroughly in Chapter 9.)

Reducing brightness ratios is a means of controlling glare and is achieved by examining a variety of factors in the environment, including the illumination levels between areas in a space and the size of the opening in the luminaire. Generally, smaller luminaire openings have a greater potential for glare than do larger apertures. Therefore, a luminaire that disperses light from a large area can help to reduce glare. In addition to glare from electrical light sources, an interior designer must also reduce brightness ratios from daylight by specifying window treatments that either prevent direct sunlight from entering the room or soften the light penetration. Exterior devices, such as awnings or roof overhangs, can also be used to reduce glare from sunlight.

Illumination Zones

An important factor in controlling brightness and glare is having appropriate illumination levels within an environment. This involves examining relative illuminance levels and the rate of change. Proper illumination levels help to manage glare by reducing high contrasts that can occur with multiple light sources. **Illumination zones** are generally divided into three areas, including the immediate task, area surrounding the task, and the background area (Figure 6.4). The background area includes the surroundings of an interior and any halls or rooms that adjoin a space.

Illumination zone
An imaginary division of space that includes three areas: the immediate task, the area surrounding the task, and the background.

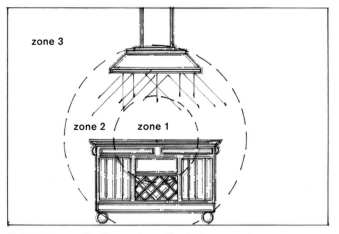

zone 3

zone 2 / zone 1

FIGURE 6.4 The three primary illumination zones in a space.

In determining the appropriate lighting levels within a space, the task area generally requires the highest illumination level, followed by the area immediately surrounding the task. The lowest illumination level is for the background. A gradual reduction in illumination levels surrounding a task allows the eye to comfortably adapt from the high level directly on the task to the other areas within a space. Ease of adaptation is important because while people are engaged in a task, their peripheral vision and eyes are constantly moving from the task to all areas of a room. Strong contrasts between the various areas will cause eye fatigue and can result in discomfort or disability glare. This is particularly problematic when an individual must spend a great deal of time performing the task. Gradual contrasts in illumination levels are especially important for critical tasks that require high illumination levels. For example, a surgeon needs appropriate illumination levels between areas in an operating room.

Between different areas illumination ratios have been identified that reduce high contrast and promote gradual changes in lighting levels. Generally, a luminance ratio between a task and its immediate area should be three to one (3:1). The luminance ratio between a task and the second zone is approximately five to one (5:1). A luminance ratio between a task and the background is generally ten to one (10:1) and should not exceed twenty to one (20:1).

There are some special conditions and factors that affect proper illumination zones. Materials and colors that have high reflectance ratings can affect illumination levels. A consistent value and intensity on a wall will make it easier to specify luminaires and lamps that meet the criteria for the proper background illumination levels. (Reflectance and illumination levels are discussed in the next section of this chapter.) Windows in a space, especially when an individual performing a task is facing a window, also affect illumination levels. Windows elicit extremes in contrast because of the high illumination levels derived from daylight and the "black hole" in the evening. Usually, windows are in the background area of a room where one should plan for the lowest illumination level. To reduce the illumination level during the day, a window treatment that controls daylight penetration, such as sheers, could be specified, or blinds to redirect light to a nonoffending direction. Electrical lighting around the window can also help to create an even distribution of illumination on a wall. In the evening, the window should have a treatment that covers it entirely, and the treatment should be a color that has a similar value and intensity as the wall surface.

Reflectance, Optical Control, and Transmission

An object's appearance, the architectural features, the quantity of illumination, and the ability to perform a task are affected by reflectance, optical control, and transmission.

Reflectance
The ratio of incident light to the light reflected from a surface or material.

Angle of incident
The rays of light emitted from a light source before they strike an object or surface.

Reflectance

Reflectance is another factor that is affected by the direction of a light source and demonstrates the interaction between lighting and surface qualities of objects and materials. Determining the reflectance from a surface or object involves examining the **angles of incident** and reflections (Figure 6.5). Changing the angle of the light source affects the angle of reflection (Figure 6.6). The type of lamp and shielding device on luminaires also affect the angle of incident. For example, a lamp with a clear glass covering allows light to travel in a straight direction.

Frosted or milky materials alter the angle of direction. Thus, light emitted from a frosted incandescent lamp will be diffused. Luminaires are designed with shielding devices that direct incident light in one or multiple directions. Some luminaires, such as a pendant globe with a white painted finish, will emit a multidirectional angle of incident. **Interreflection** occurs when light is contained within a structure and is continuously reflected from its surfaces. As discussed in Chapter 4, this occurs in fiber optics lamps that are encased in a black tube (Figure 6.7).

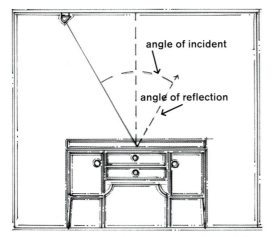

FIGURE 6.5 Angle of incident coming from a light source, striking a surface, and reflecting to the interior.

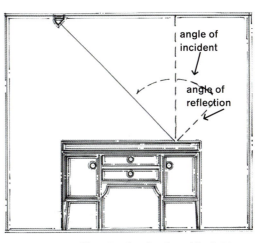

FIGURE 6.6 Changing the direction of the light source alters the angle of reflection.

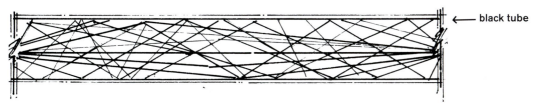

FIGURE 6.7 Interreflection is occurring by light reflecting back and forth within an enclosed area.

The color and texture of an object or surface affect reflectance qualities. Depending upon the characteristics of a material, when light strikes a surface, it is reflected or absorbed. **Specular reflectance** results when all the incident light is reflected (Figure 6.8a). This occurs when light strikes a glossy surface. When most of the incident light is reflected, **semi-specular reflectance** occurs (Figure 6.8b). This can occur when light strikes a surface that has some specular qualities but that is irregular, such as etched glass or a hammered finish. **Diffused reflectance** (Figure 6.8c) arises when the incident light is scattered in a variety of angles, such as when light strikes a matte finish. Reflection from a shiny material or bright color can cause discomfort or disability glare.

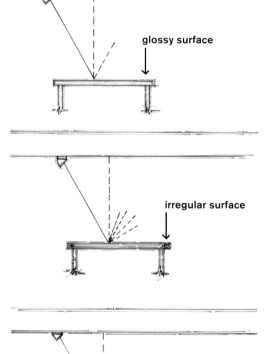

FIGURE 6.8a Angle of incident coming from a light source, striking a glossy surface, and reflecting to the interior.

glossy surface

FIGURE 6.8b Angle of incident coming from a light source, striking an irregular surface, and reflecting to the interior.

irregular surface

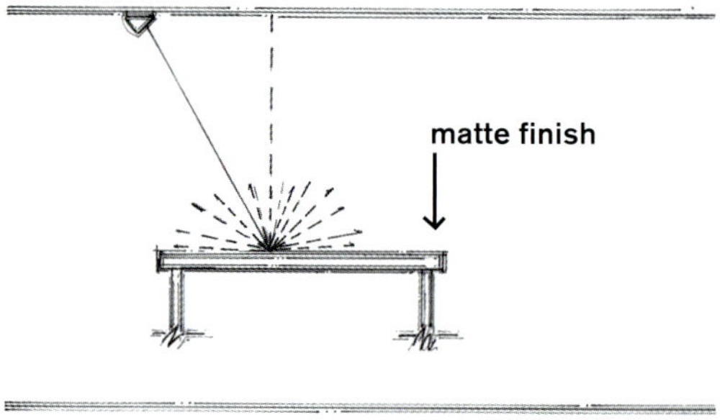

FIGURE 6.8c Angle of incident coming from a light source, striking a matte surface, and reflecting to the interior.

matte finish

Reflectance properties of materials also affect illumination levels in a space. The following formula can be used to determine the interaction between an illumination level and materials: $l = e \times \rho$, where l represents **luminance** in a space, e is the illumination level, and ρ, the Greek letter *rho*, is the reflectance percentage. For example, if the amount of light emitted from a light source is 60 foot-candles and strikes a surface with a 40 percent reflectance, the luminance of the surface will be 24 ($24 = 60 \times .40$). (Refer to Chapter 7 for more information on calculating lighting quantities.)

Reflectance values of colors and some materials are provided by a variety of resources and can be used to determine appropriate illumination levels in a space. The Munsell Color System indicates the reflectance of numerous colors. As discussed in Chapter 5, in the Munsell system white is at the top with a designation of 10, and 0 located on the bottom of the vertical axis, represents black. The luminous reflectance factor for each of the Munsell values is delineated in Table 5.2. As noted in Table 5.2, all light is reflected with white ($\rho = 1$). The following formula can be used to determine the approximate reflectance of a color (v represents value). In applying this formula the reflectance is approximately 56 percent for a color with a value of 8.

$$P \cong \frac{v(v-1)}{100}$$

$$P \cong \frac{8(8-1)}{100} = .56$$

Luminance
A unit of measurement that indicates the amount of light in the eyes of users of a space after reflection or transmission from a surface.

Materials also have luminous reflectance factors. Smooth and shiny materials will reflect more light than will rough and heavily textured materials. Reflectance values of various materials are provided in Table 6.1. In applying luminous reflectance values to an interior with light colors and smooth surfaces, the illumination level may need to be reduced. In contrast, in an environment that has dark colors and rough materials, the illumination level might have to be increased. However, before increasing or decreasing the illumination level, an interior designer must examine other environmental factors that affect reflectance values in a space, including the size of the room, the location of a surface, and light sources.

TABLE 6.1

Reflecting Materials

Material	Reflectance[a,b] (percent)	Characteristics
Specular		
Mirrored and optical coated glass	80–99	Provide directional control of light and bright-
Metallized and optical coated plastic	75–97	ness at specific viewing angles. Effective as
Processed anodized and optical		efficient reflectors and for special decorative
coated aluminum	75–95	lighting effects.
Polished aluminum	60–70	
Chromium	60–65	
Stainless steel	55–65	
Black structural glass	5	
Spread		
Processed aluminum (diffuse)	70–80	General diffuse reflection with a high specular
Etched aluminum	70–85	surface reflection of from 5–10 percent of light.
Satin chromium	50–55	
Brushed aluminum	55–58	
Aluminum paint	60–70	
Diffuse		
White plaster	90–92	Diffuse reflection results in uniform surface
White paint[b]	75–90	brightness at all viewing angles. Materials of
Porcelain enamel[b]	65–90	this type are good reflecting backgrounds for
White terra-cotta[b]	65–80	coves and luminous forms.
White structural glass	75–80	
Limestone	35–65	

[a]In as much as the amount of light transmitted depends upon the thickness of the material and the angle of incidence of light, the figures given are based on thickness generally used in lighting applications and on near-normal angles of incidence.

[b]These provide compound diffuse-specular reflection unless matte finished.

Source: Reprinted from the IESNA Lighting Handbook (9th ed.), pp. 1–22, with permission from the Illuminating Engineering Society of North America.

Because of the interreflection characteristics of lighting, reflectance levels are affected by the size of a room. In a small room, the walls are close together, so the light reflected from the walls strikes other walls and increases the reflectance level of the color. In a large room with high ceilings, the surfaces may be too far apart to cause interreflection, thus resulting in a lower reflectance level. Remember, even light-colored walls absorb some light. The location of the surface also affects reflectance levels. For instance, the location of ceilings and walls cause interreflection, while floors reflect less light. This helps to explain why in Chapter 2 it was recommended that windows be positioned close to ceilings to maximize the amount of daylight emitted in a space. Light sources that are close to a light-colored surface and have a high illumination level will elicit the greatest amount of reflection. Recommended reflectance levels for surfaces are summarized in Table 6.2. This is a guideline and can be important when energy conservation is a design criteria.

Optical Control

Some lamps and luminaires are designed for optical control. As discussed in Chapter 3, reflector lamps, such as R, PAR, and MR lamps, have an optical system designed within the lamp to control light. As described in Chapter 9, elements of luminaires that are designed to control illumination are shielding devices, reflection, refraction, and diffusion. Shielding devices for luminaires include baffles, louvers, and fascias. Light cannot penetrate the shielding units within the luminaire, thus producing light through reflection. Luminaires that are designed to control light through reflection have a material, such as shiny aluminum, on the inside surfaces. Light is emitted from the lamp and is reflected from the material to a surface or object (Figure 6.9). A luminaire with an interior surface made from a specular material, such as aluminum, can reflect a high percentage of a lamp's illumination. However, these luminaires can cause glare. Luminaires made from a specular material, but that have a brushed or etched finish, will diffuse some of the incident light rays. Matte finishes and dark colors will diffuse illumination. Some luminaires are designed with

TABLE 6.2

Recommended Reflectance for Interior Surfaces of Residences

Surface	Reflectance (percent)	Approximate Munsell Value
Ceiling	60–99	8 and above
Curtain and drapery treatment on large wall areas	35–60	6.5–8
Walls	35–60[*]	6.5–8
Floors	15–35[*]	4.0–6.5

[*] In areas where lighting for specific visual tasks takes precedence over lighting for the environment, the minimum reflectance should be 40 percent for walls, 25 percent for floors.

Source: Reprinted from the IESNA Lighting Handbook (9th ed.), pp. 18–22, with permission from the Illuminating Engineering Society of North America.

reflector contours to maximize the amount of illumination emitted from a lamp. Common shapes for these luminaires include ellipses, parabolas, and circles.

Refraction is used to control light in a luminaire by utilizing the same principle as light passing through a prism. Through refraction, the direction of a light source is altered to maximize the amount of light falling on a surface. Prismatic lenses made from glass or plastic are designed with small prisms that refract the light to the space and reduce glare. Glass and plastic lenses that do not have prisms distribute illumination through diffusion or transmission.

Transmission

Some luminaires have materials that are designed to let light through rather than control it. **Transmission** is the term that is used to describe materials that allow most of the incident light to pass through. The three types of transmission are direct, diffuse, and mixed (Figures

Reflector contour
The unit of a luminaire designed to reflect light.

Refraction
The occurence wherby the direction of a light ray changes in an oblique manner as it passes through a material.

Transmission
Materials that allow most of the incident light to pass through.

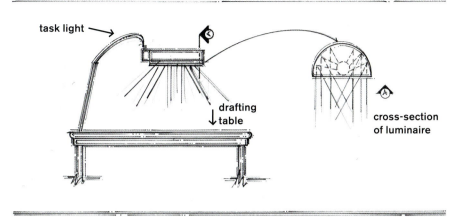

task light

drafting
table

cross-section
of luminaire

FIGURE 6.9 Light strikes the interior of a luminaire and then reflects into an interior space.

6.10 a–c). Direct transmission occurs when the majority of the light passes through the material (Figure 6.10a). Clear glass is an example of a material that allows for direct transmission. Material that creates diffused transmission, such as plastics, causes the light to be scattered in many directions (Figure 6.10b). Mixed transmission occurs with materials that allow most of the light to pass through in a semiscattered manner (Figure 6.10c). Etched and sandblasted glass are examples of materials that cause mixed transmission. Table 6.3 illustrates the transmittance percentage for various materials. Keep in mind that white plastics can be a source of glare. (For more information on the design of luminaires, see Chapter 9.)

Patterns of Light, Shade, and Shadow

Controlling the directional qualities of light sources is a key element in creating atmosphere in an environment. Patterns of light, shade, and shadow help to create an exciting space that has variety and mystery. Excellent examples of mastering these patterns are evident in film, paintings, photography, and stage lighting. (These mediums are discussed in Chapter 18.) A room with no variance in light and shade is generally flat and fails to enhance variations in textures of materials or architectural features, and such a room can feel like a dull, cloudy day.

TABLE 6.3
Transmitting Materials

Material	Transmittance[a] (percent)	Characteristics
Glass		
Clear and optical coated	80–99	Low absorption; no diffusion; high concentrated transmission. Used as protective cover plates for concealed light sources.
Configurated, obscure, etched, ground, sandblasted, and frosted	70–85	Low absorption; high transmission; poor diffusion. Used only when backed by good diffusing glass or when light sources are placed at edges of panel to light the background.
Opalescent and alabaster	55–80	Lower transmission than above glasses; fair diffusion. Used for favorable appearance when indirectly lighted.
Flashed (cased) opal	30–65	Low absorption; excellent diffusion. Used for panels of uniform brightness with good efficiency.
Solid opal glass	15–40	Higher absorption than flashed opal glass; excellent diffusion. Used in place of flashed opal where a white appearance is required.
Plastics		
Clear prismatic lens	70–92	Low absorption; no diffusion; high concentrated transmission. Used as shielding for fluorescent luminaries, outdoor signs, and luminaires.
White	30–70	High absorption; excellent diffusion. Used to diffuse lamp images and provide even appearance in fluorescent luminaires.
Colors	0–90	Available in any color for special color-rendering lighting requirements for aesthetic reasons.
Marble (*impregnated*)	5–30	High absorption; excellent diffusion; used for panels of low brightness. Seldom used in producing general illumination because of the low efficiency.
Alabaster	20–50	High absorption; good diffusion. Used for favorable appearance when directly lighted.

[a]In as much as the amount of light transmitted depends upon the thickness of the material and the angle of incidence of light, the figures given are based on thickness generally used in lighting applications and on near normal angles of incidence.

Source: Reprinted from the IESNA Lighting Handbook (9th ed.), pp. 1–22, with permission from the Illuminating Engineering Society of North America.

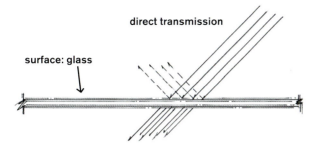

FIGURE 6.10a Direct transmission occurs by most of the incident light passing through clear glass in a straight direction.

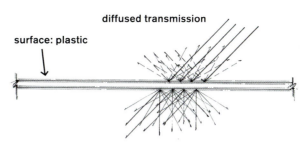

FIGURE 6.10b Diffused transmission occurs by some of the incident light passing through a plastic material in a scattered direction.

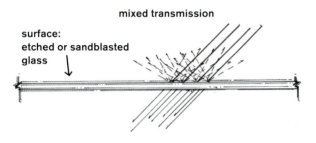

FIGURE 6.10c Mixed transmission occurs by most of the incident light passing through an etched glass in a semi-scattered direction.

Figures 6.11 a and b illustrate how interiors can be enhanced with the addition of light, shade, and shadows.

Successful applications require the identification of what should be highlighted, and which objects or areas could be in shade and shadow. Patterns of light and shadow should always reinforce elements of the interior architecture and objects of emphasis. Chapter 2 explores considerations for highlighting features of an interior, including the identification of unique features of an architectural element, rather than illuminating an entire object. It is equally important to plan lighting that does not emphasize defects in materials or quality. In identifying which areas or objects to highlight in a space, it is important to consider the patterns of light and shadows that can enhance the design or direct attention away from it. For example, a symmetrically balanced furniture arrangement can be reinforced through a symmetrical pattern of highlight and shadows. Highlighting the elements in the space that create rhythm can reinforce this aspect of design. Light and

FIGURE 6.11a
The lack of highlights and shadows create a dull lighting environment.

FIGURE 6.11b
Highlights and shadows create an interesting lighting environment.

shadow patterns can be used as wayfinding paths in a building or space. In contrast, it is important to remember that light and shadow can distract from a design; for example, when scalloped figures of light are illuminated on a patterned wall.

An important factor in identifying areas to highlight is determining which aspects of an object or area could be hidden by shade or a shadow. For example, if facial features of a sculpture are to be highlighted, it might not be desirable for shade to hide the upper torso area. Highlighting signage might result in some words not being visible because of shade or shadows created by the light source.

The intensity of a light source, the angle of direction, and its distance from an object affect the shape and length of shade and shadows. The type of shadow can affect the atmosphere of the interior. A high-intensity light source that is close to an object will create a dark shadow that has defined details. Light sources at a low angle will create elongated shadows. Shadows of trees late in the afternoon demonstrate this concept. A light source that is close to an object will create shorter shadows. Generally, dark and elongated shadows create the most dramatic effects in an interior. When planning lighting in a space with many windows, it is important to track the light and shadow patterns throughout the day and at different times of the year.

To have an environment with effective patterns of light, shade, and shadow requires control over the direction and **dispersion** of light sources, and which are affected by the type of lamp and design of the luminaire. As discussed in Chapter 2, the direction of a light source can either enhance or obliterate the textural qualities of a surface, object, or people. Objects will generally appear most attractive when a light source is positioned to the side, at an angle between 15 and 45 degrees (Figure 6.12). To help avoid glare, shiny materials should be highlighted by a light source that is positioned to the side of the object. Glass objects will generally sparkle the most when they are illuminated from above and below.

The dispersion of a light source determines the amount of area that will be illuminated. As discussed in Chapter 3, spot and flood lamps distribute beam angles in a small and broad area, respectively. Luminaires are designed to disperse light in a range from small to large. For example, some downlights have a pinhole in the center of

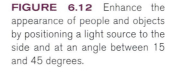

Dispersion
The distribution of light rays from a source.

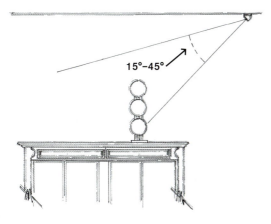

FIGURE 6.12 Enhance the appearance of people and objects by positioning a light source to the side and at an angle between 15 and 45 degrees.

15°–45°

the fixture that allows only a small amount of light to be emitted from the luminaire. A small dispersion of light, with less than a 30-degree angle of beam, will enhance form, textures, and shapes (see Chapter 15).

The directional effects of lighting explored in this chapter are one of the elements in a lighting system. In specifying a lighting plan, an interior designer must consider how the intensity and direction of a light source affects an object's appearance, the architectural features of a space, the ability of people in the space to perform a task, and quantity of illumination. The next chapter covers how to determine the quantity of illumination required in a quality lighting environment.

SUMMARY

- The ability to perform a task or view an object is affected by a variety of factors, including glare, contrast, colors, illumination levels, and the physical condition of eyes.
- The direction of a light source can affect the quantity of light required in a space.
- Properly specifying the direction of a light source, rather than increasing the quantity of lumens, can improve a dark lighting environment.
- To have a quality lighting environment, an interior designer must develop a plan that maximizes the positive attributes of brightness and that controls glare.
- Brightness is generally a subjective reaction to an environment and is dependent upon individuals' expectations, comparative contexts, and the physical condition of their eyes.
- There are a variety of factors that affect glare, including individual perceptions, condition of eyes, and extremes in illumination contrasts.
- Proper illumination levels between areas in a space help to manage undesirable brightness and glare by reducing high contrasts.
- The direction and type of light source affect angles of incident and resultant reflections.

- Reflectance is an example of the interaction between lighting and the surface qualities of objects and materials.
- Controlling the directional qualities of light sources is a key element in creating the desired atmosphere in an environment and in having effective accent lighting.
- Patterns of light, shade, and shadow help to create an interesting space that has variety.

Key Terms

angle of incident	indirect glare
brightness	interreflection
diffused reflectance	luminance
direct glare	reflectance
disability glare	reflector contours
discomfort glare	refraction
dispersion	semi-specular reflectance
glare	specular reflectance
illumination zones	transmission

Exercises

1. Identify five different commercial spaces and ask at least ten people in each space whether they perceive any of the light sources as bright. Be sure to ask people who are a variety of ages. Record their responses, the type of luminaire, lamp, footcandle level, and the location of the light sources. Analyze the data and write a report that summarizes the results and provides recommendations for future illumination applications.

2. Locate five different windows that are oriented on different sides of a building and that have a variety of sizes and shapes. On a sunny day record the footcandle level next to the windowsill and place an object under the window. Record the size of the window. Determine how close to the window one has to be in order to see

the details of the object. Record your results. Add electrical light to the area around the window to eliminate the disability glare and record the required foot-candle level. Analyze and synthesize all results in a written report. Include recommendations for future practice.

3. Measure the footcandle levels for the three illumination zones in five different office settings. Record the results and the type of luminaire, lamp, and location of each light source. Calculate the footcandle differences between the illumination zones and determine whether the transition levels are appropriate. If they are not, provide suggestions for improving the space. Write a report that summarizes the results and provides suggestions for future practice.

4. Select eight different materials that have a variety of textures. Utilizing a clamp light, direct the light source at each material and record the resultant reflection properties. Position the light source at a variety of angles and distances from the material. Record all results and write a report that provides a summary and recommendations for future practice.

5. Using the World Wide Web, locate luminaires that are designed with each of the following control devices: (a) reflection, (b) refraction, (c) diffusion, and (d) shielding unit. Print the pictures of the luminaires and mount them in a notebook. Identify the advantages and disadvantages of each.

6. Visit an art museum and two different restaurants and retail stores. For each space record the type of luminaire and lamp and the location of the fixtures. Identify any sources of brightness or glare. Examine the patterns of light, shade, and shadow. Write a report (that could include sketches and photographs) that addresses the items listed below:

   a. A summary of the illumination for each space.

   b. Recommendations for problems associated with brightness or glare.

   c. The effectiveness of patterns of light, shade, and shadow and provide any recommendations for improving the patterns.

REFERENCES

American Society of Heating, Refrigeration and Air-Conditioning Engineers (1999). *Energy efficient design of new buildings except new low-rise residential buildings, ASHRAE/IES90.1-1999.* Atlanta, GA: ASHRAE.

Benya, J., Heschong, L., McGowan, T., Miller, N., and Rubinstein, F. (2001). *Advanced lighting guidelines.* White Salmon, WA: New Buildings Institute.

Birren, F. (1969). *Light, Color and Environment.* New York: Van Nostrand Reinhold.

Boyce, P.R. (1981). *Human Factors in Lighting,* New York: Macmillan.

Boylan, B.R. (1987). *The Lighting Primer.* Ames, IA: Iowa State University Press.

Coaton, J.R., and Marsden, A. M. (1997). *Lamps and Lighting,* (4th ed.). London: Arnold.

Egan, M.D. (1983). *Concepts in Architectural Lighting.* New York: McGraw-Hill.

Gordan, G., and Nuckolls, J.L. (1995). *Interior Lighting for Designers.* New York: John Wiley & Sons.

Hill, H., and Bruce, V. (1996). The effects of lighting on the perception of facial surfaces. *Journal of Experimental Psychology: Human Perception and Performance, 22*(4), 986–1004.

Illuminating Engineering Society of North America (IESNA) (2000). *IESNA Lighting Handbook,* (9th ed.). New York: Illuminating Engineering Society of North America.

Illuminating Engineering Society of North America (IESNA) (1998). Lighting for the aged and partially sighted community. Recommended Practice for Lighting and the Visual Environment for Senior Living, RP-28-98. New York: Illuminating Engineering Society of North America.

Kaufman, J.E. (ed.) (1984). *IES Lighting Handbook Reference Volume 1984.* New York: Illuminating Engineering Society.

Lam, W.C. (1977). *Perception and Lighting as Formgivers for Architecture.* New York: McGraw-Hill.

Littlefair, P. J. (1991). Site layout planning for daylight and sunlight: a guide to good practice. *BRE Report,* BR 209.

Loe, D.L., and Rowlands, E. (1996). The art and science of lighting: A strategy for lighting design. *Lighting Research & Technology, 28*(4), 153–164.

Loe, D.L., Mansfield, J.F., and Rowlands, E. (1994). Appearance of lit environment and its relevance in lighting design: Environmental study. *Lighting Research & Technology, 26*(3), 119–133.

Moore, F. (1985). *Concepts and Practice of Architectural Daylighting.* New York: Van Nostrand Reinhold Company.

Phillips, D. (2000). *Lighting Modern Buildings.* Oxford: Architectural Press.

Rea, M.S. (1986). Toward a model of visual performance: Foundations and data. *Journal of the Illuminating Engineering Society, 15*(2), 41–57.

Rea, M.S., and Ouellette, M.J. (1988). Visual performance using reaction times. *Lighting Research & Technology, 20*(4), 139–53.

Rea, M.S., and Ouellette, M.J. (1991). Relative visual performance: A basis for application. *Lighting Research & Technology, 23*(3), 135–144.

Rosenthal, J., and Wertenbaker, L. (1972). *The Magic of Light.* Boston: Little, Brown and Company.

Rowlands, E.D., Loe, D.L., McIntosh, R.M., and Mansfield, K.P. (1985). Lighting adequacy and quality in office interiors by consideration of subjective assessment and physical measurement. *CIE Journal, 4*(1), 23–37.

Smith F.K., and Bertolone, F.J. (1986). *The Principles and Practices of Lighting Design: Bringing Interiors to Light.* New York: Whitney Library of Design.

Steffy, G.R. (1990). *Architectural Lighting Design.* New York: Van Nostrand Reinhold.

Tresidder, J. (ed.) (1983). *Mastering Composition and Light.* New York: Time-Life Books.

Veitch, J. (2000, July). Lighting guidelines from lighting quality research. *CIBSE/ILE Lighting 2000 Conference.* New York, United Kingdom.

Watson, L. (1977). *Lighting Design Handbook.* New York: McGraw-Hill.

Weale, R.A. (1961). Retinal illumination of age. *Trans. Illuminating Engineering Society (London), 26*(2), 95–100.

Wilkins, A.J., Nimmo-Smith, I., Slater, A.I., and Bedocs, L. (1989). Fluorescent lighting, headaches, and eyestrain. *Lighting Research & Technology, 21*(1), 11–18.

Wright, G.A., and Rea, M.S. (1984). Age, a human factor in lighting. *Proceedings of the 1984 International Conference on Occupational Ergonomics.* D.A. Attwood, and C. McCann, (Eds.). Rexdale, Ontario, Canada: Human Factors Association of Canada.

CHAPTER 7

Quantity of Lighting

- Describe the basic units of measurement used in lighting, including luminous intensity, luminous flux, illuminance, luminance, and luminance exitance.

- Comprehend the relationships among the basic units of measurement utilized in lighting, including luminous intensity, luminous flux, illuminance, luminance, and luminance exitance.

- Understand candlepower distribution curves, and how to apply the data they provide to lighting specifications.

- Identify key factors to consider when specifying illumination levels for a quality lighting environment.

- Determine the average illuminance for an interior using the lumen method.

- Determine illuminance levels for a point in a space.

- Evaluate characteristics of basic and advanced lighting software.

DETERMINING the appropriate quantity of illumination is a key factor in designing a quality environment. A quality lighting environment will have a flexible illumination level plan that reflects changes at different times of the day, a variety of activities, and the users of the space. It is critical to view quantity of illumination as only one consideration in a lighting system. Unfortunately, many environments are planned with only an appropriate uniform foot-candle level being considered.

Units of Measurement

International System of Units

Measuring the quantity of lighting in an environment is based upon the principles of radiometry and photometry. **Radiometry** is a scientific area that focuses on measuring an amount of radiant energy. **Photometry** is a science that is derived from radiometry but that includes the human response to a source of illumination. The worldwide standard for the units of measurement is the International System of Units (SI). The basic units of measurement include luminous intensity, luminous flux, illuminance, luminance, and luminous exitance.

A starting point for understanding photometry is the candela (cd), which is the unit of measurement of **luminous intensity**. "I" is the abbreviation for luminous intensity. One candela represents the luminous intensity from a source, pointing in a specific direction, on a solid angle called the **steradian** (Figure 7.1). Originally, a candle was used as the measurement for luminous intensity, but it was impossible to arrive at standardization with various types of candles; hence the international use of the candela. *Candlepower* and *candela* are considered interchangeable terms. The other three units of measurement are derived from the candela.

Luminous flux is the unit of measurement that indicates the total amount of illumination emitted by a source, and F is the abbreviation

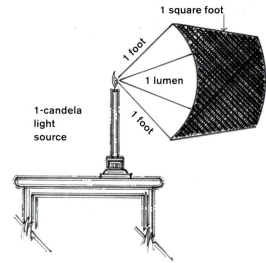

FIGURE 7.1 One candela illuminated on a solid angle, the steradian.

for this unit. Luminous flux is measured in lumens (lm). Lamp manu-facturers provide lumen information. As discussed in Chapter 3, the number of lumens produced by a lamp per watts consumed deter-mines the lamp's efficacy. The **luminaire efficacy ratio (LER)** is a ratio of the watts consumed for the entire luminaire system, which in-cludes the total lamp lumens, ballast factor, and photometric effi-ciency. (For more information on LER, refer to Chapters 9 and 12.)

The unit of measurement used to determine the total amount of light on a surface is **illuminance**. The abbreviation for illuminance is E, and it is measured in lux (lx) or footcandle (fc) in the metric and customary systems, respectively. An illumination of 1 lux is produced by 1 lumen of light illuminated on an area of 1 square meter. Ten lux equal approximately 1 footcandle. Thus, a recommendation for 400 lux of illumination on a work surface would be equivalent to 40 fc. To provide context for these measurements, the footcandle levels for a full moon and sunlight at noon are .01 and 10,000, respectively. Many work areas in homes, offices, and conference rooms utilize 30–50 fc (300–500 lx). As discussed in previous chapters, there are many fac-tors that must be considered in determining illumination levels, in-cluding the lamp, design of the luminaire, maintenance procedures, reflectance values, and distance and angle from the light source to the task.

Luminance as a unit of measurement indicates the amount of light in the eyes of users of the space after reflection or transmission from a surface. Illuminance and reflectance affect luminance. The unit of measurement is candela per square meter (cd/m^2), and L is the abbre-viation for the term. *Brightness,* a term that is synonymous with lumi-nance, is a phenomenon that describes an individual's perception of the light in a space and is not a unit of measurement. As discussed in Chapter 6, luminance affects the apparent brightness of a surface, or material, and is dependent upon the location of the user as well as col-ors, textures, and interior architecture. **Luminous exitance** is another term associated with luminance. This unit indicates the total quantity of light that is reflected and emitted in all directions from a surface or material. Luminous exitance is measured in lumens per square foot (lm/ft^2).

Luminaire efficacy ratio (LER)
A ratio of the number of watts consumed per the entire luminaire system. .

Illuminance
The total amount of light on a surface; measured in lux (lx) or footcandle (fc).

Luminous exitance
The unit of measurement that indicates the total quantity of light reflected and emitted in all directions from a surface or material.

Photometric Data

To determine the direction, pattern, and intensity of light from reflector lamps and luminaires, interior designers refer to **candlepower distribution curves**, as provided by lamp and luminaire manufacturers (see Figure 7.2). Interior designers often use the term "bat-wing graphs" when referring to specific curves that resemble the shape of a bat's wings. These curves result from a bat-wing lens. Polar candlepower distribution curves utilize zero, **nadir** (straight down), as the location of a light source. The concentric circles on the graph indicate the intensity expressed in candelas and the radiating lines are the angles of distribution.

Figure 7.2 illustrates a photometric data cutsheet of a direct fluorescent (2-T8s) luminaire with silver parabolic louvers manufactured by Prudential Lighting. Directly above the candlepower distribution graph are summary data related to the luminaire. D=100 percent and I=0 percent, which indicate that the luminaire is a direct (100 percent) fixture and does not have any indirect (0 percent) light. The lamp lumens are 2950 with input watts of 59.

The cutsheet also provides spacing criteria data. The spacing criterion (SC) is a metric measurement that provides luminaire locations for spaces requiring consistent illumination levels. The height measurement for direct luminaires is determined from the bottom of the fixture to a work surface that is 2 feet 6 inches above the floor (Figure 7.3). The measurement for indirect luminaires is from the ceiling to the work surface. Luminaire manufacturers provide SC ratio recommendations with other photometric data (see Figure 7.2). The SC for the length of the luminaire is referred to as the "parallel" or "along," and the short side of the luminaire is the "perpendicular" or "across." For the luminaire depicted in Figure 7.2, the SC along is 1.1, and the SC across is 1.3. Deviations from the recommended SC locations may result in illumination levels that are too high or in dark areas.

To maximize the amount of illumination derived from reflectance, luminaires should be installed close to walls, but not so close that they cause excessive brightness on the walls. Generally, the distance from a wall to a fixture is half the center-to-center distance between fixtures. The formula for calculating the center-to-center distances between fixtures is: Spacing Intervals (SI) = SC ratio $\times$ mounting height (MH).

photometric data

OLYP-2T8-04-SPL-TMW-D1

Report # LSI15526 D=100% I=0.0%
Spacing Criteria: Along 1.1; Across 1.3
Lamp Lumens: 2950 Input Watts: 59

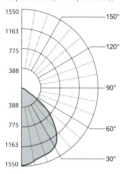

1550		150°
1163		
775		120°
388		
388		90°
388		
775		60°
1163		
1550		30°

Candlepower Summary

Vertical Angle	Horizontal Angle					Output Lumens
	0°	22.5°	45°	67.5°	90°	
0	1526	1526	1526	1526	1526	
5	1519	1513	1511	1508	1511	145
10	1480	1474	1466	1459	1458	
15	1419	1406	1400	1414	1417	397
20	1347	1329	1341	1376	1396	
25	1262	1245	1287	1347	1379	598
30	1160	1158	1233	1299	1334	
35	1045	1062	1156	1206	1241	708
40	913	956	1045	1057	1077	
45	771	830	885	866	884	651
50	605	668	678	656	684	
55	414	482	462	427	411	394
60	215	253	261	198	157	
65	103	106	106	103	105	117
70	53	49	46	70	75	
75	26	23	19	39	48	33
80	11	11	9	14	21	
85	3	3	3	5	6	5
90	0	0	0	0	0	

Zonal Lumen Summary

Zone	% Lamp	% Luminaire
0-90	51.66	100.00
90-180	0.00	0.00

Efficiency = 51.7%

Luminance Summary (cd/m^2)

Angle	0°	45°	90°
45	3612	4162	4156
55	2388	2678	2380
65	804	835	829
75	338	244	616
85	120	121	228

Coefficients of Utilization (%)

Floor	effective floor cavity reflectance = .20									
Ceiling	80				70				50	
Wall	70	50	30	10	70	50	30	10	50	30	10
RCR 0	62	62	62	62	60	60	60	60	57	57	57
1	58	56	54	53	57	55	53	52	53	52	51
2	54	51	48	46	53	50	48	46	48	46	45
3	50	46	43	40	49	45	42	40	44	42	39
4	47	42	38	36	46	41	38	35	40	37	35
5	43	38	34	31	42	37	34	31	36	33	31
6	40	34	30	28	39	34	30	27	33	30	27
7	37	31	27	25	37	31	27	24	30	27	24
8	34	28	24	21	34	28	24	21	27	24	21
9	32	25	21	19	31	25	21	19	24	21	19
10	29	23	19	17	29	23	19	17	22	19	16

installation

Adjoining Detail

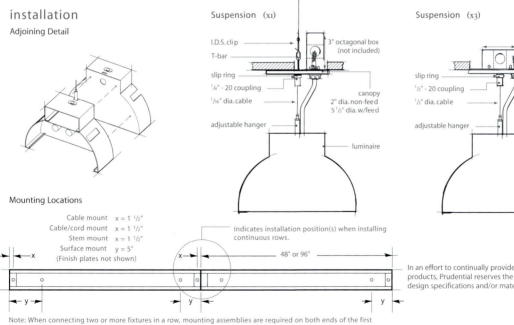

Mounting Locations

Cable mount x = 1 1/2"
Cable/cord mount x = 1 1/2"
Stem mount x = 1 1/2"
Surface mount y = 5"
(Finish plates not shown)

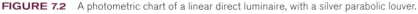

Suspension (x1)

I.D.S. clip
T-bar
slip ring
1/4" - 20 coupling
1/16" dia. cable
adjustable hanger

3" octagonal box (not included)
canopy
2" dia. non-feed
5 1/2" dia. w/feed
luminaire

Suspension (x3)

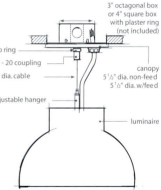

slip ring
1/2" - 20 coupling
1/2" dia. cable
adjustable hanger

3" octagonal box or 4" square box with plaster ring (not included)
canopy
5 1/2" dia. non-feed
5 1/2" dia. w/feed
luminaire

Indicates installation position(s) when installing continuous rows.

x — 48" or 96"

In an effort to continually provide the highest quality products, Prudential reserves the right to change design specifications and/or materials, without notice.

Note: When connecting two or more fixtures in a row, mounting assemblies are required on both ends of the first fixture, with only one mounting assembly required on each additional fixture.

FIGURE 7.2 A photometric chart of a linear direct luminaire, with a silver parabolic louver.

FIGURE 7.3 In calcu-
lating lighting quantities,
the height measurement
for direct luminaires is determined from the bottom
of the fixture to a work
surface that is 2'-6"
from the floor (Mounting
Height = MH).

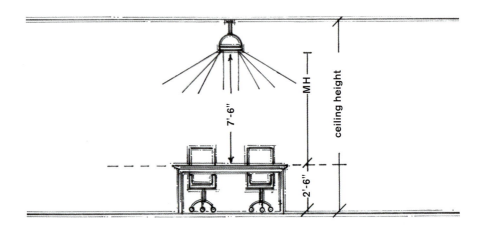

The mounting height is the distance from the bottom of the luminaire
to the work surface. The spacing interval for a luminaire that is 7 feet
6 inches from a work surface and an SC of along 1.1 and across 1.3 is
8 and 10 feet on center, respectively. This is determined by the
SI = SC × MH equation as:

$$SI = 1.1 \times 7.5 = 8.25$$

or 8 feet on center along the length of the fixture

$$SI = 1.3 \times 7.5 = 9.75$$

or 10 feet on center along the short side of the fixture

To read the candlepower distribution graph, identify a specific angle
of view and then read the associated candelas. For example, for the direct linear luminaire, illustrated in Figure 7.2, the emitted candelas at
a 30-degree vertical angle are approximately 1160. This number is also
available in the candlepower summary table. To locate the candelas at
a 30-degree vertical angle in the candlepower summary, refer to the
vertical angle column. Find 30 degrees and look to the right to locate
the horizontal angle column for 0 degrees. Continuing in the same row
and moving to the right will provide the emitted candelas at the 22.5-,
45-, 67.5-, and 90-degree horizontal angle. For example, at the 30-
degree vertical angle, the emitted candelas at the 45-degree horizontal
angle are 1233. The last column in the candlepower summary chart indicates the output in lumens at various vertical angles. For example, at
the 25-degree angle the output in lumens is 598.

The zonal lumens summary table provides a quick overview of lumens in two zones. Since the luminaire has a direct distribution of light, all the light is emitted from the 0–90-degree (downward) zone. The zonal lumens also indicate the efficiency of the luminaire and lamp combination, which is 51.7 percent. The cutsheet also provides luminance summary (cd/m^2) data. For this luminaire the luminance levels are higher at the lower vertical angles. For example, at the 45-degree vertical angle the luminance is 3612. Luminance at the 75-degree vertical angle is 338. The table containing coefficients of utilization (percentage) data is explained later in this chapter.

As illustrated in Figure 7.2, luminaires and reflector lamps with a symmetrical distribution are often illustrated on only one side of the graph, since each half will be identical. It is important to note that indirect/direct luminaires have a candlepower distribution curve above and below nadir. If the luminaire distributes a high level of illumination toward the ceiling, to avoid annoying brightness or glare it might be necessary to locate the fixture at a considerable distance from the ceiling. Luminaires that emit light from the top and sides of the fixture will have candlepower distribution graphs for vertical and horizontal light angles.

Lighting Performance Metrics

In addition to the units of measurement, three lighting performance metrics that assist in determining appropriate quantities of lighting are the **equivalent sphere index (ESI), relative visual performance (RVP),** and **visual comfort probability (VCP)**. Calculating these ratings requires sophisticated computer programs, but the ratings may be included with photometric data from luminaire manufacturers. Because of the multiple factors that affect a quality lighting environment, the author's recommendation is to use these metrics as a guide for comparing different luminaires. Since ESI and RVP are not often used in practice, the discussion will focus on VCP.

VCP ratings point out potential disability glare to users of the space; they are calculated to include a variety of factors, including the design of the luminaire, location of the fixture, angles of view, room proportions, and surface reflectance values. The VCP is the percentage of people who might experience disability glare when they are seated in

Equivalent sphere index (ESI)
A metric measurement demonstrating a comparison between an ideal illumination condition within a sphere and the results of a specific lighting system.

Relative visual performance (RVP)
A metric measurement indicating how well a task can be performed with a specific luminaire in a fixed horizontal location.

Visual comfort probability (VCP)
A rating that represents the percentage of people who might experience disability glare when they are seated in the least desirable location in a space.

the least desirable location. The higher the VCP rating, the better the luminaire is designed to prevent disability glare. IES recommends a VCP of 80 in spaces where computers are used extensively. The rating is measured at an angle below 65 degrees. To have a high VCP rating, some luminaires are designed with the lamp located high in the fixture. This reduces the likelihood of disability glare, but the interreflection that occurs within the fixture can reduce illumination levels.

Illuminance Recommendations

There are numerous factors to consider when specifying illuminance levels for a quality lighting environment, including the integration of human needs, architecture, economics, and the environment (IESNA, 2000). IESNA suggests that human needs include visibility, task performance, visual comfort, social communication, mood and atmosphere, health, safety, well-being, and aesthetics. Architectural factors include form, composition, style, codes, and standards. Economics and the environment involve issues related to installation, maintenance, operation, and energy. IESNA and several international organizations have developed recommendations for illuminance levels. Many of the IESNA recommendations have met the requirements of the American National Standards Institute (ANSI). The Chartered Institution of Building Services Engineers (CIBSE) developed recommendations for the United Kingdom. Most of the recommendations are for task lighting at a horizontal work surface that is 2 feet 6 inches above the floor.

Specifying illuminance levels should be considered a fluid practice, whereby the levels vary for each activity throughout the day. For example, during one day in an office an individual may be engaged in a variety of activities that have different lighting requirements, such as reading, working at the computer, or viewing a video. The illuminance recommendations should include a range of levels that cover each task. Daylight integration and control should also be included in the fluid illuminance specifications. (Lighting suggestions for specific tasks are discussed in Chapters 19 and 20.)

The *IESNA Lighting Design Guide* (2000) is the standard used by engineers and lighting designers. The guide was developed to recommend illuminance levels based upon specific tasks and criteria that affect the quality of lighting. To address diverse applications, the guide is composed of six sections: (1) interior, (2) industrial, (3) outdoor, (4) sports and recreation, (5) transportation, and (6) emergency, safety, and security. The "interior" section has headings in the rows of the table that include residential and commercial space, such as health-care facilities, food-service facilities, and museums. The subheadings become more specific for each type of space. For example, "offices" have subheadings for filing, open-plan office, and libraries. Some of the subheadings indicate more specific tasks or areas. For example, general lighting in the residence category includes "passage areas (circulation)," and "conversation, relaxation, and entertainment" recommendations.

The columns of the table in the *IESNA Lighting Design Guide* identify criteria to be considered when specifying illuminance levels, and, when applicable, the level of importance on a four-point scale from "Very Important" to "Not Important," or "Not Applicable." Design issues in the tables include a variety of considerations, such as "Appearance of Space and Luminaires," "Direct Glare," "Shadows," and "System Control and Flexibility." The columns on the table also provide the illuminance direction, vertical or horizontal, and an associated "Category of Value (lux)." The category range is from A to G, with A having the lowest lux illumination level. The lux and fc recommendations are based upon three major areas, orientation and simple visual tasks, common visual tasks, and specific visual tasks. The recommended lux and fc levels are provided for each category. For example, the lux recommendation for category "F—Performance of visual tasks of low contrast and small size" is 1000 lx (100 fc). In addition to analyzing the recommendations provided in the tables of the *IESNA Lighting Design Guide,* IESNA recommends reading about specific design criteria and principles of application.

Calculations

Calculations for determining illuminance can be done by hand or by using a lighting software package. This section reviews both applications. In a quality lighting environment, it is critical to consider the illuminance level identified through the calculations to be only one variable in the final specifications. All the criteria discussed throughout this textbook, and the uniqueness of a site and its users, must be synthesized for the final lighting plan.

Lumen Method

The lumen method described in this section is an abbreviated method used to determine the average illuminance on horizontal surfaces in a room. These data can be useful in the initial stages of the lighting design process. To determine more accurate illuminance calculations, refer to IESNA (2000) or advanced lighting programs.

To perform illuminance calculations, there are several elements that must be identified, including the proportions of a room, luminaire, lamps, location of work surface, distance between the work surface and the luminaires, and reflectance values of ceilings, walls, and floors. In addition, the calculations require the **room-cavity ratios (RCR), coefficient of utilization for luminaires (CU), light loss factor (LLF), lamp lumen depreciation (LLD),** and **luminaire dirt depreciation (LDD)**.

The RCR is a formula designed to accommodate the proportions of a space and the distance from the luminaires to the work surface. In the formula, H is the height of the ceiling from the work surface; L is the length of the room; and W is the width of the room.

$$RCR = \frac{5(H)\,(L + W)}{L \times W}$$

The RCR is used to determine the CU (see Figure 7.2). The CU is dependent upon the variables of the space and the design of the luminaire. The CU indicates the ratio of initial lamp lumens to the lumens on a work surface for a particular luminaire, for lamps, for the location of the task plane, and for the variable of the spaces. CU percentages are available from luminaire manufacturers (see Figure 7.2). The CU table in Figure 7.2 is based upon a floor cavity reflectance of .20. Ceiling reflectance percentages are 80, 70, and 50. Wall reflectance percentages are provided for 70, 50, 30, and 10.

LLF indicates the illuminance that is lost resulting from the type of lamp, ambient temperature of the space, time, input voltage, ballast, lamp position, interior conditions, and burnouts. There can be a 25 percent loss of lumens because of dirt, dust, and lamp depreciation. Some of the variables affecting these losses are discussed in Chapter 3. IESNA (2000) has identified recoverable and nonrecoverable LLFs. The recoverable LLFs include room surface dirt depreciation, lamp lumen depreciation, lamp burnouts factor, and luminaire dirt depreciation. Nonrecoverable factors include ambient temperature, input voltage, ballast factor, and luminaire surface depreciation.

For an abbreviated method in determining the average illuminance on horizontal surfaces in a room, LLF can be calculated by multiplying LLD by LDD. LLD is a metric measurement that examines the loss of lumens due to the design of a lamp. Table 7.1 provides a list of LLD for selected lamps. LDD accounts for the loss of light caused by dirt and dust accumulation. Important considerations for LDD are the design of the luminaire, the atmosphere of the space, and how often the lamps are cleaned. Table 7.2 and Figure 7.4 produced by IESNA (2000) illustrate maintenance categories for various luminaires, atmosphere considerations, and dirt conditions. This information serves as a reference for determining LDD. As defined by IESNA (2000) the cat-

TABLE 7.1

Lamp Lumen Depreciation (LLD) Factors for Selected Lamps

Lamps	Typical LLD Factors
Incandescent	.85
Halogen	.92
Fluorescent	
T8/730	.90
T8/830	.93
Compact fluorescent	.85
Metal halide	.73
Ceramic metal halide	.89
High-pressure sodium	.80

TABLE 7.2

Procedure for Determining Luminaire Maintenance Categories

Maintenance Category	Top Enclosure	Bottom Enclosure
I.	1. None	1. None
II.	1. None 2. Transparent with 15 percent or more uplight through apertures 3. Translucent with 15 percent or more uplight through apertures 4. Opaque with 15 percent or more uplight through apertures	1. None 2. Louvers or baffles
III.	1. Transparent with less than 15 percent upward light through apertures 2. Translucent with less than 15 percent upward light through apertures 3. Opaque with less than 15 percent uplight through apertures	1. None 2. Louvers or baffles
IV.	1. Transparent unapertured 2. Translucent unapertured 3. Opaque unapertured	1. None 2. Louvers
V.	1. Transparent unapertured 2. Translucent unapertured 3. Opaque unapertured	1. Transparent unapertured 2. Translucent unapertured
VI.	1. None 2. Transparent unapertured 3. Translucent unapertured 4. Opaque unapertured	1. Transparent unapertured 2. Translucent unapertured 3. Opaque unapertured

Source: Reprinted from the *IESNA Lighting Handbook* (9th ed.), pp. 9–20, with permission from the Illuminating Engineering Society of North America.

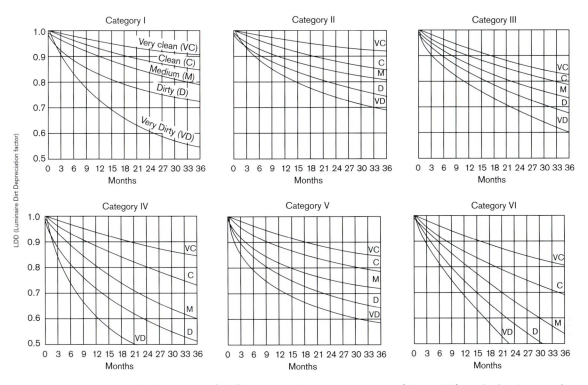

FIGURE 7.4 Luminaire Dirt Depreciation (LDD) factors for six luminaire categories (I through VI) and for five degrees of dirtiness.

egories include "very clean" (VC), "clean" (C), "medium" (M), "dirty" (D), and "very dirty" (VD). Lamps mounted in an exposed luminaire, in an environment that has a great deal of dust, such as a woodworking studio, would have to be cleaned very frequently to reduce significant light loss.

A simple method for determining average illuminance is the lumen method, or also referred to as the *zonal cavity calculation*. This method provides only the average illuminance in a space and does not factor in variances in light levels. The basic formula for determining the average maintained illuminance on a work surface is:

$$\text{Maintained fc} = \frac{\text{Number of lamps} \times \text{Initial lamp lumens} \times \text{LLF} \times \text{CU}}{\text{Area}}$$

For example, let us consider a classroom with the following factors:

- 30-foot by 30-foot space with a 10-foot ceiling and a task plane 2 feet 6 inches (AFF)
- Clean space
- Lamp cleaning twice a year
- 12 surface-mount luminaires with two F32T8 lamps in each luminaire
- 80 percent ceiling reflectance, 50 percent wall reflectance, and 20 percent floor reflectance

The average maintained illuminance on a work surface in this space is 30 fc. This is determined by performing steps one through six listed below:

1. Determine the total number of lamps by multiplying the number of lamps per luminaire (2), by the number of luminaires (12). Use the SC to determine an approximate number of luminaires. For this example the total number of lamps is 24.
2. Refer to the lamp manufacturer's catalog to determine the initial lamp lumens. For this example the approximate initial lumens for a F32T8 lamp is 2800.
3. Calculate the LLF by first identifying the LLD (see Table 7.1). In this example, the LLD for a F32T8 lamp is .93.
4. The information found in Table 7.2 and Figure 7.4 identifies the LDD. For this example, in Table 7.2, the 2-lamp parabolic louver, surface-mount luminaire is found in the maintenance category III. In Figure 7.4, for a clean room, and lamps are cleaned every six months, the LDD is approximately .92. By multiplying the LLD by the LDD, the LLF is .85 (.93 × .92 = .85).
5. The CU is determined by first calculating the RCR. For this example:

$$RCR = \frac{5(7.5)\,(30 + 30)}{30 \times 30} = 2.5 \text{ or } 3$$

Given a RCR of 3 and a space with 80 percent ceiling reflectance (pcc), 50 percent wall reflectance (pw), and 20 percent floor reflectance (Figure 7.2 assumes a 20 percent floor reflectance), the CU is approximately .46 for the luminaire in Figure 7.2.

6. To determine the average maintained illuminance on the work surface, the values determined in steps 1–5 are then inserted into the formula:

$$fc = \frac{24 \text{ lamps} \times 2800 \text{ Initial lamp lumens} \times .85 \times .46}{30 \times 30 \text{ Area}} = 29.2 \text{ or } 30$$

Note that by factoring in the LLF and the CU, illuminance levels are decreased, which reflects characteristics of luminaires, interior architecture, and environmental factors in the space. Without these two considerations the illumination level would be approximately 75 fc at the initial installation and would not reflect what could occur in the space throughout the life of the installation. This notation helps to illustrate why it is important to consider all the systemic factors that affect illuminance.

Point-by-Point Method

The basic point-by-point method determines the fc level for a focal point or enough light to keep a plant alive. This method requires using the inverse square law and cosine law, also referred to as Lambert's Law. The inverse square law is utilized only for point sources. The inverse square law formula is $E = I/d^2$ whereby E represents illumination (fc), "I" is the luminous intensity (cd) of the source and d is the distance from the light source to the work surface. Luminous intensity is determined by examining a lamp's candlepower distribution chart, which is available from lamp manufacturers (see Figure 7.5). The inverse square law is based upon the concept that the illumination level on a surface decreases the farther the work surface is from the light source. The math is the square of its distance from the source. For example, the illuminance on a surface 2 feet away from its source is one-fourth as much as the illumination 1 foot from the light source (Figure 7.6).

The inverse square law formula can be utilized for determining the illuminance on a point from a light source that is located directly above

FIGURE 7.5 A candle-power distribution chart of a reflector BR40/SP.

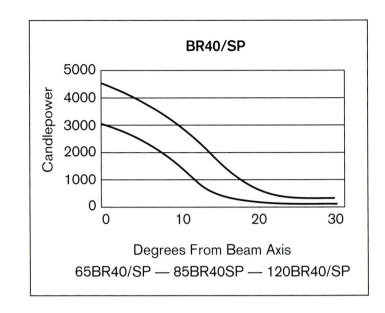

the surface (Figure 7.7). For example, for an 85-watt reflector BR40 spot lamp located directly above a surface, 7 feet 6 inches from the lamp, the approximate fc level would be 53. This is determined by the $E = I/d^2$ equation as:

$$E = 3000/7.5^2 = 53.3 \text{ or } 53 \text{ fc}$$

FIGURE 7.6 A demonstration of the inverse square law, whereby the level of illumination on a surface decreases the farther a surface is from the light source.

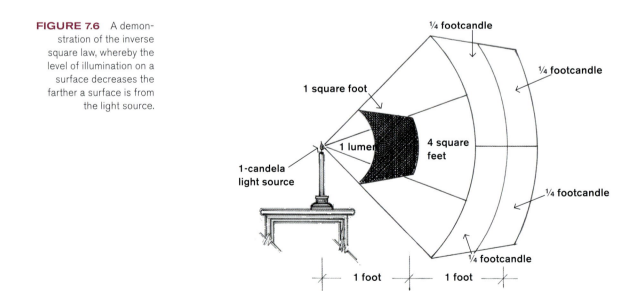

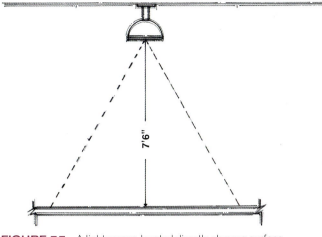

FIGURE 7.7 A light source located directly above a surface.

The formula for the cosine law is $E = I/d^2 \times \cos \theta$. θ is the angle at a point between a ray and perpendicular to the plane upon which that point is located. The cosine law indicates that the illuminance on a surface will vary according to the cosine of the angle of incident. Table 7.3 contains trigonometric functions that provide the cosine and sine for several angles. The cosine and sine are used for horizontal and vertical surfaces, respectively. The formula for determining the illuminance on a vertical surface is: $E = I/d^2 \times \sin \theta$.

Determining the illuminance for specific locations can be very complex because of the variety of areas within a space and the interdependence of the factors that affect lighting. Generally, interior designers and engineers will use lighting software to perform the calculations. A review of programs is provided at the end of this chapter. To gain a conceptual understanding of the process and the factors that are important to consider when determining illuminance for specific points, two representative examples follow.

The cosine law can be utilized to determine the illuminance on a horizontal surface when the luminaire, or the point to be lighted, is at an angle (Figure 7.8a). For example, for an 85-watt reflector BR40 spot lamp located at a 30-degree angle above a horizontal surface 7 feet

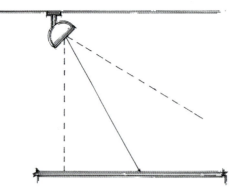

FIGURE 7.8a A light source that is located at an angle to a horizontal surface.

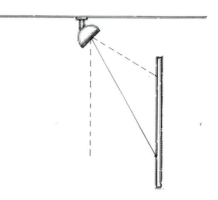

FIGURE 7.8b A light source that is located at an angle to a vertical surface.

6 inches from the lamp, the illumination level would be approximately 3 fc. This is determined by the $E = I/d^2 \times \cos \theta$ equation as:

$$E = 200 / 7.5^2 \times .866 = 3.08 \text{ or 3 fc}$$

For an 85-watt reflector BR40 spot lamp located at a 30-degree angle aimed at a vertical surface 7 feet 6 inches from the lamp, the illumination level would be approximately 2 fc (Figure 7.8b). This is determined by the $E = I/d^2 \times \sin \theta$ equation as:

$$E = 200 / 7.5^2 \times .500 = 1.77 \text{ or 2 fc}$$

Lighting Software Packages

Lighting software packages are available for basic and advanced illuminance calculations using daylight and electrical light sources. Basic programs, including Auto CAD extensions, will predict brightness of surfaces and patterns of light distribution on vertical and horizontal surfaces. Most manufacturers have software that is relatively easy to use. Gray-scaled graphic illustrations demonstrating light, shade, and shadows are provided by some of the programs (see Figure 22.10). Some of the basic programs will provide the data for ESI, RVP, and VCP. To obtain the most precise calculations, lighting programs utilize

TABLE 7.3

Trigonometric Functions:
Sines and Cosines of Angles

Θ°	Sin Θ	Cos Θ
0	0.00000	1.000
5	.0872	.996
10	.174	.985
15	.259	.966
20	.342	.940
25	.423	.906
30	.500	.866
35	.574	.819
40	.643	.766
45	.707	.707
50	.766	.643
55	.819	.574
60	.866	.500
65	.906	.423
70	.940	.342
75	.966	.259
80	.985	.174
85	.996	.0872
90	1.000	0.0000

Adapted from: Sines and Cosines of Angles Downing, D., (1990). Trigonometry. Hauppauge, NY: Barrons Educational Series, Inc.

radiosity. To perform these calculations, an interior designer must know the characteristics of the interior, including room dimensions, luminaire locations, surface reflectances, luminaire photometric data, and LLF. Basic programs are only able to calculate illuminance for rooms in traditional shapes and sizes. The results of the calculations are luminance, exitance, watts per square meter or foot, and summary illuminance statistics, including the illuminance at specific locations. Some programs will provide values derived from the unique effects from factors such as partitions, columns, furniture, and daylight.

Advanced lighting programs have radiosity and ray-tracing elements.

Radiosity
A type of radiative-transfer calculation utilized in lighting software.

FIGURE 7.9 Advanced lighting programs can calculate illuminance in rooms with unique shapes. This shower/bathing room is located in Bali, Indonesia.

These features produce faster and high-quality renderings. Advanced programs are able to calculate illuminance in rooms with unique shapes, including sloped ceilings (Figure 7.9). IESNA annually publishes a review of current lighting software in *Lighting Design + Application*. For the most current assessment refer to IESNA publications and http://www.lightsearch.com.

Interior designers conduct calculations for new construction and remodeling existing spaces. Both applications utilize the calculation methods discussed in this section. For existing spaces, an interior designer will frequently want to obtain current fc levels, which is accomplished by taking illuminance measurements in the field by using a footcandle meter (Figure 7.10a). This instrument provides the fc levels for any area within the space as well as reflectance values of surfaces. To determine a footcandle level within a room, an interior designer places the footcandle meter in the specified location and reads the result. Usually, an interior designer will want the fc levels for general and task lighting. To obtain the general illuminance, an interior designer will establish a grid, take readings at each cross-section of the grid, and then average the results. Task lighting fc readings can be

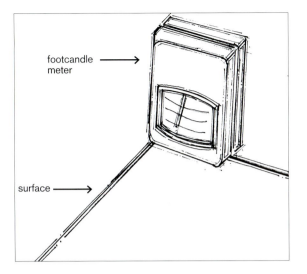

FIGURE 7.10a In the field, an interior designer can determine illumination levels by using a footcandle meter.

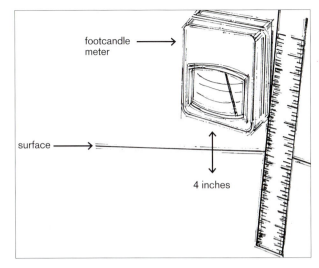

FIGURE 7.10b An interior designer can determine the reflectance of surfaces by placing a footcandle meter approximately 4 inches away from the surface to record the fc level.

obtained by placing the footcandle meter on each work surface. To determine an approximation of the reflectance of surfaces, an interior designer will place the footcandle meter approximately 4 inches from the surface and record the fc level (Figure 7.10b). (For more information regarding field measurements and analyses, see Chapters 21 and 22.)

This chapter explores the topic of determining the quantity of illumination in an interior. In determining illumination levels, many factors of the environment and about users of the space are covered, within the context of recommendations provided by IESNA and other international organizations. Quantity of lighting is only one of the factors that must be considered in designing a quality lighting environment.

SUMMARY

■ Measuring the quantity of lighting in an environment is based upon the principles of radiometry and photometry. Radiometry is a scientific area that focuses on measuring radiant energy. Photometry is a science that is derived from radiometry, whereby quantities of lighting include the human response to the source of illumination.

- The basic units of measurement for lighting include luminous intensity, luminous flux, illuminance, luminance, and luminance exitance.

- To determine the direction, pattern and intensity of light from reflector lamps and luminaires, interior designers refer to photometric data reports, such as those provided by lamp and luminaire manufacturers.

- IESNA and various international organizations have developed recommendations for illuminance levels. The *IESNA Lighting Design Guide* (2000) was developed to recommend illuminance levels based upon specific tasks and criteria that affect the quality of lighting.

- A simple method for determining average illuminance is the lumen method, also referred to as the zonal cavity calculation. This method provides only the average illuminance in a space and does not consider variances in light levels. The basic formula for determining the average maintained illuminance on a work surface is:

$$\text{Maintained fc} = \frac{\text{Number of lamps} \times \text{Initial lamp lumens} \times \text{LLF} \times \text{CU}}{\text{Area}}$$

- The basic point-by-point method determines the fc level for a focal point or enough light to keep a plant alive. Determining the illuminance for specific locations can be very complex because of the variety of areas within a space and the interdependence of the factors that affect lighting.

- Lighting software packages are available for basic and advanced illuminance calculations, using daylight and electrical light sources. Basic programs, including Auto CAD extensions, predict brightness of surfaces and patterns of light distribution on vertical and horizontal surfaces. Most manufacturers have software that is relatively easy to use. Advanced lighting programs have radiosity and ray-tracing elements to produce faster and high-quality renderings of complex spaces.

■ Interior designers conduct calculations for new construction and re-modeling of existing spaces. Both applications utilize the calculation methods illustrated in this chapter. For existing spaces, an interior designer will frequently take illuminance measurements in the field by using a footcandle meter.

Key Terms

candlepower distribution curves	luminous intensity
coefficient of utilization (CU)	nadir
equivalent sphere index (ESI)	photometry
illuminance	radiometry
lamp lumen depreciation (LLD)	radiosity
light loss factor (LLF)	relative visual performance (RVP)
luminaire dirt depreciation (LDD)	room-cavity ratio (RCR)
luminaire efficacy ratio (LER)	steradian
luminous exitance	visual comfort probability (VCP)
luminous flux	

Exercises

1. Search the World Wide Web for three luminaire manufacturers. For each manufacturer locate the photometric reports for three different luminaires. In a written report provide the following information: (a) a summary of the photometric data for each luminaire, (b) comparison of photometric information of each manufacturer, and (c) an analysis of how an interior designer would utilize the photometric data in designing a quality lighting environment.

2. Visit three different spaces and record the following information about each space: (a) size of the room, (b) size and location of windows, (c) the type of luminaires and lamps and their location, and (d) the colors and textures of the ceiling, floor, and walls. Use a footcandle meter to record the fc level for general and task

illuminance. Also record the fc levels for each wall. In a written report summarize the data collected and analyze the adequacy of illumination. Provide suggestions for improving the space, including how well the space has layered lighting.

3. Use the *IESNA Lighting Design Guide* (2000) to determine the recommended illuminance levels for five different interior tasks. Examine the ratings for the design criteria of each task. In a written report summarize the recommendations for the five tasks and include your assessment of the ratings provided by the *IESNA Lighting Design Guide* (2000).

4. Search the World Wide Web for three luminaires for which data related to spacing criterion (SC) are provided. In a written report summarize the SC for each luminaire and provide a rationale for differences between SC recommendations. Include how an interior designer would utilize the SC data for specifying luminaires.

5. Search the World Wide Web for three different lighting software packages. Write a report providing the following information for each program: (a) name of the program, (b) manufacturer, (c) computer power, (c) description of the program, (d) application suggestions, (e) price, and (f) advantages and disadvantages of the program.

6. Identify a commercial and a residential space. By applying the lumen method, calculate a recommended illuminance level for each space. Also identify the recommended illuminance level for a task surface in each space by using the basic point-by-point method. In a written report include the following items:
   a. Floor plan of the spaces.
   b. Elevations of walls with windows.
   c. Summary of materials and colors in the spaces.
   d. Calculations resulting from the lumen method and the point-by-point method.
   e. Recommendations for luminaires and lamps.

REFERENCES

Allphin, W. (1961). BCD appraisals of luminaire brightness in a simulated office. *Illuminating Engineering, 56(1)*, 31–44.

Ashdown, I. (1998). Making near-field photometry practical. *Journal of the Illuminating Engineering Society,* 27(*1*), 67–79.

Ballman, T.L., and Levin, R.E. (1987). Illumination in partitioned spaces. *Journal of the Illuminating Engineering Society,* 16(*2*), 31–49.

Benya, J., Heschong, L., McGowan, T., Miller, N., and Rubinstein, F. (2001). *Advanced Lighting Guidelines.* White Salmon, WA: New Buildings Institute.

Boylan, B.R. (1987). *The Lighting Primer.* Ames, IA: Iowa State University Press.

Bradley, R.D., and Logan, H.L. (1964). A uniform method for computing the probability of comfort response in a visual field. *Illuminating Engineering,* 59(*3*), 189-206.

Carter, D.J., Sexton, R.C., and Miller, M.S. (1989). Field measurement of illuminance. *Lighting, Research, & Technology,* 21(*1*), 29–35.

Clark, F. (1968). Light loss factor in the design process. *Illuminating Engineering,* 63(*11*), 575–581.

Clark, F. (1963). Accurate maintenance factors. *Illuminating Engineering,* 58(*3*), 124–131.

Coaton, J.R., and Marsden, A.M. (1997). *Lamps and Lighting* (4th ed.). London: Arnold.

Commission International de l'Eclairage (1994). *CIE Collections in Photometry and Radiometry.* CIE no 114. Vienna, Austria: Bureau Central de la CIE.

DeCusatis, C. (1997). *Handbook of Applied Optometry.* New York: AIP Press.

DiLaura, D.L. (1976). On the computation of visual comfort probability. *Journal of the Illuminating Engineering Society,* 5(*4*), 207–217.

Egan, M.D. (1983). *Concepts in Architectural Lighting.* New York: McGraw-Hill.

Eklund, N., Boyce, P., and Simpson, S. (2000). Lighting and sustained performance. *Journal of the Illuminating Engineering Society,* 29(*1*), 116.

Fry, G.A. (1976). A simplified formula for discomfort glare. *Journal of the Illuminating Engineering Society,* 8(*1*), 10–20.

Gaertner, A.A. (1994). Photometric and radiometric quantities. *In Course on Photometry, Radiometry, and Colorimetry.* NRC 38643. Ottawa, Ontario: National Research Council. Institute for National Measurement Standards.

General Electric (1989). *Lighting Application Bulletin.* Cleveland, OH: General Electric.

Gordon, G. (2003). *Interior Lighting for Designers* (4th ed.). New York: John Wiley & Sons.

Gordon, G., and Nuckolls, J.L. (1995). *Interior Lighting for Designers.* New York: John Wiley & Sons.

Gregory, R.I. (1979). *Eye and Brain: The Psychology of Seeing* (3rd ed.). New York: McGraw-Hill.

Greif, M. (1986). *The Lighting Book.* Pittstown, NJ: The Main Street Press.

Guth, S.K. (1966). Computing visual comfort ratings for a specific interior lighting installation. *Illuminating Engineering,* 61(*10*), 634–642.

Guth, S.K., and McNelis, J.F. (1961). Further data on discomfort glare from multiple sources. *Illuminating Engineering,* 56(*1*), 46–57.

Hopkinson, R.G. (1957). Evaluation of glare. *Illuminating Engineering,* 52(*6*), 305–316.

Hunter, R.S. (1975). *The Measurement of Appearance.* New York: John Wiley & Sons.

Illuminating Engineering Society. Committee on Recommendations of Quality and Quantity of Illumination, Subcommittee on Direct Glare (1966). Outline of a standard procedure for computing visual comfort ratios for interior lighting. Report No. 2. *Illuminating Engineering,* 61(*10*), 643–666.

Illuminating Engineering Society. Committee on Recommendations of Quality and Quantity of Illumination (1969). A statement concerning visual comfort probability. (VCP): Naïve vs. experienced observers. *Illuminating Engineering,* 64(*9*), 604.

Illuminating Engineering Society. Committee on Standards of Quality and Quantity for

Interior Illumination. (1946). The interreflection method of predetermining brightness and brightness ratios. *Illuminating Engineering, 41* (5), 361–385.

Illuminating Engineering Society. Committee on Testing Procedures. Subcommittee on Guide for Measurement of Photometric Brightness. (1961). IES guide for measurement of photometric brightness (luminance). *Illuminating Engineering,* 56(7), 457–462.

Illuminating Engineering Society. Lighting Design Practice Committee. (1964). Zonal-cavity method of calculating and using coefficients of utilization. *Illuminating Engineering,* 59(5), 309–328.

Illuminating Engineering Society. Lighting Design Practice Committee (1968). Calculation of luminance coefficients based upon zonal-cavity method. *Illuminating Engineering,* 63(8), 423–432.

Illuminating Engineering Society of North America (IESNA) (2000). *IESNA Lighting Handbook* (9th ed.). New York: Illuminating Engineering Society of North America.

Kaufman, J.E. (ed.) (1984). *IES Lighting Handbook Reference Volume 1984.* New York: Illuminating Engineering Society.

Knowles-Middleton, W.E., and Mayo, E.G. (1951). Variations in the horizontal distribution of light from candlepower standards. *Journal of the Opticians Society of America, 41*(8), 513–516.

Lam, W.C. (1977). *Perception and Lighting as Formgivers for Architecture.* New York: McGraw-Hill.

Lawrence Berkeley National Laboratory (1997). *Lighting Source Book.* Berkeley, CA: Lawrence Berkeley National Laboratory.

Levin, R.E. (1982). The photometric connection: Parts 1–4. *Lighting Design Application, 12* (*9*), 28–35; 12 (*10*), 60-63; 12 (*11*), 42–47; 12 (*12*), 16–18.

Lewis, A.L. (1998). Equating light sources for visual performance at low luminances. *Journal of the Illuminating Engineering Society, 27*(*1*), 80.

Lighting Design Lab (1998). *Daylight Models* (video). Seattle, WA: Lighting Design Lab.

Littlefair, P.J. (1991). *Site Layout Planning for Daylight and Sunlight: A Guide to Good Practice.* BRE Report BR 209.

Lynes, J.A. (1978). *Developments in Lighting.* London: Applied Science Publishers Ltd.

Moore, F. (1985). *Concepts and Practice of Architectural Daylighting.* New York: Van Nostrand Reinhold.

Murdoch, J.B. (1981). Inverse square law approximation of illuminance. *Journal of the Illuminating Engineering Society,* 10(2), 96–106.

National Bureau of Standards (1991). *The International System of Units (SI),* (6th ed.). NBS Special Publication 330. Gaithersburg, MD: National Bureau of Standards.

O'Brien, P.F., and Balogh, E. (1967). Configuration factors for computing illumination within interiors. *Illuminating Engineering, 62* (4), 169–179.

Phillips, D. (2000). *Lighting Modern Buildings.* Oxford: Architectural Press.

Rosenthal, J., and Wertenbaker, L. (1972). *The Magic of Light.* Boston: Little, Brown and Company.

Smith F.K. and Bertolone, F.J. (1986). *The Principles and Practices of Lighting Design: Bringing Interiors to Light.* New York: Whitney Library of Design.

Steffy, G.R. (2002). *Architectural Lighting Design,* (2nd ed.). New York: Van Nostrand Reinhold.

Tresidder, J. (ed.) (1983). *Mastering Composition and Light.* New York: Time-Life Books.

Veitch, J. (2000, July). Lighting guidelines from lighting quality research. *CIBSE/ILE Lighting 2000 Conference.* New York, United Kingdom.

Veitch, J., and Newsham, G. (1999, June). Preferred luminous conditions in open-plan offices: Implications for lighting quality recommendations. *CIE Proceedings*. CIE Pub No. 133, vol. 1, part 2: 4–6.

Veitch, J., and Newsham, G. (1996, August). Experts' quantitative and qualitative assessment of lighting quality. *Proceedings of the 1996 Annual IESNA Conference*. Cleveland, OH. Available at: http://fox.nrc.ca/irc/fulltext/nrcc39874.html.

Ward, L.G., and Shakespeare, R.A. (1998). *Rendering with Radiance: The Art and Science of Lighting Visualization*. San Francisco: Morgan Kaufmann.

Watson, L. (1977). *Lighting Design Handbook*. New York: McGraw-Hill.

Zhang, J.X., and Ngai, P.Y. (1991). Lighting calculations in a multi-partitioned space. *Journal of the Illuminating Engineering Society, 20(1)*, 32–43.

CHAPTER 8

Electricity

OBJECTIVES

- Understand electrical units applicable to lighting, including volts, amps, and watts.

- Describe the relationships between volts, amps, ohms, and watts.

- Understand electrical currents and circuits in lighting systems.

- Describe the electrical distribution process applicable to lighting systems.

- Perform electrical calculations for lighting systems.

ELECTRICAL energy is certainly the most versatile form of energy currently at our disposal. Electricity can be distributed easily, safely, and efficiently over great distances. Electricity can be transformed into other forms of energy, such as heat, mechanical, or light, and it produces virtually no pollution at its point of consumption. One of the premiere and most appropriate applications for electrical energy is artificial lighting. When compared with other energy forms that could be used for lighting, electrical energy is safe, efficient, reliable, convenient, and inexpensive to install and operate. An interior designer needs to have a basic awareness of electricity in order to understand how electricity affects a lighting plan. Furthermore, interior designers should have discussions with engineers and electricians with whom they work on interior projects.

Electrical Units

Electricity is a natural phenomenon that is a basic element of the living world. Lightning, a visible example of electricity, existed before life started on our planet. As a consequence, scientists for thousands of years have been intrigued by electricity and how electric energy could be used to improve civilization. One of the first scientists credited with exploring the concept of electricity is the ancient Greek Thales of Miletus. Thales found that amber, composed of the fossilized pitch from pine trees, could lift a feather after being rubbed with fur. As a consequence, the word "electricity" is derived from "electron," which is the Greek term for amber.

Volts

Volts (V)

A measure of the amount of electrical "stimulus" that enables current to flow through a circuit.

Electrical potential, measured in **volts (V)**, is a measure of the amount of electrical "motivation," or "stimulus," needed to enable current to flow through a circuit. If all other circuit factors are held constant, an increase in voltage will result in a proportionate increase in current flow. For example, if the voltage in a circuit is doubled, the current will also double. The vast majority of line-voltage lighting applications operate at 120 volts, but some large-scale commercial lighting applications may operate at 277 volts. Low-voltage lighting applications usually operate at 12 volts. The abbreviation for volts is V.

Amps

Amps (A)

A measure of the quantity of electrical particle flow in a circuit.

Electrical current, measured in **amps (A)**, is a measure of the quantity of electrical particle flow in a circuit. Current can flow only when there is a complete circuit path and a voltage, or electrical, potential source. Circuits having higher current require larger wire sizes, circuit breakers, and switches. Most lighting circuits are rated at either 15 or 20 amps but can be safely loaded only to 80 percent, of that rating (12 and 16 amps, respectively). The common abbreviation for amps is A.

Ohms (R)

A measure of a circuit's ability to resist or impede the flow of electrical current.

Ohms

Electrical resistance, measured in **ohms (R)**, is the measure of a circuit's ability to resist, or impede, the flow of electrical current. A circuit having a large amount of resistance allows little current to flow, while a circuit having a small amount of resistance allows a large amount of current to flow. An example of resistance in a lighting system would be an incandescent lamp filament. The filament of a 300-watt lamp would have about one-third the resistance of the filament in a 100-watt lamp. The common algebraic abbreviation for ohms is R. Interior designers generally have little concern for the measurement or the calculation of resistance because it is determined by the wattage of the selected lamps.

Watts

Electrical power, measured in watts (W), is the measure of an electrical circuit's ability to do work. In the context of lighting systems, "work" is the measure of the amount of light produced, plus the amount of waste heat. The common abbreviation for watts is W.

Electric Current and Circuits

An **electrical circuit** consists of a voltage source and a resistance, or load (such as a lightbulb), connected in a complete loop or circuit, using electrical conductors, such as wires. A lighting circuit also typically contains control devices, such as switches and safety devices, designed to prevent electrical overloads.

A short circuit has practically no resistance to electrical flow and hence allows a nearly infinite amount of current to flow. A short circuit has no practical application and is typically the result of a wiring error or a malfunction of an electrical component. In contrast, an open circuit is a circuit that has an infinite amount of resistance to current flow, causing current flow to cease. A good example of an open circuit is a lighting circuit when the switch is turned off or a lighting circuit that has a burned-out bulb.

Circuits are designed to function in a series, or parallel to one another (Figures 8.1a and b). In a **series circuit**, lamps operate together as one system. Therefore, if one lamp burns out, the remaining lamps

Electrical circuit
Circuit composed of a voltage source and a load, connected in a continuous loop using electrical conductors, such as wires.

Series circuit
Lamps that operate together as one system.

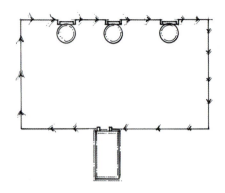

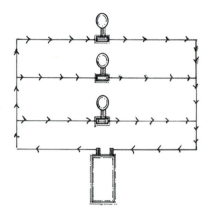

FIGURE 8.1a Lamps that are connected in a series circuit.

FIGURE 8.1b Lamps that are connected in a parallel circuit.

do not work since the complete path is broken and the circuit is therefore open. This is often observed with a string of Christmas lights. In architectural lighting applications, lamps are rarely if ever connected in series.

Electrical currents in a **parallel circuit** operate independently of one another and are not sensitive to the presence or absence of a single load. Each lamp in a parallel circuit has its own individual complete circuit path. This means that lamps will continue to operate when one of them burns out.

Circuits operate only when there is a continuous flow of electricity. A break in the flow will stop the electrical current. The function of an electrical switch is to stop the flow of electricity. Therefore, when an electrical switch is turned "on," the circuit is closed, or connected, and light is present in the space. To turn the light "off," the switch opens the circuit and breaks the flow of electricity. Relays are used for remote-control switching and for switching large lighting circuits. (For more information regarding switches see Chapter 10.)

Fuses and **circuit breakers** are safety devices designed to protect wires and electrical fixtures from excessive electrical current flow. For example, if too many luminaires are connected to a circuit, the breaker will sense the excessive load and "open" the circuit, thereby stopping the electricity flow. This guards against unsafe conditions, such as fire, electrical shock, or burns. A circuit breaker is a special on/off switch

Parallel circuit
Lamps that operate independently of one another and are not load-sensitive.

Fuse
A safety device, generally found in older structures, designed to protect wires and electrical fixtures from excessive electrical loads.

Circuit breaker
A safety device designed to protect wires and electrical fixtures from excessive electrical loads.

that senses the amount of current flowing through the switch. An overload of electrical current will cause the breaker to trip to the off position and stop electricity from entering the circuit. A fuse, used in older buildings, is a thin strip of low-temperature metal that the circuit's current must pass through. When the current flow becomes too great, this thin strip of metal melts, thus destroying the path for current flow. Most electrical installations today use circuit breakers rather than fuses.

Electrical Distribution

As illustrated in Figure 8.2, the electrical distribution process begins at a power station generator that produces *alternating current* (AC). Since the distances between a power station and consumers can be hundreds of miles, step-up transformers are used to convert the generated voltage to tens or hundreds of thousands of volts. Transmitting electricity at very high voltages reduces electrical losses and makes it possible to transmit a very large amount of energy over relatively small wires.

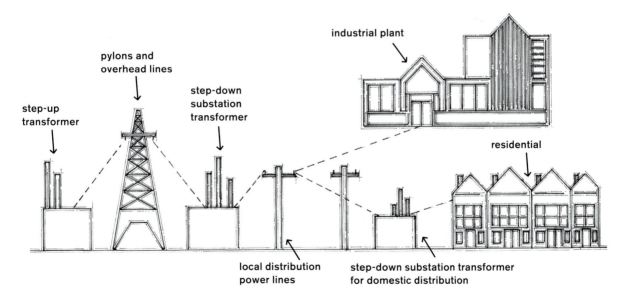

FIGURE 8.2 Electrical distribution process from the power station generator to homes and businesses.

In traveling from the step-up transformer to various communities, the high-voltage wires are strung between pylons at very high heights. The height is necessary because these high voltages are extremely dangerous. Once the wires reach a specific point of use, a step-down transformer is used to lower the voltage. For businesses that require high voltages, such as a factory, the power lines from the local distribution unit go directly to a transformer in the building. For less demanding applications, the power lines from the local distribution unit go to a step-down transformer before being attached to a residence, office, or small business.

The United States has three voltages for buildings: 480Y/277V, 208Y/120V, and 240/120V. For lighting, most interior designers work with 120V; however, some large commercial buildings have 277V. There are fluorescent and high-intensity discharge lamps that can operate with 277V or 120V, but most incandescent lamps will operate only with 120V. In other situations an electrical engineer would specify a transformer that would step down the volts from the building to the incandescent lamps.

As illustrated in Figure 8.3, service wires provided by a utility company enter a building through a service panel. The service panel distributes electrical power into circuits and has a grounding wire that is

FIGURE 8.3
Electrical distribution from a utility company through the building.

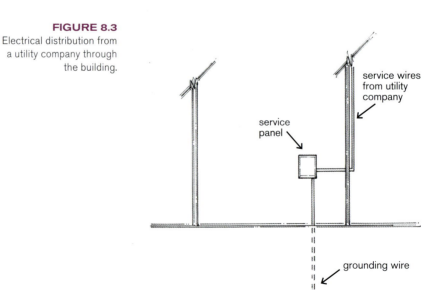

service wires from utility company

service panel

grounding wire

attached to a metal rod driven deep into the earth. The purpose of the grounding wire is to prevent electrical shocks. Insulating materials are used to cover wires that carry electrical current (Figure 8.4 a–c). For residential applications the wires are insulated with Romex, or BX, nonmetallic and metal cables, respectively. Commercial wires are insulated with a flexible metal conduit called "greenfield." To distribute wires over long distances through buildings, the cables are wrapped in nylon (N), and inserted in a rigid electrical metal conduit (EMT). A wire insulated with rubber is marked R, and T is used to designate a thermoplastic covering. Because of its flexibility, thermoplastic insulation is more desirable for luminaire wiring.

Conduits used in commercial buildings have additional designations, including temperature and moisture resistance. Wires are rated for 60, 75, and 90 degrees Celsius. The nomenclature used is H, or HH. Lighting applications require 75 degrees Celsius. A wire that has been rated to resist moisture is noted with a W for wetness. The most common conduit used for lighting in commercial interiors is THHN/THWN. This designation indicates that the wire is insulated with thermoplastic, is encased in nylon, has the ability to withstand heat at 75 degrees Celsius, and can be used in wet applications.

In specifying a lighting plan, an interior designer must be concerned with the amperage rating of the wire as designated by the number of the wire. According to the categorization system of the American Wire Gauge (AWG), the higher the number of the wire, the smaller the diameter. A No. 12 AWG, rated at 25A, is the wire that is most often used for lighting. An electric cooktop uses a No. 8 AWG wire, rated at 40A. To comply with electrical codes, a No. 12 wire must be installed with a circuit breaker that is rated for 20A but can be loaded only to 16A. Therefore, each circuit with a No. 12 AWG wire can accommodate only 16A. Electrical codes also restrict the maximum square footage for amp ratings. The maximum square footage for a No. 12 AWG wire is 500 square feet. A No. 14 AWG wire, rated at 15A, can be used to cover 375 square feet, with electrical outlets 12 feet apart. Examples of how an interior designer specifies lighting with these parameters are provided in the calculation section of this chapter.

A service panel is located at or near the location where the electrical

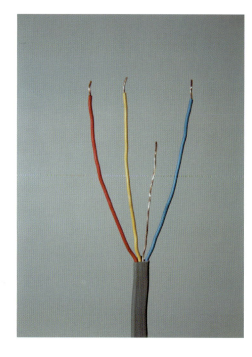

FIGURE 8.4a   Four core copper cables (showing colored, plastic insulation) permit two way switching of lighting.

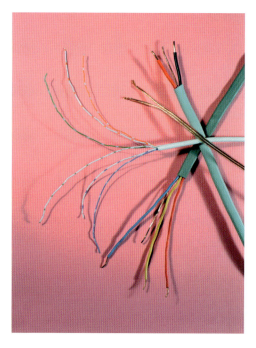

FIGURE 8.4c   Various types of PVC coated domestic cable.

FIGURE 8.4b   Conduit for electrical wiring.

service wires enter the building. A typical residential service panel is rated at 200 amps. The purpose of the service panel is to distribute electrical current safely through several lower amperage circuits within the building.

A single-phase service panel has two buses as well as circuit breakers for each individual circuit. *Buses* are vertical metal units that distribute power to the circuit breakers. Electricity flows from a circuit breaker through the red or black "hot" wires and back to the panel through the neutral white wire. Circuits can be individualized to accommodate one of two voltage requirements. For example, lighting and general-purpose electrical applications are usually distributed on 120V circuits. Individual circuits are generally installed for high-wattage appliances, such as microwaves, ranges, water heaters, and furnaces. For commercial applications, power is distributed from a main service panel to smaller subpanels located throughout a building via feeder circuits (see Figure 8.5). Branch circuits are then used to distribute power from the various panels to light switches and electrical outlets. When electricity must be distributed to long runs of open office systems, power must be located at numerous intervals.

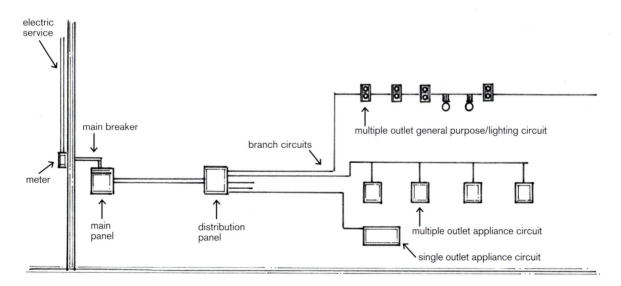

FIGURE 8.5   Power distributed through panels and circuits in buildings.

Calculations

For the interior designer, the most important algebraic equation is called the *power equation*. The general form of this equation is W = A × V where W = watts, A = amps, and V = volts. For practical use, this equation can be algebraically transformed to A = W/V. For example, if an interior designer determined a need for 2500 watts of standard 120-volt line-voltage lighting in a space, the total number of amps of current required to produce 2500 watts of light can be determined by the A = W/V equation as:

$$A = 2500/120 = 20.83 \text{ amps}$$

Given that a typical 20-amp lighting circuit can be loaded to only 16 amps and a 15-amp lighting circuit can be loaded to only 12 amps, this lighting application would require at least two 15-amp or two 20-amp circuits.

The power equation can also be used to determine the differences between using line and low voltage. For example, if an interior designer determined a need for 200 watts of illumination in a space, the amps for standard 120-volt line-voltage lighting can be determined by the A = W/V equation as:

$$A = 200/120 = 1.67 \text{ amps (at 120 volts)}$$

This lighting application would require one 15-amp or one 20-amp circuit. For the same space requiring 200 watts of illumination, the amps for 12-volt low-voltage lighting can be determined by the A = W/V equation as:

$$A = 200/12 = 16.67 \text{ amps (at 12 volts)}$$

As demonstrated in Figure 8.6, for the same 200 watts the line volts required 1.67 amps and the low-voltage circuit needed 16.67 amps.

To determine the most efficient operation for some commercial sites, an interior designer might have to compare the differences between using 120V and 277V. For example, to determine the total

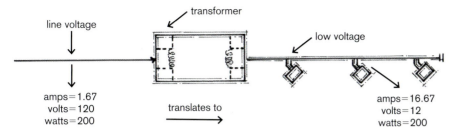

line voltage

amps=1.67
volts=120
watts=200

transformer

translates to

low voltage

amps=16.67
volts=12
watts=200

FIGURE 8.6 Comparison of amps, volts, and watts for a line and low-voltage application.

number of watts that a 20A circuit can produce at 120V and 277V, the first step is to use the $W = A/V$ equation:

$$W = 16 \times 120 = 1920 \text{ watts}$$

and

$$W = 16 \times 277 = 4432 \text{ watts}$$

The second step is to calculate the number of lamps for each circuit by dividing the maximum number of watts per circuit by the number of watts per lamp. The calculation for the number of lamps for a 120V circuit is:

$$1920/75 = 25.6 \text{ lamps}$$

The calculation for the number of lamps for a 277V circuit is:

$$4432/75 = 59.09 \text{ lamps}$$

If each luminaire has two lamps, an interior designer would round down the number of lamps. Thus, for a 120V circuit, 24 fluorescent lamps would be installed in 12 luminaires. The 277V circuit would have 58 fluorescent lamps in 29 luminaires. In practice, to have a balanced arrangement on the ceiling, an interior designer would probably specify 28 luminaires, each having 2 lamps. This example demonstrates that the 277V circuit accommodates the highest number of lamps, thus reducing the number of circuits required for a space.

In some states, an interior designer must specify a lighting design that meets energy conservation practices. For example, California's Title 24 Energy Efficiency Standards for Residential and Nonresidential Buildings has high standards for energy efficiency. The watts-per-square-foot maximums must include all energy-consuming units in a lighting system, including lamps, ballasts, and transformers. (For more information regarding energy conservation, see Chapter 12.) Use the following equation to calculate watts per square foot:

$$\text{watts per square foot} = \text{square footage/total watts}$$

For example, in an open office space with 1200 square feet and with 480 watts for the lighting system, the watts-per-square-foot calculation is:

$$1200/480 = 2.5 \text{ watts per square foot}$$

This chapter provides basic electrical theory and sample calculations that an interior designer would perform to specify lighting systems. Electricity is essential for lighting and must be understood within the context of the entire system. The principles of electricity are applied to the topics covered in the next several chapters.

SUMMARY

- The primary electrical units involved in lighting systems are *volts, amps,* and *watts.*
- Electrical potential, measured in volts, is a measure of the amount of electrical "stimulus" that enables current to flow through a circuit.
- The vast majority of line-voltage lighting applications operate at 120 volts. Low-voltage lighting applications usually operate at 12 volts.
- Electrical current, measured in amps, is a measure of the quantity of electrical particle flow in a circuit. Current can flow only when there is a complete circuit path and a voltage, or electrical potential, source.

- Most lighting circuits are rated at either 15 or 20 amps, but they can be safely loaded to only 80 percent, of that rating (12 or 16 amps, respectively).

- Electrical power, measured in watts, is the measure of an electrical circuit's ability to do work. In the context of lighting systems, "work" is the measure of the amount of light produced plus the amount of waste heat.

- An electrical circuit consists of a voltage source and a resistance, or load (such as a lightbulb), connected in a complete loop or circuit using electrical conductors, such as wires.

- Circuits are designed to function either in a series or as parallel. In a series circuit the lamps operate together as one system. Electrical currents in a parallel circuit operate independently and are not load-sensitive.

- Circuits operate only when there is a continuous flow of electricity. A break in the flow will stop the electrical current. The function of an electrical switch is to stop the flow of electricity.

- The electrical distribution process begins at a power station generator that produces alternating current (AC). From the power station a transformer is used to step-up the voltage. Once the wires are at a specific location, a step-down transformer is used to lower the voltage.

- The United States has three voltages for buildings: 480Y/277V, 208Y/120V, and 240/120V. All these voltages are available in a three-phase power. One-phase power is all that is needed for lighting.

- In a building, the service panel distributes electrical power into multiple and individual circuits and has a grounding wire that is attached to a metal rod driven deep into the earth.

- A single-phase service panel has two buses as well as circuit breakers for each individual circuit. Electricity flows from a circuit breaker through the red or black "hot" wires and returns through the neutral white wire.

- For the interior designer, the most important algebraic equation is called the "power equation." The general form of this equation is $W = A \times V$ where W = watts, A = amps, and V = volts. For practical use, this equation can be algebraically transformed to $A = W/V$.

Key Terms

amps (A)	ohms (R)
circuit breaker	parallel circuit
electrical circuit	series circuit
fuse	volts (V)

Exercises

1. Conduct a field trip to a commercial site and to a residential construction site. Survey each site after the electrical system has been installed but before the drywall is in place. At the sites photograph or sketch the building's electrical system starting at the service wires and ending at electrical outlets and light fixtures. In a written report, including drawings, summarize the electrical distribution for the commercial and residential sites. The report should include the similarities and differences between commercial and residential electrical systems.

2. Using the data collected at the commercial and residential construction sites in Exercise 1, write a report that identifies the maximum wattages for each room in the buildings.

3. A track-lighting system has a low-voltage transformer with a rating of 210 watts. How many MR16 lamps at 20 watts each can be safely installed on the track system?

4. An interior designer consults with an electrical engineer. The designer would like to use a minimum number of circuits for a school building. The designer would like to use 75-watt fluorescent lamps in a classroom that is 1500 square feet. Do the calculations for 120V and 277V. Summarize your calculations in a written report and include recommendations for the classroom, including the number of lamps and luminaires.

REFERENCES

Benya, J., Heschong, L., McGowan, T., Miller, N., and Rubinstein, F. (2001). *Advanced Lighting Guidelines*. White Salmon, WA: New Buildings Institute.

Bernstien, A., and K. Conway. (2000, March). *The Public Benefits of California's Investments in Energy Efficiency.* Prepared for the California Energy Commission by the RAND Corporation. MR-1212.0-CEC.

Carriere, L., and Rea, M. (1988). Economics of switching fluorescent lamps. *IEEE Transactions on Industry Applications* 24(3), 370–379.

Coaton, J.R., and Marsden, A.M. (1997). *Lamps and Lighting* (4th ed.). London: Arnold.

Editors of Creative Publishing International, Inc. (1998). *The Complete Guide to Home Wiring: A Comprehensive Manual, from Basic Repairs to Advanced Projects.* Minnetonka, MN: Creative Publishing International.

Egan, M.D. (1983). *Concepts in Architectural Lighting.* New York: McGraw-Hill.

Elenbass, W. (1971). *Fluorescent Lamps, Philips Technical Library* (2nd ed.). London: Macmillan

Energy Information Administration (EIA) (1996). *Annual Energy Outlook, with Projections to 2015.* Washington, DC: U.S. Department of Energy.

Energy Information Administration (EIA) (1995). *Annual Energy Review for 1995.* Washington, DC: U.S. Department of Energy.

Fielder, W.J., and Frederick, H.J. (2001). *The Lit Interior.* Boston: Architectural Press.

General Electric (1989). Lighting Application Bulletin. Cleveland, OH: General Electric.

Gibilisco, S. (1997). *Teach Yourself Electricity and Electronics.* New York: McGraw-Hill.

Gordon, G. and Nuckolls, J.L. (1995). *Interior Lighting for Designers.* New York: John Wiley & Sons.

Goulding, J.R., Lewis, J.O., and Steemers, T.C. (eds.) (1992). *Energy in Architecture. The European Passive Solar Handbook.* London: Batsford.

Illuminating Engineering Society of North America (IESNA) (2000). *IESNA Lighting Handbook,* (9th ed.). New York: Illuminating Engineering Society of North America.

Interlaboratory Working Group (1997, September). Scenarios of U.S. Carbon Reductions—Potential Impacts of Energy Technologies by 2010 and Beyond. Office of Energy Efficiency and Renewable Energy, U.S. Department of Energy.

Kaufman, J.E. (ed.) (1984). *IES Lighting Handbook Reference Volume 1984.* New York: Illuminating Engineering Society.

Lawrence Berkeley National Laboratory (1992). *Analysis of Federal Policy Options for Improving U.S. Lighting Energy Efficiency.* Berkeley, CA: Lawrence Berkeley National Laboratory.

Maniccia, D., Von Neida, B., and Tweed, A. (2000). Analysis of the energy and cost savings potential of occupancy sensors for commercial lighting systems. *Proceedings of the 2000 Annual Conference of the Illuminating Engineering Society of North America.*

Phillips, D. (2000). *Lighting Modern Buildings.* Oxford: Architectural Press.

Portland Energy Conservation. (1992). *Building Commissioning Guidelines,* (2nd ed.). Portland, OR: Bonneville Power Administration.

Rundquist, R.A., Johnson, K., and Aumann, D. (1993). Calculating lighting and HVAC interactions. *ASHRAE Journal,* 35(11), 28.

Rundquist, R.A., McDougall, T.G., and Benya, J. (1996). *Lighting Controls: Patterns for Design.* Prepared by R. A. Rundquist Associates for the Electric Power Research Institute and the Empire State Electrical Energy Research Corporation.

Smith F.K., and Bertolone, F.J. (1986). *The Principles and Practices of Lighting Design: Bringing Interiors to Light.* New York: Whitney Library of Design.

Southern California Edison (1999). Energy Design Resources Case Studies: REMO and Timberland. Available from: http://www.energydesignresources.com.

Veitch, J., and Newsham, G. (2000). Exercised control, lighting choices, and energy use: an office simulation experiment. *Journal of Environmental Psychology,* 20(3), 219–237.

Veitch, J., and Newsham, G. (1999, June). Preferred luminous conditions in open-plan offices: implications for lighting quality recommendations. *CIE Proceedings,* CIE Pub. 133, vol. 1, part 2: 4–6.

Veitch, J., and Newsham, G. (1998). Lighting quality and energy-efficiency effects on task performance, mood, health, satisfaction, and comfort. *Journal of the Illuminating Engineering Society,* 27(1), 107.

Veitch, J., and Newsham, G. (1996, August). Experts' quantitative and qualitative assessment of lighting quality. *Proceedings of the 1996 Annual IESNA Conference.* Cleveland, OH. Available at: http://fox.nrc.ca/irc/fulltext/nrcc39874.html.

CHAPTER 9

Lighting Systems: Luminaires

OBJECTIVES

- Describe the components of luminaires, including housing elements, materials, finishes, and accessories.

- Identify primary ways to distribute light: (1) direct, (2) indirect, (3) semi-direct, (4) semi-indirect, and (5) diffused.

- Understand how luminaires are designed to distribute light.

- Understand the advantages and disadvantages of the major categories of luminaires, including recessed, surface-mounted, suspended, track, structural, and furniture-integrated units.

- Apply an understanding of luminaires to the specification and placement of fixtures in an environment.

- Identify and apply selection criteria to the specification and placement of luminaires in an interior.

LAMPS and electricity are identified as elements of a lighting system earlier in this text. Another major component of the system, luminaires, is reviewed in this chapter. In addition to exploring the role of luminaires in an interdependent system, this chapter demonstrates how the selection and placement of luminaires affect the quality of lighting, quantity of illumination, and the directional effects of lighting. To successfully specify a quality lighting environment, an interior designer must understand all the interdependent elements of the lighting system and have a working knowledge of the products that are available. This chapter focuses on luminaires that require installation in ceilings, walls, floors, architectural elements, or cabinetry. Chapter 11 reviews portable luminaires, including table and floor fixtures.

Components of Luminaires

Luminaires blend science with art. They are designed to resolve many of the contrasting characteristics of illumination, such as directing light up or down, flooding a space with light, or spotlighting a small art piece on a table. Many industrial designers, architects, and interior designers have been challenged to design a luminaire that successfully addresses these issues. Luminaires and chairs are two interior elements that often define a designer. Charles Rennie Mackintosh is an excellent example of a designer who is well known for the design of his chairs and luminaires (Figure 9.1). A review of contemporary designers of luminaires is in Chapter 11.

FIGURE 9.1 An interior designed by Charles Rennie Mackintosh illustrates his custom-designed pieces, including the chairs and luminaires.

Defining Luminaires

A luminaire is an element of a lighting system that includes the light source, housing elements, ballasts, transformers, controls, a mounting mechanism, and a connection to electrical power. Other terms used for luminaires are fixtures and fittings. The housing unit includes the socket for the light source and any elements that are designed to reflect, shield, diffuse, or transmit light. Luminaires are designed for line or low voltage. Luminaires that require transformers are either *integral* or *remote*. For installation purposes, many luminaires require a *junction box*, which is a metal unit that distributes the wires for electricity. In operating as a system, all the components of the luminaire must be compatible and functioning. Thus, luminaires have specific requirements, including the type of lamp, maximum wattages, volts, and mounting restrictions.

A primary purpose of a luminaire is optical control. A bare lamp emits light in various directions and typically causes glare. A luminaire is designed to control the light and hopefully either reduce or eliminate glare. Therefore, the content covered in Chapters 6 and 7, directional effects of lighting and quantity of lighting, respectively, is critical in selecting and placing luminaires. The placement of the luminaire affects the quality of illumination on a task, object, or surface, and affects the apparent size and shape of a space. For example, luminaires can be positioned to define dining areas in a restaurant. The placement helps to divide a large restaurant into smaller, more intimate spaces and provides variety within the vertical viewing area. In addition to serving the functional purpose of providing illumination in a space, the design of a luminaire should reflect the theme of the design concept. Frank Lloyd Wright was a master at designing a luminaire that was in perfect concert with the other elements of the interior (Figure 9.2).

Design of Luminaires

The majority of luminaires are specifically designed to maximize optical control. This involves determining the optimum size and shape of the luminaire and specifying the appropriate materials and finishes.

FIGURE 9.2 The ceiling luminaire was designed to blend with all of the elements in this interior by Frank Lloyd Wright.

Frequently, the shape and size of a luminaire is a function of the type of lamp. Chapter 3 discusses some of the size requirements for electrical light sources. Incandescent lamps generally provide the greatest flexibility in the size and shape of a luminaire. The tube shape of fluorescent lamps typically requires a rectangular-shaped luminaire. Luminaire manufacturers provide lamp and wattage recommendations in their product literature. To maximize the design of a luminaire and ensure safe operation, an interior designer must specify lamps according to manufacturers' requirements.

In addition to accommodating the size and shape of a lamp, the design of the luminaire must efficiently control and direct light. The primary factors that affect the distribution of illumination are the shape of the luminaire, materials, finishes, location and size of the aperture, and mounting position. Chapter 6 provides examples of how the shape, materials, and finish affect the directional effects of lighting. The location of the aperture, materials, and mounting position determine primary ways to distribute light: (a) direct, (b) indirect, (c) semi-direct,

(d) semi-indirect, and (e) diffused (Figure 9.3). **Direct** distribution occurs when at least 90 percent of the illumination is downward. **Indirect** luminaires distribute at least 90 percent of the light toward the ceiling. **Semi-direct** luminaires distribute most of the illumination downward, and some of the light upward. **Semi-indirect** fixtures distribute most of the illumination upward, and some of the light downward. **Diffused** luminaires distribute illumination in all directions.

To compare the efficiency and effectiveness of different luminaires, an interior designer can use the luminaire efficacy rating (LER). This metric reflects how efficiently a luminaire emits light for its intended purpose. Generally, the higher the number, the more energy-efficient the luminaire. The National Electrical Manufacturers Association (NEMA) Web site provides the LER for common luminaires. In practice, the LER metric could indicate that it might be more effective to specify one lamp with superior optical control rather than several lamps that have a higher efficacy rating.

Direct light
Distribution of light when at least 90 percent of the illumination is downward.

Indirect light
Distribution of light with at least 90 percent of the light directed toward the ceiling.

Semi-direct lighting
Distribution of light with most of the illumination directed downward and some of the light directed upward.

Semi-indirect lighting
Distribution of light with most of the illumination directed upward and some of the light directed downward.

Diffused light
Distribution of light in all directions.

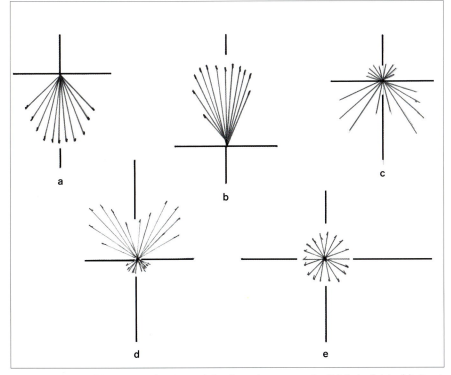

FIGURE 9.3 Photometric drawings of the five primary ways to distribute light: (a) direct, (b) indirect, (c) semi-direct, (d) semi-indirect, and (e) diffused.

Distributing Illumination

It is possible to control and direct light through devices that are designed to reflect, diffuse, refract, and shield illumination. These units are either built into the luminaire or snap onto the front of the fixture. **Reflectors** are shaped to redirect light by reflection. The amount of light emitted from an aperture can range from a wide angle to a very narrow spot. Specular materials, and parabolic and ellipse shapes, are often used to reflect light. An excellent example is the parabolic louvers used in fluorescent luminaires (Figure 9.4). Downlights often have a specular or grooved aluminum reflector. To have adequate reflection of light when a luminaire does not have an internal reflector, an interior designer might specify reflector lamps.

Diffusers scatter the light in many directions, and are made from white plastic or etched glass (Figure 9.5 a–e). Polyethylene and polycarbonate plastics must be treated to resist yellowing that can occur from UV radiation. Acrylic plastics are impervious to UV radiation; however, since the material can be manufactured in very thin sheets, the diffusers can sag. This is especially problematic in luminaires with large apertures.

Refractors are devices designed to redirect light through the scientific principle of refraction. Refractors are generally prismatic lenses made from either plastic or glass. Some refractors are designed to spread light; hence they are called a spread lens. A **fresnel refractor** is a lens composed of concentric circles with a flat or domed surface.

FIGURE 9.4 A fluorescent luminaire with parabolic louvers.

FIGURE 9.5 (a) Luminaires with diffusers that scatter light in multiple directions; (b) adjustable luminaire wih a black baffle; (c) adjustable luminaire with a MR16 lamp; (d) downlight with a slotted shield; (e) adjustable luminaire with a cube cell louver.

Units designed to shield a light source include baffles, louvers, cowls, and shades. Baffles, louvers, and cowls are usually made from an opaque material. The term **baffle** refers to a linear or round shaped unit in a luminaire designed to shield light from view. **Louver** is used to describe the shielding device in a grid or "egg crate" formation. **Cowls** are used to shield a light source on track luminaires and are available in a variety of shapes and sizes (Figure 9.6). Luminaire **shades** are either opaque or translucent. Light emitted through opaque shades is restricted to the size of the apertures, and results in a distinctive pattern on surfaces. Translucent shades produce a diffused light and can create glare with a high-intensity lamp. The quality and quantity of light emitted from a shade is dependent upon the color, texture, and thickness of the material it is made of.

Baffle
A linear or round shaped unit in a luminaire designed to shield light from view.

Louver
A grid-shaped unit of a luminaire designed to shield light from view.

Cowl
A component at the end of a track light designed to shield light from view.

Shade
A device either opaque or translucent that shields a bare lamp from view.

FIGURE 9.6 A cowl on a track head with a black baffle.

Materials and Finishes

Luminaires are primarily constructed from steel, aluminum, glass, or plastic. Steel is used primarily for structural elements of a luminaire. It is an inexpensive, strong material and requires special coatings when used for luminaires. Aluminum is used for many of the structural elements of luminaires, including housings, poles, and reflectors. Aluminum is lightweight and impervious to air and water. Aluminum can have a variety of finishes, including etched, polished, brushed, lacquered, enameled, and plastic-coated.

Glass is used in luminaires to transmit light, protect lamps, and serve a decorative purpose. Several different types of glass are used in luminaires. For example, soda-lime glass is used for lens covers. Refractors and reflectors are made from borosilicate glass. Lead glass is used for applications that require flexibility in shape, such as neon signs. Hand-blown glass, in numerous colors and textures, is used for shades on a variety of luminaires, including tracks, sconces, and pendants (Figure 9.7). Plastic is used for louvers, baffles, lenses, diffusers, switches, shades, and wire insulation. The advantages of plastic include its light weight, its relatively low cost, and its capacity for being used in a variety of shapes and colors. To avoid color discoloration, plastic can be laminated with a UV-resistant film.

FIGURE 9.7 Hand-blown glass pendant.

Luminaires are designed in a variety of finishes for functional and decorative purposes. Finishes are applied primarily to protect a surface and provide reflectance. Common finishes include coatings of lacquers, enamels, and metals. Lacquer and enamel coatings generally make reflective finishes. Metallic coatings are excellent for specular reflection. The most common finish colors are black, white, brushed nickel, polished brass, chrome, and gold. The color of surfaces that reflect light can affect the color of the light that is distributed in a space. For example, a luminaire with a gold-colored rim reflects a warmer color than does a white fixture.

Accessories and Special Considerations

Luminaire manufacturers have numerous accessories, including devices that reduce glare and create special effects. To direct light and reduce glare, some luminaires have accessories, such as barn doors, extension hoods, cowls, pinhole shields, gimbal rings, and eyeballs (Figure 9.8 a-e). Special lenses are also available that create unique ways of distributing light, such as prismatic, linear, sanded, sanded-perimeter, sanded-center, sanded-half, and sanded-key (Figure 9.9 a-g). Diffusers made of standard opal or ground glass have poor

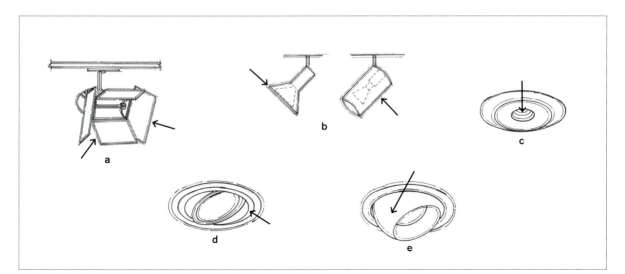

FIGURE 9.8 Accessories for luminaires: (a) barn door shutters, (b) extension hoods (right) and cowls (left), (c) pinhole rim, (d) gimbal ring, and (e) eyeball.

FIGURE 9.9 Special lenses for luminaires: (a) prismatic, (b) linear, (c) sanded, (d) sanded perimeter, (e) sanded center, (f) sanded half, and (g) sanded key.

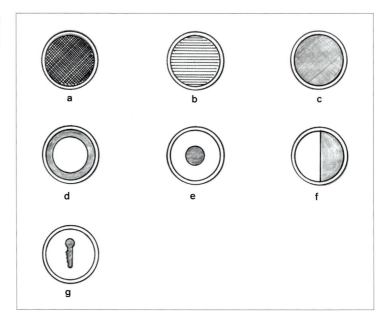

optical control and low transmissive efficiency. Accessories for special effects include projectors with framing heads, iris heads, and graphic gobo (Figure 9.10 a-c). Common applications for projection are patterns, images, logos, and mobile effects. For colored light, the accessories include colored glass lenses, colored theatrical gels, and lenses with a dichroic coating. A lens with a dichroic coating has excellent optical clarity and maintains a consistent color.

Some luminaires are designed to meet specific mechanical and installation requirements. An interior designer specifies these luminaires in order to comply with local building and electrical codes. (See Chapter 12 for more information about codes and regulations.) Some luminaires are designed to accommodate the supply and return system for heating, ventilating, and air-conditioning units.

Installation concerns include: clearance space for recessed luminaires, weight, mounting requirements, and the location of insulation. Clearances required for installing luminaires, including insulation restrictions, are found in the manufacturers' product specifications. The IC (insulated ceiling) designation indicates that the luminaire can be installed in an insulated ceiling or wall. A luminaire that is IC-AT (airtight) has the additional benefit of conserving energy by reducing air

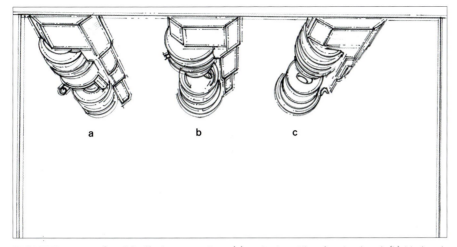

FIGURE 9.10 Special effect accessories: (a) projector with a framing head, (b) iris head, and (c) graphic gobo.

infiltration. Manufacturers also provide information on the weight of a luminaire. Large and heavy luminaires can be problematic when a space lacks the structural elements for the proper mounting mechanism and when there are suspended ceiling applications. Some applications might require waterproof luminaires.

To improve an existing lighting plan and conserve energy and natural resources, interior designers can review lighting system retrofit options, which enable an existing fixture to be converted to an updated system. *Lighting retrofits* are available for specific components of a luminaire or an entire lighting system. The most common components for retrofit are lamps, sockets, reflectors, and ballasts. Retrofits should be considered when the replacement component improves the efficacy, color, light distribution, and maintenance of the system. For example, replacing old fluorescent lamps with lamps that have high efficacy ratings might reduce the number of lamps needed in a luminaire or space. The addition of a specular reflector in a luminaire can increase the quantity of illumination emitted from the fixture and direct the light to the required location. Some manufacturers have products that retrofit incandescent lamps for compact fluorescents. The *Lighting Retrofit Manual* (EPRI, 1997) is an excellent resource for information. (See Chapter 12 for details regarding energy and conservation practices.)

Luminaire Types

Major categories of luminaires include recessed, surface-mounted, suspended, track, structural, and furniture-integrated units. These luminaires are designed primarily for incandescent, fluorescent, and HID lamps, and they are available in a variety of sizes, shapes, and materials. Most of these luminaires can be used for general, task, accent, or decorative lighting. Some manufacturers design a luminaire for multiple applications, such as a pendant, ceiling mount, and sconce. Luminaires designed for multiple applications provide for unity in the design of a fixture and meet the needs of various lighting techniques.

There are manufacturers who mass-produce luminaires, but there are numerous small companies that also produce luminaires. Some of the small companies make luminaires by hand. Italian designers have a reputation for creating some of the most creative and classical pieces. (See Chapter 11 for styles of luminaires.) The quality of construction and materials varies among manufacturers and product lines. To have a quality lighting environment, interior designers must be cognizant of the characteristics of the product they are specifying. To gain this knowledge, they must visit manufacturer showrooms, discuss product attributes with manufacturer representatives, attend educational seminars, and read current articles in trade journals.

Recessed Luminaires

Recessed downlight **luminaires** are fixtures that are installed above a sheetrock or suspended-grid ceiling. New developments in the design of recessed luminaires allow for a flangeless installation. As a result of this design, the ceiling surface is flush with the aperture of the recessed fixture. The installation has a clean appearance and helps to conceal the fixture. Recessed luminaires that have some of the housing above and below the ceiling are **semi-recessed luminaires**. A recessed luminaire generally creates direct lighting in a space. The most common recessed luminaires are troffers, downlights, wall-wash, and accent. Common sizes for recessed troffers are 6 or 8 inches by 4 feet (15–20 cm by 122 cm), 1 foot by 4 feet (31 cm by 122 cm), 2 feet by 2 feet (61 cm by 61 cm), and 2 feet by 4 feet (61 cm by 122 cm) (Figure

Recessed luminaire
Fixture that is installed above a sheetrock or suspended-grid ceiling.

Semi-recessed luminaire
Fixture that has some of the housing above and some below the ceiling.

9.11). The sizes accommodate the various lengths of fluorescent lamps. The interior of troffers is generally painted white or has a specular metal reflector. The most common devices at the apertures for fluorescent troffers are acrylic prismatic lenses and parabolic louvers. As demonstrated in Figure 7.2, the photometric distribution for a fluorescent fixture with silver parabolic louvers is direct. Parabolic louvers with large cell depths (1.5–4 in. or 4–10 cm) have higher luminaire efficiency than smaller cells because the large cells have more reflectance surfaces. **Luminous ceilings** utilize rows of lamps behind diffused lenses.

Recessed downlights are also referred to as *high hats* or *cans*. The most common shapes for recessed downlights are round and square. The size of a downlight aperture can be as small as 2 inches. The finish applied to the rim affects the efficiency of the luminaire. White and aluminum finishes provide the highest luminaire efficiency. Dark colored and black rims have lower luminaire efficiency ratings, but the reflectance values help to reduce glare. The efficiency of a downlight is also dependent upon the existence of a reflector in the luminaire. To maximize the lumens emitted from downlights without reflectors, reflector lamps should be specified.

Luminous ceiling
Lighting method on a ceiling that utilizes rows of lamps behind diffused lenses.

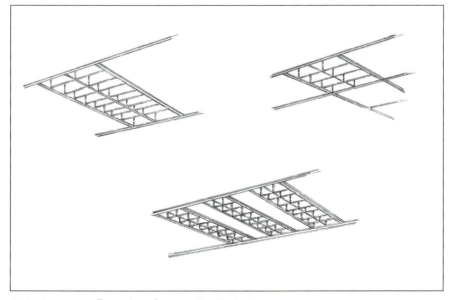

FIGURE 9.11   Examples of recessed troffer luminaires.

The type of device used at the aperture, or a bare opening, affects the photometric distribution from downlights. In general, light emitted from a downlight with a bare opening will be dependent upon the type of lamp. For example, a narrow halogen spot lamp mounted in a recessed downlight will emit a narrow beam of light. Recessed downlights with a bare opening can cause discomfort or disability glare because of the exposed lamp. There are many devices used at the aperture of recessed downlights, including baffles, louvers, and fresnel and prismatic lenses. Special recessed luminaires are designed for floor installations. These recessed uplight luminaires include a floor-mount plate and are often used to enhance architectural details.

Recessed downlights are also designed to direct light to a vertical surface. For grazing techniques, the distance from the downlight to the wall should be approximately 6–8 inches (15–20 cm). The distance between downlights depends upon whether a scalloped pattern on the wall is considered desirable. Luminaires that are close together are less likely to create a scalloped pattern. Recessed linear or round wall-washers distribute light on a wall in a large area (Figure 9.12). A typical photometric distribution of a recessed wall-washer illustrates how light strikes a vertical surface (Figure 9.13). A reflector or an angled lens

FIGURE 9.12
Recessed linear
wall-washer.

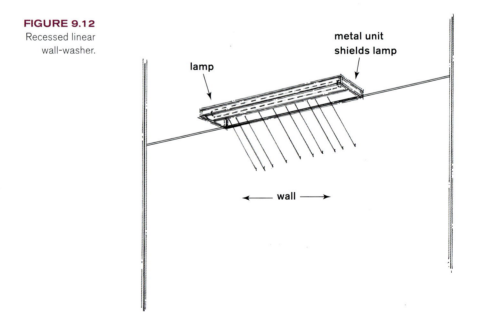

metal unit
shields lamp

lamp

←— wall —→

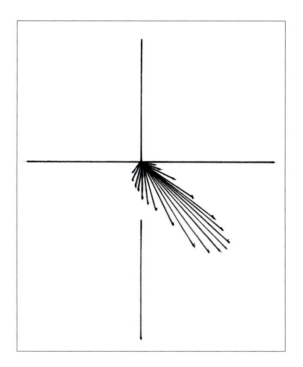

causes the light to angle to the wall. Wall-washer luminaires should be located at least 30 inches (76 cm) from the wall to prevent hot spots. To avoid scalloped patterns on the wall, the distance from the luminaire to the wall and between luminaires should be approximately one-third the height of the ceiling.

Recessed accent or spot downlights emit a narrow beam of light. Recessed accent downlights have a 30 to 45 degree aiming angle and can rotate at least 350 degrees. Common directional trims for recessed accent downlights include slotted, baffled, eyeball, and pinhole apertures (Figures 9.14 a–c). Recessed accent luminaires are either fixed or adjustable. Multiple recessed luminaires have two to six spots in one rectangular opening (Figure 9.15). These luminaires provide the flexibility of spotlighting three different points of emphasis with only one hole in the ceiling. For interiors with angled ceilings, recessed, sloped-ceiling luminaires distribute light downward, wall-wash, or spotlight objects.

An advantage to recessed luminaires is that they emit light to a variety of locations, while maintaining the appearance of a clean ceiling

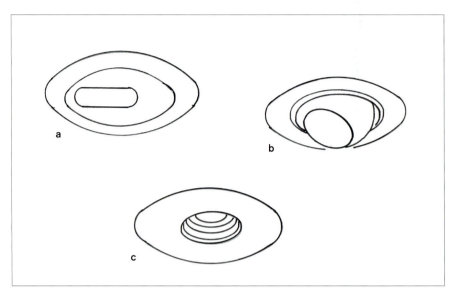

FIGURE 9.14 Directional trims for recessed accent downlights: (a) slotted, (b) eyeball, and (c) baffled pinhole.

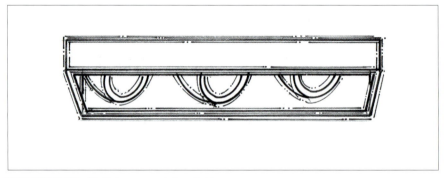

FIGURE 9.15 Multiple recessed downlights.

line, which can make a space appear larger. Recessed luminaires can provide task lighting for an area that has a decorative luminaire. Miniature recessed luminaires can be hidden to promote an element of mystery to the interior. Some of the disadvantages to recessed lighting include the clearance space required for installation, space allowances between insulation and the housing unit, and ventilation to remove heat. Recessed luminaires should always be planned early in construction, because of the mounting requirements, the need to accommodate a fire-rated ceiling, and the holes in the ceiling. In addition to the structural mounting requirements, a recessed luminaire must be placed in the proper location to avoid problems associated with direct lighting, including glare and unflattering shadows on people. The fixed distance from the ceiling to an object or surface makes it very important to select a luminaire and lamp that can perform to the parameters of the specific site. Removing recessed luminaires can be costly and disruptive to the surface of a finished ceiling. Relamping can be difficult, especially for rooms with very tall ceilings. Recessed luminaires designed for front relamping are easier to maintain.

Surface-Mount Luminaires

Surface-mount luminaires are fixtures that are installed on a ceiling, wall, floor, or under a shelf or cabinet. Surface-mount luminaires are designed for direct, indirect, semi-direct, and diffused lighting. The most common surface-mount luminaires for ceilings are troffers, downlights, wraparound lens, and **HID high-bay** (Figure 9.16). Wraparound lens luminaires emit most of the light from the sides and bottom of the fixture. Close proximity to the ceiling can maximize luminance by reflecting from the ceiling; however, these luminaires can also cause glare on computer monitors. HID high-bay luminaires accommodate metal halide and high-pressure sodium lamps. The aluminum reflector has good optical control and is often used in commercial applications with high ceilings.

Surface-mount luminaire
Fixture that is installed on a ceiling or wall or under a shelf or cabinet.

HID high-bay
A cone-shaped fixture designed to accommodate the shape of HID light sources.

FIGURE 9.16 HID high-bay luminaire.

Sconces and whiteboard luminaires are some of the most common surface-mount luminaires for walls (Figure 9.17). Sconces are often decorative light sources that provide direct, indirect, semi-direct, semi-indirect, and diffused lighting. For safety purposes, and to comply with the Americans with Disabilities Act (ADA), sconces that are mounted below 80 inches (203 cm) from the floor should project no more than 4 inches (10 cm) from the wall. (See Chapter 14 for more information about lighting safety.) The eye-level location of a sconce can easily create discomfort or disability glare. This is especially problematic when sconces are located at the bottom of stairways. An individual coming down the stairs can experience disability glare from viewing the exposed lamps. Exposed lamps can also be a problem when the shielding device for the sconce is a thin, translucent material and the illumination level is high. To help prevent glare, some sconces have diffusers, louvers, baffles, or lenses.

Whiteboard lighting is mounted on a wall, and provides direct light on a whiteboard or chalkboard. Generally, fluorescent lamps are used for whiteboard lighting. The internal reflector emits a soft light on the vertical surface without shadows or glare. Surface-mount luminaires also include fixtures that are installed under a shelf or cabinet. The

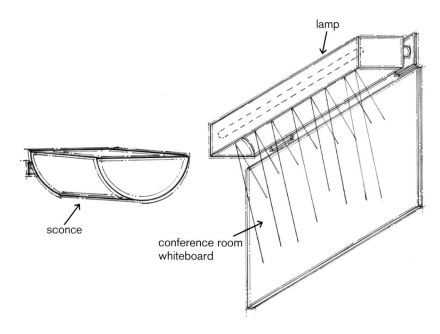

FIGURE 9.17 Surface-mount luminaires.

most common shapes are linear, round, and square. Generally, the linear luminaires have fluorescent lamps, and the round and square shapes use incandescent lamps. The punch of light emitted from miniature, surface-mount luminaires is an excellent way to highlight objects on a shelf.

Surface-mount luminaires have the advantage of simultaneously providing illumination and being a decorative piece. The potential to direct and diffuse light provides flexibility in addressing the multiple lighting requirements in an environment. Compared to recessed luminaires, surface-mount fixtures are easier to install. In specifying the location of a surface-mount luminaire, an interior designer does not have to consider clearances for insulation or mechanical and plumbing restrictions. Some of the disadvantages of surface-mount luminaires are based upon the location of the fixtures. Relamping at the ceiling level can be difficult. Removing the luminaire can result in severe damage to finishes and materials. Since a surface-mount luminaire can become a focal point in a room, selection and location of the fixtures must adhere to the principles of design. For example, luminaires should reflect the theme of the design concept, the scale must be appropriate for the shape and size of the room, and the placement of the fixtures should be balanced on the ceiling. Some surface-mount luminaires cast a light and shadow pattern on a wall or ceiling. This could negatively distort the appearance of a patterned or textured surface.

Suspended Luminaires

Suspended luminaires are fixtures that are installed on a ceiling and extend into the room via cords, chains, poles, or wires. Some luminaires have a mechanism that allows for easy cord length adjustments. Suspended luminaires can emit direct, indirect, semi-direct, and diffused lighting. The most common suspended luminaires include pendants, chandeliers, ceiling fans, linear fluorescent fixtures (indirect and bidirectional), and an element of a track system. Many of these are for decorative purposes only.

Linear fluorescent luminaires are frequently designed for task lighting. Bidirectional (direct-indirect) luminaires for general or task lighting should have materials, reflectors, baffles, or louvers that have re-

Suspended luminaire
Fixture that is installed on a ceiling and extends into the room by a cord, chain, pole, or wires.

flectances greater than 90 percent. To avoid hot spots, or glare, suspended luminaires that have indirect lighting should be mounted at least 18 inches (46 cm) from the ceiling. Suspended luminaires in a circulation area should be at least 80 inches (203 cm) from the floor. The distance from a dining table to the bottom of the luminaire should be 30 inches (76 cm) or more. An appropriate distance is determined by the height of the ceiling and the scale of the room and the luminaire.

The primary advantage to using a suspended luminaire is decorative. Therefore, the design of the luminaire must reflect the design concept of the interior and adhere to the principles of design. Generally, suspended luminaires are focal points in an interior and can visually divide the space. Thus, depending upon the location, size, and material, suspended luminaires can make an interior appear smaller. Suspended luminaires can be difficult to maintain because of their location and the high accumulation of dirt and dust. Two important considerations for mounting suspended luminaires are to avoid glare and to prevent someone from hitting the fixture. To specify an appropriate location, an interior designer should consider how the location affects people standing and sitting. Whenever possible, the location of the luminaire should not interfere with decorative focal points in an environment, such as artwork on a wall or a beautiful view from a window. For multiple, suspended luminaires in rows, care must be taken to ensure that the fixtures are hung in a perfectly straight line.

Track Luminaires

Track luminaire
Fixtures that has multiple heads mounted on an electrical raceway.

Track luminaires are fixtures that have multiple heads and are mounted on an electrical raceway (Figure 9.18). Tracks are available in a variety of lengths, and connectors are used to create shapes, such as L, T, or X. Generally, one end of the track connects to the main circuit wiring, and the other end is dead. Multitracks are available for separate switching arrangements. Low-voltage track systems are available with remote transformers. Track systems can be suspended from a ceiling by cables, recessed into the ceiling plane, or surface-mounted on a ceiling or wall. Track-mounted luminaires, or heads, are available in a

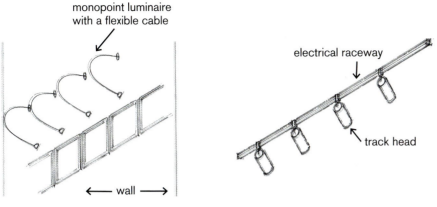

FIGURE 9.18 Examples of track luminaires.

variety of styles, colors, sizes, lamp types, and materials; they also come with built-in transformers. Some track heads are connected to the end of a long, flexible cable that can be shaped to aim light in numerous directions. A monopoint luminaire is used for installations that require only one track head. Track luminaires have evolved to designs that include low-voltage cable and rail systems (Figure 9.18). The heads on these systems are attached to a cable or rail, which can be adjusted and shaped at the site of installation. The flexibility of the system allows for designs in curves and soft angles.

Light distribution from the heads is direct, indirect, direct-indirect, and diffused. The most common applications for track systems are accent, wallwash, and downlight. Many heads are designed to hold the lamp and do not have optical control. For these heads, it is critical to select the lamp that will have the desired beam spread and intensity. To control glare, heads are available with louvers, lenses, and shielding devices that are solid or mesh. Suspension kits for the track system, and extensions for each track head, are available for tall ceilings.

The primary advantage to a track system is the flexibility, in that it is relatively simple to reaim and relocate the heads. This is why they are frequently used to highlight items on display in retail stores. Tracks also provide the flexibility of having different types of illumination from one fixture. Disadvantages to track system are the difficulties in reaching the heads, a strong potential for glare, and a high accumulation of dirt and dust. When it is difficult to reach the track heads, they are seldom reaimed or relocated. This negates the most important advantage of a track system and increases the potential for glare. To reduce the potential of glare, avoid track locations where users can see the lamps, or add a shielding device to the heads. In specifying a track system, it is important to be aware of the quality of the product. Some tracks are made of flimsy aluminum and should be avoided for applications that require frequent reaiming and relocating. There are also some safety concerns associated with track systems. Generally, components are not interchangeable from one manufacturer to another, especially for track systems that are UL-rated specifically for one manufacturer and one product line. In addition, the ease in adding heads to a track increases the potential for exceeding the maximum wattages for the system.

Structural and Furniture-Integrated Luminaires

Structural luminaires are an element of the architectural interior. The major types of structural luminaires are cove, valance, cornice, soffit, and wall brackets (Figure 9.19 a-e). Cove lighting is mounted on a wall, and the light is directed up toward the ceiling. Cove lighting is especially effective in rooms with tall ceilings, and it can be integrated with crown molding. **Valance lighting** is mounted above a window, and the light is directed up and down. Cornice lighting can be mounted on a wall or above a window, and the light is directed down. **Soffit lighting** is a built-in wall element that is close or next to the ceiling and extends 12 to 18 inches (31–46 cm) from the wall. Generally, soffit lighting directs the light down onto a task. Some units can include indirect lighting. Soffit lighting is frequently used over work areas, such as kitchen counters, desks, and bathroom sinks. Wall bracket lighting is mounted on a wall, and the light is directed up and down. A wallslot is integrated in the ceiling system and distributes light down on vertical surfaces. For example, wallslots can be used around the perimeter of a room. New developments in seamless fluorescent systems eliminate dark zones in continuous rows. This results in a continuous band of illumination on walls and ceilings.

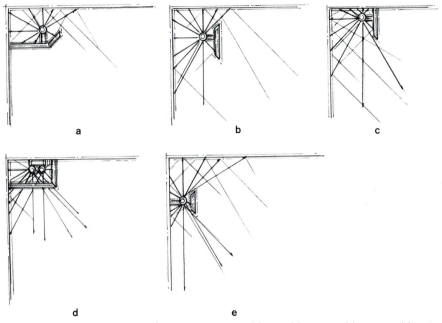

FIGURE 9.19 Examples of structural luminaires: (a) cove (b) valance, (c), cornice, (d) soffit, and (e) wall bracket.

The most common materials used to construct structural luminaires are wood, metal, and gypsum board. *Fascia* is the term for the board that is shielding the light source. To achieve the maximum amount of light from structural luminaires, the interior surfaces should be painted white, and the fascia should have an angled cutoff. Generally, linear fluorescent lamps are used in these units. To attain consistency in color and intensity level, lamps from one manufacturer should be installed in a unit. To reduce glare, some structural luminaires include a device that shields the light source, such as a baffle, lens, or louver.

The size of the unit and its location on a wall are also important to the success of structural luminaires. The unit must have the proper dimensions so as to maximize reflectance and adequately shield the lamps from multiple angles of view. The location on the wall affects reflectance, illumination levels, and the potential for glare. The dimensions that follow are applicable for cove, valance, cornice, and wall bracket lighting. Structural luminaires should be mounted at least

18 inches (46 cm) from a ceiling. The distance from the wall should be 6 to 12 inches (15–31 cm). Lamps should be mounted at least 4 inches (10 cm) from the wall and 2 inches (5 cm) from the fascia. The height of the fascia should be 8 to 12 inches (20–31 cm). Soffit luminaires should be mounted 12 to 18 inches (31–46 cm) from the wall and 6 to 12 inches (15–31 cm) high. Modifications to recommended dimensions may be necessary for rooms with high ceilings or for very large or small rooms. For example, dark areas may occur in the center of a large room that has cove lighting. Some luminaires distribute light more evenly and avoid *hot spots* from the lamps. The integration of built-in reflectors assists in distributing the light along a surface.

Structural luminaires have the advantage of enhancing the interior by being well integrated with the interior architecture. Outlining the shape and size of an interior can make a space appear larger and can serve as a means to follow the rhythm of the structure. Another advantage to this type of lighting is that the evenly distributed light resembles the positive qualities of daylight. This effect is excellent for general lighting purposes. Structural luminaires can also add an element of mystery to an environment, because the light sources are hidden from view, and so the light appears to be floating. Disadvantages to structural luminaires are the potential for glare, damage to ceiling and walls when removing the elements, and difficulties associated with cleaning lamps and relamping. For structural applications in large rooms, the center of the room might be dark. In addition, any cracks or imperfections in walls or ceilings can become very noticeable when the light grazes the surfaces. Imperfections are less likely to show with a matte finish paint.

Furniture-integrated luminaires have lamps mounted in a cabinet and are generally hidden from view. The most common furniture pieces that have integrated lighting are office systems, curio cabinets, breakfronts, and bookcases (Figure 9.20). Office-system integrated furniture have lamps for ambient and task lighting. Furniture designed for the purpose of highlighting objects generally has downlights or spots. Furniture-integrated luminaires can provide excellent light for their intended purpose. Concerns related to these luminaires focus on

Furniture-integrated luminaire
Unit that has lamps mounted in the cabinet; generally hidden from view. The most common furniture pieces with integrated lighting are office systems, curio cabinets, breakfronts, and bookcases.

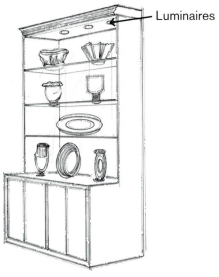

Luminaires

FIGURE 9.20 Furniture-integrated luminaires.

the amount of heat that can collect in the cabinets and the difficulties associated with relamping.

Specifying Luminaires

To specify luminaires, an interior designer must be knowledgeable about the products offered by various manufacturers of luminaires, lamps, and devices used to control fixtures.

Manufacturers' Specifications

The specification process begins with researching current products. The Internet is an excellent resource for identifying and comparing products. Web sites are being developed that have specification-driven product categories. For example, a Web site lists several product categories, such as type of fixture, lamp, and applications (Figure 9.21). A user selects the desired categories, and the Web site locates the products that fit the specifications.

In reviewing various products, it is critical to locate specification data supplied by the manufacturer. These data include installation instructions, application guides, specification sheets, photometric information, and costs. The photometric data include spacing criterion

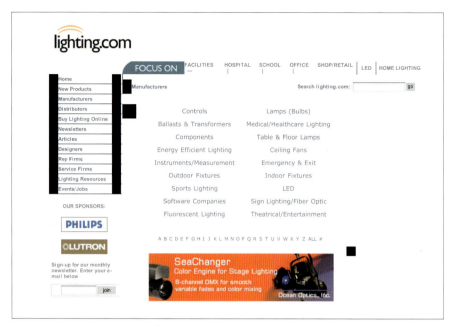

(SC), coefficient of utilization (CU), and luminaire distribution curves and tables. An interior designer needs this information in order to select and specify luminaires and lamps. Data are also used to perform calculations and provide maintenance recommendations to a client.

Selection Considerations

Selecting luminaires for a quality lighting environment begins with an analysis of the site and the users of the space. (Detailed information about the lighting design process is provided in Chapters 21 and 22.) Ideally, lighting is considered at the beginning stages of a project. A major factor that can affect the lighting plan is whether the project is new construction or work to an existing structure. Both situations can present unique challenges that an interior designer must resolve before specifying the luminaires.

In reviewing the specifics of the project, it is important for the designer to prioritize criteria associated with luminaires. For example, when an existing building has significant structural limitations, the first priority might be to select luminaires that can be installed in the rooms. Economic considerations could be a major priority for a client who has a building in a community with high electrical costs. A priority for an expensive jewelry store is to enhance the sparkle of jewels. Prioritized criteria are very helpful when specifying categories of luminaires.

Within the context of priorities, the purpose of the luminaire must be identified. How will the luminaire be integrated with the layered lighting plan? Will the luminaire provide general, task, accent, or decorative lighting? An interior designer must also determine whether the luminaire should be the focal point of the space, blend into the interior, or be completely hidden. Once these decisions have been made, the next step in selecting luminaires involves evaluating specific characteristics of lighting systems, including quality of product, photometric data, lamp characteristics, economics, installation methods, operational considerations, maintenance, and design considerations.

The desired quality of the luminaire is often dependent upon the priorities of the client. However, in order to make informed decisions, it is the responsibility of the interior designer to know the quality differences among products. Luminaires that are made from quality materials and are well constructed are always a good investment. Quality luminaires are especially important for long-term installations and when durability is critical. High-end interiors should also have quality luminaires.

Photometric data should be reviewed to determine the light distribution of the luminaire; the designer should perform the calculations necessary to make this determination. Specification data will also indicate the suggested lamps for the luminaire. Characteristics of the suggested lamps should be reviewed to determine whether they meet the objectives of the lighting plan. Some of the considerations are efficacy ratings, color characteristics, life of the lamp, aiming qualities, operating position, wattages, heat accumulation, optical control properties, control features, and availability of lamps. When designers search internationally for luminaires, it is critical that they know the plug and outlet compatibilities and the UL rating because different countries have different electrical systems and requirements. The economics associated with luminaires include the cost of the fixture, lamps, ballasts, controls, electricity, installation, and maintenance. (See Chapter 12 for more information about energy efficiency and luminaires.)

In selecting luminaires, there are many installation factors to consider. To determine the feasibility of installing a luminaire, the electrical, mechanical, plumbing, and structural components of the building must be surveyed. This process includes reviewing local building and electrical codes. Historical buildings have strict renovation codes and regulations that must be followed throughout a project. The interior must be surveyed to determine access for installation and maintenance. Space requirements may include ballasts, transformers, output boxes, and climate control. There must be adequate support in ceilings and walls for mounting luminaires. Materials such as sheetrock, plaster, wood, and acoustical tile are the most common surfaces for mounting luminaires. Masonry walls and irregular surfaces can pose installation difficulties. The surface must be appropriate for the luminaire's mounting requirements. In addition, unusual surface configurations may require a luminaire that can be modified or adjusted at the field site. The horizontal and vertical impact on the space must be considered when installing a luminaire. In addition, wall-mounted luminaires significantly affect the placement of art on the wall. A review of installation considerations should also include examining the directional effects of lighting on the space and users.

Operational considerations must be considered when specifying luminaires. Factors to examine include use of controls, adjustability, future requirements, ergonomics, environmental factors, and safety. An interior might require special controls, such as dimmers, occupancy detectors, and daylight photosensor systems. For a successful operation, a luminaire must be selected that is compatible with the specific requirements of the controls. (Controls for luminaires are covered in Chapter 10.)

Adjustability of a luminaire could be critical for lighting that is used by a variety of users and for a variety of tasks. It may be necessary to move luminaires to different locations or to completely remove the lighting system at a later date. For these situations, luminaires should be selected that allow for easy relocation and removal. Ergonomic and environmental factors should always be considered when specifying luminaires and lamps. (For more information about these topics see Chapter 12.) Safety concerns focus on fire prevention and adequate light to perform tasks. Safety issues are affected by the overall design of the luminaire. For example, a luminaire with an exposed lamp poses the danger of someone being burned or a fire occurring because of a flammable material hitting the lamp. The stability of the luminaire should also be examined, especially when children, elderly people, and pets are users of the space.

Maintenance is another important consideration for specifying a luminaire. A luminaire that cannot be easily cleaned or relamped reflects badly upon the reputation of an interior designer. A critical expense related to maintenance is the cost of labor. Luminaires mounted in a location that is easily accessed generally do not pose maintenance problems. For locations that are difficult to reach, such as 20-foot-high ceilings, the luminaire should relamp from the front, and have a shield to reduce the accumulation of dirt or dust. Lamps that have a long life should also be considered. A product that requires special tools can hamper luminaire maintenance. The material of the luminaire could also pose maintenance problems. For example, shiny aluminum scratches easily and shows fingerprints.

The luminaire must reflect the theme of the interior and reinforce the principles of design. Interior designers should approach the selection of a luminaire with the same criteria as they would for other elements in the space. To select a luminaire of a specific period often requires historical research. To be in concert with the theme of an interior, some interior designers have luminaires custom-made. This is frequently done for hotels and restaurants. (Chapter 11 provides a summary of historical and contemporary luminaires.) The principles of design should be applied to selecting and locating luminaires. Ceiling-mounted luminaires should be balanced with other elements on the ceiling, including diffusers, returns, smoke alarms, and emergency lights. Symmetrical or asymmetrical balance can be used depending upon the type of fixture and the purpose of the lighting. Luminaires should be selected that reinforce the rhythm, emphasis, unity, proportion, and scale of a space and its furnishings. When tall ceilings are emphasized in a room, luminaires should be selected that provide a vertical focus. Low-level lighting should be used in a space that is intended to be intimate. The size of the luminaire should be proportionate to the size of the room and the installation area. In addition, for nonresidential projects the type of lamps should be limited because it helps to avoid confusion when maintenance people must relamp the fixtures. When there is a variety of lamps, it is very likely that the correct lamp will not be placed in the proper luminaire when relamping is necessary.

The proper selection and placement of luminaires is essential to a quality lighting environment. To conserve energy, the design of the luminaires should emit as many lumens as possible. The key to success is having a thorough knowledge of the products, understanding the interdependence of the elements in a lighting system, and considering how luminaires affect the overall design of an interior. Controls are another important element of the system. A discussion of controls, and how they affect the performance of luminaires, is covered in the next chapter.

SUMMARY

- A luminaire is an element of a lighting system; it includes the light source, housing elements, ballasts, transformers, controls, a mounting mechanism, and a connection to electrical power. A primary purpose of luminaires is optical control.
- Maximizing optical control involves determining the optimum size and shape of the luminaire and specifying the appropriate materials and finishes.
- Primary ways to distribute light are: (a) direct, (b) indirect, (c) semi-direct, (d) semi-indirect, and (e) diffused.
- The luminaire efficacy rating (LER) formula is used to compare the efficiency and effectiveness of different luminaires. This metric reflects how efficiently a luminaire emits light for its intended purpose.
- Controlling and redirecting light occurs through devices that are designed to reflect, diffuse, refract, and shield illumination.
- Luminaires are primarily constructed of steel, aluminum, glass, and

plastic. They are produced in a variety of finishes for functional and decorative purposes.

■ Luminaire manufacturers have numerous accessories, including devices that reduce glare and create special effects.

■ Luminaire installation concerns include clearance space for recessed luminaires, weight, mounting provisions, and the location of insulation. Most of the requirements are found in the manufacturers' product specifications.

■ To improve an existing lighting plan and conserve energy and natural resources, interior designers can review lighting system retrofit options.

■ Major categories of luminaires include recessed, surface-mounted, suspended, track, structural, and furniture-integrated units. These luminaires are designed primarily for incandescent, fluorescent, and HID lamps, and they are available in a variety of sizes, shapes, and materials. Most of these luminaires can be used for general, task, accent, or decorative lighting.

■ The major types of structural luminaires are cove, valance, cornice, soffit, and wall bracket.

■ To specify luminaires, an interior designer must be knowledgeable about the products offered by various manufacturers of luminaires, lamps, and controls. It is critical to locate specification data supplied by the manufacturer.

■ Selecting luminaires for a quality lighting environment begins with an analysis of the site and the users of the space. Within the context of priorities, the purpose of the luminaire must be identified.

■ To determine the feasibility of installing a luminaire, the electrical, mechanical, plumbing, and structural components of the building must be surveyed.

■ Operational considerations include use of controls, adjustability, future requirements, ergonomics, environmental factors, and safety. Maintenance is another important matter when specifying a luminaire.

■ A luminaire must reflect the theme of the interior and reinforce the principles of design.

Key Terms

baffle	reflector
cowl	refractor
diffused light	semi-direct light
diffuser	semi-indirect light
direct light	semi-recessed luminaire
fresnel refractor	shade
furniture-integrated luminaire	soffit lighting
HID high-bay	structural luminaire
indirect light	surface-mount luminaire
louvers	suspended luminaire
luminous ceiling	track luminaire
recessed luminaire	valance lighting

Exercises

1. For each major luminaire type (recessed, surface-mount, suspended, track, and structural) identify effective applications for general, task, and accent lighting. Summarize your suggestions in a written report; you may include illustrations and sketches.

2. Locate five different commercial or residential interiors. For each interior, respond to the following items: (a) identify the overall design theme of the space, (b) identify the luminaires, (c) evaluate the luminaires according to the principles of design, including balance, rhythm, emphasis, proportion, scale, variety, and unity. In a written report summarize each interior and include the illustrations.

3. Create a product resource file. Search the World Wide Web for 20 luminaire and 5 lamp manufacturers. The products should include all the types of luminaires. Locate all specification data for each product. Compile the resources in a file that is organized by types of luminaires and lamps. For each manufacturer, locate the photometric reports for three different luminaires.

4. Interior designers must write specifications for lighting plans. Identify two interiors and write the lighting plan specifications for

the luminaires and lamps. Specifications should include all the information needed to order the luminaires and lamps. Refer to manufacturers' product data for the specification details. Specifications may be presented in a table.

5. Identify an existing commercial site. Conduct an analysis of the site, and determine the users of the environment. Develop a concept for a new lighting plan by addressing the following considerations: (a) site and users, (b) prioritized criteria, (c) purpose of the luminaires, (d) quality of the luminaires, (e) photometric data, (f) installation considerations, (g) operations, (h) maintenance, and (i) the principles of design. In a written report provide recommendations for a new lighting plan, including illustrations, photos, or sketches.

REFERENCES

Allphin, W. (1961). BCD appraisals of luminaire brightness in a simulated office. *Illuminating Engineering, 56(1)*, 31–44.

Benya, J., Heschong, L., McGowan, T., Miller, N., and Rubinstein, F. (2001). *Advanced Lighting Guidelines.* White Salmon, WA: New Buildings Institute.

Boyce, P.N., Elkund, N., and Simpson, S. (2000). Individual lighting control: Task performance, mood and illuminance. *Journal of the Illuminating Engineering Society, 29 (1)*, 131–142.

Boyce, P.R. (1981). *Human Factors in Lighting,* New York: Macmillan.

Boylan, B.R. (1987). *The Lighting Primer.* Ames, IA: Iowa State University Press.

Carter, D.J., Sexton, R.C., and Miller, M.S. (1989). Field measurement of illuminance. *Lighting, Research, & Technology, 21 (1)*, 29–35.

Clark, F. (1968). Light loss factor in the design process. *Illuminating Engineering, 63(11)*, 575–581.

Clark, F. (1963). Accurate maintenance factors. *Illuminating Engineering, 58(3)*, 124–131.

Coaton, J.R., and Marsden, A.M. (1997). *Lamps and Lighting,* (4th ed.). London: Arnold.

Ducker Research (August 1999). Lighting quality-key customer values and decision process. *Report to the Light Right Research Consortium.*

Egan, M.D. (1983). *Concepts in Architectural Lighting.* New York: McGraw-Hill.

Electric Power Research Institute (EPRI). (1997). *Lighting Retrofit Manual.* Pleasant Hill, CA: Electric Power Research Institute.

Elmer, W.B. (1980). *The Optical Design of Reflectors.* New York: John Wiley & Sons.

Gordan, G., and Nuckolls, J.L. (1995). *Interior Lighting for Designers.* New York: John Wiley & Sons.

Greif, M. (1986). *The Lighting Book.* Pittstown, NJ: The Main Street Press.

Hopkinson, R.G. (1957). Evaluation of glare. *Illuminating Engineering, 52(6)*, 305–316.

Illuminating Engineering Society. Committee on Light Control and Equipment Design

(1970). IES guide to design of light control. Part IV: Practical concepts of equipment design. *Illuminating Engineering, 65(8)*, 479–494.

Illuminating Engineering Society. Lighting Design Practice Committee. (1968). Calculation of luminance coefficients based upon zonal-cavity method. *Illuminating Engineering, 63(8)*, 423–432.

Illuminating Engineering Society of North America (IESNA) (2000). *IESNA Lighting Handbook* (9th edition).New York: Illuminating Engineering Society of North America.

Kaufman, J.E. (ed.) (1984). *IES Lighting Handbook Reference Volume 1984*. New York: Illuminating Engineering Society.

Lewis, A.L. (1998). Equating light sources for visual performance at low luminances. *Journal of the Illuminating Engineering Society*, 27(1), 80.

Loe, D.L., Mansfield, J.F., and Rowlands, E. (1994). Appearance of lit environment and its relevance in lighting design: Environmental study. *Lighting Research & Technology, 26(3)*, 119–133.

Loe, D.L., and Rowlands, E. (1996). The art and science of lighting: A strategy for lighting design. *Lighting Research & Technology, 28(4)*, 153–164.

Lynes, J.A. (1978). *Developments in Lighting—1*. London: Applied Science Publishers.

O'Brien, P.F., and Balogh, E. (1967). Configuration factors for computing illumination within interiors. Illuminating Engineering, 62 (4), 169–179.

Phillips, D. (2000). *Lighting Modern Buildings*. Oxford: Architectural Press.

Smith F.K., and Bertolone, F.J. (1986). *The Principles and Practices of Lighting Design: Bringing Interiors to Light*. New York: Whitney Library of Design.

Steffy, G.R. (1990). *Architectural Lighting Design*. New York: Van Nostrand Reinhold.

Veitch, J., and Newsham, G. (1998). Lighting quality and energy-efficiency effects on task performance, mood, health, satisfaction, and comfort. *Journal of the Illuminating Engineering Society*, 27(1), 107.

Ward, L.G., and Shakespeare, R.A. (1998). *Rendering with Radiance: The Art and Science of Lighting Visualization*. San Francisco: Morgan Kaufmann.

Watson, L. (1977). *Lighting Design Handbook*. New York: McGrawHill.

CHAPTER 10

Lighting Systems: Controls

OBJECTIVES

- Describe the role of transformers and ballasts in a lighting system.

- Differentiate between magnetic and electronic versions of transformers and ballasts.

- Describe how lighting controls can conserve energy and enhance an environment.

- Identify the primary ways in which controls can conserve energy, including scheduling, daylight integration, monitoring lamp maintenance, and load shedding.

- Describe the basic equipment for lighting controls, including switches, dimmers, timers, occupancy sensors, photosensors, and central units.

- Understand how to specify auxiliary and lighting controls for a quality lighting environment.

CONTROLS are an important component of a lighting system. In the past, controls were not a major consideration. However, advancements in digital technologies have increased the performance and options available to an interior designer. As controls become even more sophisticated, interior designers will have many ways to improve the efficiency of lighting systems and provide flexibility for users. Constant improvements in the technology of controls require that interior designers routinely read product literature and articles in professional journals.

This chapter explores auxiliary and lighting controls and how they affect a quality lighting environment. Auxiliary controls include transformers and ballasts. Lighting controls include a broad category of techniques and equipment that are designed to enhance an environment and conserve energy. Lighting controls operate either manually or automatically and include switches, dimmers, timers, occupancy sensors, photosensors, and central controls.

Auxiliary Controls

Transformers and ballasts are devices that assist in the operation of some lighting systems. These controls must be compatible with a lighting system and they consume a small amount of electricity.

Transformer
An electrical device that converts voltages in a system.

Transformers

A **transformer** is an electrical device that converts voltage in a system. *Step-up transformers* are used to transport electricity to communities, and *step-down transformers* lower the voltage for specific commercial and residential applications. For lighting purposes, a transformer is either integral to the design of the luminaire, or it is a separate unit that is concealed under a ceiling or behind a wall (Figure 10.1). The

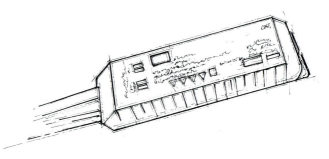

FIGURE 10.1 A 60 watt transformer utilized in lighting systems.

vast majority of line-voltage lighting applications operate at 120 volts. Low-voltage lighting applications usually operate at 12 volts. Thus, for low-voltage lighting a transformer is needed to step-down the line voltage to 12 volts. Neon lights and LEDs require a transformer in order for them to operate with a direct current.

Transformers are available in magnetic and electronic versions. Magnetic transformers have a steel core, are encased in copper wire, and are very reliable. Magnetic units are heavier, larger, noisier, and cheaper than electronic transformers. Electronic transformers are composed of an electrical circuit and generally do not last as long as a magnetic unit. The advantages to electronic transformers include a smaller size, less weight, and quieter operation. Since electricity is required to operate transformers, the energy consumed by the device must be included in determining the watts-per-square-foot calculations in a space.

Each transformer is rated with a maximum wattage; this information is provided by manufacturers. For safety purposes and proper operation of the luminaire, it is critical to specify lamps that do not exceed the maximum wattages. Also, there can be a noticeable voltage drop and reduced light output when there is a long distance from the transformer to the luminaire. Thus, the transformer should be installed as close as possible to the luminaire. The maximum distance from a luminaire to a transformer is dependent upon the wattage and the wire gauge. For example, a single-fixture luminaire with a 16-gauge wire at 12 volts can accommodate 150 watts when the transformer is 50 feet (15.24 m) from the luminaire. A single-fixture luminaire with a 12-gauge wire at 12 volts can accommodate 250 watts when the transformer is 50 feet (15.24 m) from the luminaire. A 24-volt system is available to help alleviate problems associated with distances between the transformer and luminaires. All these data are available from luminaire manufacturers.

Most transformers work with standard incandescent dimmers. There are some options available for transformers, including automatic reset, soft starting, resettable circuit breakers, thermal protection, and short-circuit protection. There are also special devices designed for unique installation requirements, such as expandable hanger bars.

Very small transformers with dimmers can be used in cabinets or display shelves. Plug-in transformers are available for 12-volt fixtures.

Ballasts

A ballast is a control device used with an electric-discharge lamp that starts a lamp; it also controls the electrical current during operation (Figure 10.2). The ballast for a lamp is either a separate control gear or an integral system. Fluorescent and HID discharge lamps require ballasts to operate. Generally, the operating life of a ballast is greater than that of discharge lamps. Ballasts are available in magnetic and electronic versions. Magnetic ballasts are made with a core of steel laminations that is wrapped with copper or aluminum wires. Magnetic ballasts may produce a humming sound that can be a problem. To determine the level of sound, ballasts have been rated on a scale from A, the quietest, to F, the loudest. The rating for A is 20 to 24 decibels, and F is greater than 49 decibels. Electronic ballasts are produced with solid-state circuitry. To improve the efficiency of lamp/ballast systems, some electronic ballasts are designed to operate on high-frequency power. Electronic ballasts can accommodate only rapid- and instant-start fluorescent lamps. Multiple-lamp ballasts are available to accommodate several lamps.

As with transformers, the electronic version is generally preferred because the unit is more energy-efficient, quieter, and weighs less than the magnetic version. Energy savings are derived from using less elec-

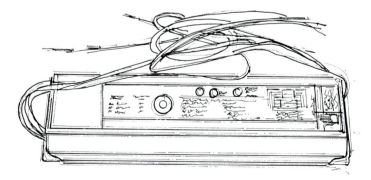

FIGURE 10.2 An electronic ballast for a fluorescent lamp.

tricity for the light output and operating at cooler temperatures. The cooler operating temperature improves lamp life and helps to reduce the energy required for air-conditioning. (For more information about energy and the environment, refer to Chapter 12.) Electronic ballasts eliminate flicker and can accommodate multiple lamp operations. The initial cost of electronic ballasts is higher than that for magnetic ballasts.

Ballasts are designed to operate in a parallel or series circuit. In a series circuit, lamps operate together as one system. If one lamp burns out, the remaining lamps do not work. Lamps operating with a parallel ballast circuit function independently and continue to operate when one of the lamps burns out.

Ballasts must always be considered as a system with specific lamps. Generally, ballasts are designed to work with the specific characteristics of lamps, such as type of source, wattage, and controls. For example, ballasts are made specifically for a metal halide lamp operating at a designated wattage. Fluorescent lamp/ballast circuits are uniquely designed for preheat, rapid start, and instant start systems. Moreover, variations among lamp manufacturers result in lamps and ballasts that may not be interchangeable.

In operating as an interdependent unit, a lamp and ballast should be selected that will maximize the performance of the system. For example, high-frequency electronic ballasts were developed to accommodate the efficacious T-8 fluorescent lamp. The unison operation of a T-8 and high-frequency electronic ballast results in low energy consumption, long lamp life, and improved maintenance. HID lamps are not more efficient operating at high frequencies. Thus, to maximize the operating potential of a lamp/ballast system, all characteristics must be reviewed, including how the individual units affect one another. Ballast characteristics and operating factors are used in determining light loss factors (LLF) and the watts-per-square-foot calculations for an interior.

Ballast power factor (BPF), ballast factor (BF), and ballast efficacy factor (BEF) are formulas developed to evaluate different lamp/ballast systems. The BPF rating reflects how efficiently electrical power is being transferred to a ballast. A desirable BPF rating is greater than

.90. The BF indicates the lumen output for a lamp/ballast system compared to the ideals of a test condition. A BF lower than 1.0 indicates that the lamp/ballast system is operating at less than optimum efficiency. A BF rating greater than 1.0 means that the lamp/ballast system is functioning at a higher than expected light output. The BEF rating is calculated by dividing the BF by the total ballast input power in watts. Federal guidelines regulate the standards for BEF ratings.

The technology of ballasts is constantly improving. The areas of development include system efficacy, control abilities, and daylight integration. The goals are to provide greater flexibility, enhance control, improve light output, and conserve energy and natural resources. Energy-saving ballast/lamp systems, such as a 32W T-8 lamp, reduce the consumption of watts. Circuits are being improved by allowing control of several lamp wattages and reading input voltages and lamp types. These enhancements reduce the number of ballasts needed for an interior, hence facilitating specification and maintenance requirements. Improvements in controls include devices, such as smart circuitry, that regulate starts and restarts. Circuits can also monitor the end-of-life of a lamp, dimming, and photocells. To protect the environment, materials used to fabricate ballasts have also been improved. Some ballasts produced prior to 1978 contained the toxic substance **polychlorinated biphenyls (PCBs).** Ballasts without PCBs are labeled "No PCBs."

Polychlorinated biphenyls (PCBs)
A toxic material that was used in ballasts produced prior to 1978.

Lighting Controls

Lighting controls are available in conventional modes, automated, or a combination of both. The newest integrated control systems allow access to interiors from anywhere. By utilizing building networks or Ethernet/Internet, lighting control systems can be monitored, programmed, and managed. System software features allow a user to customize a graphic that depicts the lighting system on floor plans, elevations, or any other illustration that helps to visualize illumination throughout a space and building. For example, via Ethernet/Internet, people sitting in their office can view a floor plan of their home and learn which lights are on or off, as well as the status of any system that is integrated with the centralized control unit, such as security and fire alarms. Via the Ethernet/Internet, an individual can also control the system, such as switching lights on or off, from the office.

Criteria for Specifying Controls

There are many criteria an interior designer should consider when specifying lighting controls, including energy considerations, economics, and aesthetics. Controls can be used to conserve energy by turning lights off when they are not needed, integrating daylight, monitoring lamp maintenance, and load shedding. Conserving energy requires examining the activity patterns of the users of the space. Based upon an analysis of how people function in a space, controls can be programmed for either predictable or unpredictable scheduling. IES (2000) estimates that predictable and unpredictable scheduling can reduce energy by up to 40 and 60 percent, respectively. Predictable scheduling is used to control the lights in a space when there is a set routine. For example, many offices have a fixed schedule for people arriving at work, taking lunch breaks, and leaving at the end of the day. A control system can be designed to automatically turn lights on and off according to the designated time and day of the week. Unpredictable scheduling is designed to accommodate unusual activities in a space. For example, a local control could be installed in a private office to turn the lights off when a person is out sick or away on vacation. Unpredictable scheduling could also be used in spaces such as retail dressing rooms, washrooms, or stacks in a library.

Controls can also conserve energy by orchestrating daylight and electrical light sources. Dimming and switching plans can be programmed to complement daylight by maintaining an appropriate illumination level regardless of the weather conditions and the time of the year. Controls can also be adjusted to ensure that areas that are far from windows have adequate illumination for the required tasks. Multiple switching plans, dimmers, and photoelectric control units are excellent techniques for conserving energy by integrating daylight.

The extent of system integration with some of the newest technology has become very sophisticated. For example, a centralized lighting control system in an office can be connected to electrical sources and shade control. Automated window shades are installed in front of windows, and a small photocell is suspended close to the window to monitor the levels of daylight illumination. As the level of daylight illumination increases, the translucent shades automatically come down and the light from electrical luminaires is reduced. Throughout the day and evening, via window shades and electrical sources, the lighting control system is constantly balancing the amount of light and glare in a room. This results in a consistent footcandle level in the space and conserves energy by eliminating or reducing electrical sources when daylight is sufficient. In addition, to customize lighting requirements for users, the system will allow for individuals to control the light level in their space.

Energy can also be conserved by programming controls to monitor lamp maintenance. For example, controls can notify users when lamps are operating at an unacceptable lumen output level. Lamps operating at less than optimum levels require more energy to function. The low lumen output could be the result of the lamp's end-of-life, or dirt and dust accumulation. Upon notice of lamp lumen depreciation, relamping procedures could be activated automatically.

Load shedding refers to reducing the electrical needs of a space. A load represents all the lights on one switch. New, centralized lighting control systems will produce power consumption reports for every fixture in a building. These control systems can also indicate the footcandle level for any surface or area in a space. Reducing illumination needs during peak times is a form of load shedding. For example, because of high air-conditioning requirements, summer is a peak electrical demand period. Thus, during the summer, one way to reduce electrical consumption could be to dim or turn lights off on sunny days. Another peak electrical period is during normal working hours. Any load shedding that can be done during the week on a regular basis will conserve energy and natural resources. *Task tuning* is another method for conserving energy. This is accomplished by having lighting systems that individualize luminaires for each person in a space.

Generally, using controls to conserve energy will result in economic savings. The cost of controls must be considered when calculating the cost of a lighting system. Control costs include the unit itself, installation, electricity, and maintenance. Generally, these expenses can be offset by proper specification, installation, and use of controls. To conserve energy, and costs for existing lighting systems, there are retrofit kits for controls.

Often controls are specified for aesthetic purposes. General, task, accent, and decorative light sources should all have controls that will enhance the purpose of the light source. Controls can be adjusted to create the mood and atmosphere required by the environment. Controls can be used to create the perfect balance for accenting a piece of artwork, or they can establish the ideal levels between illumination zones in a space. Controls also enhance an interior by balancing natural and electrical light sources. For example, when illumination levels in an existing lighting plan are not balanced, controls can be added to lower or increase light levels for specific luminaires.

Controls provide the flexibility to accommodate a variety of activities in the same space. A lighting system with properly designed controls can transform a working conference room into an evening dining area. Controls also enable individuals to take notes while watching a presentation on a screen or monitor (Figure 10.3). The proper placement of controls can assist individuals with visual impairments or challenging visual tasks. Controls can improve people's ability to see and reduce eyestrain by providing gradual adjustments in light levels. In addition, programming lights to either fade or delay off can help to provide an element of safety to a space.

Planning for controls requires a thorough analysis of the current and future needs of the space, users, and activities performed in the room. Key to successful planning is providing a system that allows for flexibility and individual control. Unfortunately, sometimes an expensive, well-planned control system may be turned off, or individuals do not know how to use the system. To inform people of how to operate and maintain controls, written materials and educational sessions are very helpful.

FIGURE 10.3 Controls can accommodate lighting requirements for different activities in the same space.

Equipment

The basic equipment for lighting controls includes switches, dimmers, timers, occupancy sensors, photosensors, and central controls. In specifying equipment, the controls must be compatible with the entire lighting system, including the specific light source. Lighting controls operate manually, automatically, or a combination of the two. The needs of the environment and users of the space should determine the type of control specified. (Chapters 21 and 22 discuss the process of designing a quality lighting environment.) To provide the greatest flexibility for users, automatic controls should have a manual-off override. In selecting controls, a consideration should be how easily individuals with disabilities can use the equipment. Because of the ever-changing technological advancements, the industry related to lighting controls is expanding. To optimize a lighting plan, an interior designer must keep current in the field and be knowledgeable regarding the interface between controls and other elements of a lighting system.

A **switch** is the easiest and oldest means of controlling lights. The

Switch

A device that controls a luminaire by regulating the flow of electricity. A circuit is closed when a light is on and is open when the light is off.

function of an electrical switch is to stop the flow of electricity. A circuit is closed when a light is on and is open when the light is off. Relays, solenoids, or contactors are used for remote-control switching and for switching large lighting loads. The most common switch is a single pole that is operated manually. Switches are available in toggles, rockers, push buttons, rotary, or touch-plate mechanisms (Figure 10.4). Generally, switches are mounted on a wall 48 inches (122 cm) above the floor, next to the opening side of a door. Arrangements with more than one switch are mounted in a multigang configuration. Multilevel or bilevel switching provides the flexibility of having different levels of illumination from the same luminaires.

Switches can be localized or mounted in a central switching system. A double pole, with a single throw, operates two different electrical devices at the same time. A three-way switch operates a circuit from two different locations. A four-way switch will turn a light on or off from three different locations. When dimming a three-way switch, the dimming function will operate on only one of the switches. (For information regarding how to draw switching arrangements on electrical plans see Chapter 23.)

Dimmers are used to conserve energy and enhance the aesthetics of an environment. Generally, reducing the power in a lamp conserves

> **Dimmer**
> An electrical device designed to decrease light output by reducing power to a lamp.

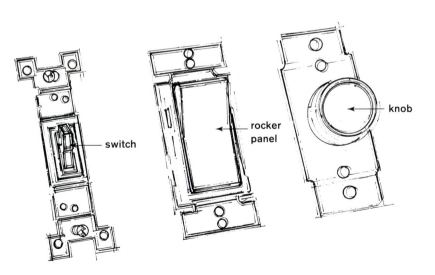

FIGURE 10.4 Different types of switches.

energy, affects color, and can extend the life of some lamps. Architectural dimming is the term that describes a system that can be reduced to a light output of 1 to 2 percent. Dimmers have maximum wattages that must be adhered to for proper performance and safe operation. Manufacturers of dimmers provide wattage maximums. Low-voltage lamps require a transformer that is designed for dimming. Generally, a rotary unit, toggle, linear slide, or touch plate operates dimmers. Plugs and adapters are available for dimming portable luminaires.

Dimming affects each light source in various ways. For incandescent and tungsten-halogen lamps, dimming results in energy savings, longer lamp life, and a warmer color. To accommodate the halogen regenerative cycle, manufacturers may suggest that periodically tungsten-halogen lamps operate at full power. Fluorescent and HID lamps are difficult to dim, and require special dimming ballasts, and there is a reduction in lamp life. At low light levels, some dimmers cause fluorescent lamps to flicker. There is a range in dimming equipment. HID lamps do not perform well with dimmers because of the required warm-up time and restrike characteristics. Moreover, the color changes resulting from dimming HID lamps are undesirable.

Multilevel ballasts for discharge lamps can be used to create a smooth transition between light levels. Sophisticated dimmers will adjust the speed of raising or lowering light levels to accommodate the adaptation function of eyes. For example, the eye takes longer to adjust from bright to dim than from dim to bright light levels. Thus, dimmers can be programmed to take a longer period of time to change the light level from bright to dark. This can be very useful in a conference room when lights need to be dimmed for viewing audiovisual presentations.

Timers control lighting systems by turning lights on and off at designated times. Timers can be very simple devices that a home owner manually sets and plugs into a wall socket, or they can be a component in very sophisticated computer programs. Some of the computer programs include astronomical data that automatically adjusts when lights turn on or off according to the amount of daylight at a particular time of the year for a specific geographical location. Timers are available with backup systems for power outages. Timers are useful for predictable schedules in areas of high use or for HID lamps that should

Timer
A device designed to control lighting systems by turning lights on and off at designated times.

not be switched frequently. Timers can also be used in spaces that are not used often, such as restrooms or storage facilities. Unless there is supplementary lighting, timers should not be used in areas where there is concern for safety or security.

Occupancy sensors are designed to turn lights on or off based upon whether there are people in a room. Research indicates energy savings from occupancy sensors (Jennings, Rubenstein, and DiBartolomeo, 2000; Maniccia, Von Neida, and Tweed, 2000). Generally, occupancy sensors are practical in spaces for people with unpredictable schedules or few people. They are also useful for security purposes. Sensors detect people in a space by discerning sounds, movements, or body heat. Ultrasonic sensors analyze changes in wave patterns to detect movements. Interiors with a high degree of air movement can interfere with the operation of ultrasonic sensors. Passive infrared (PIR) sensors are used to detect body heat. To function properly, PIR sensors require an unobstructed view of all areas of a room. Generally, ultrasonic sensors are more successful than PIR units. There are also dual-technology sensors that combine the technologies of ultrasonic and PIR. Occupancy sensors can be used with switches, dimmers, timers, photosensors, and central controls, which provides the maximum amount of flexibility in designing a system for a variety of spaces and users.

The success of occupancy sensors is dependent upon a thorough analysis of the interior and how people function in the space. Physical characteristics of the space and the users will determine the appropriate sensor and the mounting location. Generally, PIR sensors are effective in open spaces that are free of obstructions, rooms with ceilings higher than 14 feet (427 cm), and remote areas. Ultrasonic or dual-technology sensors should be used in rooms with ceilings lower than 14 feet (427 cm), partitions, and large furniture.

Occupancy sensors are available in a variety of mounting configurations. They can be mounted on the ceiling, on walls, or in the corners of a room. They are also available for wall switches; they can be plugged into electrical outlets; and there are portable units that can be located next to an individual. Each sensor technology has a designated angle of coverage and an effective range. Manufacturers' literature provides the performance characteristics. In determining the location of

Occupancy sensor
A device designed to turn lights on or off depending on whether people are present in a room.

the sensor, the most important consideration is to maintain an unobstructed view. The wrong type of sensor or an inappropriate location will cause a false on or off. For example, when a PIR sensor is unable to detect a person working behind a high partition, the lights will automatically turn off. When this continues to happen, users of the space become frustrated and eventually may deactivate the system. To help avoid false readings, installations should include commissioning adjustments. This involves testing and adjusting the occupancy sensor to accommodate any nuances present in an interior.

Photosensors are devices that detect the amount of illumination in a space and then send signals that control electrical light sources by switching lights on and off or by adjusting illumination levels to reach the optimum point. Photosensors are used often for daylight integration applications, and research indicates an energy savings (Jennings, Rubenstein, and DiBartolomeo, 2000; Pacific Gas & Electric Company, 1999; Rundquist, McDougall, and Benya, 1996). By using photosensors, electrical light sources can be adjusted to accommodate fluctuations in the quality and quantity of daylight in a space or on a task. Photosensors are available as separate units or may be integrated in a luminaire.

As with occupancy sensors, an important element of success with photosensors is a proper mounting location. Photosensors can be mounted on a ceiling close to a task, directly on the surface of a work area, or next to a window or skylight. Locating a photosensor close to exterior openings can be accomplished by an inside or outdoors mount. For the most accurate readings, a photosensor should not be mounted in direct view of electrical sources or sunlight. In addition, each photosensor should be connected to luminaires that have the same lighting requirements. For example, in a large classroom the general perimeter lighting has a lower illumination level than the task lighting located above desks. Therefore, an individual photosensor should be connected to the general and task luminaires.

A **central control system** uses a microprocessor to monitor, adjust, and regulate lighting in many areas or zones within a building. Some units are designed to integrate lighting with other electrical units, including mechanical, energy, and security systems. Electrical units can

Photosensor
Device that detects the amount of illumination in the space and then sends signals to control electrical light sources.

Central control system
An electronic device that uses a microprocessor to monitor, adjust, and regulate lighting in many areas or zones within a building.

include motorized window treatments, whirlpool jets, ceiling fans, kitchen appliances, sprinkler systems, garage door openers, security systems, skylights, sound systems, and audiovisual equipment. Mechanical systems can include heating, ventilation, air-conditioning, and plumbing. Central control systems can be connected to switches, dimmers, timers, occupancy sensors, and photosensors. For flexibility and safety purposes, central control systems should always have manual options for operating the luminaires.

Central control systems can be programmed for preset scenes. Each scene is designed for a specific space and its illumination requirements. Scenes can be programmed for security, entertainment, exterior lights, relaxation, or work. For example, by hitting the button labeled "work" in a conference room, the central control system will adjust the luminaires to the programmed illumination levels. Striking the "video" button will automatically adjust the luminaires for the task of viewing a video. Central control systems have become very sophisticated in residential buildings. For example, someone driving home from work can telephone the system and direct it to start the bath water at a specific fill level and temperature, warm the towel bars, heat the tile floor, close the blinds, play music, and dim the lights. Central controls are activated by keypads, touch screens, computers, telephones, and handheld infrared remotes. Keypad buttons and faceplates are available in a variety of finishes and can be custom engraved for labeling purposes (Figure 10.5). Control units are available in humid and waterproof versions to accommodate mild moisture and water damage, respectively.

Computer network control systems for lighting will continue to improve in the future. For digital lighting control the focus is digital addressable lighting interface (DALI). DALI is a means of communicating through low-voltage wires. The communication ability allows DALI to distribute information to the lighting system, and the luminaires can report back to DALI. DALI controls individual luminaires, groups of fixtures, occupancy sensors, dimming, photosensors, timers, scenes, transition fades, and other networked systems. Luminaires communicate with DALI when a lamp is close to burning out, has low lumen output, or has ballast irregularities.

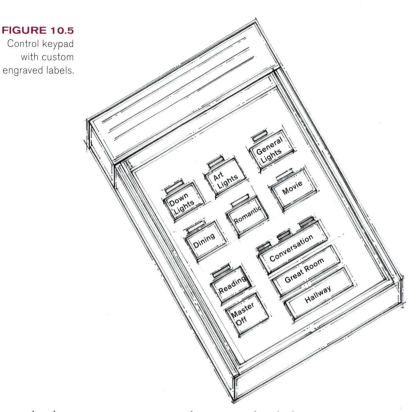

FIGURE 10.5
Control keypad with custom engraved labels.

Controls play a very important role in a quality lighting environment by fine-tuning the system. Effective use of lighting controls can conserve energy and natural resources, provide users with the flexibility to regulate luminaires, vary illumination with the same fixtures, and create an atmosphere that fulfills the purpose of the space. Controls can also help to support safety and security systems. The progressive nature of the technology associated with controls requires that interior designers stay abreast of the field.

SUMMARY

- Magnetic and electronic transformers convert voltages in a system. For lighting purposes, a transformer is either integral to the design of the luminaire or is a separate unit that is concealed under a ceiling or behind a wall.
- Magnetic and electronic ballasts are control devices used with electric discharge lamps; they start lamps and control the electrical current during operation.

- Generally, electronic transformers and ballasts are preferable to magnetic units because they are more energy-efficient, quieter, and weigh less.
- The ballast power factor (BPF), ballast factor (BF), and ballast efficacy factor (BEF) are formulas developed to evaluate different lamp/ballast systems.
- Lighting controls operate either manually or automatically, and include switches, dimmers, timers, occupancy sensors, photosensors, and central controls.
- Controls can be used to conserve energy by turning lights off when they are not needed, integrating daylight, monitoring lamp maintenance, and load shedding.
- Generally, using controls to conserve energy will result in economic savings. The cost of controls includes the unit itself, installation, electricity, and maintenance.
- Controls can be adjusted to create the mood and atmosphere required by the environment.
- The function of an electrical switch is to stop the flow of electricity. A circuit is closed when a light is on and is open when the light is off.
- Dimmers can conserve energy and enhance the aesthetics of an environment. Generally, reducing the power to a lamp conserves energy, affects color, and can extend the life of some lamps.
- Timers control lighting systems by turning lights on and off at designated times.
- Occupancy sensors are designed to turn lights on or off based upon whether there are people in a room.
- Photosensors are devices that detect the amount of illumination in the space and then send signals to control electrical light sources. Photosensors are often used for daylight integration applications.
- Research indicates energy savings from using occupancy sensors and photosensors.
- Proper mounting location is key to the success of occupancy sensors and photosensors.
- A central control system uses a microprocessor to monitor, adjust, and regulate lighting in many areas or zones within a building.

Some units are designed to integrate lighting with other electrical units, including mechanical, energy, and security systems.

Key Terms

central control system	polychlorinated biphenyls (PCBs)
dimmer	switch
occupancy sensor	timer
photosensor	transformer

Exercises

1. Review the literature for the past two years to identify the newest developments in transformers and ballasts. In a written report summarize the results and identify how to apply the findings to lighting systems.
2. Develop a plan for a client to conserve energy by using lighting controls. The plan should address scheduling patterns, daylight integration, maintenance, load shedding, and economics. In a written report outline the energy savings plan and include a prioritized time line.
3. Identify effective methods for applying controls to general, task, accent, and decorative lighting. Provide the suggestions in a written report that could include illustrations and drawings.
4. Review current literature regarding lighting controls. For each major type of lighting control, including switches, dimmers, timers, occupancy sensors, and photosensors, provide recommendations for effective interior applications. Write a report that includes your research and effective applications.
5. Identify three commercial and two residential spaces that will use central controls. For each space, develop preset scenes that integrate lighting with other systems. In a written report describe the preset scenes and indicate how the programming will enhance the quality of the lighting environment.

REFERENCES

American Society of Heating, Refrigeration and Air-Conditioning Engineers (1999). Energy efficient design of new buildings except new low-rise residential buildings. *ASHRAE/IES90.1-1999*. Atlanta, GA: ASHRAE.

Ander, G. (1997). *Daylighting Performance & Design*. New York: John Wiley & Sons.

British Standards Institution (1992). *Code of Practice for Daylighting. British Standard BS 8206*, Part 2.

Benya, J., Heschong, L., McGowan, T., Miller, N., and Rubinstein, F. (2001). *Advanced Lighting Guidelines*. White Salmon, WA: New Buildings Institute.

Bernstien, A., and Conway, K. (2000, March). The public benefits of California's investments in energy efficiency. Prepared for the California Energy Commission by the RAND Corporation. MR-1212.0-CEC.

Bierman, A., and Conway, K. (2000). Characterizing daylight photosensor systems performance to help overcome market barriers. *Journal of the Illuminating Engineering Society, 29(1)*, 101–115.

Boyce, P.N., Elkund, N., and Simpson, S. (2000). Individual lighting control: Task performance, mood and illuminance. *Journal of the Illuminating Engineering Society, 29(1)*, 131–142.

Carriere, L., and Rea, M. (1988). Economics of switching fluorescent lamps. *IEEE Transactions on Industry Applications, 24 (3)*, 370–379.

Clark, F. (1963). Accurate maintenance factors. *Illuminating Engineering, 58(3)*, 124–131.

Coaton, J.R., and Marsden, A.M. (1997). *Lamps and Lighting* (4th ed.). London: Arnold.

Elenbass, W. (1971). *Fluorescent Lamps, Philips Technical Library* (2nd ed.). London: Macmillan.

Energy Information Administration (EIA) (1996). *Annual Energy Outlook, with Projections to 2015*. Washington, DC: U.S. Department of Energy.

Energy Information Administration (EIA) (1995). *Annual Energy Review for 1995*. Washington, DC: U.S. Department of Energy.

Gordan, G., and Nuckolls, J.L. (1995). *Interior Lighting for Designers*. New York: John Wiley & Sons.

Heschong Mahone Group (HMG) (August 1999). *Skylighting and Retail Sales, and Daylighting in Schools*. For Pacific Gas & Electric. http://www.pge.com.pec/daylight.

Heschong Mahone Group (HMG). (1997, May). *The Lighting Efficiency Technology Report, Vol. I: California Lighting Baseline*. For the California Energy Commission.

Illuminating Engineering Society, Committee on Light Control and Equipment Design (1970). IES guide to design of light control. Part IV: Practical concepts of equipment design. *Illuminating Engineering, 65(8)*, 479–494.

Illuminating Engineering Society of North America (IESNA) (2000). *IESNA Lighting Handbook* (9th ed.). New York: Illuminating Engineering Society of North America.

Interlaboratory Working Group (1997, September). *Scenarios of U.S. Carbon Reductions— Potential Impacts of Energy Technologies by 2010 and Beyond*. Office of Energy Efficiency and Renewable Energy. U.S. Department of Energy.

Jennings, J.F., Rubinstein, R., and DiBartolomeo, D.R. (2000). Comparisons of control options in private offices in an advanced lighting controls test bed. *Journal of the Illuminating Engineering Society, 29(29)*, 39–60.

Ji, Y., Davis, R., and Chen, W. (1999). An investigation of the effect of operating cycles on the life of compact fluorescent lamps. *Journal of the Illuminating Engineering Society, 28(2)*, 57–62.

Lawrence Berkeley National Laboratory (1992). *Analysis of Federal Policy Options for Improving U.S. Lighting Energy Efficiency.* Berkeley, CA: Lawrence Berkeley National Laboratory.

Littlefair, P.J. (1991). Site layout planning for daylight and sunlight: A guide to good practice. *BRE Report BR 209.*

Maniccia, D., Rutledge, D., Rea, M., and Morrow, W. (1999). Occupant use of manual lighting control in private offices. *Journal of the Illuminating Engineering Society, 28(2),* 42–56.

Maniccia, D., Von Neida, B., and Tweed, A. (2000). Analysis of the energy and cost savings potential of occupancy sensors for commercial lighting systems. *Proceedings of the 2000 Annual Conference of the Illuminating Engineering Society of North America.*

Mistrick, R., Chen, C., Bierman, B., and Felts, D. (2000). A comparison of photosensor-controlled electronic dimming systems. *Proceedings of the 2000 Annual Conference of the Illuminating Engineering Society, 29(1),* 66–80.

Narendrean, N., Yin, T., et al. (2000). A lamp life predictor for the frequently switched instant-start fluorescent systems. *Proceedings of the 2000 Annual Conference of the Illuminating Engineering Society of North America.*

National Lighting Product Information Program (NLPIP) (1998, March). *Specifier Reports: Photosensors.*

Pacific Gas & Electric Company (1999). *Daylighting Initiative Case Study.* http://www.pge.com/pec/daylight.

Phillips, D. (2000). *Lighting Modern Buildings.* Oxford: Architectural Press.

Portland Energy Conservation, I (1992). *Building Commissioning Guidelines* (2nd ed.). Portland, OR: Bonneville Power Administration.

Rundquist, R.A., McDougall, T.G., and Benya, J. (1996). *Lighting Controls: Patterns for Design.* Prepared by R A. Rundquist Associates for the Electric Power Research Institute and the Empire State Electrical Energy Research Corporation.

Rundquist, R.A., Johnson, K., and Aumann, D. (1993). Calculating lighting and HVAC interactions. *ASHRAE Journal, 35(11),* 28.

Southern California Edison (1999). *Energy Design Resources Case Studies: REMO and Timberland.* Available from: http://www.energydesignresources.com

U.K. Department of the Environment (1998, March). Desktop guide to daylighting for architects. *Good Practice Guide 245.* Oxfordshire, United Kingdom: ETSU.

Van Bogaert, G. (1996). Local control system for ergonomic energy-saving lighting. *Special IAEEEL Edition.*

Veitch, J., and Newsham, G. (2000). Exercised control, lighting choices, and energy use: An office simulation experiment. *Journal of Environmental Psychology, 20(3),* 219–237.

Portable Luminaires and Styles of Fixtures

OBJECTIVES

■ Identify characteristics and components of portable luminaires, including techniques for distributing light.

■ Compare and contrast the characteristics and components of portable luminaires.

■ Describe and evaluate the relationship between portable luminaires and elements of an interior.

■ Identify the proper task locations for portable luminaires.

■ Describe fixtures for stationary and portable candles, oil, gas, and early electricity, including chandeliers, lanterns, and wall lights.

■ Identify classical luminaires and the names of the pieces and the designers.

■ Describe the reasons for custom luminaires and provide a brief overview of the process.

INTERIOR designers must have an understanding of the characteristics of portable luminaires and a history of the evolution of fixtures. Portable fixtures are the most common luminaire purchased throughout the world, and they are the oldest means of providing illumination in an interior. Nonelectrical fixtures have been evolving for centuries; however, designs for electrical sources started only about

100 years ago. As a new technology, there is a great deal still to be learned about materials and process technology and how these affect a quality lighting environment.

To select a portable luminaire that meets the intended purpose, an interior designer must understand the characteristics of fixtures, how they affect the design of an interior, and how to place them properly. In addition, the design of a portable luminaire should be in unity with the overall theme and style of an interior. A historical review of light fixtures, including contemporary designs, provides a basis for specifying a luminaire that meets the needs of the overall design concept. This is an ideal time to begin a historical perspective of luminaires; there are many classics that must be recognized.

Portable Luminaires

Portable luminaires are important in layering light and they can provide what is needed for general, task, accent, and decorative techniques.

> *Portable luminaire*
> *Table and floor fixtures,*
> *generally plugged into*
> *a wall socket.*

Characteristics and Components

Portable luminaires include table and floor fixtures and are used primarily in residential interiors, hotels, restaurants, and private offices. Often portable luminaires are the only light source in a space. In contrast to the hard wiring required for the fixtures discussed in Chapter 9, portable luminaires generally are plugged into a wall socket. Some fixtures are battery-operated or they use a flame for illumination. Portable luminaires are available in a variety of styles, sizes, and price ranges. These fixtures are extremely popular because they are easy to install, provide instant illumination, have a wide range of lighting effects, and can have a relatively inexpensive initial cost. However, operating expenses can be high because of the frequent use of incandescent lamps in these fixtures.

Portable luminaires are an innovation that uniquely blends technology and art. As with the luminaires discussed in Chapter 9, portable fixtures are made by hand or mass-produced in factories. There are a variety of professions involved in designing fixtures, including industrial designers, lighting designers, architects, and interior designers. Many designers work independently, while others are associated with a furniture manufacturer. Professionals, such as Frank Lloyd Wright and Charles Rennie Mackintosh, design a luminaire for a specific site. Most designers create luminaires that can be used in any location. In designing a luminaire, considerations include the purpose of the fixture, light distribution, source of illumination, materials, construction methods, controls, and price range.

Portable luminaires are used often for general lighting because the fixtures can be placed in background locations, and the wide range of fixtures available allows for a variety of atmospheres in a space. Portable luminaires are excellent for task lighting because users can easily position and adjust the fixture to meet their needs. As an accent lighting technique, portable luminaires are ideal because small fixtures can easily be mounted in positions to highlight objects while they remain hidden from view. A significant role for portable luminaires is decorative lighting. The next two sections in this chapter cover some of the most important decorative designs used in period, traditional, and contemporary interiors.

Portable luminaires distribute light in the following ways: (a) direct, (b) indirect, (c) semi-direct, (d) semi-indirect, and (e) diffused. The purpose of the fixture determines the appropriate distribution pattern. Generally, luminaire manufacturers do not provide candlepower distribution curves for portable fixtures, so an interior designer must visualize the illumination pattern. Through practice, this becomes fairly easy to do, unless a space has unusual features or extreme proportions. For example, it might be unsatisfactory to illuminate a 20-foot (609 cm) ceiling with an indirect floor luminaire. To determine the best luminaire for unusual spaces, an interior designer can experiment with several fixtures.

An important consideration in analyzing distribution patterns is glare. Discomfort or disability glare can occur when an exposed lamp is in a direct line of view or when a shade is too translucent. To determine problems associated with glare, the location of the fixture must be analyzed in relation to the users. An interior designer must analyze all the positions of users in a space in order to eliminate glare. For example, the location of a table luminaire might be perfect for people seated next to the fixture. However, people standing in the room might experience glare because they are able to see the top of the lamp. In contrast, an individual sitting next to a table fixture that is on a high table might experience glare, but people standing in the space may not be affected by the brightness. An indirect floor fixture placed at the bottom of a stairway might cause severe glare for people walking down the steps.

The type of shielding device used affects glare and distribution patterns. An opaque shade distributes light in a directional manner that is determined by the location of the opening. For example, a metal shade with an opening at the bottom provides direct illumination. An opaque shade with an opening at the top and bottom produces either semi-direct or semi-indirect light. In addition, a high-wattage lamp used with an opaque shade can be problematic because of the extreme contrasts between the emitted light and the dark shade. A translucent shade provides a diffused form of illumination, and a bright lamp shining through thin material can cause glare. The location of the lamp in the fixture also affects distribution patterns. For example, a lamp in a high position primarily distributes indirect light; a lamp in a low location produces more direct light.

Portable luminaires are designed to accommodate electrical and nonelectrical light sources. The most common lamps used for portable electrical fixtures are incandescent, tungsten-halogen, and compact fluorescents in arbitrary, tubular, or circular shapes. For low-voltage luminaires, an integral transformer accommodates the adjustments in current. To conserve energy and natural resources, lamp and luminaire manufacturers have been developing fixtures that are more efficient light sources than the traditional incandescent lamp. For example, some portable luminaires are produced for metal halide lamps. (Chapter 12 provides recommendations for energy conservation.) Nonelectrical sources include flames from candles, oil, or gas.

Generally, the type of light source affects the design of the luminaire. For example, a luminaire for a candle-shaped incandescent lamp is dramatically different from a metal halide lamp. The major parts of a portable luminaire include the base, wiring, lamp socket, and perhaps a shielding device. As illustrated in Figure 11.1, some luminaires have finials, harps, and harp extenders for larger lamps, such as CFLs. Most portable luminaires have basic on/off switches for controls. Luminaires that are designed for three-way switching should have a three-way incandescent lamp to save energy and provide flexibility for the user. However, a three-way lamp should not be used in a luminaire that does not have a three-way switch because fixtures that operate the lamp at only the highest wattage waste energy. Some portable luminaires have dimmers, timers, photosensors, or occupancy sensors. These are either built into the luminaire or are a separate device. Because of technological differences, CFL lamps should not be used in a fixture that is designed to dim incandescent sources.

In selecting a luminaire, the interaction between the light source and any material the light will strike is very important. The type of material affects the quality of the light and the atmosphere in the space. For centuries people have explored various materials that will enhance light. Initially, materials were selected to maximize the quantity of light emitted from a flame, and then, for decorative purposes, materials

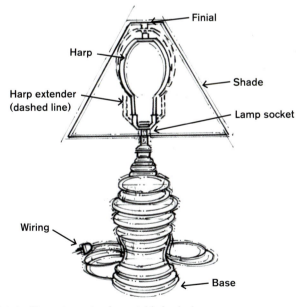

FIGURE 11.1 The major parts of a portable luminaire.

such as crystal and glass were added to fixtures. Portable luminaires are manufactured in the materials identified in Chapter 9, as well as many others, in order to accommodate the decorative purpose of the fixtures. The type of material used often reflects the time period that the original luminaire was made. For example, silver luminaires were made for the wealthy during the seventeenth and eighteenth centuries. Tin fixtures were typical during American colonial times. Examples of the various materials are illustrated in the next two sections of this chapter. The base of portable luminaires is made of metals, porcelain, enamel, crystal, wood, pottery, marble, or glass. Metals include brass, silver, gilded bronze, tin, bronze, copper, iron, pewter, and wrought iron.

A variety of materials are used to shade and distribute the light source. Traditional materials include fabric, paper, glass, and metal. Silk is an excellent fabric for a soft and diffused lighting effect. Light filtered through paper can reveal interesting textures and emit a warm tone. For example, interesting effects are derived from parchment paper and papers that are treated with boiled linseed oil. A variety of colors, textures, finishes, and patterns are used for glass shades. Louis Comfort Tiffany designed some of the most beautiful luminaires ever created by using glass. Some of the most significant examples of glass used in luminaires includes cut glass, cameo, favrile, and transparent ruby. Hollophane pressed glass uniquely refracts light to reduce glare. Metals for shades can be solid, pierced, or mesh. The most common metals used for mesh are fine stainless steel, bronze, and brass. Shades are available to completely surround the fixture; half-shades are available for wall luminaires. The interior of a shade should be white when the purpose of the luminaire is to illuminate a task. In addition to the materials discussed in this text, to create unique effects, an interior designer may explore a variety of elements that could be used to shield, filter, and diffuse light.

Design Considerations

In specifying portable luminaires, interior designers must consider the design of the fixture, the relationship of the fixture to other elements in the space, and the appropriate location for the intended purpose. In addition to satisfying the purpose of the lighting, the design of the fixture should be analyzed according to the elements and principles of design. For example, the base should be in proper proportion to the shade. The shade should be the proper size and shape for the overall fixture. The texture, lines, and color of the luminaire should be appropriate for the style. The design of quality luminaires supports the function of illumination. In contrast, many portable luminaires have a design that is not related to lighting. For example, there are many portable luminaires that have an animal as the base (Figure 11.2). This type of design can fail to support the purpose of lighting, and there is no sense to having a shade on top of an animal's head. For safety reasons the fixture should be physically balanced, and the cord should be away from walkways. To help conceal cords, whenever possible floor outlets should be specified.

The fixture should be the appropriate style, size, shape, and color for the interior and to create the desired atmosphere. Generally, a portable luminaire becomes one of the focal points in a space. Hence, as an important element of the space, the location of the fixture must be appropriate to the interior's furnishings, fabrics, wallcoverings, and

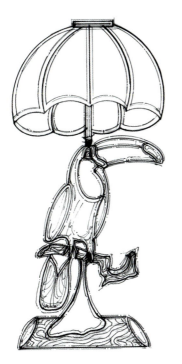

FIGURE 11.2 The design of the luminaire should support the function of illumination. An animal wearing a shade can fail to support the purpose of lighting.

accessories. This is especially important for the area immediately surrounding the fixture. For example, a luminaire placed on a table next to a sofa must be the appropriate size, shape, and color for the table, the sofa, accessories on the table, and any artwork on the wall. As illustrated in Figure 11.3, the luminaire is too large for the table and is placed too high in relationship to the chair. Furthermore, someone seated on the chair would experience glare when looking at the luminaire. In contrast, Figure 11.4 shows a luminaire that is a part of the total composition of its adjacent elements. The placement of fixtures can be used to define small areas in a room and balance lighting during day and evening hours.

In addition to specifying a location that addresses the elements and principles of design, there are specific requirements to support tasks. Effective task lighting has been a problem for centuries. The ideal location provides direct light on the task, with no shadows or glare. To accommodate an individual seated in a chair or on a sofa, the

FIGURE 11.3 The luminaire is too large for the table and is placed too high in relationship to the chair. The user would most likely experience glare.

FIGURE 11.4 The luminaire is part of the total composition of its adjacent elements.

luminaire should be placed to the side and slightly behind the person. To avoid shadows on a task, the luminaire should be placed on the left side for right-handed individuals and on the opposite side for left-handed people. The bottom of the shade should be at about eye level, which generally translates to 38 to 42 inches (97–107 cm) from the floor (Figure 11.5). This height emits light directly on the task, and the individual does not experience glare from the lamp. The location of a fixture for an individual working at a desk should be approximately 15 inches (38 cm) from the individual and 12 inches (30 cm) from the front edge of the desk. The bottom of the shade should be about 15 inches (38 cm) above the desk. The location of the luminaire might have to be adjusted to avoid reflections on a computer monitor.

Historical Luminaires

As discussed in Chapter 1, fire is the most primitive source of light, and designing fixtures that controlled fire provided the origin of interior lighting. In addition to fulfilling the need to see during times of

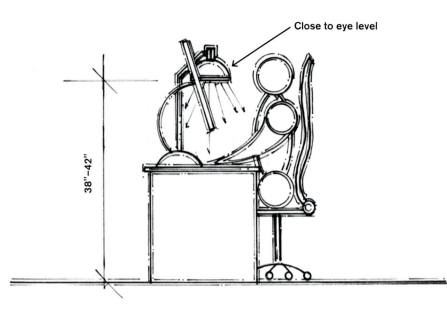

FIGURE 11.5 An effective location for a portable task luminaire.

Close to eye level

38"–42"

darkness, luminaires have become a decorative element in an interior. Knowledge of the history and development of fixtures is essential when designing period interiors. To specify a luminaire that is the proper style for an interior requires research and an awareness of fixtures that were developed throughout history. The following sections provide a brief historical overview of fixtures. It can provide guidance in selecting styles and advance an understanding of the use of lighting in interiors.

Oil and Candles

To establish a history of styles, researchers have studied paintings, personal diaries, estate inventories, letters, drawings in books, postcards, and eventually photographs. Paintings in particular provide considerable details for documenting interior materials, furniture, accessories, space arrangements, and lighting, as well as information on how people functioned in a space. Analyzing a complete interior helps to understand the relationship between the elements in a space within the context of social, economic, and cultural factors. A specific analysis of historical interior lighting provides an understanding of lighting techniques that have been used for centuries and how to apply the techniques to current environments. Historic settings also demonstrate the importance of daylight in interiors and provide inspiration for successful applications. For example, to accommodate task lighting, furniture was placed close to walls with large windows (Figure 11.6). In France, the stained glass in Chartres Cathedral is an excellent example of how daylight was used to help people learn about the Bible, while creating extraordinary decorative lighting; this is accomplished by illustrating the stories of the Bible in the stained glass windows.

Flame as a light source led to portable fixtures, chandeliers, lanterns, and wall lights. The earliest version of a floor fixture was a candlestick resting on top of a stand or torchère. The location of fixtures was dependent upon the task, surrounding elements, and architectural features. Generally, portable fixtures, such as candleholders, were placed on a table or desk next to the task. Many paintings illustrate how people used flames from oil and candles for task lighting. Frequently, lighting was balanced by having the fixtures placed throughout the room and located to accommodate the tasks, such as

FIGURE 11.6 *Le Déjeuner* (*The Luncheon*), c. 1739, by François Boucher, shows how daylight was a major element of illumination prior to electrical light sources. Desks and tables were often placed close to walls with large windows. The candles on the wall are also a light source.

sewing or reading. To illuminate as much of the room as possible, chandeliers were located in the center of a room. Wealthy people, churches, and public buildings used chandeliers in large rooms with tall ceilings. The low ceilings in rooms of the common people could not accommodate a chandelier.

To prevent flames from going out, lanterns were used in areas that were exposed to winds, such as entries and hallways. Frequently wall lights were located next to windows, mirrors, and doorways. Placement of lights next to windows substituted for daylight during the evening hours. Placing wall lights close to reflective surfaces, such as mirrors, increased the level of illumination (Figure 11.6). For safety purposes, wall lights were placed on the wall above the heads of people standing in the space and were located close to doors in order to illuminate the space when people entered the room.

The earliest lighting fixtures are Greek and Roman oil lamps. In addition to the basic fixtures identified in Chapter 1, some antique oil lamps had unusual shapes and configurations (Figure 11.7). Oil lamps were designed to rest on tables or pedestals or to hang from the ceiling. The bronze oil lamp in the *Portrait of Madame Récamier* painting by Jacques-Louis David in 1800 illustrates the continued use of oil as a fuel for lighting, (Figure 11.8).

FIGURE 11.7 Many different designs were created for oil lamps.

FIGURE 11.8 The *Portrait of Madame Récamier* by Jacques-Louis David shows the use of the bronze oil lamp in 1800.

The late eighteenth and early nineteenth centuries introduced hanging bowl lamps and a table lamp design that deviated from the traditional spout lamp. Ami Argand developed a major improvement in oil lighting in the late eighteenth century. The Argand lamp had significant levels of illumination because concentric tubes allowed a great deal of air to travel through the wick (Figure 11.9). The glass chimney added to the lamp also improved the level of illumination. Unfortunately, the high placement of the container for oil produced a shadow on work surfaces. Eventually, the invention of the mechanism for adjusting the wick allowed the oil container to be placed in any position on a fixture. As a significant source for quality task lighting, the overall shape of the Argand lamp has influenced the design of many fixtures used for reading.

Pendant oil lights and large table fixtures became popular during the early nineteenth century. Some pendant lights had holders for candles and oil. Many of the table lights had engraved glass shades. To eliminate the shadow created by the Argand lamp, the sinumbra lamp was designed with a ring to hold the oil and the shade (Figure 11.10).

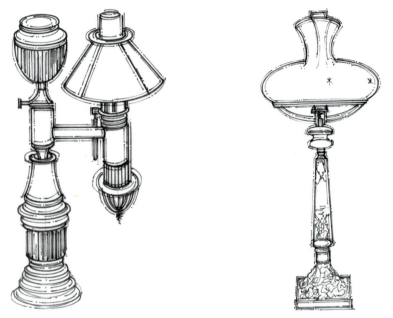

FIGURE 11.9 An Argand lamp.

FIGURE 11.10 A sinumbra lamp.

The translation for *sinumbra* is "without shadow." The invention of paraffin oil in the mid-nineteenth century led to the development of various table and pendant oil lights.

In addition to oil, candles were an extremely important source of lighting for interiors. During the sixteenth century candles became an important lighting source for residences. The most popular method for manufacturing candles was dipping. By the seventeenth century molds were used to make candles. By the eighteenth century candles became a clean and bright light source. In the nineteenth century, the discovery of paraffin wax created a quality of light that was similar to beeswax. Today, quality candles are made from 100 percent stearin, or 75 percent stearin and 25 percent beeswax. Candles are used in candlesticks, candelabrum, candelabra, chandeliers, lanterns, wall-lights, and furniture (Figure 11.11 a–d). **Candlesticks** are units that hold a single candle and are the most common design for candles. A **candelabrum** is a unit that has more than one holder for candles, and **candelabra** is the plural. **Chandeliers** are suspended from the ceiling and have multiple holders for candles. The translation for the French term

Candlestick
A unit that holds a single candle and are the most commonly designed holder for candles.

Candelabrum
A unit that has more than one holder for candles.

Candelabra
A term for a pair of candelabrum.

Chandelier
Unit that is suspended from the ceiling and has multiple holders for candles.

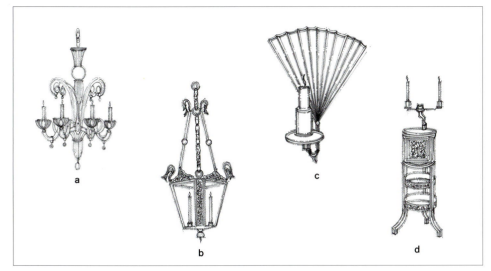

FIGURE 11.11   Candles used in a (a) chandelier, (b) lantern, (c) wall light, and (d) furniture.

chandelier is "tallow candle". A **lantern** can be either a suspended or a portable fixture. **Wall-lights** are mounted on a wall and have one or multiple holders for candles. To provide task lighting, some furniture was designed to include holders for candles. One of the most significant pieces of furniture designed for candles is the writing desk created by Jean-François Oeben in 1760 and finished by Jean-Henri Riesener in 1769 for Louis XV of France (Figure 11.12). To provide

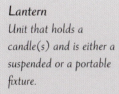

Lantern
Unit that holds a candle(s) and is either a suspended or a portable fixture.

Wall-light
Unit that is mounted on a wall, with one or multiple holders for candles.

FIGURE 11.12 Louis XV's writing desk was designed with multiple candle holders.

additional task lighting, candles have been integrated in such items as serving pieces, mirrors, and clocks (Figure 11.13). To accommodate candle maintenance, snuffers were designed in a variety of styles, including some with the same motifs as the candlesticks.

Figure 11.14 illustrates representative examples of candlesticks from the sixteenth century to the early twentieth century. The illustrations are intended to provide a general overview of the evolution of styles. A list of books that provide detailed descriptions of historical styles is found in the reference section of this chapter. Early candlesticks were made from bronze, brass, copper, iron, and tin, and they

FIGURE 11.13   Candles integrated in a serving piece.

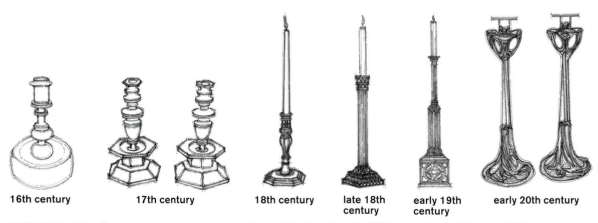

| 16th century | 17th century | 18th century | late 18th century | early 19th century | early 20th century |

FIGURE 11.14   Representative examples of portable candleholders from the 16th century through the early 20th century.

often had drip pans to collect wax residue. The seventeenth century introduced candlesticks made of silver, pewter, and glass. The eighteenth century added gilded bronze, gold, and porcelain to the materials used for candlesticks. Decorative shades were added to candlesticks and candelabra to prevent melting of the wax makeup on the faces of women (Figure 11.15).

Craft and designs constantly improved through the centuries. As with furniture, craftspeople designed candlesticks that were unique to their country. The designs of sixteenth-century candlesticks were simple, and they were fairly small in size. The overall shape was round with a series of rings that surrounded the base. The mid-seventeenth century introduced candlesticks with a column that was supported on a square base. Many of the candlesticks had detailed engraving. Candlesticks designed in the latter part of the seventeenth and early eighteenth centuries became simple in design and returned to some of the same shapes used during the sixteenth century. The mid-eighteenth century had candlestick designs in the rococo style, with an asymmetrical balance. This time period also focused on human figures supporting the candleholder and intricate porcelain designs. Candlestick

FIGURE 11.15 Decorative shade on a candelabrum.

designs in the late eighteenth century returned to antiquity, including classical Greek and Roman designs. Egyptian and gothic influences were reflected in candlestick designs of the nineteenth century, and wood torchères became popular. Candelabra and candleholders that were integrated with centerpieces became popular during the late eighteenth and early nineteenth centuries. By the end of the nineteenth century, fundamentally new designs for candlesticks were not prevalent because of improvements in oil and gas and because of the beginning of electrical sources.

The development of chandeliers started in the sixteenth century; however, significant pieces were not developed until the eighteenth century. These designs were made from silver, gilded wood, brass, gilded bronze, glass, cut glass, and rock crystal. Designs for lanterns also became important in the eighteenth century. Chandeliers in the late eighteenth and early nineteenth centuries were predominantly made of cut glass and gilded bronze.

Frequent use of wall-lights started in the seventeenth century, and they were generally made of brass and silver. Some of the designs had elaborate carving, and the substantial backplate beautifully reflected candlelight. Designs in the early eighteenth century eliminated the large backplate and created a more linear form that included a curved extension for the candleholder. Wall-lights in the eighteenth century typically were made from gilded bronze and were designed to accommodate multiple candles. Designs in the mid-eighteenth century were organic in outline, and during the late eighteenth century the shape changed to a straight-linear form. In the early nineteenth century, wall-lights became very popular in the United States and often were made from tin. Generally, the designs had a large backplate for the reflection of light.

Gas and Early Electricity

The Industrial Revolution in the nineteenth century introduced gas lighting. However, it was available only to buildings that were in the service area, and installation was expensive. Gas lighting required gas mains under the streets and piping in walls and ceilings. Pipes distributed gas to the burner in the fixture, and a gas cock regulated the flame. The type of burner determined the quality of light. For example, a bats-wing gas burner distributes flame in the shape of a bat's wing. The required connection to pipes significantly affected furniture and wall arrangements in rooms. Thus gas is the first lighting source that fundamentally restricted the location of light in a space.

The most common fixtures were chandeliers, later called **gaseliers**, and wall brackets (Figure 11.16 a and b). Gaseliers had several arms that distributed the gas to the burner, and they often had etched glass shades. In the late nineteenth century the arms were often embellished with art nouveau castings. Fixtures were generally made of brass, and common designs were classical and colonial revival. The progressive improvements in gas lighting resulted in its being widely used. People had a fondness for a light source that could be turned on or off with a switch and that provided a high level of illumination. The primary problem, as with all flame sources, was maintenance. On a regular basis, wicks had to be maintained, shades cleaned, soot removed from surfaces, and fuel replenished. At the end of the nineteenth and early twentieth centuries, fixtures for kerosene lighting were used to supplement gas fixtures to provide good illumination for

Gaselier
A suspended unit that has several arms to distribute gas to a burner; often has etched glass shades.

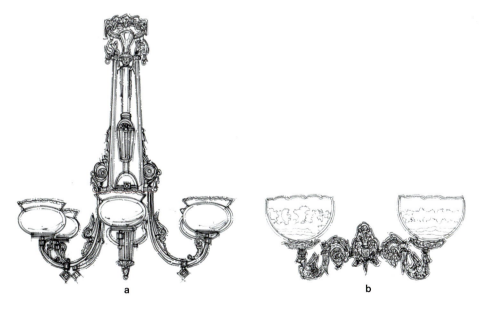

FIGURE 11.16 A (a) Gaselier and (b) gas wall bracket.

people who did not have access to gas main lines. Portable kerosene fixtures were the most popular, but pendant and wall styles were available (Figure 11.17). Kerosene fixtures are identifiable by their large glass shade, sizable fuel reservoir, and wide opening with a screw cap for filling the fixture.

The invention of the incandescent carbon-filament lamp in the late nineteenth century introduced electrical light. For the first time in lighting history, the incandescent lamp provided a clean and consistent light source that could be focused in a variety of directions. Flexibility in direction was a significant improvement in lighting. Generally, previous sources could provide light that was directed only toward the ceiling. The incandescent lamp allowed light to be aimed in any direction, including downward toward a task.

During the early development years, the incandescent lamp had problems associated with reliability and duration. Initial lamps lasted only about 40 hours and produced sporadic levels of illumination. In addition, advertisements reveal that people also worried about the safety and strength of the lamp. As a result, many fixtures were designed to accommodate gas and electricity until about 1910 (Figure 11.18 a and b). These **gaselier-electrolier** and gas-electric wall lights

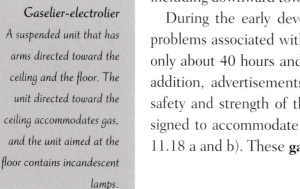

Gaselier-electrolier

A suspended unit that has arms directed toward the ceiling and the floor. The unit directed toward the ceiling accommodates gas, and the unit aimed at the floor contains incandescent lamps.

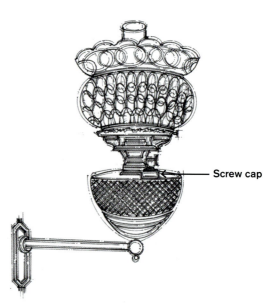

Screw cap

FIGURE 11.17 A kerosene fixture.

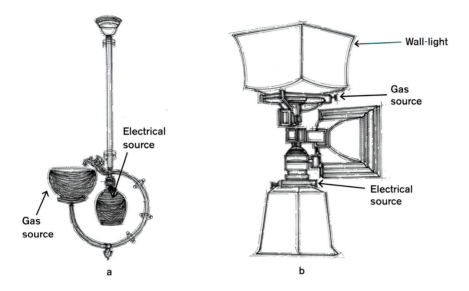

FIGURE 11.18 A (a) gaselier-electrolier and (b) gas-electric wall-light.

are unique because they had arms directed toward both the ceiling and the floor. The indirect light aimed at the ceiling accommodated gas, and the direct light was provided by incandescent lamps. A combination of gas and electricity helped people make the transition to a new way of lighting.

Early electric fixtures resembled many of the designs for gas lighting, and they generally used the same materials. Fixture types included electroliers and wall lights, and could be mounted on the ceiling or be portable. These fixtures used the carbon-filament bulb, which required clear glass for optimum illumination. A variety of factors converged at the same time that resulted in new designs for light fixtures. The flexibility and cleanliness of the incandescent lamp eventually allowed designers of the decorative arts to create fixtures in a variety of shapes, sizes, and materials. The lack of fear of open flames enabled designers to experiment with new materials. In addition, designers revolted against historical styles. This style revolution brought about naturalistic forms and floral motifs and led to the development of an important period in lighting design, the art nouveau style.

Art glass represents the most significant characteristic of light fixtures in the art nouveau style. Emile Gallé, Jean Daum, and Tiffany were three of the most talented glass craftsmen. For the first time in lighting history, the high level of illumination produced by the incandescent lamp allowed craftsmen to create glass in sophisticated patterns and in dark colors. Fixtures were made primarily in pendant and portable styles. The base and structural elements were made generally of bronze. In the early twentieth century Gallé founded the school of Nancy for the purpose of producing glass for fixtures. Gallé, Daum, and the work produced in Nancy were best known for intaglio-carved and cameo glass. Tiffany's primary contributions to art glass were favrile glass and leaded glass shades with colored glass. Other movements that occurred during the early twentieth century were *L'Art Moderne,* De Stijl, Bauhaus, and art deco.

Restoration and Reproduction Considerations

The choices for specifying lighting for period interiors are original fixtures, restorations, or reproductions. Types of fixtures are a controversial issue in historic preservation. Some historians feel that to create a period interior requires fixtures that are true to the original style. The other perspective is that restoration should reflect the evolutionary changes that occur with technology and time. Often interior designers develop personal beliefs that can be influenced by their clients and by the style and location of the interiors they are designing.

Original fixtures often require restoration work, especially in situations where the original design was for gas lighting and then modified for electricity. Generally, restoration work involves refinishing, structural repairs, rewiring, and replacing parts. Glass shades are the most frequent replacement unit and one of the most difficult parts to replace when the original was produced by one of the famous glass craftsmen. Problems associated with reproductions include the expense of handcrafted work, access to materials, authenticity of the original design, and compliance with current building codes. (For more information regarding codes, see Chapter 12.) Some of the best reproductions are licensed by professional historic organizations or museums.

In addition to selecting a period fixture, designers must also take into account the proper location of a fixture in a room within the context of the era. The proper fixture and location requires an analysis of the type of space and furnishings as well as how people lived in the space. For example, the low illumination level produced by candles and oil required fixture placement in several locations. Fabrics and any other flammable material had to be far away from open flames. In addition, a period interior requires specifications for walls, fabrics, tapestries, and floor coverings. How lighting affected colors and textures are important considerations in selecting these materials. Original materials were selected by using a flame light. Lighting in a fabric showroom, which is often where interior designers select materials, is not the same quality or quantity as produced by oil, candles, or gas. Thus, to provide an authentic reproduction, an interior designer should consider how the materials look under the light of a flame. To accommodate the need for higher illumination levels, additional luminaires are sometimes specified in period interiors. For these situations, mounting and installation of fixtures should always be conducted in a manner that minimizes damage to the original architecture.

Contemporary Luminaires

A variety of professions are responsible for designing contemporary fixtures, including industrial designers, lighting designers, architects, and interior designers.

Luminaires and Designers

Continued improvements in electricity and the incandescent lamp led to an increase in the demand for luminaires. Consumer interest in and fascination with a new source of illumination were motivating factors in designing luminaires. There were few luminaire designs before 1920; many fixtures were designed during the 1920s and 1930s. There were very few luminaires designed during the 1940s, which were dominated by World War II. Many luminaires were designed during the 1960s, 1970s, and 1980s, and developments tapered off during the 1990s. The early twenty-first century should experience a resurgence in styles because of the technological developments of fiber optics and LEDs.

Designers from Italy, Denmark, Sweden, the United States, France, Germany, and Great Britain created many of the most significant luminaire designs during the twentieth century. In particular, Italian designers and manufacturers were tremendous innovators and extensively influenced lighting design. This foundation is still influencing furniture and lighting designs. The annual trade shows in Milan, Italy, receive international attention and often are used to present prototypes of new luminaire designs.

In the early twentieth century, designers were influenced by the design of fixtures for candles, oil, and gas, and they had to develop a unit that accommodated a fixed lamp, a socket, wiring, and perhaps a shade. The design of the luminaire also had to direct the light for the purpose of the fixture, avoid glare, and diffuse the heat. Today these criteria are obvious, but in the early twentieth century these were all new considerations that designers had to factor in so that they could create luminaires for electricity. Some of the luminaires created in the early twentieth century by designers such as Josef Hoffmann, Jacob Jacobsen, Mariano Fortuny, and Eileen Gray have become classics and are still produced today (Figure 11.19 a–d). Designers who worked on initial luminaires should be appreciated for their vision and their enormous contributions to quality environments. As the twentieth century advanced, improvements in materials and technology and the

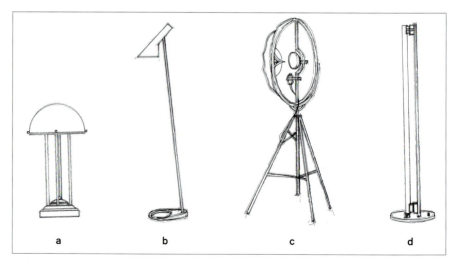

FIGURE 11.19 Reproductions of luminaires designed by (a) J. Hoffmann, (b) J. Jacobsen, (c) M. Fortuny, and (d) E. Gray.

development of other light sources, including fluorescent and HID, led to new luminaire designs. Designers also started to be inspired by developments in other fields, such as automobiles, space, products for industrial use, and the theater. Achille and Pier Giacomo Castiglione are known for designing the "Toio" luminaire from spare parts in a garage. Thus, their luminaire is made primarily from a fishing pole and an automobile's headlight.

During the twentieth and early twenty-first centuries, thousands of luminaires have been designed by hundreds of people. A thorough analysis of contemporary lighting designers is beyond the scope of this book. Criteria for selecting classic design can be fixtures that have been produced for decades, designs that influenced many designers, luminaires that have been recognized by museums, and conceptual innovations. Generally, these luminaires are designed to effectively provide light for the intended purpose, reflect integrity in the application of materials, and use classical proportions. Some of the luminaires are available in different versions of the same styles including table, floor, and wall-mounted. An analysis of luminaires reveals that, early in the development of luminaires, designers appeared to be intrigued with creating a fixture that maximized the ability to finally control a light source. Examples of these luminaires include table lamps by Gerrit Rietveld for Shroder House in 1918, Fortuny in 1929, and E. Bucquet in 1930. E. Bucquet's task luminaire was a tremendous influence on the design of George Carwardine's "Anglepoise" in 1932, Jacobsen in 1937, Paolo Rizzatto and Alberto Meda's "Berenice" in 1985, and in 1998 Philippe Starck's "Archimoon" series. Early designs of floor lamps that provide control and flexibility include Boris Lacroix's designs in 1950, 1952, and 1953 and Gino Sarfatti's luminaire in 1950. As lamps became cooler and new materials were developed, designers were able to experiment with paper, fabric, and plastics. Ingo Maurer's "Wo bist du, Edison?" is an excellent example of incorporating the technology of holograms in a suspended luminaire.

Designers often titled their pieces the way painters do. Eventually simply stating the name of a piece was enough to identify the luminaire. For example, interior designers discuss and specify Philippe Starck's *Sissy Lamp*. Knowledge of designers' titles of pieces is critical in communicating in the design field. In specifying luminaires, an interior designer may use the classics as a basis for comparison and apply the elements and principles of design.

Custom Luminaires

In addition to having a wide assortment of luminaires available from manufacturers, interior designers have the option of designing custom fixtures. Fundamentally, the reasons for custom designing a luminaire focus on the need for a unique fixture or on special installation requirements (Figure 11.20). A custom luminaire may be appropriate when a client wants a piece designed for a specific application or the need for a fixture that is not commercially available in a specific color, finish, size, shape, or material. The latter situation often occurs in historic renovation projects. Because very few are available from manufacturers, the need for lamps can frequently precipitate the design of a cus-

FIGURE 11.20 The luminaire has cherry wood display panels with bronze suspension rods and Plexiglas glazing. Low-voltage current passes from a transformer concealed in the ceiling through the suspension rods and frames to the cantilevered lamps. The result is the appearance of "floating" artwork.

tom luminaire. Special installation conditions that may require a custom fixture include unique room dimensions, space limitations, electrical limitations, or building code restrictions.

Allowing adequate time for the process is a critical element in designing custom luminaires. A major reason for the long time it takes is the number of people involved in the process. Generally, the team includes the client, architects, interior designers, general contractors, electrical contractors, electrical distributors, the luminaire manufacturer, materials suppliers, lamp manufacturers, UL approvals, and possibly a lighting designer. The process starts with rough sketches, preliminary drawings, and possibly **prototypes**. For complicated lighting plans, often **mock-ups** of the luminaires are created. Upon approval of the drawings, an order is sent to the manufacturer and detailed drawings are developed. Once the design and specifications are approved again, the luminaire is created. A custom fixture can be the focal point of an interior, thus justifying the time and patience devoted to the process. In addition, generally the quality of custom fixtures is impeccable because the manufacturers have to employ craftspeople who have the skills to assemble luminaires with complicated designs, finishes, and materials. This high level of skill and quality is also necessary for the innovators in the field of lighting.

Custom fixtures are a unique component of lighting a quality environment, and they represent one of the many choices available to interior designers. Portable luminaires are an important element of an interior; thus it is critical to have a thorough awareness of the products that are available on the market and the advantages and disadvantages of each. The luminaire selected should be in concert with the design concept and the interior elements of the space. Knowledge of historical fixtures and contemporary designs provides a resource foundation for selecting the appropriate luminaire for the specific setting.

Prototype
A model of a new product, or a new version of an existing lighting system.

Mock-up
A full-size model of a proposed lighting system, and its structural elements.

SUMMARY

- Portable luminaires are important in layering light and can fulfill the needs for general, task, accent, and decorative lighting. To select a portable luminaire that meets the intended purpose, an interior designer must understand the characteristics of fixtures, the affect on the design of an interior, and proper placement.

- Portable luminaires include table and floor fixtures and are used primarily in residential interiors, hotels, restaurants, and private offices.

- There are a variety of professions responsible for designing fixtures, including industrial designers, lighting designers, architects, and interior designers.

- Portable luminaires distribute light in the following ways: (a) direct, (b) indirect, (c) semi-direct, (d) semi-indirect, and (e) diffused. The purpose of the fixture determines the distribution pattern that is appropriate.

- The base of portable luminaires is made of metals, porcelain, enamel, crystal, wood, pottery, marble, or glass. Metals include brass, silver, gilded bronze, tin, bronze, copper, iron, pewter, and wrought iron. Traditional materials for shades include fabric, paper, glass, and metal.

- The fixture should be the appropriate style, size, shape, and color for the interior, and it should enhance the desired atmosphere.

- The location of a fixture should address the elements and principles of design; it should also support tasks. The ideal location provides direct light on the task, with no shadows or glare.

- Historical knowledge about the development of fixtures is essential when designing period interiors. To specify a luminaire that is the proper style for an interior requires research and an awareness of fixtures that were developed throughout history.

- Using flame as the light source led to portable fixtures, chandeliers, lanterns, and wall lights.

- Some of the earliest lighting fixtures were Greek and Roman oil lamps.

- Candles were used in candlesticks, candelabra, chandeliers, lanterns, wall-lights, and furniture. To provide additional task lighting, candles were integrated into serving pieces and mirrors and for illuminating clocks.

- The most common fixtures for gas were gaseliers and wall brackets.

- Fixture types for electricity included electroliers and wall-lights and both portable and ceiling-mounted fixtures.
- Lighting choices for period interiors are original fixtures, restorations, or reproductions.
- The dominant decades in the twentieth century for luminaire designs were the 1920s, 1930s, 1960s, 1970s, and 1980s.
- Designers from Italy, Denmark, Sweden, the United States, France, Germany, and Great Britain created many of the most significant luminaire designs during the twentieth century. Italian designers and manufacturers were tremendous innovators and extensively influenced lighting design.
- A custom luminaire may be appropriate when a client wants a piece designed for a specific application or needs a fixture that is not commercially available in a specific color, finish, size, shape, or material.
- Special installation conditions that may require a custom fixture include unique room dimensions, space limitations, electrical limitations, or building code restrictions.
- Allowing adequate time for the process is a critical element in designing custom luminaires.

Key Terms

candelabra	lantern
candelabrum	mock-up
candlestick	portable luminaire
chandelier	prototype
gaselier	wall-light
gaselier-electrolier	

Exercises

1. Select five portable luminaires and analyze each in relationship to the function, elements, and principles of design. In addition, evaluate how well the design of the luminaire accommodates the lamp that is specified for the fixture. Present your evaluations in a written report and include illustrations of the luminaires.

2. Visit three buildings or select three photographs of interiors. For each space identify the luminaires and their placement. Analyze the design and location of the luminaire in relationship to the other elements in the space. Summarize the results in a written report and include illustrations, photographs, or sketches.

3. Conduct an analysis of several paintings from the sixteenth to the eighteenth century. Prepare a written report that provides a summary of the following items for each century:
    a. Type of fixture, approximate size, and fuel source
    b. Location of the fixture
    c. Apparent purpose of the fixture
    d. Daylight integration
    e. Overall effect on the users of the space

4. Search on the World Wide Web for several restoration and reproduction manufacturers. Identify the type of products and their quality and price range. Compile the resources in a file.

5. Select one of the designers identified in this chapter. Write an essay that includes a biographical profile of the designer, illustrations of their luminaires, and how the designer has influenced the field of lighting. The luminaire illustrations should include an analysis of how the designs evolved over time.

6. Select a commercial space and design a luminaire specifically for the interior. The following items must be submitted for the project:
    a. Sketches of the custom luminaire
    b. Detailed drawings
    c. Prototype of the luminaire constructed from materials of your choice
    d. Material specifications
    e. Plan for executing the project, including time lines, team members, and required steps

REFERENCES

Albers, J. (1963). *Interaction of Color*. New Haven: Yale University Press.
Alton, J. (1995). *Painting with Light*. Berkeley, CA: University of California Press.
Baroni, D. (1983). *The Electric Light: A Century of Design*. New York: Van Nostrand Reinhold.
Bascot, H.P. (1987). *Nineteenth Century Lighting, Candle Powered Devices: 1783–1883*. Exton, PA: Schiffer.

Benya, J., Heschong, L., McGowan, T., Miller, N., and Rubinstein, F. (2001). *Advanced Lighting Guidelines*. White Salmon, WA: New Buildings Institute.

Birren, F. (1969). *Light, Color and Environment*. New York: Van Nostrand Reinhold.

Bourne, J., and Brett, V. (1991). *Lighting in the Domestic Interior*. London: Sotheby's.

Bowers, B. (1998). *Lengthening the Day: A History of Lighting Technology*. Oxford: Oxford University Press.

Boyce, P.R. (1981). *Human Factors in Lighting*. New York: Macmillan.

Boylan, B.R. (1987). *The Lighting Primer*. Ames, IA: Iowa State University Press.

Butler, J.T. (1967). *Candleholders in America, 1650–1900*. New York: Crown Publishers.

Chandler, D. (1936). *Outline of History of Lighting by Gas*. London: South Metropolitan Gas Company.

Conran, S., and Bond, M. (1999). *Somabasics Lighting*. San Francisco: Soma Books.

Cook, M.L., and Ferro, M.L. (Spring 1983). Electric lighting and wiring in historic American buildings. *Technology and Conservation*, 28–48.

Cuffley, P. (1973). *A Complete Catalogue and History of Oil and Kerosene Lamps in Australia*. Victoria, Australia: Pioneer Design Studio.

D'Allemagne, H.R. (1891). *Historie du luminaire*. Paris.

Dietz, U.G. (1892). *Victorian Lighting: The Dietz Catalogue of 1860*. Reprint. Watkins Glen, NY: American Life Foundation.

Dinkel, J. (1989). *The Royal Pavilion Brighton*. London: Tourism, Museums and Entertainments Committee of the Brighton Borough Council.

Duncan, A. (1978). *Art Nouveau and Art Deco Lighting*. New York: Simon and Schuster.

Eveleigh, D.J. (1985). *Candle Lighting*. Aylesbury, England: Shire Publications.

Ferro, M., and Cook, M.L. (1984). *Electric Wiring and Lighting in Historic American Buildings: Guidelines for Restoration and Rehabilitation Projects*. New Bedford, MA: AFC.

Fielder, W.J., and Frederick, H.J. (2001). *The Lit Interior*. Boston: Architectural Press.

Gledhill, D. (1981). *Gas Lighting*. Aylesbury, England: Shire Publications.

Gordan, G. and Nuckolls, J.L. (1995). *Interior Lighting for Designers*. New York: John Wiley & Sons.

Gould, G.G. (1928). *Period Lighting Fixtures*. New York: Dodd, Mead.

Greif, M. (1986). *The Lighting Book*. Pittstown, NJ: The Main Street Press.

Grove, J.R. (1967). *Antique Brass Candlesticks, 1450–1750*. Queen Anne, MD.

Harvey, E.N. (1957). *A History of Luminescence from the Earliest of Times until 1900*. Philadelphia: America Philosophical Society.

Illuminating Engineering Society of North America (IESNA) (2000). *IESNA Lighting Handbook* (9th ed.). New York: Illuminating Engineering Society of North America.

Laing, A.D. (1982). *Lighting*. London: Victoria & Albert Museum.

Lam, W.C. (1977). *Perception and Lighting as Formgivers for Architecture*. New York: McGraw-Hill.

Lynes, J.A. (1978). *Developments in Lighting—1*. London: Applied Science Publishers.

Maril, N. *American lighting 1840–1940*. Exton, PA: Schiffer.

Meadows, C.A. (1972). *Discovering Oil Lamps*. Aylesbury, England: Shire Publications.

Miller, M. (1981). *Chartres: The Cathedral and the Old Town*. Great Britain: Garrod and Lofthouse.

Moss, R.W. (1988). *Lighting for Historic Buildings*. Washington, DC: The Preservation Press.

Myers, D.P. (1989). *Gaslighting in America: A Guide for Historic Preservation*. Washington, DC: National Park Service, U.S. Department of the Interior, 1978. Reprint. New York: Dover Publications.

O'Dea, W.T. (1958). *The Social History of Lighting*. London: Routledge and Kegan Paul.

Phillips, D. (2000). *Lighting Modern Buildings*. Oxford: Architectural Press.

Poese, B. (1976). *Lighting through the Years*. Des Moines, IA: Wallace-Homestead Book Company.

Praz, M. (1983). *An Illustrated History of Interior Decoration: From Pompeii to Art Nouveau*. London: Thames and Hudson.

Russell, L.S. (1968) *A Heritage of Light*. Toronto: University of Toronto Press.

Schroder, M. (1969) *The Argand Burner: Its Origin and Development in France and England, 1780–1803*. Copenhagen: Odense University Press.

Thornton, P.K. (1984). *Authentic Décor, the Domestic Interior 1620–1920*. London.

Thornton, P.K. (1978). *Seventeenth Century Interior Decoration in England, France, and Holland*. New Haven, CT: Yale University Press.

Thuro, C.M. (1976). *Oil Lamps*. Des Moines, IA: Homestead Book Company.

Thuro, C.M. (1983). *Oil Lamps II*. Toronto: Thorncliffe House.

Thwing, L.L., and Daniels, J. (1952). *A Dictionary of Old Lamps and Other Lighting Devices*. Cambridge, MA: C. E. Tuttle.

Van der Kemp, G., Hoog, S., and Meyer, D. (1984). *Versailles*. New York: Éditions d'Art Lys Vilo, Inc.

Watson, L. (1977). *Lighting Design Handbook*. New York: McGraw-Hill.

CHAPTER 12

Energy and the Environment

OBJECTIVES

- Describe international energy requirements through 2020.

- Analyze the energy required for lighting, including consumption by type of building and practices described by producers, conveyors, and consumers.

- As prescribed by energy codes and standards, understand minimum requirements for energy-efficient design of new and existing buildings.

- Determine the factors that should be considered in an economic analysis.

- Define sustainable design and apply an understanding of it to lighting systems.

- Identify the factors that should be considered when specifying a sustainable lighting system.

INTERIOR designers have an ethical responsibility to safeguard the health, safety, and welfare of the occupants of the interiors they specify. As our planet experiences increases in population and a depletion of natural resources, protecting the environment has become increasingly essential for the health and welfare of future generations. As global citizens, interior designers can play an active role in educating consumers and making a conscious effort to specify products and materials that minimize the impact on the environment.

During the past several years, the field of interior design has become more focused on the environment than it had been previously. This is evident by the emergence of sustainable design. **Sustainable design** is design that focuses on products and processes that protect the environment while conserving energy for future generations. Whenever possible, lighting specifications should reflect the principles embodied in sustainable design. This involves selecting lighting systems that conserve energy and comply with standards, codes, and regulations. In specifying sustainable lighting systems, information reviewed in previous chapters of this textbook must be incorporated into the design of the environment. The topics most germane are daylight integration, characteristics of lamps, directional effects of lighting, design of luminaires, electricity, and controls. These areas and the principles of sustainable design are also to be considered in a lighting system's energy and maintenance management plan.

Energy

A quality lighting environment requires luminaire systems that protect the environment and conserve energy; they should also be cost effective.

Global Energy Consumption

The Energy Information Administration (EIA) of the U.S. Department of Energy (DOE) issued a report titled *International Energy Outlook 2002* that provides an analysis and forecast of international energy requirements through 2020. For the purpose of the report the EIA divided the world into the following six groupings: (1) industrialized countries, (2) Eastern Europe/former Soviet Union (EE/FSU), (3) developing Asia, (4) Middle East, (5) Africa, and (6) Central and South America (Figure 12.1). The projections were based on 2002 U.S. and foreign government policies. The report includes a forecast of electrical needs, which is very helpful in determining the energy demands for lighting in the future.

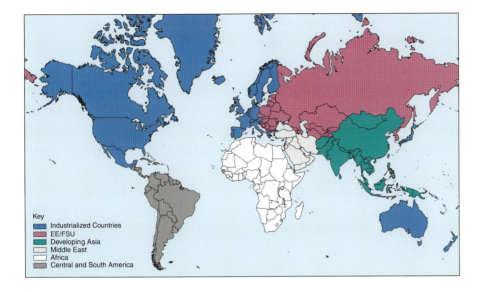

FIGURE 12.1 Map of the following six country groupings: industrialized countries, Eastern Europe/Former Soviet Union (EE/FSU), developing Asia, Middle East, Africa, and Central and South America.

Key
- Industrialized Countries
- EE/FSU
- Developing Asia
- Middle East
- Africa
- Central and South America

According to the EIA (2002), by the year 2020 world energy consumption will be 612 quadrillion British thermal units (Btu). The developing countries, primarily those in Asia and Central and South America, will experience the greatest demands for energy. In reviewing energy consumption by type of fuel, the EIA reports that the greatest increase in demand is for natural gas (Figure 12.2). Most of the increase in the consumption of natural gas is attributed to using gas turbine power plants for the generation of electricity. This technology is appealing to producers and consumers because natural gas has many

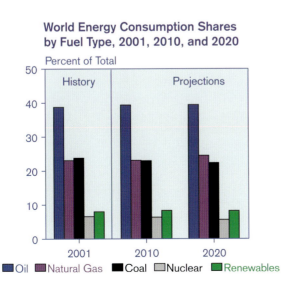

World Energy Consumption Shares by Fuel Type, 2001, 2010, and 2020

Percent of Total

History | Projections

2001   2010   2020

■ Oil ■ Natural Gas ■ Coal □ Nuclear ■ Renewables

FIGURE 12.2 World energy consumption by fuel type for 2001, 2010, and 2020.

environmental and economical benefits. Natural gas burns more cleanly than do fossil fuels, thus reducing the ill effects derived from gas emissions.

Table 12.1 illustrates the history and projections for electrical consumption by region. The EIA postulates that electrical consumption for developing Asia and Central and South America will increase by 4.5 and 3.9 percent per year, respectively. Currently, some areas in developing countries do not have electricity. Thus, the EIA anticipates that the increase in electrical usage will be primarily derived from improvements in the standard of living in these countries. The EIA also estimates the demands for the type of fuel that would be used to

TABLE 12.1

World Net Electricity Consumption by Region, 1990–2020
(Billion Kilowatt hours)

Region	History		Projections				Average Percent Change 1999–2020
	1990	1999	2005	2010	2015	2020	
Industrialized Countries	6,385	7,517	8,620	9,446	10,281	11,151	1.9
United States	2,817	3,236	3,793	4,170	4,556	4,916	2.0
EE/FSU	1,906	1,452	1,651	1,807	2,006	2,173	1.9
Developing Countries	2,258	3,863	4,912	6,127	7,548	9,082	4.2
Developing Asia	1,259	2,319	3,090	3,900	4,819	5,858	4.5
China	551	1,084	1,523	2,031	2,631	3,349	5.5
India	257	424	537	649	784	923	3.8
South Korea	93	233	309	348	392	429	3.0
Other Developing Asia	357	578	724	872	1,012	1,157	3.4
Central and South America	449	684	788	988	1,249	1,517	3.9
Total World	10,549	12,833	15,182	17,380	19,835	22,407	2.7

Note: EE/FSU = Eastern Europe and the former Soviet Union.

Sources: History: Energy Information Administration (EIA), *International Energy Annual 1999,* DOE/EIA-0219(99) (Washington, DC, February 2001). *Projections:* EIA, World Energy Projection System (2002).

generate electricity (Figure 12.3). The report indicates that coal will continue to be in high demand through 2020, but the largest increase will be for natural gas.

Energy Consumption for Lighting

The EIA report does not provide a historical profile or projection of electrical demands by use, such as meeting the needs for lighting. However, some of this information is available from the U.S. Environmental Protection Agency (EPA) and the International Association of Energy-Efficient Lighting (IAEEL). The EPA has determined that lighting consumes approximately 23 percent of the electricity used in buildings. In addition, approximately 20 percent of the electricity required for air-conditioning results from the heat generated by lamps. Most of the lighting needs occur during weekdays, which is the peak demand time period for electricity. The purpose of the building affects the percentage of the electricity that is used for lighting. For example, a large percentage of the electricity consumed by a retail store is dedicated to lighting. In contrast, the percentage of electricity used for lighting by a factory is very small, because the highest demands are for operating machinery. Approximately half the electricity used in

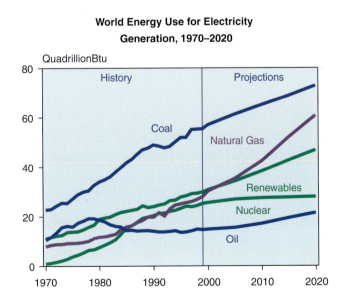

World Energy Use for Electricity Generation, 1970–2020

QuadrillionBtu

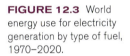

FIGURE 12.3 World energy use for electricity generation by type of fuel, 1970–2020.

commercial buildings is for lighting systems, and about 10 percent of the electricity consumed in residences is used for lighting.

The design of a building also affects the percentage of electricity that is used for lighting. Generally, buildings that have a small percentage exposed to daylight require more electricity for lighting. Effective daylight integration can conserve energy and resources. The amount of illumination from a window approximately 3 feet by 5 feet is equivalent to 100 60-watt incandescent lamps. Software is available to generate a simulation of the electrical needs for lighting in proposed buildings.

Based upon a study of thirty eight countries, the IAEEL reports that "globally, electric lighting accounts for more than 2000 TWh electricity and 2900 million metric tons of carbon dioxide emissions (CO_2) per year" (2000, p. 1). The IAEEL study reveals that global electrical lighting needs are the highest in the service and residential sectors. Thus, this study suggests that in order to reduce the energy needed for lighting in the future, the focus should be on efficient lighting systems designed for service and residential environments.

To analyze lighting practices and attitudes, the American History Museum of the Smithsonian Institution is collecting a written history of responses from producers, conveyors, and consumers. The study defines *producers* as individuals involved in making lamps and lighting devices. *Conveyors* are people who distribute lamps and lighting devices. The *consumer group* represents anyone who purchases or uses lighting. Questions and their responses are available on the museum's Web site (http://americanhistory.si.edu/). Questions primarily focus on issues related to energy conservation. For example, one of the producer's questions is: "Has your involvement with energy-efficient lighting led you to consider energy issues when you think about other products? Can you give examples?" (2003, p. 6). A conveyor question is: "Efficient lighting is increasingly seen as a system involving many integrated components. From your experience, how has this affected adoption of the technology?" (2003, p. 4). Consumers are asked: "Have you replaced entire lighting fixtures in order to use more efficient bulbs? If not, would you consider doing so?" (2003, p. 3).

The Web site includes selected responses to the questions. Since this is an ongoing study, findings and conclusions are not available at the time of publication of this text. However, by reading the responses from producers, conveyors, and consumers, an interior designer can gain insight into problems associated with making and distributing efficient lighting systems. For example, in response to the conveyor question identified in the previous paragraph, one respondent, who is a designer and specifier, noted, "This is a great concept that has only begun to crawl. I am currently working on a very complex project where we [lighting, HVAC, security and IT designers] have integrated wide and local control of all systems with cross-compatibility. The various industries involved have yet to recognize the complexity of cross-compatibility and many say they have gone there, but have [actually] only scratched the surface. Once the walls are broken down and the various disciplines truly work together in development, only then will we see some highly efficient and sophisticated technologies" (2003, pp. 6–7). An understanding of the issues can facilitate discussions with industry representatives and lead to more energy-efficient lighting systems.

Understanding the perspectives of consumers can be invaluable in developing strategies to convince people to purchase energy-efficient lighting systems. For example, in response to being asked about using energy-efficient lighting equipment, a consumer commented, "Unfortunately, as a consumer I have no economic incentive to purchase energy-efficient fixtures. The premium for these types of bulbs is usually such that it is very hard to rationalize [buying them] as you are in the aisle of your local hardware store or Wal-mart" (2003, p. 1). A homeowner responded, "It's a good idea but how much of our energy budget is consumed by lighting?" (2003, p. 2).

Energy Standards and Codes

To promote energy efficiency and sustainable development, standards and codes have been established worldwide. Because standards and codes are continuously being updated, an interior designer must always refer to the most current versions. Generally, changes in energy standards and codes focus on requiring lighting systems that reduce energy consumption. Standards delineate minimum energy efficiency for lighting equipment and limit power for special interior applications. States and local communities must have laws that comply with federal standards. Codes are laws that have been created at either the federal, regional, state, or local level. Many states or localities adopt the federal standards as their codes with no modifications. However, some states, such as California, have codes that exceed federal standards. Interior designers must always refer to the state and local codes that regulate their clients' buildings. This is especially important when designers have a project that is located in a different state or country from their own. Most standards and codes prescribe requirements according to the type of structure and existing or new construction.

Important energy standards and codes that affect lighting efficiency are ASHRAE/IESNA 90.1-2001 (American Society of Heating, Refrigeration, and Air Conditioning Engineers/Illuminating Engineering Society of North America), MEC-95 (Model Energy Code), IECC-03 (International Energy Conservation Code), and NFPA (National Fire Protection Act) 5000. Energy standards for lighting started in 1974 with a publication titled *Energy Conservation Guidelines for Existing Office Buildings* developed by the General Service Administration and the Public Building Services (GSA/PBS). During this time period the ASHRAE worked with the IES to write a chapter on lighting in the standards document, titled "ASHRAE 90-75." This chapter focuses on lighting-power budget-determination procedures and energy standards for specific applications. This standard has had several revisions. The most current edition is ASHRAE/IESNA 90.1-2001 for commercial buildings except low-rise residential buildings, and ASHRAE/IESNA 90.2-2001 for low-rise residential buildings. The standard specifies minimum requirements for the energy-efficient design of new buildings, and additions or alterations to existing buildings.

The "Energy Conservation Standards for New Building Act of 1976" mandated lighting efficiency standards. As a result of this legislation, and ASHRAE 90-75, the Model Code for Energy Conservation in New Building Construction (MCEC 77) was developed by several professional organizations. In 1983 the title of MCEC was changed to Model Energy Code (MEC). The International Code Council is responsible for the IECC. This code has a lighting section that is derived from ASHRAE/IESNA 90.1. The National Fire Protection Association

(NFPA) 5000 Building Code is NFPA's complete building code and includes ASHRAE/IESNA 90.1 and 90.2 as the standard for energy provisions.

Since most lighting codes and regulations are based upon ASHRAE/IESNA 90.1, an interior designer should know this document well. Section 9 in ASHRAE/IESNA 90.1 is dedicated to lighting. Section 9.1 reviews general lighting applications. Section 9.2 encompasses mandatory provisions, including lighting controls, tandem wiring, exit signs, installed interior lighting power, and luminaire wattage. The prescriptive path for interior lighting power allowance (ILPA) is described in Section 9.3. The ILPA is calculated by the building area and space-by-space methods. The building area method involves the entire building and is determined by multiplying the gross lighted area by allowances provided in the standard's table of lighting power density. The ILPA is based upon maximum watts per square foot and the type of building. For example, the maximum watts per square foot for a retail store is higher than an office. By the year 2005, most office buildings in the United States will be limited to 1.1 watts per square foot.

The space-by-space method is a more flexible and accurate means to calculate the ILPA, because each area of the building is identified. The ILPA is determined by adding up all the lighting power allowances room by room. For example, in a school building, the ILPA would include the lighting power for classrooms, hallways, offices, restrooms, cafeteria, and gymnasium.

Compared to previous versions of the standard, ASHRAE/IESNA 90.1-2001 has more stringent interior lighting power requirements and mandatory control requirements. Installed interior lighting power calculations include lamps, ballasts, and controls for all permanent and portable luminaires. Some of the lighting power exemptions include luminaires for safety, exit signs, theatrical lighting, educational demonstration systems, areas for the visually impaired, plant growth, museum exhibits, medical/dental procedures, retail display windows, and registered historic landmarks. Except for safety and security lighting, controls must be accessible and mounted in a location that can be seen by users. Control devices are restricted to 2500 square feet in spaces less than 10,000 square feet. In spaces greater than 10,000 square feet, control devices are limited to an area of 10,000 square feet. Automatic shutoff controls are required for spaces greater than 5000 square feet. To simplify energy code compliance, the DOE has free software designed to perform the calculations. RES*check* and COM*check* are the compliance tools for residential and commercial buildings, respectively (http://www.energycodes.gov).

The U.S. Energy Policy Act of 1992 (EPAct-92) has significantly affected energy-efficient lighting. The EPAct focuses on standards for lighting, window energy-efficient rating systems, and demand-side-management (DSM) programs. The EPAct mandates that all states must have codes that meet or exceed the standards in ASHRAE/IESNA 90.1. The EPAct energy code also requires lamp manufacturers to stop producing many lamps that are not energy-efficient, including standard 40-watt fluorescent lamps and some incandescent reflector and PAR lamps. Lamps for special applications, such as emergency, safety, and cold temperature service, are excluded from meeting efficiency standards. As a result of the EPAct, lamp manufacturers have developed many energy-efficient lamps, including the T-8 and T-5/HO (high output). Figure 12.4 illustrates efficacy standards for selected lamps. The Federal Trade Commission (FTC) has developed an energy-efficient labeling program that must be used by all

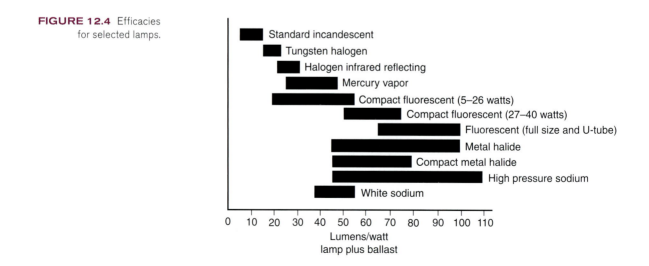

FIGURE 12.4 Efficacies for selected lamps.

lamp manufacturers. The label includes energy ratings for lamps and estimated operating costs per year.

In addition to standards and codes, there are voluntary programs sponsored by the EPA and DOE that include recommendations for energy-efficient lighting practices. The EPA supports the Energy Star Building, and the DOE established Building America and Rebuild America. Energy Star is a program "helping businesses and individuals protect the environment through superior energy" (www.energystar.gov, p. 1). The program provides energy management strategies for businesses and recognizes buildings that perform efficiently. Energy Star has a residential voluntary labeling program to inform consumers of which products meet strict energy-efficiency guidelines. The purpose of Building America is to provide energy solutions for production housing. The program is based upon a systems engineering approach to create homes that consume less energy, improve builder productivity, and implement innovative technologies. Rebuild America encourages energy-efficiency improvements in existing commercial, new education, and existing high-rise residential buildings.

Energy Management and Economics

Interior designers can assist their clients in developing a strategy for lighting energy management and for conducting a cost analysis. Sound advice regarding lighting energy management and economics demonstrates to a client that an interior designer's focus is on a quality lighting environment that includes specifying a lighting system that is energy-efficient and profitable to the business while helping to protect the environment. Financial savings can include reductions in electrical costs, rebates from utility companies, and increases in worker productivity. Approximately 80 percent of a company's expenses are associated with people. Many studies have demonstrated that a quality lighting environment can enhance productivity. Therefore, money invested in a quality lighting system can be returned by increases in employee accomplishments. (See Chapter 13 for more information on human factors and lighting.) Furthermore, the image of a company can be enhanced by its promoting energy-efficiency and sustainable development.

Lighting energy management should be initiated during the planning process of an interior project. (Chapters 21 and 22 provide detailed information related to the design process.) Energy performance should be an element in decisions related to lighting, daylight integration, other building systems, and the overall design of the space. Energy Star has a software package called Target Finder that allows a client to set an energy performance goal for a new building design and then compare the estimated energy consumption to the target (www.energystar.gov). By using Target Finder during the planning process, changes that enhance energy efficiency can be made prior to construction. For commercial leased buildings, Energy Star's QuikScope software can demonstrate the financial viability associated with improvements in energy performance.

An economic analysis of lighting should include all expenses associated with an installed system, including lamps, luminaires, ballasts, transformers, controls, electricity, maintenance, disposal, and labor. A lighting system is approximately 5 percent of the total cost of a building. Generally, these capital costs are distributed over a ten-year period. Factors that affect the operation of a lighting system include the daylight factor, lamp life, and the efficiency of lamps and luminaires.

Generally, a lighting economic analysis can be conducted by examining simple payback or the life-cycle cost-benefit analysis (LCCBA). The LCCBA is complex and beyond the scope of this textbook. Chapter 25 in *IESNA Lighting Handbook,* 9th edition, provides a detailed illustration of how to conduct a LCCBA. Calculations include initial costs, annual power, maintenance costs, and the time value of money. IESNA recommends that LCCBA be used for large and complex projects. Many software tools are available to determine the costs and benefits of proposed energy conservation projects. The simple payback method is a quick estimate of the number of years required to pay back the money invested in a lighting system. This is a convenient method to use when comparing different lighting systems. For example, the payback period is five years for a lighting system that saves $3000 in energy costs per year and costs $15,000 to purchase and operate.

$$\text{Payback} = \text{cost of system/savings per year}$$

$$5 \text{ years} = \$15{,}000/\$3000$$

The Environment and Sustainable Design

Interior designers are in a unique position to encourage sustainable design because they specify millions of products and materials each year.

Sustainable Design

The U. S. Office of Technology Assessment (1992) indicates that sustainable design consists of two major components: (1) waste prevention by reducing weight, toxicity, and energy use; and (2) better materials management by facilitating remanufacturing, recycling, composting, and energy recovery. The Environmental Protection Agency (2001) has determined that the issues related to sustainable design include pollution prevention, multiple and systematic effects, an environmental life-cycle assessment (LCA), magnitude of impact (local and global), and specification of environmental attributes. The EIA study (2002) cited earlier in this chapter also examines world energy use and environmental issues. Figure 12.5 illustrates historical and projected world carbon dioxide emissions by region. The EIA reports that "the United States is currently the largest energy consumer in the industrialized world, accounting for the majority of its energy-related carbon dioxide emissions" (2002, p. 164).

All these areas are important when an interior designer specifies a lighting system. The manufacturing process, operations, and the disposal required for lighting systems consume resources, use energy, and cause pollution. In specifying lighting systems the goals should be to: (1) reduce the use of nonrenewable resources, (2) control the use of renewable products, (3) minimize air, water, and soil pollution, (4) protect natural habitats, (5) eliminate toxic substances, and (6) reduce light pollution.

There are many public and private energy and sustainable programs that are valuable resources (Table 12.2). The EPA, DOE, National

FIGURE 12.5 Historical and projected world carbon dioxide emissions by region, 1990–2020.

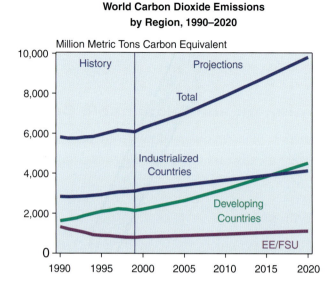

World Carbon Dioxide Emissions by Region, 1990–2020

Wildlife Federation, and the National Science Foundation (NSF) all sponsor programs that encourage environmental conservation, minimize waste, and maximize energy. The former Green Lights Program has been subsumed by the Energy Star Program. The U.S. Green Building Council developed the Leadership in Energy and Environmental Design (LEED) system. The LEED system is quickly becoming the energy and environmental standard throughout the building industry. LEED is a voluntary, national standard for developing high-performance, sustainable buildings. LEED was founded to: "define 'green building' by establishing a common standard of measurement; promote integrated, whole-building design practices; recognize environmental leadership in the building industry; stimulate sustainable competition; raise consumer awareness of sustainable building benefits; and transform the building market" (www.usgbc.org/LEED, p. 1).

In addition to building rating systems, voluntary labeling programs help to identify sustainable products. In the United States the eco-label and other labels developed by businesses and government-sponsored programs designate sustainable products (Figure 12.6). Many countries throughout the world have created labels for sustainable products; they are used on lamps, materials, equipment, appliances, and floor coverings.

TABLE 12.2

Energy and Sustainable Programs

Resources	Internet Address
Agencies	
U.S. Department of Energy	http://www.energy.gov
U.S. Environmental Protection Agency	http://www.epa.gov
Offices	
Office of Energy Efficiency and Renewable Energy	http://www.eere.energy.gov
National Fenestration Rating Council (NFRC)	http://www.nrfc.org
Programs and Research Laboratories	
Advanced Buildings	http://www.advancedbuilding.org
ASHRAE/IESNA 90.1-2001 (American Society of Heating, Refrigeration, and Air Conditioning Engineers/Illuminating Engineering Society of North America),	http://www.ashrae.org
Building America Program	http://www.eere.energy.gov/buildings/ building_america
Building Industry Research Alliance	http://www.bira.ws
Building Science Consortium	http://www.eere.energy.gov/buildings/ building_america/bsc.shtml
Consortium for Advanced Residential Buildings (CARB)	http://www.carb-swa.com
Dark Sky International	http://www.darksky.org
DesignLights Consortium	http://www.energyace.com/ energy_star_program.htm
Energy Star Program	
Environmental Energy Technologies Division (EETD)	
Energy Information Administration	http://www.lbl.gov
Industrialized Housing Partnership	
Integrated Building and Construction Solutions (IBACOS)	http://www.ibacos-ba.com
International Association of Energy-Efficient Lighting (IAEEL)	http://www.iaeel.org
General Service Administration and the Public Building Services (GSA/PBS)	http://www.gsa.gov/Portal/home.jsp
IECC-03 (International Energy Conservation Code)	http://www.bocai.org/index.html
Lawrence Berkeley National Laboratory	http://www.lbl.gov
Leadership in Energy & Environmental Design	http://www.usgbc.org/LEED/LEED_main.asp
Lighting Systems Research Group	http://eetd.lbl.gov/btp/lsr
MEC-95 (Model Energy Code)	http://www.energycodes.gov
NFPA (National Fire Protection Act) 5000	http://www.nfpa.org/catalog/home/index.asp
National Renewable Energy Laboratory (NREL)	http://www.nrel.gov
National Science Foundation (NSF)	http://www.nsf.gov
National Wildlife Federation	http://www.nwf.org
Oak Ridge National Laboratory (ORNL)	http://www.ornl.gov
Rebuild America	http://www.rebuild.org
U.S. Green Building Council	http://grove.ufl.edu/~usgbc

FIGURE 12.6 The eco-label used in the United States to designate a green product.

Design for the Environment

U.S. EPA

Disposal Regulations

The primary goals of sustainable disposal practices are to reduce the environmental impact and decrease waste. To improve solid-waste disposal methods, the Solid Waste Disposal Act was enacted in 1965. In 1976 this act was amended to establish the Resource Conservation and Recovery Act (RCRA). The RCRA was created to: (1) protect human health and the environment, (2) reduce and/or eliminate the generation of hazardous wastes, and (3) conserve energy and natural resources (Department of Energy, 2003, p. 1). The RCRA regulates hazardous waste associated with mercury, lead, and sodium. Several agencies have responsibilities associated with the RCRA. Guidelines and regulations from the EPA significantly affect the field of lighting. EPA regulates the "proper management of solid and hazardous wastes, oversees and approves the development of state waste management plans, and provides financial aid to agencies and firms performing research on solid waste" (Department of Energy, 2003, p. 1). The Toxic Substances Control Act (TSCA) and the Superfund Law (the Comprehensive Environmental Response, Compensation and Liability Act or CERCLA) regulate proper disposal of PCBs at the federal level.

To test the mercury content of lamps, in 1990 the EPA developed the **toxicity characteristic leaching procedure (TCLP)**. To pass the TCLP test, the range of mercury content in a lamp should be between

Toxicity characteristic leaching procedure (TCLP)

A test developed by the EPA to test, the mercury content of lamps. To pass the TCLP test, the range of mercury content must be between 4 and 6 milligrams without additives.

4 and 6 milligrams without additives. Some lamp manufacturers include additives in lamps with mercury levels that exceed the TCLP test. The additives alter the material composition in the lamps in a manner that allows them to pass the TCLP test even though the mercury content is high. Local laws and regulations specify the maximum levels of mercury in lamps. Some states, such as California, have laws that mandate lower mercury levels than the TCLP. A new law was created titled Land Disposal Program Flexibility Act of 1996, which addresses adjustments to land disposal restriction provision and water monitoring at solid-waste landfill units.

As a result of this legislation, there are many regulations that affect handling, removal, storage, transport, and disposal of lighting devices. Environmental regulations exist at the federal, regional, state, and local levels. The most current regulations should always be reviewed when lighting systems need to be removed. A building owner can be held liable for failing to comply with environmental regulations. An interior designer should encourage a client to maintain records of lamps and ballasts operating in a building and subsequent disposal processes.

Primary concerns related to removing lighting systems are toxic leaks and lamp breakage. Thus, once a lighting system has been determined to contain toxic materials, removal requires strict handling requirements, including the wearing of special protective clothing, gloves, and goggles. The equipment must be contained in special packaging, labeled as prescribed, and transported by means that will help ensure safe delivery with no breakage. Materials can be transported to recycling facilities, hazardous waste landfills, or incinerators. Each of the methods of disposal has various cost options, which should be included in the price of lighting systems. Contact the EPA to obtain the most current methods for hazardous waste disposal.

Many companies specialize in lamp and ballast disposal. The appendix provides a list of firms associated with recycling and processing lamps and ballasts. In selecting a disposal company, research should be conducted to ensure that the company has updated permits, good standing with the EPA, proper training in hazardous waste handling, and adequate liability insurance. The EPA publishes a list of companies associated with lighting waste disposal.

Electricity

Saving energy helps to prevent pollution. In reviewing the impact of lighting on the environment, all processes and resources in its life cycle must be assessed, starting at the production of electricity, resources consumed for manufacturing lighting products, energy used for the operation of lighting systems, and disposal practices. Electricity is used to produce the components in a lighting system, including lamps, luminaires, and controls. Electricity is then used to operate lighting systems. In addition, the heat that is produced by lamps taxes air-conditioning units.

The substantial use of electricity for lighting systems requires a thorough analysis of the energy's impact on the environment. Coal, oil, and natural gas are used to produce electricity. These fossil fuels are finite resources. Thus, at some point in the future the world will no longer have these nonrenewable resources. In addition, the production of electricity causes air pollution and acid rain. As a result, global warming, habitat destruction, and the extinction of species affect the world's ecosystems. Selecting efficient lamps and luminaires that last a long time diminishes electrical use by decreasing the amount of electricity used to operate the system and reducing the amount of electricity required to manufacture new components of lighting systems.

Components of Lighting Systems

The environmental impact of the components of lighting systems includes the type of materials used for the products, the manufacturing process, delivery, use, and disposal practices. Information related to materials and delivery modes are available from manufacturers. Some manufacturers have made a conscious effort to create sustainable products and be sustainable companies. Unfortunately, some manufacturers only appear to be sustainable; their claims prove to be superficial. Until formal standards have been developed that clearly define sustainable products and company practices, interior designers must apply their knowledge of sustainable design to information provided by manufacturers.

Ideally, materials used for the components of lighting systems should be derived from renewable resources, reused products, or recycled materials. In addition, the materials should contain little or no toxic substances. A primary area of concern is the use of mercury in fluorescent, HID, and neon lights. Currently, light for these lamps cannot be produced without mercury. Mercury is **PBT (persistent, bioaccumulation, toxic)**. This classification means that mercury is poisonous, remains in water or land indefinitely, and accrues in the world's ecosystems. For example, when a fluorescent lamp is deposited in a landfill and breaks, mercury leaks into the ground. Water from rain can transport mercury to the air, lakes, and rivers. Once the mercury is in the water system, fish ingest the mercury, plant life is affected, and eventually people can develop high doses of mercury by eating fish. To reduce the environmental impact, lamps should be specified that have a long life and a low mercury content. Lamp life and mercury content information is available from lamp manufacturers. Federal and state laws regulate the disposal of lamps containing mercury.

Another area of concern is the toxic material **polychlorinated biphenyls (PCBs)**. This chemical was used in ballasts produced prior to 1978. Ballasts without PCBs are labeled "No PCBs." Federal and state laws also regulate the disposal of ballasts with PCBs. In addition to examining the mercury content and PCBs in products, materials used to manufacture other components of lighting systems should be examined. This includes the housing unit, transformers, and controls. These components should be reviewed to determine the toxicity of materials and the source of origin. To specify a sustainable environment, the products should be made from renewable resources, reused products, or recycled materials.

In addition to examining the materials used for lighting systems, sustainable design includes the manufacturers' production processes and delivery of goods. A sustainable manufacturing company will promote energy efficiency and sustainable development by reducing electrical usage, using renewable resources, recycling, and preventing toxic waste. These practices should be evident throughout the life cycle of the manufacturing process, packaging, and delivery. Packaging should be made from recycled materials and on the smallest scale possible,

Persistent, bioaccumulation, toxic (PBT)
A classification that indicates a material is toxic, remains in water or land indefinitely, and accrues in the world's ecosystem.

which lowers resources needed to create the packaging and the space required in delivery trucks. A sustainable focus on delivery is important because there are a lot of nonrenewable resources used for transportation. A sustainable manufacturer will focus on minimizing the number of trucks needed to transport products and the distances each vehicle must travel.

Sustainable Practice

A life-cycle assessment includes an examination of the lighting plan, specifications, daylight integration, consumer use, maintenance, and disposal practices. Sustainable lighting systems must be used in a manner that enhances the quality of illumination while conserving energy. Sustainable practice requires proper placement and selection of appropriate lamps, luminaires, auxiliary components, and controls. Successful sustainable practice requires teamwork and developing systems and procedures that maximize the efficiency and effectiveness of an entire building's system. For existing buildings, an assessment of the lighting system should be conducted. The assessment should include an inventory of lamps, ballasts, luminaires, portable fixtures, controls, and daylight integration. The number of hours of being turned on and times during the day and week should be recorded. Effective sustainable practice demonstrates the interdependency of lighting and all the elements of the interior and architecture. Thus, the assessment should include the purpose of luminaires, room finishes, colors, materials, architectural features, electrical usage, air-conditioning loads, maintenance, and disposal policies.

Sustainable design includes proper placement of luminaires as well as colors and materials that maximize the reflectance of illumination. The location of luminaires should provide effective lighting for specific tasks. Luminaire layouts that have a uniform "blanket" distribution often waste energy. Specifying too many luminaires causes unnecessary natural resources to be consumed during the manufacturing and delivery processes. The lighting layout must be appropriate for the purpose of the luminaires and must control glare. The coefficient of utilization (CU) for the space is an important calculation in determining how the room proportions and the reflectances of walls, ceiling, and floors affect the quantity of lumens on a task. Colors of ceilings and walls should be light in value and have at least a 90 and 70 percent reflectance, respectively. Textures should be carefully chosen to avoid glare, while enhancing the reflectance of light.

Sustainable design requires lamps that conserve energy and that have a high efficacy rating, excellent light output, long life, high lumen maintenance, high color rendering, color stability, low mercury levels, and flexible disposal options. They should also be TCLP-compliant and contain no additives. Lamps with high efficacy often are advertised as "energy-saving," "ultimate performance," or "long life." Discharge lamps, including fluorescent, metal halide, and high-pressure sodium are the most efficient white light sources. Since incandescent lamps are not efficacious, they should be used only for special applications. CFLs are a good substitute for incandescent lamps, because they consume approximately 70 percent less electricity, and last six to ten times longer. CFLs are available in several different shapes and in a variety of color temperatures. For warm or cool light, specify a color temperature of 2700–3000K, and 4500–6000K, respectively. To conserve energy and reduce maintenance costs, CFLs are starting to be used in recessed downlights, wall sconces, and structural lighting. For applications that require excellent color rendition and precise optical control, such as for accent lighting, halogen or halogen infrared (HIR) are good choices because they are more efficient than incandescent lamps.

Compared to incandescent lamps, fluorescent lamps produce the same light output but use one-third the energy. Fluorescent lamps also last approximately 10 times longer than incandescent ones, and they utilize less hazardous materials. T8 and T5 fluorescent lamps are becoming very popular because they are energy-efficient, have improved color properties, and are a small size. The super-T8 is efficacious, and the T5/HO (high output) has a lumen level that equals some HID lamps. The F32T8 operated with an electronic ballast is a very popular retrofit system for the banned F40T12 with a magnetic ballast. Generally, this retrofit reduces the number of ballasts and lamps required for an installation. Thus, energy is saved by the reduction in the number of lamps and ballasts, and in the wattage consumed per lamp. By substituting the F32T8 for the F40T12, the energy savings is 8 watts per lamp. Eliminating magnetic ballasts for electronic units will further reduce the watts required for operation. To determine the efficiency of a lamp/ballast system, three ratings should be reviewed: ballast power factor (BPF), ballast factor (BF), and the ballast efficacy factor (BEF). A desirable BPF rating is greater than .90. A BF rating greater than 1.0 indicates a system that is functioning at a higher than expected light output. The BEF rating is calculated by dividing the BF by the total input power in watts. High BEF ratings indicate an efficient lamp/ballast system.

HID lamps are efficacious sources, and, generally, the higher wattages produce more lumens per watt. HPS is the most efficacious, followed by metal halide, and mercury vapor. High-pressure sodium or metal halide lamps should be substituted for mercury vapor lamps. Standard metal halide lamps should be replaced with energy-efficient metal halide lamps. The pulse-start metal halide (PSMH) lamp is efficacious because it uses approximately 30 percent less wattage than a standard metal halide lamp. Metal halides are available in warm (3000K) and cool (4000K) colors, and the CRI ranges are 85 to 96. LEDs are an excellent lighting source for exit signs. The Lawrence Berkeley National Laboratory (LBNL) is developing a fiber optic illuminator that will absorb most of the light produced by the lamp and transport the lumens to the fiber optics. Once this is accomplished, fiber optics will be an energy-efficient light source.

The focus on sustainable design has encouraged some luminaire designers to create fixtures made from recycled products. This practice represents a transformation of the conceptual design process. Prior to sustainable design, a designer developed a concept for a luminaire based upon using new materials, and then businesses identified products that could be made from recycled materials. Starting the conceptual process with recycled products stimulates new designs for luminaires and conserves resources. Interiors of luminaires should be semi-specular, low iridescent, or white. Beyond the material composition of a luminaire, a sustainable fixture is designed to be energy-efficient. This is accomplished primarily by maximizing the lumen output. The luminaire efficacy rating (LER) can be used to compare the efficiency and effectiveness of different luminaires. Generally, the most efficient luminaires have high LERs. To reduce the accumulation of dirt and dust on lamps, luminaires should be sealed.

For existing buildings, the luminaires should be evaluated to determine whether the fixtures should be replaced or retrofitted. The most common retrofit application is to add a reflector to the interior of a luminaire. A reflector can enhance the lumen output by 20 to 30 percent. To improve optics, diffusers should be replaced with prismatic lenses made from either plastic or glass. "Egg crate" louvers should be replaced with parabolic louvers because the contour parabolic shape maximizes lumen output and provides an effective means of controlling glare.

Energy consumed in a space is based upon the wattage and the amount of time the energy is used. Controls are the element of a lighting system that can affect the length of time electricity is used in a space. Thus, to promote energy efficiency and sustainable development, a quality lighting environment has effective controls that have been installed with a thorough commissioning process which ensures that a building system performs according to the specifications. Ideally, as controls are operating in a space, users of the space should not notice changes in the illumination levels. Many studies have been conducted to determine the energy savings and practices of controls. Pacific Gas and Electric Company (PG&E) (2000) conducted a study to examine the technology, current practice, and economics of lighting controls in relationship to Title 24, California's Energy Efficiency Standards for Nonresidential Buildings. The study reviewed controls for single and bilevel dwellings, occupancy sensors, areas with daylight, automatic shut-off, and manual switches. As required by Title 24, most spaces must have "controls to reduce lighting." This generally involves bilevel controls and can be accomplished by "switching that turns off half the lights in a space; dimmers that reduce the entire space's light level by half; individual switches for two or more groups of luminaires in a space; or switching off the middle lamp of three-lamp luminaires" (PG&E, 2000, p. 1). There is little documentation to suggest the energy-effectiveness of Title 24. However, research studies provide support for saving energy by installing individual controls, and people seem to demonstrate more satisfaction with a lighting system that allows flexibility (Boyce, Eklund, and Simpson, 1999; Jennings, Rubenstein, DiBartolomeo, and Blanc, 2000; Rea, 1998).

Many studies conclude that occupancy sensors save energy and have a short payback period (Floyd, Parker, and Sherwin, 1996; Jennings, Rubenstein, DiBartolomeo, and Blane, 2000; Maniccia, Rutledge, Rea, and Morrow, 1999; PG & E, 1998; Rea, 1998; Richman, Dittmer, and Keller, 1996; Southern California Edison, 2000). The energy savings range from 19 to 90 percent, depending upon the purpose of the building and space. Generally, the least energy savings were demonstrated in private offices, open-plan spaces, classrooms, and conference rooms. Warehouses, restrooms, hotel meeting rooms, corridors, small storage areas, and hospital rooms appeared to have the greatest energy savings in using occupancy sensors. These results appear to indicate that occupancy sensors should be used in spaces that are not continuously being used, such as corridors, restrooms, and small storage areas. Occupancy controls with maximum sensitivity and adequate delay times appear to have the greatest success. The maximum energy savings will be derived from properly commissioned occupancy sensors. The range of payback periods was from 1.1 to 3 years.

Research further indicates that daylight controls save energy. Heiser (1998) found that ballasts with load shedding and daylight harvesting demonstrated a 76 percent energy savings. Smiley (1996) concluded that daylight controls reduced the air-conditioning load by 10 percent, and energy consumption decreased from 22 to 64 percent. An advanced technology for switching lighting systems is the Integrated Building Environmental Communications System (IBECS). Rubinstein and Pettler designed, built, and demonstrated an Internet addressable light switch system "that can provide multiple levels of light which can be triggered either from specially designed wall switches or from a digital communications network" (2001, p. 1). The system can be installed in existing buildings.

Sustainable design emphasizes the importance of incorporating daylight in spaces. Daylight integration reduces energy consumption and helps to improve the overall health of the atmosphere in buildings.

Energy savings are derived from switching patterns, window glazings, and window treatments and by adding skylights, light pipes, and light shelves. Daylight switching plans include automatic switching or dimmers (Figure 12.7). These technologies make it possible for lights next to windows to be turned off or dimmed, while luminaires away from the windows are turned on. Heat gain or loss through windows can be controlled by an efficient U-factor rating. The lower the U-value, the greater the resistance to heat transfer and the greater the insulation value. The National Fenestration Rating Council (NFRC) provides U-value ratings for windows.

Research suggests that the next energy-efficient window technologies are photovoltaic cells and electrochromic glazings (Lee, DiBartolomeo, and Selkowitz, 2000; Selkowitz, and Lee, 1998). Devices for windows, such as motorized shading systems and window coatings, can reduce peak electric loads by 20 to 30 percent in commercial buildings (Lee, Selkowitz, Levi, Blanc, McConahey, McLintock, Hakkarainen, Sloar, Myser, and May, 2002; NREL, 1998). Photovoltaic cells convert daylight energy into electricity. Electrochromic glazings alter optical properties, depending upon the voltage that is applied to the glass. This allows the tint of the windows to be adjusted based upon climatic conditions and the time of the day. To maximize energy efficiency, in addition to adding new skylights, light pipes, and

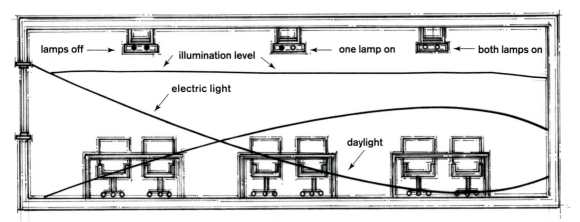

FIGURE 12.7 Daylight switching plan that illustrates lights that can be turned on or off depending upon the amount of daylight entering a space.

light shelves, old skylights should be evaluated to determine if they should be replaced with those incorporating the newest technologies.

Sustainable practice must include a thorough maintenance plan that includes cleaning instructions, a relamping program, and disposal guidelines. Dirt, dust, and age affect lumen output. The IESNA reports, "the combined effect of equipment age and dirt depreciation can reduce illuminance by 25 to 50% depending on the application and equipment used" (2000, p. 28-1). To enable maintenance workers to clean and relamp fixtures, the luminaires should be easily accessible. Cleaning instructions should include the proper detergent and how often luminaires, lamps, ceilings, walls, and windows should be cleaned. Abrasive detergents can scratch reflectors, which can cause a decrease in lumen output. To determine the proper cleaning detergent and method, consult manufacturers' product literature. Generally, the most energy-efficient time to relamp is 70 percent of rated life. Lamps burning beyond this time generally consume a high amount of electricity for the lumen output. To save labor costs, group relamping should be specified.

Light pollution
The excessive glow of light in the evening sky.

Light Pollution and Trespass

Emerging sustainable concerns are light pollution and light trespass. **Light pollution** is the excessive glow of light in the night sky (Figure 12.8). Light pollution is the result of excess lighting and sources aimed in inappropriate directions. As illustrated in the satellite photograph, light pollution is evident in large cities. Light becomes visible at night because light strikes water vapor and pollution.

Light trespass
The result of excess lighting and light sources aimed in inappropriate directions.

Light trespass occurs when the glare from a light source annoys an individual at an adjacent property. For example, people living in an apartment building could experience light trespass from the bright lights of a gas station that is located close to their bedroom window. Light trespass could also come from a bright light inside a home that is aimed at a neighbor's window.

Light pollution and light trespass are derived primarily from exterior lighting, which is a topic that is beyond the scope of this textbook. These topics are mentioned briefly to bring awareness to another

sustainable issue related to lighting systems. Knowledge of these concerns will assist the interior designer in discussing environmental lighting systems with clients and other professionals who are specifying exterior lighting, such as engineers, architects, or landscape architects. In addition, there could be commercial applications that require high levels of illumination close to windows in the interior of a building. This situation could contribute to light pollution and cause light trespass. For more information regarding light pollution and light trespass, contact the Dark Sky Association (DSA).

By specifying energy-efficient lighting systems, interior designers can conserve energy and natural resources for future generations. Key to this accomplishment is taking an integrated approach to lighting and keeping abreast of laws, standards, and codes. All individuals and resources must be involved in promoting energy efficiency and sustainable development. Most important, the users of a space must receive information and training about efficient use of lighting systems. An evaluation plan of the lighting system should be included with specifications. To utilize the most efficient technology, an interior designer should read current literature, attend seminars, and discuss improvements with manufacturers' representatives.

SUMMARY

- According to the EIA (2002), by the year 2020 world energy consumption will be 612 quadrillion British thermal units (Btu).

- The EIA estimates that electrical consumption for developing Asia and Central and South America will increase by 4.5 and 3.9 percent per year, respectively.

- The EPA has determined that lighting consumes approximately 23 percent of the electricity used in buildings.

- Based upon a study of 38 countries, the IAEEL reports that "Globally, electric lighting accounts for more than 2000 TWh electricity and 2900 million metric tons of carbon dioxide emissions (CO_2) per year."

- To promote energy efficiency and sustainable development, standards and codes have been established worldwide. An interior designer must always refer to the most current standards and codes because they are continuously updated.

- Important energy standards and codes that affect lighting efficiency are ASHRAE/IESNA 90.1-2001, MEC-95, and IECC-03.

- The U.S. Energy Policy Act of 1992 (EPAct-92) has significantly affected energy-efficient lighting. EPAct focuses on standards for lighting, window energy-efficient rating systems, and demand-side-management (DSM) programs.

- An economic analysis of lighting should include all expenses associated with an installed system, including lamps, luminaires, ballasts, transformers, controls, electricity, maintenance, disposal, and labor.

- An economic analysis of lighting can be conducted by examining the simple payback, or the life-cycle cost-benefit analysis (LCCBA). Many software tools are available to determine the costs and benefits of proposed energy conservation projects. The simple payback method is a quick estimate of the number of years required to payback the money invested in a lighting system.

- The Environmental Protection Agency (EPA) has determined that the issues related to sustainable design include pollution prevention, multiple and systematic effects, an environmental life-cycle assessment (LCA), magnitude of impact (local and global), and specification of environmental attributes.

- In specifying lighting systems the goals should be to: (1) reduce the use of nonrenewable resources, (2) control the use of renewable products, (3) minimize air, water, and soil pollution, (4) protect natural habitats, (5) eliminate toxic substances, and (6) reduce light pollution.
- The primary goals of sustainable disposal practices are to reduce the impact on the environment and decrease waste.
- In reviewing the impact of lighting on the environment, all processes and resources in the life cycle must be assessed, starting at the production of electricity, resources consumed for manufacturing lighting products, energy used for the operation of lighting systems, and disposal practices.
- A life-cycle assessment includes an examination of the lighting plan, specifications, daylight integration, consumer use, maintenance, and disposal practices.
- Sustainable design requires lamps that conserve energy and have high efficacy ratings, excellent light output, long life, high lumen maintenance, high color rendering, color stability, low mercury levels, and flexible disposal options. They should also be TCLP-compliant without additives.

Key Terms

light pollution

light trespass

persistent, bioaccumulation, toxic (PBT)

sustainable design

toxicity characteristic leaching procedure (TCLP)

Exercises

1. Locate the study of the written history of responses from lighting producers, conveyors, and consumers conducted by the American History Museum of the Smithsonian Institute. Analyze and summarize the results in a written report. Include how the results of

the study can influence energy-efficient lighting practices in the future.

2. Research local state laws and regulations affecting sustainable design and energy-efficient lighting systems. In a written report summarize the findings and discuss how the laws and regulations affect lighting systems.

3. Research international sustainable policies and regulations. In a written report compare and contrast policies, and provide suggestions for improving the sustainable regulations in your hometown.

4. Visit an office and a department in a retail store. For each space, conduct an analysis of the lighting systems from a sustainable and energy conservation perspective. Develop recommendations for improving the lighting systems, including retrofit applications. Summarize the results in a written report and include illustrations, photographs, or sketches.

5. Interview facility managers to determine sustainable and energy conservation lighting practices. In a written report summarize your findings and provide suggestions for improving energy efficiency and sustainable development.

REFERENCES

American History Museum of the Smithsonian Institute (2003). *Lighting the Way: A Project at the Smithsonian.* http://americanhistory.si.edu/.

American Society of Heating, Refrigeration and Air-Conditioning Engineers (1999). Energy efficient design of new buildings except new low-rise residential buildings, *ASHRAE/IES90.1-1999.* Atlanta, GA: ASHRAE.

Ander, G. (1997). *Daylighting Performance & Design.* New York: John Wiley & Sons.

BCAP. (1999, January). *Energy Conservation and Code Updates: Status of State Energy Codes.* Building Codes Assistance Project, last updated January 1999. http://www.energycodes.org/states/states.htm.

Barnes, P.R., Van Dyke, J.W., McConnell, B.W., and Das, S. (1996, July). *Determination Analysis of Energy Conservation Standards for Distribution Transformers.* Oak Ridge, TN: Oak Ridge National Laboratory. ORNL-6847.

Benya, J., Heschong, L., McGowan, T., Miller, N., and Rubinstein, F. (2001). *Advanced Lighting Guidelines.* White Salmon, WA: New Buildings Institute.

Bernstien, A., and Conway, K. (2000, March). The public benefits of California's investments in energy efficiency. Prepared for the California Energy Commission by the RAND Corporation. MR-1212.0-CEC.

Bierman, A., and Conway, K. (2000). Characterizing daylight photosensor systems performance to help overcome market barriers. *Journal of the Illuminating Engineering Society, 29(1),* 101–115.

Boyce, P.N., Elkund, N., and Simpson, S. (2000). Individual lighting control: Task performance, mood and illuminance. *Journal of the Illuminating Engineering Society, 29(1),* 131–142.

Boyce, P.N., Eklund, N., and Simpson, S. (1999). Individual lighting control: Task performance, mood and illuminance. *IESNA Conference Proceedings, 1999.* New York: Illuminating Engineering Society of North America.

Boylan, B.R. (1987). *The Lighting Primer.* Ames, IA: Iowa State University Press.

BSI (1992). *Code of Practice for Daylighting.* British Standard BS 8206, Part 2.

California Energy Commission (1999, July). *Building Energy Efficiency Standards.* Title 24 Pt. 6. California Energy Commission.

Carriere, L., and Rea, M. (1988). Economics of switching fluorescent lamps. *IEEE Transactions on Industry Applications, 24 (3),* 370–379.

CIBSE (1987). *Window Design.* CIBSE Applications Manual.

Clark, F. (1963). Accurate maintenance factors. *Illuminating Engineering,* 58(3), 124–131.

Coaton, J.R., and Marsden, A.M. (1997). *Lamps and Lighting* (4th ed.). London: Arnold.

DeCanio, S J. (1998, April). The efficiency paradox: Bureaucratic and organizational barriers to profitable energy-saving investments. *Energy Policy,* 26(5), 441–454.

Delene, J.G., Sheffield, J., Williams, K. A., Reid, R.L., and Hadley, S. (1999, September). *An Assessment of the Economics of Future Electric Power Generation Options and the Implications for Fusion,* ORNL/TM-1999-243, Oak Ridge National Laboratory.

Department of Energy (DOE) (2003) Research conservation and recovery act. http://tis.eh.doe.gov/oepa/law_sum/RCRA.HTM.

Energy Information Administration (EIA) (2002) *International Energy Outlook 2002,* Washington, DC: U.S. Department of Energy.

Energy Information Administration (EIA) (December 1998a), *Annual Energy Outlook 1999 with Projections to 2020,* DOE/EIA-0383(99), http://www.eia.doe.gov/oiaf/aeo99/homepage.html, Washington, DC: U.S. Department of Energy,

Energy Information Administration (EIA). (1996). *Annual Energy Outlook, with Projections to 2015.* Washington, DC: U.S. Department of Energy.

Energy Information Administration (EIA) (1995). *Annual Energy Review for 1995.* Washington, DC: U.S. Department of Energy.

Environmental Protection Agency (EPA) (March 1999). *Analysis of Emissions Reduction Options for the Electric Power Industry,* Washington, DC: U.S. Environmental Protection Agency, Office of Air and Radiation. http://www.epa.gov/capi/multipol/mercury.htm.

Erwine, B., and Heschong, L. (2000, March/April). Daylight: healthy, wealthy & wise. *Architectural Lighting Magazine.*

Floyd, D.B., Parker, D.S., and Sherwin, J.R. (1996, August). *Measured Field Performance and Energy Savings of Occupancy Sensors: Three Case Studies.* Florida Solar Energy Center, online publication FSEC-PF309.

Goulding, J.R., Lewis, J.O., and Steemers, T.C. (eds.) (1992). *Energy in Architecture: The European Passive Solar Handbook.* London: Batsford.

Henderson, S.T. (1977). *Daylight and Its Spectrum* (2nd ed.). Bristol, England: Adam Hilger.

Heiser, S. (1998). Controllable ballast retrofit using load shedding and daylight harvesting strategies: powerline.com.

Heschong Mahone Group (HMG) (August 1999). *Skylighting and Retail Sales, and Daylighting in Schools.* For Pacific Gas & Electric. http://www.pge.com.pec/daylight.

Heschong Mahone Group (HMG) (1997, May). *The Lighting Efficiency Technology Report, Vol. I: California Lighting Baseline.* For the California Energy Commission.

Illuminating Engineering Society, Lighting Design Practice Committee. (1968). Calculation of luminance coefficients based upon zonal-cavity method. *Illuminating Engineering,* 63(8), 423–432.

Illuminating Engineering Society of North America (IESNA) (2000). *IESNA Lighting Handbook* (9th ed.). New York: Illuminating Engineering Society of North America.

Interlaboratory Working Group. (2000, November). *Scenarios for a Clean Energy Future* (Oak Ridge, TN: Oak Ridge National Laboratory and Berkeley, CA: Lawrence Berkeley National Laboratory), ORNL/CON-476 and LBNL-44029.

Interlaboratory Working Group (1997, September). *Scenarios of U.S. Carbon Reductions—Potential Impacts of Energy Technologies by 2010 and Beyond.* Office of Energy Efficiency and Renewable Energy, U.S. Department of Energy.

International Association of Energy-Efficient Lighting (IAEEL) (2000). Global lighting: 1000 power plants. *IAEEL Newsletter,* 1-2/00, 1–4.

International Dark-Sky Association (IDA) (1996). *Information Sheets 10 and 20.* http://www.ida.org.

Jennings, J.F., Rubinstein, R., and DiBartolomeo, D.R. (2000). Comparisons of control options in private offices in an advanced lighting controls test bed. *Journal of the Illuminating Engineering Society,* 29(29), 39–60.

Koomey, J., Sanstad, A. H., and Shown, L.J. (1996, July). Energy-efficient lighting: market data, market imperfections, and policy success. *Contemporary Economic Policy.* Vol. XIV, no. 3 (Also LBL-37702.REV). 98-111.

Lawrence Berkeley National Laboratory (1997). *Lighting Source Book.* Berkeley, CA: Lawrence Berkeley National Laboratory.

Lawrence Berkeley National Laboratory. (1992). *Analysis of Federal Policy Options for Improving U.S. Lighting Energy Efficiency.* Berkeley, CA: Lawrence Berkeley National Laboratory.

Lee, E.S., DiBartolomeo, D.L., and Selkowitz, S.S. (2000, August). Electrochromic glazings for commercial buildings: Preliminary results from a full-scale testbed. *ACEEE 2000 Summer Study on Energy Efficiency in Buildings, Efficiency and Sustainability.* CA: Pacific Grove.

Lee, E.S., Selkowitz, M.S., Levi, S.L., Blanc, E., McConahey, M., McLintock, P., Hakkarainen, N.L., Myer, M.P., and May, (2002, August). Active load management with advanced window wall systems: Research and industry perspectives. *ACEEE 2002 Summer Study on Efficiency in Buildings.* CA: Pacific Grove.

Lewin, I. (1999, August). Light trespass: Research, results, and recommendations. *IESNA Annual Conference Proceedings,* 107.

Lewis, I. (2000, April). *Light Trespass Research, Final Report: TR-114914.* Electric Power Research Institute.

Lighting Design Lab (1998). *Daylight Models* (video). Seattle, WA: Lighting Design Lab.

Littlefair, P.J. (1991). Site layout planning for daylight and sunlight: A guide to good practice. *BRE Report BR 209.*

Maniccia, D., Rutledge, D., Rea, M., and Morrow, W. (1999). Occupant use of manual lighting control in private offices. *Journal of the Illuminating Engineering Society,* 28(2), 42–56.

Maniccia, D., Von Neida, B., and Tweed, A. (2000). Analysis of the energy and cost savings potential of occupancy sensors for commercial lighting systems. *Proceedings of the 2000 Annual Conference of the Illuminating Engineering Society of North America.*

Mistrick, R., Chen, C., Bierman, B., and Felts, D. (2000). A comparison of photosensor-controlled electronic dimming systems. *Proceedings of the 2000 Annual Conference of the Illuminating Engineering Society,* 29(1): 66–80.

Moore, F. (1985). *Concepts and Practice of Architectural Daylighting.* New York: Van Nostrand Reinhold.

National Lighting Product Information Program (NLPIP) (1998, March). *Specifier Reports: Photosensors.*

NREL (1998, September). *Photovoltaics and Commercial Buildings—A Natural Match.* Golden, CO: Produced for the U.S. Department of Energy by the National Renewable Energy Laboratory.

Office of Fossil Energy (1999, May). *Coal and Power Systems: Strategic Plan & Multi-Year Program Plans.* U.S. Department of Energy, Washington, DC.

Pacific Gas & Electric Company (2000). *Lighting Controls: Codes and Standards Enhancement (CASE) Study.* San Francisco, CA: Pacific Gas & Electric Company.

Pacific Gas & Electric Company (1999). *Daylighting Initiative Case Study.* http://www.pge.com/pec/daylight.

Pacific Gas & Electric Company (1998). Case study—occupancy sensor commissioning. *1998 Building Commissioning and Building Performance Tools Program.*

Phillips, D. (2000). *Lighting Modern Buildings.* Oxford: Architectural Press.

Portland Energy Conservation, I. (1992). *Building Commissioning Guidelines* (2nd ed.). Portland, OR: Bonneville Power Administration.

Rea, M.S. (1998). The quest for the ideal office controls system. *LRC Lighting Futures, 1998* 3 (3).

Richman, E.E., Dittmer, A.L., and Keller, J.M. (1996, Winter). Field analysis of occupancy sensor operation: Parameters affecting lighting energy savings. *Journal of Illuminating Engineering Society.*

Rubinstein, F., and Pettler, P. (2001). Final report on Internet addressable light switch. *High Performance Commercial Building Systems.* CA: California Energy Commission.

Rundquist, R.A., Johnson, K., and Aumann, D. (1993). Calculating lighting and HVAC interactions. *ASHRAE Journal,* 35(11), 28.

Rundquist, R.A., McDougall, T.G., and Benya, J. (1996). *Lighting Controls: Patterns for Design.* Prepared by R.A. Rundquist Associates for the Electric Power Research Institute and the Empire State Electrical Energy Research Corporation.

Selkowitz, S., and Lee, E.S. (1998, May). Advanced fenestration systems for improved daylight performance. *Daylighting E98 Conference Proceedings,* Canada: Ottawa, Ontario.

Slater, A., Bordass, B., and Heasman, T. (1996, March). Give people control of lighting controls. *IAELL Newsletter.*

Smiley, F. (1996, February). Durant middle school. *Architectural Lighting Magazine.*

Steffy, G.R. (1990). *Architectural Lighting Design.* New York: Van Nostrand Reinhold.

Southern California Edison (1999). *Energy Design Resources Case Studies: REMO and Timberland.* http://www.energydesignresources.com.

U.K. Department of the Environment (1998, March). Desktop guide to daylighting for architects. *Good Practice Guide 245.* Oxfordshire, England: ETSU.

U.S. Environmental Protection Agency (EPA) (2001). *Design for the Environment.* http://www.epa.gov/.

U.S. Office of Technology Assessment (1992). *Green Products by Design: Choices for a Cleaner Environment.* Washington, DC: Office of Technology Assessment.

Van Bogaert, G. (1996). Local control system for ergonomic energy-saving lighting. *Special IAEEEL Edition.*

Van den Beld, G.J., Begemann, S.H.A., and Tenner, A.D. (1997). Comparison of preferred lighting levels for two different lighting systems in north-oriented offices. *Light and Engineering, 5(3),* 48–52.

Veitch, J. (2000, July). Lighting guidelines from lighting quality research. *CIBSE/ILE Lighting 2000 Conference.* New York, U.K.

Veitch, J., and Newsham, G. (2000). Exercised control, lighting choices, and energy use: An office simulation experiment. *Journal of Environmental Psychology, 20(3),* 219–237.

Veitch, J., and Newsham, G. (1999, January). Individual control can be energy efficient. *IAEEL Newsletter.*

Veitch, J., and Newsham, G. (1998). Lighting quality and energy-efficiency effects on task performance, mood, health, satisfaction, and comfort. *Journal of the Illuminating Engineering Society, 27(1),* 107.

Webber, C.A., and Brown, R.E. (1998). Savings potential of ENERGY STAR voluntary labeling programs. *Proceedings of the 1998 ACEEE Summer Study on Energy Efficiency in Buildings.* Asilomar, CA: American Council for an Energy Efficient Economy, Washington, DC (also LBNL-41972).

CHAPTER 13

Illumination and Human Factors

OBJECTIVES

- Describe the results of research that indicate both negative and positive effects of lighting on a person's health.

- Understand how light affects the body's circadian rhythm.

- Describe the effects of age and disease on eyes.

- Apply an understanding of visual impairments to a lighting environment.

- Understand the behavioral and psychological effects of light on people.

- Understand how lighting affects people's emotions and perceptions of an environment.

- Apply the principles of universal design to a lighting environment.

RESEARCH indicates that lighting can affect the health, behavior, and psychological well-being of people. The fundamental basis for this research is the concept of the interaction between people and the environment. According to Wapner and Demick, the person-in-environment system assumes that the individual is "comprised [sic] of mutually defining *physical/biological* (e.g., health), *psychological* (e.g., self-esteem), and *sociocultural* (e.g., role as worker) aspects; and the environment is comprised [sic] of mutually defining aspects, including *physical* (natural and built), *interpersonal* (e.g., friend, spouse), and *socio-cultural* (rules of home, community, and culture) aspects" (2002, p. 5). An awareness of the interaction between a person and the environment is key to understanding how illumination can affect people. In designing a lighting system, the interior designer must know the users of the space within the context of the specific environment.

A quality lighting environment is planned to optimize the person-in-environment system. This involves a knowledge of current research and a thorough assessment of the project. Early lighting research focused on visual aspects of illumination as it related to workplace performance and perceptions of the environment. Current research still explores behavioral and psychological effects of illumination, but the emerging topic is how lighting affects biological processes in people. An assessment of a project includes the purpose of the space and the characteristics of the users of the space. (Chapter 22 reviews the client and project assessment process.) Understanding the effects of illumination on people can assist an interior designer in fulfilling the purpose of the environment. By knowing the specific characteristics of people, through observation, lighting can be designed to accommodate special needs of individuals within the context of the environment.

The effect of illumination on people includes physiological and psychological factors. Physiological aspects are related to health, vision, and the needs of special populations. Illumination can affect the psychological well-being of people by altering behavior and eliciting subjective impressions of an environment. The physiological and psychological effects of lighting on people should be applied to the design of the environment. Considerations should include the design of a layered lighting system, layout, physical attributes of the space, and ergonomic factors.

The effects of illumination on vision are discussed in previous chapters in this textbook and should serve as background to the information covered in this chapter. An overview of the vision process is presented in Chapter 1. (Chapter 5 reviews vision and color perceptions, followed by the subjective nature of brightness in Chapter 6.) Generally, the effects of illumination are dependent upon subjective responses, the context of the situation, personal vision attributes, light sources, directional qualities, and characteristics of elements of the design.

Physiological Factors

The person-in-environment system examines the interaction between an individual's health and the natural and built environments. Daylight and electrical light are elements of the natural and built environment, respectively, that can affect health.

Lighting Effects on Health

Photobiology is the science that examines the interactions of light and living organisms (http://www.pol-us.net, 2003). Research indicates that lighting has negative and positive effects on a person's health. Some of the negative effects from lighting include eyestrain, headaches, dizziness, skin cancer, and premature aging of skin and eyes. Research is exploring the effects of lighting on the growth and development of infants (Giradin, 1992; Miller, White, R., Whitman, O'Callaghn, and Maxwell, 1995; Quinn, Shin, Maguire, and Stone, 1999; Phelps and Watts, 1997; Reynolds, Hardy, Kennedy, Spencer, van Heuven, and Fielder, 1998). For example, individuals with epilepsy may experience seizures when exposed to flickering lights. Only a very small percentage of the population can detect flicker in a properly operating discharge lamp. Some populations have difficulties with fluorescent lamps. Kleeman (1981) found that fluorescent lighting affected hyperactive children by causing nutritional problems and a reduced attention span. Some diseases or medications can cause an individual to be extra sensitive to high illumination levels.

Photomedicine is the name of the science that is dedicated to using light to improve human health. Some of the positive effects of light on people are derived by the body's production of Vitamin D, which aids in the absorption of calcium. This can result in helping to prevent osteoporosis and rickets. Ultraviolet light is used to cure jaundice in infants. In addition, the medical profession is exploring light therapy as a means of curing certain forms of cancer, leukemia, and skin conditions. Light is also being used to regulate hormones, improve growth in children, and enhance the immune system. Research is examining the possibility that light can affect biological functions through means other than vision. A newly discovered photoreceptive mechanism in

Photobiology
The science that examines the interaction of light and living organisms.

the eye could lead to a better understanding of the effects of illumination on biological and psychological functions.

Light therapy has been successful in helping to regulate the biological clock that is associated with the body's circadian rhythm (National Mental Health Association, 2003; Rea, 2002; Rea, Bullough, and Figueiro, 2002; Rea, Figueiro, and Bullough, 2002). The circadian rhythm coordinates bodily functions for being awake and sleeping. The cycle affects hormone levels and metabolic processes. High levels of illumination are required to initiate the circadian process, and lower light levels trigger the production of melatonin, a hormone required for sleeping. People who experience jet lag or work night shifts often have difficulty regulating their circadian rhythms. Circadian effects of light was a major area of discussion at the 2002 LRO (Lighting Research Office) Symposium. Topics included human cancer development, productivity, and jet lag (Figueiro and Stevens, 2002; Lockley, 2002; Stevens, 2002). For the most part, problems associated with regulating circadian rhythms did not exist prior to electrical lighting because people functioned with the earth's natural clock of daylight and evening hours. Electrical lighting allows people to maintain high levels of illumination 24 hours a day, every day of the year. Most of the effects resulting from this unnatural cycle are still unknown.

> **Seasonal affective disorder (SAD)**
> A condition seemingly associated with an individual's inadequate exposure to sunlight.

However, problems related to circadian rhythms are associated with **seasonal affective disorder (SAD)**, which is a condition associated with an individual's inadequate exposure to sunlight. Some of the effects of SAD are depression, weight gain, lack of concentration, and sleeplessness. Many people experience SAD during the time of the year when the days are the shortest. This is especially problematic for people living in the northern region of the northern hemisphere, because of the few hours of sunlight. Research indicates that females are more likely to experience SAD than males. To help cure SAD, people are encouraged to spend more time outdoors, preferably on sunny days, early in the day. Some physicians will prescribe light therapy to eliminate SAD. Generally, this treatment involves exposure to high levels of illumination at the start of the day. Light therapy has also been helpful in regulating sleep patterns with dementia patients (Mishimia, Okawa, Hiskikawa, Hozumi, Hori, and Takashi, 1994; Satlin, Volicer,

Ross, Herz, and Campbell, 1992). People who have a severe case of SAD need a professional diagnosis of the disease, since medication, as well as light therapy, might be needed. SAD can be very serious, even resulting in suicide.

Vision Impairments

People with vision impairments require special lighting accommodations. This population includes all age groups, but is dominated by the elderly. The Bureau of the Census (1997) estimates that 16 million people in the United States have a visual impairment. The elderly population, defined as people over the age of 65, is growing at a fast pace. Projections by the Department of Health and Human Services (1997) indicate that the United States will have approximately 70 million elderly people by the year 2030. To specify lighting environments that support people with visual impairments requires an understanding of the vision process and the effects of age and disease on eyes.

All the functions of vision deteriorate with age. The most common changes in vision include a reduction in the size of the pupil, decreased elasticity of muscles, and a yellowing and thickening of the lens. The decrease in the eye's elasticity and the thickening of the lens results in *presbyopia*. This condition affects visual acuity and the ability to see objects at close range. Age-related macular degeneration affects central vision and is a common reason for vision impairment in elderly. In addition, crystallizing of the lens increases sensitivity to glare. The natural aging process on eyes affects visual acuity, color identification, the adaptation process, peripheral vision, depth perception, motion detection, and tolerance of glare. Visual impairments also affect eye-hand coordination.

In addition to the effects of age on vision, the elderly are prone to diseases of the eye, including cataracts, glaucoma, and diabetic retinopathy. *Cataracts* are a clouding over the lens of the eye and occur very frequently in the elderly. The extent of vision loss resulting from cataracts ranges from no affect to blindness. Cataracts cause blurring and increase sensitivity to bright lights and glare. Clouding can affect color identification, especially colors in the cool spectrum.

Glaucoma is actually several diseases that are caused by the lack of fluid draining from the eye. The pressure created from the lack of drainage damages the optic nerve. Without proper treatment, blindness can occur. Glaucoma can cause blind spots, blurred vision, and a loss of peripheral vision followed by central vision. Diabetes is common in the elderly, and it affects vision by contributing to cataracts and diabetic retinopathy. High levels of sugar in the bloodstream cause diabetic retinopathy. Eyesight can be affected by a change in the central field of vision and color identification. For more information regarding vision impairments, refer to the National Eye Institute (http://www.nei.nih.gov/) or the Lighthouse National Center for Vision and Aging (http://www.aoa.gov/directory/127.html).

Psychological Factors

Wapner and Demick (2002) indicate that the person-in-environment system includes an individual's psychological well-being as well as interpersonal attributes of the environment. Lighting research has focused on the effects of illumination on these factors. Generally, the topics include characteristics of natural and electrical light sources and their behavioral and psychological effects on people. For example, Veitch, Gifford, and Hine (1991) conducted a research study, "Demand Characteristics and Full Spectrum Lighting Effects on Performance and Mood." Chapter 2 discusses research studies that found positive effects of daylight on activities in hospitals, schools, and retail stores (Heschong, 1999; Heschong, 1997, Littlefair, 1996; Littlefair, 1991; Wu and Ng, 2003). In addition, Beauchemin and Hays (1996) found that individuals in psychiatric units who had rooms with natural daylight stayed approximately three days less than patients living with electrical sources.

Researchers have been interested in understanding which characteristics of electrical light sources affect people. The topics include specific lamps, color rendering index, color temperatures, quantity of light, intensity, spectral composition, and distribution patterns. Some studies have explored lighting effects on special populations, including individuals with Alzheimer's disease, cancer, AIDS, infants, and the elderly (Figueiro, Eggleston, and Rea, 2002; Graham and Michel, 2003; Miller, 2002; Noelle-Waggoner, 2002).

In examining lighting effects on behavior, research has focused on the performance of office workers, on cognitive processes, and on wayfinding. The effect of lighting on psychological factors includes attitudes, stress, satisfaction, interpersonal communication, perceptions of space, motivation, control, and stimulation. The following two sections provide a summary of lighting effects on the behavior and psychology of people. For additional research studies, refer to the reference list at the end of this chapter.

Lighting Effects on Behavior

Some of the earliest lighting research investigated the effects of quantity of light on productivity in the workplace (Blackwell, 1946; Boynton and Boss, 1971; Boyce, 1973; Hughes and McNelis, 1978; Simonson and Brozek, 1948; Weston, 1962). At that time, electrical light sources were relatively new, and the lighting industry tried to get employers to invest in lighting systems. The cost-benefit approach served as a rationale for purchasing lighting. Research studies demonstrated that quality lighting improved worker productivity, and the increase in performance offset the cost of the lighting system.

Owing to the many interdependent factors that can affect performance, including noise, stress, ambient temperature, and daylight, current research regarding the effect of lighting on productivity is inconclusive. Some studies have demonstrated that instead of a direct relationship between lighting and productivity, improved performance may be the result of a higher level of satisfaction with working conditions (Boyce, Akashi, Hunter, and Bullough, 2003; Ducker, 1999; Isen, Daubman, and Nowicki, 1987). Research has indicated that control over one's environment, including lighting, is a significant factor in employee satisfaction (Boyce, Eklund, and Simpson, 2000; Hedge, Erickson, and Rubin, 1992; Sherrod and Cohen, 1979; Veitch and Newsham, 1998; Veitch and Newsham, 1999).

To determine the effect of illumination on performance, research studies have examined specific characteristics of lighting systems, including fluorescent lamps, ballasts, and type of luminaire. Full-spectrum fluorescent lamps have been researched extensively to determine their effect on performance. Generally, research indicates no effect on performance or mood (Berry, 1983; Boray, Gifford, and Rosenblood, 1989; Food and Drug Administration, 1986; Veitch, 1997; Veitch and McColl, 1995; Veitch, Gifford, and Hine, 1991). However, research does indicate that fluorescent light flicker can increase headaches and stress (Veitch and McColl, 2001; Kuller and Laike, 1998; Wilkins, Nimmo-Smith, Slater, and Bedocs, 1989). Veitch and Newsham (1998) found improved performance in clerical work by using electronic, rather than magnetic, ballasts in the workplace. Moreover, the use of electronic ballasts reduced headaches (Wilkins, et al., 1989).

In addition to eliminating light flicker, electronic ballasts might be preferred because they operate more quietly than magnetic ballasts. Many studies have shown a significant relationship between noise and quality of performance (Banbury, Macken, Tremblay, and Jones, 2001; Evans and Cohen, 1987; Gawron, 1982; Hygge, 1991; Hygge and Knez, 2001; Nelson, Nilsson, and Johnson, 1984). The type of luminaire might contribute to noise in an environment. Fixtures that are made from hard materials and have relatively large areas with flat surfaces can reflect sound.

Generally, research indicates that the type of luminaire and its light distribution patterns does not affect worker performance (Eklund, Boyce, and Simpson, 2000; Veitch and Newsham, 1998). However, research demonstrates that proper lighting for the computer's visual display terminal (VDT) is required to enhance worker productivity (Clark, 2001; National Lighting Bureau, 1988). To reduce eyestrain and dry eyes, physicians recommend frequent eye movement. This can be accomplished by creating an interesting environment around the VDT screen and varying illumination levels.

Emotions and Perceptions

Everyone's emotions have been affected by illumination. A bright, sunny day can make someone feel cheerful and outgoing. In contrast, a dark and gloomy day can elicit feelings of depression and sadness. The lighting in the United States Memorial Holocaust Museum in Washington, D.C., was specifically planned to simultaneously evoke feelings of compassion, sadness, and outrage in the viewers. The permanent exhibit begins with two images that have an immediate impact on viewers (Figure 13.1). A large photograph of people who were killed is directly in front of people when they leave the elevator. The words "THE HOLOCAUST," carved in black steel, next to the photograph, bring an immediate connection to the tragic event. Lighting plays a significant role in reinforcing the impact; only the words and the photograph are illuminated in a very dark space. Another powerful use of lighting at the museum is the method used to illuminate a railroad car, which was used to transport victims (Figure 13.2). A spotlight was

FIGURE 13.1 One of the first images seen in the permanent exhibition space of the Holocaust Museum in Washington, D.C. The high-contrast lighting emphasizes the images and enhances emotional responses from visitors of the museum.

FIGURE 13.2 The railroad car used to transport victims of the Holocaust. The lighting technique emphasizes the horrible conditions.

used on one of two small windows. The interior of the car is completely dark, except for a small streak of light along the wall and floor. This light emphasizes the extremely low levels of light that people had while traveling to a prison camp. Furthermore, the small area of light on the floor reinforces the minute space people had for the journey. Over one hundred people were crammed into each small car.

Research indicates that light affects emotions, cognitive processes, memory, communication, and perceptions (Baron, Rea, and Daniels, 1992; Knez, 2001; Knez, 1995). A great deal of research has been directed at the effect of lighting on moods, including differences in moods for men and women. In lighting preference studies by Flynn (1977), the results indicate that people prefer warm and dim lights, compared to cool and bright sources. Knez (1995) experimented with the effects of various electrical light sources on mood and cognition of males and females. The findings demonstrate that women's negative moods and problem-solving skills decreased in the warm (3000K) light and increased under cool (4000K) sources. Men's negative feelings and problem-solving skills increased in the warm, compared to cool lighting. Knez and Enmarker (1998) found that office lighting affects mood differently in men and women. Warm light generated positive moods for both genders.

Mood can also be affected by the lighting patterns in a space. Generally, uniform lighting patterns are viewed as monotonous and boring. Their effect on people becomes more pronounced when tasks being performed are repetitive and require a long period of time to complete. Generally, nonuniform lighting at low illumination levels is perceived as romantic, intimate, and relaxing (Flynn, 1977). Nonuniform lighting at low levels is often specified to meet the restorative needs of people who are easily agitated or dealing with stress. Views of nature, candlelight, and a fire in fireplaces are also therapeutic lighting solutions. Generally, people tend to stay in a space longer when lighting improves their appearance. Therefore, people tend to engage in more social interaction when they perceive that lighting enhances their physical features.

Stimulation is a psychological need that can be met by appropriate lighting. Some research has found a connection between stimulation and the spectral distribution of a light source. Rea (1999) reported that a blue spectrum stimulates the rods in eyes, and Navvab (2000) suggests that bluer light should be used in the workplace. The proper amount of stimulation can increase attentiveness, reduce fatigue, alter perceptions of time, and promote positive moods. A stimulating environment can increase the satisfaction of performing boring tasks by providing interest and reducing the perception of time (Gawron, 1982; Hughes and McNelis, 1978). Varying light levels, using nonuniform lighting patterns, and having windows with views can achieve stimulation in an environment. Windows in an office are so important in the Netherlands that the country has enacted laws requiring desks to be located no farther than 16 feet from a window.

Stimulation is a factor in attracting attention to objects or areas in a room. Creating contrast and specifying the best angle are key to attracting attention to an object. An illumination level that is the same for the surrounding area and the accent object will not effectively emphasize the item. One approach to achieving contrast is to illuminate the object of attention at a higher level than its surrounding area. (See Chapter 2 for a discussion on accent lighting.)

Too much stimulation can cause anxiety and stress in people. Excessive stimulation from lighting can be derived from glare, flickering, unnatural light patterns, noise, or color distortions. These conditions can make people feel uncomfortable, unsafe, irritable, and generally dissatisfied with the environment. People with visual impairments and individuals with dementia are even more inclined to be adversely affected by stressful lighting environments. The uncertainty associated with an inability to adequately see objects or architectural elements in a space increases anxieties to the extent that people with visual impairments may alter their lifestyle. For example, people with visual impairments tend to avoid restaurants with low levels of lighting or visit only familiar places. People with dementia often have visual impairments and are challenged by a lack of memory and a disorientation of time and space. Lighting can provide visual cues that can assist with memory loss and wayfinding. Exposure to daylight and exterior views can help to alleviate problems associated with disorientation.

Some individuals with dementia experience a phenomenon termed *sundowning,* which is associated with behavior problems during the late afternoon and early evening (Cohen-Mansfield, Werner, and Freedman, 1995; Graham and Michel, 2003; Martin, Marler, Shochat and Ancoli-Israel, 2002). Individuals experiencing sundowning can be confused and agitated easily. Researchers suggest that behavior problems associated with this time of the day could be related to lower levels of illumination. Therefore, to help reduce confusion and anxiety, especially in unfamiliar environments, effective lighting is essential.

People can also feel stressed when they are in a dark space, a building that is unfamiliar to them, or in an emergency situation. To help alleviate stress in public spaces, wayfinding lighting and adequate signage should be well planned. Adequate orientation systems are especially important in emergency conditions. In a fire or any other type of disaster, people are extraordinarily stressed. One approach to reducing panic is to provide easy, visible cues for exiting buildings. (Refer to

Chapter 14 for more information about lighting and safety issues.) To reduce anxieties, adequate illumination should always exist in confined spaces, such as hallways and stairways.

There are many ways lighting can affect perceptions of an environment. Lighting can alter perceptions of the architectural elements of an interior. As discussed in Chapter 5, lighting can also affect perception of colors in an environment. The placement of light, the intensity of light, and the type of luminaire can affect perceptions of spatial volume. Generally, vertical lighting defines the volume in a space. Illuminating walls and ceilings can make a space appear larger. A nonuniform distribution of light, such as an application with downlights, can reduce the apparent size of a room. Lighting can also change the perception of depth in a space. For example, a hallway can appear to be shorter if a bright light is placed at the end of it (Figure 13.3).

Lighting can create many subjective reactions to an environment and is dependent upon individuals' expectations of the purpose of the space. Researchers have asked people in a variety of environments to describe their perceptions of the lighting. Generally, people have been asked to determine if the space is bright, dim, warm, cool, gloomy, or cheerful. Figure 13.4 illustrates how perceptions of a room can be altered by changing the location and type of luminaire. Many research studies have indicated that when walls and ceilings are illuminated in

FIGURE 13.3 The perceptual depth of space is affected by the lighting placement at the end of the hallway.

FIGURE 13.4
Research results indicate
that when walls and ceilings
are illuminated in a space,
people perceive the room
as bright and pleasant.

a space, people perceive the room as bright and pleasant (Carter, Slater, Perry, Mansfield, Loe, and Sandoval, 1994; Hill and Cook, 2003; Loe, Mansfield, and Rowlands, 1994). Spaces that focus only on horizontal lighting are perceived to be dark and gloomy. Subjects indicated the most preferred interiors had illumination on vertical surfaces and directly on a task.

Research has also indicated gender differences regarding perceptions of lighting in a space (Knez, 1997; Knez and Enmarker,1998; Knez and Kers, 2000; Knez, 2001; Nelson, et al., 1984; Belcher and Kluczny, 1987). Based upon several research studies, Knez concluded, "Females and males were found to show differing levels of emotions (levels of positive and negative mood) to colour of light and combinations of colour of light and illuminance and/or CRI levels" (2001, p. 202). In addition, females were more expressive in their views of lighting and tended to perceive illumination as more intense and glaring than did males (Brody and Hall, 1993; Dimberg and Lundqvist, 1990; Knez, 1995; Knez and Enmarker, 1998; Kenz and Kers, 2000). Knez (2001) also found that short-term memory was improved for individuals working with warm (3000K) lighting. Long-term memory for males was most successful using daylight (5500K).

Universal Design

Lighting systems should be planned to accommodate all people, whenever possible, without modifications. This can be accomplished by specifying a lighting plan that meets the physical and psychological needs of the users of the space.

Physical Environment

A quality lighting environment reflects the principles of **universal design**. In designing environments that meet the needs and abilities of people of all ages, an interior designer should review the current literature. Research studies are invaluable in providing guidance and recommendations for effective environments.

There are many aspects of lighting that should be considered when applying the principles of universal design, including visual acuity, manual dexterity, and placement of luminaires, switches, and outlets. Visual acuity is effected by illumination level, type of lamp, distribution, color temperature, color rendering, ballast, and the ability to control lighting. Visual acuity requires addressing the needs of individuals with visual impairments and diseases. Specifying value contrasts for tasks can also enhance visual acuity. (This information is discussed in the next section of this chapter.)

Wall switches and luminaires should be intuitive to use and easy to operate. Generally, rocker or touch switches are the easiest. Devices that have to be pinched or twisted should be avoided. Switches and dimmers should be accessible and easy to operate. Portable luminaires that have the switching mechanism on the cord should be avoided. Luminaires that allow the user to change the direction of the light source should be weighted, and the shade should be designed to prevent

Universal Design
An approach to the physical environment that is focused on accommodating the needs of all people, whenever possible, without modifications.

burns from the heat from the lamp. The Research Group for Inclusive Environments (RGIE) (2002) conducted a study with the elderly to determine which portable luminaire was the most satisfactory for people with visual impairments in an office environment. The results indicated a preference for the "Anglepoise" luminaire with a 60W tungsten pearl lamp primarily because of ease of use (Figure 13.5). The model has a reach of 43 inches (1100 mm), and the shade had an 8-inch (200 mm) diameter. According to RGIE, people reported that the Anglepoise luminaire was "easy to use, easy to get the light where it was wanted, quite flexible" (2003, p. 1).

Placement of luminaires, switches, and outlets should be accessible to people with disabilities, including individuals in wheelchairs. Luminaires should always be positioned to eliminate shadows on work surfaces. Portable luminaires that are designed to allow the user to adjust the direction or control the level of illumination should be located at a convenient distance to the user. The average range of reach is 24 inches (610 mm). The American Disability Act (ADA) (2003) specifies that wall-mounted luminaires mounted between 27 and 80 inches (685 mm and 2030 mm) above a finished floor (AFF) should not

FIGURE 13.5 People with visual impairments in an office environment selected the Anglepoise tungsten luminaire as the preferred portable luminaire, primarily because of ease of use.

extend more than 4 inches (100 mm) from the wall. Luminaires at or below 27 inches (685 mm) AFF may protrude any amount. The lowest element of a suspended luminaire should allow for 80 inches (2030 mm) of clear headroom. Freestanding luminaires mounted on posts may overhang 12 inches (305 mm) horizontally and 27 to 80 inches (685 mm to 2030 mm) AFF.

Wall switches and outlets should be mounted at a level that is accessible to people standing or sitting in a wheelchair. Universal access is 15 to 48 inches (380 mm to 1219 mm) AFF. ADA specifies that electrical receptacles on walls shall be mounted no less than 15 inches (380 mm) AFF. However, in following the principles of universal design, a convenient location for wall switches and outlets is 38 and 18 inches (965 and 457 mm) AFF, respectively. Regarding illumination requirements, ADA requires signage in the 100 to 300 lux range (10 to 30 footcandles), and elevator thresholds should be a minimum of 50 lux (5 fc).

Special Populations

Effective environments reflect knowledge of the specific needs of individuals. Understanding the characteristics of the users requires observations, interviews, and often researching special situations. For example, when designing a space for a person with AIDS, programming should include researching the disease to discover how it affects an individual's physical, behavioral, and psychological aspects. The lighting should then be planned to accommodate these specific needs. (Chapters 21 and 22 provide detailed information about programming and project assessment.)

People with visual impairments require special lighting considerations. This is especially important in public spaces, such as medical centers, restaurants, museums, and retail stores. Generally, illumination levels should be approximately 20 percent higher for people with visual impairments, with a special emphasis on quality task lighting. Increases in the intensity of light must be accomplished without glare. People with visual impairments are often excessively sensitive to glare. Matte finishes on work surfaces and walls will help to reduce glare. Indirect light can be a good solution for general illumination. Lamp sources must be properly shielded, and windows should have a means to diffuse sunlight. To increase the level of illumination in a space, light-colored materials and finishes should be specified. Walls and ceilings should be illuminated in a uniform distribution pattern. Even illumination levels also help individuals who experience a lack of depth perception. This is especially important in transition areas, such as stairways and doorways. Lights should be located on steps, and value contrasts can help an individual to determine the size of a step. Audible alarm systems should be installed, and occupancy sensors could be considered.

The RGIE (2002) study indicated that people with visual impairments need a luminaire that is easy to adjust, remains fixed in the desired position, distributes light over a large area, and conceals the lamp from view. Ceiling-mounted spotlights are not satisfactory, because they are difficult to adjust and the light was too dim for task lighting. Many people expressed concerns with lamps, such as tungsten-halogen, that emit heat. Often the heat generated by the lamp makes it difficult to hold the device that is provided to adjust the direction of the light source.

Elderly people often have visual impairments resulting from the effects of age on eyes. In addition to the recommendations provided earlier in this section, there are some other suggestions for designing lighting for the elderly. Because of the yellowing and thickening of the lens, veiling reflections should be avoided, and light sources should be in the bluish-white range (4100k). In addition, to assist in color identification, yellow in interior spaces should be avoided and illumination levels need to be higher than normal, but without glare. Ensuring gradual light level changes, especially in areas immediately next to outdoor space, should accommodate the decrease in the adaptation ability of the eyes.

Elderly people experience other physical changes that should be considered when designing a lighting environment. Generally, reaction time to light and sound is reduced, and there is a decline in motor skills. Luminaires and switches should be selected that are easy to operate because of the loss of dexterity. The degradation in vision and physical skills affects the safety of the elderly and can lead to feelings of insecurity. Thus, it is critical to have excellent illumination in areas of potential danger, such as exterior doors, kitchens, bathrooms, and at the top and bottom of stairways. (Chapter 14 covers issues related to safety and security.) Most elderly people experience a decline in hearing. To compensate for this, many depend upon reading lips and interpreting body language. To successfully do these things requires adequate lighting on people, especially in locations of high interaction, such as dining tables or conversational areas in a living room. Fluorescent lighting systems with magnetic ballasts can cause interference in hearing aids. Lamps and ballasts that elicit noise or flickering should be avoided.

The high increase of people diagnosed with dementia, most notably Alzheimer's disease, has precipitated many research studies that have focused on identifying appropriate physical attributes for their environments (Passini, Pigot, Rainville, and Tetreault, 2000; Winchip, 1990; Zeisel, 2000). Dementia affects memory and brings about personality changes in people. Research indicates that people with Alzheimer's disease are prone to agitation when exposed to flickering lights (Hiatt, 1991). A lack of daylight has been linked to depression, fatigue, and hyperactivity. As a result of memory loss, people often experience disorientation with time and space. Windows help to provide a time reference, and a view of the sky and ground can assist in space orientation for people in bed. Wayfinding is a significant problem for people with dementia. Lighting cues can help such people find their way through a building. Different illumination levels can designate changes in spaces. In a long-term care center, a personalized light fixture outside the door of patients' apartments can help them to recognize their unit. Because of their memory loss, whenever possible, portable luminaires should not be moved.

The results of research should be applied. The key to success is understanding that lighting research is a relatively new field of study and is continuously improving and expanding. Thus, to specify a lighting environment that addresses the health, behavior, emotions, and perceptions of people, an interior designer should always refer to the most current research. In analyzing research, it is critical to scrutinize the specifics of a study. Each study is conducted with specific subjects and parameters. To apply the research to practice, there should be similarities between the research study and an interior project. The material discussed in this chapter and the preceding chapters in this textbook should be applied to the lighting design process that is covered in the next unit.

SUMMARY

- The person-in-environment system examines the interaction between an individual's health and the natural and built environment.
- Research indicates that lighting has negative and positive effects on a person's health. Some of the negative effects from lighting include eyestrain, headaches, dizziness, skin cancer, and aging of skin and eyes.
- Light therapy has been successful in helping to regulate the biological clock that is associated with the body's circadian rhythm.
- The Bureau of the Census (1997) estimates that 16 million people in the United States have a visual impairment.
- The Department of Health and Human Services (1997) indicates that the United States will have approximately 70 million elderly by the year 2030.
- All the functions of vision deteriorate with age. The most common changes in vision include a reduction in the size of the pupil, less elasticity of muscles, and a yellowing and thickening of the lens.
- Lighting research has focused on the characteristics of natural and electrical light sources and their behavioral and psychological effects on people. The topics include specific lamps, CRI, color temperatures, quantity of light, intensity, spectral composition, and distribution patterns.
- To determine the effect of illumination on performance, research studies have examined specific characteristics of lighting systems, including fluorescent lamps, ballasts, and types of luminaire.
- Research indicates that light affects emotions, cognitive processes, memory, communication, and perceptions.
- Lighting can alter perceptions of the architectural elements of an interior.

■ A quality lighting environment reflects the principles of universal design. Lighting systems should be planned to accommodate all people, whenever possible, without modifications.

Key Terms

photobiology   universal design
seasonal affective disorder
   (SAD)

Exercises

1. Visit three buildings or select three photographs of interiors. For each space, identify the characteristics of the illumination and how these characteristics affect emotions and perceptions. Provide recommendations for improving the spaces. Summarize your results in a written report, and include illustrations, photographs, or sketches.

2. Interview people in an office, restaurant, retail store, and healthcare facility to determine their perceptions of the interior. Analyze the results, and determine the positive and negative attributes of each space. Summarize the results in a written report, and include illustrations, photographs, or sketches.

3. Select five photographs of the interiors of public places. For each space identify the purpose of the space, the most frequent users, and the anticipated behavioral response to the lighting environment. Summarize your results in a written report, and include photographs.

4. Research the psychological and physical needs of a special population. Write an essay that includes specific lighting requirements for that population. Illustrations of luminaires should be included.

5. Research a disease that affects the psychological and physical needs of the afflicted individuals. Write an essay that includes specific lighting requirements for individuals with the disease. Illustrations of luminaires should be included.

REFERENCES

Ander, G. (1997). *Daylighting Performance & Design.* New York: John Wiley & Sons.

Archea, J. (1985). Environmental factors associated with stair accidents by the elderly. *Clinics in Geriatric Medicine, 1,* 555–569.

Arendt, J., and Broadway, J. (1987). Light and melatonin as zeitgebers in man. Chronobiology International, 4, 273–282.

Averill, J.R. (1973). Personal control over aversive stimuli and its relationship to stress. *Psychological Bulletin, 80,* 286–303.

Banbury, S., Macken, W., Tremblay, S., and Jones, D. (2001). Noise distraction affects memory. *Human Factors, 43(1),* 12–29.

Barnes, R.D. (1981). Perceived freedom and control in the built environment. In J.H. Harvey, (ed.), *Cognition, Social Behavior, and the Environment.* Hillsdale, NJ: Erlbaum, pp. 409–422.

Baron, R.A., and Rea, M.S. (1991). Lighting to soothe the mood. *Lighting Design and Application, 12,* 30–32.

Baron, R.A., Rea, M.S., and Daniels, S.G. (1992). Effects of indoor lighting (illuminance and spectral distribution) on the performance of cognitive tasks and interpersonal behaviors: The potential mediating role of positive affect. *Motivation and Emotion, 16,* 1–33.

Beach, L.R., Wise, B.K., and Wise, J.A. (1988). The human factors of color in environmental design: A critical review. *Technical Report,* NASA Ames Research Center, Moffett Field, CA.

Beauchemin, K.M., and Hays, P. (1996). Sunny hospital rooms expedite recovery from severe and refractory depressions. *Journal of Affective Disorders, 40,* 49–51.

Begemann, S.H.A., Aarts, M.P.J. and Tenner, A.D. (1994, November). *Daylight, Artificial Light, and People.* Paper presented at the 1994 Annual Conference of the Illuminating Engineering Society of Australia and New Zealand, Melbourne, Australia.

Belcher, M.C., and Kluczny, R. (1987, June). The effects of light on decision making: Some experimental results. *Proceedings of CIE 21st Session,* Venice, Italy: Central Bureau of CIE.

Benya, J., Heschong, L., McGowan, T., Miller, N., and Rubinstein, F. (2001). *Advanced Lighting Guidelines.* White Salmon, WA: New Buildings Institute.

Berry, J.L. (1983). Work efficiency and mood states of electronic assembly workers exposed to full-spectrum and conventional fluorescent illumination. *Dissertation Abstracts International, 44,* 635B.

Bierman, A., and Conway, K. (2000). Characterizing daylight photosensor systems performance to help overcome market barriers. *Journal of the Illuminating Engineering Society, 29(1),* 101–115.

Birren, F. (1969). *Light, Color and Environment.* New York: Van Nostrand Reinhold.

Blackwell, H.M. (1946). Contrast thresholds of the human eye. *Journal of the Optical Society of America, 36,* 624–643.

Blehar, M.C., and Rosenthal, N.E. (eds.) (1989). *Seasonal Affective Disorders and Phototherapy:* New York: Guilford Press.

Boray, P., Gifford, R., and Rosenblood, L. (1989). Effects of warm white, cool white and full-spectrum fluorescent lighting on simple cognitive performance, mood and ratings of others. *Journal of Environmental Psychology, 9,* 297–308.

Boubekri, M., Hull IV, R.B., and Boyer, L.L. (1991). Impact of window size and sunlight penetration on office workers' mood and satisfaction: A novel way of assessing sunlight. *Environment and Behavior, 23,* 474–493.

Bowmaker, J.K., and Dartnall, H.J. (1980). Visual pigments of rods and cones in human retina. *Journal of Physiology,* 298, 501–511.

Boyce, P.N., Elkund, N., and Simpson, S. (2000). Individual lighting control: Task performance, mood and illuminance. *Journal of the Illuminating Engineering Society,* 29(1), 131–142.

Boyce, P.N., Eklund, N., and Simpson, S. (1999). Individual lighting control: Task performance, mood and illuminance. *IESNA Conference Proceedings, 1999.* New York: Illuminating Engineering Society of North America.

Boyce, P.R. (1973). Age, illuminance, visual performance, and preference. *Lighting Research and Technology,* 5, 125–139.

Boyce, P.R. (1981). *Human Factors in Lighting,* New York: Macmillan.

Boyce, P.R. (1987). Lighting research and lighting design: Bridging the gap. *Lighting Design and Application,* 17(5), 10–12 and 50–51; 17(6), 38–44.

Boyce, P.R., Akashi, Y., Hunter, C.M., and Bullough, J.D. (2003). The impact of spectral power distribution on the performance of an achromatic visual task. *Lighting Research and Technology,* 35(2), 141–161.

Boynton, R.M., and Boss, D.E. (1971). The effect of background luminance and contrast upon visual search performance. *Illuminating Engineering,* 66, 173–186.

Bradley, R.D., and Logan, H.L. (1964). A uniform method for computing the probability of comfort response in a visual field. *Illuminating Engineering,* 59(3), 189–206.

Brainard, G.C., and Bernecker, C.A. (1995, November). The effects of light on physiology and behavior. *Proceedings of CIE 23rd Session,* Vol. 2. New Delhi, India: Central Bureau of CIE.

Brody, L.R., and Hall, J.A. (1993). Gender and emotion. In M. Lewis and J.M. Havilands, (eds.), *Handbook of Emotions.* New York: Guilford, pp. 447–460.

Bureau of the Census (1997). *Statistical Abstract of the United States: 1997,* Vol. 117. Washington, DC: Bureau of the Census, p. 143.

Butler, D.L., and Biner, P. M. (1990). A preliminary study of skylight preferences, *Environment and Behavior,* 22, 119–140.

Butler, D.L., and Biner, P.M. (1989). Effects of setting on window preferences and factors associated with those preferences. *Environment and Behavior,* 21, 17–31.

Campbell, S.S., and Murphy, P.J. (1998). Extraocular circadian phototransduction in humans. *Science,* 279, 396–399.

Carter, D.J., Slater, A.I., and Moore, T. (1999, June). A study of occupier-control lighting systems. *Proceedings of the 24th Session of the Commission Internationale de l'Eclairage,*
Warsaw, Poland. Vol. 1, Part 2. Vienna, Austria: CIE Central Bureau, pp. 108–110.

Cohen, S., Evans, G.W., Stokols, D., and Krantz, D.S. (1986). *Behavior, Health, and Environmental Stress.* New York: Plenum.

Cohen-Mansfield, J., Werner, P., and Freedman, L. (1995). Sleep and agitation in agitated nursing home residents: An observational study. *American Sleep Disorders Association and Sleep Research Society,* 18(8), 674–680.

Collins, K.W. (1980). Effects of conversational noise, coping techniques, and individual differences on the performance of academic tasks. *Dissertation Abstracts International,* 41, (1-B), 386–387.

Dalgleish, T., Rosen, K., and Marks, M. (1996). Rhythm and blues: The theory and treatment of seasonal affective disorders. *British Journal of Clinical Psychology,* 35, 163–182.

DeCusatis, C. (1997). *Handbook of Applied Optometry.* New York: AIP Press.

Delay, E.R., and Richardson, M.A. (1981). Time estimation in humans: Effects of ambient illumination and sex. *Perceptual and Motor Skills,* 53, 747–750.

Department of Health and Human Services (1997). *A Profile of Older Americans: 1997.* Washington, DC: Department of Health and Human Services, p. 5.

Ducker Research. (1999, August). Lighting quality—key customer values and decision process. *Report to the Light Right Research Consortium.*

Eklund, N., Boyce, P., and Simpson, S. (2000). Lighting and sustained performance. *Journal of the Illuminating Engineering Society, 29(1),* 116.

Ellis, H.C., and Ashbrook, P.W. (1991). The "state" of mood and memory research: A selective review. In D. Kuiken, (ed.), *Mood and Memory, Theory, Research and Applications.* London: Sage Publications, pp. 1–21.

Erwine, B., and Heschong, L. (2000, March/April). Daylight: healthy, wealthy & wise. *Architectural Lighting Magazine.*

Evans, G.W. (1997). Environmental stress and health. In A. Baum, T. Revenson, and J.E. Singer, (eds.), *Handbook of Health Psychology.* Hillsdale, NJ: Earlbaum.

Evans, G.W. (ed.) (1982). *Environmental Stress.* Cambridge: Cambridge University Press.

Evans, G.W., and Cohen, S. (1987). *Environmental Stress.* In D. Stokols and I. Altman, (eds.), Handbook of Environmental Psychology. New York: John Wiley & Sons, pp. 571–610.

Figueiro, M.G., Eggleston, G., and Rea, M.S. (2002). Effects of light exposure on behavior of Alzheimer's patients: A pilot study. Paper presented at the Fifth International LRO Lighting Research Symposium, Orlando, FL.

Figueiro, M.G., and Stevens, R. (2002). Daylight and productivity: A possible link to circadian regulation. Poster Session at the Fifth International LRO Lighting Research Symposium, Orlando, FL.

Flynn, J.E. (1977). A study of subjective responses to low energy and nonuniform lighting systems. *Lighting Design and Application, 7,* 6–15.

Flynn, J.E., and Spencer, T.J. (1977). The effects of light source color on user impression and satisfaction. *Journal of the Illuminating Engineering Society, 4,* 167–179.

Food and Drug Administration. (1986, September). Lamp's labeling found to be fraudulent. *FDA Talk Paper* (No. T86-69). Rockville, MA: U.S. Department of Health and Human Services.

Garling, T., Book, A., and Lindberg, E. (1986). Spatial orientation and wayfinding in the designed environment: A conceptual analysis and some suggestions for postoccupancy evaluation. *Journal of Architectural and Planning Research, 3,* 55–64.

Gawron, V.J. (1982). Performance effects of noise intensity, psychological set, and task type and complexity. *Human Factors, 24,* 225–243.

Gifford, R. (1988). Light, décor, arousal, comfort and communication. *Journal of Environmental Psychology, 8,* 177–189.

Giradin, B.W. (1992). Lightwave frequency and sleep-wake frequency in well, full-term neonates, *Holistic Nursing Practice, 6(4),* 57–66.

Glass, D.C., and Singer, J.E. (1972). *Urban Stress.* New York: Academic Press.

Graham, R., and Michel, A. (2003). Impact of dementia on circadian patterns. Lighting and circadian rhythms and sleep in older adults (Technical Memorandum 1007708) Palo Alto, CA: Electric Power Research Institute (EPRI).

Graham, R., and Michel, A. (2003). Sundowning. Lighting and circadian rhythms and sleep in older adults (Technical Memorandum 1007708) Palo Alto, CA: Electric Power Research Institute (EPRI).

Gregory, R.I. (1979). Eye and brain: *The Psychology of Seeing,* 3rd ed. New York: McGraw-Hill.

Hall, E.T. (1966). *The Hidden Dimension.* New York: Doubleday.

Hedge, A., Erickson, W., and Rubin, G. (1992). Effects of personal and occupational factors on sick building syndrome reports in air conditioning offices. In J.C. Quirk, L.R. Murphy, and J.J. Hurrell, (Eds.) Stress and well-being at work. Washington, DC: American Psychological Association, pp. 286-298.

Heschong Mahone Group (HMG). (1999, August). Skylighting and retail sales, and daylighting in schools. For Pacific Gas & Electric. URL: http://www.pge.com.pec/daylight.

Henderson, J. (1986). Light as nutrient: a design update. Interiors, 146, 50.

Heschong Mahone Group (HMG). (1997, May). The lighting efficiency technology report, vol. I: California Lighting Baseline. For the California Energy Commission.

Hiatt, L. (1991). Nursing home renovation designed for reform. Boston: Butterworth.

Hill, H., and Bruce, V. The effects of lighting on the perception of facial surfaces. *Journal of Experimental Psychology: Human Perception and Performance, 22(4),* 986–1004.

Hughes, P.C. (1980). The use of light and color in health. In A.C. Hastings, J. Fadiman, and J.S. Gordon (eds.), *The Complete Guide to Holistic Medicine: Health for the Whole Person.* Boulder, CO: Westview Press, pp. 294–308.

Hughes, P.C., and McNelis, J.F. (1978). Lighting, productivity, and the work environment. *Lighting Design and Application, 8(12),* 32–38.

Hygge, S. (1991). The interaction of noise and mild heat on cognitive performance and serial reaction time. *Environment International,* 17, 229–234.

Illuminating Engineering Society of North America (IESNA) (2000). *IESNA Lighting Handbook,* 9th edition. New York: Illuminating Engineering Society of North America.

Illuminating Engineering Society of North America. (1998). Lighting for the aged and partially sighted committee. *Recommended Practice for Lighting and the Visual Environment for Senior Living,* RP-28-98. New York: Illuminating Engineering Society of North America.

Isen, A.M., Daubman, K.A., and Nowicki, G.P. (1987). Positive affect facilitates creative problem solving. *Journal of Personality and Social Psychology, 52(6),* 1122–1131.

Kleeman, W.B. (1981). *The Challenge of Interior Design.* Boston: CBI Publishing.

Knez, I. (2001). Effects of colour of light on nonvisual psychological processes. *Journal of Environmental Psychology, 21(2),* 201–208.

Knez, I. (1997, November). Changes in females' and males' positive and negative moods as a result of variations in CCT, CRI and illuminance levels. *Proceedings of Right Light: 4th European Conference on Energy Efficient Lighting,* Copenhagen, Denmark, 1, 149–154.

Knez, I. (1995). Effects of indoor lighting on mood and cognition. *Journal of Environmental Psychology,* 15, 39–51.

Knez, I., and Enmarker, I. (1998). Effects of office lighting on mood and cognitive performance and a gender effect in work related judgment. *Environment and Behavior,* 4, 553–567.

Knez, I., and Hygge, S. (in press). The circumplex structure of affect: A Swedish version. *Scandinavian Journal of Psychology.*

Knez, I., and Kers, C. (2000). Effects of indoor lighting, gender and age on mood and cognitive performance. *Environment and Behavior,* 32, 817–831.

Kwallek, N., and Lewis, C.M. (1990). Effects of environmental colour on males and females: A red or white or green office. *Applied Economics,* 21, 275–278.

Lam, R.W., Kripke, D.F., and Gillin, J.C. (1989). Phototherapy for depressive disorders: A review, *Canadian Journal of Psychiatry,* 34, 140–147.

Lam, W.C. (1977). *Perception and Lighting as Formgivers for Architecture.* New York: McGraw-Hill.

Lewy, A.J., Wehr, T.A., Goodwin, F.K., Newsome, D.A., and Markey, S.P. (1980). Light suppresses melatonin secretion in humans. *Science,* 210, 1267–1269.

Lockely, S. (2002). Light and human circadian regulation: Night work, day work, and jet lag. Paper presented at the Fifth International LRO Lighting Research Symposium, Orlando, FL.

Maas, J.B., Jayson, J.K., and Kleiber, D.A. (1974). Effects of spectral differences in illumination on fatigue. *Journal of Applied Psychology,* 59, 524–526.

Marans, R.W., and Yan, X. (1989). Lighting quality and environmental satisfaction in open and enclosed offices. *Journal of Architectural and Planning Research,* 6, 118–131.

Martin, L.E., Marler, M., Shochat, T., and Ancoli-Israel, S. (2000). Circadian rhythms of agitation in institutionalized patients with Alzheimer's disease. *Chronobiology International,* 17(3), 405–418.

McClaughan, C.L.B., Aspinall, P.A., and Webb, R.S. (1996, March/April). The effects of lighting upon mood and decision making, *Proceedings of CIBSE National Lighting Conference,* University of Bath, Bath, England, pp. 237–245.

Megaw, E. (1992). The visual environment. In A.P. Smith and D.M. Jones, (eds.), *Handbook of Human Performance, Volume 1: The Physical Environment.* London: Academic Press, pp. 261–296.

Miller, C.L., White, R., Whitman, T.L., O'Callaghn, M.F., and Maxwell, S.E. (1995). The effects of cycled versus noncycled lighting on the growth and development in preterm infants. *Infant Behavior and Development,* 18(1), 87–95.

Miller, N. (2002). Lighting for seniors: Obstacles in applying the research. Paper presented at the Fifth International LRO Lighting Research Symposium, Orlando, FL.

Mishimia, K., Okawa, M., Hiskikawa, Y., Hozumi, S., Hori, H., and Takashi, (1994). Morning bright therapy for sleep and behavior disorders in elderly patients with dementia. *Acta Psychiatry Scandinavia,* 89, 1–7.

National Lighting Bureau (1988). *Office Lighting and Productivity.* Washington, DC: National Lighting Bureau.

National Mental Health Association (2003). *Seasonal Affective Disorders.* http://www.nmha.org. Retrieved May 8, 2003.

Navvab, M. (2000). A comparison of visual performance under high and low color temperature fluorescent lamps. *Proceedings of the 2000 Annual Conference of the Illuminating Engineering Society of North America.* Washington, D.C.

Nelson, T.M., Nilsson, T.H., and Johnson, M. (1984). Interaction of temperature, illuminance and apparent time of sedentary work fatigue. *Ergonomics,* 27, 89–101.

Noelle-Waggoner, E. (2002). Let there be light, or face the consequences: A national concern for our aging population. Paper presented at the Fifth International LRO Lighting Research Symposium, Orlando, FL.

Passini, R. (1984). *Wayfinding in Architecture,* New York: Van Nostrand Reinhold.

Passini, R., Pigot, H., Rainville, C., and Tetreault, M.H. (2000). Wayfinding in a nursing home for advanced dementia of the Alzheimer's type. *Environment and Behavior,* 32(5), 684–710.

Passini, R., Rainville, C., Marchand, N., and Joanette, Y. (1998). Wayfinding and dementia: Some research findings and a new look at design. *Journal of Architectural and Planning Research,* 15(2), 133–151.

Phelps, D.L., and Watts, J.L. (1997). Early light reduction for preventing retinopathy of prematurity in very low birth weight infants. Cochrane Library Issue 2.

Quinn, G.C., Shin, M., Maguire, M., and Stone, R. (1999, May). Myopia and ambient lighting at night. Nature, 113.

Rea, M.S. (1986). Toward a model of visual performance: Foundations and data. *Journal of the Illuminating Engineering Society,* 15(2), 41–57.

Rea, M.S. (1988). Population data on near field visual acuity for use with the vision and lighting diagnostic (VALiD) Kit (report no. CR5544.3). Ottawa, ON: National Research Council of Canada.

Rea, M.S. (2002). Light—much more than vision. (Keynote). Light and Human Health: EPRI/LRO5 International Lighting Research Symposium. Palo Alto, CA: The Lighting Research Office of the Electric Power Research Institute, 1–15.

Rea, M.S., Bullough, J.D., and Figueiro, M.G. (2002). Phototransduction for human melatonin suppression. *Journal of Pineal Research,* 32, 209–213.

Rea, M.S. Figueiro, M.G., and Bullough, J.D. (2002). Circadian photobiology: An emerging framework for lighting practice and research. *Lighting Research and Technology,* 34(3), 177–190.

Rea, M.S., and Ouellette, M.J. (1988). Visual performance using reaction times. *Lighting Research & Technology,* 20(4), 39–53.

Rea, M.S., and Ouellette, M.J. (1991). Relative visual performance: A basis for application. *Lighting Research & Technology,* 23(3), 135–144.

Research Group for Inclusive Environments (RGIE). Task lighting for visually impaired people in an office environment. *Research Group for Inclusive Environments (RGIE).* http://www.rdg.ac.uk. Retrieved: December 18, 2002.

Reynolds, J.D., Hardy, R.J., Kennedy, K.A., Spencer, R., van Heuven, W.A.J., and Fielder, A.R. (1998). Lack of efficacy of light reduction in preventing retinopathy of prematurity. *The New England Journal of Medicine,* 338(22), 1572–1576.

Rothman, M. (1987). Designing work environments to influence productivity, *Journal of Business and Psychology.* 1, 390–550, 395.

Rowlands, E.D., Loe, D.L., McIntosh, R.M., and Mansfield, K.P. (1985). Lighting adequacy and quality in office interiors by consideration of subjective assessment and physical measurement. *CIE Journal,* 4(1), 23–37.

Saegert, S. (1976). Stress-inducing and stress-reducing qualities of environment. In H.M. Proshansky, W.H. Ittelson, and L. Rivlin, (eds.), *Environmental Psychology,* 2nd edition. New York: Holt, pp. 218–223.

Sanders, P.A., and Bernecker, C.A. (1990). Uniform veiling luminance and display polarity affect VDU user performance. *Journal of the Illuminating Engineering Society,* 19(2), 113–123.

Satlin, A., Volicer, L., Ross, V., Herz, L., and Campbell, S. (1992). Bright light treatment of behavioral and sleep disturbances in patients with Alzheimer's disease. *American Journal of Psychiatry,* 149(8), 1028–1032.

Sherrod, D., and Cohen, S. (1979). Density, personal control, and design. In J. Aliello and A. Baum (eds.), *Residential Crowding and Design.* New York: Plenum, pp. 217–228.

Simonson, E., and Brozek, J. (1948). Effects of illumination level on visual performance and fatigue. *Journal of the Optical Society of America,* 38, 384–397.

Skwerer, R.G., Jacobsen, F.M., Duncan, C.C., Kelly, K.A., Sack, D.A., Tamarkin, L., Gaist, P. A., Kasper, S., and Rosenthal, N.E. (1989). Neurobiology of seasonal affective disorders and phototherapy. In M.C. Blehar and N.E. Rosenthal, (eds.), *Seasonal Affective Disorders and Phototherapy.* New York: Guilford Press, pp. 311–332.

Smith, A.P., and Broadbent, D.E. (1980). Effect of noise on performance on embedded figures tasks. *Journal of Applied Psychology,* 2, 246–248.

Sommer, R. (1969). *Personal Space.* Englewood Cliffs, NJ: Prentice-Hall.

Stevens, R. (2002). Epidemiological evidence indicating light exposure is linked to human cancer development. Paper presented at the Fifth International LRO Lighting Research Symposium, Orlando, FL.

Stokols, D., and Altman, I. (1987). Introduction. In D. Stokols and I. Altman, eds., *Handbook of Environmental Psychology*, Vol. 1, pp 1–4, New York: John Wiley & Sons.

Taylor, R.B. (1988). *Human Territorial Functioning*. New York: Cambridge University Press.

Veitch, J. (2000, July). Lighting guidelines from lighting quality research. *CIBSE/ILE Lighting 2000 Conference*. New York, United Kingdom.

Veitch, J.A., and Gifford, R. (1996a). Assessing beliefs about lighting effects on health, performance, mood and social behavior. *Environment and Behavior, 28*, 446–470.

Veitch, J.A., and Gifford, R. (1996b). Choice, perceived control, and performance decrements in the physical environment. *Journal of Environmental Psychology, 16*, 269–276.

Veitch, J.A., Gifford, R., and Hine, D.W. (1991). Demand characteristics and full spectrum lighting effects on performance and mood. *Journal of Environmental Psychology, 11*, 87–95.

Veitch, J.A., and McColl, S. (1995). On the modulation of fluorescent light: Flicker rate and spectral distribution effects on visual performance and visual comfort. *Light Research and Technology, 27*, 243–256.

Veitch, J.A., and McColl, S. (2001). Evaluation of full-spectrum fluorescent lighting. *Ergonomics, 44(3)*, 255–279.

Veitch, J.A., and Miller, N., McKay, H., and Jones, C.C. (1996, August). Lighting System Effects on Judged Lighting Quality and Facial Appearance. Paper presented at the 1996 Annual Conference of the Illuminating Engineering Society of North America, Cleveland, OH.

Veitch, J., and Newsham, G. (2000). Exercised control, lighting choices, and energy use: An office simulation experiment. *Journal of Environmental Psychology 20(3)*, 219–237.

Veitch, J.A., and Newsham, G.R. (1999, June). Preferred luminous conditions in open-plan offices: implication for lighting quality recommendations. Proceedings of the Commission Internationale de l'Eclairage (CIE) 24th Session, Vol. 1, Part 2. Warsaw, Poland, Vienna, Austria: CIE Central Bureau, pp. 4–6.

Veitch, J., and Newsham, G. (January, 1999). Individual control can be energy efficient. IAEEL Newsletter.

Veitch, J.A., and Newsham, G.R. (1998a). Experimental Investigations of Lighting Quality, Preferences and Control Effects on Task Performance and Energy Efficiency: Experiment 2, Primary Analyses—Final Report (IRC Internal Report No. 767/Client Peport No. A3546.5). Ottawa, ON: National Research Council Canada, Institute for Research in Construction.

Veitch, J.A., and Newsham, G. (1998). Consequences of the perception and exercise of control over lightings. 106th Annual Convention of the American Psychological Association, August 1998. San Francisco, CA.

Veitch, J., and Newsham, G. (1996, August). Experts' quantitative and qualitative assessment of lighting quality. Proceedings of the 1996 Annual IESNA Conference. Cleveland, OH. Available at: http://fox.nrc.ca/irc/fulltext/nrcc39874.html.

Veitch, J., and Newsham, G. (1999, June). Preferred luminous conditions in open-plan offices: implications for lighting quality recommendations. CIE Proceedings, CIE Pub no. 133, vol. 1, part 2: 4–6.

Veitch, J.A. (1997). Revisiting the performance and mood effects of information about light and fluorescent lamp type. Journal of Environmental Psychology, 17(1), 253-262.

Veitch, J.A., and Newsham, G.R. (1996). Determinants of Lighting Quality II: Research and Recommendations. Paper presented at the 104th Annual Convention of the American Psychological Association. Toronto, Ontario, Canada (ERIC Document Reproduction Service No. ED408543).

Veitch, J., and Newsham, G. (1998). Lighting quality and energy-efficiency effects on task performance, mood, health, satisfaction, and comfort. *Journal of the Illuminating Engineering Society, 27(1),* 107.

Veitch, J.A., and Newsham, G.R. (1988b). Lighting quality and energy-efficiency effects on task performance, mood, health, satisfaction and comfort. *Journal of the Illuminating Engineering Society, 27(1),* 107–129.

Wapner, S., and Demick, J. (2002). The increasing *contexts* of *context* in the study of environment behavior relations. In R. Bechtel and A. Churchman (eds.), *Handbook of Environmental Psychology.* New York: Wiley.

Weisman, G. (1981). Evaluating architectural legibility. *Environment and Behavior,* 13, 189–204.

Weston, H.C. (1962). *Sight, Light, and Work,* 2nd edition. London: Lewis.

Wilson, S., and Hedge, A. (1987). *The Office Environment Survey.* London: Building Use Studies Ltd.

Winchip, S.M. (1990). Dementia health care facility design. *Journal of Interior Design Education and Research, 16(2),* 39–46.

Wineman, J.D. (1982). The office environment as a source of stress. In G.W. Evans, (ed.), *Environmental Stress.* New York: Cambridge University Press, pp. 256–285.

Wright, G.A., and Rea, M.S. (1984). Age, a human factor in lighting. *Proceedings of the 1984 International Conference on Occupational Ergonomics.* D.A. Attwood and C. McCann (eds.). Rexdale, Ontario, Canada: Human Factors Association of Canada.

Wu, W., and Ng, E. (2003). A review of the development of daylighting in schools. *Lighting Research and Technology, 35(2),* 111–125.

Zeisel, J. (2000). Environmental design effects on Alzheimer symptoms in long term care residences. *World Hospitals and Health Service, 36(3),* 27–31.

UNIT II

LIGHTING DESIGN APPLICATIONS

CHAPTER 14

Safety and Security

OBJECTIVES

- Apply an understanding of the results of disaster research to a quality lighting environment.

- Describe safety and security concerns in the built environment.

- Understand how to plan lighting to help create safe buildings.

- Identify organizations and codes associated with building safety.

- Describe safety issues related to lamps, luminaires, and installation locations.

- Comprehend how to plan lighting for wayfinding under normal and emergency conditions.

CONCEPTS and elements of a quality lighting environment are explored in Unit I. The content serves as a foundation for specifying lighting for residential and commercial applications. The information covered in Unit I provides the options and considerations an interior designer reflects upon in determining the appropriate lighting plan for the users of the space in a specific environment. Unit II provides information and factors that are pertinent to specific applications. An interior designer specifies a lighting environment by combining the information presented in Unit I with the fundamentals of interiors provided in Unit II.

Unit I concluded with an analysis of how illumination affects human factors. This serves as an excellent starting point for examining the important topics of health and safety covered in this chapter. Interior designers have always had a responsibility to design interiors that optimize the health, safety, and welfare of the users. Recent disasters, including the terrorist attack on the World Trade Center in New York City and nightclub fires in Chicago and West Warwick, Rhode Island, serve to underscore the importance of designing an environment that is as safe as possible and of planning an effective means of egress. This chapter explores the role of lighting in designing a safe and secure environment that includes how lighting affects human behavior and architectural elements and wayfinding. All these components are integrated in residential and commercial interiors.

Health and Safety

Understanding how people function in a space under normal conditions and in times of disaster is key to planning interiors that are as safe as possible.

Disaster Research

In designing safe interiors, the environment should be planned to account for extreme events caused by natural disasters, such as tornadoes and intentional destruction initiated by people. As discussed in Chapter 13, effective interiors always reflect the interaction between an individual and the built environment. In designing a safe environment, an interior designer must study a site and the users of the space and then anticipate human behavior. The field of environmental psychology, and more specifically disaster research, examines human behavior within the context of natural traumatic events.

Peek and Mileti define a disaster as "the consequence of the interaction between the natural, social, and constructed environments and are initiated by some extreme event in the natural world" (2002, p. 512). Gilbert White is credited with initiating natural disaster research in the 1940s. Subsequently, many disciplines, including sociology and psychology, have studied hazards and their impact on people. Currently, a holistic and interdisciplinary approach involving professionals from a variety of disciplines collaboratively conduct disaster research. Results of disaster research can be applied to designing lighting for safe environments. The most relevant areas that can be applied to lighting include a hazards adjustment paradigm, preparedness activities, and warning systems.

Peek and Mileti (2002) identify a *hazards adjustment paradigm* as involving the following steps: (1) assess hazard vulnerability, (2) examine possible adjustments, (3) determine the human perception and estimation of the hazard, (4) analyze the decision-making process, and (5) identify the best adjustments, given social constraints, and evaluate their effectiveness. These steps serve as an excellent outline for planning lighting that will result in a safer environment. For a specific site, an interior designer should identify the areas that are potentially hazardous, make adjustments whenever possible, and then specify a lighting system that will minimize risks for the users of the space. A continuous evaluation of lighting effectiveness will help to create a safe and secure environment. This chapter covers some of the most vulnerable areas and identifies lighting systems and layouts designed to minimize personal injury.

Research reveals that preparing for emergencies helps save lives and reduces property damage. In summarizing factors that influence preparedness and responses, Peek and Mileti report that "broad social, political, economic, cultural, and institutional contexts shape disaster preparedness and response. At the personal and household levels, ethnic and minority status, gender, language, socioeconomic status, social attachments and relationships, economic resources, age, and physical capacity all have an impact on the propensity of people to take preparedness actions, to evacuate, and to take further mitigation measures" (2002, p. 519). Peek and Mileti (2002) further note that residential preparedness is more likely to occur when people are familiar with current events, have personally experienced disaster damage, have school-age children involved, demonstrate a long-term commitment to the community, and have received disaster education.

Generally, organizations, businesses, and governments initiate disaster preparedness programs in response to mandates and legal incentives (Peek & Mileti, 2002). The Homeland Security Act is an excellent example of a governmental preparedness program that was established after the terrorist attack on the World Trade Center. All the factors that affect preparedness and response should be considered when designing a lighting plan for a safe environment. For the most advanced perspectives regarding disaster issues, an interior designer should review current research.

Several research studies have focused on the effectiveness of warning systems and variables that influence responses. According to Peek and Mileti (2002, p. 517), a public warning response is a process that includes the following stages: "(1) hearing the warning, (2) believing the warning is credible, (3) confirming that the threat does exist and others are heeding it, (4) personalizing the risk to oneself, (5) determining if protective action is needed and if it is feasible, and (6) deciding what action to take and then taking it." Peek and Mileti (2002) summarize the variables influencing responses that include the credibility of the source, consistency, accuracy, clarity, clear guidance, frequency, and perceived confidence and certainty. Furthermore, the general physical decline associated with the aging process affects reaction time to light and sound. To help create a safe environment, the lighting plan should reflect a public warning response process and the variables that influence actions. This information is applied to the content discussed later in this chapter.

In addition to research related to disasters, a great deal of insight regarding how people perceive the safety of buildings, and personal reactions to life-threatening experiences, can be attained by interviewing survivors of a disaster and reading descriptions of a tragic event. An interior designer might not be able to interview survivors of a disaster; however, a substantial amount of information can be gleaned from articles in newspapers and news magazines. For example, numerous articles have been written about the World Trade Center attack and the 2003 nightclub fires at the E2 in Chicago and The Station in Rhode Island. In reviewing the articles, an interior designer can gain insight regarding the warning systems, physical conditions, human responses, psychological states, and problematic areas. This information can serve as a way of understanding what occurs in a panic situation and then how to improve the safety of buildings. Many of the safety suggestions identified in the next sections of this chapter reflect an analysis of the articles that were written about the World Trade Center and the nightclub fires.

As a follow-up to the two nightclub fires in 2003, the *Chicago Tribune* published an article that focused on safety issues during emergencies in buildings with many people (Deardorff, Haynes, Mihalopoulos & Mendell, 2003). The article discussed panic research and provided suggestions for improving safety from experts in the field. The authors reported that in facilities with a large number of people, individuals tend to exhibit irrational behavior, model the actions of others, and expect other people to help the injured (Deardorff, et al., 2003). Alcohol, invasion of personal space, and fear of terrorism are factors that increase panic (Deardorff, et al., 2003).

Figure 14.1 is an illustration, which was based upon research conducted at the Dresden University of Technology and demonstrates behavior during normal and panic conditions (Rust & Muñoz, 2003). As shown in the panic situation, the congestion of people at one exit suggests that people need to be informed that they can use other exits. David Hollingsworth, a nightclub consultant, commented that "it's natural for people to try to go out the way they came in. They ignore other exits that are closer" (Deardorff, et al., 2003, p. 10). The *Tribune*

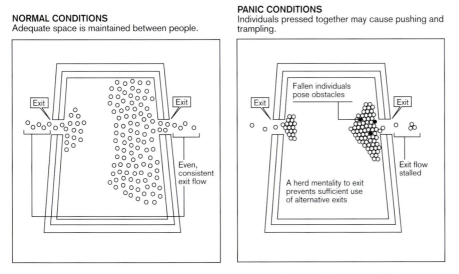

NORMAL CONDITIONS
Adequate space is maintained between people.

PANIC CONDITIONS
Individuals pressed together may cause pushing and trampling.

FIGURE 14.1   Based upon research conducted at the Dresden University of Technology, a simulation of behavior during normal and panic conditions.

article also reported that "Brian Humphrey, a spokesman for the Los Angeles Fire Department, said newly constructed nightclubs and restaurants are required to have exit signs at the floor level so that people can better see them during a fire when smoke rises. 'This helps people to better survive a fire by being able to feel their way out of the nearest exit,' Humphrey said" (Deardorff, et al., 2003, p. 10). The *Tribune* article stressed the importance of training staff in safe evacuation practices, including knowing where people should exit and how to effectively communicate the information during an emergency.

Built Environment Safety Concerns

The overall design of an interior and operational policies affect how safely people can evacuate a building. One of the first steps in safety preparedness should be to examine which areas in a building are vulnerable to hazards and elicit feelings of insecurity. Buildings should be analyzed during normal operating conditions, and an interior designer should try to envision how people would react to the environment in a crisis situation, such as a fire or tornado. It is especially important to plan an interior for a disaster, because people behave differently in a panic situation. An environment that works well during normal conditions may become dysfunctional in a crisis. For example, during normal operations of the E2 nightclub, people were able to enter and leave the building with ease. However, once the fire started, people, in a panic state, rushed to the stairs that led down to the front entrance. The stampede of people in the staircase resulted in people being crushed and killed. A similar situation occurred when people were trying to leave the World Trade Center buildings. The high number of people going down the stairs encountered firemen, including firefighting equipment, moving up the stairs. Sandy Truetler-King, a survivor from the 50th floor of the South Tower, described the conditions: "I will never forget the firefighters, struggling their way up, past us, to the stricken floors above. They encouraged us, telling us that we were handling it well, and to keep going down in an orderly fashion. They walked to certain death" (Sottardi & Tuma, 2002).

Passageway problems can be further exacerbated by smoke, debris, and total darkness. *Chicago Tribune* reporters presented a description, provided by one of the survivors, of the World Trade Center: "Gorry could see paper and debris coming down from the North Tower. He and others got about halfway down when they were told they could return to work. Gorry, however kept going down" (Sottardi & Tuma, 2002).

Smoke poses unique challenges in designing a lighting system (Figure 14.2). Emergency lighting that is easily visible during normal conditions can be very difficult or impossible to see through smoke. Unfortunately, predicting the characteristics of smoke is impossible because the source of the fire determines the density and color of the smoke. Researchers have studied the type of smoke that results from common interior materials; however, smoke can result from materials that are not normally present in a space. For example, a great deal of smoke in the World Trade Center was derived from fumes from jet fuel. Given all the uncertainties associated with emergencies, an interior designer must be aware of the visibility problems caused by smoke and develop a lighting plan that includes a variety of light sources in many locations, including ceilings, floors, and the top and lower sections of walls.

FIGURE 14.2   View of lighting during smoky conditions.

Installing many light sources is also important, in the likelihood that walls might collapse during an emergency. Many of the walls, including some staircase walls, were destroyed as people were trying to evacuate the World Trade Center buildings. If all the emergency lighting is installed on damaged walls, complete darkness will result. A reduction or loss of lighting during an emergency evacuation affects the psychological state of people. Two survivors of the World Trade Center recall the conditions. Peter Gorry, from the 62nd floor of the North Tower, recounted, "We got to about the 7th floor and there was a loud bang and the lights went off. That was about the only time I got really scared" (Sottardi & Tuma, 2002). Aaron Goldsmith, from the 40th floor in the South Tower, said, "Everything shook. The lights dimmed. I saw a hundred people, some of them panicking" (Sottardi & Tuma, 2002).

In addition to the effects of an emergency condition, all interiors have the potential for disability glare, dark areas, and shadows. These conditions can be safety issues and cause feelings of insecurity. Chapter 6 discussed areas of concern regarding disability glare. Dark areas and shadows can cause problems with wayfinding, reading signage, seeing people, and noticing potentially hazardous areas, such as stairs. Dark areas are especially problematic for people with visual impairments and individuals prone to disorientation. Dark areas may include any space that requires eyes to engage in significant adaptation, such as entrances from the outdoors. Adjusting from bright to dark always requires the most amount of time. In addition, dark areas in a building can create a fear of being attacked. Long corridors, with various areas in shadows, are especially prone to provoking feelings of insecurity.

Light sources directed at objects, architectural elements, and people can create shadows. Shadows can be a problem with adaptation and visibility and can elicit feelings of fear in people walking through a public building during times of low occupancy. People who are unfamiliar with an environment are especially prone to being fearful during times of disorientation or an emergency. To help alleviate fear experienced while trying to open a door at night, lighting next to exterior doors should be at an adequate level and installed in a location that prevents shadows. Sufficient lighting around exterior doors and windows also helps to deter crime.

Generally, areas in a building that are vulnerable to hazards include staircases, bathrooms, kitchens, and any space that involves potentially dangerous tasks. Staircases should be illuminated in a manner that allows a clear distinction between the risers and treads. Effective lighting eliminates shadows on every step, especially the last steps at the bottom of the staircase. Recommendations for illuminating staircases include luminaires at the top and bottom of staircases and lighting each step from a light source that is located in a wall next to the steps or along the treads (Figure 14.3). To help eliminate disability glare, a lamp in a luminaire located at the bottom of a staircase should always be hidden from view.

Tall buildings, even under normal conditions, can evoke feelings of fear and insecurity. Some people have a fear of heights and are not comfortable in tall buildings. Some people are uncomfortable with the natural swaying that occurs in tall buildings, especially on windy days. Swaying has become a greater concern as a consequence of the tragedy at the World Trade Center because people working in tall buildings have reported that when the building sways, they are uncertain whether the movement is the result of high winds or a terrorist attack. Occupants report that when a building sways, many objects

FIGURE 14.3 Suggestions for illuminating staircases: place a luminaire at the top of the staircase and two fixtures on each step.

move in a space, including wands on window treatments, desk doors, and water in toilets. To help reduce movement in a space caused by the building's swaying, light fixtures should be selected that prevent movement. Therefore, pendant fixtures and portable luminaires that easily move should be avoided.

The primary safety area in bathrooms is the bathtub/shower. Falls in showers and tubs are a major cause of death in people over 50 years of age. All bathrooms should have lighting for the shower. For people requiring assistance in the bathroom, it is helpful to have a light switch located in the room and outside the door leading to the bathroom. Kitchen safety concerns focus on the use of knives and burns from cooking. To help prevent injuries, task lighting should be designed to provide an adequate amount of illumination without shadows. (Refer to Chapter 19 for more information regarding lighting for bathrooms and kitchens.) Effective lighting on horizontal surfaces is important in any environment where someone could get injured from a potentially dangerous activity, such as drilling, cutting, or operating machinery.

Safety issues related to electricity must be considered in a quality lighting environment. Faulty wiring, frayed cords, and overloaded circuits have caused deaths and fires in homes and commercial buildings. The National Fire Protection Association (NFPA) and the U.S. Consumer Product Safety Commission (CPSC) report that between 1994 and 1998, residential fires caused an average of 860 deaths, 4785 injuries, and nearly $1.3 billion in property damage annually. Approximately 17 percent of the residential fires were related to electrical distribution, appliances, and equipment. Furthermore, 9 of the 440 total accidental electrocutions in 1999 were related to lighting. Overloading extension cords and electrical outlets and inserting a lamp with a higher wattage than the luminaire's rating are major safety concerns. Electrical wiring in homes 40 years and older can have significant fire hazards. Extension cords should be considered only a temporary arrangement. A serious electrical problem could exist if one can hear crackling from outlets, if lamps flicker, or if switch plates and outlets feel hot.

To help prevent injury and deaths, the 2002 edition of the National Electric Code (NEC) indicates: "All 125-volt, single-phase, 15- and

20-ampere receptacles in the locations specified in (1) through (8) shall have ground fault circuit interrupters [(GFCIs)] protection for personnel" (2002, p. 75). One through eight refers to designated areas in bathrooms, garages, outdoors, crawl spaces, unfinished basements, kitchens, wet bar sinks, and boathouses. Refer to the NEC guidelines for specific installation requirements. **Ground fault circuit interrupters (GFCIs)** protect people by shutting off power to an appliance when there is an interruption in the electrical current, such as when a hair dryer falls into a bathtub full of water. Wall receptacles within 6 feet (1829 mm) of water must have GFCIs. Portable GFCIs are available. **Arc fault circuit interrupters (AFCIs)** stop an electrical current when an arc is detected in defective electrical equipment or wiring. AFCIs can be installed on circuit-breaker panels. The NEC requires AFCIs in the bedroom circuits of new residential buildings. The CPSC (http://www.cpsc.gov), and the Electrical Safety Foundation International (ESFI) (http://www.esfi.org) are excellent resources concerning the most current safety practices.

Special populations, including the elderly, children, and people with disabilities, require additional safety considerations. The elderly, especially individuals with Alzheimer's disease, are prone to burns from hot lamps and forgetting to turn off luminaires. Luminaires that are designed with lamps in a sealed unit can help to prevent burns. Controls can help to manage when lights are on or off. Infants and young children should not be able to reach an electrical cord or luminaires. Childproof electrical sockets should be installed in all rooms. Individuals with visual impairments might require special illumination levels and aiming angles. Emergency lighting should be equipped with visual and auditory signaling. Persons with fine motor disabilities might need luminaires that are designed to accommodate their specific condition. For example, a luminaire operated by a foot control might be easier to use than a switch that requires a hand to twist a knob.

Lighting Systems and Safety

The safe specification, installation, and maintenance of lighting systems are regulated by national codes and local ordinances.

Ground fault circuit interrupters (GFCI)
A device that shuts off power to an appliance when there is an interruption in the electrical currents.

Arc fault circuit interrupter (AFCI)
A device used to stop an electrical current when sparks occur from defective electrical equipment or wiring.

Safety Codes

Governmental agencies and organizations dedicated to the safety of buildings include the NFPA, CPSC, U.S. Uniform Building Code (UBC), International Building Code (IBC), Building Officials and Code Administrators International (BOCA), Underwriters Laboratories (UL), Americans with Disabilities Act (ADA), and Occupational Safety and Health Administration (OSHA). In addition to these sources, local fire officials and licensed electricians are excellent contacts for interior designers planning a safe lighting system because they are familiar with all the laws specific to the community. All lighting systems must adhere to the local ordinances, which may include requirements more stringent than national codes.

The NFPA publishes the *National Electric Code Handbook* (2002) and the *NFPA 101, Life Safety Code, 2003 Edition*. The National Electric Code (NEC) has guidelines that directly affect lighting systems, including "Article 410 Luminaires (Lighting Fixtures), Lampholders, and Lamps." Article 410 regulates the installation and production of luminaires, and the Life Safety Code stipulates the type, location, and number of exit and emergency lighting fixtures. According to the NFPA Life Safety Code, Section 7.8.1.1, illumination for exits should include designated stairs, aisles, corridors, ramps, escalators, and passageways leading to an exit (2003, 101: p. 66).

General illumination for exits has the following requirements: "The floors and other walking surfaces within an exit and within the portions of the exit access and exit discharge designated in 7.8.1.1 shall be illuminated as follows: (1) During conditions of stair use, the minimum illumination for new stairs shall be at least 108 lux (10 ft-candle), measured at the walking surfaces. (2) The minimum illumination for floors and walking surfaces, other than new stairs, shall be to values of at least 10.8 lux (1 ft-candle), measured at the floor. (3) In assembly occupancies, the illumination of the floors of exit access shall be at least 2.2 lux (0.2 ft-candle) during periods of performances or projections involving directed light. (4) The minimum illumination requirements shall not apply where operations or processes require low lighting levels" (2003, 101: p. 66).

Lamps

Safety issues related to lamps include considerations under normal conditions and emergency lighting as well. This section of the textbook provides an awareness of only some of the problems associated with lamps and luminaires. For the safe operation of lighting systems, it is essential that interior designers follow codes and manufacturers' instructions and that they contact the CPSC for a listing of safety problems involving lamps. CPSC also provides a list of products recalled for safety violations. Safety problems associated with lamps include fires, explosions, toxic chemicals, overwattages, and incompatible lamp/luminaire systems. High-wattage lamps, especially in the incandescent family, can cause fires or burns when placed too close to flammable objects. To avoid overheating, all lamps should always be securely screwed into the socket. A serious problem has occurred with high-wattage halogen lamps installed in torchière floor luminaires. The significant amount of heat released by the lamp has caused burns or fires. Currently, to comply with UL standards, the lamps used in these luminaires must be less than 300 watts. For additional safety, UL stipulates that protective glass or a wire guard protect the lamp.

In addition to protecting people and property from the heat emitted by lamps, some lamps can burst or rupture. HID lamps can rupture at the end of life, which is another reason for a protective glass shield. A cloth should be used for handling halogen lamps because the oil from hands can cause the lamp to shatter. As discussed in Chapter 13, lamp-handling requirements are very prescriptive for lamps and ballasts containing mercury and PCBs, respectively.

Manufacturers design luminaires for specific lamps, and this information is provided in their product literature. Lamp type and wattages should always comply with manufacturers' specifications. Recent problems have occurred when CFLs were installed in luminaires that were designed *only* for incandescent lamps. This can be especially problematic when the luminaire has an incandescent dimming control. A luminaire manufacturer will indicate if the fixture can operate using an incandescent and a CFL lamp. Luminaires are rated for maximum wattages. Installing a lamp with a higher wattage can cause a fire in the electrical wiring. To adhere to manufacturers' specifications for luminaires with multiple lamps, such as track lighting, the total wattage of all of the lamps must be calculated.

Lamps for emergency and exit lighting have special considerations. Emergency lighting operates in the event of a power failure. The new NFPA 101 Life Safety Codes require a chevron-type directional indicator that is "located outside of the EXIT legend, not less than 9.5 mm (⅜ in.) from any letter" (2003, 101: p. 69). Exit lighting operates at all times and the lamps illuminate the word "EXIT." The most important considerations in specifying lamps for emergency fixtures are reliable performance, appropriate illumination levels, and long life. Emergency lighting must be planned so that it has the proper illumination level for the amount of time required to exit a space and building. Thus, emergency lighting must be site-specific and must be based upon the purpose of the space, users, and activities. Generally, emergency lighting is required for medium to large-sized buildings. Lamps for emergency and safety purposes are excluded from meeting efficiency standards.

According to the *NFPA 101, Life Safety Code, 2003 Edition,* "Emergency illumination shall be provided for not less than 1½ hours in the event of failure of normal lighting. Emergency lighting facilities shall be arranged to provide initial illumination that is not less than an average of 10.8 lux (1 ft-candle) and, at any point, not less than 1.1 lux (0.1 ft-candle), measured along the path of egress at floor level. Illumination levels shall be permitted to decline to not less than an average of 6.5 lux (0.6 ft-candle) and, at any point, not less than 6.5 lux (0.06 ft-candle) at the end of the ½ hours. A maximum-to-minimum illumination uniformity ratio of 40 to 1 shall not be exceeded" (2003, 101: p. 67). The code states that "battery-operated emergency lights shall use only reliable types of rechargeable batteries provided with suitable facilities for maintaining them in properly charged condition. Batteries used in such lights or units shall be approved for their intended use and shall comply with NFPA 70, *National Electric Code* (2003, 101: p. 67). The code also requires periodic testing of emergency lighting equipment.

As specified by Section 7-10 of the *NFPA 101, Life Safety Code, 2003 Edition,* "Exits, other than main exterior exit doors that obviously and clearly are identifiable as exits, shall be marked by an approved sign that is readily visible from any direction of exit access" (2003, 101: p. 68). The signage can be illuminated externally, or internally, or it can be photoluminescent. The level of illumination requirements are "externally illuminated signs shall be illuminated by not less than 54 lux (5 ft-candles) at the illuminated surface and shall have a contrast ratio of not less than 0.5" (2003, 101: p. 69). Refer to the *NFPA 101, Life Safety Code, 2003 Edition* for all restrictions and requirements. For excellent reliability, and to address economic and environmental concerns, many exit signs are illuminated with LEDs. Generally, LEDs used in exit signage are between 5 and 8 watts.

Safety and Luminaires

Luminaires also have safety issues under normal and emergency conditions. All rooms should have emergency lighting, including spaces used infrequently, such as restrooms and storage facilities. As with lamps, key to the safe operation of lighting systems is to follow electrical codes and manufacturers' instructions and to contact the CPSC for a listing of safety problems involving luminaires. In addition, UL and the Canadian Standards Association provide information regarding the safety of luminaires, flammability standards, and installation requirements. Safety problems associated with luminaires include people tripping over cords, fixtures falling down, and improper use of lamps and controls. In addition, luminaires that are placed too close to a flammable material can cause burns and fires. UL testing approval will be violated if a luminaire has been altered in a manner that deviates from the condition of the fixture as originally purchased. For example, as noted in Chapter 9, components are not interchangeable among manufacturers, especially for track systems that are UL-rated specifically for one manufacturer and one product line. All custom-made luminaires should be tested by UL. Emergency lighting systems can be controlled centrally or built into a standard luminaire. Centrally controlled systems are connected to many luminaires.

Regarding controls associated with illumination as a means of egress, the *NFPA 101, Life Safety Code, 2003 Edition* stipulates,

"Automatic, motion- sensor-type lighting switches shall be permitted within the means of egress, provided that the switch controllers are equipped for fail-safe operation, the illumination timers are set for a minimum 15-minute duration, and the motion sensor is activated by any occupant movement in the area served by the lighting units" (2003, 101: p. 66). (For more information regarding controls and safety refer to Chapter 10.)

Some special features related to safety that can be integrated into the design of luminaires include antivandalism devices and protection from weather and ultraviolet radiation. Besides the destruction of a luminaire, a broken fixture can be an electrical hazard, and a nonfunctioning lamp could jeopardize the safety of people in dark spaces. To protect luminaires in high-activity areas, such as a basketball court or in crime-prone settings, tamperproof luminaires are available (Figure 14.4). These luminaires require special tools to open the fixtures for maintenance purposes.

Luminaires require special design features so that they will operate under wet or cold conditions. These fixtures should be watertight and corrosion-resistant. Often cast aluminum or stainless steel is used for the housing material. Shatterproof glass or plastic diffusers are used to shield the lamp. UL categorizes these luminaires according to the degree of protection they provide from the elements. A luminaire designated as "weather location" means that the fixture can be installed in a location that is fully exposed to wet or cold conditions. A "damp

FIGURE 14.4 An example of a tamperproof luminaire.

location" luminaire must have some type of shelter from the elements, such as a porch. Shower stalls should always have fixtures designed for wet locations.

For safety purposes, luminaires should be located so that they provide appropriate visibility under normal and emergency conditions. Uniform, open spaces present the greatest challenges because there are fewer surfaces in or onto which luminaires can be installed. Generally, lighting for safety purposes is more successful when multiple luminaires, closely spaced, at moderate illumination levels are specified rather than fewer, brightly lit fixtures. Multiple luminaires help to provide adequate illumination throughout a space, and they supply a light source when a lamp fails. Luminaires should be specified for various conditions that might occur in the space, including power failures or large numbers of people. Luminaires should be specifically planned to illuminate fire equipment. A high number of people, in any space, reduces the visibility of lights. To help people see emergency lighting, many light sources in a variety of locations should be installed in rooms that accommodate high numbers of people. National and local codes should be consulted for minimum recommendations; however, depending upon the site and users of the facility, additional lighting might be necessary.

Special considerations related to the installed location of a luminaire include contrast extremes. Daylight can create disability glare for persons walking toward windows or glass doors. An especially problematic situation can occur when daylight is seen when people are walking down stairs. Color or value contrasts on floor and wall surfaces can present safety concerns, especially for individuals with visual impairments. Luminaires, such as floor-mounted fixtures, that are positioned directly under a ceiling fan can produce a strobe effect, which can trigger seizures in some individuals. The location of wall-mounted luminaires must comply with ADA requirements. Sconces that are mounted below 80 inches (203 cm) AFF should project no more than 4 inches (10 cm) from the wall.

A safe lighting system requires appropriate operational procedures. In commercial interiors, an interior designer should work with management, employees, and the building service workers to create policies and procedures related to safety and security. This involves educational and training programs, which might include videos, handouts, demonstrations, interactive media, and emergency drills. Employers might want to consider implementing a buddy system, which involves everyone being responsible for designated individuals during an emergency evacuation. A buddy system can be especially critical for assisting people with disabilities. Policies and procedures should include regular maintenance, evaluation, and testing of emergency lighting.

Wayfinding and Communication Systems

Lighting for wayfinding and communication systems must accommodate activities that occur under normal and emergency conditions. Poor lighting can pose safety and security issues in both situations.

Normal Conditions

To successfully plan lighting for wayfinding, an interior designer must examine all the elements involved with the project, including characteristics of the site, users of the space, physical constraints, safety codes, and operational policies. Wayfinding lighting should be planned to accommodate the needs of people with diverse needs, including individuals with visual, auditory, and physical disabilities. In addition, many people in public buildings are unfamiliar with the space so they require a clear understanding of how to navigate through the space in a fairly quick manner. Feelings of frustration and insecurity can arise when people are lost in a building.

To develop a lighting plan for wayfinding requires an understanding of how people move through a space. In analyzing behavioral elements of the users of a space, Weisman (1982) identified the following means of wayfinding demonstrated by people: (1) identifying one's destination and moving toward the site, (2) following a path that leads to the destination, (3) using signage and landmarks along the path, and (4) creating a mental image of the path to the destination. Lighting should play an important role in assisting with each of these approaches.

Under normal conditions, lighting for wayfinding should be planned to provide the visibility necessary to safely walk through the building and to read directional, identification, and informational signage. Computerized directory and information systems can greatly assist with wayfinding. Lighting should be planned to enhance the design characteristics of the signage and its location. The lamp, luminaire, and aiming angles should improve the overall visibility of the sign from a distance, including the typeface and the contrast between the letters and their background. The type of lighting will affect the visibility of raised images, such as braille and graphic images. A grazing lighting technique might enhance the visibility of raised images. However, this type of lighting could cause the raised character to cast a shadow and make it more difficult to read. Signage that is made from a glossy material or that is shielded behind glass will need a lighting system that reduces glare. Variations in illumination levels can help to prioritize signage throughout a space and building. The illumination levels of signage should be planned to accommodate visual adaptation adjustments.

The type and location of luminaires for signage should always be site-specific, even within one space or building. For example, lighting that is effective for a sign located in a dark area might not be effective in a room filled with daylight. The same sign in rooms with 20-foot (6096 mm) and 8-foot (2438 mm) ceilings may require different lighting techniques. Generally, signage that is perpendicular to pathways will be the most visible. Thus, luminaires are often aimed at signage from a distance or are installed directly above the sign. The location of luminaires and signage should not interfere with exit signs and emergency lighting.

Under normal conditions, there can be a variety of ways people use space, and the number of individuals in a room can vary. For example, wayfinding through a museum can be easy with few people in the space and very difficult when large numbers of people are trying to move together. Temporary displays in a museum can present unique wayfinding challenges because directional signage might be hidden. Thus, whenever possible, lighting should be planned to accommodate the needs of people in a variety of conditions.

A significant amount of wayfinding involves walking through hallways. Generally, these spaces have very little ceiling area compared to the wall space, and thus most of the lighting should be planned to illuminate walls. Walls with glass that admit daylight have to be evaluated to determine if disability glare occurs. Unique locations in a building that require special lighting considerations include intersections of corridors, staircases, steps, exits, and any obstructions (Figure 14.5). A good rule of thumb is to plan effective lighting at any point in a pathway that requires the user of the space to make a decision.

Integrating lighting with other elements in rooms and hallways helps to orient people in a building. For example, variations in illumination levels or different styles of luminaires can provide cues for different areas in a building. A major space in a building, such as an information desk in a hospital, could have a higher illumination level than the hallways leading to the space. Any landmark in a building, such as artwork or dramatic architectural elements, should have lighting that emphasizes the piece. The new illuminated walls, synchronized with music, in the Northwest Airline terminal building in Detroit, Michigan, have such a tremendous impact on people that it is easy for them to remember that they must go through the lighted area

FIGURE 14.5 Effective lighting should be planned in locations that require special lighting considerations, such as intersections of hallways and staircases.

to reach their gate destination (Figure 14.6). The entertainment in watching the light show also helps to reduce the perceived time that it takes to walk through a long tunnel.

Effective wayfinding lighting techniques are especially important in dark spaces or when the intent is to direct large numbers of people through a space. The United States Memorial Holocaust Museum in Washington, D.C., has an excellent example of lighting used to guide people through an exhibit space. A great deal of the space on the permanent exhibit floors is very dark. This is effective for creating feelings of reflection, contemplation, and reverence for all the exhibits that demonstrate the atrocities of the Holocaust. The low levels of illumination contribute to a quiet environment and encourage people to walk slowly through the space in order to learn as much as possible about the victims, survivors, and events.

The overall darkness of the rooms of the museum provides an excellent contrast to the video presentations and the illuminated photographs, special quotes, personal belongings, and written documents. The majority of the passage lighting is the result of the illuminated displays along the walls and reflections spilling into the walkways. The

FIGURE 14.6 Northwest Airline terminal building in Detroit, Michigan.

illuminated displays serve as the cues for moving through the space and provide the historical depiction of the Holocaust. The illuminated cues are especially important in finding one's way through the floors because the architect, James Ingo Freed, designed the floor plan and building to deliberately create feelings of disorientation and deception in people. Freed wanted people viewing the exhibits to experience, as much as possible, some of the same feelings of deception experienced by the victims and survivors of the Holocaust. Thus, the lighting cues help to orient one through spaces that are built with strange oblique angles. In addition, a bright source of daylight, located at the end of every major dark exhibit, helps to guide people to the floor or exhibit area. Daylight also helps to provide a visual change from the dark areas and an emotional relief from the overwhelming impact of the exhibits. The planned movements from dark to light also evoke feelings of hope within despair.

Emergency Conditions

Wayfinding in an emergency condition is critical in order to save lives. The toxic fumes from smoke can kill people quickly. Lighting plays an important role in helping to immediately inform people of the fastest way to evacuate a space and building. The *NFPA 101: Life Safety Code, 2003 Edition,* Section 7-10 addresses marking means of egress: "Access to exits shall be marked by approved, readily visible signs in all cases where the exit or way to reach the exit is not readily apparent to the occupants. New sign placement shall be such that no point in an exit access corridor is in excess of the rated viewing distance or 30 m (100 ft), whichever is less, from the nearest sign (2003, 101: p. 68)."

Section 7.10.1.7 of the 2003 code also provides valuable information regarding floor proximity egress path marking. "Where floor proximity egress path marking is required in Chapters 11 through 42, a listed and approved floor proximity egress path marking system that is internally illuminated shall be installed within 455 m (18 in.) of the floor. The system shall provide a visible delineation of the path of travel along the designated exit access and shall be essentially continuous, except as interrupted by doorways, hallways, corridors, or other such architectural features. The system shall operate continuously or at any time the building fire alarm system is activated." The code indicates that the general illumination of signs for exit "shall be suitably illuminated by a reliable light source. Externally and internally illuminated signs shall be legible in both the normal and emergency lighting mode" (2003, 101: p. 68).

Engineers in Hungary, Germany, and Japan recently studied the effects of smoke and panic on egress. Helbing, Farkas, and Vicsek summarized current research related to the following characteristics of escape panics: "(i) People move or try to move considerably faster than normal. (ii) Individuals start pushing, and interactions among people become physical in nature. (iii) Moving and, in particular, passing of a bottleneck becomes incoordinated. (iv) At exits, arching and clogging are observed. (v) Jams are building up. (vi) The physical interactions in the jammed crowd add up and cause dangerous pressures up to 4450 Newtons per meter, which can bend steel barriers or tear down brick walls. (vii) Escape is further slowed down by fallen or injured people turning into 'obstacles.' (viii) People show a tendency of mass behaviour, i.e., to do what other people do. (ix) Alternative exits are often overlooked or not efficiently used in escape situations" (2000, p. 2).

In the same article, Helbing, Farkas, and Vicsek (2000) provide the results of a simulation study they conducted to examine the dynamic conditions associated with escape panic. They conclude that "it is, therefore, imperative to have sufficiently wide exits and to prevent counterflows, when big crowds want to leave. Our results suggest that the best escape strategy is a certain compromise between following of others and an individualistic searching behavior. We find that pedestrians tend to jam up at one of the exits instead of equally using all available exits, if the panic parameter is large" (Helbing, Farkas, and Vicsek, 2000, p. 12 and 16).

In another study, Isobe, Helbing, and Nagatani (2003) created simulations of the evacuation process under conditions in which there was no visibility. To simulate evacuating a smoke-filled room, students were asked to exit an empty classroom wearing an eye mask. The researchers videotaped the room to observe their behavior. The research involved different conditions, including trying to exit a room with one and two doors. To study the individual and collective behavior of people, the simulation in the room with one door first involved a student alone and then a group of ten students.

The results of the study (Isobe, Helbing, & Nagatani, 2003) suggest that when people were told to find the exit, they turned slightly at first, and then moved toward one of the walls. They used their hands to move along the wall in either the right or left direction. When one or two of the students exited the room, the remaining students noticed the direction and followed. This resulted in a lower evacuation time for the group of ten students, as compared to the person who was alone. A similar situation occurred in the simulation with two doors at opposite sides of the room. As soon as one of the individuals found the exit, it appears the other students recognized the location of the exit acoustically and moved to the same exit. This resulted in unnecessary jamming because the other exit was basically unused. The researchers indicate, "First, the average escape time becomes minimal for a specific finite number of people, who are initially in the room. Second, adding more exits does not increase the efficiency of evacuation in the expected way" (Isobe, Helbing, & Nagatani, 2003, p. 1).

Current research, descriptions provided by survivors of disasters, and the unpredictability of each emergency suggest that multiple means must be considered to help people evacuate a building. Frequently, elements planned to assist with evacuation focus on only lighting and signage. Clearly, more research needs to be conducted to consider how lighting can play a role in safe emergency evacuations. The following suggestions should serve as a stimulus for designers to think about ways lighting can make buildings safer.

Research indicates that in conditions without visibility, people use other senses to help them exit a room. For example, in the Isobe, Helbing, and Nagatani (2003) study, it was found that when blindfolded, people touched the walls to guide them to the door. Furthermore, in a group situation, the sound of people exiting the room helped others to locate the exit door. Thus, in addition to lighting, other means, such as audio and textured surfaces, might be considered to help guide people to exits. Since moving quickly actually slowed evacuation, perhaps researchers should study the effectiveness of emergency lighting. For example, a bright, flashing red or white light with a loud buzzing sound might contribute to panic and cause people to move faster. Perhaps a well-seen modulated light source might accomplish the task of alerting people that they must exit the building while reducing panic and the speed of exit. The light source might also have a recording of a calm voice that informs people to exit the building and describes the quickest path. If the spoken directions are site-specific, people would be told to go to the closest exit. Perhaps, this could encourage people to use multiple exits and exits other than the one used when they first entered the space.

Textured, directional signage and using photoluminescent paints could provide supplemental emergency information. Some of the survivors of the World Trade Center disaster reported that the staircases were black, which made it very difficult to know when they had reached the last step. This uncertainty contributed to increasing the evacuation time. To help people know when they have reached a landing, perhaps staircases should have a texture along the walls that changes when people reach the last step, or perhaps the last step could be illuminated and the luminaire could have a noticeable texture change that is detectable by feet.

Lighting for safety and security purposes is very serious, essential, and critical. Some of the recent emergency situations and research studies serve as a stimulus to create safer buildings. An interior designer should explore all current resources when planning a safe environment. The most successful applications involve multiple professionals, such as engineers, researchers, electricians, fire officials, manufacturers, and behavioral scientists working together.

SUMMARY

- Understanding how people function in a space under normal conditions and during disasters is key to planning interiors that are as safe as possible.
- Based upon research and interviews with experts in the field, a *Chicago Tribune* article stressed the importance of training staff in safe evacuation practices, including knowing where people should

exit and how to effectively communicate information during an emergency.

- One of the first steps in safety preparedness should be to examine which areas in a building are vulnerable to hazards and cause feelings of insecurity. Buildings should be analyzed under normal operating conditions, and one should try to envision what might occur in a crisis.

- Passageway problems can be further exacerbated by smoke, debris, and total darkness.

- In addition to the effects of an emergency condition, all interiors have the potential for disability glare, dark areas, and shadows. These conditions can be safety issues and cause feelings of insecurity.

- Generally, areas in a building that are vulnerable to hazards include staircases, bathrooms, kitchens, and any space that involves potentially dangerous tasks. The primary safety area in bathrooms is the bathtub/shower. Safety issues related to electricity must be considered in a quality lighting environment.

- Tall buildings under normal conditions can evoke feelings of fear and insecurity.

- The safe specification, installation, and maintenance of lighting systems are regulated by national codes and local ordinances.

- The National Electric Code (NEC) is a document sponsored by the NFPA. The NEC has guidelines that directly affect lighting systems, including Article 410 and *NFPA 101: Life Safety Code, 2003 Edition*.

- Key to the safe operation of lighting systems is following codes and manufacturers' instructions and contacting the CPSC for a listing of safety problems involving lamps, luminaires, and controls.

- Lamps for emergency and exit lighting have special considerations. Emergency lighting must operate in the event of a power failure. Exit lighting operates at all times, and the lamps illuminate the word "exit."

- Some special features related to safety that can be integrated into the design of luminaires include antivandalism devices and protection from weather and ultraviolet radiation.

- A safe lighting system requires appropriate operational procedures. In commercial interiors, an interior designer should work with management, employees, and the building service workers to create policies and procedures related to safety and security.

■ To successfully plan lighting for wayfinding, an interior designer must examine all the elements involved in a project, including characteristics of the site, users of the space, physical constraints, safety codes, and operational policies.

■ Under normal conditions, lighting for wayfinding should be planned to provide the visibility necessary to safely walk through the building and to read directional, identification, and informational signage.

■ Wayfinding in an emergency is critical to saving lives. The toxic fumes from smoke can kill people quickly. Lighting plays an important role in helping to immediately inform people of the fastest way to evacuate a space and building.

■ Current research, descriptions provided by survivors of disasters, and the unpredictability of each emergency suggest that multiple means must be considered to help people evacuate a building. More research needs to be conducted to consider how lighting can play a role in safe emergency evacuations.

Key Terms

arc fault circuit interrupters (AFCIs)

ground fault circuit interrupters (GFCIs)

Exercises

1. Visit three different commercial buildings. For each site identify which features of the space could become a hazard in a panic situation. Provide suggestions for how lighting could improve the safety and security of the space. Summarize your results in a written report and include illustrations, photographs, or sketches.

2. Research a recent disaster that occurred in a building. Write a written report that addresses the following issues:

   a. Describe the characteristics of the built environment.

   b. Analyze what occurred in the emergency.

c. Identify what we can learn from the emergency that can help to improve the safety of buildings.

3. Research emergency lighting systems from at least three different manufacturers. In a written report compare and contrast the characteristics of the lighting systems. Include illustrations, photographs, or sketches.

4. Research at least four organizations or agencies related to the safety of buildings. In a written report summarize information related to lighting systems.

5. Visit three different commercial buildings. For each site, identify the wayfinding techniques and the lighting designed for wayfinding. Summarize the techniques and provide suggestions for how the wayfinding techniques could be improved under normal and emergency conditions. Include illustrations, photographs, or sketches.

REFERENCES

Allphin, W. (1961). BCD appraisals of luminaire brightness in a simulated office. *Illuminating Engineering,* 56(1), 31–44.

Ander, G. (1997). *Daylighting Performance & Design.* New York: John Wiley & Sons.

Archea, J. (1985). Environmental factors associated with stair accidents by the elderly. *Clinics in Geriatric Medicine,* 1, 555–569.

Ashdown, I. (1998). Making near-field photometry practical. *Journal of the Illuminating Engineering Society,* 27(1), 67–79.

Benya, J., Heschong, L., McGowan, T., Miller, N., and Rubinstein, F. (2001). *Advanced Lighting Guidelines.* White Salmon, WA: New Buildings Institute.

Blackwell, H.M. (1946). Contrast thresholds of the human eye. *Journal of the Optical Society of America,* 36, 624–643.

Boyce, P.R. (1973). Age, illuminance, visual performance, and preference. *Lighting Research and Technology,* 5, 125–139.

Brainard, G.C., and Bernecker, C.A. (1995, November). The effects of light on physiology and behavior. Proceedings of CIE 23rd Session, New Delhi, India: Central Bureau of CIE.

BSI (1992). *Code of Practice for Daylighting.* British Standard BS 8206 Part 2.

Coaton, J.R., and Marsden, A.M. (1997). *Lamps and Lighting,* 4th edition. London: Arnold.

Deardorff, J., Haynes, V., Mihalopoulos, D., and Mendell, D. (2003, February 23). Club safety takes center stage: Tragedies put spotlight on procedures at nightspots. *Chicago Tribune,* pp. 1, 10.

Environmental Protection Agency (EPA) (1999, March). *Analysis of Emissions Reduction Options for the Electric Power Industry,* Office of Air and Radiation, U.S. Environmental Protection Agency, Washington, DC. http://www.epa.gov/capi/multipol/mercury.htm.

Erwine, B., and Heschong, L. (2000, March/April). Daylight: Healthy, wealthy & wise. *Architectural Lighting Magazine.*

Evans, G.W. (1997). Environmental stress and health. In A. Baum, T. Revenson, and J.E. Singer (eds.), *Handbook of Health Psychology.* Hillsdale, NJ: Earlbaum.

Evans, G.W. (ed.) (1982). *Environmental Stress.* Cambridge: Cambridge University Press.

Evans, G.W,. and Cohen, S. (1987). Environmental stress. In D. Stokols and I Altman (eds.), *Handbook of Environmental Psychology.* New York: John Wiley & Sons, pp. 571–610.

Food and Drug Administration. (1986, September 10). Lamp's labeling found to be fraudulent. *FDA Talk Paper* (No. T86-69). Rockville, MA: U.S. Department of Health and Human Services.

Fry, G.A. (1976). A simplified formula for discomfort glare. *Journal of the Illuminating Engineering Society,* 8(1), 10–20.

Garling, T., Book, A., and Lindberg, E. (1986). Spatial orientation and wayfinding in the designed environment: A conceptual analysis and some suggestions for postoccupancy evaluation. *Journal of Architectural and Planning Research,* 3, 55–64.

Gawron, V.J. (1982). Performance effects of noise intensity, psychological set, and task type and complexity. *Human Factors,* 24, 225–243.

Gregory, R.I. (1979). *Eye and Brain: The Psychology of Seeing,* 3rd edition. New York: McGraw-Hill.

Guth, S.K., and McNelis, J.F. (1961). Further data on discomfort glare from multiple sources. *Illuminating Engineering,* 56(1), 46–57.

Hedge, A., Erickson, W., and Rubin, G. (1992). Effects of personal and occupational factors on sick building syndrome reports in air conditioning offices. In J.C. Quirk, L.R. Murphy, and J.J. Hurrell (eds.), *Stress and Well-Being at Work.* Washington, DC: American Psychological Association, pp. 286–298.

Helbing, D., Farkas, I., and Vicsek, T. (September 28, 2000). Simulating Dynamical Features of Escape Panic. Web site: arXiv:cond-mat/0009448 v1.

Hopkinson, R.G. (1957). Evaluation of glare. *Illuminating Engineering,* 52(6), 305–316.

Illuminating Engineering Society of North America (IESNA) (1998). Lighting for the aged and partially sighted committee. *Recommended Practice for Lighting and the Visual Environment for Senior Living,* RP-28-98. New York: Illuminating Engineering Society of North America.

Illuminating Engineering Society of North America (IESNA) (2000). *IESNA Lighting Handbook,* 9th edition. New York: Illuminating Engineering Society of North America.

Isobe, M., Helbing, D., and Nagatani, T. (2003, June). Many-particle simulation of the evacuation process from a room without visibility. Web site: arXiv:cond-mat/0306136 v1.

Lindell, M., and Perry, R. (1992). *Behavioral Foundations of Community Emergency Planning.* Washington, DC: Hemisphere.

Mileti, D.S., and Sorensen, J.S. (1990). *Communication of Emergency Public Warnings: A Social Science Perspective and State-of-the-Art Assessment.* Oak Ridge, TN: Oak Ridge National Laboratory.

National Fire Protection Association (NFPA) (2003). *NFPA 101: Life Safety Code, 2003 Edition.* Quincy, MA: National Fire Protection Association.

National Fire Protection Association (NFPA) (2002). *National Electrical Code Handbook,* 9th edition. Quincy, MA: National Fire Protection Association.

Passini, R. (1984). *Wayfinding in Architecture,* New York: Van Nostrand Reinhold.

Passini, R., Pigot, H., Rainville, C., and Tetreault, M.H. (2000). Wayfinding in a nursing home for advanced dementia of the Alzheimer's type. *Environment and Behavior,* 32(5), 684–710.

Passini, R., Rainville, C., Marchand, N., and Joanette, Y. (1998). Wayfinding and dementia: Some research findings and a new look at design. *Journal of Architectural and Planning Research,* 15(2), 133–151.

Peek, L.A., and Mileti, D.S. (2002). The history and future of disaster research. In R.B. Bechtel and A. Churchman (eds.), *Handbook of Environmental Psychology,* pp. 511–524.

Phillips, D. (2000). *Lighting Modern Buildings.* Oxford: Architectural Press.

Research Group for Inclusive Environments (RGIE). Task lighting for visually impaired people in an office environment. *Research Group for Inclusive Environments (RGIE).* http://www.rdg.ac.uk. Retrieved December 18, 2002.

Rust, M., and Muñoz, D. (2003, February 23). Club safety takes center stage; Tragedies put spotlight on procedures at nightspots. In Deardorff, J., Haynes, V., Mihalopoulos, D., and Mendell, D. *Chicago Tribune,* pp. 1, 10.

Sottardi, D., and Tuma, R. (2002, September 8) How survivors got out of the towers. September 13, 2001. Reprinted on a CD-ROM, *Chicago Tribune.*

U.S. Environmental Protection Agency (EPA) (2001). *Design for the Environment* http://www.epa.gov/.

U.S. Office of Technology Assessment (1992). *Green Products by Design: Choices for a Cleaner Environment.* Washington, DC: Office of Technology Assessment.

Veitch, J.A., and Newsham, G.R. (1996). *Determinants of Lighting Quality II: Research and Recommendations.* Paper presented at the 104th Annual Convention of the American Psychological Association. Toronto, Ontario, Canada (ERIC Document Reproduction Service No. ED408543).

Wapner, S., and Demick, J. (2002). The increasing *contexts* of *context* in the study of environment behavior relations. In R. Bechtel and A. Churchman (eds.), *Handbook of Environmental Psychology.* New York: John Wiley & Sons.

Weale, R.A. (1961). Retinal illumination of age. *Illuminating Engineering Society,* 26(2), 95–100.

Weisman, G. (1981). Evaluating architectural legibility. *Environment and Behavior,* 13, 189–204.

Weston, H.C. (1962). *Sight, Light, and Work,* 2nd edition. London: Lewis.

Winchip, S.M. (1990). Dementia health care facility design. *Journal of Interior Design Education and Research,* 16(2), 39–46.

Wright, G.A., and Rea, M.S. (1984). Age, a human factor in lighting. *Proceedings of the 1984 International Conference on Occupational Ergonomics.* D.A. Attwood and C. McCann (eds.). Rexdale, Ontario, Canada: Human Factors Association of Canada.

Zeisel, J. (2000). Environmental design effects on Alzheimer symptoms in long term care residences. *World Hospitals and Health Service,* 36(3), 27–31.

CHAPTER 15

Illuminating Visual Art

OBJECTIVES

■ Identify the characteristics of objects and the contextual factors that are important for illuminating visual art.

■ Describe the characteristics of lamps, luminaires, and controls that are important for illuminating visual art.

■ Understand how lighting can be designed to help conserve artwork.

■ Apply an understanding of the characteristics of objects, contextual factors, and lighting systems to lighting visual art.

■ Compare and contrast the three major presentation formats for visual art, including vertical surfaces, three-dimensional pieces, and display cases.

■ Understand the relationships among visual art, lighting systems, presentation formats, the environment, and users of the space.

ILLUMINATING visual art is one of the most challenging techniques in designing a quality lighting environment. Accent lighting for visual art is the layer of light that can create drama in an interior. Every residential and commercial interior has some piece of visual art or an object of personal significance that should be illuminated. Unfortunately, many spaces have no lighting on visual art or the lighting does not adequately enhance the piece. The lighting system selected for illuminating objects can range from very inexpensive to museum quality.

Knowledge of the lighting systems and techniques that enhance visual art will allow an interior designer to specify a lighting plan that is appropriate for the purpose of the space, characteristics of the object, geometry of the space, and the project's budget. A working knowledge of effective visual art illumination can be a tremendous asset to an interior designer's portfolio and distinguish his or her work from other designers in the field.

Many of the topics addressed in Unit I should be applied to the information presented in this chapter. An understanding of illuminating visual art must include an understanding that light is part of the electromagnetic spectrum and an understanding of the physics of color, characteristics of daylight, and electrical sources. The directional effects of lighting are critically important in avoiding glare and understanding optical control and patterns of light, shade, and shadow on three-dimensional objects. Quantity of lighting plays a critical role in the preservation of visual art. A fundamental understanding of the various types of luminaires and controls is applied to selecting equipment that enhances visual art. Illuminating visual art must also take into account energy conservation, human factors, and safety concerns.

Object and Contextual Considerations

To illuminate visual art, an interior designer must understand the characteristics of the object and the contextual factors that can affect the appearance of the object.

Object Characteristics

In lighting visual art the goals should be to preserve the piece, provide clarity of expression, and enhance the aesthetics of an environment. To accomplish these goals requires an understanding of the object being displayed and its inherent characteristics. This often requires research and collaborating with curators and conservators. Working with experts in the field is imperative because of the enormous variety of items that might be highlighted with lighting. Pieces to illuminate may include paintings, sketches, line drawings, watercolors, pastels, photographs, art glass, murals, and sculptures. Objects to highlight can also include specialist collections consisting of manuscripts, books, coins, crystal, figurines, stamps, paperweights, and furniture. Some pieces, such as tapestries, costumes, rugs, and textile wall hangings, have a highly worked surface that requires special illumination techniques.

Objects are made from a variety of materials with distinctive characteristics. For example, brushwork done with glossy oils is not as fragile as pastels and watercolors. Artwork on paper, such as posters and prints, is more susceptible to damage than artwork done on canvas. Key to the conservation of visual art is knowing the inherent characteristics of materials, because they can be irreversibly damaged by visible light, ultraviolet (UV), and infrared (IR) radiation.

Generally, artwork is made from organic, inorganic, and composite materials. Organic materials are items made from plants or animals, such as paper, textiles, leather, wood, grasses, and lacquers. Organic materials are especially sensitive to light. Examples of inorganic materials are metal, stone, glass, and ceramics. Generally, inorganic materials are not damaged by light; however, some glasses are sensitive to light. Objects made from composite materials are composed of a combination of organic and inorganic matter. For example, a mural could be made from wood, grasses, and ceramics. To know the inherent characteristics of a specific piece, the best advice is to consult with a curator or conservator.

Objects to be illuminated are not restricted to valuable artwork. Every environment has interesting, everyday items that can be illuminated to create drama in a room. Generally, the best objects to illuminate have interesting textures or shapes or are meaningful to the users of the space. For example, heavy, textured draperies or brick on a fireplace grazed with lighting can create interesting highlights and shadows. Highlighting a bouquet of flowers, water, or the foliage of plants and trees can create excellent accents in a room. Illuminating family photographs, children's artwork, a corporate logo, awards, or the original cornerstone of a building can provide accent lighting and become a topic of conversation. Interior designers should work with their client to determine significant objects in the space and then specify the most effective lighting system to highlight the objects.

The variety of objects that could be illuminated is further complicated by the diversity in materials, sizes, colors, and shapes. These characteristics and the contextual setting must be considered in determining the appropriate lighting system. As discussed in Chapter 5, the perceived color of an object or a surface is determined by numerous factors, including the object, texture of the object, surrounding background, lamp, light fixture, eyes, color constancy, the brain, geometry of the room, light direction, intensity of the lamp, and the distance of the light fixture from an object. All these factors must be considered to create the contrast necessary for highlighting an object.

Some objects have unique characteristics that require special attention. For example, illuminating objects requires a close examination of the angles of incident and reflections. A piece that has a variety of materials, colors, and textures can be difficult to illuminate. Thus, an object that consists of both shiny and rough textures may require multiple light sources to accent the variation in reflectances. A specular surface is especially complicated to illuminate because the material reflects a light source like a mirror, which can create discomfort or disability glare. A change in the angle of incident can make the object appear dark, or even black. The darkness could prevent a viewer from seeing fine details in a piece, such as engraving on a silver urn. Thus, some pieces need special consideration and may require mock-ups or prototypes so that designers can see how the lighting works and eliminate problems with visibility. A mock-up is a full-size model of the proposed lighting system and structural elements. A prototype is a model of a new product or a new version of an existing lighting system.

In determining the appropriate technique for illuminating visual art, a consideration should be given to the conditions that existed when the artist created the piece. Most artwork was created prior to the existence of electrical light sources. Thus, the colors, textures, and materials chosen for a piece were based upon the effects and spectral qualities of daylight or candlelight. Perhaps the artist expected the colors and textures of a piece to be enhanced by the natural variations that occur in daylight. A marble sculpture that was originally created for an outdoor courtyard can look dramatically different when placed under electrical light sources. During the evening hours, a painting might look more interesting illuminated by candlelight rather than by an incandescent spotlight. Some contemporary artists create the setting that will enhance their artwork. For example, a piece by Richard Prince at the Barbara Gladstone Gallery in New York City incorporates a large source of daylight to enhance his artwork (Figure 15.1). Conservation guidelines must be practiced when illuminating artwork, but considering the artist's intent is critical to enhance the piece.

Contextual Factors

There are a variety of contextual factors that affect illuminated objects, including characteristics of the environment and users of the space. Contextual elements in an interior include the geometry of the space, material compositions, the location of the piece, color of surrounding surfaces, reflectance values, and illumination dispersion. In planning lighting to highlight objects, all these factors must be considered. Previous chapters in this text review these topics; however, there are some additional considerations that should be examined when specifying an environment that enhances visual art.

FIGURE 15.1 In the Barbara Gladstone Gallery, New York City daylight transmitting through the large opening creates a lighting effect that enhances the texture, color, and dimensional qualities of Richard Prince's artwork.

Creating emphasis on visual art requires an orchestrated harmonization among the object, environment, users of the space, and lighting system. In addition, artwork often changes in a space by the addition of new pieces or when new arrangements are created. Every time there are changes to the artwork, environment, or lighting system, the lighting for the art must be reevaluated and, if necessary, adjusted.

The geometry and components of a space can affect the quality of illumination aimed at an object. For example, rooms with very tall ceilings, unusual angles, and significant historical architectural elements pose unique lighting challenges. Some of the problems focus on the complexities of installation and preventing glare. In rooms with tall ceilings, the luminaire and lamp must be able to project a small beam at a far distance and prevent glare. People tend to focus a great deal of attention on a ceiling in a tall space. Therefore, the lighting plan and color of the ceiling must avoid visual noise. The color of the ceiling in a tall room also affects the visual noise of exposed lamps. A black ceiling creates the greatest contrast with a light source; hence, the lamps should be shielded from view. Lamps installed on a white ceiling are not as noticeable. Unusual angles in a room can create installation difficulties and may compete with the artwork for emphasis. The lighting plan should not destroy significant architectural elements in a space. In addition, some lighting installations might be prohibited if a building is listed on the National Register of Historic Places.

Generally, illuminating visual art will be most successful when there is simplicity in the surroundings. Elements such as large patterned wallcoverings or intense colors should be avoided. Any surface that can alter the color of an object due to its reflectance properties should be carefully selected. For example, a white sculpture could appear to be pink when it is placed next to a red wall. The pink could be intensified when the piece is located in a semicircular niche. A mixture of daylight and electrical sources in one space complicates the resulting colors. All surfaces, including the floor material, capable of reflecting color onto an object should be carefully selected. Light colors and matte finishes often work well in enhancing visual art.

An object's color, the background color, and the shadows created by a light source can affect its visibility. As shown in Figure 15.2, the

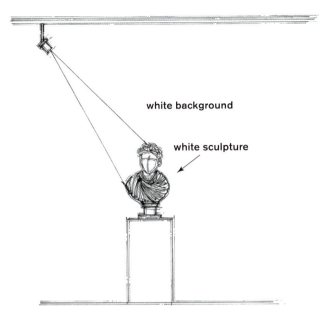

FIGURE 15.2 The shadows on the white sculpture help to emphasize its dimensional qualities.

white background

white sculpture

shadows below the white object with a white background help to define the piece and emphasize its dimensional qualities. In contrast, the shadows of a black object with a dark background hinder our ability to discern the shape of a form. Reducing the lumen output of a lamp and adding **fill light** to the piece can reduce the intense blackness of a shadow. Techniques used to create fill light include adding an additional light source that is aimed at the shadow or interreflection that strikes the shadow from the object's surrounding light sources. In addition, increasing the distance from the lamp to the object, or expanding the aiming angle (i.e., 30 to 45 degrees), can also help to reduce dark shadows.

Any highly specular material, such as mirrors or metallic finishes, can affect the quality of lighting on visual art. The dispersion of a light source determines the amount of area that will be illuminated. Surfaces perpendicular to or across from an object should be examined to determine undesirable reflective qualities. For example, in Figure 15.3, the window's reflection on the photograph creates visual noise on the piece. Potential reflections should be reviewed from a variety of positions, including the height of people seated in wheelchairs and the height differences between adults and children.

Fill light
Direct and/or indirect light that helps to reduce the intensity of dark areas.

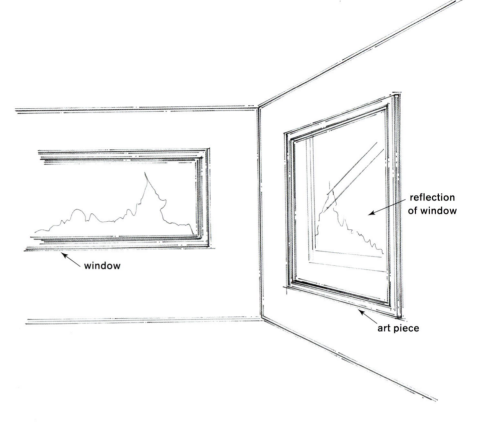

FIGURE 15.3 The window's reflection is causing glare on the artwork. To avoid veining reflections on artwork, light from a variety of sources and directions must be considered.

window

reflection of window

art piece

In a museum or an educational setting, there are other elements in the environment related to visual art that should be illuminated. The lighting for wayfinding through the spaces should be at an intensity level that does not interfere with highlighted pieces. The lighting should also help guide viewers through the gallery areas and floors. Effective lighting should be planned for the text and graphics that are necessary for wayfinding and educational purposes. Lighting might also have to be planned for audiovisual equipment and interactive systems.

Physical characteristics of people and subjective perceptions affect the success of illuminated visual art. Lighting should be planned to accommodate a variety of different heights, abilities, and visual impairments. Since effective illumination of visual art often involves contrasts for emphasis, the sequential experience within and between spaces must always be carefully planned. Adaptation is a particular concern because often a space with artwork has a low level of illumination in order to enhance the pieces and to limit their exposure to the deterioration effects of light. Therefore, it is critical to have a transition space with moderate light levels adjacent to a dark room. This is especially important when a dark room adjoins areas illuminated by daylight. In planning to accommodate visual adaptation, the anticipated time for viewing and illumination intensity on visual art should be considered. For example, an intense light source aimed at a dark painting might not be disturbing when people are casually walking through the room, as in a museum setting. However, the strong contrast might be offensive to people looking at a piece for a long time while they are having dinner in a restaurant.

Subjective perceptions of artwork can be affected by psychology, cultural meanings, and life experiences. Lighting used to highlight visual art should not be disturbing to viewers and their expectations. Flickering lights or color distortion from an electrical source can affect the subjective perceptions of a viewer. Flickering lights in a disco are expected, but this lighting technique would be disturbing to most people viewing the "Mona Lisa." Accurate color rendition is essential in illuminating visual art. A light source that creates an unexpected color can have a profoundly negative psychological effect on viewers. Work from Picasso's blue period must not appear to be green because of an inappropriate electrical light source. As discussed in Chapter 5, the range of cultural meanings associated with color must also be considered when illuminating artwork.

Lighting Systems

All of the components of a lighting system, including the light sources, luminaires, and controls, should enhance visual art.

Light Sources

A light source used to illuminate visual art should have optimum color, beam spread, projection distance, and intensity level, and it must conserve the organic material of the piece. Depending upon the object and the effect desired, the light source can be diffused, or it can be a concentrated beam of light. By using ultraviolet filtering devices, a light source can be daylight, electrical sources, or a combination of the two. To maximize the appearance of art and provide a connection to the outdoors, many museums blend daylight with electrical sources. Daylight is a desirable light source for illuminating art because of its ever-changing spectral qualities. Using daylight to illuminate art also tends to reflect the intent of the artist. Artists living in the northern hemisphere frequently work in rooms facing north, because light from this direction renders colors comparable to those seen in daylight and provides clarity to details. In the southern hemisphere, south-facing windows are the most desirable. (The various ways to protect visual art from the ill effects of light are discussed at the end of this section.)

The most common electrical sources used for illuminating visual art are incandescent filament, tungsten-halogen, metal halide, and fiber optics. Common lamps include PAR 16, 20, 30, 32, 46, 56; MR 11, 16; and R 14, 20, 25. Low-voltage lamps are often used because of their white color, energy efficiency, precise beam control, and long life. Refer to luminaire manufacturers' product literature to determine which lamps have been approved by UL. Lamps with a continuous spectrum are excellent for illuminating art. To balance the warm colors of incandescent lamps, a pale blue filter can be installed over the front of the lamp. This can be especially important when the lamp is dimmed, because the color becomes warmer at lower light levels.

To select a lamp that enhances the colors in visual art, refer to manufacturers' chromaticity ratings and color rendering index. Generally, a preferred range in chromaticity ratings is 3000 to 4100K. When daylight is not used with electrical sources, art frequently will look best when lit by lamps with lower chromaticity ratings. Generally, lamps with higher chromaticity ratings should be used when electrical and daylight sources are combined. The primary reason for the different chromaticity ratings is that a warmer electrical source helps to balance the naturally cooler color of daylight. A lamp's CRI rating should be a minimum of 85, and, whenever possible, the CRI should be 100.

Some other characteristics of lamps that are important for illuminating visual art include the beam spread, projection distance, and level of intensity. This information is available from lamp manufacturers, and examples are provided in the Appendix. The beam spread is critical for highlighting only the elements of a piece that should be illuminated. Optical control can be derived from the lamp or luminaire or a combination of the two. As discussed in Chapter 3, reflector lamps, such as R, PAR, and MR lamps, have an optical system designed within the lamp to control light. Some luminaires are specifically designed to disperse light in a range from narrow to wide. An important consideration in calculating the location of the beam spread is the location of the luminaire. Generally, the beam spread of a lamp installed far from an art piece will be wider than a beam emitted from a luminaire that is close to the object (see Figure 15.4). The lamp's projection, or **throw distance**, affects the beam spread and the quantity of light that will fall on an object. This is especially important in rooms with tall ceilings. For example, in a ten-story atrium area, it would be important to specify a lamp that has a long projection distance if the luminaire is installed in the ceiling and the art piece is at ground level.

The illumination level on visual art is important in order to adequately see details of the piece, eliminate glare, and create the contrast required for emphasis. It is also important to maintain a maximum level for conservation purposes, without damaging the work of art. To clearly see the details of an object requires an orchestration of all the elements of the lighting system and environment. Unfortunately, when

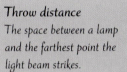

Throw distance
The space between a lamp and the farthest point the light beam strikes.

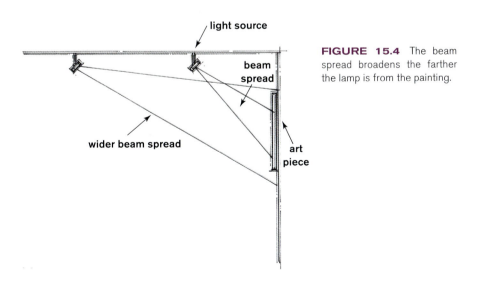

FIGURE 15.4 The beam spread broadens the farther the lamp is from the painting.

it is difficult to see details, a common solution is to increase illumination levels, which may result in viewer discomfort or disability glare. To improve a lighting environment, the entire system must be analyzed and evaluated. Often making details visible requires that factors be combined. Highlighting visual art requires an appropriate illumination ratio between the object and its background. Generally, a 5 to 1 ratio focuses attention to an object, and a ratio of 15 to 1, or greater, creates drama. In the name of conservation 10 to 1 can be effective.

Illumination levels affect the condition of visual art. Higher illumination levels increase photochemical and thermal damage to an object. The more light energy that strikes an object, the greater the rate of deterioration. Damage to an object is dependent upon the light level and the amount of time the object is exposed to the light. Therefore, if it is necessary to illuminate an object with high levels of illumination, then the time of exposure should be short. To protect visual art, the goal should be to use the lowest level of illumination possible for the shortest period of time. Table 15.1 provides a list of recommended standards for visible light levels (National Park Service, 1999). A visible light meter measures light levels, and an ultraviolet meter monitors UV radiation. Lights should be turned off whenever possible.

Not only does visible light adversely affect the condition of artwork but UV rays also can cause damage. In fact, UV rays can cause the greatest damage to materials. Daylight and all electrical sources have some level of UV radiation. However, using the proper filters, equipment, and techniques can eliminate UV radiation. Artwork should never be in direct contact with daylight. Indirect daylight can enter a space in a variety of ways, including *clerestories*, or light wells. Paints containing titanium dioxide pigment or zinc can help to absorb UV radiation. Ceilings, walls, and any other surfaces that are in contact with direct sunlight should be covered with paints containing these elements. Window treatments, including shutters, draperies, blinds, and shades, can filter UV radiation. Some devices, such as mechanized louvers, are controlled by sunlight. UV filtering film can be installed on windows, lamps, and glass that protect artwork. UV filters that are made from acrylic and other plastics should be replaced when they yellow or crack.

TABLE 15.1
Standards for Visible Light Levels

50 lux maximum	200 lux maximum	300 lux maximum*
Light-sensitive materials	*Less light-sensitive materials*	*Other materials that are not light-sensitive*
Dyed organic materials	Undyed organic materials	Metals
Textiles	Oil and tempera paintings	Stone
Watercolors	Finished wooden surfaces	Ceramics
Photographs and blueprints		Some glass
Tapestries		
Prints and drawings		
Manuscripts		
Leather		
Wallpapers		
Biological specimens		
Furs		
Feathers		

*Note: "In general don't use levels above 300 lux in your exhibit space so that light level variation between exhibit spaces is not too great" (1999, p. 4:36).

Adapted from: National Park Service, *Museum Handbook,* Part I (1999), Chapter 4: Museum Collections Environment.

All electrical lamps emit some UV radiation. The level of emission depends upon the type of lamp. Incandescent lamps emit the lowest level of UV radiation, followed by tungsten-halogen lamps. Fluorescent and HID lamps emit high levels of UV radiation, so these lamps should always have a filter. UV and IR reduction filters are available for many luminaires. Dichroic glass is excellent for absorbing UV radiation. For special applications, fiber optics can be an excellent solution, because the light source does not come in direct contact with an object.

To help protect artwork, conservation requirements should always be included in lighting specifications. For maintenance purposes, the variety of lamps, wattages, and color rendering properties should be minimized. This will help to ensure that the correct lamp is installed during relamping procedures. Whenever possible, the lamps selected should conserve energy. This is especially important because, generally, the most effective lamps for illuminating visual art consume high levels of energy. To conserve energy, recent legislation has prohibited many of the lamps that were formerly used to illuminate visual art.

Luminaires and Controls

Luminaires and controls specified for artwork should preserve and enhance the objects. To protect artwork, luminaires should be selected that have a high luminaire efficacy rating (LER) and UV and IR filters. To reduce the amount of heat striking an object and the intensity of a light source, luminaires should not be mounted close to artwork. Lamps should be turned off when they are not needed. Thus, to provide flexibility in switching lamps on and off, luminaires should be wired to separate control circuits. In addition, dimmers, timers, occupancy sensors, and photosensors can help to reduce the time of exposure and illumination levels. To instantly provide the perfect lighting plan, art scenes can be programmed using central control units.

Selecting a luminaire requires an assessment of the purpose of the fixture, characteristics of the visual art, architectural features, installation choices, and maintenance considerations. The lighting layers for visual art should include ambient, task, and accent sources. Daylight, electrical sources, or a combination of the two can provide the illumination for each of these techniques. Ambient lighting is important for visual art because it provides the background lighting needed for people to walk through the space, and because it can contribute to fill light. Task lighting should enable a viewer to clearly see an object and read any related text. Accent lighting should enhance the excitement and drama of visual art. A luminaire should be selected to specifically enhance the purpose of each layer of lighting.

In addition to having an understanding of the inherent characteristics of the materials of an object, interior designers must know the dimensions, colors, form, texture, and lines of a piece. These details help in identifying the appropriate luminaire, the number of fixtures, and an appropriate location for the fixtures. A critical factor in selecting luminaires is the permanence of the artwork. In settings in which the art is frequently changed or moved, such as art museums, luminaires should be selected that maximize the flexibility in aiming angles, lamps, and sources.

Luminaires should be selected that enhance the architectural features of a space. The style, scale, color, and proportions of the luminaires should be unified with the characteristics of the room. To focus attention on the visual art, the luminaires should blend with the architecture of the space or be concealed from view. An excellent example of blending luminaires with architecture is in some of the galleries at the Museum of Contemporary Art in Chicago (Figure 15.5). The grid pattern of the luminous ceiling was designed to accommodate the dimensions and proper location for the track system's electrical raceway. In older museums, track systems had to be installed on ceilings that were not designed for contemporary fixtures. Thus, designers were not able to achieve a harmonious blending of the architecture and lighting

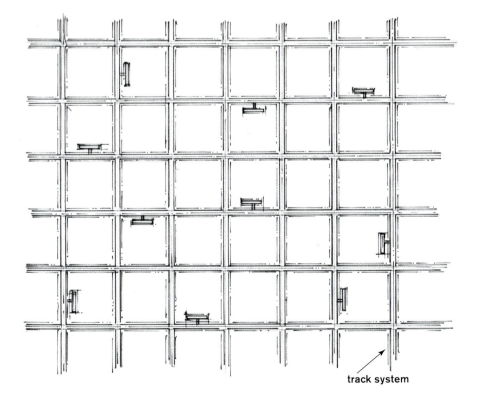

track system

FIGURE 15.5 An adaption of a reflected ceiling plan of a gallery at the Museum of Contemporary Art in Chicago. The grid pattern of the ceiling accommodates the dimensions and proper location for the track system's electrical raceway.

systems. For buildings listed on the National Register of Historic Places, preserving the architecture and the integrity of the space is essential. For these projects designers should consult the guidelines provided by the National Park Service.

The type of visual art, architectural details, installation options, and maintenance factors must simultaneously be considered in selecting a luminaire. For example, the best lighting technique for a sculpture might be recessed fixtures, located to the sides of a piece. The architectural details and installation options must be analyzed to determine if it is feasible to install a recessed fixture. For example, the proper location for the recessed fixture might damage significant architectural elements. Furthermore, the ideal position for illuminating the sculpture might not have the clearance space or access to electrical power. The location of the fixture must also be accessible for maintenance purposes, including cleaning and relamping. After a thorough analysis of the visual art, architectural details, and installation and maintenance has been conducted, the luminaires can be selected.

Generally, luminaires for visual art are recessed, structural, furniture-integrated, and surface-mounted on ceilings or walls. Ceiling-mounted track systems are frequently used because of their flexibility; it is easy to reaim them, change lamps, and relocate the heads. Some portable luminaires are available for accent and uplights. For illuminating visual art, the most effective types of luminaires are individual spot, projector optics, flood, and wall-wash. Individual spot and projector optics may be used to highlight a specific piece or unique details. Generally, flood and wall-wash units are used for display and ambient lighting. To maximize control of the light, most luminaires are designed for lamps with an integral reflector, such as R, PAR, and MR.

There are features and accessories for luminaires that can be helpful in illuminating visual art. Luminaire devices for holding accessories are either integral to the housing unit or require special holders that have to be ordered. All luminaire manufacturers will have unique attributes of their product. Therefore, an interior designer should review the catalogs of several manufacturers, understand the characteristics of the product, compare performance data, and then specify the luminaires that are best for the objectives of the project. Some of the features of luminaires important to consider for illuminating visual art include the type of lamp, characteristics of the housing, adjustment features, accessory options, and maintenance.

In selecting a luminaire, it is critical to examine the type of lamps that can be installed in the fixture. A luminaire style might not be able to accommodate specific characteristics required of a lamp. Luminaire manufacturers will list the type of lamp, voltage, and maximum wattages for each luminaire. The specific characteristics of a lamp should be researched to determine the best color, energy-efficiency ratings, beam spread, throw distance, heat emission, and life.

Manufacturers' product literature will provide all the specifications of a luminaire. Some of the features that are important for illuminating visual art include the ability to control light and eliminate spill light and glare. **Spill light** is undesirable light emitted from an opening. Quality lighting on visual art requires accurate control of light on an object and the surrounding area. A luminaire designed for accent lighting should project the light at the appropriate distance, illumination level, and beam spread. Wall-washing and flood luminaires should have a uniform, smooth distribution of light over an entire wall. An anodized aluminum kick reflector in the head of a track system distributes light evenly from ceiling to floor (Figure 15.6). Some wall-wash luminaires have an asymmetrical reflector device that can direct maximum illumination at eye level.

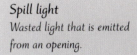

Spill light
Wasted light that is emitted from an opening.

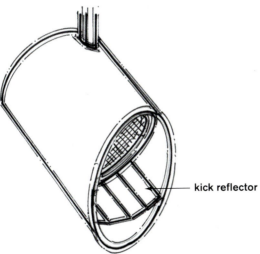

kick reflector

FIGURE 15.6 A track head with an anodized aluminum kick reflector.

Optical systems in luminaires can provide accurate, long throw distances that range from very narrow to very wide beam spreads. Proper control of illumination also involves eliminating undesirable light, such as glare and spill light. Undesirable light has to be controlled from the aperture and the luminaire's housing unit. Some other inherent characteristics that can be important for visual art are a compact size, location of electronic transformers, dimming capabilities, ability to dissipate heat, and variability of intensity.

Often illuminating visual art requires precision techniques and frequent changes of the object. To accommodate these needs, luminaires should be selected that have pan and tilt adjustments. These units should be self-locking in the horizontal and vertical planes. Some luminaires have 360-degree rotation for pan adjustments. Units are available with up to 45-degree tilt adjustments. A locking focus can also be an important feature of a luminaire because the unit can be cleaned and relamped without someone inadvertently changing the initial focus position.

Since the lighting for visual art can change frequently, ease of maintenance is an important consideration. Generally, a luminaire that is accessible from the front and has a hinged opening to the aperture is the easiest for changing accessories and relamping. Mounting slots that are integrated into the housing unit are convenient for changing accessories. Ideally, tools should not be required to relamp or change the accessories.

Luminaire accessories are important in creating quality lighting for art. The most important accessories are optical lenses, filters, baffles, louvers, and barn doors (Figure 15.7 a–d). Optical lenses help to shape and control light and are available in a variety of styles. Many of the lenses help smooth the imperfections emitted from electrical light sources. A diffused or sand-blasted spread distributes light in a smooth, consistent pattern (see Figure 9.9). An elongated or linear spread lens creates a strip of light (Figure 15.7 a). A prismatic spread distributes light in a wide, even pattern. Asymmetrical and symmetrical spread lenses distribute light in an uneven and even pattern, respectively. The most useful filters for illuminating visual art are color, light reduction, and UV and IR reduction. Color filters are used for chromatic effects and replicating daylight. Light reduction filters pro-

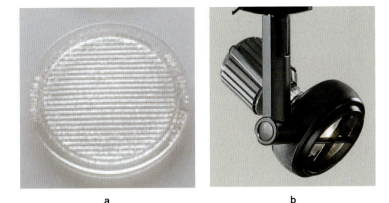

a   b

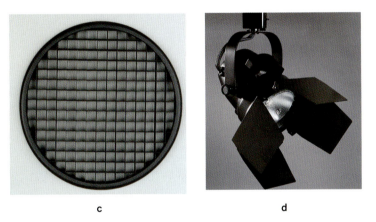

c   d

FIGURE 15.7 A variety of luminaire accessories: (a) linear lens; (b) cross baffle; (c) cube cell louver; (d) barn door shutters.

vide variability in lighting intensities. UV and IR reduction filters are used for conservation purposes.

There are many accessories available to eliminate glare and spill light. Some heads have a snoot (extended metal tube) that provides a full cutoff of glare. A cross baffle eliminates frontal glare and spill light (Figure 15.7 b). Louvers help to shield the lamp and reduce glare. The various types of louvers are hex cell (honeycomb), cube cell, concentric rings, and parabolic (Figure 15.7 c). Each type distributes light in varying intensities and patterns. A solid lamp shield will totally eliminate glare from the back of the lamp. Perforated or mesh lamp units reduce the level of intensity of light. Barn doors are very effective for illuminating art because they help to eliminate glare and to shape the light beam (Figure 15.7 d). Extended barn doors eliminate spill light. Stainless steel light-blocking screens reduce light without changing the color or beam distribution.

Presentation Formats

The characteristics of a piece of visual art affect the selection of its appropriate location.

Vertical Surfaces

An interior designer should anticipate that projects could include highlighting a variety of materials and objects. For example, at the United States Memorial Holocaust Museum in Washington, D.C., a special exhibit was done on the writing abilities of Anne Frank. Thus, the focal point of the exhibit was words, so the lighting had to enhance quotes from Frank's diary. One way of accomplishing this effectively was using multiple light sources and a computerized projector. An open-weave fabric was stretched approximately 6 inches (15.24 cm) in front of the wall that displayed Frank's quotes. The wall was softly washed with uplights, which were placed behind a fascia along the floor. To soften the illumination intensity, a light-filtering fabric was placed over the lights. The illuminated quotes were printed in white text, which created an excellent contrast to the dark wall and the dark room. The quote that a viewer first sees when walking into the room is permanent; however, the other quotes fade on and off. The combination of the lighting and the words fading in and out behind the soft fabric creates a provocative setting that makes the viewer feel that Frank's thoughts of the past are still alive today. The Anne Frank exhibit is an excellent example of how accent lighting can involve a variety of objects or concepts and that uncommon elements can often inspire creative solutions.

The visual art, interior, and lighting should be viewed as a system that has to be planned simultaneously in order to create a quality lighting environment. The proper location for visual art includes identifying the best room and the ideal spot within the room. In selecting the right room, an important consideration is daylight. Visual art made from organic materials that are very sensitive to daylight, such as textiles, tapestries, and watercolors, should be located in a room without daylight, or with only indirect daylight. Generally, sculptures made from inorganic materials are enhanced in a room with daylight.

The room's geometry and the scale of a piece affect how well lighting can enhance the art. For example, illuminating a very small object could be challenging in a space with very tall ceilings. Thus, the small object might look better in a smaller room or in a display case. The location of windows and openings on a wall also affect the harmonization of lighting and visual art. For instance, an art piece might be too large to fit on the wall that can be illuminated. Windows next to a wall that has a painting could cause disability glare. The reflection of a window on an adjacent wall could cause veiling reflections on the visual art. Therefore, the interior designer must analyze all the characteristics of spaces and, whenever possible, select the room that best allows the lighting to enhance the visual art.

Many of the elements that are considered in selecting the ideal room become important criteria in determining the best location within the space. In addition, the purpose of the space, characteristics of the piece, and primary location of viewing should be considered when identifying the installation spot. For example, in a dining room people view things primarily from a seated position. Thus, visual art and the lighting should be located in a position that looks best when seen by someone sitting on a dining room chair. In a living room, the seat height of the sofa is lower than a dining chair. Thus, the visual art and lighting should be adjusted to a lower viewing angle. The location of the visual art and lighting should be at a higher level when people are viewing the pieces while they are walking through a space, such as in an art museum or hallway. In general, eye level in a standing position is estimated at 5 feet 3 inches (160 cm) AFF.

Generally, the characteristics of an art piece will determine whether it is located on a vertical or horizontal plane. Most two-dimensional visual art looks best when mounted on a vertical surface. A horizontal surface can enhance some objects, such as pages from a rare book. In selecting the luminaires for a vertical surface, the number of pieces and size of the objects are important considerations. For example, one large object on a wall requires several points of light. A gallery display that changes frequently also needs several light sources. On the other hand, a small painting over a fireplace might need only one light source. In planning multiple light sources, the pattern of light must be determined. A uniform pattern of illumination will create an even distribution of light on art, without emphasis on a piece or on a detail of an object. A nonuniform distribution of light creates the emphasis needed to highlight visual art.

In designing for emphasis, it is critical to plan appropriate intensity levels for the illumination zones of the piece. The illumination level surrounding an art piece should be of a lower intensity than that of the visual art. Frequently, only a painting is illuminated, and the wall area surrounding it is dark. Generally, severe contrast does not enhance an object, and a strong intensity can cause difficulties with visual adaptation. Thus, the lighting must be planned to enhance the visual art and its surrounding area. One approach is to wash the wall with a soft, ambient light and then use accent lighting for the visual art.

Generally, the best way to illuminate visual art on a vertical surface is to aim the light from the ceiling. In order to do this well, important factors to consider are the viewing position, the aiming angle, the height of the ceiling, and the distance between the light fixture and the wall. For lighting systems that have multiple sources, such as tracks, the location between fixtures is also important. Figure 15.8 illustrates a significant problem with a painting for which the appropriate calcu-

FIGURE 15.8
Accurate calculations will help to assure that the light beam strikes a painting in the desired location.

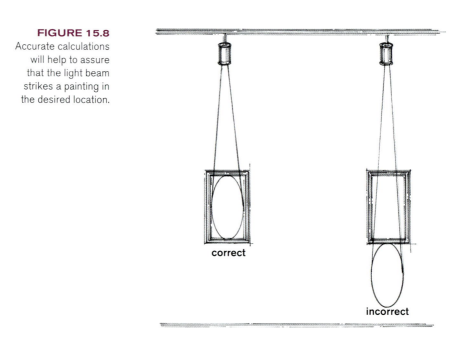

correct

incorrect

lations were not performed. Furthermore, the aiming angle must not create a shadow from the frame onto the art. The best way to calculate the ideal mounting location is to refer to the luminaire's performance data charts. The Appendix contains an example of a manufacturer's chart for accent lighting. The chart includes all the critical data needed to effectively light visual art on a wall, including the intensity of the light source, aiming angle, viewing position, and distances. Complete tables for grazing, accent, and wall-washing techniques are provided in the Appendix.

In selecting an appropriate aiming angle, it is important to consider the reflective properties of the art piece. For art with a flat surface, the preferred aiming angle is between 30 and 45 degrees nadir in the vertical plane. For very tall paintings, cross lighting might be effective (Figure 15.9). To avoid problems with glare on glossy surfaces, such as oil paint or glass, the aiming angle might have to be increased. Using non-reflective glass or angling the piece slightly toward the floor can also help to reduce glare. When daylight is used as one of the light sources, the aiming angle associated with the aperture is important. For example, the angle of light emitted from a skylight affects visual art differently from the way it is affected when daylight comes through a window. Furthermore, because of the aiming angle, light from a window located next to a piece will create a different effect from when the window is directly across from the visual art. Electrical light sources can be used to balance the different effects created by daylight.

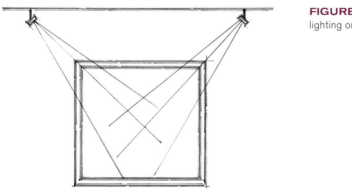

FIGURE 15.9 Cross lighting on a tall painting.

Three-Dimensional Pieces

Three-dimensional art objects can include sculpture, ceramics, crystal, furniture, flowers, trees, or water. Lighting should be designed to enhance the volumetric form of the object. Determining the expectations of sculptors is an excellent approach to understanding how to design the optimum lighting scheme for a sculpture. Many of the first sculptures were made for an outdoor setting, such as a courtyard, not a dark room in a building. Thus, it appears that people had an incredible understanding of what type of lighting would best enhance three-dimensional art. A sculpture placed outdoors looks different every hour and day and at different times of the year. On a cloudless day, the intense beams of light highlight the dominant elements of the piece and create interesting patterns of shade and shadows. Reflected light provides the fill light needed for people to view the entire sculpture. Clouds introduce interesting modulation patterns on the piece and enable a viewer to clearly see carving details. As the sun rotates around the piece throughout the day, the dimensionality of the visual art is reinforced. Thus, an understanding of lighting techniques that enhance three-dimensional pieces must include a close examination of the qualities of daylight.

The object's inherent characteristics should be considered when the lighting system is designed. Objects that are solid masses, such as marble sculptures, require different lighting techniques from pieces that have light moving through or around the surfaces. Lighting for specular materials has to be planned to eliminate glare. The characteristics of the piece affect the proper aiming angle. For example, backlighting can be an effective technique for illuminating glass objects because the silhouette of the object can be enhanced while glare is eliminated (Figure 2.15). An excellent method for highlighting water coming out of a fountain is to locate luminaires at an angle that will illuminate the point where the spray strikes the water's surface. Objects with transparent qualities, such as glass or some foliage on plants or trees, should be illuminated from the top or bottom. Opaque objects look best with front or backlighting techniques.

The overall shape of the object can affect the appropriate location of the light sources. Generally, objects that have a vertical shape look best when primarily illuminated from the side. Forms that have an overall horizontal line generally look best when the primary light source is above them. The contours, color, and the surrounding area of an object must be considered when planning the lighting system. For objects with deep, recessed crevices, adequate fill light must be included in the lighting scheme. To create modeling and provide clarity to the piece, lighting must differentiate between the object, shade, and shadows. This is especially important with dark objects. Shade and shadows on light-colored objects can be used to define the form. To see the details of a three-dimensional object placed in front of a window, there must be an illuminance balance between the front of the piece and the bright daylight behind the object. Techniques used to create the balance include supplementing daylight with electrical sources and/or diffusing the daylight by using a transparent window treatment.

It should be possible to view three-dimensional pieces from all directions. However, in many situations, an object is placed close to a wall, so someone can see only three sides. Each location requires different lighting techniques. Unfortunately, often the lighting technique used to illuminate a three-dimensional object is more appropriate for two-dimensional visual art. To enhance the three-dimensional quality of the piece, appropriate background lighting must be included in the lighting plan. Color changes are another concern related to the placement of visual art. Objects that are close to surfaces, such as walls, ceilings, and floors, can be affected by the reflectance of colors.

Objects that are illuminated on all sides are very challenging to light because the potential for glare is very high. Successful applications include proper aiming angles and effective glare elimination devices on the luminaires. Another important lighting consideration related to its location of the object is its position in the vertical plane. Different lighting techniques should be employed for a piece that is resting on the ground and an object that is on a pedestal. A lighting technique that includes uplighting might be effective for a piece that is on the floor. An object on a pedestal can be illuminated from a variety of angles, including uplights built into the top of the pedestal (Figure 15.10). The height of the pedestal and the location of the lighting should be at a level that best enhances the most emphatic elements of

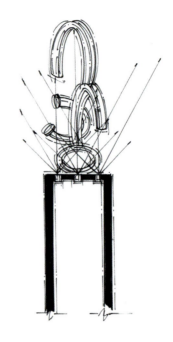

FIGURE 15.10 The object is illuminated by uplights built in the top of the pedestal.

the piece. This is especially critical for large pieces, because there are many surfaces to explore. Thus, the element of the piece that is at eye level becomes the focal point.

An effective lighting plan for three-dimensional pieces includes a lighting source for each zone of illumination. The illumination for three-dimensional pieces should be designed to accommodate three to four zones, depending upon the location of the piece. When an object is next to a wall, there are three different illumination zones (Figure 15.11 a). The first zone comprises the elements of the piece that are accented. The second zone should be the fill light that softens the shadows and provides general illumination on the piece. The third zone is the lighting that illuminates the wall behind the piece. For visual art that can be viewed on all sides, four illumination zones exist (Figure 15.11 b). The first and second zones are the accent and fill lights, respectively. The third zone is the lighting immediately surrounding the piece, and the fourth zone is the background illumination. A combination of various light sources will provide the most effective form delineation. However, as with sunlight, the light source that creates the shadows should come from one overall direction. Shadows coming from conflicting angles can be confusing to a viewer.

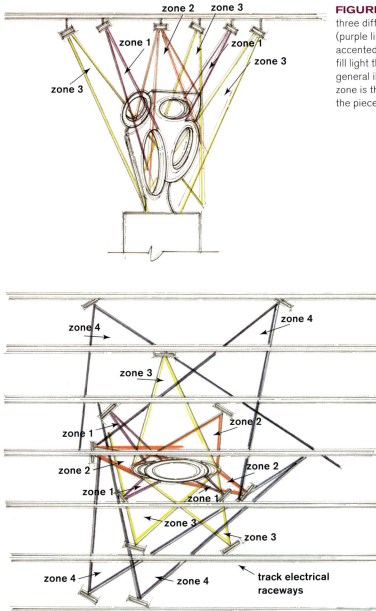

FIGURE 15.11 a Front view of a sculpture and three different illumination zones: a) the first zone (purple lines) is the elements of the piece that are accented; b) the second zone (orange lines) is the fill light that softens the shadows, and provides general illumnation on the piece; and c) the third zone is the lighting that illuminates the wall behind the piece (yellow lines).

FIGURE 15.11 b Plan view of a sculpture and four different illumination zones: a) the first zone (purple lines) is the elements of the piece that are accented; b) the second zone (orange lines) is the fill light that softens the shadows, and provides general illumination on the piece; c) the third zone (yellow lines) is the lighting immediately surrounding the piece; and d) the fourth zone (blue lines) is the background illumination.

Many lighting techniques can be used to create the illumination zones. All the methods include a variation of intensities, aiming angles, and distances from the object. Figure 15.12 a and b illustrates a variety of ways to illuminate three-dimensional pieces. Depending upon the

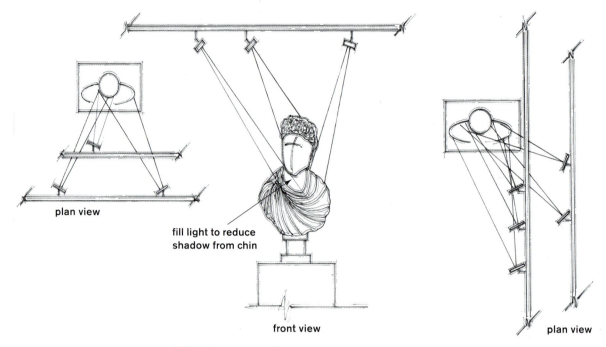

plan view

fill light to reduce
shadow from chin

front view

plan view

FIGURE 15.12 a Plan and side views of illuminating a three-dimensional piece. Fill light is used to
reduce shadows from the chin.

FIGURE 15.12 b Plan view of illuminating a three-dimensional piece
using tracks that are perpendicular to
the artwork.

piece and the geometry of the space, the accent light source can be directly above, in front, or to the side of the piece. For sculptures with
heads; adequate fill light should be added to the area below the chin.
Frequently, shadows from the accent lighting are cast on the upper
torso of the piece, which visually distorts the shape of the body and
could potentially hide interesting carved details at the neckline (Figure
15.12 a). The lighting techniques with two tracks are effective for providing overall lighting for such pieces or the background. Ideally, a
track system should be set up parallel to visual art; however, for applications when this is not possible, multiple heads on a track that is perpendicular to the visual art can be effective (Figure 15.12 b).

Display Cases

Display cases are ideal for fragile and small pieces. In a retail or museum setting, they provide security from theft. Advancements in fiber
optics make display cases even more desirable for artifacts, because

objects can be illuminated without deterioration effects from UV and IR radiation. In addition, the versatility and small size of fiber optic systems allow incredible precision of placement with a light beam.

The lighting techniques used for items in display cases are determined by the inherent characteristics of the objects and the type of case being used. Figure 15.13 (a–c) provides several examples of ways to illuminate objects in a display case. Generally, objects in display cases are three-dimensional pieces. Thus, many of the techniques discussed in the previous section apply to objects in a display case. In addition, the walls of display cases must be carefully planned so as to avoid dark areas on the upper walls, shadows on objects, and scalloped patterns that might interfere with viewing. Colors of the surfaces in a display case must also be carefully selected because the strength of the

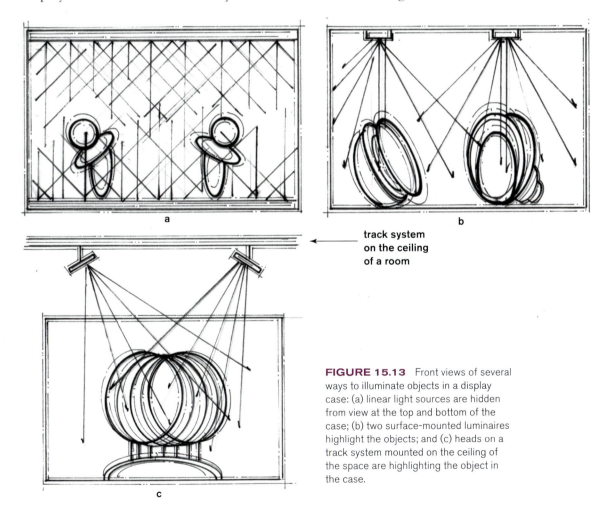

a

b

track system
on the ceiling
of a room

c

FIGURE 15.13 Front views of several ways to illuminate objects in a display case: (a) linear light sources are hidden from view at the top and bottom of the case; (b) two surface-mounted luminaires highlight the objects; and (c) heads on a track system mounted on the ceiling of the space are highlighting the object in the case.

color contrast between an object and its surroundings affects the proper level of illumination. This phenomenon is intensified in small display cases, because the close proximity of surfaces causes a great deal of interreflection to occur with light and color.

Small objects and pieces that sparkle require special illumination techniques. For example, jewelry is very challenging to illuminate because the pieces are small and jewels always look best when they sparkle. Two excellent examples of illuminating jewelry are at the Art Institute in Chicago and the Smithsonian's Museum of Natural History. Both exhibits use fiber optics and custom-designed display cases. The display at the Art Institute is effective because the fiber optics are integrated into the three-dimensional openings that display the suspended jewelry (Figure 15.14). The oval openings and the effective patterns of light and shadow derived from the fiber optics immediately attract the viewer's attention to the pieces. At the Smithsonian, the magnificent Harry Winston exhibit of jewelry, including the Hope diamond, has been beautifully displayed in cases illuminated by fiber optics. Using end-emitting fiber optics highlights the jewelry in each small case (Figure 15.15). To create the greatest sparkle possible, each

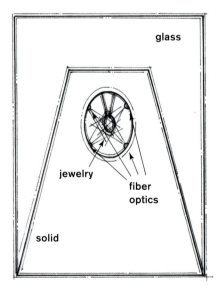

FIGURE 15.14 Drawing of a display at the Art Institute in Chicago. Fiber optics were used to illuminate the jewelry that was suspended by an invisible thread.

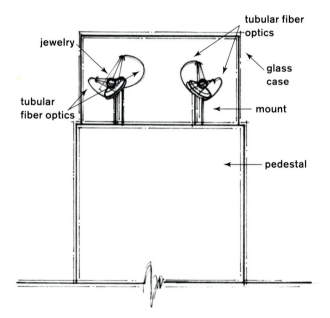

FIGURE 15.15 Drawing of displays at the Harry Winston jewelry exhibit at the Smithsonian Museum. Fiber optics were used to illuminate the jewelry.

light head is at the perfect angle. In addition, to camouflage the fiber optics as much as possible, the color of the sheathing used around the cable is matched perfectly with the colors used in the background surfaces of the display case.

Display cases can be freestanding, recessed in a wall, or an extension of a wall with exposure on three sides (Figure 15.16 a–c). Illumination of the objects can be installed internally, externally, or a combination of both. Internal lighting can be recessed in the case **light attic**, or concealed vertically or horizontally at any edge of the case (Figure 15.17). The location of recessed lighting in the light attic is determined by the size of the display case. Generally, the larger the case, the greater the distance should be from the light source to the illuminated objects. For optical control, a diffusing or shielding device should be used over the light sources. Freestanding cases should have lighting that enhances the piece from all angles. For a silhouette effect, the display case should have a luminous back. For fiber optic installations, the illuminator box should be placed in a remote location that allows for easy maintenance access. To provide an appropriate level of

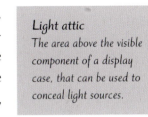

Light attic
The area above the visible component of a display case, that can be used to conceal light sources.

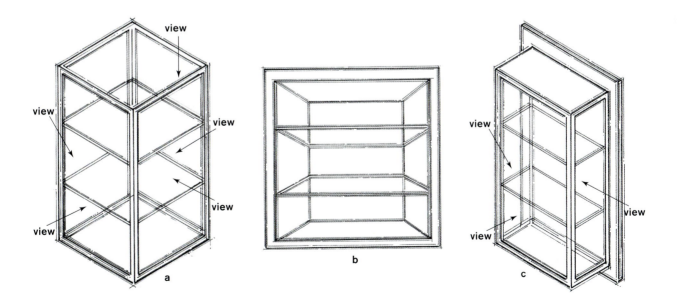

FIGURE 15.16 Examples of types of display cases: a) free standing, b) recessed in a wall, and c) an extension of a wall with exposure on three sides.

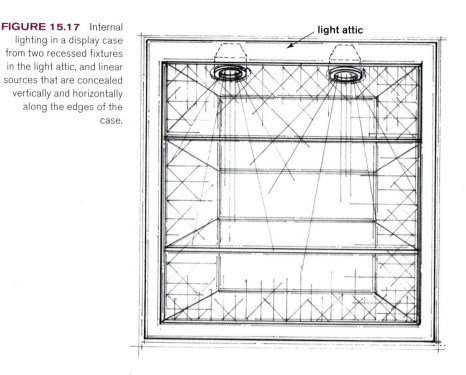

FIGURE 15.17 Internal lighting in a display case from two recessed fixtures in the light attic, and linear sources that are concealed vertically and horizontally along the edges of the case.

light attic

illumination on visual art, the length of cable should not exceed the manufacturer's specifications. Adequate ventilation to dissipate the heat from lamps should always be an important consideration.

Light sources located outside display cases must be designed to enhance the visual art and avoid glare that could easily occur when the light beam strikes the surface of the case. For cases designed to display pieces in the vertical position, the light source should be aimed at the front of the glass at an angle between 45 and 60 degrees (Figure 15.18). For cases that display objects on a horizontal plane, such as manuscripts, the light source should be approximately 30 degrees to the right and left of the viewer so as to prevent shadows (Figure 15.19). In addition, an appropriate balance between the level of illumination inside and outside the display case must be created in order to prevent viewers from seeing their reflection in the surface of the case. A window or an illuminated display case located across from an exhibit case can create veiling reflections. In order to determine when a light source will create glare on glass, place a mirror in front of the display case and note any fixture that can be seen in the mirror. These fixtures are the sources of possible veiling reflections.

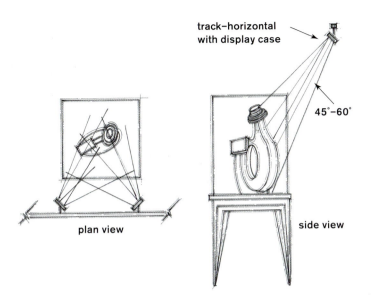

FIGURE 15.18 Plan and side views of external lighting on an object in a vertical-shaped display case. The light source is aimed at the front of the glass at an angle between 45 and 60 degrees.

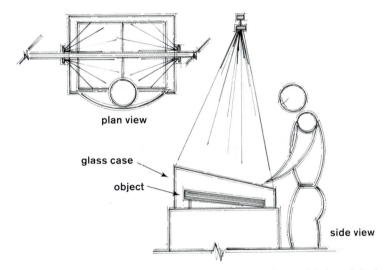

FIGURE 15.19 Plan and side views of external lighting on a horizontal-shaped display case. The plan view shows light sources located to the left and right of a viewer.

The four illumination zones are also important in display cases. However, since most display cases are fairly small, interreflection is likely to occur, which can affect the illumination zones. This factor, and the frequent need to have very precise lighting on small objects, prompts many lighting professionals to create prototypes or mock-ups of display cases. These tests can provide special insight when new lighting techniques or sources are used. Designs of new display cases should be developed in consultation with an electrician, a cabinet-maker, and, if necessary, a curator.

Designing quality lighting for visual art is exciting and challenging. Accent techniques can be used for a variety of objects in commercial and residential buildings. An interior designer must assess all the elements of the environment and characteristics of the objects. This requires collaboration with conservators, curators, cabinetmakers, electricians, and architects. To help ensure the best lighting system, mock-ups and/or prototypes should be fabricated. In addition, after the installation is complete, the lighting system will need fine-tuning, including adjusting the focus and aiming angles.

SUMMARY

- In lighting visual art, the goals should be to preserve the piece, provide clarity of expression, and enhance the aesthetics of an environment. To accomplish these goals requires an understanding of the object and its inherent characteristics.
- Key to conservation of visual art is knowing the inherent characteristics of materials, because they can be irreversibly damaged by visible light and ultraviolet (UV) and infrared (IR) radiation.
- Contextual elements in an interior include the geometry of the space, material compositions, location of the piece, color of surrounding surfaces, reflectance values, and illumination dispersion.
- Physical characteristics of people and subjective perceptions affect the success of illuminated visual art. Lighting should be planned to accommodate a variety of different heights, abilities, and visual impairments.
- A light source used to illuminate visual art should have the optimum color, beam spread, projection distance, and intensity level, and it should conserve the organic material of the piece.
- The illumination level on visual art is important to enable viewers to adequately see details of the piece, eliminate glare, create the contrast required for emphasis, and maintain a maximum level for conservation purposes.

- Luminaires and controls specified for visual art should preserve and enhance the objects. To protect visual art, luminaires should be selected that have a high luminaire efficacy rating (LER) and UV and IR filters.
- To select a luminaire for aesthetic reasons requires an assessment of the purpose of the fixture, characteristics of the visual art, architectural features, installation choices, and maintenance considerations. The lighting layers for visual art should include ambient, task, and accent sources.
- Luminaires should be selected that enhance the architectural features of a space. The style, scale, color, and proportions of the luminaires should be unified with the characteristics of the room.
- The type of visual art, architectural details, installation options, and maintenance factors must simultaneously be considered in selecting a luminaire.
- The specific characteristics of a lamp should be researched to determine the best color, energy-efficiency ratings, beam spread, throw distance, heat emission, and life.
- The luminaire's accessories are important in creating quality lighting on art. The most important accessories are optical lenses, filters, baffles, louvers, and barn doors.
- The visual art, interior, and lighting should be viewed as a system that has to be planned simultaneously in order to create a quality lighting environment.
- The purpose of the space, characteristics of the piece, and primary location of viewing should be considered when identifying the installation spot.
- Generally, the best way to illuminate visual art on a vertical surface is to aim the light from the ceiling. For this lighting technique, important factors to consider are the viewing position, the aiming angle, the height of the ceiling, and the distance between the light fixture and the wall.
- Lighting should be designed to enhance the volumetric form of the object. An effective lighting plan for three-dimensional pieces includes a lighting source for each zone of illumination.
- Display cases can be an effective technique for illuminating art pieces and collectibles. They are ideal for fragile and small pieces.

Illumination of the objects can be installed internally, externally, or a combination of both.

Key Terms

fill light	**spill light**
light attic	**throw distance**

Exercises

1. Search the World Wide Web for five manufacturers of the luminaires that could be used to highlight visual art. Locate all specification data for each luminaire. Compile the resources in a file, and include all performance data related to illuminating visual art.

2. Identify an existing commercial site. Conduct an analysis of the site and identify all visual art in the space. Evaluate the effectiveness of the lighting by addressing the following considerations: (a) characteristics of the visual art, (b) contextual factors, (c) light sources, (d) luminaires, (e) controls, and (f) presentation format. In a written report summarize the effectiveness of the lighting plan and provide recommendations for improving the plan. Include relevant illustrations, photos, or sketches.

3. Visit an art museum and conduct an analysis of several galleries. Be sure to look at a variety of materials and presentation formats. Evaluate the effectiveness of the lighting by addressing the following considerations: (a) characteristics of the visual art, (b) contextual factors, (c) light sources, (d) luminaires, (e) controls, and (f) presentation format. In a written report summarize the effectiveness of the lighting plan and indicate how the techniques could be applied to practice.

4. Observe, sketch, or photograph a sculpture in an outdoor setting, under various conditions of the sky and at various times of day. Write a report that summarizes how the light affects the appearance of the sculpture. Include in the report your impressions

regarding the most desirable lighting conditions and viewing angles. Include photographs and/or sketches.

5. Design a display case that uses fiber optics to illuminate the objects. The drawings should include a plan view and front and side elevations. Include the fiber optic manufacturer's product data and a description of the objects in the display case.

REFERENCES

Albana, C., and Gurlino, P.E. (November 4, 1991). *Creative Light.* Museum (UNESCO, Paris), Vol. XLIII, No. 172.

Albers, J. (1963). *Interaction of Color.* New Haven, CT: Yale University Press.

Alton, J. (1995). *Painting with Light.* Berkeley, CA: University of California Press.

Applebaum, B. (1991). *Guide to Environmental Protection of Collections.* Madison, CT: Sound View Press.

Beach, L.R., Wise, B.K., and Wise, J.A. (1988). *The Human Factors of Color in Environmental Design: A Critical Review.* Technical Report, NASA Ames Research Center, Moffett Field, CA.

Begemann, S.H.A., Aarts, M.P.J., and Tenner, A.D. (November, 1994). *Daylight, Artificial Light, and People.* Paper presented at the 1994 Annual Conference of the Illuminating Engineering Society of Australia and New Zealand, Melbourne, Australia.

Benya, J., Heschong, L., McGowan, T., Miller, N., and Rubinstein, F. (2001). *Advanced Lighting Guidelines.* White Salmon, WA: New Buildings Institute.

Birren, F. (1969). *Light, Color and Environment.* New York: Van Nostrand Reinhold.

Boyce, P.R. (1973). Age, illuminance, visual performance, and preference. *Lighting Research and Technology,* 5, 125–139.

Boyce, P.R. (1981). *Human Factors in Lighting,* New York: Macmillan.

Boynton, R.M., and Boss, D.F. (1971). The effect of background luminance and contrast upon visual search performance. *Illuminating Engineering,* 66, 173–186.

British Standards Institution. (1992). *Code of Practice for Daylighting.* British Standard BS 8206 Part 2.

Brown, G.Z. (1985). *Sun, Wind, and Light: Architectural Design Strategies.* New York: John Wiley & Sons.

Clark, F. (1963). Accurate maintenance factors. *Illuminating Engineering,* 58(3), 124–131.

Flynn, J.E., and Spencer, T.J. (1977). The effects of light source color on user impression and satisfaction. *Journal of the Illuminating Engineering Society.* 4, 167–179.

Fry, G.A. (1976). A simplified formula for discomfort glare. *Journal of the Illuminating Engineering Society,* 8(1), 10–20.

Garling, T., Book, A., and Lindberg, E. (1986). Spatial orientation and wayfinding in the designed environment: A conceptual analysis and some suggestions for postoccupancy evaluation. *Journal of Architectural and Planning Research,* 3, 55–64.

Gifford, R. (1993). Scientific evidence for claim about full-spectrum lamps: Past and future. *IRC Internal Report No. 659.*

Gregory, R.I. (1979). *Eye and Brain: The Psychology of Seeing,* 3rd edition. New York: McGraw-Hill.

Guth, S.K. (1966). Computing visual comfort ratings for a specific interior lighting installation. *Illuminating Engineering, 61(10),* 634–642.

Halse, A.O. (1968). *The Use of Color in Interiors.* New York: McGraw-Hill.

Halstead, M.B. (1997). Colour. In J.R. Coaton and A.M. Marsden (eds.), *Lamps and Lighting.* New York: John Wiley & Sons.

Harriman, M.S. (October, 1992). Designing for architecture. *Architecture,* p. 89.

Henderson, S.T. (1977). *Daylight and Its Spectrum,* 2nd edition. Bristol, England: Adam Hilger.

Hopkinson, R.G. (1957). Evaluation of glare. *Illuminating Engineering, 52(6),* 305–316.

Hunt, R.W.G. (1991). *Measuring Colour,* 2nd edition. Chichester, England: Ellis Horwood.

Hunter, R.S. (1975). *The Measurement of Appearance.* New York: John Wiley & Sons.

Illuminating Engineering Society of North America (IESNA) (2000). *IESNA Lighting Handbook,* 9th Edition. New York: Illuminating Engineering Society of North America.

Illuminating Engineering Society of North America (IESNA) (1998). Lighting for the aged and partially sighted committee. *Recommended Practice for Lighting and the Visual Environment for Senior Living,* RP-28-98. New York: Illuminating Engineering Society of North America.

Illuminating Engineering Society of North America (IESNA) Committee on Testing Procedures. Subcommittee on Guide for Measurement of Photometric Brightness (1961). IES guide for measurement of photometric brightness (luminance). *Illuminating Engineering, 56(7),* 457–462.

Itten, J. (1961). *The Art of Color.* New York: Van Nostrand Reinhold.

Kay, G.N. (1999). *Fiber Optics in Architectural Lighting.* New York: McGraw-Hill.

Kay, G.N. (1996). *ASTM Standards for Preservation and Rehabilitation.* Philadelphia: American Society for Testing and Materials.

Kay, G.N. (1992). *Mechanical/Electrical Systems for Historic Buildings.* New York: McGraw-Hill.

Knowles-Middleton, W.E., and Mayo, E.G. (1951). Variations in the horizontal distribution of light from candlepower standards. *Journal of the Opticians Society of America, 41(8),* 513–516.

Lam, W.C. (1977). *Perception and Lighting as Formgivers for Architecture.* New York: McGraw-Hill.

Lam, W.M. (1986). *Sunlighting as Formgivers for Architecture.* New York: Van Nostrand Reinhold.

Lawrence Berkeley National Laboratory (1997). *Lighting Source Book.*

Lawrence Berkeley National Laboratory (1992). *Analysis of Federal Policy Options for Improving U.S. Lighting Energy Efficiency.*

Lewis, A.L. (1998). Equating light sources for visual performance at low luminances. *Journal of the Illuminating Engineering Society, 27(1),* 80.

Lighting Controls Association (1999). *The National Dimming Initiative.* Rosslyn, VA: Advance Transfer Co.

Lighting Design Lab (1998). *Daylight Models* (video). Seattle, WA: Lighting Design Lab.

Littlefair, P.J. (1996). *Designing with Innovative Daylighting.* London: CRC, Garston.

Megaw, E. (1992). The visual environment. In A.P. Smith and D.M. Jones (eds.), *Handbook of Human Performance, Volume 1: The Physical Environment.* London: Academic Press, pp. 261–296.

Miller, J.V. (1993). *Evaluating Fading Characteristics of Light Sources.* Seaford, DE: NoUVIR Research Company.

Moore, F. (1985). *Concepts and Practice of Architectural Daylighting.* New York: Van Nostrand Reinhold.

Montaner, J. *New Museums.* Princeton, NJ: Princeton Architectural Press.

National Park Services (1999). *National Park Services Museum Handbook, Part I.* Washington DC: National Park Services.

O'Brien, P.F., and Balogh, E. (1967). Configuration factors for computing illumination within interiors. *Illuminating Engineering, 62(4),* 169–179.

Pacific Gas & Electric Company (2000). *Lighting Controls: Codes and Standards Enhancement (CASE) Study.* San Francisco: Pacific Gas & Electric Company.

Pacific Gas & Electric Company (1998). Case study: Occupancy sensor commissioning. *1998 Building Commissioning and Building Performance Tools Program.* San Francisco: Pacific Gas & Electric Company.

Passini, R. (1984). *Wayfinding in Architecture,* New York: Van Nostrand Reinhold.

Phillips, D. (2000). *Lighting Modern Buildings.* Oxford: Architectural Press.

Phillips, D. (1997). *Lighting Historic Buildings.* New York: McGraw-Hill.

Reid, F. (1993). *The Stage Lighting Handbook,* 4th edition. London: A&C Black.

Rundquist, R.A., Johnson, K., and Aumann, D. (1993). Calculating lighting and HVAC interactions. *ASHRAE Journal, 35(11),* 28.

Schott Fibre Optics (1997). *Lighting Designers' Handbook for Fibre Optic Systems.* Doncaster, South Yorkshire, UK: Schott Fibre Optics.

Thomson, G. (1986). *The Museum Environment.* London: Butterworths.

Timson, P., and Gregson, B. (1993). *Fibre-Optic Lighting and Sensing Technology.* London: Eurotec.

Tresidder, J. (ed.) (1983). *Mastering Composition and Light.* New York: Time-Life Books.

Varley, H. (1980). *Color.* Los Angeles,: Knapp.

Veitch, J.A., and McColl, S. (2001). Evaluation of full-spectrum fluorescent lighting. *Ergonomics, 44(3),* 255–279.

Ward Larson, G., and Shakespeare, R.A. (1998). *Rendering with Radiance: The Art and Science of Lighting Visualization.* San Francisco: Morgan Kaufmann.

Weisman, G. (1981). Evaluating architectural legibility. *Environment and Behavior,* 13, 189–204.

Wyszecki, G., and Stiles, W.S. (1967). *Color Science.* New York: John Wiley & Sons.

CHAPTER 16

Light Art

■ Describe light art and understand the evolution of the medium.

■ Identify characteristics of stained and leaded glass and apply an understanding of these characteristics to light art.

■ Describe characteristics of wall relief, sculpture, and installations associated with light art.

■ Describe equipment and forms of dynamic light art.

■ Identify artists of wall relief, sculpture, installations, and dynamic art associated with light art.

TECHNIQUES used for illuminating artwork are discussed in Chapter 15. This chapter examines how artists have explored using light as an art form. Generally, light art does not require any of the accent lighting covered in Chapter 15. In fact, additional lighting would obliterate the effect artists have created in their pieces. Specifying light art for an interior is an aesthetic choice of a client. Clients who are familiar with contemporary art might be aware of specific artists or mediums. However, often an interior designer has to educate a client about various options, including light art, that would enhance an environment. Therefore, in order to make informed recommendations to a client, an interior designer must be aware of new products and concepts. Furthermore, in order to successfully design an environment, all elements of the space must be considered. This must include any special requirements of a light art installation, including specific colors for adjacent surfaces, electrical power, equipment, adequate ventilation, and adequate space to view the art.

The purpose of this chapter is to provide an overview of the various ways artists have used light as a medium for their artwork. The examples represent a small sample of what has been done in the field, but the techniques are representative of significant concepts. Many of the artists, such as James Turrell, Chyrssa, Dan Flavin, Bruce Nauman, Robert Irwin, Margaret Benyon, and Keith Sonnier, discussed in this chapter are considered innovators of the art form. The importance of this medium is evident in light art exhibits such as "The Magic of Light: Artists Focusing on Non-Traditional Media" at the Hudson River Museum in Yonkers, New York, in 2002, the 2002 "Rays of Light Art Exhibition" at the *Lightology* showroom in Chicago, and the 2000–2001 "Venice/Venezia: California Art from the Panza Collection" at the Guggenheim Museum in New York City. Some of the examples presented in this chapter were shown at these exhibits. Light art is a constantly changing field that requires frequent exposure to the work of new and emerging artists. Reading current magazines and books, visiting art galleries, and attending special museum exhibits and lighting conferences are excellent ways to stay current.

Conceptualization of Light Art

Specifying light art requires an understanding of the medium and how to select the appropriate lighting system.

Defining Light Art

Light art utilizes illumination as the artwork. It can sculpt an object, space, or environment. A combination of light, sound, and movement (often integral to light art) can prompt a range of sensory reactions in a viewer. Light art can be simple or require sophisticated computer programs to control the medium. Light art can be mounted on a wall, suspended from a ceiling, or positioned on a floor; it can be site-specific, kinetic, or illusionary. A person can either view or be a participant in

Light art
A medium that utilizes illumination as the artwork. Light art can sculpt an object, space, or environment. A combination of light, sound, and movement, which often is integral to light art, may prompt a range of sensory reactions in a viewer.

light art. Light for the art piece can be daylight, any electrical source, or a combination of sources. The most common sources are daylight, neon, fluorescent, fiber optics, LEDs, and laser beams. Light sources may be exposed or hidden from view. Some of the illusions created in light art are successful because of people's perceptions of light, space, color, and movement. The possibilities are endless, and with significant technological advancements in fiber optics and LEDs, the future of this medium is incredibly exciting.

Artists have always had a fascination with light. Many painters, such as Rembrandt, Renoir, Monet, and Vermeer, tried to capture the magical qualities of reflected light. Chapter 18 analyzes how light affects the composition of a painting. Chapter 15 explores the various ways light can enhance three-dimensional pieces.

Throughout history, artists have always used whatever materials were available to them to create their pieces. Sculptors experimented with marble because the material was easily accessible. Paint was accessible and relatively inexpensive; thus, it has been used for centuries. When plastic was invented, many artists explored it in creating art. Electrical lights are another resource that artists can use to express themselves. The potential of using electrical light as art could be viewed as starting at the 1893 Columbian Exposition in Chicago. The fair had the first major demonstration of electric lamps. In writing about the fair, Erik Larson (2003, p. 254) said:

> If evenings at the fair were seductive, the nights were ravishing. The lamps that laced every building and walkway produced the most elaborate demonstration of electric illumination ever attempted and the first large-scale test of alternating current. The fair alone consumed three times as much electricity as the entire city of Chicago. These were important engineering milestones, but what visitors adored was the sheer beauty of seeing so many lights ignited in one place, at one time. Every building, including the Manufactures and Liberal Arts Building, was outlined in white bulbs. Giant searchlights—the largest ever made and said to be visible sixty miles away—had been mounted on the Manufactures' roof and swept the grounds and surrounding neighborhoods.

Large colored bulbs lit the hundred-foot plumes of water that burst from the MacMonnies Fountain.

For many visitors these nightly illuminations were their first encounter with electricity. Hilda Satt, a girl newly arrived from Poland, went to the fair with her father. "As the light was fading in the sky, millions of lights were suddenly flashed on, all at one time," she recalled, years later. "Having seen nothing but kerosene lamps for illumination, this was like getting a sudden vision of Heaven."

Lighting Systems

The enchantment experienced by people attending the fair introduced the concept of using light as an aesthetic medium. After the fair, exposed incandescent lamps were used to highlight objects, buildings, and signage. Some of the first billboards in New York City were illuminated with incandescent lamps. The creation of neon lamps in 1910, by Georges Claude in Paris, presented a colorful, reliable, and flexible means to use light. A Parisian barber is credited with displaying the first neon sign in front of his shop in 1912. In the United States, neon signage was first used in the 1920s, to illuminate the word "Packard" in front of car dealerships. The depression stifled the production of neon products until the Chicago Century of Progress Exposition in 1933–1934. Entire buildings were outlined in neon, which renewed excitement in the technology. This continued until the fluorescent lamp became popular in the 1940s.

Neon, as a form of art, started in the 1960s by the Greek artist Chyrssa. The first pieces were a series of neon boxes that contained stylized letters that flashed on and off. During this same time period, other artists started creating visual art using various light sources, including fluorescent lamps and laser beams. Natural and electrical light sources were then used to create kinetic (motion) art by blending light, movement, color, and viewer participation.

As technology progressed, new light sources, techniques, and equipment have been used for light art. Some artists today use technology that is typically used for stage lighting, such as gels, strobes, and projectors for effects, patterns, and framing applications. Special effects can be achieved by using rotating heads, scanners, color changers, and screens. **Rotating heads** control a light beam through panning and tilting of the housing unit. **Scanners** reflect light off a moving mirror to create the appearance of movement. All the technology can be orchestrated by sophisticated control systems, which can be programmed to fade, be synchronized with music, link scenes during various time periods, be activated by viewers, and change colors or effects.

Rotating heads
Equipment that controls a light beam through panning and tilting the housing unit.

Scanner
Equipment that reflects light off a moving mirror to create movement.

Dimensional Qualities of Light Art

Light art is created in a variety of formats, including stained glass, wall relief, sculptures, and installations.

Stained and Leaded Glass

Generally, light as an art form is viewed as a medium that was created with the invention of electrical light sources. However, to fully appreciate light art requires an analysis of how daylight has been used to create visual art. For 2,000 years glass has been used to radiate color and enhance light. Light through beveled glass shimmers and produces light through refraction. Sandblasted or etched glass creates diffused light.

Stained glass for churches in the late twelfth and early thirteenth centuries is an excellent example of light art. Quality stained glass gives the impression that the lead outlining the glass does not exist, so the walls appear to be illuminated paintings. The purposes of stained glass were to provide illumination, educate the parishioners by depicting teachings of the Bible, and elicit feelings of inspiration. A great deal of illumination was provided through stained glass because advancements in construction techniques made it possible to have rows of large windows on exterior walls. Sainte Chapelle in Paris is an excellent example of a church with walls of stained glass (Figure 16.1).

The designs created in stained glass were based upon paintings, tapestries, and illustrated manuscripts. The images primarily depicted religious subjects, but some windows illustrated everyday life in the village.

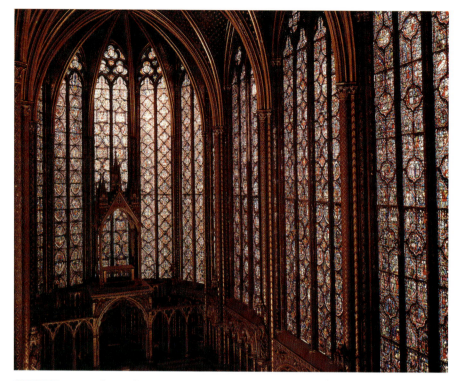

FIGURE 16.1 Sainte Chapelle Cathedral in Paris is an excellent example of a church with walls of stained glass.

Colors were selected to be intense and evoke emotions in people. One of the most famous colors is the cobalt blue in the stained glass of Chartres Cathedral in France. The beautiful colors of stained glass create magical effects on the surrounding walls of stone. (As discussed later in this chapter, this effect is similar to some of the current lighting techniques created by computer-generated programs.)

In the late nineteenth century, the work of Louis Comfort Tiffany and John La Farge prompted a resurgence of interest in colored glass and light as an art form. In particular, people appreciated the beauty of opalescent glass, which was created by Tiffany and La Farge. The magnificent Tiffany Chapel at the 1893 Columbian Exposition in Chicago impressed people throughout the world and contributed to Tiffany's fame (Figure 16.2). Tiffany and La Farge designed leaded glass for windows, murals, ceilings, vases, and luminaires. Their pieces were installed in churches and the mansions of wealthy people. As a result of its beauty and diversity in applications, stained glass was made for a variety of

FIGURE 16.2 The Tiffany Chapel was created for the 1893 Columbian Exposition in Chicago. The Chapel has been reconstructed at the Morse Museum in Winter Haven, Florida.

buildings, including schools, libraries, railway stations, and commercial buildings. Furthermore, it became fashionable to include at least one leaded window in many traditional homes. The most common location was transoms, doorways, and stairway landings.

The leaded glass windows created by Frank Lloyd Wright are also excellent examples of light art. An exhibit, "Light Screens: The Leaded Glass of Frank Lloyd Wright," was in the Renwick Gallery, at the Smithsonian Museum in 2003. Wright used the term "light screens" for his windows: because his windows were arranged in a manner similar to the Japanese *shoji* screens (Sloan, 2002). In the early years of Wright's career, he was not fond of windows: "Often I used to gloat over the beautiful buildings I could build if only it were unnecessary to cut holes in them" (Sloan, 2002, p. 2). This attitude changed dramatically as Wright became a master at designing leaded glass windows, doors, clerestories, and skylights.

The curator of the exhibit, Julie Sloan (2002), organized the exhibit to explain three overlapping phases of Wright's work: (1) his earliest work, "A Vocabulary of Form" (1885–1899), (2) "A Language of Pattern" (1900–1910), and (3) "A New Poetics" (1911–1923). Windows designed in Wright's first phase used Victorian-style pressed glass with patterns of vertical lines and squares. In the second phase the leaded glass was clear and in earthy colors and largely symmetrical patterns. The sumac patterns of the windows designed for the Susan Lawrence Dana house in Springfield, Illinois, were some of Wright's most famous windows (Figure 16.3). The third phase had a more contemporary appearance and was exemplified in the windows designed for the Avery Coonley Playhouse in Riverside, Illinois (Figure 16.4).

An interest in the work of Tiffany and the art of making glass was rediscovered in the 1960s and 1970s. This is evident in the ceiling of the Metropolitan Cathedral in Brasilia, Brazil (Figure 16.5). Artists also started exploring the relationship between light, movement, and new forms of glass, such as dichroic glass (Figure 16.6). As artists educate one another about the interplay of light, new fabrication techniques, and materials, the future of stained glass is an exciting one.

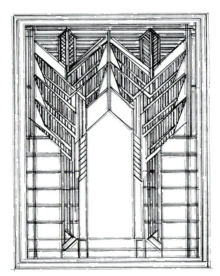

FIGURE 16.3 An illustration of a leaded glass window designed by Frank Lloyd Wright for the Susan Lawrence Dana house in Springfield, Illinois.

FIGURE 16.4 A leaded glass window designed by Frank Lloyd Wright for the Avery Coonley Playhouse in Riverside, Illinois.

Wall Relief and Sculpture

Light art uses a variety of sources and has multiple dimensions and forms. Neon is one of the most common sources for light art and is used in a variety of applications, including signage, interior decor, and

FIGURE 16.6 This light dome uses dichroic glass to create the shimmer and reflections.

illuminating buildings. The lumen output of neon lamps is low; therefore, when higher illumination levels are required, the light source will frequently be a cold cathode lamp. Originally, neon signage was made for advertising purposes and was not considered visual art. However, some of the signs had such a significant level of creativity and skill that they were considered visual art. Neon lamps still require a master glass-bending craftsperson to create the shapes and forms. Today, many people consider these craftspeople artists. Often a light artist will hire a glass bender to make a piece because many artists working with the medium do not have the skills to bend, pump, and mount neon lamps.

Some of the artists who work with neon are Keith Sonnier, Kathleen Williamsen, Stephanie Andrews, Joseph Kosuth, Stephen Antonakos, Paul Seide, Bruce Nauman, Dale Chihuly, James Carpenter, Kenny Greenberg, and Pietro Costa. Many of the wall relief art pieces done by Bruce Nauman and Joseph Kosuth use neon lamps to express concepts through drawing words. In a discussion of his work, *Window or Wall Sign* (1967) (Figure 16.7), Bruce Nauman explained, "Once written down, I could see that the statement, 'The true artist helps the world by revealing mystic truths' was on the one hand a totally silly idea and yet, on the other hand, I believed it" (1982, p, 20). As a conceptual artist, Joseph Kosuth uses a linguistic approach to analyze images and words.

Stephen Antonakos, Kathleen Williamsen, Keith Sonnier, and Pietro Costa use neon to create shapes and outline forms. In an interview

FIGURE 16.7 Bruce Nauman's *Window or Wall Sign,* 1967, uses neon lamps to express concepts through drawing words.

Stephen Antonakos described how he started using neon lamps: " I have lived in New York since I was four, surrounded by its exciting lights, and there I discovered neon. Its colors are unbelievable, and I saw that it could be manipulated into any form" (2001). In Keith Sonnier's *Lit Square* (1969) (Figure 16.8), he explains, "The neon element in *Lit Square* is arranged around the perimeter of the glass sheet to maximise the play of neon-generated light and partially lit reflected image" (1986).

Paul Seide, Kenny Greenberg, Stephanie Andrews, Dale Chihuly, and James Carpenter utilize neon to either create, or enhance sculptures (Figure 16.9). Paul Seide is well known for his creativity in experimenting with shapes other than the traditional linear tube. To explore the interactions between movement, glass, and light, Seide uses remote radio oscillators. In 1999, Chihuly described his perspective of glass and light: "And so when you're working with transparent materials, when you're looking at glass, plastic, ice, or water, you're looking at light itself. The light is coming through, and you see that cobalt blue, that ruby red, whatever the color might be—you're looking at the light and the color mix together. Something magical and mystical, something we don't understand, nor should we care to understand. Sort of like trying to understand the moon. Water has magical powers, and glass has magical powers. So does plastic, and so does ice" (Rose, 2002, pp. 155–156).

Other artists are known for their work in light sources other than neon. The illumination qualities of fluorescent lamps are used in Robert Thurmer's *Light Ladder*, Critz Campbell's *Eudora* (Figure

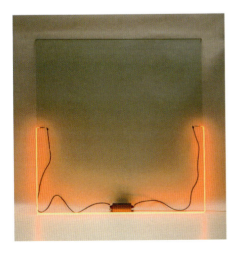

FIGURE 16.8 *Lit Square,* 1969, by Keith Sonnier is an example of how an artist uses neon lamps to create shapes and outline forms.

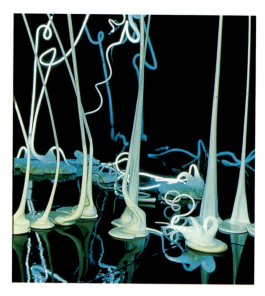

FIGURE 16.9 Dale Chihuly and James Carpenter's *Glass Forest, 1971,* is a good example of how artists use neon to create or enhance sculptures.

16.10), and Zane Coleman's *Light Marbles.* In Christian Boltanski's *Pourim Réserve* (1989), incandescent lamps and all the electrical wires participate in the composition. Tatsuo Miyajima and Sheila Moss have explored LEDs and phosphorescent paint (Figure 16.11). Cork Marcheschi, in collaboration with James Nowak, uses inert gas and illuminated frequency in glass forms. (Figure 16.12). Susan Chorpenning's *Backtrack* (1995) uses projected light and phosphorescent

FIGURE 16.10 In Critz Campbell's *Eudora,* 2002, light is emitted from a source that was installed in the chair.

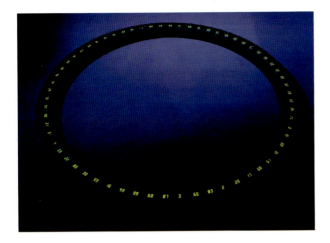

FIGURE 16.11 Tatsuo Miyajima's explored the use of LEDs and phosphorescent paint in this work, *Counter Circle. No. 17.*

paint. Helen Maria Nugent uses illuminated, hand-etched, dichroic glass to create colorful patterns on walls (Figure 16.13).

Installation Art

Installation art (a genre of art that uses a variety of media in a specific space) is an excellent format for exploring the relationships between light, space, and forms and how they involve the viewer physically and emotionally. Artists creating installation art have the advantage of determining the context for the piece. This control enables them to specify all the components of the lighting system and the ideal location within the space. Some of the artists who have created light art in an installation medium are Dan Flavin, James Turrell, Robert Irwin, Christian Boltanski, Ron Haselden, Joost van Santen, and Dale Chihuly.

FIGURE 16.12 These blown glass forms are filled with inert gas and illuminated frequency, installed in the Monterey Bay Aquarium.

FIGURE 16.13 Helen Maria Nugent employed illuminated hand-etched, dichroic glass to create colorful patterns on the wall.

Dan Flavin, James Turrell, and Robert Irwin are well known for using light to create illusions of color and space. Dan Flavin has gained recognition by exploring the relationship between light, color, line, and space. Many of his installations utilize commercial fluorescent lamps in standardized colors (blue, green, pink, red, yellow, and four different whites), and sizes (2-, 4-, 6-, and 8-foot lengths). Reflections of light and color on viewers elicit feelings of participation with the art. *Greens crossing greens (to Piet Mondrian who lacked green)* (1966) is an excellent example of Flavin's use of fluorescent lamps, color, and space (Figure 16.14). Flavin describes his art as "a sequence of implicit decisions to combine the traditions of painting and sculpture in architecture, with acts of electric light defining space" (1999, p. 26). James Turrell's art involves a viewer's perception of space, color, and light. Turrell's art uses light, color, and empty rooms to create illusions. *Lunette* (1974) gives the appearance of either a sunrise or a sunset. In reality the light is derived from hidden neon lamps.

An installation at the Dia Center for the Arts in New York City illustrates how Robert Irwin uses space, light, form, and viewer's participation to create art light. In *Part 1: Prologue: x18³* (1998), daylight and light from fluorescent lamps mounted on the ceiling radiate through several panels of fine white mesh scrim (Figure 16.15). As people walk

FIGURE 16.14 Dan Flavin, *greens crossing greens (to Piet Mondrian who lacked green)*, 1966, shows the use of fluorescent lamps, color, and space.

through the space, shadows evolve and the intensity and clarity of light changes. Light, shadow, and perceptions of space and objects are creatively explored with Christian Boltanski's *Théatre d'ombres* (Figure 16.16). In Ron Haselden's *Coliseum* (1989), flickering LEDs are used to give the perception that the spheres are moving.

Joost van Santen's *Emmen: Ordnance Survey Building* provides an interesting study of how daylight changes the appearance of a space at various times of the day. The installation includes red and blue mirror objects that reflect sunlight on the walls and panels. Dale Chihuly is internationally known for his extensive installations. Chihuly also seeks viewer participation with light, color, glass, and space. For example, Chihuly designed an installation that allows people to walk under a ceiling of glass art. In passing through the space, viewers experience an array of reflections and radiant colors over their entire body. In recent exhibits at the Garfield Park Conservatory in Chicago and at the Franklin Park Conservatory, the gardens served as the environment for the glass art. Natural and electrical sources illuminate the forms, colors, water, and foliage (Figure 16.17).

FIGURE 16.15 In *Part 1: Prologue: x18³* by Robert Irwin, 1998, daylight and light from fluorescent lamps mounted on the ceiling radiate through several panels of fine white mesh scrim.

FIGURE 16.16 Light, shadow, and perceptions of space and objects are creatively explored with Christian Boltanski's *Theatre d'ombres*, 1984–1997.

Dynamic Light Art

The beauty of movement, light, and color can be expressed in many ways. The magic can come from the flicker of candlelight or sunlight refracting light through a prism.

Kinetic Art

For centuries, artists have been intrigued with how movement affects art. Impressionistic artists tries to capture the color changes that occur as the sun moves throughout the day. In *Nu Descendant un Escalier* (1912), Marcel Duchamp painted the movements of someone walking

FIGURE 16.17 For a major installation at the Garfield Park Conservatory, Dale Chihuly used natural and artificial sources to illuminate the forms, colors, water, and foliage.

FIGURE 16.18 An example of lumia.

down stairs. Alexander Calder's mobiles are a study of movement, light, balance, shapes, sizes, and colors. This textbook focuses on luminous movements.

Various techniques are used to achieve movement in art, including natural, mechanical, electrical, and chemical techniques. Kinetic art can be two- or three-dimensional, which naturally occurs or may be controlled by mechanical or computer means. A kinetic art piece can be actual or virtual and often requires viewer participation. In analyzing the aesthetic experience of movement, Popper created the following classifications: "those which are stable but stimulate physiological reactions in the spectator, those which challenge the spectator to physical action, and finally those which are themselves in movement" (1968, p. 96).

The origins of the luminous movement can be credited to Thomas Wilfred. In the early 1920s, Wilfred invented a means to blend color and music to create art. This resulted in the technique termed **lumia**, which is a composition of movement and light art (Figure 16.18). To achieve the color and music projections, Wilfred created the console instrument, **clavilux** (color organ). Wilfred performed many lumia concerts in New York City. To widely distribute lumia, Wilfred developed the lumia box, which looked like a television set. In the 1950s, Frank Malina, who created the *lumidyne*, renewed Wilfred's work with light and music. The lumidyne creates lumia by projecting a light source through a moving rotor. Nino Calos used a lumidyne to re-create the traditional stained glass rose windows of cathedrals.

Lumia
A form of light art that blends light, color, and movement.

Clavilux
A console instrument used to create lumia.

Other techniques used to create luminous movements include sunlight, simple optics, and chemicals. P. K. Hoenich creates lumia by using sunlight and wind. Hoenich describes his technique, "The 'Robot-Picture'—This is a moving and changing sunlight projection system which repeats itself yearly. The artist can fully control this technique and pre-determine a year's programme. The 'Robot-Painter'—This too, is a moving and changing sunlight projection system, but it never repeats itself. With this system the artist cannot foresee the individual pictures that will be produced, but he determines the style of the pictures by choosing the shapes and motion of the reflecting elements in the 'robot'" (Malina, 1974, p. 23).

Julio Le Parc and John Healey use beams of light and optics to create lumia. In *Continual Lumiere Cylindre,* LeParc has a moving beam of light reflect from cylindrical metal mirrors. To create a light show, D.R. Wier projects light through liquid chemicals. Larry Albright uses krypton, rare gases, and an electrical charge between 5,000 and 80,000 volts to create an explosive form of lumia. The electrically charged globe changes patterns when someone touches the glass.

Advancements in computers and technologies associated with lighting and multimedia have inspired many artists to create new forms of

FIGURE 16.19 Paul Friedlander created an eight-meter high kinetic light sculpture installation for the Interface Media Arts festival with viewer participation.

lumia. In the 1970s artists such as Richard Land and Ben F. Laposky started working with kinetic art and computers. John Scarpa and Joan Truckenbrod use technology to create a variety of theatrical effects. Truckenbrod is inspired by nature, and her images depict tensions that exist in families. Paul Friedlander creates virtual installations with viewer participation (Figure 16.19). Many architects and interior designers are using color, light, movement, and computer programs to change the appearance of objects and surfaces. Frequently, these installations are found in restaurants, bars, and airport terminals.

Brad Koerner creates interactive luminous spaces, which are a combination of media, light, and architecture in an interactive environment (Figure 16.20). Dilouie describes the design: "Sensors detect occupancy and direction through ultrasonic passive-infrared and touch methods. Input signals are sent to a control system, which includes a web-based hit counter and statistics package, then distributed

FIGURE 16.20 A conceptual model by Brad Koerner. The artist created a luminous space with a combination of media, light, and architecture in an interactive environment.

to lighting controllers and video playback machines, which produce light, sound, and video as instructed" (2002, p. 14). In discussing his work, Koerner indicates, "It is my belief that architects and lighting designers will need to be able to design environments as conceptual interfaces that communicate a narrative. These spaces will have a living presence with their dynamic fusion of light and the human body, blending two seemingly disparate worlds together and reinvigorating the significance of our tangible experiences" (2002, p. 18).

Lasers and Holography

Several scientists were working on the development of the laser in the 1960s, but Theodore Maiman is credited with its invention. A **laser** (light amplification by stimulated emission radiation) is a device that stimulates emission radiation in order to amplify coherent light. A coherent light source is monochromatic and very directional. A laser produces a beam of light that is extremely bright and thin, is one pure color, and can project long distances. Thus, lasers are often used for shows that are outdoors or in large auditoriums.

Artists who have created light art using lasers are R. Whitman,

FIGURE 16.21 Michael J. Campbell uses laser beams to create light art in his piece, *Laser Beam: Fantasia,* 1969.

Michael J. Campbell, John M. Peterson, and Richard Lefrak. Campbell's piece titled *Laser Beam: Fantasia* is an excellent example of lumia (Figure 16.21). The dots and linear images displayed on a 25-foot (7620 mm) wall change according to the music. Peterson experimented with a variety of materials, including wooden boxes, plastic, helium-neon lasers, mirrors, and speakers. In *Experiment No. 2* (1969), Peterson directed a beam into an opening of a box that was filled with moving pebbled plastic. The light that was reflected to screens created constant changes in the visual art.

The invention of the laser was required in order to develop holography, because the method requires coherent light. Specifically, holograms need the combination of one color and extreme directionality. **Holography** is a method of photography that records an image, or **hologram**, without an image-forming lens. The word *hologram* has Greek origins that translate into "whole thing" or "whole image". Denis Gabor invented holography in 1947, but the method was very rudimentary because the laser had not been invented.

To see the virtual object requires an understanding of making and viewing a hologram (Figure 16.22). The first step in making a hologram is to split a laser into two beams of light. One beam (object beam) is

Holography
A method of photography that records an image, or hologram, without an image-forming lens.

Hologram
A photographic plate that records an image in holography. The word hologram, has Greek origins that translates into "whole thing," or "whole image".

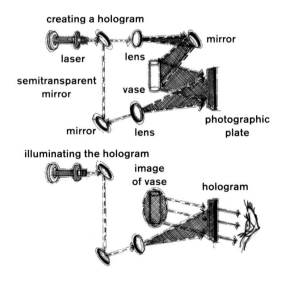

FIGURE 16.22 The holography process, which involves making and viewing a hologram.

FIGURE 16.23 Margaret Benyon uses the holography process to create light art in her piece, *Penetrate the Emulsion.*

aimed at a mirror and passes through a lens to the object. The other beam (reference beam) is reflected off another mirror, passes through a lens, and then strikes the photographic plate, or hologram. A hologram of the object is then created. To view the image, a light beam that follows the same direction of the reference beam strikes the hologram. The hologram alters the direction of light waves, which results in a perfect replication of the original object. The three-dimensional image appears to float in space. Using a white light source, such as sunlight, will create an image with streaks of colors from the rainbow. The monochromatic properties of a laser eliminate the color variation.

Advancements in technology have improved the quality of holograms and reduced the costs. An important achievement has been the pulsed laser, which enables movement to be captured without blurring. In the past, any movement captured by a hologram resulted in blurred images. The development of an embossing technique allows for the mass production of holograms. Some of the most prominent artists using holography are Margaret Benyon, Harriet Casdin-Silver, Rudie Berkhout, Bruce Nauman, Anait Stephens, Dan Schweitzer, Ruben Nunez, Dieter Jung, Sam Moree, and Edward Lowe (Figure 16.23). The innovators of artistic holography focused on demonstrating how the method works. Contemporary artists have advanced the aesthetic experience and continue to evoke enormous fascination with virtual images.

As more artists create exciting light art pieces, this new medium gains appreciation in the art world. This is evident by recent exhibits, acquisitions by major museums, and expanded gallery space. As technology advances and new approaches to using light as an element in a work of art are developed, light art will gain even more popularity. As a result, there will be a greater need for interior designers to understand how to incorporate this dynamic medium into commercial and residential spaces.

SUMMARY

- Light art utilizes illumination as the artwork. Light art can sculpt an object, space, or environment. A combination of light, sound, and movement can prompt a range of sensory reactions in a viewer.
- Neon, as a form of art, started in the 1960s by the Greek artist Chyrssa.
- Some artists today use technology that is typically used for stage lighting, such as gels, strobes, and projectors, for effects, patterns, and framing applications. Special effects can be achieved by using rotating heads, scanners, color changers, and screens.
- To fully appreciate light art requires an analysis of how daylight emitted through stained and leaded glass has been used to create visual art.
- In the late nineteenth century, the work of Louis Comfort Tiffany and John La Farge prompted a resurgence of interest in colored glass and light as an art form.
- The leaded glass windows created by Frank Lloyd Wright are excellent examples of light art.
- Light art uses a variety of sources and has multiple dimensions and forms. Neon is one of the most common sources for light art and is used in a variety of applications, including signage, interior decor, and illuminating buildings.
- Installation art is an excellent format for exploring the relationships between light, space, forms, and the physical and emotional involvement of the viewer.
- Various techniques are used to achieve movement in art, including natural, mechanical, electrical, and chemical techniques. Kinetic art can be two- or three-dimensional, which naturally occurs, or is controlled by mechanical or computer means. A kinetic art piece can be actual or virtual and often requires viewer participation.
- Several scientists were working on the development of the laser in the

1960s, but Theodore Maiman is credited with its invention. A laser (light amplification by stimulated emission radiation) is a device that stimulates emission radiation in order to amplify coherent light.

■ Holography is a method of photography that records an image, or hologram, without an image-forming lens. The word *hologram* has Greek origins that translate into "whole thing" or "whole image."

Key Term

clavilux	**light art**
hologram	**lumia**
holography	**rotating heads**
laser	**scanners**

Exercises

1. Select one of the forms of light art identified in the chapter. Write an essay that includes a historical profile, illustrations of the visual art, and recommendations for installing the art in commercial and residential interiors.

2. Select one of the artists identified in the chapter. Write an essay that includes a biographical profile of the artist, illustrations of his or her art, and how the artist has influenced the medium of light art.

3. Search the World Wide Web for five manufacturers of lighting systems, including controls, that could be used for light art. Identify the type of products, quality, and price range. Compile the resources in a file.

4. Research light art that has been done in the past two years. Write an essay that includes an analysis of current light art, type of technology, artists, and how the artwork is integrated into interiors. Include photographs, sketches, or illustrations.

5. Write an essay that identifies and analyzes factors that should be considered when installing light art. Issues that should be included

in the essay are: (a) site and users, (b) geometry of the space, (c) elements of the space, including colors, textures, and furniture, (d) ambient and task lighting, (e) technology and equipment requirements, (f) installation considerations, (g) operations, and (h) maintenance. In a written report provide recommendations for specifying light art, including illustrations, photos, or sketches.

REFERENCES

Archer, M. (1994). *Installation Art*. London: Thames and Hudson.

Berner, J. (1980). *The Holography Book*. New York: Avon Books.

Brisac, C. (1986). *A Thousand Years of Stained Glass*. Garden City, NY: Doubleday & Company.

Cincinnati Art Museum and the Laser Laboratory of the University of Cincinnati Medical Center (1969). *Laser Light: A New Visual Art*. Cincinnati, OH: Cincinnati Art Museum.

Dilouie, C. (March 2002). Getting a response: Interactive spaces. *Architectural Lighting*, pp.14, 16, 18.

Dobbins, N, and Dobbins, R. (1998). *Etched Glass: Techniques and Designs*. Madison, WI: Hand Books Press.

Doty, R. (1968). *Light: Object and Image*. New York: Whitney Museum of American Art.

Duncan, A. (1982). *Tiffany Windows*. New York: Simon and Schuster.

Hodges, N. (1993). *Installation Art*. Deerfield Beach, FL: VCH Publishers.

Larson, E. (2003). *The Devil in The White City*. New York: Crown Publishers.

Malina, F.J. (1974). *Kinetic Art: Theory and Practice*. New York: Dover Publications.

Museu d'Art Contemporani de Barcelona (2000). *Force Fields: Phases of the Kinetic*. Barcelona, Spain: Museu d'Art Contemporani de Barcelona.

Popper, F. (1968). *Origins and Development of Kinetic Art*. New York: New York Graphic Society.

Porcelli, J. (1998). *Stained Glass: Jewels of Light*. New York: Friedman/Fairfax Publishers.

Ragheb, J.F. (1999). *Dan Flavin: The Architecture of Light*. Berlin, Germany: Deutsche Guggenheim.

Rose, B. (2002). *Chihuly Gardens and Glass*. Seattle WA: Portland Press.

Rosenthal, J., and Wertenbaker, L. (1972). *The Magic of Light*. Boston: Little, Brown.

Sloan, J.L. (2002) *Light Screens: The Leaded Glass of Frank Lloyd Wright*. New York: Rizzoli International Publications.

Stern, R. (1988). *The New Let There Be Neon*. New York: Harry N. Abrams.

Tovey, J. (1971). *The Technique of Kinetic Art*. New York: Van Nostrand Reinhold.

Walton, P. (1982). *Space Light: A Holography and Laser Spectacular*. London: Routledge & Kegan Paul.

Webb, M. (1984). *The Magic of Neon*. Salt Lake City, UT: Gibbs M. Smith.

Wylie, E., and Cheek, S. (1997). *The Art of Stained and Decorative Glass*. New York: Todtri Productions.

CHAPTER 17

Light and Interior Architecture

OBJECTIVES

- Describe architectural elements that are designed to enhance illumination.

- Understand how architectural elements can control and manipulate sunlight.

- Describe how light can enhance interior architecture.

- Understand how to enhance vertical planes and the volumetric space of interiors.

- Apply an understanding of the integration of light and architecture to contemporary interiors.

ARTISTS such as Dan Flavin, James Turrell, and Robert Irwin, who have focused on the relationships between light, color, line, and space are discussed in Chapter 16. Viewing their installations helps to achieve an understanding of how light can alter perceptions of space. This phenomenon can be used to illuminate residential and commercial interiors. In addition, a quality lighting environment integrates natural and electrical light sources with interior architecture. Light, shade, and shadow are essential to creating form. As stated by Le Corbusier, "The elements of architecture are light and shade, walls, and space." (Jenjer, 1996)

A lighting system should be responsive to the architect's vision of the interior. Light and architecture should have an interdependent relationship in which the structure is designed to maximize the positive qualities of illumination, and the lighting sources enhance the architectural elements of spaces. This chapter analyzes this interrelationship by focusing on how light and shade affect planes, forms, and volume in interiors.

Architecture to Enhance Daylight

An excellent approach to understanding the relationship between light and architecture is to study masterpieces of architecture.

Power of the Sun

Most structures were built prior to the invention of electricity, so the architects had to design the structures to accommodate the characteristics of sunlight. The primary purpose of sunlight was to provide illumination in all the spaces of a building. This was especially challenging in large structures. In addition, architects designing buildings in hot and humid regions of the world had to subdue the severe glare from direct sunlight.

The materials, skills, and engineering capabilities available to the architects then affected how buildings were designed and constructed. For example, ancient Rome had the skills, technology, and materials available to construct buildings from brick, stone, and stucco. In Greece, the material used to build the Parthenon and Acropolis was marble because the stone was available and the cities had artisans who possessed the skills to carve the detailed ornamentation. These factors become important in studying how daylight was integrated with architecture. For example, advancements in construction and materials have provided the means for daylight to enter an oculus in a dome, reflect from a vault, penetrate stained glass windows, and eventually be transmitted through entire walls of glass.

Many architectural masterpieces demonstrate how light can be manipulated to enhance structural elements and have emotive effects on the users of the space. Dramatic examples of how a structure can be designed to demonstrate the power of a ruler by controlling sunlight are the temples of Ramesses and Nefertari, in Abu Simbel, Egypt (~1260 B.C.) (Figure 17.1). To proclaim the power of Egypt, the temples were carved into the side of a mountain. The interior of the temples has a series of passageways that eventually lead to a room deep in the mountain. The purpose of the room is to display several statues of the gods. The entrance of the temples was precisely designed to project sunlight on the statues only two times a year. The first illumination is on Ramesses's birthday, and the second date is the anniversary date of his coronation. Controlling sunlight with such precision demonstrates an incredible knowledge of the geometry of the solar system and an awareness of the psychological effect the sun can have on people. People were in awe because the sun illuminated Ramesses statues on two specific days.

The Pantheon, in Rome, Italy, is another example of a building commissioned by a ruler who used the sun and architectural forms to express supremacy. In A.D. 120–127, Emperor Hadrian directed the design and construction of the Pantheon. For political reasons, Hadrian wanted a building that would demonstrate his power and the

FIGURE 17.1 The entrance of the Temples of Ramesses and Nefertari was precisely designed to project sunlight on the statues only two times a year.

vitality of the Roman civilization. As an amateur architect, Hadrian was instrumental in designing a building that would evoke awe in people by its scale and technological advancements. To emphasize these characteristics, light and darkness were strategically planned. The entrance from the portico is a dark space of relatively common dimensions. From this space, one moves through tall bronze doors to the immense 144 feet (43 m) rotunda, filled with daylight, from the oculus at the center of the dome.

At that time, construction of a huge rotunda with a large opening at the top demonstrated extraordinary expertise. The quantity of daylight in the space is maximized by direct sunlight streaming through the oculus and indirect light reflecting from the interior surfaces of the dome. The coffers in the dome create interesting light, shade, and shadow patterns and serve the functional purpose of reducing the weight of the concrete. The experience of moving from a dark, small space to a bright, enormous space emphasized the significance of the construction feat while creating feelings of astonishment and trepidation.

Emperor Justinian I was another ruler who created a monumental building primarily for political reasons. In 532, the emperor ordered the construction of Hagia Sophia, or Christ as Holy Wisdom, in Istanbul, Turkey (Figure 17.2). In the Byzantine style, the massive dome, 102 feet

FIGURE 17.2 In the interior of Hagia Sophia, direct illumination is derived primarily from the round-headed windows at the base of the central dome and the lower half-domes.

(31 m) in diameter and 185 feet (56 m) above the floor, rests on a pendentive. Direct illumination is derived primarily from the round-headed windows at the base of the central dome and the lower half-domes. Daylight penetrating through the clear glass windows causes the gold mosaic tiles and other richly decorated materials to glisten. Indirect light in the nave is emitted through the openings between columns in the screen walls. The variety of apertures and angles of direction produces a quality of light that is diverse in color, intensity, and inspiration.

Gothic cathedrals and churches constructed during the seventeenth and eighteenth centuries are also excellent examples of using scale, architectural elements, and light to evoke emotional responses. As discussed in Chapter 16, Gothic cathedrals are well known for the beautiful colors of their stained glass windows that allow sunlight into the interiors. The tall, vertical windows create harmony within the space and emphasize the soaring height. The plan of such churches and cathedrals enhances and intensifies natural daylight (Figure 17.3). Functionally, light must be directed to areas where worshippers gather, the nave and transepts. Spiritually, light should provide emphasis on the altar, toward heaven, and on the windows that contain images from the bible. As illustrated in Figure 17.4, a common approach for

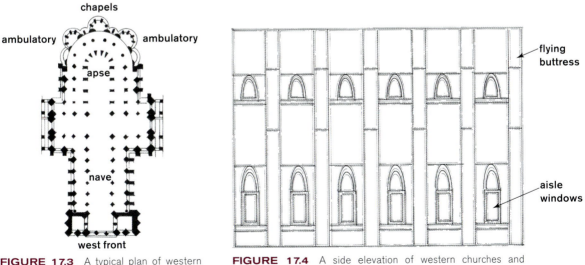

FIGURE 17.3 A typical plan of western churches and cathedrals.

FIGURE 17.4 A side elevation of western churches and cathedrals, including clerestories and flying buttresses.

illuminating the nave and transepts was to locate rows of windows along the outside perimeter wall, and then to install clerestories high on the screen walls that separate the nave from the aisles. The light from the perimeter walls enters the nave through the arched openings of the screen wall. The taller the structure, the more light in the space.

To maximize the amount of daylight that entered cathedrals, flying buttresses were added to the structures. Prior to the development of flying buttresses, perimeter walls supported most of the weight of the structure. Thus, the area for windows had to be relatively small. Located outside the building, flying buttresses significantly helped to support the structure, especially the top external walls of the nave. By shifting a great deal of structural weight to the flying buttresses, the external walls could be filled with windows. In the vertical plane, windows on multiple levels provide illumination with a variety of intensities.

A variety of architectural elements developed to manipulate light provide the emphasis on the altar and toward heaven. Often an enormous dome lined with windows is located above the altar area. This creates a high level of illumination directed toward heaven. The windows in the dome transmit a large quantity of light because the extreme height of the structure enables unobstructed daylight to strike all the surfaces. In addition, indirect light is created by daylight, that is reflected from the dome's interior surfaces. The quantity of light emitted by the dome appears to be even brighter when there is a significant illumination contrast between the altar and the nave, where worshippers pray.

Emphatic lighting for the altar is also derived from windows in the surrounding chapels and ambulatory. Locating the windows at the approximate height of the altar and using walls that have a semicircular arrangement contribute to creating the emphasis on the altar. The semicircular shape of the wall enables light to strike the altar from three directions. Indirect light is derived from surfaces that surround windows. Often windows are recessed in a deep wall and are surrounded by light-colored surfaces, which are angled to reflect daylight into the interior space. As a result, a high level of illumination is emitted from windows that are surrounded by deep, vertical surfaces.

In contrast to the stained glass that was used in Gothic cathedrals, clear glass windows were specified for the church of Vierzehneiligen, in Banz, Germany (designed by Johann Balthasar Neumann, 1743–1772). The type of glass used in windows can affect the integration of light sources and architecture. For example, colors emitted from stained glass are emphasized when the light shining through the colors strikes plain, stone walls with few ornamental details. Interiors with surfaces that are highly decorated are enhanced by natural daylight. Natural daylight provides the highlights and shadows required to emphasize the forms of surfaces with high relief, and it causes colors to gleam. Vierzehneiligen is an excellent example of a highly decorated interior that is enhanced by natural light. Natural light is especially effective because the windows are placed close to the ornamental surfaces, thus creating a grazing effect across the detailed carvings.

Light emitted from above can have a spiritual effect and can provide illumination throughout the space. Saint Mary's Cathedral in Tokyo, Japan (designed by Kenzo Tange), is an excellent example of a building designed to use light for emotive responses (Figure 17.5). The light emphasizes the soaring vertical planes surrounding the altar and shadow

FIGURE 17.5 Daylight enhances the soaring vertical planes surrounding the altar at Saint Mary's Cathedral in Tokyo, Japan.

created by natural daylight. The powerful integration of architecture and light evokes a response in worshippers that is similar to the reactions people have when they enter the Pantheon, Hagia Sophia, and Gothic cathedrals.

For architectural interest and the enhancement of illumination, there are a variety of different materials and shapes that are used in domes and adjacent surfaces. To intensify light in a room, John Soane placed mirrors on the interior of the dome in his house in Lincoln's Inn Fields, in London (1792). Hundreds of mirrors are integrated in the stalactite vault of the Sotoun Palace in Isfahan, Iran (Figure 17.6). Colors, light, and architectural forms are emphasized in the magnificent glass ceiling in the center of Baron Victor Horta's Van Eetvelde House (1895) (Figure 17.7). The Art Nouveau building was constructed in a very narrow space in Brussels, Belgium. To provide the maximum amount of natural light throughout all of the floors in the building, Horta designed a beautiful glass ceiling, which is suspended over the central hall, and then placed large windows on the street side of the façade.

To intensify the level of illumination and create higher structures, some buildings, such as St. Paul's Cathedral in London and the U.S. Capitol, have three structures in the central dome, each consisting of a dome with an oculus, a middle dome or cone, and a cupola at the top

FIGURE 17.6 Mirrors in the stalactite vault of the Sotoun Palace in Isfahan, Iran create a twinkling effect in the space.

FIGURE 17.7 Colors, light, and architectural forms are emphasized in the beautiful stained glass dome in the center of the Baron Victor Horta's Van Eetvelde House.

(Figure 17.8). The San Lorenzo, a church in Turin, Italy (1668), designed by architect Guarino Guarini, also has an extensive dome formation (Figure 17.9). The interior of the dome has a series of ribs in the shape of a six-sided star. Natural light casts a shadow on the rib formation, which results in complex patterns being cast on the floor of the cathedral. With respect to the following, it is critical to examine how the various shapes and adjacent surfaces enhance illumination (Figure 17.10a and b). The architect Jan Courtvriendt designed a six-sided dome in the nave of Notre Dame-du-Bon-Secours, in Brussels, Belgium (1664). A star-patterned dome fills a vault in the Chapel of the Constable in Burgos, Spain (1482) (Figure 17.10a). The central tower of the Ely Cathedral (1300s) has an octagon-shaped dome, which is illuminated by a wooden lantern and is lined with windows. In 1632, François Mansart designed domes next to each other for Sainte Marie-de-la-Visitation in Paris (Figure 17.10b). The round dome is placed above the nave, and the oval dome covers one of the chapels.

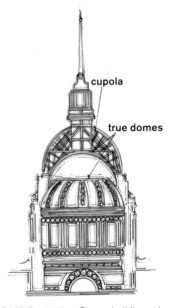

FIGURE 17.8 Some buildings have three structures in the central dome. The lower structure is a dome with an oculus. The center section has a middle dome or cone, and the third structure is a cupola at the top.

FIGURE 17.9 The San Lorenzo in Turin, Italy, designed by architect Guarino Guarini has a dome with a series of ribs in the shape of a six-sided star.

As demonstrated in Figures 17.10a and b, surfaces surrounding an aperture affect the quantity of illumination that enters the space and reinforce architectural forms. In addition, the shade and shadows created by natural light articulate the shapes and forms of the structures. St. Stephen's Walbrook, in London (1672–1679), designed by Christopher Wren, has some unique formations projected from windows, which emphasize the shape of the windows and increase illumination levels (Figure 17.11). All the apertures on the lower level

FIGURE 17.10a The shade and shadows created by natural light articulate the shape and structure of the dome in the Chapel of the Constable in Burgos, Spain.

FIGURE 17.10b In the domes of Sainte Marie-de-la-Visitation in Paris, the surfaces surrounding the apertures affect the quantity of illumination that enters the space.

FIGURE 17.11 In St. Stephen's Walbrook in Great Britain, unique formations projected from windows emphasize the shape of the windows and increase illumination levels.

have deep recesses in the shape of the windows. These extend the ceiling surfaces until they reach the center of the rounded arch, which emphasizes the windows in the vault at the center of the photograph. The ceiling appears to be an extension of the windows, which visually expands the area of illumination. Light and shade create the forms in the vault. The windows on the upper level, next to the center vault, also have adjacent surfaces that follow the flow of light and form.

The concept of blending vertical and ceiling planes is evident in the Natural History Museum, London (Figure 17.12), designed by Alfred Waterhouse (1868–1881), and Benjamin Woodward's Museum of Science, in Oxford, England (1854–1860). Both these museums have a glass roof that flows into the vertical planes of the structures. Natural light is used to unify the converging planes. Iron and glass are seamlessly integrated in the Romanesque and Gothic arches. The successful integration results in an environment that dramatically illustrates how light can emphasize the technology of iron and glass.

Controlling Sunlight

In designing architecture to enhance light, architects have had to, in a sense, control sunlight. The functional necessity for controlling glare

FIGURE 17.12 Iron and glass are seamlessly integrated in the Romanesque arches of the Natural History Museum in Great Britain.

and the heat of the sun resulted in buildings that are excellent examples of how architecture is integrated with sunlight. The architectural elements used to control light were interesting architectural enhancements, and they affected the quality and quantity of lighting in spaces. Generally, to reduce glare, indirect lighting was necessary. This resulted in interiors with low illumination levels and a variety of colors and patterns, depending upon the characteristics of the reflective surfaces. For example, many ancient buildings have walls painted with colorful frescoes. Light striking these walls illuminates colors of the paintings, and they reflect a variety of hues on surfaces adjacent to the frescoes.

Some excellent examples of enhancing and controlling light are evident in ancient Egyptian, Greek, and Roman structures. A common practice with these buildings was to construct the primary rooms around a central courtyard, which was open to the sky. The Temple of Amon at Karnak (2000 B.C.) is well known for its tremendous Hypostyle Hall that was built in the roofless courtyard. The dramatic shadows produced by the enormous pillars create an imposing light and shadow pattern on the ground.

Natural light from a courtyard was a major source of illumination in the rooms of residences. The exterior walls on the first floor often had no windows, or perhaps clerestories were positioned high on the wall. Some structures had ventilators on the roof, which allowed in light and air. The inward spatial orientation resulted in natural light penetrating the rooms, while providing privacy and reducing the noise levels from the streets. To reduce glare in rooms, atriums often were enclosed with a peristyle. This arrangement provided shade and created an interesting pattern on vertical planes. For example, the large Palace of Knossos, in Knossos, Crete, (1700–1380 B.C.) was arranged around a large courtyard. In viewing the courtyard from the Queen's Hall, an extremely interesting pattern is created by the light penetrating the apertures in the wall. The silhouette lighting effect articulates the forms and details of the columns and helps to reduce the appearance of the mass of the structure. The interesting contoured ceiling is enhanced by colors reflected from the dolphin fresco and the light and shadow patterns from the columns. In addition, the extremely thick walls help reduce glare from the sun. The outer wall absorbs the heat and intense glare and then reflects light into the interior space.

FIGURE 17.13 The grand staircase in the Palace of Knossos is illuminated by a light well.

Providing natural light throughout the Palace of Knossos was especially challenging because the royal apartments were originally four stories high. To resolve this problem, light wells were strategically located in the building. For example, the grand staircase and royal guardroom was located in the courtyard and was illuminated by a light well (Figure 17.13). Some light wells had decorative ornamentation. The House of the Vettii, in Pompeii, Italy (first century A.D.), is another excellent example of a structure designed to provide high levels of illumination and eliminates glare (Figure 17.14). This residence has two atriums with impluviums (shallow basins in the floor) holding rainwater in the center of the rectangles. One atrium and various rooms have

FIGURE 17.14 This structure, House of the Vettii at Pompeii, is designed to provide high levels of illumination and eliminates glare.

picturesque frescoes lining the walls. The peristyle's deep roof over-hang prevents direct sunlight from striking the frescos. This results in the frescos being illuminated by a resplendent quality of light and helps to reduce fading. Painted windows in the trompe l'oeil (literally French for "fool the eye," photographically realistic depiction) wall decoration created the impression of more light in rooms.

The Greeks and Romans also used natural light to guide people through a building and to emphasize the axial arrangement of a structure (Figure 17.15). Alternating horizontal and vertical architectural elements enhanced vistas. To create drama in a building, the sequence of spaces was altered by varying room sizes, ceiling heights, and illumination levels. Light and darkness were manipulated to provide visual interest, accentuate volumetric space, define areas, and distinguish between public and private rooms. For example, when entering a residence from the street, the vestibule was often a dark small room with a low ceiling. From the vestibule, one would often walk into an atrium that was open to the sky. Sunlight striking the water in the impluvium created shimmering reflections on surfaces. The adjoining private spaces were dark and small and had low ceilings. The number of

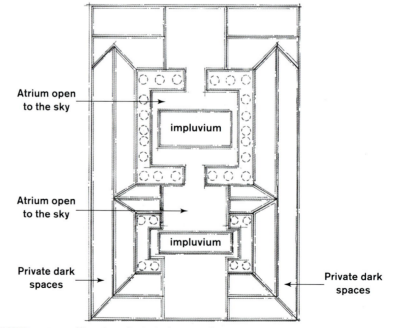

FIGURE 17.15 Plan view of a typical ancient Roman residence.

alternating spaces was dependent upon the size of the dwelling. People walking through larger residences progressed through many rooms with alternating characteristics. For visitors, the overall objective was to enter from the dark public side of a residence and then proceed to the bright activity area. Family members had the same sequential experience, but the private rooms were dark and small. A similar sequential arrangement can be found in the plans of the Italian Renaissance palazzo. Many palazzi (palaces) have an arcaded cortile (enclosed courtyard) open to the sky, which serves as the atrium.

There are other architectural elements designed to subdue bright sunlight and reduce the intense heat in arid countries. These structures can affect the quality and quantity of illumination in rooms. Many buildings in the Islamic style are designed to protect the interiors from the harsh sun. For example, double-tiered archways surround the Imam Mosque, an enormous square in Isfahan, Iran (Figure 17.16). The deep recesses articulate the form of the pointed arches and shade the interior spaces. The Taj Mahal, in Agra, India, also has deep, recessed archways surrounding the structure.

The contemporary architect Louis Kahn went to Africa to study the climatic conditions there for a potential architectural project. To

FIGURE 17.16
Double-tiered archways surrounding the Imam Mosque in Isfahan, Iran.

contend with the hot glare of the sun, Kahn designed architectural elements that he ultimately incorporated into many buildings in a variety of geographic locations. In studying Kahn's philosophy, Tyng (1984) identified many of these elements. For example, the **keyhole window** was developed to allow light to enter a room at all levels, but to reduce glare the greatest amount of light is emitted in the area above where people work (Figure 17.17). Kahn also designed a **glare-shielding wall** that exists on the outside of a building. This exterior wall absorbs most of the glare and heat from the sun, while reflecting light into the interior space. The concept of the glare-shielding wall is similar to the extremely thick walls of the Palace of Knossos.

The hollow columns designed for Kahn's Mikveh Israel Synagogue, in Philadelphia, demonstrate another example of integrating natural light with architectural elements (Figure 17.18). As described by Tyng, "Here he [Kahn] inserted hollow columns into the exterior walls at intervals. These nonstructural cylinders act as diffusion chambers. Daylight shines through their exterior openings, ricochets around inside the columns, and filters subtly through openings into the synagogue" (1984, p. 145). Tyng also provided a quote that helps to explain Kahn's philosophy of silence and light: "Inspiration is the feeling of beginning at the threshold where Silence and Light meet: Silence, with its desire to be, and Light, the giver of all presences. This, I believe, is in all living things; in the tree, in the rose, in the microbe" (Tyng, 1984, p. 169).

Light to Enhance Architecture

An interdependent relationship between architecture and illumination is essential for a quality lighting environment.

Planes of Interior Architecture

Ideally, architecture should enhance light, and light should enrich architecture. Some of the most inspiring examples of this symphonic relationship are found in churches and museums. In many of these buildings, natural and electrical light sources have been carefully

Keyhole window

A window shape that allows light to enter a room at all levels, however, to reduce glare, the greatest amount of light is emitted in the area above where people sit and stand.

Glare-shielding wall

An exterior wall that absorbs most of the glare and heat from the sun, while reflecting light into the interior space.

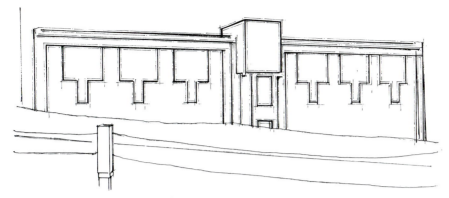

FIGURE 17.17 An illustration of Kahn's keyhole windows shows an uneven distribution of daylight in the interior.

orchestrated with the architecture to elicit emotional responses. Many architects use light as the natural element that connects heaven and earth. Generally, light that enhances architecture exists in the ambient and accent layers; however, there are also decorative examples.

Developing a lighting plan that enhances architecture requires a thorough understanding of the architect's conceptual design and

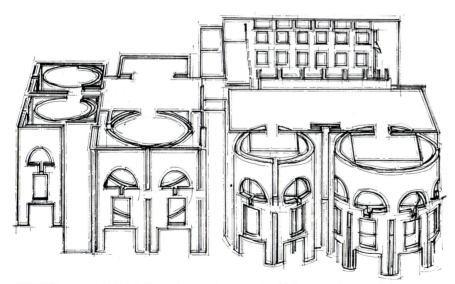

FIGURE 17.18 Kahn's hollow columns integrate natural light and architectural elements.

objectives. This includes understanding the context of the environment and the overall mood the architect wants to create. The lighting for a building designed for quiet reflection will be dramatically different from the lighting for a nightclub. Within the context of the plan, dominant architectural elements and features should be identified and prioritized. This includes an examination of planes, geometric volume, and unique architectural details. The planes of a space include the vertical and horizontal surfaces of walls, floors, and ceilings. Geometric volume encompasses the overall shape of a room and its dimensional qualities. Architectural features could include columns, a magnificent staircase, or hand-carved wood moldings.

Once the emphatic elements of the architecture are identified and prioritized, the lighting should be planned to enhance the forms, lines, colors, and textures. Unless a space must be dark, as in a movie theater, illumination should include natural and electrical sources. Illuminating architectural elements requires an examination of three major considerations: (1) lighting systems and techniques that will specifically enhance a plane, space, or feature; (2) how the emphatic lighting identified in item 1 will affect other architectural elements in a space; and (3) how other light sources affect the emphatic lighting. This simultaneous conceptualization requires a thorough analysis of color and the directional qualities of illumination, including incident and reflected light.

The effects of all three conditions can enhance or obliterate architectural features. For example, an emphatic technique in a space might be interesting shadows cast on a floor from the grid in a skylight. Given this intent, the shadows will be most successful when the proper illumination contrast is established, the distance between the skylight and floor is appropriate, and characteristics of the floor do not interfere with the pattern of shadows cast by the grid. The desired effect might be significantly altered by high illumination levels from direct or indirect light from other sources in the space. Shadows might not appear on a dark or patterned floorcovering. Shadows that overlap each other will not be visible; the darkest shadow is all that will be seen. Therefore, darker shadows from other elements in the space may eliminate the lighter shadows that are cast by the grid in the skylight.

Many of the examples that follow include an analysis of how simultaneous conditions in a space affect interior architecture.

In planning light to enhance architecture, walls are an important consideration because they consume a high percentage of surface area in a room, and they support the windows that let in natural light. Thus, walls can have a dramatic effect on the architectural composition of a space and elicit a psychological reaction in people. Illuminating vertical planes should include niches, passageways, arches, and pilasters. Emphasis on a vertical plane can be derived from electrical illumination that is directed toward a wall or from natural light transmitted through windows or a combination of both primary sources. As discussed in Chapters 9 and 11, a variety of electrical lighting techniques can be used to illuminate walls, including recessed and surface-mounted fixtures and structural elements, such as cornices, soffits, valances, and wall brackets.

The placement and shape of a window affects the overall composition of a vertical plane and can define the space. An excellent example of integrating light, color, texture, shape, and forms to enhance a vertical plane is evident in Le Corbusier's (Charles Edouard Jeanneret) Chapelle Notre Dame du Haut, built high on a hilltop in Ronchamp, France (Figure 17.19). As described by Le Corbusier, the chapel is "of silence, of prayer, of peace, of spiritual joy." The chapel is simple, serene, and incredibly complex. In responding to the design of the chapel, Le Corbusier explained, "The key is light, and light illuminates shapes, and shapes have emotional power." The chapel has an overall sculptural form that has been reinforced by the creative use of natural light. For example, inside the main chapel, the east wall is emphasized by the interplay of light, form, color, and texture. This is accomplished by the overall abstract design of the wall, which is created by the light and dark contrast of the apertures and the vertical plane. The light and dark contrast is reinforced by the shadow-box formation created by the extraordinarily thick walls. The walls have the surface depth required to reflect the entire design of a window on the bottom splay. Using light to emphasize the walls is especially meaningful for this chapel because concrete was blended with the stones from the previous chapel, which was destroyed in World War II.

The splays around the windows artfully reflect the colors and patterns of the glass, which were painted by Le Corbusier. The use of clear and colored glass results in a visual display that is constantly changing. The variability of natural daylight transmitting through the clear glass provides an array of colors and creates movement in the space. Light passing through the clear glass forms an illuminated frame for the patterns, that are created by the intense hues and designs of the painted glass. Concrete textures are strategically placed to enhance the effect of the illumination. For example, the texture of the concrete on the sides and top of the window is rough. As a result of this placement, light emitted from the sides and top of the window grazes the surfaces to create light and shadow patterns on the walls. The texture on the bottom splay is smooth. An even texture is ideal for mirroring the details of the paintings of the windows.

As a piece of sculpture, each wall in the main chapel is dramatically different. To unify the four planes, Le Corbusier designed a band of light between the walls and the roofline. The placement of the light leads the eye around the perimeter of the room and creates the illusion that the roof is floating. This effect is explained by Le Corbusier's belief: "Good architecture walks and moves inside as well as outside. It is living architecture." Light, architecture, and movement are also apparent in Le Corbusier's Villa Savoye (1929–1931) in Poissy, France (Figure 17.20). The alternating horizontal lines of the wall surfaces and strip windows emphasize the illuminated planes in the residence. The natural and artificial bands of light appear to merge together horizontally. Moving up and down the ramps allows the eye to follow the horizontal images created by the light and dark patterns of the perimeter walls.

The Church of the Light in Osaka, Japan (1987–1989), designed by Tadao Ando, is another example of the use of natural light to create a focus on the vertical plane (Figure 17.21). This is accomplished by slicing daylight through a wall to create the form of an enormous cross. The shape of the cross is accentuated by the high contrast between the sunlight and dark surfaces. The cross is reinforced by its reflection on the ceiling and floor. Reflections from the smooth surface of the ceiling give the impression that the cross is glowing above the worshippers. Symbolically, the power of the cross touches the worshippers when the light illuminates the floor and pews.

A simple use of light and form is also present in a room created for contemplation and designed by Claudio Silvestrin (1997) in Frankfurt, Germany (Figure 17.22). The streaks of light that move across the floor and slightly up the wall create the serenity required for quiet reflection. The single light source at the end of the room emphasizes the

FIGURE 17.20 Light, architecture, and movement are visible in Le Corbusier's Villa Savoye.

FIGURE 17.21 Church of the Light in Osaka, Japan, uses natural light to create a focus on the vertical plane.

majestic height of the room. This scale can make people feel uncomfortable; however, the streaks of light help to create a setting of more human proportions. This can be understood by following the surfaces that are illuminated by the lines of light. For example, streaks of sunlight cross the floor, lead the eye to the seating area, and then progress up the wall for a short distance. To encourage meditation, light is manipulated to emphasize the benches. This is accomplished by the long

FIGURE 17.22 A simple use of light and form is used in this room that was designed for contemplation.

streaks of light that lead to the benches and the immediate transition that occurs when the light moves from a vertical plane to the horizontal surface of the seats. The location on the wall where the light eventually stops is critical in creating the impression that the reflective area has a human scale. Illumination stopped at a low level across the entire wall gives the illusion that another ceiling exists. The appearance of a low ceiling provides the human proportions that are needed to welcome people to such a tall room.

As demonstrated by these examples, patterns created by light and shadow can have a powerful impact on people and on interior architecture. The type and location of the pattern in a room must always be planned in a quality lighting environment. Patterns created by stained glass are derived from the colors and the designs. Beautiful patterns of light and shadow can be created by pierced openings in carved stones. For example, at the Taj Mahal fascinating patterns are created by light passing through pierced marble screens. A similar extraordinary effect occurs in the lacy, Gothic arches of the Batalha Abbey (1388– 1530s) in Batalha, Portugal, and the magnificent stalactite vaults of the Alhambra Palace in Granada, Spain (Figure 17.23a and b). The constantly moving metal diaphragms of the L'Institut du Monde Arabe (1987) in Paris create astonishing patterns on the floors of every level in the building (see Figure 2.4). To maximize the beauty of these

a   b

FIGURE 17.23 Interesting patterns and shadows are created from light passing through (a) the intricate gothic arches at the Batalha Abbey in Portugal and (b) the stalactite vaults of the Alhambra Palace in Granada, Spain.

designs, the colors and textures of the surfaces, which display the shadows, should be an appropriate texture and pattern.

An illuminated pattern in a room can be cast on various surfaces and objects. Often the pattern strikes floors and ceilings. These designs can be integrated into other elements and features of the space. For example, in the Neue Staatsgalerie in Stuttgart, Germany (1978–1984), designed by James Stirling, the shadow pattern created by the horizontal elements of the window is repeated in the shape of the suspended ceiling (Figure 17.24). The shadows of the window's vertical elements are reiterated in the electrical sources recessed in the ceiling. In the Capuchinas Sacramentarias del Purisimo Corazon de Maria in Tlalpan, Mexico, Luis Barragán artistically created different effects from the basic grid motif. As illustrated in Figure 17.25, both windows have light passing through a grid. However, the rigid and informal grids create very different illumination effects through the wall and on the reflections on the floor.

Creative lighting on vertical and horizontal planes can be integrated in passageways. These areas are an excellent location for stimulating lighting because these spaces often lack furniture or other decorative objects. In addition, a focus on intriguing lighting can make the journey through a passageway seem shorter. The cryptoportico in

FIGURE 17.24 The horizontal elements of the window are repeated in the shape of the suspended ceiling at the Neue Staatsgalerie in Germany.

FIGURE 17.25 In these windows, Luis Barragán uses the basic grid motif, which creates different effects through the wall and on the reflections of the floor.

Hadrian's Villa in Tivoli, Italy, and the roof of the chapter house of Wells in England are excellent examples of dramatic effects that can be created by carefully considering the shape of apertures, textures, and characteristics of the surface that reflects the light (Figure 17.26).

In addition to the stunning lighting effects that can be created by domes, a variety of lighting techniques can be integrated with architecture to illuminate ceilings. For example, in the Kimbell Art Museum in Fort Worth, Texas (1966–1972), Louis Kahn innovatively illuminated galleries with daylight by installing a reflecting device in the barrel vault (Figure 17.27). To provide accent lighting on paintings and sculptures, electrical light fixtures were mounted on the edges of the reflecting device. Indirect daylight simultaneously enhances the form of the vault and provides excellent illumination for viewing visual art.

Frank Lloyd Wright also specified lighting for the purpose of enhancing ceilings and forms. Light penetrating through the ceiling of the Johnson Wax building in Racine, Wisconsin (1936–1939 and 1944), provides excellent general lighting and accents the form of the lily pad columns (Figure 17.28). The integration of light with the mass of the lily pads results in a fascinating alternating pattern on the ceiling. A similar effect is demonstrated in Wright's Unity Temple, in Oak

FIGURE 17.26 A passageway in Hadrian's Villa, Italy, has a dramatic lighting effect, which can make the journey through it feel shorter.

FIGURE 17.27 This gallery in the Kimbell Art Museum is illuminated with daylight and a reflecting device that was placed in the barrel vault.

Park, Illinois (1904–1908). The primary space for worship is filled with light emitted through a stained glass skylight that covers the entire seating area. The square shapes of the skylight are repeated throughout the temple. Placing custom designed suspended pendants in each corner of the space reinforces the overall form of the skylight. Wright also specified corner pendant placement in the dining room of the Susan Lawrence Dana house in Springfield, Illinois (1902) (Figure 17.29). The precise location of the art glass fixtures causes shadows of butterflies to appear on the walls of the room. Furthermore, the stained glass pendants visually define the dining area.

Another example of using electrical light sources to illuminate a ceiling is the entrance hall of the Daily Express building in London, designed by Ellis Clarke, Robert Atkinson, and Owen Williams (Figure 17.30). The concealed light sources artfully enhance every form, color, and texture of the round ceiling. The integration of light and the center element of the ceiling gives the impression that the room is illuminated with fireworks.

FIGURE 17.28 The ceiling in the Johnson Wax building in Racine, Wisconsin (1936-50) by Frank Lloyd Wright.

FIGURE 17.29 The dining room in the Susan Lawrence Dana house in Springfield, Illinois (1902), by Frank Lloyd Wright. The stained glass of the luminaires creates shadows of butterflies on the walls of the dining room.

FIGURE 17.30 The lobby of the Daily Express building in London by Ellis Clarke, Ronald Atkinson, and Owen Williams (1932).

Volumetric Space and Movement

Using light to define volumetric space is challenging. One of the first attempts to create an interior that demonstrates light was conceptualized by Etienne-Louis Boullée in the 1700s (Figure 17.31). As a memorial to the scientific work of Isaac Newton, Boullée imagined a

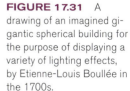

FIGURE 17.31 A drawing of an imagined gigantic spherical building for the purpose of displaying a variety of lighting effects, by Etienne-Louis Boullée in the 1700s.

gigantic spherical building for the purpose of displaying a variety of lighting effects. In theory, upon entering the building, people would experience multiple effects of day and night illumination. This imaginary structure represents the potential of integrating light and volume to evoke emotional responses in people.

An artistic approach to using illumination in defining volumetric space can be achieved by having shafts of light penetrate a room. As shown in Figure 17.32, multiple shafts of sunlight are slicing through the main concourse of Grand Central Station in New York City (designed by Whitney Warren, 1903–1913). The streaks of visible light enable people to see the actual length and width of direct light. Thus, people are able to follow the path of a light source. The rays of daylight can simultaneously define the volume of a space and create imaginary spaces that approach human proportions. For example, the long distance from the windows to the floor emphasizes the enormous height of the space. The broad width of the beams reinforces the wide windows of the massive wall. At floor level, the rays of light divide the large floor area into several bright and dark spaces. The dark areas between the pools of light create imaginary private spaces for people to convene. People feel more comfortable in the dark areas because they are not exposed to the glare of direct sunlight. Also, compared to the huge size of the concourse, these spaces appear to be on a human scale.

FIGURE 17.32 Multiple shafts of light penetrate the main concourse of Grand Central Station in New York City.

Illuminating vertical architectural members, such as columns, pillars, decorative moldings, and staircases, can also help to define the volume of a space. This phenomenon occurs because the eye can easily follow a line, which delineates the height of a space. For example, the emphasis on the lily pad columns in the Johnson Wax building reinforces the great volume of the office space. As with rays of sunlight, vertical members help to divide a large space into smaller dimensions. Viewing smaller spaces within the context of a large room helps people to understand volumetric space. In addition to providing clarity to volume, illuminating vertical members can also create interesting focal points in an environment. For this to be effective, the lighting must enhance the three-dimensional form of the member. Recommendations for illumination techniques for three-dimensional pieces appear in Chapter 15.

Staircases are an elegant way to emphasize the volume of an interior and integrate light with movement. Some of the most effective techniques for illuminating staircases involve concealed light sources, because the steps can appear to float in midair. The Guggenheim Museum in New York City, designed by Frank Lloyd Wright (1956–1959), is an excellent example of integrating light with an enormous ramp to reinforce the organic shape of the building and enable people to physically sense the volume of space. Complementary natural and electrical lighting techniques illuminate the spiral path on the walls of which is displayed the visual art. The interplay between architecture and light is so intriguing at the Guggenheim that Dan Flavin designed a multicolored neon lamp installation to emphasize the spiral form. Figures 17.33a and b illustrate some other extraordinary examples of how light can emphasize the exquisite form of a spiral design and create an emotional response for people who are looking or ascending up.

A quality lighting environment includes an effective illumination of interior architecture from all prospective views, including the appearance of the interior space from the exterior during evening hours. Interior lighting can help people to understand volume and form of interior architecture while they are in the space and when they are viewing a building from the outside during the evening. Naturally, most lighting plans are designed to accommodate the needs of people who are in the

FIGURE 17.33a Stained glass windows follow the curves of the spiral tower in the Thanks-Giving Square in Dallas, Texas.

FIGURE 17.33b Light emphasizes the unique shape and form of this staircase.

space. However, some buildings should have a lighting plan that also includes specific applications for highlighting the interior architecture when viewed from the street. For example, the interior illumination enhances the forms and volume of the Vitra Fire Station in Weil Am Rhein, Germany (designed by Zaha Hadid, 1989–1993), and the National Commercial Bank, in Jeddah, Saudi Arabia (designed by Gordon Bunshaft) (Figure 17.34 a and b).

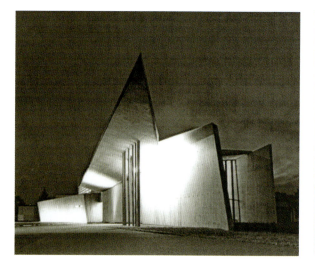

FIGURE 17.34a Interior illumination enhances the exterior views of the Vitra Fire Station building in Germany.

FIGURE 17.34b The lighting plan of this National Commercial Bank highlights the interior architecture when viewed from the street.

The integration of lighting and architecture is essential in a quality lighting environment. Analyzing architectural masterpieces is an excellent way to understand how to create interiors that enhance the elements of a space, including planes, volume, and forms. In addition, a successful integration of lighting and architecture can cause emotional responses from the users of the space. As with all lighting plans, the key to success is collaboratively developing the integration during the conceptual phase of a project.

SUMMARY

- The materials, skills, and engineering capabilities that were available to architects in the past affected how buildings were designed and constructed. These factors become very important in studying how daylight was integrated with architecture.
- Many architectural masterpieces demonstrate how light can be manipulated to enhance structural elements and have emotive effects on the users of the space.
- Gothic cathedrals and churches constructed during the seventeenth and eighteenth centuries are also excellent examples of using scale, architectural elements, and light to evoke emotional responses.
- For architectural interest and the enhancement of illumination, there are a variety of different materials and shapes that are used in domes and adjacent surfaces.
- In designing architecture to enhance light, people had to control sunlight in order to control glare and the heat of the sun. This resulted in buildings that are excellent examples of integrating architecture with light.
- An interdependent relationship between architecture and illumination is essential for a quality lighting environment. Ideally, architecture should enhance light, and light should enrich architecture.
- Developing a lighting plan that enhances architecture requires a thorough understanding of the architect's conceptual design and objectives. This includes understanding the context of the environment and the mood the architect wishes to create.

- Once the emphatic elements of the architecture are identified and prioritized, the lighting should be planned to enhance the forms, lines, colors, and textures.
- Illuminating architectural elements requires an examination of three major considerations: (1) lighting systems and techniques that will specifically enhance a plane, space, or feature; (2) how the emphatic lighting identified in item 1 will affect other architectural elements in a space; and (3) how other light sources affect the emphatic lighting.
- The placement and shape of a window affects the overall composition of the vertical plane and can define the space.
- Patterns created by light and shadow can have a powerful impact on people and interior architecture. The type and location of the pattern in a room must always be planned in a quality lighting environment.
- An artistic approach to using illumination in defining volumetric space can be achieved by shafts of light penetrating a room.
- Illuminating vertical architectural members, such as columns, pillars, decorative moldings, and staircases, can also help to define the volume of a space.
- A quality lighting environment includes an effective illumination of interior architecture from all prospective views, including the appearance of the interior space from the exterior during evening hours.

Key Terms

keyhole window	glare-shielding wall

Exercises

1. Research five examples of how architecture was designed to enhance natural light. Compile the examples in a file. Write an essay

that includes an analysis of the integration of natural light and the architecture. Include photographs, sketches, or illustrations.

2. Develop a conceptual design for axial planning that includes variations in illumination levels, size of spaces, and ceiling heights. Submit drawings of the floor plan and a cross-sectional view. Include an essay that explains how the variations in space and lighting will affect users of the environment.

3. Write an essay that identifies and analyzes factors that should be considered when illuminating architectural elements. Issues that should be included are (a) lighting systems and techniques that will specifically enhance a plane, space, or feature; (b) how the emphatic lighting identified in *a* will affect other architectural elements in a space; and c) how other light sources affect the emphatic lighting. The essay should include a thorough analysis of color and the directional qualities of illumination, including incident and reflected light. In a written report provide recommendations for illuminating architectural elements, including illustrations, photos, or sketches.

4. Identify three examples that demonstrate how lighting can enhance vertical and horizontal planes. Compile the examples in a file. Write an essay that includes an analysis of the examples and how the integration of natural and electrical light is dealt with. Include photographs, sketches, or illustrations.

5. Identify three examples that demonstrate how architecture can enhance volumetric space. Compile the examples in a file. Write an essay that includes an analysis of the examples and how the integration of natural and electrical light is dealt with. Include photographs, sketches, or illustrations.

REFERENCES

Bagenal, P., and Meades, J. (1980). *The Illustrated Atlas of the World's Great Buildings*. New York: Galahad Books.

Barford, G. (1986). *Understanding Modern Architecture*. Worcester, MA: Davis Publications.

Beazley, M. (1984). *The World Atlas of Architecture*. Boston: G. K. Hall & Co.

Bergdoll, B. (2000). *European Architecture: 1750–1890*. New York: Oxford University Press.

Blakemore, R.G. (1997). *History of Interior Design and Furniture: From Ancient Egypt to Nineteenth-Century Europe*. New York: John Wiley & Sons.

Borras, M.L. *Antonio Gaudi: Casa Batllo, Barcelona, Spain. 1905–07; Casa Mila, Barcelona, Spain. 1905–10.* Tokyo: Global Architecture.

Ching, F. (1996). *Architecture: Form, Space, & Order,* 2nd Edition. New York: John Wiley & Sons.

Cruickshank, D. (ed.) (2000). *Architecture: The Critics' Choice.* New York: Watson-Guptill Publications.

Glancey, J. (1998). *20th Architecture: The Structures That Shaped the Century.* New York: The Overlook Press.

Hale, J. (1994). *The Old Way of Seeing.* Boston: Houghton Mifflin.

Harwood, B., May, B., and Sherman, C. (2002). *Architecture and Interior Design through the 18th Century.* Upper Saddle River, NJ: Prentice Hall.

Jacquet, P. *History of Architecture.* London: Leisure Arts.

Jenjer, J. (1996). *Le Corbusier: Architect, Painter, Poet.* New York: Harry N. Abrams.

Kostof, S. (1995). *A History of Architecture: Settings and Rituals.* New York: Oxford University Press.

Lam, W.M. (1977). *Perception and Lighting as Formgivers for Architecture.* New York: McGraw-Hill.

Lam, W.M. (1986). *Sunlighting as Formgivers for Architecture.* New York: Van Nostrand Reinhold.

Linton, H. (1985). *Color Model Environments: Color and Light in Three-Dimensional Design.* New York: Van Nostrand Reinhold.

Macaulay, D. (2000). *Building Big.* Boston: Houghton Mifflin.

Mahnke, F.H. (1996). *Color, Environment, and Human Response.* New York: Van Nostrand Reinhold.

McCarter, R. (ed.) (1991). *Frank Lloyd Wright: A Primer on Architectural Principles.* New York: Princeton Architectural Press.

Meier, R. *Le Corbusier: Villa Savoye, Poissy, France. 1929–31.* Tokyo: Global Architecture.

Murray, P. (1971). *Renaissance Architecture.* New York: Harry N. Abrams.

Nappo, S. (1998). *Pompeii: A Guide to the Ancient City.* New York: Barnes & Noble Books.

Otto, C.F. (1979). *Space into Light.* New York: The Architectural History Foundation; and London: The MIT Press.

Puppi, L. (1989). *Palladio Drawings.* New York: Rizzoli.

Raeburn, M. (1975). *Architecture of the World.* New York: Galahad Books.

Rand McNally (1991). *Wonders of the World.* New York: Rand McNally.

Risebero, B. (2001). *The Story of Western Architecture.* Cambridge, MA: The MIT Press.

Summerson, J. (2000). *Inigo Jones.* London: Yale University Press.

Sutton, I. (1999). *Western Architecture.* London: Thames and Hudson.

Thorne, M. (ed.) (1999). *The Pritzker Architecture Prize: The First Twenty Years.* New York: Harry N. Abrams, in association with The Art Institute of Chicago.

Time-Life Guides (2000). *The World's Greatest Buildings: Masterpieces of Architecture and Engineering.* New York: Time-Life Books.

Tyng, A. (1984). *Beginnings: Louis I. Kahn's Philosophy of Architecture.* New York: John Wiley & Sons.

Whiton, S., and Abercrombie, S. (2002). *Interior Design & Decoration,* 5th edition. Upper Saddle River, NJ: Prentice Hall.

Yoshizaka, T. (1989). *Le Corbusier: Chapelle Notre Dame du Haut Ronchamp, France. 1950–54.* Tokyo: Global Architecture.

Zevi, B. (1974). *Architecture as Space.* New York: Horizon Press.

CHAPTER 18

Inspirational Mediums

- **Understand the observational skills related to lighting for artists, photographers, and directors.**

- **Understand how artists, photographers, and directors use lighting to evoke emotional responses and create unique visual effects.**

- **Determine the relationships between the effects of direct lighting and paintings, photographs, and stage scenes.**

- **Determine the relationships between the effects of reflected light and multiple sources and paintings, photographs, and stage scenes.**

- **Apply an understanding of lighting techniques used in the visual and performing arts to commercial and residential interiors.**

QUALITY lighting environments reflect a thorough understanding of the effects of lighting in interiors and on people. Chapter 17 examines the relationship between interior architecture and lighting. This chapter expands the content in Chapter 17 by exploring how artists have interpreted lighting on people and the environment. We will analyze the work of artists in the visual and performing arts, specifically, the mediums that include paintings, photography, stage, and film. An understanding of how artists manipulate light to accomplish the intent of a piece or performance can provide valuable inspiration for illuminating interiors.

The illustrations presented in this chapter represent the results of processing lighting from an artistic perspective. Artists have learned how to work with light by engaging in detailed observations of illumination on people, surfaces, colors, and objects. Their expertise is invaluable to an understanding of how to use lighting to provide clarity to an environment. For quality lighting environments, interior designers must develop the same seeing skills and then apply the knowledge gained to illuminating interiors.

Visual and Performing Arts

To learn from artists' observational skills requires a thorough analysis of the effects of lighting in their work. Several paintings, photographs, films, and stage scenes illustrate how to use light to create emphasis and to enhance people, objects, and spaces. In addition, these mediums demonstrate the powerful ability of light to evoke emotional responses in viewers. The captured view of a painting, photograph, or stage set provides the opportunity for designers to understand how the type of lighting, angle, intensity, and location of natural and electrical sources affect people and the environment. In addition, the mediums illustrate which lighting techniques create specific emotional responses. Each medium offers its own techniques for capturing the effects of lighting and demonstrating the artists' powers of observation. Interior designers can learn to recognize the effects of lighting by examining the observations of artists in these mediums and then producing similar effects in their own medium.

Painting

Long before the invention of electricity and electrical light sources, artists studied the effects of lighting on people, objects, interiors, color, and moods. The first paintings to include shades and shadows demonstrate an early understanding of the effects of lighting. The invention of oil paintings by the Flemish in the fifteenth century enabled artists to paint interior scenes with incredible detail and precision. Because of the photographic, or realistic, quality of these paintings, many of them demonstrate, with complete accuracy, the effects of lighting. In addition to artistic skills, to accomplish this level of accuracy requires incredible observation skills. An interest in painting light and its effects continued through the impressionist period in the late nineteenth century. Therefore, this chapter primarily focuses on paintings from the Renaissance to the impressionist period. Still life, portraits, and **nocturnes** (or painting in darkness) are excellent genres for examining the effects of lighting.

The painting by Hendrick van Steenwyck is an excellent example of what can be learned about lighting by studying a painting (Figure 18.1). The furniture, objects, surfaces, textures, and colors in the room are affected by the warm, natural daylight emitted through the leaded glass windows. The size and location of the windows affects how light illuminates the space. The large surface area of the windows emits a high level of illumination in the room. The location close to the ceiling and adjacent wall results in illumination primarily on the ceiling beams, the wall in the foreground, and the three individuals. Several factors contribute to the interesting highlights and shadows, which are

Nocturne
An artistic genre that involves painting or drawing in darkness.

FIGURE 18.1 Hendrick van Steenwyck's painting, *Jesus in the House of Martha and Mary*, c. 1620, is an excellent example of what can be learned about lighting by studying a painting. Furniture, objects, surfaces, textures, and colors in the room are affected by the daylight.

created by the forms of the beams. The highlights and shadows are visible because the level of illumination is high, the windows are close to the beams, and the direction of the sunlight is parallel to the horizontal lines of the beams. The window's close proximity to the wall, in the background, results in a warm color on the surface and an interesting texture derived from the plaster material. The painting demonstrates the length and shape of the table's shadow, which is cast on the floor. This detail provides good information regarding the amount of space that is required between objects when there is a need to avoid shadows on an image.

Photography

In 1888, George Eastman invented the roll-film Kodak camera. This technological development allowed anyone to capture images on film. People were no longer dependent upon painters for preserving memories. However, during the early days of photography, pictures resembled painted portraits. As the art form developed, photographers used the camera as an expressive medium. As a result, there are numerous examples of photographs that effectively use lighting to suggest a mood, communicate to viewers, and enhance people, forms, and spaces. Black-and-white photographs in particular provide excellent insight into understanding how to distribute dark, light, and midtones. The tonal subtleties of black-and-white photographs illustrate the importance of strategically locating lighting to emphasize highlights and shadows. The grays moderate the contrasting extremes of black-and-white. Moreover, the lack of color enables a viewer to better analyze how lighting has been used to enhance the principles of design, including balancing the composition and delineating forms and positive and negative space.

The Performing Arts

We analyze stage and film lighting from the perspective of how illumination creates moods, communicates to viewers, enhances aesthetics, facilitates timing, reinforces movement, and emphasizes three-dimensional objects and interiors. The performing arts demonstrate how to integrate lighting with people, objects, interiors, costumes, music, and stories. Fundamentally, directors or cinematographers in film and lighting designers on stage begin the development of a scene in total darkness. To see anything on the stage, lighting must be added to the space. Starting the lighting process in total darkness causes a lighting designer to plan methodically the best illumination for the desired intent of a scene. When working in a black space, lighting has to be specified for every element and person in the space. Without this type of meticulous planning, important objects, expressions, or gestures might be ignored or unseen by the audience. The technique of adding light to darkness can provide a fresh approach to illuminating commercial and residential space. Generally, interior designers begin a lighting plan by conceptualizing how to add light to dark areas. In contrast, stage and film lighting illustrates how light can take darkness away from a space. This is a fascinating and provocative approach to illuminating interiors.

Facilitating timing and creating the illusion of movement are important characteristics of stage and film lighting that can be applied to interiors. Lighting directors have learned that an audience can get restless when the same illumination effect remains on a stage for a long period of time. Thus, stage and film lighting is changed frequently to prevent boredom and produce stimulating scenes. This same phenomenon should be applied to interior space. Interiors that do not have multiple layers of illumination, a range of intensities, and a variety of lighting techniques can be unexciting to the users of the space.

Light, in films and on stage, is also used to provide orientation to a scene. The various lighting effects that are required to establish different times of the day and year provide a profile of how the quality and quantity of lighting affect the mood and overall impression of people and interiors. Scenes provide the opportunity to study the various lighting effects of electrical sources, sunlight through fog, the moon, or a sunset. Most important, these effects can be studied as people and activities are occurring in a space. Thus, film and theater scenes come as close as possible to replicating existing interiors. Observing movement through spaces allows an interior designer to better understand how images and people change as they move toward or away from lighting sources. Movement is also important in studying light and the three-dimensional aspects of objects and a space. To reveal dimensional qualities, light and shadows must be accurately positioned within the scene. As is explored in this chapter, many of these techniques can be applied to commercial and residential interiors.

Emotional and Visual Effects

Many lighting concepts can be learned by studying visual and performing arts. This study involves an understanding of the psychology of lighting and the elements and principles of design. Chapter 13 discusses the psychology of lighting. To understand how lighting elicits emotive responses in viewers, analyze a painting, photograph, or stage scene and then determine reactions to the context of what you are viewing. Would it make people feel happy, sad, sober, confused, shocked, or complacent? The next thought process should be to analyze the scene to determine how lighting contributed to the response. For example, most people would feel a sense of fear and mystery when viewing a scene in the film *The Spiritualist* (Figure 18.2). Light and shadows contribute to this response. For example, illumination on the face of the woman reinforces the trance she appears to be experiencing from looking at the shadowed figure. Moreover, the black wall emphasizes the outline of the ominous eye. The strategic placement of light, shade, and shadows contributes to the mystery of the forms.

Visual and performing arts can also help designers to understand how lighting in an interior can be used to enhance the elements and principles of design. This exploration requires a distinction between two different ways lighting is used in paintings, photographs, or stage scenes. Lighting can be represented realistically, or light can exist unnaturally. As illustrated in Figure 18.3, Balthasar van der Ast meticulously painted the effects of light on the objects, surfaces, and space. The highlights and shadows in the painting give the impression that a single warm light source, at a low intensity level, was used to illuminate the composition. The light appears to be emitted from the right side, at a low angle. As a result of the characteristics of the light source,

FIGURE 18.2 This stage scene from the film *The Spiritualist*, illustrates how lighting affects emotive responses in viewers. Most people would feel a sense of fear and mystery when viewing this film. Illumination and shadows contribute to this response.

FIGURE 18.3 In *Still Life with Basket of Fruit*, Balthasar van der Ast meticulously painted the effects of light on the objects, surfaces, and space.

the flowers, shells, and fruit in the foreground are highlighted, and objects in the middle and background become progressively darker. Van der Ast's precision with painting the effects of light is evident in the exact replication of the highlights, shade, and shadows that would be created by a light source located at a low angle. For example, as illustrated in the basket, van der Ast painted all the shadows created by the fibrous material, and he illustrates how the variance in darkness changes as the basket is farther away from the light source. Realistic painting is also evident in the true colors of objects, based upon the characteristics of the light source. For example, the flowers and fruit in warm hues are painted in rich yellows and reds because the natural light source is primarily in the warm spectrum.

Representational paintings, like the still life illustrated in Figure 18.3, can provide insight into how a specific type of light source and its directional angle affect objects and the overall composition of an area in a space. By analyzing van der Ast's painting, an interior designer would learn that a soft light source, at a low angle, from the side, highlights only objects in the foreground. The warm light source enhances the warm hues and deemphasizes cool-colored objects. In addition, the low angle creates long shadows. Thus, to avoid shadows that would hide objects, adequate space must be allotted between items. This precise replication of actual lighting conditions also illustrates the calming effect that can result from low illumination levels.

Often, light is illustrated unnaturally, when the intent is to enhance one of the principles of design, such as emphasis, rhythm, balance, unity, or variety. For example, in Figure 18.4, Sandro Botticelli did not depict light realistically. It appears that the canopy of trees in the dark forest is shielding sunlight from the figures in the painting. However, each figure is brightly illuminated from head to toe. An unrealistic, uniform distribution of light was painted on every object of emphasis, including the figures, peaches in the trees, and flowers on the ground. The slight shadows on the figures exist for the purpose of creating a perspective rather than for depicting the true shadows that would be cast by sunlight. The very unrealistic blue-toned color of Zephr, the west wind of spring, is another example of how Botticelli's intent with the painting was to manipulate color and light for symbolic reasons.

Botticelli's control of light results in an enhancement of the principles of design. For example, illuminated figures, items, and spaces develop rhythm in the composition, establish balance, and create emphasis. The repeated illuminated figures, peaches, flowers, and back-

FIGURE 18.4 In this work, *Primavera*, Sandro Botticelli did not depict light realistically. Illumination is used to enhance many of the principles of design.

ground establish rhythm in the painting. The scale of the illuminated objects directs the eye through the composition. Thus, a viewer first notices the large illuminated figures, then moves to the bright blue sky in the background, the peaches in the trees, and then briefly examines the small flowers in the grass. Placement of the illuminated objects also creates the asymmetrical balance in the painting. The severe contrast between the bright figures and objects and their background contributes to the emphasis on the subject of *Primavera*. The light and dark contrast also provides variety to the unified illuminated objects and figures.

An interior designer can analyze paintings such as *Primavera* to learn how to place lighting strategically in a room for the purpose of creating rhythm, balance, emphasis, variety, and unity. For example, rhythm and balance can be achieved by establishing multiple lighting levels throughout a space. Emphasis can be derived from the size of a light source, its intensity level, or its location in the room. Highlight and shadow contrast can provide the variety of repeated illumination patterns within the unity. Illumination distribution can also affect proportion in the space. The ideal lighting distribution should reflect the geometrical divisions of the golden mean.

Effects of Direct Illumination

There are many examples in paintings, photographs, and stage scenes that help to inform an interior designer of how to manipulate light effectively. The designer should look for the elements of illumination and the special effects that are produced in various artistic mediums by skillful use of these elements.

Elements of Illumination

In analyzing the effects of lighting, important considerations include the type of light, number of sources, illumination intensity, directional angle, and distance from objects, people, or surfaces. Frequently, the light source is not visible, so it must be inferred from what is provided in the scene.

Mediums should be studied to determine the effect of light on people, objects, surfaces, colors, and spaces, including shadows. Specifically, mediums can be analyzed to determine how the lighting provides clarity to details and objects. This can be important for highlighting products in a retail environment. Furthermore, mediums provide the unique opportunity to study the complicated interplay of shadows and reflections. How lighting can contribute spatial organization and composition can also be observed in the visual and performing arts.

In Figure 18.1, the location of windows in relationship to the objects in the room affects the appearance of colors, shapes, and textures. For example, the tall, wooden bench is illuminated at a fairly high level because this surface is in full sunlight. Most of the bottom section of the bench and table are below the window sill, thus these surfaces are darker. The wall surrounding the windows is also fairly dark. However, the entire vertical plane has variable darkness, because the reflected light from the light colored background wall and other surfaces are providing some illumination on the area under the window. These sources of illumination are not striking the wall surface between the windows. The proximity and angle of the daylight also enhances the warm colors and textures of the clothing.

The angle and location of a light source is very critical in recessed areas of a wall, such as a niche. Figures 18.5a and 18.5b demonstrate the illuminative differences that varying lighting angles produce on objects placed in niches. The objects in Figure 18.5a are illuminated by a light source that is directed toward the niche, from the right side. In Figure 18.5b, the light source grazes the wall because the window is very close to the wall. The light source directed at the niche, in Figure 18.5a, results in most of the objects being illuminated and interesting shadows of the pages in the open book. The angles of light accentuate the niches by creating a delineating line that surrounds the openings. This is achieved by alternating the illuminated and shaded surfaces of the wall and niche. For example, on the left side of the niche opening in Figure 18.5b, the wall is illuminated and the niche is dark. On the right side, the opposite effect occurs; the wall is in darkness, and the niche surface is illuminated. The angle of illumination in Figure 18.5b primarily highlights the objects that are extended from the niche. The grazing effect enhances the textures of the fabric, brass candlestick holder, clock, ribbon, and brass curtain rings. Objects located in the niche receive only reflected light, which results in their appearing dark.

FIGURE 18.5a Compare the lighting effects of Charles Bird King's painting, *Poor Artist's Cupboard*, with Figure 18.5b. King uses a light source that is directed toward the niche from the right side.

FIGURE 18.5b In comparison to King's approach in Figure 18.5a, Gerard Dou uses a light source to graze the wall in his painting, *Still Life with Candlestick and Pocket Watch*.

A light source's angle, direction, intensity, and color significantly affect faces and complexions. In most situations, lighting should enhance the way people look. Therefore, in areas where people will be sitting or standing, an interior designer should closely examine the way light strikes facial features. Portrait artists, photographers, and film and stage directors are very much aware of the effects of lighting on people. In analyzing portrait paintings and photographs, there are many variables to consider, including the pose, lighting characteristics, and distance between the light source and the individual. The most flattering portraits use lighting that enhances the selected pose. For example, in *Bernardini Luini,* by Michelangelo, the soft lighting is coming from a high angle apparently above the figure's head. The light source and angle enhance her complexion and facial features and minimize shadows that can create unflattering distortions on a face. A similar result is evident in the photograph (Figure 18.6). The high angle of the dim lighting demonstrates the natural beauty of generations of women. This technique renders an elusive touch to the portrait. Rembrandt's painting of an old woman (*An Old Woman Reading*), reflected light is directed up toward her face, thus reinforcing wrinkles and facial shadows to emphasize her age. Intense lighting directed up toward faces at

FIGURE 18.6 The high angle of the dim lighting enhances the natural beauty of generations of women.

an unnatural angle was used to reinforce the criminal nature of the activities conducted by the actors in Figure 18.7. Similar lighting techniques were used to create frightening images in the Boris Karloff film *The Mummy*.

As illustrated in Figure 18.8, the lighting variables and a frontal pose can significantly affect which facial features are highlighted. The high lighting angle and low illumination level in Figure 18.8a reveals most of Rembrandt's facial features, with a specific emphasis on his eyes. In contrast, a low and side illumination angle hides Rembrandt's eyes in his self-portrait painted when he was 23 years of age (Figure 18.8b). It is interesting to note that Rembrandt used a more flattering lighting technique for the self-portrait when he was 34 years of age compared to the one painted when he was 23.

A profile introduces new situations that must be dealt with by lighting. In Figure 18.9 both women are in profile and are illuminated by natural light emitted through a window that is located in front of them. Due to a slight angle change, the woman's facial features are enhanced in Figure 18.9a, but in Figure 18.9b the woman's face is in a shadow. The aforementioned examples demonstrate the importance of understanding the relationship between lighting and the locations of

FIGURE 18.7 In scenes from the movie *T-Men*, the apparent criminal nature of these activities is reinforced by intense lighting directed up toward faces at an unnatural angle.

a   b

FIGURE 18.8 Lighting variables and frontal pose can significantly affect which facial features are highlighted. Compare the lighting effects in (a) *Self-Portrait at the Age of Thirty-four* to the painting (b) *Self-Portrait*, when the artist was 23 years of age.

a   b

FIGURE 18.9 Lighting variables and side profiles can significantly affect which facial features are highlighted. Compare the lighting effects in Jan Vermeer's paintings (a) *Woman Holding a Balance* and (b) *Young Woman with a Pearl Necklace*.

illumination and people. Some of the examples illustrate artists' manipulation of light for intrigue and aesthetic purposes. The lighting in these portraits might not be appropriate for illuminating people, but perhaps they can provide inspiration for illuminating sculptures.

Special Effects

In addition to facial features, lighting variables should be considered when materials are being illuminated. As discussed in Chapter 6, lighting affects materials in various ways depending upon the colors, textures, surface qualities, and reflection factor. Reflective materials, such as glass or silver, are difficult to illuminate. Many artists manipulate light to enhance the shimmer of glass. Specific lighting characteristics contribute to the sparkle of glass in Figure 18.10a. A close examination of the highlights reveals that most of the sparkle is a result of seeing the reflection of the large windowpanes in the glass. Thus, the surface area of a light source can affect the reflective qualities of glass, as can the shape of the glass object. Adding another highly reflective medium, such as liquid in a glass, can provide additional glossy surfaces to show the interplay of light and shiny materials. Light-colored liquids can be even more effective, because the hues can create a transparent surface to display variations in light and shadow. A dark background in a painting can provide an excellent color to contrast the light-colored liquid and the sparkle from the glasses.

Silver is also a challenging material to illuminate. Heda and Desportes approach highlighting silver from two different perspectives. In Heda's *Still Life,* to reveal the forms of the silver pieces and the detailed engravings, the light source appears to be striking the objects from a fairly high angle, and a low illumination level was used throughout the space. The reflected light, from the wall behind the table, provides additional soft illumination to the shiny surfaces (Figure 18.10a). In Desportes's still life, direct light from a high angle delineates the details of the edges of the tureen and platters (Figure 18.10b). The reflection of peaches, with their soft texture and warm hues, enhances the polish of the silver in the smooth-surfaced centers of the platters. In contrast to Heda, Desportes used a background devoid of light to provide the emphasis to the bright silver pieces. An instructive element of Desportes's painting is the angle of lighting in relationship to the reflective surfaces of the silver platters. Desportes precisely coordinated both elements so as to eliminate disability glare, which could easily occur when light strikes a shiny surface.

Still life paintings can provide interior designers with excellent

FIGURE 18.10a William Heda used light to enhance the forms of the silver pieces and the detailed engravings in this painting *Still Life.*

FIGURE 18.10b In *Silver Tureen with Peaches* by Alexandre-Francois Desportes, light is directed from a high angle to delineate the details of the edges of the tureen and platters.

insight into how to best enhance the appearance of specific forms, colors, and textures used in interiors. For example, in Coorte's *Still Life with Shells,* light, which is directed only at the edges of the shells, creates a grazing effect that reveals the diverse forms, curves, colors, and crevices of each shell. The extremely dark surrounding area emphasizes the illuminated shells (Figure 18.11a). Figure 18.11b is a dramatic illustration of how fabric can be highlighted. The intense direct light causes the silk to glisten, and the sleek texture is enhanced by the dark contrasting shadows (Figure 18.11b).

Direct light behind objects or people can create disability glare (see Chapter 6) or delineate a form of a silhouette. Visual and performing arts often use a diffused light source behind an object or scene to create drama and emphasis and to communicate to viewers. Fog is used frequently to create the white contrast required for emphasizing a silhouette. For example, in the film *Manhattan,* Woody Allen uses an elusive fog to serve as the background for emphasizing forms and their developing relationship. In Orson Welles's film *Citizen Kane,* a bright light source is used to emphasize the power of Kane, and the reflected light provides enough illumination to enable the viewer to notice that an employee is in awe of the man (Figure 18.12).

FIGURE 18.11a Adriaen Coorte's *Still Life with Shells* shows how light is directed only at the edges of the shells and reveals the diverse forms, curves, colors, and crevices of each shell.

FIGURE 18.11b There is an intense and direct light source in this painting, *Trompe – l'oeil Still Life with a Flower Garland and a Curtain*, by Adriaen van der Spelt and Frans van Mieris, which causes the silk in the curtain to glisten.

FIGURE 18.12 In the film *Citizen Kane*, Welles uses a bright light source to emphasize the power of Kane.

In Woody Allen's film *Shadows and Fog,* the mysterious murderer is concealed by darkness and fog. Most of the scenes in the movie are in fog. Fog and indoor shots were alternated throughout the film. This technique provides a relief for the audience, because it can be frustrating to view objects and people constantly in distorted, low levels of lighting. The visual breaks required in the film demonstrate to the interior designer how important it is to vary lighting techniques and intensity levels.

Photographs have captured many images in London, a city known for having many foggy days. Fog is used to emphasize unique forms by providing tonal contrasts, and the atmospheric conditions nearly obliterate the background (Figure 18.13). The blank canvas created by fog contributes to an emphasis on the silhouette. These exterior photographs can help an interior designer to understand how backlighting in interiors can enhance the form of objects.

FIGURE 18.13 Fog creates the emphasis on the man's unique form by providing tonal contrasts.

Nocturne paintings can also demonstrate how providing lighting at an appropriate level can emphasize intriguing forms and maximize reflected light. The nocturne genre can educate interior designers about differences between lighting effects for black spaces and those used for dark spaces. Black is the total absence of light. People do not work or live in black spaces. Thus, as illustrated in nocturne paintings, black spaces should never exist in interiors. In comparison, dark spaces have some level of illumination. For example, theaters during a performance are in darkness, but the environment has some illumination. Nocturne paintings reveal how to effectively illuminate spaces that are primarily in darkness and create artistic forms. For example, in Georges de La Tour's *The Penitent Magdalen,* candlelight provides direct and indirect illumination on the woman (Figure 18.14). The indirect light is de-

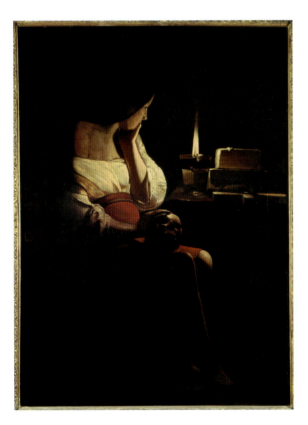

FIGURE 18.14 The candlelight in Georges de La Tour's *The Penitent Magdalen,* c.1638–43, provides direct and indirect illumination on the woman.

rived from candlelight striking the frame and reflecting a diffused illumination on the woman. The silhouette of the woman is emphasized by the contrast between the darkened background and her illuminated body. Thus, as illustrated in nocturne paintings, interiors that need to be dark should never be black, and reflected light can be effective for providing illumination without harsh contrasts. For this to be successful, light sources should not be at a high level and should be preferably dispersed throughout a space.

The artistic use of silhouettes in the visual and performing arts can be applied to interior spaces as well. Silhouette lighting techniques can emphasize any interesting form or focal point. For example, the techniques used to highlight the lines and curves of photographed people could be applied to a flowing staircase or an elegant chaise lounge. Silhouettes in nocturnes illustrate how objects can be emphasized in dark areas, such as theaters, restaurants, or nightclubs. An important consideration for creating artistic silhouettes is using a soft lighting effect behind the object that is to be emphasized. A low level of illumination must be directed at the object.

An interesting aspect of silhouette lighting is generally the use of hidden light sources. This technique can often add a sense of mystery and intrigue to an illuminated room or object. For example, in the still life painting by Isaac Soreau, it appears that the primary light source is aimed at a high angle toward the plate of fruit (Figure 18.15). However, a close examination of the red grapes in the center of the arrangement reveals that the glow emitted by the fruit must be derived from a light source located under the grapes. The glowing red grapes in this painting is an excellent example of using a hidden lighting source and how a beautiful effect can result from passing light through a colorful, transparent material. The illumination effect on the red grapes would be very different if light was aimed at the fruit rather than passing through it. Light aimed at the grapes can highlight the shiny surfaces, but the beauty of the transparent nature of the grapes and the associated luminous effect would not occur.

Often, the effect of a hidden source is revealed only by shadows. As discussed in previous chapters, shade and shadows can add an artistic element to an interior. Shade and shadows can be used creatively to communicate a story or be part of a symbolic composition. For

FIGURE 18.15 In Isaac Soreau's *Still Life of Grapes in a Basket*, the center of the arrangement reveals a glow emitted by the fruit. It appears the light source is located under the grapes.

example, in the 1968 photograph of Turkoman and Uzbek workers in Samarkand, Russia, the shadows from mountains cast patterns on the faces of the workers (Figure 18.16). The scattered distribution of light and shadow could symbolically represent a sense of hope within de-

FIGURE 18.16 This 1968 photograph shows Communist Turkoman and Uzbek workers in Samarkand, Russia. Shadows from muntins cast an array of patterns on the faces of the workers. The distribution of light and shadow appear to have symbolic meaning.

spair. An especially poignant use of shade is illustrated in the shaded painting of Lenin, who appears to be overseeing the workers.

Figure 18.16 not only illustrates how lighting and its effects can communicate to viewers but it also demonstrates how shadows can create images in a space. Some of the shade and shadows might be desirable, but the interior designer needs to be aware of and control the effects of lighting on the environment. One shadow effect that can create magic in a space is **dappled lighting.** Impressionist artists frequently used this technique to demonstrate the effect of sunlight shining through leaves and branches of trees. For example, in Renoir's painting *Le Moulin de la Galette,* a magical touch is added to the people and objects in the garden by the dappled light running throughout the setting (Figure 18.17).

Dappled lighting
An effect that creates multiple, irregular spots of light and shadow on objects and in a space. An example is when light filters through leaves and branches of trees.

Effects of Reflected Light and Multiple Sources

Reflected light and the use of multiple light sources affect the appearance of people, colors, surfaces, objects, and a space. Visual and performing arts provide excellent examples of the effects.

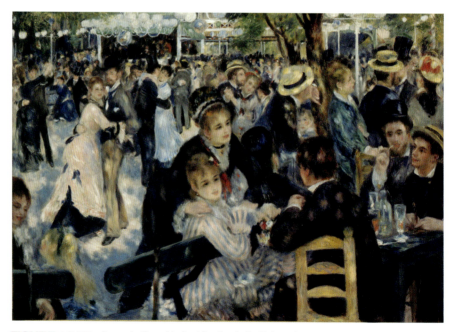

FIGURE 18.17 Auguste Renoir's *Le Moulin de la Galette* has a variety of playful lights and shadows that are created by the dappled lighting effect.

Effects of Reflected Light

As noted in the previous section, direct light can enhance or distort facial features. On the other hand, most reflected light enhances facial features, including the texture of complexions. Important factors that affect the quality of reflected light include textures and colors of surfaces that receive direct and reflected illumination. Many examples are provided in Chapters 5 and 6. This section examines techniques used by artists, photographers, and directors to enhance their subjects.

A 1998 National Geographic photograph of a young dancer on a boat, by John Chao, is an excellent example of how a soft, reflected light enhances a woman's face. The magnificent quality of light on the dancer is derived from the diffused sunlight coming through the haze and the reflected light from the lake. An important factor in the development of this beautiful lighting effect is a diffused light source reflecting off a smooth surface. On a bright, sunny day, the sunlight reflecting from the lake would create a harsher quality of light, which would have resulted in dark shadows throughout the boat.

There are other conditions in the environment that contribute to the exquisite lighting on her face. The roof of the boat shields her face from the potential negative effects of direct illumination. This technique is reminiscent of a historical period when women used parasols to prevent direct sunlight from striking their faces. The translucent fabric of the parasols created a soft, diffused light that illuminated and enhanced facial features. Another condition that enhances the dancer's face is the dim, diffused light in all the areas that surround her head. Specifically, a continuous, mellow light is horizontal to her face. Thus, facial features and complexions will generally look the best when a soft, diffused light is directed at a face at approximately eye level.

The effects of reflected light on color and its surrounding objects and surfaces is an effect of lighting that needs to be carefully analyzed by interior designers. Many still life and portrait paintings are excellent genres to analyze when considering how reflected light can change the color of an object. Louise Moillon's painting is an instructive example for examining the effects of reflected light because of the close proximity of the fruits and vegetables to each other (Figure 18.18). An examination of the colors on the fruit indicates that the hues change because of the reflections of the objects next to them. For example, when the red-orange color of a peach is reflected on the yellow side of an adjacent peach, the resultant color appears to be orange. An object that has a low value and intensity reflects a dark hue on objects that are light-colored. For example, the plums reflect a dark hue on the bright-colored peaches.

The reflected color on an object can either improve the design or obliterate the intent of a composition. Key to a successful quality lighting design is the awareness of the effects of reflected colors and to manipulate lighting sources for the most advantageous display.

Effects of Multiple Sources

Visual and performing arts use natural and electrical light sources to illuminate the subjects in their mediums. Most of the examples in this chapter are of subjects illuminated by natural light. Where an artist or photographer works affects the lighting. When standing outside, an artist painting realistically reveals all the subtle changes that result from variability of natural light. Monet's series of atmospheric paintings of the Cathedral of Rouen is an excellent example of how various illuminative effects can change the form and colors of a structure. Working indoors introduces a variety of lighting sources that can affect

FIGURE 18.18 The close proximity of fruits and vegetables in this still life painting by Louise Moillon provides the context for observing effects of reflected light on adjacent objects.

elements in a space. In analyzing paintings, photographs, or stage scenes for the purpose of learning more about lighting effects, it is important to try to determine the type of light source. For example, a photograph of faces illuminated by candlelight illustrates the beautiful, warm color that results from this type of light (Figure 18.19). Paintings and photographs using daylight can be analyzed from the perspective of learning how the light from a sunset differs from sunlight at high noon. Moreover, artistic mediums should be examined to determine how changing a lighting effect alters the mood of the setting.

In addition to studying lighting effects from various sources, artistic mediums should be examined to learn how lighting from multiple sources affects people, colors, surfaces, objects, and interiors. Multiple light sources can be effective approaches to illuminating people. For example, the multiple light sources in a publicity photograph of Greta Garbo taken by Clarence Sinclair Bull creatively enhance the striking profile of her face, neckline, and hair (Figure 18.20). A soft light is directed at her neckline, which emphasizes the elegant form of her neck, and some reflected light warmly strikes her face. The extremely soft texture of her complexion appears to be the result of a diffused light source, which is located above her. To create highlights in her hair, a relatively bright light source is aimed directly at her head.

The photograph of Garbo also illustrates an intriguing approach to creating emphasis in a composition by altering lighting intensities and

FIGURE 18.19 The warm colors of candlelight enhance facial features and complexions of people.

FIGURE 18.20 Clarence Sinclair Bull uses light creatively to enhance the profile of Greta Garbo's face, neckline, and hair. To create emphasis on her face, Bull alternated lighting intensities and background colors.

background colors. For example, the actress's face is the primary focal point of the photograph, and her hair is the secondary point of emphasis, followed by the beads in her dress. Lighting contributed to this prioritization; the photographer used a moderate level of illumination on her face and a black background. Without this combination the photograph would not work as well. For example, the moderate level of illumination is excellent for enhancing Garbo's facial features. A bright light source could create unflattering shadows on her face. To create the extreme contrast that is needed to have an emphatic image, the moderate illumination level required a black background. The light source and background value contribute to making Garbo's hair the second point of emphasis in the photograph. This is accomplished by having a gray-colored background only behind her hair. Moreover, on the back wall, the line that separates gray from black exists exactly where the light and dark areas in her hair are divided. Generally, the brightest light source will be the emphatic area in a composition. Thus, to avoid this situation, the gray background behind her hair is used to subdue the intense contrast that would have occurred with the combination of the black wall and bright light source. The sequins on her dress become the last emphatic area, because light is reflecting off small beads. However, there had to be many beads to create the rhythm and unity required to draw attention to the area.

Multiple light sources are often used in film and stage productions to create emphasis. Generally, in these mediums, lighting techniques help to guide the viewer to various aspects of the story. For example, in *Citizen Kane*, Welles used lighting to communicate the story by prioritizing people and elements in the rooms of his mistress's apartment (Figure 18.21). Illumination levels and contrast of backgrounds contribute to the eye first seeing the mistress, then moving to Kane, and ending in the bedroom. The contrast between the illumination from the bedroom lights and the dark draperies that frame the opening emphasizes the bedroom. In addition, illuminating the object and using a dark background emphasize the statue, which is located next to Kane. This statue is significant to the story, because the piece is a miniature version of a large statue that exists at his mansion.

Using light to reinforce three-dimensional objects and multiple rooms is frequently used in the visual and performing arts. In Diego Velazquez's painting *Las Meninas*, alternating light and shade contribute to the depth of the spaces (Figure 18.22). In the foreground,

FIGURE 18.21 In the film *Citizen Kane*, Welles uses multiple illumination levels and contrast of backgrounds to guide the audience through the rooms and storyline.

the girls are illuminated by daylight, and the space behind them is dark. To create a transition to the background, the paneled door is illuminated. The angle of the door leads the eye to the illuminated staircase wall. A similar technique was employed in one of the scenes in *Citizen Kane* (Figure 18.23). Toward the end of the movie, a series of rooms in Kane's mansion is used to illustrate his dwindling power. Light and shade between spaces is used to emphasize the progression of rooms. This effect resembles the ancient Romans' techniques for axial planning, which was discussed in Chapter 17. The light dims as one travels from the foreground to the background but, to reinforce the perspective in the scene, a contrast created by shaded surfaces is always maintained between the rooms.

Light at the end of a large area or multiple spaces is an effective means to guide people through a space, and it provides visual interest in transitional areas. Photographs of two scenes in London demonstrate how a viewer is drawn to the light in the background (Figure 18.24a and b). Both photographs demonstrate how light at the end of a walkway can move people toward the light. However, the quantity of light within the two streets can contribute to different emotive responses.

FIGURE 18.22 Diego Velazquez alternated light and shade in *Las Meninas* to add depth to the rooms and lead the viewer to various areas in the painting.

FIGURE 18.23 In the film, *Citizen Kane*, Welles planned light and shade between spaces to emphasize the progression of rooms as Kane's power dwindled. This effect resembles the ancient Roman's techniques for axial planning.

The dark, narrow space in Figure 18.24a creates a more ominous impression than the street in Figure 18.24b, which has light reflecting from taller buildings (Figure 18.24b). The gloomy effect in an interior could cause anxiety in people who are unfamiliar with a building. In both photographs, the interplay of fog, light, and shade demonstrates how common elements can become artistic forms.

Artists, photographers, and directors have mastered an understanding of light, color, intensity, directional angles, contrast, emphasis, and emotive power on people. The mediums in which they work can serve as inspirations for illuminating interiors. The key to success is practicing and developing observation skills. The concepts and information gained through critical examination can then be transferred to commercial and residential interiors. Analyzing interiors and nontraditional settings can provide insight into which lighting effects work and which do not. This chapter should be viewed as a starting point for understanding unique and innovative lighting effects.

FIGURE 18.24a A photograph that demonstrates how light at the end of a walkway can move people in that direction. In comparison to the lighting effect in Figure 18.24b this dark, narrow space creates an ominous impression.

FIGURE 18.24b In comparison to the lighting effect in Figure 18.24a, this space does not appear to be as depressing due to an increase in reflected light from the taller buildings.

SUMMARY

- Several paintings, photographs, films, and stage scenes illustrate how to use light to create emphasis and enhance people, objects, and spaces. In addition, these mediums demonstrate the powerful ability of light to evoke emotional responses in viewers.

- Photographic or realistic paintings can demonstrate with complete accuracy the effects of lighting.

- Black-and-white photographs, in particular, provide excellent insight into understanding how to distribute dark, light, and midtones.

- Stage and film lighting create moods, communicate to viewers, enhance aesthetics, facilitate timing, reinforce movement, and emphasize three-dimensional objects and interiors.

- Visual and performing arts can contribute to an understanding of how lighting in an interior can be used to enhance the elements and principles of design. Lighting can be represented realistically or light can exist unnaturally.

- Often light is illustrated unnaturally, when the intent is to enhance one of the principles of design, such as emphasis, rhythm, balance, unity, or variety.

- In analyzing the effects of lighting, important considerations include the type of light, number of sources, illumination intensity, directional angle, and distance from objects, people, or surfaces.

- A light source's angle, direction, intensity, and color significantly affect faces and complexions.

- In addition to facial features, lighting variables should be considered when illuminating materials. Lighting affects materials in various ways depending upon the colors, textures, surface qualities, and reflection factor.

- Direct light behind objects or people can create disability glare or delineate a beautiful form of a silhouette.

- Nocturne paintings can demonstrate how providing lighting at an appropriate illumination level can emphasize intriguing forms and maximize reflected light.

- An interesting aspect of silhouette lighting is generally the use of hidden light sources. This technique can often add a sense of mystery and intrigue to an illuminated room or object.

- One shadow effect that can create magic in a space is the use of dappled lighting.
- Reflected light has an effect on people, colors, surfaces, objects, and a space. Important factors that affect the quality of reflected light include textures and colors of surfaces, that receive direct and reflected illumination.
- Where an artist or photographer works influences the lighting effects. When standing outside, an artist painting realistically reveals all the subtle changes of natural light.
- Multiple sources to create levels of emphasis are often used in film and stage productions. Generally, in these mediums, lighting techniques help to guide the viewer to various aspects of the story.
- Light to reinforce three-dimensional objects and multiple rooms is frequently used in the visual and performing arts.

Key Terms

dappled lighting	nocturne

Exercises

1. Visit two art museums and study the lighting effects used by artists and photographers. In a written report describe the artwork's lighting techniques and your emotional responses to the works. Determine how some of the illumination effects could be applied to interiors. Include illustrations, photographs, or sketches of the artwork.

2. View two black-and-white films and study the lighting effects. In a written report describe the lighting techniques and your emotional responses to them. Determine how some of the illumination effects could be applied to interiors. Include illustrations, photographs, or sketches of scenes.

3. Interview artists, photographers, or theater directors to determine their perspective on lighting and the importance of illumination in their medium. In a written report summarize the interviews and

provide suggestions for applying the information to illuminating interiors.

4. Draw a perspective of an interior without windows, lighting, or furniture. Place a sheet of black construction paper over the drawing. Using a mat knife, cut holes where you want to position furniture in the space. Determine where you want layered lighting and windows to exist. Cut holes in the paper that represent the rays of light coming in from luminaires and windows. In a written report describe how your design provides for a quality lighting environment and enhances the principles of design. Submit your drawing and construction paper with the cutouts.

5. Use an existing drawing of multiple rooms to develop a lighting plan that has alternating light and shadow treatments. Determine the human response elicited from the space, and identify the lighting techniques that contribute to the response. In a written report describe the space and the anticipated emotive responses. Recommend lighting techniques. Include illustrations, photographs, or sketches.

REFERENCES

Albers, J. (1963). *Interaction of Color.* New Haven, CT: Yale University Press.

Alton, J. (1995). *Painting with Light.* Berkeley, CA: University of California Press.

Anderson, N.K. (2003). *Frederic Remington: The Color of Night.* Washington DC: National Gallery of Art.

Bailey, M. (1995). *Vermeer.* Ann Arbor, MI: Borders Press.

Barnet S. (2003). *A Short Guide to Writing about Art.* New York: Longman.

Beckett, S.W. (1994). *The Story of Painting.* New York: Dorling Kindersley.

Beckett, S.W. (1999). *Sister Wendy's 1000 Masterpieces.* New York: Dorling Kindersley.

Birren, F. (1969). *Light, Color and Environment.* New York: Van Nostrand Reinhold.

Brode, D. (1992). *The Films of Woody Allen.* New York: Citadel Press.

Brookman, P. (ed.) (2003). *Robert Frank—London/Wales.* Zurich, Switzerland: Scalo.

Corsellis, J. (1982). *Painting Figures in Light.* New York: Watson-Guptill.

Doty, R. (1968). *Light: Object and Image.* New York: Whitney Museum of American Art.

Ebert-Schifferer, S. (1998). *Still Life: A History.* New York: Harry N. Abrams.

Goldberg, V., and Silberman, R. (1999). *American Photography: A Century of Images.* San Francisco: Chronicle Books.

Halse, A.O. (1968). *The Use of Color in Interiors.* New York: McGraw-Hill.

Hills, P. (1987). *The Light of Early Italian Painting.* New Haven, CT and London: Yale University Press.

Itten, J. (1961). *The Art of Color*. New York: Van Nostrand Reinhold.

Lebo, H. (1990). *Citizen Kane*. New York: Doubleday.

Linton, H. (1985). *Color Model Environments: Color and Light in Three-Dimensional Design*. New York: Van Nostrand Reinhold.

Mahnke, F.H. (1996). *Color, Environment, and Human Response*. New York: Van Nostrand Reinhold.

Mannoni, L. (2000). *The Great Art of Light and Shadow: Archaeology of the Cinema*. Exeter, Great Britain: University of Exeter Press.

National Gallery of Art (June 29–September 28, 2003). *Small Wonders: Dutch Still Lifes by Adriaen Coorte*. Washington, DC: National Gallery of Art Exhibition.

National Geographic (1998). *National Geographic Photographs: Then and Now*. Washington, DC: The National Geographic Society.

Pescio, C. (1995). *Masters of Art: Rembrandt and Seventeenth-Century Holland*. New York: Peter Bedrick Books.

Reid, F. (1993). *The Stage Lighting Handbook*, 4th ed. London: A&C Black.

Reid, F. (1995). *Lighting the Stage*. Jordan Hill, Oxford, United Kingdom: Focal Press.

Rosenthal, J., and Wertenbaker, L. (1972). *The Magic of Light*. Boston: Little, Brown and Company.

Sayre, H. (1999). *Writing about Art,* 3rd edition. Upper Saddle River, NJ: Prentice Hall.

Schama, S. (1999). *Rembrandt's Eyes*. New York: Alfred A. Knopf.

Schlemm, B.L. (1978). *Painting with Light*. New York: Watson-Guptill Publications.

Tresidder, J. (ed.) (1983). *Mastering Composition and Light*. New York: Time-Life Books.

Willis-Braithwaite, D. (1993). *VanDerZee Photographer: 1886–1983*. New York: Harry N. Abrams.

Zuffi, S., and Castria, F. (1998). *Modern Painting: The Impressionists—and the Avant-Garde of the Twentieth Century*. New York: Barron's.

CHAPTER 19

Case Studies: Residential Applications

OBJECTIVES

■ Understand positive and negative historical lighting practices and apply the information to designing quality residential lighting environments.

■ Apply an understanding of the content covered in previous chapters to lighting residences.

■ Understand how to use anthropometric data for determining effective task lighting.

■ Identify and apply criteria that are important for illuminating transitional spaces.

■ Identify and apply criteria that are important for illuminating activities that occur in multifunctional and dedicated spaces.

RESIDENTIAL design encompasses an enormous variety of structures throughout the world. Interior designers work with clients' residences in cities, suburbs, small towns, and even dwellings that float on water. Residences have been constructed in every conceivable style, in an extremely broad range of sizes, and an amazing array of configurations. The complexity increases when you factor in the diversity of furniture, floor coverings, wall coverings, colors, materials, equipment, and accessories, which are unique to every residence. The tremendous diversity creates an exciting challenge for interior designers and emphasizes the importance of specifying lighting systems that are tailored to every client and his or her residence.

A quality lighting plan accommodates the specific needs of the client within the context of the characteristics of the residence. Analyzing and reflecting upon the content presented in previous chapters should provide the basis for designing lighting for every client. Quality lighting requires an approach that integrates the users of the space with activities and the specific elements in an environment, including orientation, colors, textures, materials, furniture, accessories, and the geometry of the space. Lighting must also be designed to accommodate the client's budget, preferred taste, lifestyle, and the installation limitations of the residence.

Background Perspectives

Designing a quality lighting environment in residences requires a fundamental understanding of the history of lighting interior spaces.

Historical Insights

As noted in Chapters 1 and 3, electrical light sources became a reality with the invention of the incandescent carbon-filament lamp in 1879. Amazingly, soon after the introduction of this new technology, two books were written to address electrical lighting in homes. In 1884 Robert Hammond wrote *The Electric Light in Our Homes,* followed by J. E. H. Gordon's book, *Decorative Electricity,* published in 1891. Both these books were written before the worldwide introduction of electricity at the 1893 World's Fair in Chicago. Hammond's book is technical and primarily focuses on explaining the operating principles of the incandescent lamp, electricity, and installation methods. Gordon's book provides an insightful and comprehensive approach to lighting every room in a house, including halls, stairs, dining rooms, libraries, boudoirs, drawing rooms, bedrooms, school rooms, nurseries, and "servants' departments." Gordon also includes chapters on installation and "Lighting of Shops, Concert-Halls, etc." In an attempt to convince people that electricity was safe in their homes, Gordon's husband wrote a chapter titled "Fire Risks."

Gordon's incredible vision and insight provide an excellent starting point for examining residential lighting. Many of her lighting concerns and suggestions are relevant and applicable today. For example, she begins the book by describing how electrical lighting in homes can help to relieve stress in our lives:

> As business and pleasure become year by year more closely crowded into our lives, and as life itself becomes more full of excitement and events, the importance of rest and home comfort increases, and what were the superfluous luxuries of our ancestors become necessities to the overstrained nerves of men and women of today. In our English climate and with our English habits so large a proportion of our lives is passed by electrical light, that the nature of that light becomes an all-important factor in matters of comfort and discomfort, rest and fatigue."
>
> (Gordon, 1891, pp. B-1).

Similarly, in 2001, interior designer Clodagh wrote: "Begin by recognizing that everything about an environment affects you—the placement of walls, the flow of rooms, the quality of light, the texture of the floor beneath your feet. The rushed tempo of our lives lures us into following conventions that do not necessarily suit us. Carefully questioning these preconceptions creates an opportunity to celebrate many facets of life that have fallen by the wayside as casualties of routine." (2001, p. 15)

Similarities despite the two distant centuries continue with Gordon's concerns about the complexities of interacting with electricians, installing electricity in existing homes, dealing with high costs, and hiding unsightly wires and switches. Gordon focused on the importance of daylight, reflectance, and balancing illumination in a space. She also provided suggestions for specifying **electrical standards**, or fixtures for each task, and selecting the appropriate color to enhance

Electrical standard
An early term for a luminaire.

people and interiors. Gordon should be credited with the concept of layered lighting. In the chapter on dining rooms, Gordon recommends a specific electrical standard for ambient, task, and accent lighting. Ambient lighting is provided by "three or four ceiling lights"; a "dinner-table pendant" and standards on the table supply the task illumination. Accent lighting is achieved by highlighting dinnerware (Figure 19.1): "Cabinets filled with silver and old china can be illuminated by electric lamps hidden within" (1891, p. 55).

Gordon explains, "The object of this book is to consider how far the new illuminant, electricity, can aid us in our hours of work, and conduce to the comfort and peace of our hours of rest and recreation" (1891, p.2). This objective is still relevant and provides the focus for the topics discussed in this chapter. Throughout the world, one's residence is the place for self-expression, contentment, personal relationships, and self-renewal. A quality residential lighting environment enhances the way people live in their homes by fulfilling functional and aesthetic needs. As noted by Le Corbusier in 1923, "a house is only habitable when it is full of light and air."

FIGURE 19.1
A very early concept for illuminating a dining room table was to use a pendant luminaire and electrical standards.

Past to Future Practices

A historical review of the development of residential lighting helps to provide an understanding of some detrimental practices that have basically never changed. For example, Gordon notes, "most of the electric light dinner-table pendants look like old gas pendants adapted for the electric light" (1891, p. 48). Many current luminaires are based upon designs that were suitable for gas illumination, but are not appropriate for electrical energy. To distribute the highest illumination level possible throughout a room, gas pendants were frequently placed in the center of a ceiling. This practice continued with the invention of electricity and had negative consequences. "Most of the electric light found at present in dining-rooms is very glaring and disagreeable" (Gordon, 1891, p. 60). Many homes today still have a surface-mounted fixture in the center of the ceiling. Often, this is the only electrical light source in the room. As a result, to provide an adequate level of illumination in the room, the lamp becomes a "glare bomb." Interior designers must recognize applications that have become practice throughout the years and evaluate the appropriateness for today's interiors and technologies. As new lighting technology develops, designs and applications must be developed that respond to the medium.

In contrast to installing too much light in one location, many builders have eliminated fixtures in residential rooms and spaces. For example, today it is common to visit an apartment or single-family residence that has one luminaire in the entryway, hallway, dining room, and in each bathroom. The kitchen might have a fixture in the center of the room and another over the sink. If the home has a family room, the fireplace may perhaps be highlighted with recessed spots. Generally, switched outlets substitute for luminaires in living rooms and bedrooms. No luminaires exist in closets, and basements have exposed incandescent lamps. Furthermore, many newly constructed residences are built with few windows. Often, the structure is built to meet the minimum code requirements, which results in little natural illumination. And, from the exterior perspective, most elevations have unbalanced fenestration arrangements. Frequently, windows are placed at the front and back of a two-story dwelling, and no windows, or only one small window in a corner, are built on the sides.

Unfortunately, many people have grown accustomed to ineffective lighting. Often clients do not notice bad lighting or the lack of illumination when they are looking at places to purchase. An interior designer is in the position to educate people about the need for effective natural and electrical light sources. Once clients become aware of poor lighting and learn how it can be improved, they understand how quality illumination can benefit their environment.

Quality residential lighting environments are complex to design, but the integration of the lighting with the interior elements should appear to be seamless. The holistic approach involves content covered in the previous chapters, including daylight integration, layered lighting, illumination zones, color, directional effects of illumination, and lighting systems. Designers of residential lighting should also consider energy conservation, sustainable practice, safety, security, and human factors related to physiology and psychology. The chapters related to illuminating visual art and interior architecture can be applied to every room in a residence. The work of artists, photographers, and directors can provide insight and inspiration for creative applications, including the possibility of installing light art.

Within the context of applying previous content, residential lighting should take an integrated approach, which involves designing the lighting at the beginning of a project. For existing structures, an interior designer might be restrained by the attributes of the rooms, and when needed, the client's acceptance of new electrical installations. Planning provides the designers with the opportunity to determine exactly what type of lighting will be installed and where. Often a builder does a generic lighting plan. Then after the residence is constructed, an interior designer is retained to enhance the lighting. This approach greatly reduces the options available, because site-specific lighting solutions require easy access to power and space for installing housing units or structural elements.

An integrated approach also involves analyzing various lighting options within the context of the users of the space, their activities, daylight, architectural elements, furniture design, materials, reflectance, and decorative accessories. As with set design in films and theater, residential lighting is a major element in the total composition.

Layered lighting is important for every room in a residence, including bathrooms. Frequently, residential rooms only have one layer of lighting, such as a task light over a bathroom mirror. Layered lighting does not have to be expensive and can be accomplished with portable luminaires. The challenge is remembering to plan layered lighting in every room. In determining lighting techniques and the lighting system, all options should be considered for every room. Frequently, lighting in residences has the same type of luminaire for a specific room or task. For example, a popular approach for a kitchen is a surface-mounted fluorescent fixture in the center of the ceiling. An entryway will often have a glass and brass pendant suspended on a chain. There may be rooms where these luminaires might be perfect. However, assuming that these luminaires are always appropriate in prescribed places is a mistake. A quality residential lighting environment is designed expressly for the unique needs of clients, their style of living, and all the elements of each room.

As discussed in previous chapters, interior designers can choose from an enormous range of lighting techniques and luminaires. Electrical lighting does not have to be uniform and stagnant. A goal for electrical lighting should be to imitate the same wonderful variability of daylight. In determining the ideal lighting approach, an interior designer should examine all options, including daylight, recessed, surface-mounted, suspended, track, cable, portable, structural, and furniture-integrated luminaires. In addition, it is critical to plan lighting controls. Controls can help to create variability in the effects of lighting. In addition, controls should be planned to accommodate the way a person functions in a space. For example, for the client who likes to read in bed, a switch for the luminaire should be located next to the bed. Frequently, the only location for switches is next to the door of the bedroom.

A client might not be able to afford an expensive central control system. However, dimmers on every switch are inexpensive to install and can provide tremendous flexibility in illumination levels. A comprehensive control plan includes dimmers for bathroom and kitchen lighting. A low illumination level is effective when people use the bathroom in the middle of the night or when getting up on a dark morning.

Dimmers in kitchens can provide flexibility for the various activities that can occur throughout the room. In addition, because of the typically high wattages needed for critical tasks performed in kitchens, dimmers can help to conserve energy.

Controls also can play an important role in establishing a desired mood. People have definite mood preferences, which can vary according to the time of the day, week, month, or season. A mood or atmosphere in a residence can be relaxed, formal, stimulating, calming, cozy, or airy. A residence provides the opportunity for self-expression. Thus, an interior designer must understand the mood preferences of their clients and then plan the lighting to enhance the desired atmosphere.

Custom-designed lighting plans are essential to accommodate the multiple activities that can occur in residential interiors. Many rooms are multipurpose or multifunctional. Thus, an interior designer must learn from their clients which activities they perform in specific rooms. (A description of a complete site and client assessment is in Chapter 22.) The lighting design should provide the ideal illumination for the specific needs of the users who are performing a task or activity. Therefore, rather than focusing on specific lighting for each room of a residence, the next section is organized by delineating special lighting considerations in dedicated spaces, and reviewing lighting requirements for tasks or activities that are typically conducted in residences. This approach provides essential residential lighting considerations and presents the content in a format that allows information to be applied to a variety of rooms, users, and lighting systems.

Transitional Spaces

The transitional spaces in residences includes entryways, foyers, hallways, and staircases.

Entryways and Foyers

Often the terms *entryway* and *foyer* are used interchangeably. For the purpose of this section, *entryway* or *entry* is the term referring to the space located immediately outside the front entrance of a residence, and *foyer* is the interior area. Often, entry lighting includes one or two luminaires located next to the front door. This may provide adequate safety and security lighting; however, this location should also have lighting that sets the tone for the overall design concept of the residence. (Refer to Chapter 14 regarding safety and security considerations.) This is the first impression people have when approaching a residence. Thus, the lighting should reflect the desired image. Some clients may want a very dignified, formal feeling to the entrance, and other people may want a casual, informal atmosphere. Lighting can reinforce the desired impression by the design of the luminaires, illumination levels, and highlighted elements.

Luminaires for the entryway should reflect the architectural style of the home, and the size of the fixture should be an appropriate scale for the size of the door, entry, and home. When a designer selects exterior luminaires, the entire elevation of the residence must be analyzed. Frequently, a luminaire next to a door is too small for the surrounding elements. A common practice is to use the same entry light on a residence regardless of whether the entrance has one door or double doors. To achieve good proportions, the residence with double doors needs larger entry luminaires. Frequently, exterior luminaires next to garage doors are far too small. Often, the fixture is the same as the one located next to the front door. An 18-foot-wide (549 cm) door should not have the same size fixture as a 3-foot-wide (91 cm) door.

The entry and foyer are major transition areas from the outside to the interior. As a result, the illumination level of the entry and foyer must accommodate daylight and evening light. To have a smooth adaptation transition during the day, the foyer should have natural light, and supplemental electrical lighting for cloudy days or if the windows are too small to provide adequate levels of daylight. For the evening hours, the entry and foyer lighting should provide a smooth transition. Landscape lighting can help to ease the illumination level differences between the outdoors and interior. Adaptation light levels must be considered when people come to the residence and are moving from a dark environment to a lighter setting. In addition, appropriate levels should be planned for when guests leave the residence, moving from a bright setting to a dark environment. As mentioned in Chapter 13, the eye takes longer to adapt when going from a bright to a dark setting. A transitional lighting plan should accommodate the variabilities of both situations.

The design of the entry's luminaire, location, and lamp wattage should be carefully specified. The extreme contrast between the light source and the darkness can easily create disability glare. Also, a bright light source during the evening hours can be annoying and can prevent someone from reading the residence's address or seeing the path leading to the entrance. The luminaire and installation location must be evaluated to determine whether there is glare from multiple positions. This involves evaluating the lighting effect from the street, the pathway to the front door, and the entrance. For residences with steps leading to the front door, it is important to determine if glare occurs when people look up while ascending the stairs.

Foyer lighting must be coordinated with the exterior illumination and the rooms adjacent to the space. To balance lighting and provide transitional light levels, a minimum level of illumination should exist in all rooms adjoining the foyer. As an introduction to the interior of a residence, lighting can help to establish first impressions. Clients may have various privacy needs associated with the foyer. Lighting in the foyer and the surrounding spaces can be designed to help provide privacy. For example, accent lighting on an expensive art collection could be dimmed or turned off when the owner learns there is a stranger at the door. The location of the foyer in relationship to the other spaces in the residence often provides an opportunity for designing interesting axial plans. As discussed in previous chapters, one technique for creating interesting vistas is to alternate lighting levels between spaces. A foyer also serves as the transitional point for people who live in the residence. Thus, lighting in the foyer can help people forget the stress and strain of the external world. It can also encourage individuals to focus on relaxing and spending quality time alone or with others.

Typically people do not spend a great deal of time in the foyer. Thus, lighting must be designed to quickly attract attention to the most desirable elements in the space. The mood must also be immediately apparent. Space restraints often limit the layered lighting of luminaires mounted on the ceiling and walls. Unfortunately, a frequent approach to foyer lighting is a single pendant in the center of the room. Most pendants, or chandeliers, should be considered only decorative lighting. Thus, ambient, task, and accent lighting should be planned in the space. A pendant luminaire should always be the appropriate scale and style for the space. Frequently, luminaires are too large or small for the dimensions of the foyer. The height of the ceiling is also important when selecting the size of a luminaire. The height of the luminaires should be commensurate with the distance between the floor and the ceiling. In confined spaces, make certain that the luminaire does not interfere with the area required for the door swing. In addition, a suspended luminaire should be in the center of large windows that might exist above the front door so that it will be visible from outside.

Hallways and Staircases

Hallways and staircases are also transitional areas in a residence. Therefore, typically little time is spent analyzing elements in the areas, including architectural details or artwork on the walls. Moreover, since people are moving through a hallway or staircase, their concentration is often diverted from the interior elements. Most people are in a standing position as they walk through a hallway or progress up and down stairs. The combination of minimal time, movement, and a standing position creates unique lighting challenges that must be addressed for quality lighting environments.

Hallway challenges include layered lighting techniques, attracting attention to interesting elements that might exist on vertical planes, reducing the apparent length of long hallways, avoiding dark areas, creating safe passage during sleeping hours, and providing convenient switching arrangements. Layered lighting often does not exist in hallways because people feel the only illumination necessary is task lighting. Illumination should be planned so that people can safely walk through hallways; however, ambient and accent lighting are also important considerations. Variations in lighting, including accent lighting, can help to reduce the apparent length of a hallway and can help to avoid dark areas. For layered lighting, all vertical and horizontal planes should be considered, including structural luminaires in the ceiling, transoms above doors, and interior windows. Since hallways rarely have natural light, transoms and interior windows on walls adjoining hallways can provide excellent illumination during the day.

As a passageway from bedrooms to bathrooms, hallways need illumination that creates a safe environment during the sleeping hours. To assist the eye with adaptation, lighting during this time period should be low. The illumination level and location of the fixtures should be determined by the visual abilities of the users of the residence. Controls play an important role in safety and convenience. Switches for luminaires should be accessible at various locations in the hallway, including the end of the space and next to bedroom and bathroom doors. To ensure adequate illumination at the appropriate location, hallways can have occupancy sensors or photosensors.

The combination of movement and changes in elevation pose safety issues for vertical circulation. As discussed in Chapter 14, staircases should be illuminated in a manner that provides a clear distinction between the risers and treads. The projecting edges of the treads should be visible. This can be accomplished in a variety of ways, including locating luminaires at the top and bottom of staircases and lighting each step. Generally, lighting at the top of a staircase should be brighter than the luminaire located at the bottom. Recessing light sources along the wall or in the treads or using low-voltage strip systems along the edges of the treads can illuminate each step. Integrating lighting in the railing can also illuminate steps. Accent lighting should highlight interesting elements on walls that adjoin a staircase, such as architectural moldings or artwork. Often, a staircase is a beautiful focal point in a residence; thus, accent lighting should highlight the most intriguing elements of the design. As mentioned in Chapter 18, silhouette lighting can be an effective technique for emphasizing an elegant staircase.

Task-Specific Illumination

Quality lighting environments enhance the way people live and work in their residences. This involves lighting that is client- and site-specific.

Tasks Performed in Multiple Spaces

A thorough assessment needs to be conducted to determine who performs which activities where in the residence. (Chapter 22 provides a detailed description of the assessment process.) In determining lighting approaches, a distinction should be made between guests and people living in the residence. People who are not familiar with an interior, especially overnight guests, might require special lighting techniques.

To design a lighting plan that is client- and site-specific requires an assessment of all the variables associated with performing a task. This includes an analysis of the task, characteristics of the user, reflectance, illumination source, luminaire performance data, and dimensions of furniture. As discussed in Chapter 13, the needs of special populations must always be addressed. Tasks that are visually demanding or require special accuracy require very precise illumination. Information must be collected regarding the visual abilities and anthropometric data of the users of the residence. *Anthropometric data,* or detailed measurements of the human body, are valuable information for determining the proper location of luminaires, switches, and outlets. For example, to have a light source at the proper location for reading requires knowing the vertical distance from the seat to the eyes. Measuring the user, or referring to anthropometric charts, can determine the torso and head dimensions. The Appendix includes anthropometric charts for children, women, and men comparisons. Sections that follow in this chapter identify criteria that are important for specific tasks, including appropriate dimensional factors. This information can be applied to the specific needs of users within the context of their environment.

People read in numerous locations in a residence; however, effective lighting should be planned for areas where frequent and prolonged reading occurs. To have effective illumination for reading requires the proper integration of the individual and the layers of lighting, the task light source, and the parameters of the furniture. The layers of lighting should have illumination levels that are appropriately balanced with the intensity of the light for reading. Since lighting for reading is often at a high illumination level, appropriate levels throughout the room will help to avoid extreme contrasts and the eye fatigue that often accompanies these adverse conditions.

The task light source should be directed at the reading material and should distribute the appropriate illumination level. The lamp should be concealed from the eyes of the reader. Luminaires with translucent shades in white or a bone color can be effective because they provide direct and indirect illumination on the task. Opaque or dark-colored shades restrict the quantity and distribution of illumination on a task. The diameter of the shade's bottom affects the area of illumination. Generally, to help ensure that light will strike the reading material, the bottom diameter of a shade should be approximately 16 inches (40 cm). The top of the shade should be open in order to help diffuse illumination around the reading area.

Ideally, the bottom of the shade should be at the eye level of the reader. To accomplish this requires that the designer know specific characteristics of the luminaire and have several measurements. Lighting for reading can be provided by a light source located next to an individual, above an individual, or slightly behind an individual. The luminaires can be portable, surface-mounted, or recessed. The goals with any location or luminaire are to eliminate glare, avoid shadows on the reading material, and provide illumination directly on the task.

The measurements needed to provide effective light for reading with a portable luminaire on a table next to a chair are the vertical distances of the user's eye level from the floor, the sizes of the fixture, and the furniture (Figure 19.2). The ideal condition is for the bottom of the shade to be level with the reader's eyes. Thus, the total distance from the floor to the reader's eye level must equal the distance from the floor

FIGURE 19.2 Determining the appropriate location of a luminaire for reading requires multiple measurements of people, furniture, and the fixture. To place the luminaire at the ideal position for reading, the total distance from the floor to reader's eye level must equal the distance from the floor to the bottom of the shade.

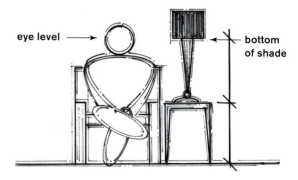

eye level ⟶   ← bottom of shade

to the bottom of the shade. A change in any of the elements can affect the effectiveness of the lighting. For example, the situation shown in Figure 19.2 was created for a female adult with a seat-to-eye measurement of 32 inches (80 cm). If a child sits in the chair, the lighting is no longer effective because his or her eyes would be exposed to a bare lamp. An adult using a chair with a lower seat or a higher table would have the same result. A recessed luminaire above a reader should be located so that the reader's head does not cast a shadow on the reading material. The critical issue is to consider all the parameters of the elements that are used for task lighting. Figures 19.3 a and b provide additional examples of measurements that are needed for various approaches to task lighting for reading.

Effective task lighting should also be planned for writing. People write in a variety of rooms in a residence, but most writing occurs on a horizontal surface. A luminaire that is mounted on the surface should be approximately 12 inches (30 cm) from the individual and 15 inches (38 cm) to the right or left of the paper (Figure 19.4). To avoid shadows on the task, the luminaire should be located to the left of a right-handed person and on the right side of a left-handed individual. The bottom of a shade should be level with the eyes of the writer. The other criteria described in the discussion related to reading can be applied to the writing task.

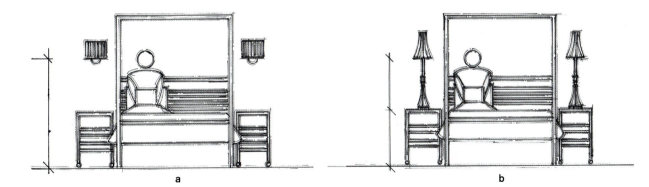

a

b

FIGURE 19.3 Various approaches to task lighting for reading: (a) a wall mounted luminaire next to the bed; and (b) a portable luminaire on a table next to the bed. The placement for *a* requires the measurements of the eye level of the user while seated in bed. The placement for *b* requires the measurements of the height of the fixture base to the bottom of the shade, the table height, and the eye level of the user while seated in bed.

FIGURE 19.4

Plan view of the placement of a luminaire on a desk or table for the purpose of reading and writing. To avoid shadows on the task the luminaire should be located to the left, of a right-handed person, and on the right side of a left-handed individual. The bottom of a shade should be level with the eyes of the user.

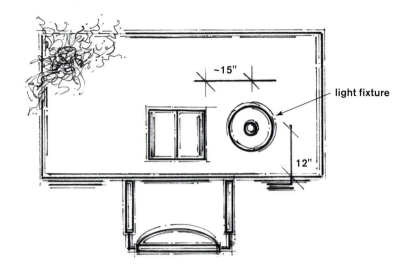

Frequently, a surface that is used for writing is also used for operating a computer. Unfortunately, the two tasks have different illumination requirements because writing is performed on a horizontal surface, and computer work is conducted on a vertical plane. The solution is to employ multiple luminaires, techniques, and controls. An effective method for illuminating a work surface with a computer is to locate diffused luminaires above the user either in front or to the sides of the individual (Figure 19.5). Illumination zones must be planned to avoid dark areas behind the VDT screen.

Appropriate illumination zones also become important for viewing a television screen or playing video games on a computer. People should not watch a screen in the dark. A television screen can emit a high level of illumination, which contrasts significantly with dark surroundings. Illumination should exist in all areas of a room, including behind the television, next to the screen, and surrounding the viewer. As more residences are creating media rooms or home theaters, effective layered lighting techniques must be used to accommodate these unique illumination requirements. Furthermore, the illumination relationship between a very dark space and adjacent areas becomes very important. During the day, room-darkening window treatments must be used to prevent sunlight from entering the space. Illumination in interior rooms adjoining a media room must be coordinated to avoid potentially bright and dark extremes.

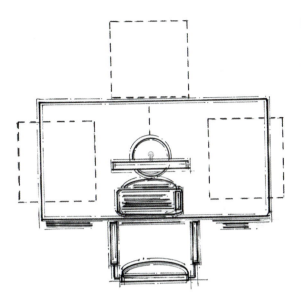

FIGURE 19.5 Plan view of the suggested placement of luminaires for working at a computer.

Task lighting in residences must also be planned for hobbies or other activities perhaps related to an individual's profession. These tasks can include painting or sewing or playing the piano, games, and cards. Figure 19.6 provides an example of the measurements that are important to consider when designing illumination for a variety of tasks. For all these activities, the lighting must be planned to avoid glare in the eyes of the users and prevent shadows of heads or hands from being cast on the tasks. The areas surrounding the tasks should always have lighting that creates smooth transitions between illumination levels.

For creating artwork, most artists prefer natural daylight with a northern orientation. When electrical light sources are necessary, lamps with high CRI ratings should be specified, and illumination should have a uniform distribution pattern. For hand sewing, the light source should be located beside or behind the person. As with writing, the luminaire should be located on the right or left side of the person doing the sewing, depending upon whether the person is right- or left-handed. To effectively read sheet music, the light source should be aimed at the music rack at an approximate 90-degree angle. Surfaces used for playing games or cards should have a fairly uniform distribution of illumination over the entire area.

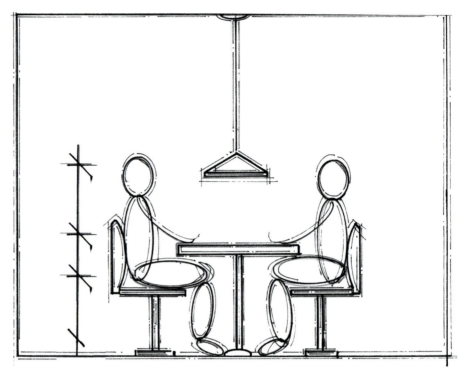

FIGURE 19.6 Suggested placement of a luminaire for playing cards or games.

Formal and informal conversation occurs throughout a residence; however, in rooms where conversations often occur, lighting should be designed to encourage and enhance the activity. Therefore, based upon the lifestyle of the client, prime conversational areas could be the living room, kitchen, dining room, or bedrooms. Generally, lighting conducive for conversation is relaxing and enhances the facial features of people (Figure 19.7). Frequently, this involves soft, indirect lighting at low to moderate illumination levels. Illumination on people can be derived from reflected surfaces, diffused through a soft fabric, or a combination of the two. Direct illumination that grazes the front of people's faces or is aimed at their eyes should always be avoided. Bright light sources behind people should also be avoided, because the silhouette effect can make it impossible to see individuals seated across from one another.

Other important considerations for conversational lighting include illumination within other areas of the room and any adjacent spaces.

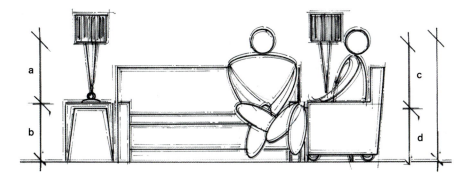

FIGURE 19.7 Suggested placement of luminaires for a conversation area. To enhance facial features of people the centers of the shades of luminaires should be approximately level with the faces of individuals. This placement requires the following measurements: (a) height of the fixture base to the center of the shade; (b) table height; (c) eye level of users; and (d) seat height.

Eye movement is a constant activity. Therefore, lighting should be designed to avoid extreme contrasts and provide visual interest. Illumination zones should be appropriately planned to have a smooth transition from the immediate seeing area to other areas within the room and beyond. Highlighting special artifacts in a room can provide variety in the environment and perhaps stimulate conversation. In planning accent lighting, the directional angles should be analyzed to ensure that people, when they are sitting, are not exposed to bare lamps. For example, frequently, paintings are located on a wall for viewing from a standing position. As a result, accent lighting might be perfect for people standing, but people who are sitting might get a glare. A careful assessment of the lighting environment must include an analysis of the effects of illumination from multiple positions. This is especially critical in multifunctional spaces.

Tasks Performed in Dedicated Spaces

Food preparation and cleanup require special lighting considerations because of the danger of burns and cuts. Areas to consider include counters, ranges, and the sink. A variety of lighting techniques can be employed for the specific tasks done in kitchens. The horizontal nature of these tasks requires illumination that is located directly above the work area. Luminaires and their locations must be carefully planned to eliminate glare and shadows cast on tasks. To see the colors of food accurately, lamps should be selected with high CRI ratings. Layered lighting becomes very important in kitchens, because direct illumination at a fairly high intensity level is needed for critical tasks, and ambient lighting helps to moderate the contrasts resulting from bright and dark areas. Accent lighting provides visual interest to a work environment, especially in kitchens that are also used as a primary gathering place. Controls with a range of variability are useful for accommodating the multiple activities and tasks conducted in kitchens.

Illumination on counters, including islands, can be derived from luminaires mounted under wall cabinets or fixtures installed in soffits or the ceiling (Figure 19.8 a–c). Luminaires under wall cabinets can be located at the front or back edge of the cabinetry. Glare can pose a problem with this technique when the counter and/or the backsplash have a shiny or glossy finish. Luminaires installed in soffits or the ceiling can be recessed or surface-mounted. The point of installation must be carefully planned to avoid having an individual's shadow cast on the task and to allow adequate clearance space for cabinet doors.

Luminaires located above a cooktop or sink can be an effective method for providing illumination. The light source should be

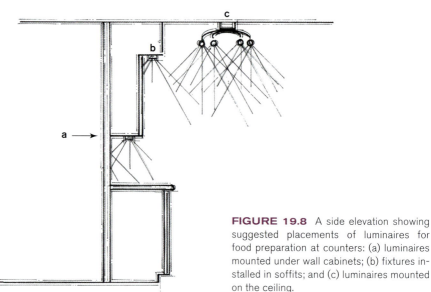

FIGURE 19.8 A side elevation showing suggested placements of luminaires for food preparation at counters: (a) luminaires mounted under wall cabinets; (b) fixtures installed in soffits; and (c) luminaires mounted on the ceiling.

positioned to eliminate glare and avoid having someone work in his or her shadow. Glare can be especially problematic for the work conducted at the cooktop because frequently the surfaces are made up of highly reflective materials. Light directed from the right and left of the worker can help to eliminate shadows on a task (Figure 19.9). This **cross-lighting** technique can be effective because each light source simultaneously serves as direct and fill lighting. To help deal with cleaning associated with grease, luminaires surrounding the cooktop should have sealed covers and surfaces that are easy to wash.

There are many methods for illuminating kitchen cabinetry, and many techniques involve hiding sources within the structural elements of the cabinets. Whenever possible, the interior of cabinets in the food-preparation areas should be illuminated. This is especially important for corner and base cabinets. The light source should be positioned to illuminate most of the items in the cabinet, including the products in the back. For ambient or accent lighting, luminaires can follow the lines of cabinetry along the kick space or a cornice board at the top of the cabinets. To highlight items on shelves, frequently, small recessed fixtures are located at the top of a cabinet, and the illumination distributes light on several shelves. Unfortunately, some applications prevent light from striking the items on the bottom shelf. When highlighting

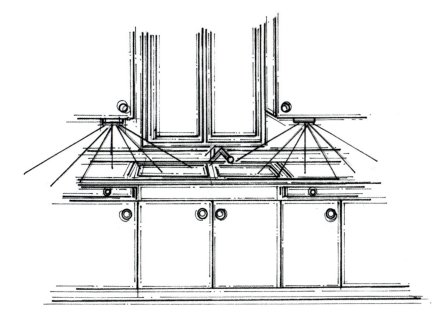

FIGURE 19.9
Cross-lighting technique used over a sink. Each light source can serve as direct and fill lighting. The proper placement will help to eliminate shadows on the task.

objects on shelves, adequate illumination must be planned for the whole cabinet.

Illumination for eating can also be accomplished with a variety of techniques and types of luminaires. Frequently, a pendant fixture is located over a table. This can be an effective approach; however, other methods should always be considered. Furthermore, one fixture is never the answer for an entire room. In a dining room luminaires should be expressly selected for the task of eating. Task lighting does not have to be located above the center of a table. For example, illuminating the four corners of a table can provide excellent task lighting and soft illumination on the faces of people seated at the table, especially if the table is relocated or expanded with table leaves (Figure 19.10). In a dining room, furniture that serves a task, such as sideboards or buffets, should also have adequate illumination. Accent lighting can include highlighting any crystal or silver on the table.

The size and location of luminaires should be carefully planned in a dining room. For a pendant fixture, the size must be appropriate for the dimensions of the table and room. Frequently, a dining room fixture is too small or too large for the table and the size of the room. An appropriate size should be determined by following the principles of the

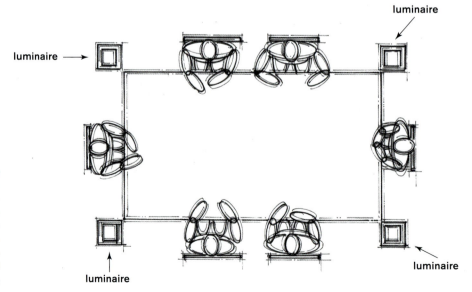

FIGURE 19.10
Plan view of a dining room with illumination close to the four corners of a table. This technique can provide excellent task lighting and soft illumination on the faces of people seated at the table.

golden section. Frequently, a contractor will install a pendant in the center of the room, without considering the location of the dining table. The table might not be in the center of the room because of other furniture in the space, such as breakfronts or buffets. To avoid having people hit their head on a pendant fixture when they stand up, the luminaire should be approximately 6 inches (15 cm) from the edges of the table. A pendant should not interfere with artwork on a wall or a beautiful view. For these situations, the space between a table and the ceiling should be unobstructed. This might be accomplished by concealed light sources.

Rooms for sleeping and playing have some unique lighting considerations. The ages of the occupants are an important issue. Lighting and electrical outlets must be safe for children of all ages and the elderly. Cords on portable luminaires should not be accessible from any location in a room. Luminaires that can easily fall over should be avoided. All outlets should be covered with protective seals. To promote eye development, young infants should have some level of illumination at all times of the day. The lighting in rooms for children should be planned to accommodate the changing activities that occur in the space as they become older. Playing with blocks on the floor requires different illumination from studying at a desk or working at a computer. Whenever possible, projecting future needs of children's spaces should occur during the construction phase of a project.

People of all ages need adequate illumination to move through rooms during the evening hours. Low levels of illumination turned on throughout the night or occupancy sensors or photosensors can provide sufficient evening illumination. People who share a room often awaken in the morning at different times. Separate lighting systems can provide illumination for the person who must get up, while maintaining a fairly dark environment for the person still sleeping. Frequently, in residences built during the past several years, there is no lighting in closets. Illumination in closets is essential not only to enable people to see what they're doing but also to prevent accidents when belongings fall. The bare incandescent lamp, which was a common approach for closets, should be avoided. The brightness can cause disability glare, and the lamp poses a fire hazard. Adequate clearance around a light source should always be provided in a confined space. To illuminate items on shelves and hanging on rods, an effective approach is to locate a light source at a high position on the wall across from the objects (Figure 19.11). Low, supplementary lighting should be provided to illuminate objects on the floor.

Effective illumination is critical in grooming areas. Many accidents occur in bathrooms, so illumination is required that can help to promote a safe environment. The combination of water and slick surfaces creates a treacherous situation. Lighting should illuminate all areas in a bathroom, including steps, bathtubs, showers, and locations likely to have standing water. Illumination on handrails and grab bars can be very helpful. Luminaires in the shower must be rated for wet locations and should be positioned to minimize shadows and eliminate glare not only in the shower but throughout the bathroom. And glare should be determined based on sitting and standing positions of residents.

Illumination for applying makeup and for shaving has special requirements. Some of the most important criteria include accurate color rendering properties, clarity in seeing details, and a uniform distribution of illumination. Lamps for facial grooming should have a CRI

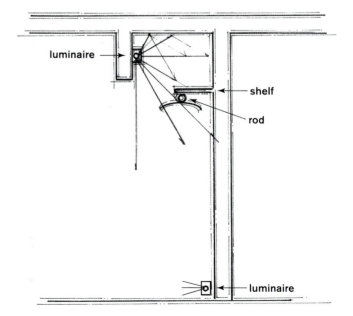

FIGURE 19.11 A side elevation of a suggestion for providing illumination in a closet. Adequate clearance should be provided between the luminaire and objects in the closet. The luminaire should have an element that covers a bare lamp.

rating of 100. The desired color temperature of the lamp can vary with ethnicities. Generally, Western and Eastern cultures prefer warm and cool light sources, respectively. All shadows on a face must be eliminated. To accurately see facial details, illumination should be diffused and located next to the face. The quality of illumination is affected by the interaction between the characteristics of a lamp and the type of diffuser used on a luminaire. For example, an effective combination for facial grooming is an opal diffuser and fluorescent lamps. To determine the best lighting effect, various lamps and diffusers should be tested. Ideally, luminaires should surround a face from above and the sides (Figure 19.12). At a minimum, luminaires should be located next to both sides of a face. Lamps or the center of shades should be located at cheek level. A fixture mounted above the mirror should illuminate full-length mirrors.

Creative lighting methods in bathrooms can focus on maximizing the beautiful reflective qualities of water. Water that is illuminated can generate dancing reflections on walls and ceilings. A tranquil and stunning effect can be created by illuminating water that is cascading down a smooth-surfaced wall. Large bathtubs or hot tubs that are installed above the floor can visually consume a great deal of space. To reduce

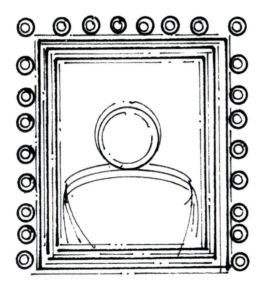

FIGURE 19.12 A suggested placement of luminaires for facial grooming: place illumination on the top and both sides of a mirror surrounding the face of a person who is standing or seated in a chair. Lamps or the center of shades should be located at the cheek level of a face.

the apparent size of large bathing units, one approach is to give the impression that the bathtub is floating. One method to accomplish this effect is to outline the lower form with a continuous light source.

Quality residential lighting should be unique to every individual, activity, and environment. Too often, prescribed lighting solutions have been applied to residences. An interior designer should specify a lighting plan that incorporates relevant issues presented in previous chapters of this textbook within the context of the needs of their client. All the lighting techniques, lamps, and luminaires should be considered when specifying the ambient, task, and accent lighting for every room of a residence.

SUMMARY

- In *Decorative Electricity,* published in 1891, many of Gordon's lighting concerns and suggestions are relevant and applicable today. Some examples include the complexities of installing electricity in existing homes, dealing with high costs, hiding unsightly wires, and the importance of daylight.
- Many current luminaires are based upon designs that were suitable for gas illumination but are not appropriate for electrical energy.
- Many homes today still have a surface-mounted fixture in the center of the ceiling. Often, this is the only electrical light source in a room, and the lamp becomes a "glare bomb." In contrast to installing too much light in one location, many builders have eliminated fixtures in residential rooms and spaces.
- Quality residential lighting environments are complex to design, but the integration of the lighting with the interior elements should appear to be seamless. The holistic approach involves content covered in the previous chapters in this textbook.
- Residential lighting should be an integrated approach, which involves designing the lighting at the beginning of a project.
- An integrated approach considers the users of the space, activities, daylight, architectural elements, furniture designs, materials, reflectance, and decorative accessories.

- Layered lighting is important for every room in a residence, including bathrooms.

- Residential lighting should not be prescribed. Interior designers should make their selections from an enormous range of lighting techniques and luminaires.

- Electrical lighting does not have to be uniform and stagnant. A goal for electrical lighting should be to imitate the same wonderful variability of daylight.

- Custom-designed lighting plans are essential to accommodate the multiple activities that can occur in residential interiors.

- Luminaires should reflect the architectural style of the home, and the size of the fixture should be an appropriate scale for the size of the door, entryway, and home.

- The entryway and foyer are major transition areas from the outside to the interior. As a result, the illumination level of the entry and foyer must accommodate daylight and evening hours.

- Foyer lighting must be coordinated with the exterior illumination and the rooms adjacent to the space.

- Hallways and staircases are transitional areas in a residence. The combination of minimal time, movement, and passing through these areas in a standing position create unique lighting challenges, which must be addressed for quality lighting environments.

- Hallway challenges include layered lighting techniques, attracting attention to interesting elements that might exist on vertical planes, reducing the apparent length of long hallways, avoiding dark areas, creating safe passage during sleeping hours, and providing convenient switching arrangements.

- Staircases should be illuminated in a manner that allows a clear distinction between risers and treads.

- Quality lighting environments enhance the way people live and work in their residences. This involves lighting that is client- and site-specific. A thorough analysis needs to be conducted to determine who performs which activities where in the residence.

- To design a lighting plan that is client- and site-specific requires an assessment of all the variables associated with performing a task. This includes an analysis of the task, characteristics of the performer of the task, reflectance, illumination source, luminaire performance data, and dimensions of furniture.

■ Anthropometric data, or detailed measurements of the human body, are valuable information for determining the proper location of luminaires, switches, and outlets.

■ Food preparation and cleanup require special lighting considerations because of the dangers of burns and cuts.

■ In a dining room luminaires should be expressly selected for the task of eating.

■ Rooms for sleeping have some unique lighting considerations. The ages of the occupants are an important issue.

■ Effective illumination is critical in grooming areas. The high number of accidents that occur in bathrooms requires illumination that can help to promote a safe environment.

Key Terms

| cross-lighting | electrical standard |

Exercises

1. Research the history of residential lighting since the invention of the incandescent lamp. Identify types of luminaires and common practices. In a written report describe the evolution of residential lighting, including an analysis of how social, political, and economic conditions affected practice. Photographs, illustrations, and drawings may be included.

2. Select photographs of entries, foyers, hallways, and staircases. Identify the electrical luminaires in the spaces and determine which category (general, task, accent) of lighting the luminaire is being used for. If a luminaire does not exist for a category of lighting, provide a suggestion for a luminaire that would be effective for the specific lighting technique. The identification and analysis should be submitted in written form. Photographs must be included.

3. Select photographs that include areas for reading, conversation, writing, working at a computer, and watching television. Identify the lighting for the task and determine the effectiveness of the illumination. When necessary, provide suggestions to improve the effectiveness of the lighting for the specific activity. The identification and analysis should be submitted in written form. Photographs must be included.

4. Select photographs of kitchens, dining rooms, bedrooms, and bathrooms. Identify the ambient, task, and accent lighting and determine the effectiveness of the illumination. When necessary, provide suggestions to improve the effectiveness of the lighting for a specific purpose. The identification and analysis should be submitted in written form. Photographs must be included.

5. Record the measurements of anthropometric data, luminaires, and furniture for the following activities: (a) reading in a chair and in bed, (b) facial grooming standing and seated, (c) writing at a table, and (d) working at a computer. Based upon the measurements, determine the appropriateness of the location of furniture and luminaires in relationship to the users. Analyze the data and write a report summarizing your results and that provides recommendations for future illumination applications.

REFERENCES

Albers, J. (1963). *Interaction of Color.* New Haven, CT: Yale University Press.

American Institute of Architects (2000). Architectural Graphics Standards, 10th ed. New York: John Wiley & Sons.

Ander, G. (1997). *Daylighting Performance & Design.* New York: John Wiley & Sons.

Archea, J. (1985). Environmental factors associated with stair accidents by the elderly. *Clinics in Geriatric Medicine,* 1, 555–569.

Baron, R.A., and Rea, M.S. (1991). Lighting to soothe the mood. *Lighting Design and Application,* 12, 30–32.

Benya, J., Heschong, L., McGowan, T., Miller, N., and Rubinstein, F. (2001). *Advanced Lighting Guidelines.* White Salmon, WA: New Buildings Institute.

Blakemore, R.G. (1997). *History of Interior Design and Furniture: From Ancient Egypt to Nineteenth-Century Europe.* New York: John Wiley & Sons.

Bradtmiller, B., and Annis, J. (1997). *Anthropometry for Persons with Disabilities: Needs for the Twenty-First Century.* Washington, DC: U.S. Architectural and Transportation Barriers Compliance Board (http://www.access-board.gov/research&training/Anthropometry/anthro.htm).

Clark, C. (2001). Computers are causing health problems. *Journal of End User Computing, 13(1),* 34–45.

Clodagh (2001). *Total Design: Contemplate, Cleanse, Clarify, and Create your Personal Space.* New York: Clarkson/Potter Publishers.

Deason, V. (1997). Anthropometry: The human dimension. *Optics and Lasers in Engineering, 28,* 83–88.

Diffrient, N., Tilley, A.R., and Bardagjy, J.C. (1974). *Humanscale 1/2/3.* Cambridge: The MIT Press.

Diffrient, N., Tilley, A.R., and Harman, D. (1981). *Humanscale 4/5/6.* Cambridge: The MIT Press.

Diffrient, N., Tilley, A.R., and Harman, D. (1981). *Humanscale 7/8/9.* Cambridge: The MIT Press.

Dreyfuss, H. (1960). *The Measure of Man-Human Factors in Design.* New York: Whitney Publications.

Fry, G.A. (1976). A simplified formula for discomfort glare. *Journal of the Illuminating Engineering Society, 8(1),* 10–20.

General Electric (1989). *Lighting Application Bulletin.* Cleveland, OH: General Electric.

Gordon, J.E.H. (1891). *Decorative Electricity.* London: Sampson Low, Marston, Searle, & Rivington.

Grandjean, E. (1987). *Ergonomics in Computerized Offices.* Philadelphia: Taylor & Francis.

Hall, E.T. (1966). *The Hidden Dimension.* New York: Doubleday.

Halse, A.O. (1968). *The Use of Color in Interiors.* New York: McGraw-Hill.

Halstead, M.B. (1997). Colour. In J.R. Coaton and A.M. Marsden (eds.), *Lamps and Lighting.* New York: John Wiley & Sons.

Hammond, R. (1884). *The Electric Light in Our Homes.* New York: R. Worthington.

Hill, H., and Bruce, V. The effects of lighting on the perception of facial surfaces. *Journal of Experimental Psychology: Human Perception and Performance, 22(4),* 986–1004.

Hopkinson, R.G. (1957). Evaluation of glare. *Illuminating Engineering, 52(6),* 305–316.

Human Factors Society (1988). *American National Standard for Human Factors Engineering of Visual Display Terminal Workstations* (ANSI/HFS 100-1988). Santa Monica, CA.

Illuminating Engineering Society of North America (IESNA) (1998). Lighting for the aged and partially sighted committee. *Recommended Practice for Lighting and the Visual Environment for Senior Living,* RP-28-98. New York: Illuminating Engineering Society of North America.

Illuminating Engineering Society of North America (IESNA) (2000). *IESNA Lighting Handbook,* 9th edition. New York: Illuminating Engineering Society of North America.

Lam, W.M. (1986). *Sunlighting as Formgivers for Architecture.* New York: Van Nostrand Reinhold.

Lighting Controls Association (1999). *The National Dimming Initiative.* Advance Transfer Co.

Littlefair, P.J. (1996). *Designing with Innovative Daylighting.* London: CRC, Garston.

McClaughan, C.L.B., Aspinall, P.A., and Webb, R.S. (March 31–April 13, 1996). The effects of lighting upon mood and decision making, *Proceedings of CIBSE National Lighting Conference,* University of Bath, pp. 237–245.

Miller, C.L., White, R., Whitman, T.L., O'Callaghn, M.F., and Maxwell, S.E. (1995). The effects of cycled versus noncycled lighting on the growth and development in preterm infants. *Infant Behavior and Development, 18(1),* 87–95.

Mistrick, R., Chen, C., Bierman, B., and Felts, D. (2000). A comparison of photosensor-controlled electronic dimming systems. *Proceedings of the 2000 Annual Conference of the Illuminating Engineering Society, 29(1),* 66–80.

Mount, C.M (1992). *Residential Interiors.* Glen Cove, NY: P.B.C. International.

NASA (1978). *Anthropometric Source Book.* NASA Reference Publication 1024. Washington, DC: U.S. National Aeronautics and Space Administration.

Nielsen, J. (1993). *Usability Engineering.* Boston: Academic Press.

O'Dea, W.T. (1958). *The Social History of Lighting.* London: Routledge and Kegan Paul.

Panero, J., and Zelnik, M. (1979). *Human Dimension, Interior Space.* New York: Whitney Library of Design.

Pheasant, S. (1996). *Bodyspace: Anthropometry, Ergonomics and the Design of Work,* 2nd ed. Bristol, England: Taylor & Francis.

Phillips, D. (1997). *Lighting Historic Buildings.* New York: McGraw-Hill.

Raschko, B. (1982). *Housing Interiors for the Disabled and Elderly.* New York: Van Nostrand Reinhold.

Rowlands, E.D., Loe, D.L., McIntosh, R.M., and Mansfield, K.P. (1985). Lighting adequacy and quality in office interiors by consideration of subjective assessment and physical measurement. *CIE Journal, 4(1),* 23–37.

Rundquist, R.A., McDougall, T.G., and Benya, J. (1996). *Lighting Controls: Patterns for Design.* Prepared by R.A. Rundquist Associates for the Electric Power Research Institute and the Empire State Electrical Energy Research Corporation. Northampton, MA.

Smith F.K., and Bertolone, F.J. (1986). *The Principles and Practices of Lighting Design: Bringing Interiors to Light.* New York: Whitney Library of Design.

Society of Automotive Engineers (1977). *Anthropometry of Infants, Children and Youths to Age 18 for Product Safety Design.* SP-450. Warrendale, PA.

Sommer, R. (1969). *Personal Space.* Englewood Cliffs, NJ: Prentice-Hall.

Steffy, G.R. (1990). *Architectural Lighting Design.* New York: Van Nostrand Reinhold.

Stoudt, H.W. (1981). Anthropometry of the elderly. *Human Factors Society Bulletin, 23,* (1).

U.K. Department of the Environment (March 1998). Desktop guide to daylighting for architects. *Good Practice Guide 245.* Harwell, Oxfordshire, England: ETSU.

U.S. Department of Health, Education, and Welfare (1966). Weight, height, and selected body dimensions of adults: United States, 1960–1962. *Vital and Health Statistics, Series 11, no. 8.* Washington, DC.: U.S. Government Printing Office.

U.S. Department of Health, Education, and Welfare (1979). Weight and height of adults 18–74 years of age: United States, 1971–1974. *Vital and Health Statistics, Series 11, no. 211.* Washington DC: U.S. Government Printing Office.

U.S. Department of Housing and Urban Development (1972). *A Design Guide for Home Safety.* Washington D.C.; U.S. Government Printing Office.

U.S. Department of Justice (1991). Americans with disabilities act-Title III. *Federal Register* [28 CFR Part 36], vol. 56, no. 144. Washington, DC: U.S. Government Printing Office.

Veitch, J., and Newsham, G. (January 1999). Individual control can be energy efficient. *IAEEL Newsletter.*

Whiton, S., and Abercrombie, S. (2002). *Interior Design & Decoration,* 5th edition. Upper Saddle River, NJ: Prentice-Hall.

Woodson, W., Tillman, B., and Tillman, P. (1992). New York: McGraw-Hill.

Wright, G.A., and Rea, M.S. (1984). Age, a human factor in lighting. *Proceedings of the 1984 International Conference on Occupational Ergonomics.* D.A. Attwood and C.McCann (eds.). Rexdale, Ontario, Canada: Human Factors Association of Canada.

CHAPTER 20

Case Studies: Commercial Applications

OBJECTIVES

■ Determine the relationship between the dynamics of organizations and designing a quality lighting environment.

■ Describe common lighting considerations in commercial facilities, including structural elements, needs of the end users, principles of universal design, and public areas.

■ Identify salient characteristics of commercial lighting systems.

■ Identify and apply important lighting considerations in offices, educational facilities, and healthcare institutions.

■ Identify and apply important lighting considerations in the hospitality industry and retail stores.

IMPORTANT considerations in lighting residential interiors are discussed in Chapter 19. This chapter explores the most frequent commercial interiors designers are commissioned to work on. As with residential interiors, commercial environments have common areas and considerations, which are discussed in the first section of this chapter. Some of the most important issues affecting all commercial structures include designing for diverse populations, safety concerns, protecting the environment, and energy conservation. People with multiple abilities, communication skills, and perceptions work in or visit commercial buildings. Therefore, the principles of universal design are a critical component in designing a quality lighting environment. The application of the principles is important in creating an environment that is as safe as possible for all users. Commercial interiors consume tremendous amounts of resources and electricity. As a result, energy codes are becoming more stringent every year. By implementing effective conservation practices, an interior designer can comply with the codes and help make a positive impact on our planet.

The principles of a quality lighting environment must be applied to all types of commercial structures and to every space within a building. This chapter focuses on how lighting affects the end users in offices, schools, healthcare institutions, hospitality interiors, and retail establishments. Designing the lighting for commercial interiors requires a thorough understanding of the goals of the organization and the characteristics of the end users. The environment must be responsive to the needs of the client, people who work in the building, and people who visit for a limited amount of time. Creating functional and aesthetic designs requires interacting with users of the environment and applying observational skills. (Chapter 22 explores methodology in detail.) Efforts involve collaborating with multiple professionals engaged in the construction process, including architects, engineers, contractors, electricians, building inspectors, acoustical experts, and fire-prevention specialists.

Commercial Design Factors

To design a quality light environment in commercial interiors requires an examination of the organization, typical commercial considerations, and an understanding of the most effective lighting systems.

Dynamics of Organizations

Effectively designing the lighting for a commercial interior requires an understanding of an organization's mission, goals, and objectives. Most organizations have this information recorded in documents, such as annual reports, strategic plans, or informational brochures. This analysis should be completed in the planning or programming phase of the project. (See Chapter 21 for more information on the phases of the design process.) In addition to knowing the goals of a client's organization, it may be helpful to have a good understanding of the industry's current issues and concerns. For example, in designing the lighting for a new restaurant, an analysis of the restaurant industry can provide valuable insight about profitable operating practices. Frequently, many of the concepts that are crucial for profitability can be transferred to the design of an interior, including lighting.

Elements contributing to profits and significant returns on investments (ROI) should be considered in the design of a lighting environment. For example, offices must have lighting that accommodates the functional requirements of performing tasks and creates an aesthetic environment that motivates people to do their best work. Commercial buildings designed to serve the public, such as retail stores, must have lighting that attracts people to the business and then prompts sales. Appropriate and efficient lighting systems affect the ROI. Frequently, a business will examine the length of time it takes to earn back the initial investment in a lighting system. An energy-efficient lighting system can result in a short time period for the ROI.

The cost of salaries and benefits are the largest expenses of an organization. Therefore, a critical component of lighting is addressing the needs of the users. As discussed in Chapter 14, lighting affects the safety, health, and welfare of people. In addition, effective lighting can help to eliminate errors, retain employees, and reduce absenteeism. To accommodate the lighting needs of the users, the assessment process must determine characteristics of the individuals, the tasks, and the environment. People interact with an environment and are affected by lighting. Effective lighting includes illumination that evokes specific emotions, moods, and responses. Every business has an image that can be reinforced by its lighting. Illumination can give the impression that a business is sophisticated, trendy, frugal, traditional, or expensive.

Helping an organization to be successful often requires an examination of past lighting practices and policies. As with residential interiors, lighting in many commercial environments has not changed with improvements in lamps, luminaires, controls, and enhanced knowledge of the principles of quality lighting. This situation becomes even more complex when changes in management philosophies, contemporary work/life practices, technological advancements, and worldwide interactions of people are factored in. Therefore, designing quality lighting environments requires constant scanning of the worldwide environment. This involves studying technological changes, business policies, global economics, political influences, social conditions, and cultural issues.

Progressive lighting approaches reflect a blend of knowing the future directions of an industry and understanding how current events affect lighting environments. For example, for years interior designers have tried to find the best method of illumination for people working at a computer. By monitoring the advancements of lighting systems and computers, an interior designer can specify a lighting environment that successfully integrates both technologies. Interior designers should also monitor new interior products and materials. Changes in the size, shape, color, or texture of a product can affect a lighting environment. For example, products manufactured by ceiling tile companies dramatically affect a lighting system. Therefore, it is imperative that an interior designer be knowledgeable about new products and apply innovations to lighting systems. Crises in the worldwide energy supply have traditionally impacted the field of lighting. Thus, keeping abreast of events that affect energy supplies can prepare an interior designer to specify lighting systems that meet or exceed energy codes.

In addition to responding to worldwide conditions and technological advancements, quality commercial lighting environments should be sufficiently flexible to accommodate a variety of organizational changes. To stay progressive and maintain a competitive edge, organizations create new policies and procedures that can affect the interior environment. For example, the continuous escalating cost of real estate has prompted organizations to consolidate space and create more multifunctional areas. This affects the lighting environment because multiple approaches to illumination need to exist to accommodate the needs of a variety of users performing diverse tasks. To accommodate diverse activities and changes in the number of employees, many organizations want interiors that can be easily reconfigured. To address this issue, lighting must correspond to the geometry of new spaces, furniture, and equipment.

Common Commercial Considerations

Lighting for commercial interiors must be planned, installed, and evaluated within the parameters of the project, including the budget and schedule. This requires an extensive collaborative effort with the client, end users, and professionals who work the project. Approaches to lighting can be affected by whether the building is owned or leased. A leased space might restrict the lighting environment. For example, the contract might prohibit lighting that is integrated into the interior architecture. In reviewing parameters associated with the construction of a building, it is critical to determine access to power. The location of power sources affects lighting techniques and the type of luminaires that may be installed. In commercial structures, power for lighting may be accessed from walls, soundproof partitions, floors, or ceilings. Power accessed from horizontal planes could be direct, a raised floor, or a suspended ceiling. Vertical access can be available along walls or through furniture.

Ceilings in commercial buildings must accommodate a variety of devices related to structural support, HVAC, safety, and security. Thus, luminaires on a ceiling plane must be planned in coordination with many elements, including beams, columns, diffusers, return grilles, sprinkler heads, loudspeakers, smoke alarms, emergency fixtures, and fire and wayfinding signage (Figure 20.1). (Chapter 23 describes typical drawings for lighting plans.) A well-designed ceiling plane is especially important in spaces with high ceilings because the horizontal plane exists at a comfortable viewing angle for users of the room. As a result, ceilings can become a focal point of an interior. Glare from ceiling luminaires must be controlled, and illumination should be designed to avoid a dirty appearance on ceiling surfaces.

Cave-like
Referring to undesirable dark areas, caused by improper distribution of illumination.

Side elevations of interiors can illustrate how suspended elements affect the space. Specifically, the location of luminaires or other elements should not interfere with emergency fixtures and signage. Elevations can demonstrate the vertical relationships among architectural elements, luminaires, and furniture. The height of suspended luminaires must not interfere with people and furniture. Side elevations can also help to expose illumination distribution patterns derived from natural and electrical sources. Since most commercial spaces are large, illumination must be distributed so that undesirable dark areas or a **cave-like** appearance is avoided. This is likely to occur in corners and at the center of wide spaces. Dark areas or striations on walls can occur when the cutoff angle for a ceiling luminaire prevents light from striking vertical surfaces close to the ceiling.

The distribution of illumination in a space can affect the users' abilities to define the boundaries of spaces, including the size and shape of rooms. Lighting should be positioned to provide the visual clarity needed for wayfinding and to make it possible for people to understand the parameters of rooms. Often this requires illuminating the perimeter walls of a room. Orientation is especially important for commercial spaces serving people who are not familiar with the building. For example, guests are not familiar with the layout of a hotel. This can be a serious life safety issue in an emergency. Many hotels have a maze of hallways leading to guest rooms. A guest who is unfamiliar with the layout could easily get lost trying to exit the building during an emergency. The same situation could occur in large ballrooms or casinos where it is difficult to locate the exit signs under crowded conditions.

In designing lighting for a variety of users, it is critical to incorporate the principles of universal design. (Refer to Chapter 13 for information regarding universal design.) In addition, content discussed in the previous chapters should be applied to commercial spaces. As discussed in Chapter 19, it is critical to design illumination that specifically addresses the needs of users, activities, the site, interior architecture, furniture, equipment, and characteristics of the elements of the space. Even within the context of commercial spaces used for the same purpose, such as restaurants, every commercial building has unique requirements that must be addressed in the lighting.

Custom lighting approaches include designing unique lighting for areas that are common spaces in most commercial interiors, such as lobbies, elevators, staircases, and hallways. Chapter 19 discusses special lighting considerations relative to most of these areas; however, there are additional illumination concerns that should be applied to commercial interiors. In the past, lobbies were designed to present a positive image to employees and visitors. To reinforce a corporate image, frequently illumination in lobbies relied upon an abundance of daylight, and electrical sources promoted the image of a corporation. Many businesses and corporations are still interested in projecting these images; however, the increase in terrorism throughout the world has forced organizations to incorporate significant security checkpoints in the lobbies of commercial structures. Security machines and equipment, which in the past were primarily used in airports, are now being used in commercial buildings, including museums (Figure 20.2). This significant change of activities in lobbies requires new methods to illuminate the spaces. Lighting must enable people to see clearly. To accurately inspect purses, luggage, and bags, lighting must be at adequate illumination levels, and the distribution patterns should eliminate glare and shadows. Frequently, when a high number of people are moving through a security checkpoint, inspections must occur in a variety of locations. Thus, it is critical for effective lighting to exist in and around the security checkpoint area.

FIGURE 20.2
Effective lighting should be planned for any area that requires security machines and equipment.

Elevators require special illumination strategies because of people who are unfamiliar with a building and a variety of environmental conditions that can exist in areas surrounding elevators. An important consideration for effective elevator illumination is to carefully plan the lighting in the areas adjacent to the openings of the elevator doors (Figure 20.3). When people leave an elevator, lighting should help to orient them to the layout of the floor. Lighting can help to inform visitors which direction to go in order to arrive at their desired location. Effective lighting is also important to help people see the transition area between the elevator and the floor of the building. To efficiently see signage and the geometry of the space, illumination levels used in the elevator and adjoining areas must be comparable. To help people feel safe when leaving an elevator, dark areas, especially corners, should be avoided. In addition to wayfinding, safety, and security issues, the area people see when they leave an elevator can be the first impression of a business or merchandise. Thus, lighting in these areas should be designed to reinforce the desired image and mood.

Generally, staircases for commercial buildings exist for emergency situations. Thus, lighting for staircases must be focused on helping people to safely exit a building and providing effective illumination for emergency personnel who may be assisting in the evacuation process. Chapter 14 examines safety and security lighting methods. Lighting in hallways must also accommodate safety and security issues. However,

unlike staircases that are intuitive to use, configurations of hallways can be very confusing to people, especially in emergencies. In addition, the length of many hallways contributes to the complexity of providing effective illumination when people are trying to quickly leave a building.

Quality illumination in hallways must help people locate exit doors, understand the layout of a floor, and enhance an area in a building that can often be dull. Locating exit doors requires adequate illumination in a variety of locations, including light sources that are directed at the door and various levels along walls. To help people who are crawling out of a building, emergency lighting should be located close to the floor. Illumination levels could also escalate in intensity as one gets closer to the exit door. (See Chapter 14 for more information on exit lighting methods.) Orienting people to the layout of a floor requires quality illumination at key decision points and can include a lighting prioritization scheme. Effective lighting must illuminate directional signage and, when available, views of the floor. Hallway intersections that force people to decide on a direction should have effective illumination. A lighting prioritization scheme can assist with this process and can help to provide variety in monotonous hallways. A common approach to establishing priority areas is to vary the intensity of illumination, whereby the most important locations have the brightest light. Varying colors of lights or using different luminaires can also create

visual prioritization in spaces. The key to success of prioritization is establishing a scheme and being consistent.

The geometry of hallways can present lighting challenges. Long and narrow hallways give people the impression that they will need a long time to walk to their destination. It is possible to reduce the apparent length of a hallway by using a bright light source at the end of the space, varying illumination levels, or incorporating light art. The shape and the location of luminaires can also alter the impression of the geometry of hallways. For example, generally, long hallways with rows of rectangular-shaped fixtures parallel to the walls will make the space appear longer (Figure 20.4). Illuminating walls can help to increase the apparent width of hallways. To create a sense of human scale, hallways with very tall ceilings can have illumination located closer to the level of people. This can be accomplished with pendant luminaires or by using wall illumination techniques that create an imaginary ceiling line on walls.

Lighting Systems

Lighting systems for commercial interiors should enhance visual comfort, while accommodating the functional and aesthetic requirements of the space. A goal for the lighting plan should always be to have a minimal impact on the local and global environment. Daylight integration,

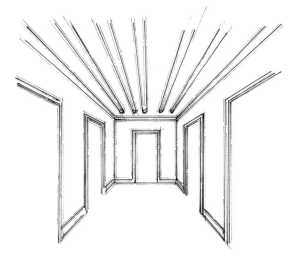

FIGURE 20.4
Luminaires in the same shape as a long hallway will make the space appear longer.

electrical sources, luminaires, and controls should be energy-efficient, conserve natural resources, and promote the health and safety of people with diverse abilities. The enormous demand for commercial lighting systems stimulates extensive product research and development. This results in lighting systems that are constantly changing and improving. To specify the most efficient and effective lighting, an interior designer must stay abreast of technological advancements. Some of the most important criteria to monitor are improved optical control, energy efficiency, lumen output relative to the size of the source, color rendition, lumen maintenance, and flexibility in controls. Technological enhancements can occur by improving various elements of lighting systems, including materials and finishes. Therefore, a new lens with a plastic or metal finish could increase the distribution of lumens on a work surface or significantly reduce glare.

Staying current in the field of lighting systems includes reading relevant research studies. The expansive nature of commercial interiors has led to many studies that have focused on analyzing the relationships between user behavior, lighting systems, and environmental conditions. For example, many studies have examined how lighting affects the productivity of people using VDT screens in offices. When studying research findings, it is very important to closely examine specific characteristics of the interior, such as the lighting system, equipment, furniture, space configuration, reflectance, and environmental conditions. The rapid technological changes associated with lighting systems and equipment can make studies outdated. Therefore, before applying the results of a study, the interior designer should find out whether the parameters of the study are appropriate for the project.

Commercial lighting systems must comply with building codes, including energy regulations. Refer to state and local energy codes regarding power limits for commercial spaces. To meet the watts-per-square-foot requirements of many energy codes, effective daylight integration is becoming increasingly important. Harvesting daylight is especially important for commercial interiors, such as offices and schools, which are primarily used during the day at peak power times. Natural and electrical lighting must be designed to reduce the energy consumption required for heating and cooling. Many commercial interiors have rooms with no natural light. To improve the psychological well-being of the end users, conserve energy, and create a more pleasing environment, whenever possible, interiors should have daylight integration. This can be accomplished through a variety of methods, including atriums, skylights, clerestories, light wells, tubular skylights, and light shelves. Effective interior and exterior shading should be installed. To allow sunlight to penetrate spaces without windows, glass in partitions should be considered. To resolve the variability of daylight, especially on overcast days, electrical sources should be energy-efficient. (See Chapter 2 for information on daylight integration.)

Lamps, ballasts, and luminaires for commercial interiors should be energy-efficient and easy to maintain. Lamps should have excellent efficacy and long life, and maintain a lumen output of about 90 percent. Efficient ballasts should work in tandem with controls, such as daylight, or motion sensors. Automatic controls should be calibrated with time delays for cloud covers with short durations. Photometric reports should be analyzed to determine which luminaire distributes the most lumens possible for a task. To compare the efficiency and effectiveness of different luminaires, refer to the luminaire efficacy rating (LER). Less efficient luminaires should be used for only special applications, such as in lobbies or to highlight a special collection. To maximize the efficiency of lighting systems, interior surfaces should have a matte finish and have high reflectance. This is especially critical for surfaces that are used to reflect light into a space, such as ceilings and the upper sections of walls. To maximize the quantity of illumination in rooms with direct lighting, the floor covering should be a light color.

In selecting the design of the luminaire, the style, size, color, and material should complement the interior architecture and the program's design concept. To conserve natural resources and prevent an outdated appearance, trendy luminaires should be avoided in many commercial interiors. This is especially important in buildings that require a high number of fixtures. Replacing trendy luminaires is expensive for a client, and, unless the components are recyclable, fixtures can add considerable bulk to our planet's landfills. To optimize efficiency and help create a clean environment, luminaires and lamps must be properly maintained. Labor for maintenance of commercial buildings is costly. Therefore, to help reduce costs, the lighting plan should have a maintenance program that includes calibrating controls, group relamping, and routine cleaning of lamps and luminaires.

Efficient and well-calibrated controls are essential for commercial interiors. Energy consumed is determined by power multiplied by the amount of time. Thus, tremendous savings can occur by reducing the amount of time lights are turned on. For example, the high levels of illumination that are required to accommodate the needs of hundreds of people during the day is the same lighting that is used by a few building service workers who clean the rooms in the evening. The goal is to ensure adequate illumination for tasks when needed and to turn lights off at other times. In an effort to force owners to conserve energy, many codes require automatic shut-off controls for commercial structures.

Task-Oriented Commercial Interiors

The most common task-oriented commercial interiors are offices, educational facilities, and healthcare institutions.

Offices

Lighting for offices is affected by management philosophies and the technology used by employees. Management is always interested in operating a profitable business by producing quality work and retaining good employees. Throughout the history of office interiors, managers have attempted to identify the specific conditions that would ensure success and reflect the corporate culture. This includes the design of office space, furniture, equipment, and lighting. In the late nineteenth century, Frederick Taylor, an industrial psychologist, convinced managers that the best approach to attain high productivity in the workplace was to use operational procedures that were utilized in factories. Thus, every person was given exactly the same space, furniture, equipment, and lighting. The expectation was that with all employees having the same environment and tools they would produce the same quality and quantity of work. Management assumed that high quantities of illumination were needed to reduce errors and stimulate productivity. In addition, management believed that the heat generated by lamps supplemented the climatic needs of buildings. Therefore, at a time when electricity was relatively inexpensive, excessive quantities of illumination filled office interiors (Figure 20.5).

A rigid approach to managing people, the design of offices, and lighting remained relatively unchanged until the 1960s, when Japan became successful by using a management philosophy based upon collaborative work environments. In a quest to match the accomplishments of Japanese businesses, Western managers initiated a quality management philosophy. This new approach to business required an office environment that encouraged collaboration. As a result, status-free (nonhierarchical) offices were created. To respond to the new configurations, lighting had to change from the illumination methods used for individual offices to light being distributed throughout very large spaces. High quantities of illumination with inefficient lamps became a significant problem during the energy crisis in the 1970s. In the 1980s, task/ambient lighting, integrated in furniture systems, became a popular solution for reducing illumination quantities and providing direct light for tasks being done at a desk.

Currently, a common management philosophy is to create an environment that is flexible to the changing needs of a business. This fre-

FIGURE 20.5
An interior with excessive quantities of illumination.

quently involves downsizing, reducing excess, eliminating categories of workers, and instituting shared spaces. In addition, as a consequence of the 9/11 attack, many corporations are decentralizing their organizations. To reduce absenteeism and retain quality employees, management has focused on the personal needs of employees. For example, to create a homelike environment, "living rooms" in an office serve as locations for meetings or casual conversation. Many employees have flexible schedules, work in a variety of locations, and are telecommuting. These individuals often need hotels and work space when they come to the office. Customized lighting in these spaces helps to individualize an office that is shared by many people. Managers believe collaboration is still important, thus, the office needs space for interaction, such as *touchdown* areas. To encourage spontaneous collaborative activities, *touchdown* spaces are distributed throughout a building. To reduce travel expenses, many managers have elected to invest in videoconferencing facilities. All these changes in management philosophies require unique approaches to illuminating the office.

In addition to understanding how management philosophies affect lighting, it is important to review how the technology that people use in an office helps to determine appropriate lighting environments. In the earliest offices, employees performed most of their work on the horizontal plane of a desk. The work involved writing, using a typewriter, and reading a variety of documents, including carbon copies. The lack of strong contrast and the importance of speed and accuracy prompted management to install lighting fixtures that emitted high quantities of illumination. In addition, to ensure bright illumination on a task, direct light sources were used without adequate shielding.

The next major development in technology used by office workers was the portable computer. Researchers are still developing the optimum lighting system that can provide effective illumination for people working at a computer and writing at a desk. Since manufacturers of computers are dramatically improving the surfaces of VDT screens, problems associated with glare and veiling reflections should eventually become obsolete.

The use of videoconferencing technology poses unique lighting challenges. The interaction between the camera, transmission, and lighting are extremely complex. (The variables to consider when designing lighting for videoconferencing are discussed later in this chapter). The progression of wireless technology enables employees to work in various locations throughout a building. Effective task lighting in a variety of locations will have to be planned to accommodate these new ways of working.

The earlier discussions on how lighting is affected by management philosophies and technology serve as the foundation for understanding components critical to quality illumination in an office environment. Another major element is the relationship between ergonomics and lighting. Tasks performed in an office can cause problems with vision and repetitive stress injuries, such as carpal tunnel syndrome (CTS). Office workers report problems of eyestrain, visual fatigue, and blurred vision. In addition, people have indicated that problems associated with vision have indirectly caused other physical ailments, such as headaches. Musculoskeletal injuries can occur when people work in unnatural positions or engage in repetitive motions. For example, one cause of CTS is repetitive wrist motions that occur when people work at a keyboard for long periods of time.

Lighting has a role in helping to reduce vision problems and musculoskeletal injuries. Task lighting in offices should be designed to accommodate the specific needs of each end user. Even though employees might be engaged in the same tasks, each individual has different vision requirements. Therefore, an employee should be able to control the type of lighting he or she needs in order to perform tasks. This can be accomplished by specifying luminaires and controls that are operated by the end user. **Localized lighting** techniques allow an employee to position light sources where they are needed and at the appropriate illumination level. Vision problems should be reduced when people can create the optimum lighting for their tasks and work environment.

Ineffective lighting can contribute to musculoskeletal injuries. For example, to avoid glare and veiling reflections an end user may move to an unnatural position. An individual working in an awkward position for a long period of time can develop back or neck problems. To prevent CTS, individuals are encouraged to vary their working positions. This might involve alternating between standing and sitting positions.

Localized lighting
A technique, that allows a user to position light sources where they are needed, and at the appropriate illumination level.

For multiple positions to be successful, lighting must be designed to accommodate various locations. Localized lighting, controlled by the end user, can provide the flexibility required for changing lines of sight. Allowing the end users to determine their lighting needs should also help resolve the problems associated with too much light in an office environment. Currently, many offices have high illumination levels, because of the historical belief that bright lights improve productivity and stimulate the work environment. Luminous VDT screens provide some of the illumination for working at a computer. Effective lighting for computer tasks includes appropriate illumination levels between the VDT screen, the immediate work area, and the surrounding areas. Glare and veiling reflections can be avoided by eliminating a direct angle of light distribution from luminaires and windows. Some luminaires are designed to project illumination below screen and eye levels. Frequently, indirect or direct/indirect pendants can provide effective illumination without creating disabling reflections on a VDT screen. Generally, for proper distribution of illumination throughout a space, indirect pendants require ceiling heights between 9 and 10 feet (274–305 cm).

One of the most complicated factors in planning lighting for offices is having effective illumination in all the various locations where people are doing their work. In the past, office buildings had dedicated spaces for categories of workers and tasks. Most companies still have private offices for managers, open areas for other employees, and conference facilities. However, effective task lighting must be included in every location where people are working. Private offices, open offices, *touchdown* areas, "living rooms", "hotel spaces", and conference facilities need lighting that enables people to read reports, work at computers, and interact with other people. Since most of these spaces are used by multiple end users, lighting must accommodate the variable vision needs of people. In addition, to accommodate changes in partitions and workstation configurations, luminaires should be specified that are easy to relocate, and power should be accessed in a variety of locations. Light sources should provide illumination for a variety of positions, tasks, and working hours. The significant technological improvements in controls can help to provide users with an easy way to customize a work environment. For example, addressable ballast technologies allow people to program specific lighting requirements for designated spaces and tasks.

Office environments have a variety of users, daylight conditions, configurations, furniture styles, and interior materials. Lighting should be customized to the unique requirements and needs of each client. Layered lighting should be designed for every space. Many of the same tasks are performed in private offices and open-plan areas. For the tasks that are performed in offices, lighting should be designed to eliminate glare on work surfaces, avoid severe contrasts in the distribution of lighting, illuminate vertical surfaces, diminish shadows, and provide effective localized lighting for end users. Open-plan offices can be complicated to illuminate because the potential for glare and veiling reflections is significant. To determine visual problems associated with multiple luminaires located throughout a large area, work areas for every station in the space must be analyzed. To maximize illumination, reflectance of interior surfaces should be 80 to 90 percent on ceilings, 40 to 60 percent on walls, and 20 to 40 percent on floors. Daylight integration is critical, and lamps should be selected that enhance the colors of the interior and of people. Some partitions or office furniture can prevent daylight from penetrating some spaces. In analyzing daylight patterns, directional angles should be reviewed in all spaces.

Lighting controls must be calibrated to accommodate the needs of people, furniture heights, and the configuration of spaces. To detect subtle motions, such as working at a keyboard, occupancy controls should be ultrasonic and calibrated for maximum sensitivity. In smaller spaces, occupancy controls can usually be located on walls. Generally, in open-plan offices, ceiling-mounted controls are most effective. Storage bins and high partitions can affect illumination levels on work surfaces. Refer to the manufacturers' literature regarding calibration techniques and specific partition heights. Manual-on switching should be installed in all spaces; however, large areas should also have wall switches that automatically turn lights off in specified areas when the space is not being used. Delays on occupancy controls should be determined by the size of the room and any impairment of the users of the space. Rooms with daylight should have automatic dimming controls calibrated for climatic conditions.

Controls are essential to conserving energy and providing flexibility in the quantity of illumination provided. The IESNA recommends 40 to 50 fc (400–500 lux) in private and open-plan offices (IESNA, 2000). Energy-efficient lighting systems must be used in most office spaces. (See Chapter 12 for information on energy and the environment.) Some of the most frequently specified luminaires include parabolic troffers, direct/indirect pendants, wall-wash units, wall sconces, and downlights. Spacing must be planned to prevent bright and dark areas on ceilings and walls and in corners of rooms. Energy-efficient sources for these luminaires are tubular, U-shaped, and compact fluorescent lamps. Less efficient sources and luminaires might be used to enhance public areas, where it is important to use controls calibrated to reduce energy usage during unoccupied times.

Technology has significantly influenced the design of conference rooms. In addition to being the traditional place where meetings are held, conference rooms have become the location for viewing audiovisual presentations, working at computers, and conducting teleconferences. Lighting for such multifunctional spaces must accommodate the range of activities, which occur at varying times of the day. Lighting must be specifically planned for every activity and end user. Lighting for discussion purposes should be designed to enhance facial features, enable participants to view a whiteboard, and provide task lighting for note-taking on paper or on a computer. When the purpose of the room changes to viewing an audiovideo presentation, perimeter lighting should be soft throughout the room and the area surrounding a screen or television monitors. In addition, task lighting for taking notes should be provided for every person in the room.

Effective lighting for videoconferencing requires a coordinated effort between the interior designer and an audiovisual specialist. Many of the lighting approaches for videoconferencing are designed to facilitate the functional requirements of specific camera equipment and the process of transmitting images. Quality image transmission requires a careful orchestration of the location of people, camera equipment, lighting, furniture, presentation boards, surface colors, and patterns on the walls. The primary goal of videoconferencing is to have effective communication among people who may be located throughout the world. Lighting and environmental conditions must provide clarity to enable participants to see people's expressions and gestures, which are captured by cameras and electronically transmitted. To accurately see the person who is talking, cameras are placed throughout the room. Lighting must be coordinated with the location of cameras in order to highlight the speaker and eliminate shadows on faces. To encourage a conversational atmosphere, the preferred camera location is at eye level.

To create attention, the highest level of illumination should be on the person who is speaking. As different people talk, the lighting should be adjusted accordingly. To eliminate glare, luminaires should be hidden from the view of the camera. The quantity of light should be determined by the requirements of the camera and reflectance of interior surfaces. Reflectance of interior surfaces should be 70 to 80 percent on ceilings and 40 to 60 percent on walls. Effective image transmission requires appropriate contrast ratios between the speaker, the immediate area around the person, and the surfaces in the background. To prevent the appearance of gloomy spaces, perimeter walls should have uniform illumination, including lamps with the same CRI and CCT ratings.

An important element in videoconferencing is the reduction in the complexity of the images that must be transmitted. For example, patterns add complexity to the transmission process. Furniture surfaces and interior materials should not have patterns. In addition, to reduce patterns of illumination in a room, variations in light levels should be gradual. The complexity of designing spaces for effective videoconferencing often requires mock-ups, which should include the specific equipment, lighting, and environmental conditions. Lighting specifications for videoconferencing will change as the technology becomes more advanced. To ensure the most effective lighting plans, an interior designer must consult with audiovisual specialists.

Educational Facilities

Lighting for educational facilities should be efficient and support philosophies of learning. Prior to the 1950s, daylight was viewed as an excellent source of illumination in the classroom (Figure 20.6). This

FIGURE 20.6
Prior to the 1950s large
windows were specified in
classrooms to provide
daylight.

was to be expected since schools primarily operated during the day.
Task illumination was needed for desks and to see writing on a black-
board or easel. The broad distribution patterns of daylight provided excellent illumination on horizontal and vertical surfaces. In the 1960s
architects and engineers were asked to provide air-conditioning in
school buildings. To promote efficient air-conditioning systems, most
schools were designed with few, if any, windows. Many classrooms became exclusively dependent upon electrical light sources. The practice
of eliminating windows in classrooms was reinforced during the energy
crisis of the 1970s. Engineers argued that eliminating windows reduced heat loss in the winter and heat gain in the summer. Furthermore, from an educational perspective, some teachers believed that
views of the outdoors encouraged students to daydream, so windows
were seen as a distraction.

In more recent years, many research studies and reports have
demonstrated the importance of daylight to learning (Benya, 2001;
Duro-Test Lighting, 2003; Heschong, 1999; Lane, 1996; Plympton,
Conway, and Epstein, 2000; Ravetto, 1994; Thayer, 1995). As discussed in Chapter 2, daylight enhances visual acuity, which provides
better light for reading and writing. Daylight also has positive psychological and physiological effects on people by reducing stress, satisfying circadian rhythms, and encouraging positive attitudes. The
Heschong Group (1999) found that students in classrooms that had

significant daylight had higher test scores than students working in classrooms with little or no daylight. The Alberta Department of Education in Canada and schools in Raleigh, North Carolina, reported health and educational benefits to children who were exposed to daylight. Research also found that absenteeism was lower in educational facilities illuminated by daylight.

A variety of activities occur in classrooms. Many educators believe that the best learning occurs when students are exposed to different approaches to teaching. These include lectures, discussion, interactive media, or team collaboration. Many classrooms are designed to accommodate a lecture format and collaborative small-group activities. Classroom activities can occur at desks, tables, or on the floor. Technology has had a tremendous impact on presenting students with a variety of ways to learn. Educators can present information to students by using computers, television monitors, screens, flip charts, chalkboards, or whiteboards.

As demonstrated in research studies, daylight is important in the classroom. Every attempt should be made to incorporate some daylight into every space, including corridors. For existing structures, this could include adding skylights, light wells, clerestories, roof monitors, light shelves, and tubular skylights. (See Chapter 2 for more information on daylight integration.) To accommodate times when a classroom needs to be dark, effective shading devices must be installed at every window in a room, including glazing on partition walls. To supplement daylight, electrical lighting systems must be energy-efficient, easy to maintain, have a long life, and retain a lumen output of around 90 percent. Tubular and compact fluorescent lamps with a CRI of 80 or better are excellent light sources for classrooms and most other areas in a school building. Rooms with very high ceilings, such as gymnasiums, should have metal halide lamps. For accent lighting, efficient sources are ceramic metal halide or halogen IR lamps.

Indirect/direct pendant luminaires provide an excellent diffused quality of illumination, and when properly spaced, a uniform distribution pattern, which can help to eliminate dark areas in a classroom. Efficient ballasts should work in tandem with controls, such as daylight or motion sensors. Multilevel switching with user override for automatic controls can be coordinated to respond to daylight contours. The quantity of light in classrooms should follow the recommendations provided by the *IESNA Lighting Handbook.* The 9th edition recommends 40 to 50 fc (400–500 lux) in classrooms and 20 to 40 fc (200–400 lux) for computer classrooms. To maximize illumination, reflectance of interior surfaces should be 90 percent on ceilings, 70 percent on walls, and 40 percent on floors.

To accommodate the range of activities that are performed by people with varied abilities, classroom lighting should be localized and flexible. For children who have visual impairments, lighting requirements must be discussed with vision specialists. Layered lighting should be used throughout the school building. To conserve energy, accent lighting should be limited, and lamps should be energy-efficient. When classrooms are used for lectures, lighting should be directed on the speaker, task luminaires should be aimed at desks to enable students to write notes, and uniform, perimeter illumination should exist throughout the room. Illumination on the speaker should not be bright, and there should be no shadows on facial features. Task lighting should prevent shadows on work surfaces for students who are right- or left-handed. Perimeter lighting in a classroom is very important, because students must read material that is often on vertical surfaces, such as whiteboards, chalkboards, or bulletin boards. Luminaires must be carefully selected and installed to eliminate glare on the shiny surfaces of whiteboards. Perimeter lighting is also important for appropriate luminance ratios, assisting the eye with adaptation, and creating a pleasing environment. Specific lighting might have to be included to illuminate the walls surrounding windows. During the day, these vertical surfaces will be dark, unless light is directed at the area. Frequently, teaching materials are located around windows; therefore, without additional illumination, students could have difficulty seeing the materials (Figure 20.7). Perimeter lighting may also be used to eliminate shadows in dark spaces, especially in corners.

Educators often combine a lecture with audiovisual presentations. Many classrooms are not planned to accommodate the variable lighting needed to take notes in a dark environment. For these conditions, low levels of illumination should exist in the area around the speaker,

the surface used to hold the speaker's notes, at desks for note-taking, and at the perimeter of the room. Illumination that is close to a monitor or screen must be strategically planned to avoid washing out images. Luminance ratios must also be carefully coordinated to assist the eye with adaptation. A dark setting can be problematic because of the bright and dark contrasts. This is a concern in a classroom environment because students must constantly shift their eyes to various areas in the room as they take notes, watch a speaker, and view an audiovisual presentation.

Computers are located in different settings throughout a school building. For example, some classrooms are dedicated to computer work. Many students use laptop computers in lecture halls while the teacher is using a computer to access relevant materials and personal files. Every setting where computers are used must have lighting that supports the task. Illumination considerations for computers, discussed earlier in this chapter and textbook, must be applied to classrooms. Rooms should be glare-free and have a diffused, uniform distribution pattern of illumination.

For situations in which students work in groups in a classroom, a different lighting effect should be planned. To encourage discussions and stimulate creative thinking, illumination for group discussions could be similar to the lighting conditions used for casual conversation in a living room. Changing the lighting environment is important in a classroom because the variance in illumination can be a psychological stimulus, and the lighting transition can reinforce a different subject or activity. One of the reasons for supporting windows in the classroom is based upon the knowledge that the brain is stimulated by the variability associated with climatic conditions and outdoor views.

Healthcare Institutions

Healthcare institutions encompass a variety of facilities, such as hospitals, medical offices, clinics, and residential long-term care units. As with other commercial structures, current medical practices and policies affect lighting. Early healthcare facilities primarily focused on the needs of doctors, rather than on patients and their families. Thus, rooms in buildings were designed primarily for medical purposes, and support facilities for family members did not exist. As the medical profession gained a better understanding of the importance of family and the environment on the recovery of patients, healthcare facilities improved patient rooms and provided for the needs of family and friends. New facilities focus on empowering patients, such as birth rooms, hospice centers, healing gardens, and age-in-place residential units. In addition to providing effective lighting for medical procedures, interiors need lighting that improves the psychological well-being of patients and meets the needs of family members.

Many of the patients in a healthcare facility have temporary or permanent disabilities. Thus, it is imperative that the principles of universal design be applied to the lighting plan. Illumination must help people who have problems associated with vision, hearing, cognition, and mobility. This is especially critical in areas where accidents are likely to occur, such as bathrooms, stairways, and stairway landings. Children and people with dementia have unique needs, which must be accommodated by the lighting plan. Hot lamps should not be used in fixtures that are accessible to patients. To eliminate glare, luminaires with exposed lamps must be analyzed from various locations in a room. To help prevent seizures, flickering lamps should be removed.

To assist people in finding rooms, especially in a crisis, illumination can help in wayfinding (Figure 20.8). Thus, lighting must be effectively

FIGURE 20.8
To assist people
in moving through interiors,
lighting must be effectively
integrated with signage.

integrated with signage. For safety, security, and aesthetic purposes, dark areas should not exist. Visitors often use reception areas and waiting rooms when they are waiting to hear about the results of surgery or a medical procedure. A serene lighting environment can help to reduce stress and anxiety associated with people who are waiting to hear about medical results. Lighting should also help to create some level of privacy for people who may have emotional responses to results. Some approaches to providing privacy include not using direct illumination on people's faces and using small pools of light, which can give the impression that a large room is divided into smaller, private areas.

Quality lighting is important in these settings because many of the tasks being performed demand accuracy. Glare and shadows must be eliminated, while an environment that projects a professional and positive impression must be created. Research indicates positive effects that daylight produces on patients in healthcare facilities. As noted in Chapter 2, Littlefair (1996) reported on the positive effects of using reflected daylight in hospital rooms. Daylight can help significantly in creating a healthy and pleasing environment. The variability of daylight can serve as a stimulus for people who must stay in one location for a long period of time, and natural light can assist with the body's circadian rhythm. Coordinating the body's circadian rhythm is especially important for people who are disoriented resulting from a long surgery or recovery period. Natural light can also be helpful in seeing skin tones.

Electrical lighting in healthcare facilities must enable medical personnel to accurately see tasks involved with medical procedures, reading reports, recording health information, and performing tests. In addition, lighting should help to promote a healthy, professional, and clean impression of the facilities. Layered lighting should be included in most spaces, especially in public areas and patient rooms. Some medical procedures require specialist lighting fixtures. Specification of these fixtures must be done in consultation with medical personnel. Excellent lighting must be available for reading and recoding medical information. These tasks are performed in a variety of locations, including nursing stations, patient rooms, laboratories, or corridors. Some medical personnel are seated at desks or standing at portable carts, which hold laptop computers. Lighting specifications should be made after an analysis is conducted to determine where medical personnel need task illumination. Lighting must accommodate the variety of tools used for recording and reading medical records. The means of communication also affects the type of lighting. For example, medical reports may be recorded by using handheld devices, laptop computers, or pencil and paper.

The most energy-efficient electrical sources should be specified for a specific task. Highly specialized lighting and illumination in highly critical areas might require less efficient lighting systems. However, most areas in healthcare facilities should have efficient lighting systems because many spaces require illumination 24 hours a day seven days a week. To ensure illumination at the appropriate quantity, cleaning and maintenance guidelines for lighting systems must be strictly enforced. Medical personnel must be able to accurately detect skin tones and examine someone without disturbing shadows obstructing details. Lamps with CRI ratings of 100 should be used for activities that require color rendition accuracy, such as examination rooms, recovery rooms, and laboratories. In addition, the colors of surfaces that may reflect light on people must be carefully selected. For example, illumination reflecting off bright green walls might cast green light on a patient lying in bed.

Lighting must accommodate the needs of patients and medical personnel. Lighting must be flexible to accommodate a variety of positions and locations in a room. Controls should be accessible from a variety of positions, including when someone is lying in bed or sitting in a chair. For patients in bed, lighting should be adjustable for sitting and lying positions. Illumination must also be planned for tasks performed in a chair, for someone walking through the room, and for bathroom activities. The medical profession has become very specialized, and many members of the medical staff work with patients in their room. For example, physical and occupational therapists often work with patients soon after surgery. Illumination must accommodate the tasks involved with their procedures and equipment.

Customer-Oriented Commercial Interiors

Interior designers are hired to design a variety of customer-oriented commercial interiors. The most common projects are hotels, restaurants, and retail spaces.

Hotels

The history of the hotel industry begins with innkeepers. These individuals were committed to providing clean, safe, and comfortable rooms for their guests. The industry has experienced major growth and changes in facilities; however, the overall focus on providing excellent service is still the guiding principle for hotel operators today. The hotel industry is one of the largest retail businesses in the world. Hotels have a variety of amenities, prices, and room sizes, and they exist in a variety of locations, including on highways, in suburban and urban settings, and in resort areas. Hotels are operated as chains, franchises, or independents. Frequently the design of chains and franchises is dictated by corporate standards. To reflect a sense of the community and reinforce a theme, some hotel designs are influenced by location. These variable traits of the hotel industry are important criteria for specifying a quality lighting environment.

In designing hotel lighting, it is important to understand concerns of the hotel industry and the client's corporate philosophy. Hotels are part of the service industry; therefore, customer satisfaction is the primary focus. People who are happy with the facilities and service become loyal customers and communicate their satisfaction to friends who may become future guests. Repeat guests represent profits to a hotel. To make people want to return, hotels must provide consistency in the quality of the facilities and amenities, including lighting. Illumination in guest rooms and public areas must enhance the impression of cleanliness and comfort. And it must be installed in locations that are convenient to reach by the end users. To maintain friendly and efficient service for guests, the hotel industry is also concerned with employee productivity. Lighting can affect guests' and employees' psychological impression of the environment. In addition, the effectiveness of task lighting for the hotel staff can affect productivity. Risk management is another major concern of the hotel industry. Effective lighting for safety and security can help to reduce injuries to guests and employees.

Lighting should reinforce the uniqueness of a particular hotel and accommodate the specific needs of guests. Hotels have a targeted clientele and a specific price point. Lighting must reflect the identifiable image and value being offered. To attract customers, hotels must distinguish their facilities and services from those of their competitors. This can be accomplished by extraordinary architectural details, spectacular views, special amenities in guest rooms, state-of-the-art technology, corporate discounts, and personalized services. Whatever the hotel is trying to do to establish a market niche, lighting must support and enhance it. Key to this success is to understand the needs of guests and monitor changes in the hotel industry. In a profile of the people who stayed in hotels during 2002, the lodging industry found a fairly even distribution among business travelers, attendees at conference/group meetings, and people traveling for leisure and other personal reasons (American Hotel & Lodging Association, 2003). However, as a consequence of the economic decline that occurred after 9/11, the hotel industry has experienced a reduction in the number of business travelers, which is a highly profitable segment of the industry. As a result, many hotels have increased amenities in guest rooms that appeal specifically to business travelers, such as workstations with complete technological connections. Some hotels have enhanced access to technology by providing e-butlers, who are able to assist a guest with technical difficulties. To accommodate these business-related tasks, guest rooms must have the appropriate lighting systems.

People want a hotel to have a comfortable sleeping environment, clean bathrooms, and effective security. To exceed minimum expectations, many hotels are implementing a variety of personalized services that require special lighting. Guests must have a good night's sleep or they will not consider future visits. According to the Sleep Foundation, sleep deprivation can have a negative affect on the physical and psychological health of people. The elderly, especially those with dementia, experience disruptions in their sleep. Sleep deprivation can become more pronounced when people travel because circadian rhythms are altered. Bright lights in guest rooms can disturb sleep and make it difficult for someone to adjust to a new time zone. Variable illumination levels and room-darkening window treatments in guest rooms can help to normalize biological clocks.

To create a calm and relaxing environment, some hotels are adding spas in guest rooms. These can include oversized bathtubs, multiple pulsating showerheads, mood music, aromatherapy scents, and candles. Electrical lighting in guest bathrooms can contribute to the ambience by reinforcing the mood and enhancing the appearance of people (Figure 20.9). This requires a bathroom lighting system with the flexibility to have low levels of illumination for the bathing area and bright sources around mirrors for facial grooming.

In the commercial sector, lodging is the fourth most intensive consumer of energy in the United States. Bornholdt (2001) indicates that lighting can consume 40 percent of the property's overall electrical costs. To reduce energy consumption and conserve resources, lighting systems in hotels must be efficient and be maintained on a regular basis. Daylight should supplement and replace electrical sources as often as possible. In comparing all the rooms in a hotel, guest rooms and meeting spaces consume the greatest amount of energy. Therefore, these spaces should have energy-efficient lighting systems and should be considered first in a retrofit operation.

In research on end-user practices and energy-consumption patterns,

FIGURE 20.9
A bathroom designed for a spa experience should have a lighting system with the flexibility to have low levels of illumination for the bathing area and bright sources around mirrors for facial grooming.

it has been learned that lights remaining on in unoccupied spaces waste a great deal of energy in hotels. For example, at the Lawrence Berkeley National Laboratory, research focused on identifying which luminaires were used, how often, and the amount of time they were on in guest rooms and guest bathrooms. The findings indicate that luminaires are primarily used in the morning from six to ten o'clock, and after five in the evening. Bathroom fixtures and table luminaires in the guest room were on the most, an average of 8 and 5 hours, respectively. The study recommends that occupancy sensors in guest bathrooms would help to conserve energy. To avoid upsetting guests, occupancy sensors should be calibrated with long set times of approximately two hours. Hotel staff should be told to turn off lights in unoccupied guest rooms and bathrooms.

To conserve energy, Green Suites International added more efficient lamps in guest rooms, corridors, and public areas with an anticipated "payback in six months or less" (2001, p. 2). Recessed can fixtures and spotlights are some of the most common luminaires in hotels. To use the most energy-efficient CFLs and PAR lamps, old luminaires should be retrofitted or replaced. Old ceiling systems in bathrooms should also be updated with the most efficient sources possible. Luminaires with LED lamps are excellent energy-efficient nightlights in guest rooms, bathrooms, and exit signs.

Controls can play an important role in conserving energy in hotels. In addition to installing occupancy sensors in guest bathrooms, stairways and corridors should have motion detector controls or timers. Controls can be calibrated to automatically change lighting in areas that fluctuate with activities and illumination needs. For example, typically a reception desk is busy with check-ins and checkouts at the early part of the day. During the rest of the day, the reception area does not need high quantities of illumination at every station. Corridors surrounding meeting rooms can also vary in usage patterns. Thus, controls should reduce the level of illumination when people are in meetings and when the corridors are unoccupied.

There are a variety of different methods to systematically control lights, including an interface with the hotel's energy management system (EMS). Real-time energy systems can instantly communicate space usage to electronic controls systems. Some hotels have an electrical system that notifies the front desk when the status of a door lock changes, or a room key card can activate electrical circuits. These mechanisms can automatically turn off lights in unoccupied spaces, and advanced systems can program a specific scene for when guests enter a room. As hotels increase the level of personalization to their guests, a scene can be programmed to the exact specifications of the needs of a returning guest. Remote-control systems in guest rooms and meeting rooms can be connected to lighting, window treatments, audiovisual equipment, laptops, and multipoint videoconferencing.

Several organizations (Open Doors Organization; the Travel Industry Association of America; the Society for Accessible Travel and Hospitality) associated with accessibility and travel have indicated that a significantly higher number of people with disabilities would travel if accommodations were better suited to their needs. Most hotels have only a few rooms designated for people with disabilities. As the hospitality industry improves facilities to attract this market segment, lighting will play an important role in meeting the needs of people with disabilities. (See Chapter 13 for more information on lighting and universal design.) Feeling safe is important for guests staying at a hotel. A study conducted by Harris Interactive indicates that 94 percent of travelers view hotel safety as a critical factor when they select a hotel

(Fannin, 2003). (Chapter 14 discusses approaches to using illumination that can help people feel safe in an environment.)

Most hotels have a theme or an image that is projected in the design of the facilities. Lighting can reinforce the theme in various ways. The most obvious method is to select luminaires that reflect the theme and are integrated with the environment. For example, many of the luminaires at Walt Disney World have been custom-designed to blend with the overall design concept (Figure 20.10). Illumination levels and special lighting effects should support the desired mood of the hotel at various times of the day. Some hotels may use a specific element of a design as the overall theme. For example, a hotel in the mountains might have rough textures as the dominating concept. For this situation, lighting techniques that specifically enhance rough textures should be selected. Fabulous views of a city skyline or a sunset over the ocean are often focal points of a hotel. To maximize guests' ability to see the views, sunlight must be shielded from end users, and, in the evening, light sources must be carefully planned to avoid reflections of fixtures on the glass.

Communicating the theme of a hotel should begin at the outside entrance and remain consistent throughout the public areas and in guest rooms as well. Lighting at the entrance of a hotel should give a safe and secure impression to guests. As people enter the hotel, lighting

FIGURE 20.10 An illustration of a custom-designed luminaire that reinforces the theme of a Disney World hotel.

should immediately help with wayfinding. Many people are first-time users of the facilities, so lighting can direct people to the reception desk, public areas, and guest rooms. Lighting for the reception desk area should provide excellent illumination for people reading hotel statements and signing bills. To meet the needs of the hotel staff and guests, task illumination must be well planned on both sides of a desk. People use the lobby area for a variety of activities, including reading the fine print of maps, conversation, and as a meeting location. Lighting in lobbies should be flexible enough to accommodate the range of activities. Task lighting must serve the needs of reading, and the faces of people should be easily seen from a variety of angles. To respond to diverse moods and activities, lighting in the lobby should have a different atmosphere during the day from that in evening hours.

A primary goal of hotel operators is to create a homelike environment in guest rooms. This includes providing lighting that can accommodate the diverse tasks that are performed in guest rooms in various locations. Technology has provided the opportunity for people to use guest rooms for a variety of purposes, including working at a computer, playing video games, and watching movies. A focus on work-related amenities has included 24-hour business centers and executive technology suites and floors. Lighting for work-related activities must be appropriate for laptops, reading, and meetings. Illumination should also provide the appropriate atmosphere for relaxation, including creative applications involving the interplay of light with water in bathrooms.

Large public areas in hotels are used for a variety of activities, including conferences, meetings, receptions, and weddings. Frequently, these spaces can be arranged into various configurations with the use of soundproof partitions. Lighting must accommodate the various tasks, including working at computers, viewing audiovideo presentations, taking notes, listening to a speech, dining, and dancing. Every possible room configuration should have lighting that will accommodate the various activities. In addition, corridor areas surrounding meeting rooms are often used to conduct business. Therefore, to have illumination that meets the needs of work-related tasks, these areas should have luminaires that can be controlled by end users.

Restaurants

Restaurants, lounges, and bars are located in a variety of structures, including hotels, offices, and stand-alone facilities. The concept of restaurants started in France in the late eighteenth century. From the beginning, successful restaurants reflected a connection between the customer and the owner, who could also be the head chef. In addition to food quality and service, this relationship may make the difference between customers coming back again and again. As a result of this personalization, many restaurants are designed to reflect the taste of the owner. Therefore, interiors of restaurants, including lighting, should be planned in close consultation with the owner(s). As with hotels, the lighting must reinforce the thematic concept of restaurants.

Restaurants can be found everywhere, in a variety of different sizes, configurations, and market bases. The restaurant business is very challenging, which is reflected in the fact that approximately 75 percent of restaurants fail in their first year of operation. In an attempt to achieve success, many owners conduct a market analysis to determine the feasibility of their plan. Ideally, to develop a comprehensive restaurant plan, lighting should be considered in the early stages. (Chapter 21 reviews design strategies for lighting environments.) All restaurants share the common goal of attaining profits through customer satisfaction. People who are happy with the quality of food, service, and ambience become repeat customers and can further increase profits by communicating the positive attributes of the business to friends and family members. Consistency is a valued commodity for a successful restaurant. Once this is attained, any changes to the restaurant, including the lighting, may be perceived as altering the quality of the food. Lighting is often considered the most important element in the design of a restaurant. Thus, it is important to be sure that the lighting is ideal from the start.

The perfect lighting approach provides the appropriate illumination for tasks and creates the atmosphere. Lighting plays an important role in attracting people to a restaurant and how comfortable people feel while dining. Lighting on the outside of the restaurant must highlight characteristics outside that would entice people to come in. Lighting can help to inform the customer about the degree of formality and price range. Generally, understated lighting techniques are used for more formal and expensive restaurants. Bright, theatrical lighting schemes often reflect a more casual and moderate price range. Lighting that helps to communicate proper dress expectations and prices is especially useful for potential customers who are unfamiliar with the restaurant.

Lighting in the reception area should be exceptional, because this is the first impression customers have of the interior of the restaurant. As a transitional area from the outside, the reception area should have appropriate illumination levels, which assist with the adaptation function of eyes. A positive reaction will encourage people to stay and may reduce anxieties associated with waiting for a table. Lighting should help to create the desired emotional response to the thematic concept of the restaurant. A fine restaurant often has soft, warm illumination. Restaurants catering to people who are looking for an adventurous evening have lighting that is bright, colorful, and perhaps synchronized with music.

Lighting for walking through the restaurant should serve several purposes. For safety reasons, effective illumination must be provided in the pathway, especially transitional areas involving steps. However, lighting should not emphasize pathways. As people walk through the restaurant, illumination levels should change to emphasize the focal points in the space. Since people are drawn to light, emphatic areas on walls should have the highest level of illumination. Lighting levels should be lower in areas surrounding dining tables and pathways. Illumination for dining tables must fill several purposes. In large dining rooms, lighting can help to create an imaginary canopy over a table. This technique can help to create intimate areas within the context of dehumanizing spaces. Illumination should be adequate for people to be able to read menus. This is especially important for the elderly, who are likely to have vision problems. Lighting should enhance the appearance of food and people seated at the table. It is critical that lighting render the colors of food accurately. Deviations from true colors may be interpreted as spoiled food. Many chefs today consider presentation an important aspect of dining. Clear and concise lighting aimed at plates can enhance these presentations.

Restaurant lighting should enhance facial features and skin tones. This is especially important in restaurants that seek to have customers stay for a long period of time. People do not feel comfortable staying in an environment that makes them look bad. Lighting for dining tables should not be positioned to create ghoulish shadows on people's faces. This can frequently occur with downlights, which are a common luminaire used in restaurants. Often, downlights are positioned above the center of a table. In this location, shadows will not be cast on faces. However, tables are frequently moved in restaurants to accommodate different numbers of people seated at a table. These changes significantly affect the relationship between the downlights and the center of the table. In restaurants that have changeable floorplans, luminaires must be flexible. In addition to eliminating shadows on faces, the color rendering rating of lamps should enhance skin tones.

To accommodate all the purposes of lighting in restaurants, various sources should be coordinated by layered lighting techniques. Whenever possible, daylight is a wonderful source of illumination for restaurants serving breakfast, lunch, and brunch. Electrical sources should have a warm temperature, and, whenever possible, energy-efficient sources should be specified. To enhance the appearance of food and skin tones, incandescent lamps are frequently used in lighting systems. For some applications, CFLs would serve as an excellent energy-efficient alternative, and fluorescent lamps help to reduce heat generated by incandescent lamps. To help servers do their jobs efficiently, illumination at service stations should provide adequate lighting on beverages, utensils, and dishes while not creating an annoying source of brightness to patrons in the dining room.

Displays of fresh food should be illuminated by lamps with high CRI ratings and specialized designations. For example, cold and warm foods should be illuminated with cool beams and heat lamps, respectively. Protective shielded lamps should be specified for exposed food and cleaning areas. LED lamps and fiber optic sources can provide excellent illumination for menu boards, for areas under cabinets, and for architectural details. Accent lighting can highlight artwork and the sparkle of glassware. Light art can often create a remarkable focal point in a dining room or reception area (Figure 20.11). Colored lighting

FIGURE 20.11
A restaurant that has light art that serves as a focal point.

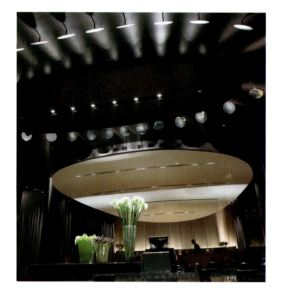

schemes should be used selectively, because of the potential distortion of food and skin tones.

Luminaires throughout a restaurant should be consistent in style and vary in relationship to the size of a room and its surroundings. The lighting system should provide variable settings for various times of the day. For example, illumination at lunchtime should be different from lighting in the evening hours. Lighting for each application should accommodate activities, the mood of the customers, and cultural influences. For example, the lighting system should easily shift from lunch conditions to quiet ambience in the evening. Frequently, during lunch hour in the United States, people discuss work and have little time for leisurely dining. Thus, some lighting techniques for lunchtime dining include fairly bright levels aimed at tabletops. People in other countries spend a much longer period of time eating lunch. Lighting in these restaurants should be conducive to a more casual and leisurely setting. Generally, dining in the evening has a relaxed and comfortable atmosphere. Thus, the lighting should reinforce this mood, by being warm and soft.

Technology and work-related tasks have started to become lighting considerations in restaurants. People are working at their computers in food service establishments, such as cyber cafés, Internet cafés, and Wi-Fi designated restaurants. "Hot spots" enable end users to surf the Web and execute data uploads/downloads. Lighting for these environments has many of the same criteria used in offices. In addition, illumination must be flexible to accommodate technology users, conversation, eating, and reading.

Retail Stores

The earliest retail stores were located at street level in residential buildings. Later designs included bazaars and arcades. These structures were dependent upon daylight for their operations. Thus, many of the stores had large glass windows lining the front of the building. The development of the large department store in the nineteenth century posed a lighting challenge. Engineers and architects had to design a structure that allowed daylight to penetrate the inner core of the building. A decorative approach to integrating daylight was to install skylights covered with beautiful stained glass (Figure 20.12). In addition, the perimeter of early department stores was lined with large windows. As electricity and electrical sources advanced, many retailers opted for eliminating the penetration of daylight, preferring being able to control the environment by manipulating electrical lights.

Currently, many retail stores, especially in shopping malls, do not have any interior daylight and are completely dependent upon electrical

FIGURE 20.12
An Art Nouveau style stained glass in a cupola of Au Printemps department store in Paris. Designed by Brière, the unit has over 3,000 individual pieces of glass.

illumination. However, recent research has indicated an increase in sales in retail stores that have daylight. The Heschong Mahone Group found that "skylights were found to be positively and significantly correlated to higher sales. All other things being equal, an average non-skylit store in the chain would likely have 40% higher sales with the addition of skylights, with a probable range between 31% and 49%" (1999, p. 2). In addition to creating a pleasant atmosphere, daylight integration can also help to reduce energy costs. This can be significant for a retail store because high-energy-consuming lamps are often used to enhance merchandise, people, and ambience.

Quality lighting is critical in retail stores and should be determined by the quality and type of merchandise. The quantity of lighting can be affected by the norms of a country. People living in countries outside the United States may prefer higher levels of illumination in retail stores. Effective lighting can help to promote sales and motivate customers to return to the store. Poor lighting can discourage people from entering the store and dampen sales. The goals of retailers are to project an image to consumers, attract customers to the store, focus attention on merchandise, reduce or eliminate returns, and create a memorable experience, which translates into future visits. Lighting has a major role in accomplishing all these goals. Lighting must reinforce the store's image. There is an enormous range of retail stores at every price range with a variety of products and services. Generally, lighting for a discount retail store has uniform, bright illumination from industrial luminaires. Higher-end stores have lower ambient light levels and spotlights that create the contrast required to highlight products. Each of these lighting techniques reflects an image and promotes a value statement. In addition, the quality of lighting supports the type of service in each establishment. Customers in discount stores require higher levels of illumination because such establishments are usually self-service. Higher-end retail stores provide personalized sales assistance, which transfers the primary product knowledge to the sales staff. Since employees are familiar with the store and its merchandise, customers do not need high levels of illumination to find products. To increase sales, especially of higher-priced items, higher-end retail stores are also interested in having an environment that encourages people to linger. The best lighting for this is a lower level of illumination and excellent color rendition.

As with the hospitality industry, a well-designed entrance is critical to presenting the first image to a customer. The entrance can help to differentiate a store from its competitors, attract the targeted customer, and create a sense of identity. A retail store in a shopping mall is especially challenged because there are many other stores nearby in competition for the same business. Thus, every retailer wants a storefront that will attract customers to their merchandise and then motivate them to come into the store to make purchases. A store's entrance should maintain consistency with the store image. Therefore, lighting must reinforce the image at the entrance and ensure adequate visibility of the merchandise. Seeing products can be problematic for stores exposed to the street. During the day, people looking at the merchandise in a window may experience significant glare from objects behind them. Reflected images cause the disability glare. The level of illumination from reflected images is much lower than the intensity of sunlight. To prevent glare on windows, the illumination levels in the window display must be greater than the level of reflected images. Exterior awnings can help to reduce glare.

Lighting for store windows is dependent upon the layout of the area. Window displays are designed with and without backs. The window display environment with backs is more controlled, and so lighting can be planned specifically for the merchandise within the confined space. This setting creates a situation in which spotlights can direct eyes to a product. Window displays without backs can be confusing to viewers because merchandise and lighting in the background create a diversion. However, many retailers prefer a window display with an open back because people walking by the store are able to see a lot of merchandise. To emphasize products in window displays without backs, illumination contrasts between the various areas should be carefully monitored, and other methods of attraction may be considered, such as using colored lights in the window or lighting with movement.

Once a customer has entered a store, lighting has a significant role in the overall plan of the space, circulation, and visual merchandising. As always, lighting should accommodate people with visual disabilities and help to assist in factors that involve other aspects of the principles of universal design. Layered lighting techniques must support the plan of the space and the objectives of merchandising. Frequently, lighting is used to designate various areas within a store. For example, in a department store, the cosmetics, shoe, and women's departments might have different levels of illumination and luminaires. Retailers often use different ceiling heights, surfaces, and colors to designate different areas or products.

Lighting can help significantly with the store's circulation plan. As customers enter a store or a different floor within the building, illumination should help people to quickly understand product categories and to find the easiest path to the area they want. Accurate identification of products requires excellent visual merchandising and strategic prioritization. Prioritization of departments and products must be determined by the client. Products that are impulse purchases are frequently a priority within a store. Lighting must be planned to reinforce the most important departments and products. This can be accomplished by a variety of methods, including varying illumination levels, altering the degree of focus, and using colored lighting schemes or different luminaires. For hierarchical lighting to be successful, there must be a concise and consistent strategy for prioritized departments and products throughout the store. Effective patterns of illumination can also assist with establishing a rhythm, that helps to guide customers' eyes to merchandise.

Lighting can assist in wayfinding, by illuminating the path to departments and merchandise. Frequently, light from ambient and accent sources can help to provide illumination for aisles. Illumination should assist customers in finding merchandise and contribute to their safety by highlighting changes in elevations, surface materials, and sharp corners of displays. Since customers walk through aisles from a variety of directions, to ensure a glare-free setting, lighting must be carefully analyzed from multiple points. This includes monitoring reflections from shiny finishes on walls and floors. For example, a highly polished marble floor can cause annoying glare from ceiling fixtures.

In addition to illumination in aisles, perimeter lighting can help customers to understand the size and shape of the store and to locate merchandise. Quickly comprehending the store's configuration encourages customers to explore the entire store. Customers unconsciously want simplicity in the design of the store and lighting. Extreme contrasts associated with luminaires mounted on dark-colored ceilings may be uncomfortably bright to customers. A confusing layout or disorganized lighting arrangement on the ceiling may discourage customers from shopping. Light fixtures, such as large track heads, that dominate a store distract from merchandise. Therefore, lighting should appear to be seamlessly integrated with architectural elements and retail fixturing equipment. Perimeter lighting can easily be integrated into vertical planes and must effectively illuminate signage and products found in the extreme areas of the store. Since people are drawn to light, perimeter wall illumination encourages customers to walk to all areas within a store. Customers will avoid dark spaces; therefore, a store plan must be carefully analyzed to determine the location of these areas. In addition, for security purposes, to help curtail theft, the sales staff must be able to see all areas within a store.

Quality lighting is critical to visual merchandising. Effective lighting must start with the product and an understanding of how to illuminate the most appealing characteristics of the merchandise. In stores with a lot of products in various colors, textures, and sizes, this is a significant challenge. Lighting must put the focus on a product or a detail of a product within a setting that has many items in close proximity. This requires an understanding of the characteristics of the product and a visualization prioritization scheme. Obviously, products are made from a variety of materials, colors, textures, shapes, and sizes. Lighting must be sufficiently flexible to accommodate the variables and changes in displays throughout the year. This becomes especially important when a retailer elects to highlight a specific area or characteristic of a product, such as the texture of a woolen sweater. Lighting flexibility can include a variety of factors, such as aiming angles, illumination intensities, color temperatures, and degree of focus. To enhance products and provide excellent visibility for evaluating merchandise, light sources should be as close to the merchandise as possible.

Some of the most challenging aspects of retail lighting are simultaneously illuminating horizontal and vertical surfaces within an environment of high contrast ratios. Successful applications include knowing the elements of the environment and the retail fixturing equipment. Retailers use stock or custom-designed fixturing. Custom-designed fixturing provides more opportunities for integrating lighting within the unit. This is especially important for equipment with dark finishes. Fixturing that requires horizontal illumination, such as tables, counters, and gondolas or aisle units, must have lighting that provides consistent illumination for all the products that might be on multiple shelves.

Frequently, merchandise located on a bottom shelf is in darkness. A variety of methods can help to illuminate shelves, including specifying internally lit units or aiming spotlights directly at shelves. Spotlighting merchandise on tables or gondolas is easier to accomplish with tiered units, which expose merchandise on every shelf (Figure 20.13). To maximize illumination, the interiors of fixturing units should be white or a light color. To illuminate products on counters or in cases made of glass, the best approach is to locate light sources in the units. Fiber optic systems are rapidly becoming popular for display cases. (Chapter 15 provides information about illumination methods for display cases.) Merchandise displayed on walls or racks requires lighting methods used for illuminating vertical surfaces, such as cornices, soffits, or wall brackets. Lighting must be positioned to illuminate all the merchandise displayed on the walls, from products located close to the ceiling to those down near the floor.

FIGURE 20.13
The tiered shelving unit enables light to strike merchandise on each shelf.

Serious consideration should be given to the areas within a store that are typically point-of-purchase locations. Important areas are dressing rooms and the sales transaction counter. Frequently, illumination in dressing rooms is derived from industrial types of luminaires, with light sources that have low color rendering ratings. Lighting in dressing rooms should enhance the appearance of the merchandise and the customers, because this is one of the most critical decision points for a consumer. Lighting should surround mirrors and provide excellent color rendition. Lighting should also be excellent at the point where people are purchasing merchandise because customers can easily change their mind and not buy the product.

Quality lighting for retail stores must balance the goals of the retailer, energy codes, and environmental concerns. To enhance merchandise and increase sales, frequently, retailers use high-energy-consuming lamps, such as incandescent and halogen lamps. However, to comply with energy codes and maximum watts-per-square-foot requirements, energy-efficient lighting systems with the lowest life cycle costs should be considered. The watts-per-square-foot maximums prescribed by energy codes are based upon the type of retail spaces. For example, mass merchandising buildings have more stringent requirements than do boutiques. Daylight integration can help to satisfy energy code requirements.

Energy-efficient lighting systems for retail stores also include selecting the appropriate luminaire and electrical source. For example, in a retail environment that requires multiple highlighted areas, low-voltage track systems are more energy-efficient than line-voltage tracks. Highlights should be done with narrow beam spots rather than with flood lamps. Lamps in a retail environment should have long life, excellent color rendition, and high light output. Currently, halogen, fluorescent, and metal halide lamps are the most energy-efficient sources. Tremendous technological improvements in metal-halide lamps have precipitated great interest in using this source for multiple retail applications. Improvements in LEDs and fiber optics will provide more energy-efficient solutions in the future.

Color rendition will always be critical in retail stores. Ideal sources have CRI ratings of 100 and warm color temperatures between

3000 to 3200 Kelvin. Specific attention should be given to the phenomenon associated with metamerism. In particular, colors of products must be consistent in display areas, dressing rooms, and the sales transaction counter. Returns frequently occur because customers are not happy with a color after they leave the store. Thus, lighting should depict the color as true as possible, and daylight is an excellent source for this. Some retailers use colored lights to attract attention to products and to differentiate departments within the store. Light art has become a popular method for attracting consumers; however, neon lights have always been used in retail settings, especially in trendy, theatrical settings.

As with all commercial environments, controls have a significant role in conserving energy and creating various settings for different moods. Retail stores should have automatic controls that are calibrated with the store's operating hours. For limited applications, occupancy sensors could be set to dim lights when departments are unoccupied and to increase illumination levels when someone enters a space. Generally, occupancy sensors are only effective in retail establishments with low traffic. Controls can be programmed for various scenes in different departments at various times of the day. This should include a special arrangement for evening maintenance. Efficient lamp maintenance is critical in a retail environment because products in the dark do not sell. Lamps should be fast to replace, accessible, and easy to change. Such lamps help the maintenance staff and sales associates who often must replace lamps during store hours. The number of types of lamps should be kept to a minimum, because relamping can be very confusing when multiple sources are used in various locations in the store.

Creating a quality lighting environment for commercial structures is a complex process. Quality lighting environments do not have prescriptive solutions. All clients should be provided with a lighting plan that is unique to the needs of their users, interior elements, and the site. Illumination must accommodate a variety of people performing numerous tasks in very diverse settings. Interior designers must be cognizant of how world events can affect corporate and institutional philosophies, because such occurrences will affect interiors and lighting. Continuous changes in technology significantly influence lighting systems. Therefore, improvements in the field of lighting should be constantly monitored in order for the designer to specify the most energy-efficient technologies. This is especially critical for commercial buildings, because of the enormous consumption of electricity.

SUMMARY

- Effectively designing the lighting for a commercial interior requires an understanding of the organization's mission, goals, and objectives.
- Progressive lighting approaches reflect a combination of knowledge of the future directions of the industry and an understanding of how current events affect lighting environments.
- Lighting for commercial interiors must be planned, installed, and evaluated within the parameters of the budget and time line.
- Elevators require special illumination strategies because people who use them may be unfamiliar with a building and because a variety of environmental conditions can exist in areas surrounding elevators.
- Quality illumination in hallways must help people to locate exit doors, understand the layout of a floor, and enhance the appearance of an area in a building that can often be dull.
- Lighting systems for commercial interiors should enhance visual comfort while accommodating functional and aesthetic requirements. A goal for the lighting plan should always be to have a minimal impact on the local and global environment.
- Lighting for offices is affected by management philosophies and technology used by employees. Management is always interested in operating a profitable business by producing quality work and retaining excellent employees.
- Tasks performed in an office can cause problems with vision and musculoskeletal injuries, such as carpal tunnel syndrome (CTS).
- Lighting for educational facilities should be efficient and support philosophies of learning.
- Healthcare facilities include hospitals, medical offices, clinics, and

residential long-term care units. In addition to providing effective lighting for medical procedures, interiors need lighting that improves the psychological well-being of patients and meets the needs of family members.

- ■ In designing hotel lighting, it is important to understand the concerns of the hotel industry and the client's corporate philosophy. Hotels are part of the service industry; thus, customer satisfaction is the primary focus.

- ■ Lighting plays an important role in attracting people to a restaurant and how comfortable people feel while dining. To accommodate all the purposes of lighting in restaurants, various sources should be coordinated in layered lighting techniques.

- ■ Quality lighting is critical in retail stores and should be determined by the quality and type of merchandise. The goals of retailers are to project an image to consumers, attract customers to the store, focus attention on merchandise, reduce or eliminate returns, and create a memorable experience, which translates into future visits. Lighting has a major role in accomplishing all these goals.

Key Terms

cave-like	localized lighting

Exercises

1. Search the World Wide Web for three corporations and institutions. Locate their mission statement and/or business philosophy. In a written report describe how corporate philosophies can be applied to lighting design.

2. Search the World Wide Web for current energy codes and the most energy-efficient lamps, luminaires, and controls for commercial buildings. Locate all specification data for each product. Compile the resources in a file that is divided into energy codes, luminaires, lamps, and controls.

3. Identify an office, school classroom, and a public area in a healthcare facility to observe during various times of the day and week. In a written report that may include sketches and photographs, address the items listed below:
   a. Determine if the space meets all the criteria for a quality lighting environment. How can the lighting be improved?
   b. Determine how well the space addresses current industry practice and the corporate mission statement.
   c. Given the users and elements of the space, identify special vision needs.
   d. Determine the human response elicited from the space and identify the lighting techniques that contribute to the response.
   e. Evaluate the energy efficiency of the lighting system, including daylight integration. How can the space be improved to conserve energy and natural resources?
4. Identify a restaurant, retail store, and a public area in a hotel and observe them during various times of the day and week. In a written report that may include sketches and photographs, address the items listed below:
   a. Determine if the space meets all the criteria for a quality lighting environment. How can the lighting be improved?
   b. Determine how well the space addresses current industry practice and the corporation's mission.
   c. Given the users and elements of the space, identify special vision needs.
   d. Determine the human response elicited from the space and identify the lighting techniques that contribute to the response.
   e. Evaluate the energy efficiency of the lighting system, including daylight integration. How can the space be improved to conserve energy and natural resources?

REFERENCES

Abercrombie, S. (1998). *Corporate Interiors, No. 2.* New York: Retail Reporting Corporation.
Allphin, W. (1961). BCD appraisals of luminaire brightness in a simulated office. *Illuminating Engineering, 56(1),* 31–44.

American Hotel & Lodging Association (2003). *2003 Lodging Industry Profile.* Washington, DC: American Hotel & Lodging Association.

Ander, G. (1997). *Daylighting Performance & Design.* New York: John Wiley & Sons.

Archea, J. (1985). Environmental factors associated with stair accidents by the elderly. *Clinics in Geriatric Medicine, 1,* 555–569.

Ballman, T.L., and Levin, R.E. (1987). Illumination in partitioned spaces. *Journal of the Illuminating Engineering Society, 16(2),* 31–49.

Baraban, R.S., and Durocher, J.F. (2001). *Successful Restaurant Design.* 2d edition, New York: John Wiley & Sons.

Barr, W., and Broudy, C. (1985). *Designing to Sell: A Complete Guide to Retail Store Planning and Design.* New York: McGraw-Hill.

Beauchemin, K.M., and Hays, P. (1996). Sunny hospital rooms expedite recovery from severe and refractory depressions. *Journal of Affective Disorders, 40,* 49–51.

Benya, J.R. (December 1–6, 2001). *Lighting for Schools.* Washington, DC: National Clearinghouse for Educational Facilities.

Benya, J., Heschong, L., McGowan, T., Miller, N., and Rubinstein, F. (2001). *Advanced Lighting Guidelines.* White Salmon, WA: New Buildings Institute.

Bernstien, A., and Conway, K. (March 2000). *The Public Benefits of California's Investments in Energy Efficiency.* Prepared for the California Energy Commission by the RAND Corporation. MR-1212.0-CEC.

Bornholdt, D. (2001). *Green Suites International & GE Lighting Team to Bring Solid Energy Savings to Light.* http://www.hospitalitynet.org.

Boubekri, M., Hull, IV, R.B., and Boyer, L.L. (1991). Impact of window size and sunlight penetration on office workers' mood and satisfaction: A novel way of assessing sunlight. *Environment and Behavior, 23,* 474–493.

Boyce, P.N., Eklund, N., and Simpson, S. (1999). Individual lighting control: Task performance, mood and illuminance. *IESNA Conference Proceedings, 1999.* New York: Illuminating Engineering Society of North America.

Boyce, P.N., Elkund, N., and Simpson, S. (2000). Individual lighting control: Task performance, mood and illuminance. *Journal of the Illuminating Engineering Society, 29(1),* 131–142.

Boykin, P.J. (1991). *Hotel Guestroom Design.* Dubuque, IA: Kendall/Hunt Publishing.

British Standards Institution (1992). *Code of Practice for Daylighting.* British Standard BS 8206 Part 2.

Building Codes Assistance Project (January 1999). *Energy Conservation and Code Updates: Status of State Energy Codes.* Last updated January 1999. http://www.energycodes.org/states/states.htm.

Bush-Brown, A. (1992). *Hospitable Design for Healthcare and Senior Communities.* New York: Van Nostrand Reinhold.

California Energy Commission (July 1999). *Building Energy Efficiency Standards.* Title 24 Pt. 6.

Chartered Institution of Building Services Engineers (1987). *Window Design.* CIBSE Applications Manual. London: CIBSE.

Clark, C. (2001). Computers are causing health problems. *Journal of End User Computing, 13(1),* 34–45.

Coaton, J.R., and Marsden, A.M. (1997). *Lamps and Lighting,* 4th Edition. London: Arnold.

Cohen, E.L., and Emery, S.R. (1984). *Dining by Design.* New York: Van Nostrand Reinhold.

Dorf, M.E. (August 1992). *Restaurants that Work.* New York: Whitney Library of Design.

Ducker Research (1999). *Lighting Quality—Key Customer Values and Decision Process.* Report to the Light Right Research Consortium.

Duro-Test Lighting (2003). *Importance of Lighting in Schools.* http://www.full-spectrum-lighting.com. 1–3.

Fannin, J. (2003). Hotel safety: Consumer demand presents a marketing opportunity. *HSMAI Marketing Review,* Spring, 27–33.

Fitch, R., and Knobel, L. (1990). *Retail Design.* New York: Whitney Library of Design.

Flynn, J.E. (1977). A study of subjective responses to low energy and nonuniform lighting systems. *Lighting Design and Application,* 7, 6–15.

Flynn, J.E., and Spencer, T.J. (1977). The effects of light source color on user impression and satisfaction. *Journal of the Illuminating Engineering Society.* 4, 167–179.

Garling, T., Book, A., and Lindberg, E. (1986). Spatial orientation and wayfinding in the designed environment: A conceptual analysis and some suggestions for postoccupancy evaluation. *Journal of Architectural and Planning Research,* 3, 55–64.

Gosling, D., and Maitl, B. (1976). *Design and Planning of Retail Systems.* New York: Whitney Library of Design.

Grabois, E., Nosek, M., and Rossi, C. (1999). Accessibility in physician's offices. *Archives of Family Medicine,* 8(1), 44–51.

Green Suites International (2001). *Green Suites International & GE Lighting Team to Bring Solid Energy Savings to Light.* http://www.hospitalitynet.org.

Herzog, T., Black, A., Fountaine, K., and Knotts, D. (1997). Benefits of restorative environment. *Journal of Environmental Psychology,* 17(2), 165–170.

Heschong Mahone Group (HMG) (May 1997). *The Lighting Efficiency Technology Report, vol. I: California Lighting Baseline.* For the California Energy Commission.

Heschong Mahone Group (HMG) (August 1999). *Skylighting and Retail Sales, and Daylighting in Schools.* For Pacific Gas & Electric. http://www.pge.com.pec/daylight.

Hiatt, L. (1991). *Nursing Home Renovation Designed for Reform.* Boston: Butterworth.

Hill, H., and Bruce, V. The effects of lighting on the perception of facial surfaces. *Journal of Experimental Psychology: Human Perception and Performance,* 22(4), 986–1004.

Howell, S., and Ira C. (1987). *Designing for Aging: Patterns of Use.* Cambridge, MA: MIT Press.

Hughes, P.C. (1980). The use of light and color in health. In A.C. Hastings, J. Fadiman, and J.S. Gordon (eds.), *The Complete Guide to Holistic Medicine: Health for the Whole Person.* Boulder, CO: Westview Press, pp. 294–308.

Hughes, P.C., and McNelis, J.F. (1978). Lighting, productivity, and the work environment. *Lighting Design and Application,* 8(12), 32–38.

Illuminating Engineering Society of North America (IESNA) (2000). *IESNA Lighting Handbook,* 9th edition. New York: Illuminating Engineering Society of North America.

Institute of Store Planners (2001). *Stores and Retail Spaces.* Cincinnati, OH: ST Publications.

Institute of Store Planners (2002). *Stores and Retail Spaces.* Cincinnati, OH: ST Publications.

Kreith, F., and West, R.E. (1996). *CRC Handbook of Energy Efficiency.* London: CRC Press.

Kuller, R., and Laike, T. (1998). The impact of flicker fluorescent lighting on well-being, performance and physiological arousal. *Ergonomics,* 4, 433–447.

Kwallek, N., and Lewis, C.M. (1990). Effects of environmental colour on males and females: A red or white or green office. *Applied Economics,* 21, 275–278.

Lamarre, L. (1995). Lighting the office environment. *EPRI Journal,* 20(3), 22–27.

Lane, M. (1996). *School Classrooms.* Lighting Design Lab. http://www.lightingdesignlab.com. 1–2.

Lang, S. (2003). Good lighting for healthcare buildings. *Business Briefing: Hospital Engineering & Facilities Management.* Berkeley, CA: Lawrence Berkeley National Laboratory.

Lawrence Berkeley National Laboratory. (1992). *Analysis of Federal Policy Options for Improving U.S. Lighting Energy Efficiency.* Berkeley, CA: Lawrence Berkeley National Laboratory.

Lawrence Berkeley National Laboratory (2003). *Lighting Energy Savings Opportunities in Hotel Guest Rooms: Results from a scoping study at the Redondo Beach Crown Plaza.* http://lighting/lbl.gov.

Leibrock, C.A. (2000). *Design Details for Health: Making the Most of Interior Design's Healing Potential.* New York: John Wiley & Sons.

Lerum, V., and Buvik, K. (2000). Sun, light, and air: Monitoring the energy performance of the new Grong school building. *ASES Solar 2000 Conference,* Madison, WI. 493–497.

Littlefair, P.J. (1991). *Site Layout Planning for Daylight and Sunlight: A Guide To Good Practice.* BRE Report BR 209.

Littlefair, P.J. (1996). *Designing with Innovative Daylighting.* London: CRC, Garston.

Lodging Magazine. (March, 1–4, 2003). Lodging trends. *Lodging Magazine,* http://www.lodgingmagazine.com, 1-4.

Malkin, J. (1992). *Hospital Interior Architecture: Creating Healing Environments.* New York: Van Nostrand Reinhold.

Malkin, J. (2002). *Medical & Dental Space Planning: A Comprehensive Guide to Design, Equipment, & Clinical Procedures.* New York: John Wiley & Sons.

Maniccia, D., Rutledge, D., Rea, M., and Morrow, W. (1999). Occupant use of manual lighting control in private offices. *Journal of the Illuminating Engineering Society 28(2),* 42–56.

Maniccia, D., Von Neida, B., and Tweed, A. (2000). Analysis of the energy and cost savings potential of occupancy sensors for commercial lighting systems. *Proceedings of the 2000 Annual Conference of the Illuminating Engineering Society of North America.*

Marans, R.W., and Yan, X. (1989). Lighting quality and environmental satisfaction in open and enclosed offices. *Journal of Architectural and Planning Research,* 6, 118–131.

Mattila, A.S. (2001). Creating customer loyalty in restaurants. *Cornell Hotel and Restaurant Administration Quarterly,* 42(6), 73–79.

Mazzurco, P. (1986). *Bath Design.* New York: Whitney Library of Design.

McGowan, J. (2002). Buildings online. *Energy User News.* http://www.energyusernews.com.

Mishimia, K., Okawa, M., Hiskikawa, Y., Hozumi, S., Hori, H., and Takashi, M. (1994). Morning bright therapy for sleep and behavior disorders in elderly patients with dementia. *Acta Psychiatry Scandinavia,* 89, 1–7.

National Lighting Bureau (1988). *Office Lighting and Productivity.* Washington, DC: National Lighting Bureau.

Northeast Energy Efficiency Partnership (2002). *Combining Quality Design and Energy Efficiency for Private Offices, Open-Plan Offices, Office Corridors.* www.neep.org.

Northeast Energy Efficiency Partnership (2000). *Combining Quality Design and Energy Efficiency for Small Retail Lighting.* www.neep.org.

Northeast Energy Efficiency Partnership (2000). *Combining Quality Design and Energy Efficiency for Retail and Grocery Daylighting.* www.neep.org.

Northeast Energy Efficiency Partnership (2002). *"Energy Effective" Lighting for Classrooms: Combining Quality Design and Energy Efficiency.* www.neep.org.

Novak, A. (1977). *Store Planning and Design.* New York: Lebhar Friedman.

Passini, R. (1984). *Wayfinding in Architecture,* New York: Van Nostrand Reinhold.

Passini, R., Pigot, H., Rainville, C., and Tetreault, M.H. (2000). Wayfinding in a nursing home for advanced dementia of the Alzheimer's type. *Environment and Behavior,* 32(5), 684–710.

Pegler, M.M. (2001). *Stores of the Year, No.13.* New York: Visual Reference Publications.

Pile, J. (1978). *Open Office Planning: A Handbook for Interior Designers and Architects.* New York: Whitney Library of Design.

Piotrowski, C., and Rogers, E. (1999) *Designing Commercial Interiors.* New York: John Wiley & Sons.

Plympton, P., Conway, S., and Epstein, K. (2000). Daylighting in schools: Improving student performance and health at a price schools can afford. *ASES Solar 2000 Passive Conference,* Madison, WI., 487–492.

Ravetto, A. (1994). Daylighting schools in North Carolina. *Solar Today, 8(2),* 22–24.

Rea, M.S. (1998). The quest for the ideal office controls system. *LRC Lighting Futures 1998, (3).*

Research Group for Inclusive Environments (RGIE). Task lighting for visually impaired people in an office environment. *Research Group for Inclusive Environments (RGIE).* http://www.rdg.ac.uk

Rothman, M. (1987). Designing work environments to influence productivity. *Journal of Business and Psychology.* 1, 390–550.

Russell, B. (1981). *The Interiors Book of Shops and Restaurants.* New York: Watson-Guptill.

Siguaw, J.A., and Enz, C.A. (1999). Designing hotel restaurants for profitability. *Cornell Hotel and Restaurant Administration Quarterly, 40(5),* 50–57.

Simeonova, M. (2003). Healthy lighting. *The Center for Health Design.* http://www.healthdesign.org. 1-3.

Slater, A., Bordass, B., and Heasman, T. (March 1996). Give people control of lighting controls. *IAELL Newsletter.*

Sleep Foundation (2003). *The Impact of Sleep Problems.* http://www.sleepfoundation.org, 1-12.

Sorcar, P.C. (1987). *Architectural Lighting for Commercial Interiors.* New York: John Wiley & Sons.

Thayer, B. (1995). A daylight school in North Carolina. *Solar Today, 9(6),* 36–39.

Thompson, G.M. (2002). Planning restaurant seating. *Cornell Hotel and Restaurant Administration Quarterly, 43(4),* 48–57.

United States Environmental Protection Agency (EPA) (2001). *Design for the Environment.* http://www.epa.gov/.

Veitch, J., and Newsham, G. (2000). Exercised control, lighting choices, and energy use: An office simulation experiment. *Journal of Environmental Psychology* 20(3), 219–237.

Veitch, J.A., and Newsham, G.R. (June 24–30, 1999). Preferred luminous conditions in open-plan offices: Implications for lighting quality recommendations. *Proceedings of the Commission Internationale de l'Eclairage (CIE) 24th Session, Warsaw, Poland,* Vol. 1, Part 2, Vienna, Austria: CIE Central Bureau, pp. 4–6.

Veitch, J., and Newsham, G. (January 1999). Individual control can be energy efficient. *IAEEL Newsletter.*

Weinhold, V. (1988). *Interior Finish Materials for Health Care Facilities.* Springfield, IL: Charles C Thomas.

Weishar, J. (1992). *Design for Effective Selling Space.* New York: McGraw-Hill.

Whitehead, R. (2002). *Lighting Design Sourcebook.* Gloucester, MA: Rockport Publishers.

LIGHTING DESIGN PROCESS

CHAPTER 21

Lighting Design Process: Initial Phases

OBJECTIVES

■ Identify the activities involved in the seven phases of the lighting design process.

■ Describe important elements and activities of the planning phase.

■ Identify the information that should be collected during the comprehensive programming phase and then be applied to developing the lighting criteria.

■ Understand relevant lighting-related information that should be collected by interviewing, surveying, and observing end users of an interior.

■ Understand relevant lighting-related information that should be recorded by analyzing the physical attributes of an interior.

■ Identify investigations that should be conducted to determine current codes, lighting systems, and research studies.

BASIC concepts and elements of a quality lighting environment, including components of lighting systems, daylight integration, directional effects of illumination, energy considerations, environmental factors related to lighting, and human factors are explored in Unit I. This content serves as the foundation for exploring specific applications in Unit II. Interior applications focus on safety, security, illuminating visual art, light art, interior architecture, inspirational mediums, and residential and commercial interiors. Unit III serves as the culminating experience of the textbook. The primary purpose of Unit III is to explain the lighting design process within the context of the content in Units I and II. Lighting design is performed by architects, interior designers, and lighting designers. Frequently, a lighting designer develops the lighting design for an architect or interior designer.

To provide a thorough analysis of the lighting design process, the information is broken down into three chapters. Chapter 21 covers project management and provides specific details regarding the project planning process and methods for conducting the comprehensive programming phase. Chapter 22 explains the lighting design phases related to schematic design and design development. As the concluding chapter in Unit III, Chapter 23 delineates contractual documents, contract administration, and evaluation.

Project Management

Managing a lighting project involves a series of phases and extensive planning.

Phases of the Lighting Design Process

Successful lighting designers must have excellent business and management skills. Many talented lighting designers have not been able to sustain a business because they did not give adequate attention to operational functions, such as managing finances or project administration. Successful management of a business includes planning the details of a project. The planning process can help to identify most of the factors that are critical to the success of the project, including costs, code restrictions, installation requirements, maintenance factors, and professional expertise. Thus, a lighting designer, in consultation with other team members, should always dedicate the time to thoroughly plan every project. The lighting design process may be divided into the following seven phases: (1) project planning, (2) comprehensive programming, (3) schematic design, (4) design development, (5) contract documentation, (6) contract administration, and (7) evaluation (Figure 21.1). Client involvement is essential at every phase of the lighting design process to ensure satisfaction with and approval of the elements of the program, including illumination plans, schedules, and budget.

This chapter discusses project planning and comprehensive programming. As a result of gathering data through programming, the criteria of the lighting project are used as the foundation for developing schematic designs. As a conceptual phase, many schematics of the lighting environment are explored with the client and the team of professionals involved in the project. Some of the schematic drawings include bubble diagrams, lighting distribution diagrams, and task/lighting relationship sketches. A successful schematic design is expounded and detailed in the design development phase. At this stage in the lighting design process, specific illumination methods, lighting systems, and layouts are presented to a client for discussion and evaluation. Upon

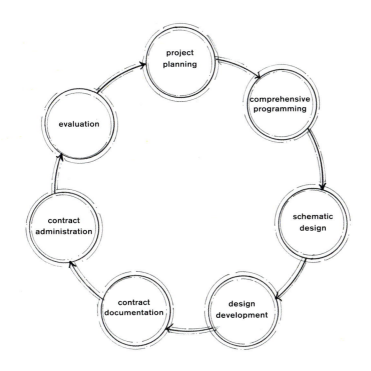

FIGURE 21.1
The lighting design process as divided into seven phases: (1) project planning, (2) comprehensive programming, (3) schematic design, (4) design development, (5) contract documentation, (6) contract administration, and (7) evaluation. As a cyclical process the evaluation phase provides useful information to improving the lighting environment for the existing client and future projects.

approval by the client, registered professionals, such as architects and engineers, enter the contract documentation phase and begin developing working drawings, specifications, sections, cut sheets, and purchase orders. A lighting designer develops lighting specifications and submits them to registered professionals for review and final determination.

The contract administration phase is the implementation stage of the project. To complete the project as specified, including within the prescribed time line and budget, a lighting designer should work closely with vendors and professionals involved in construction and installation. The evaluation phase takes place after people are using a space or a building. Often referred to as postoccupancy evaluation, the purpose of this phase is to determine user satisfaction with the lighting design. The data gathered in this phase should be used to improve any design problems. As illustrated by the directional arrows in Figure 21.1, information learned in the evaluation phase should be used to benefit plans for future clients. A process focusing on continued improvement will result in the best possible quality lighting environments.

Project Planning

The primary purposes of planning are to develop a profile of the project and to determine resources that will be needed to achieve the objectives. A lighting designer may be hired by a variety of people associated with residential and commercial interiors. Therefore, the lighting designer's client might be the owner(s), an architect, an engineer, or a contractor.

To develop the best possible lighting plan, a lighting designer should be involved in the planning stage of the entire project. Within the context of the project's objectives and time line, a lighting designer develops a plan for the lighting. The objectives of the lighting project are determined in consultation with the client and other professionals. Most lighting projects will have objectives related to users, tasks, interior elements, spatial geometry, technology, illumination methods, codes, time lines, budgets, and maintenance. Well-defined objectives outline the project and serve as the basis for the planning process.

The profile of the project, for planning purposes, should include a preliminary understanding of the needs of the owner, end users, and elements of the property. Understanding the scope of the work helps to determine the amount of time and resources needed to execute the project. This is critical information the lighting designer should acquire during the planning stages, because a client may have unreasonable expectations concerning the amount of time needed for construction, the feasibility of a design, or the cost of lighting systems. Clarifying the parameters of the project at the start of the project helps a client to understand the reality of a construction project and establish priorities, and it can serve as the basis for the lighting designer's consultation fee schedule. As discussed in Chapters 19 and 20, a client may have multiple goals for an interior, including meeting the needs of residents, employees, or customers. For planning purposes, a lighting designer should learn the client's priorities for the site and get an overall profile of the end users. The designer should also find out about other professionals involved with the project, the projected schedule, the estimated budget, and conservation practices. The programming phase, discussed in the next section of this chapter, provides suggestions for attaining detailed information from end users and about the site.

The enormous diversity associated with interior projects mandates a thorough understanding of a specific assignment. For example, a lighting project could be in an existing space or a new construction. A project could be one small room in a cottage or an entire hotel. The end user(s) might be one person or hundreds with a variety of disabilities. Each situation has specific factors that significantly affect the planning process. Therefore, initial discussions with a client must include specifics related to the parameters of the project. For planning purposes, a lighting designer must know the location of the property and whether the project involves an existing building, new construction, or speculative construction. Developing a lighting design for an existing structure might involve minor adjustments to an installation, retrofitting, or a completely new lighting scheme for an interior project with extensive renovation. For new construction, the planning phase significantly affects the lighting plan. Ideally, the lighting plan should be developed in concert with the architectural concept. Planning at this stage provides the opportunity for the designer to successfully integrate daylight and to create a design that enhances the appearance of the interior. The range of lighting possibilities diminishes as construction proceeds. Once walls, ceilings, and floors are finished, integrating structural and portable luminaires can be difficult and costly to install. Speculative construction projects require a lighting plan that appeals to a variety of people.

Early in the planning process, a lighting designer should visit a site with the client. A walk-through with the client provides an excellent opportunity for discussing existing lighting problems and constraints and the initial ideas. In consultation with the owner, it should be determined whether luminaires should be replaced, eliminated, remain in the space, or retrofitted. Initial visits should also include recording significant architectural details, preliminary measurements of rooms, existing luminaires, and location of electrical outlets. Daylight integration should be noted, as should reflectance characteristics of interior surfaces. Photographs of the interior should be taken. Information regarding end users should also be obtained, including the number of people and the type of work conducted in each location. This information becomes important in determining the scope of the project. Two different projects might have the same square footage, but a building that has many identical rooms in which a specific task is performed will generally require less time to design than a structure with different activities occurring in every room.

Information gathered during initial discussions with the client and site visits is very useful in identifying professionals who are needed to plan and implement the project. As members of the project team, these individuals should be involved as early as possible. Every project requires expertise from a variety of disciplines, including architects, interior designers, lighting designers, engineers, contractors, electricians, building inspectors, manufacturers' representatives, and craftspeople. Frequently, consultants are hired to provide advice regarding acoustics, safety, security, restoration, and energy conservation. Projects with many professionals should have a communication plan, which outlines an information dissemination process and procedures for changing orders. The communication plan should delineate who is involved in every scheduled meeting through all phases of the lighting design process. The plan should indicate who is responsible for final decisions and delineate spending authorization policies.

A clear process for communication is especially important when changes occur in a project. A change in program requirements can dramatically affect many aspects of a project. For example, late in the project, a lighting designer might be notified by a manufacturer that a luminaire has been discontinued. This can trigger multiple problems for a project. A replacement luminaire will have to be selected and then be approved by the client. The new luminaire might be smaller or larger than the original fixture. Depending upon the construction stage, reconfiguring an installation may be extremely costly. A new CRI rating of a lamp or the finish of the fixture might not be compatible with the furnishings and interior materials that were originally specified. Changes in a project cause delays, increase construction costs, and reduce the ROI. A communication plan that outlines procedures for changing orders can expedite the process and help to control overrun costs.

In consultation with the client, the team members should develop a comprehensive plan, which includes the list of activities, responsible individuals, time line, required resources, estimated costs, and billing dates (Table 21.1). Many software packages are available for program management. As illustrated in Table 21.1, a project schedule indicates the time line for activities, including important start/finish dates. Start/finish dates are critical to the success of completing a project on time and within the budget. For example, a project activity schedule should include dates for ordering and installing luminaires. The date for installing the luminaires is dependent upon electrical wiring. In addition, electricians are dependent upon the delivery dates of luminaires. Start/finish dates that are not followed can cause excessive delays and increase costs. The time line for ordering products and installations must be carefully planned. The timing for ordering lighting systems should be planned to ensure delivery when installation will occur. Generally, deliveries that arrive too early can be problematic because storage can be expensive, and the supplier will demand payment

TABLE 21.1

Project Activity Schedule

Project:			Location:			
Client:						

Phase/Activities	Start Date	Finish Date	Individual(s) Responsible	Special Considerations	Estimated Cost	Billing Date
Phase II: Comprehensive programming						
Phase III: Schematic design						
Phase IV: Design development						
Phase V: Contract documents						
Phase VI: Contract administration						
Phase VII: Evaluation						

before the client can be billed. Creating an activity schedule that successfully balances the contingencies and variables requires effective communication among all the professionals involved in the project, including product manufacturers' representatives and installers.

Comprehensive Programming

The comprehensive programming phase includes interviews, observations, and an assessment of lighting systems and research initiatives.

Interviews and Field Observations

Preliminary information gleaned from the project planning phase provides the foundation for determining the type of data needed to design a quality lighting environment. It is during the comprehensive programming phase that data are collected about the end users, the physical characteristics of the space, a review of the literature, and the applicable codes, ordinances, and regulations. To obtain information about end users and the interior, effective methodologies are interviews, surveys, and field observations. In addition, a review of research related to lighting should be conducted. The results of research can provide excellent insight and may be used to supplement data gathered in this phase. Interviews should be conducted with the client and, whenever possible, end users of the space. End users in task-oriented commercial interiors are generally employees and perhaps visitors. In customer-oriented commercial interiors, end users are employees and customers. For large organizations, it might not be possible to interview all end users. In these situations, sample interviews may be conducted with representative groups. The results of these interviews may be used to develop surveys, which would then be distributed to the remaining end users. Generally, it is impossible to gather data from all end users of large commercial interiors. The goal is to collect enough information to be able to make generalizations about the lighting environment.

Interviews and surveys provide good information regarding how the lighting design is perceived. However, it is difficult for people to describe in detail how they work or live in a space. Interviews and surveys cannot prompt all the questions that might be relevant to understanding behavior in a space. The best solution is to combine information learned from interviews and surveys with the results of field observations. Multiple methodologies provide the greatest insight into human behavior and help to validate results by reinforcing data derived from various methods. For example, during an interview a client might indicate that spotlights help to attract customers to a specific display. However, in observing customers in the store, it might be revealed that customers rarely look at the highlighted merchandise. Conflicting data need to be resolved in discussions with the client and perhaps engaging in more observation.

Effective interviews and surveys require research and preparation. Information learned from initial site visits and preliminary interviews with the client serve as the foundation for more specific questions. Questions can be written in a structured or semistructured format.

A structured arrangement is a list of questions without flexibility for asking follow-up questions. This format may be necessary when interviewing or surveying many end users. A semistructured format includes a list of questions that enables the interviewer to ask additional questions for clarification purposes or to obtain more information. In order to develop a list of questions that will generate the most useful information, the questions should be pretested with a sample group of end users and revised if necessary.

Interview and survey questions should always include an assessment of the present situation and anticipated future needs. Interview questions for a residential client should focus on the needs of individuals who live in the residence and the specific activities that take place in rooms. Table 21.2 provides examples of questions that might be asked at interviews or surveys of residential clients. Questions may be divided into the following: (1) characteristics of the end users, including physiological and psychological attributes, (2) activity assessment, (3) perceptions of lighting, and (4) anticipated changes in the future. The survey or interview questions should be modified to accommodate the unique needs and characteristics of each client. This is especially important when designing the lighting for international clients. Different culture and life experiences can affect expectations and perceptions of a lighting environment. Therefore, understanding the end users' perceptions of lighting is important in planning an environment that will meet their needs.

Understanding various perceptions of a lighting environment is important in commercial interiors as well as in residences. A demographic profile will help to identify characteristics of the end users. To determine perceptions of lighting, interview questions for commercial clients should be tailored for specific end users. For example, in designing the lighting for a restaurant, different questions should be written for the owner(s), hostess, servers, maintenance crew, new customers, and returning patrons. Each group is engaged in different activities in the restaurant; hence, their satisfaction, expectations, and perceptions of the lighting environment may vary and should be taken into account in the new design. Table 21.3 provides examples of questions that may be used as a guide for developing a questionnaire for commercial interiors.

TABLE 21.2

Residential Client Questionnaire

Name: **Age:**

Health Concerns (e.g., dementia, Alzheimer's disease, SAD, cognitive processing, hearing)

Visual Impairments	**Yes**	**No**
Cataracts	☐	☐
Glaucoma	☐	☐
Diabetic retinopathy	☐	☐
Difficulty seeing contrasts	☐	☐
Difficulty with visual acuity	☐	☐
Difficulty detecting motion	☐	☐
Difficulty with depth perception	☐	☐
Reduced field of vision	☐	☐
Colorblindness	☐	☐
Problems with glare	☐	☐
Problems with flickering lights	☐	☐

Anthropometric Data (provide measurements in a range)

Distance from seat to eye level (inches or mm) _____

Distance from floor to eye level (inches or mm) _____

Reach distance (inches or mm) _____

Activity Assessment

Room	Location in Room	Activity	Special Lighting Needs	User(s)	Day(s) of Week	Time of Day	Duration	Technology	Furniture	Luminaire(s)

(Continued)

TABLE 21.2 *(Continued)*

Residential Client Questionnaire

Perceptions of Lighting Assessment in Existing Spaces*

Client: **Room:**   **Lighting Method:**

Perceptions of Lighting	Yes	No	Details
Appropriate level of illumination			
Appropriate mood and atmosphere for activities			
Appropriate amount of daylight			
Appropriate energy conservation			
Appropriate environmental conservation			
Appropriate accent lighting for artwork or a special collection			
Problems with distribution of light on a task			
Problems with glare			Time of day: Time of year:
Problems with shadows			Time of day: Time of year:
Problems with reflections on task surfaces			
Problems with flickering			
Problems with color accuracy			
Problems with the apparent color of a room			
Problems with seeing objects			
Problems with seeing people			
Problems with reaching controls			
Problems with manipulating controls			
Problems with heat from lamps			
Problems with electrical outlets			
Problems with the apparent size of the room			
Problems with safety			
Problems with security			
Additional comments			

* To be completed with the assistance of a lighting designer.

(Continued)

TABLE 21.2 *(Continued)*
Residential Client Questionnaire

Anticipated Changes in the Future

1. Changes in individuals living in the residence:

2. Changes in number of rooms:

3. Changes in activities:

4. Anticipated renovation:

5. Furniture changes:

6. Changes in interior elements (floorcovering, wallcovering, ceilings, window treatments):

The topics include business-related information, property data, end-user characteristics, activity assessment, and perceptions of lighting.

As noted earlier, interviews and surveys should elicit basic information about perceptions of the lighting environment. However, the ideal situation is to combine the results of surveys and interviews with field observations. Observing in a residence may be fairly awkward and rarely occurs. In addition, observations in a residence are generally not all that informative because the frequent, personal contact with residential clients allows a lighting designer to acquire necessary information. The arrangement of commercial interiors often enables a lighting designer to conduct field observations of human behavior. Therefore, whenever possible, observations should be conducted in the interior that will be renovated. With new construction, sites similar to the proposed project should be observed. Research related to the project may be reviewed and integrated into plans.

The primary purpose of field observations is to watch how people behave in a specific lighting environment. Table 21.4 provides a guide that can be used for conducting field observations. As with all the

(Continued on page 617)

TABLE 21.3

Commercial Client Questionnaire

Project: **Location:**
Name: **Role (owner, employee, customer):**

Business–Related Data

Purpose of the business/organization:

Mission/goals/objectives of the business/organization:

Image of the business/organization:

Elements contributing to profits and ROI (return on investment):

Energy and environmental conservation policies and practices:

Current critical issues related to the industry:

Current societal events affecting the business/organization:

Anticipated changes in personnel:

Anticipated changes in activities:

Demographic profile of employees (sex, age, ethnic and cultural background):

Property Data

Geographic location:

Building owned or leased:

Anticipated changes in space needs:

Anticipated renovation:

Anticipated furniture changes:

Anticipated changes in interior elements (floor coverings, wall coverings, ceilings, window treatments):

(Continued)

TABLE 21.3 *(Continued)*

Commercial Client Questionnaire

Client Profile	Yes	No
Cataracts	☐	☐
Glaucoma	☐	☐
Diabetic retinopathy	☐	☐
Difficulty seeing contrasts	☐	☐
Difficulty with visual acuity	☐	☐
Difficulty with detecting motion	☐	☐
Difficulty with depth perception	☐	☐
Reduced field of vision	☐	☐
Colorblindness	☐	☐
Problems with glare	☐	☐
Problems with flickering lights	☐	☐

Anthropometric Data (provide measurements in a range)

Distance from seat to eye level (inches or mm) _____

Distance from floor to eye level (inches or mm) _____

Reach distance (inches or mm) _____

Activity Assessment

Room	Location in Room	Activity	Special Lighting Needs	User(s)	Day(s) of Week	Time of Day	Duration	Technology	Furniture	Luminaire(s)

(Continued)

TABLE 21.3 *(Continued)*
Commercial Client Questionnaire

Perceptions of Lighting Assessment in Existing Spaces*
Client: **Room:**   **Lighting Method:**

Perceptions of Lighting	Yes	No	Details
Appropriate level of illumination			
Appropriate mood and atmosphere for activities			
Appropriate amount of daylight			
Appropriate energy conservation			
Appropriate environmental conservation			
Appropriate accent lighting for artwork or a special collection			
Problems with distribution of light on a task			
Problems with glare			Time of day: Time of year:
Problems with shadows			Time of day: Time of year:
Problems with reflections on task surfaces			
Problems with flickering			
Problems with color accuracy			
Problems with the apparent color of a room			
Problems with seeing objects			
Problems with seeing people			
Problems with reaching controls			
Problems with manipulating controls			
Problems with heat from lamps			
Problems with electrical outlets			
Problems with the apparent size of the room			
Problems with safety			
Problems with security			
Additional comments			

* To be completed with the assistance of a lighting designer.

TABLE 21.4
Commercial Observations

Project: **Location:**
Observation Date: **Observation Start Time:**   **Observation Finish Time:**

Describe people in the space (number of people, employee, customer, approximate ages, special needs):

Describe activities in the space:

Describe the role of lighting in conducting activities:

Describe unnatural movements that could be the result of poor lighting (e.g., shielding eyes, hesitations):

Describe any modifications or adjustments to the environment conducted by end users that could be the result of poor lighting:

Describe any problems associated with lighting and the principles of universal design:

Identify preferred area(s):

Identify any unoccupied area(s):

guides included in this chapter, this document should be modified to address the specifics of a site, a lighting system, and the end users. Observations should occur at different times of the day, on different days of the week, and perhaps at different seasons of the year. For example, in observing behavior in a retail store, activities are different on Monday mornings, Saturday afternoons, and during the Christmas season. Therefore, to gain the most insight regarding the interaction between lighting and behavior, a site should be visited at the times that are germane to the project. The frequency of visits is dependent upon the consistency of the results. A site should be observed enough times for the observer to be able to conclude that specific behavior is fairly constant. For example, in observing behavior in a restaurant, it might be noted that someone trips on a step located at the entrance. On subsequent visits, if many people trip on the step, then it would be recorded as a significant problem and might be addressed by adding illumination to the edge of the tread. However, if only one person trips, and interviews with the employees reveal that they never noticed anyone having problems with the step, then perhaps additional illumination does not have to be installed at the entrance. As a note of caution, a ramp must be provided to comply with Americans with Disabilities Act (ADA) and International Building Code (IBC) regulations.

In observing how people interact with lighting, the most important behavior to note is when people seem to have difficulty moving and working in a space. A lighting design should seamlessly disappear within the context of how people interact with and perform tasks in the space. Problems with lighting can be detected by noticing when people move unnaturally through a space or make adjustments to either their position, the location of a task, or other interior elements. All unnatural movements should be observed, such as walking, sitting, and activities required performing a task. For example, people walking slowly upon entering a building during the day might mean that eyes are taking a long time to adapt to the contrast in illumination. If this is the problem, then illumination close to the entrance might have to be adjusted to provide a smooth transition for the eye's adaptation function. People may walk slowly through a hallway because of low illumination levels. Hesitancy exhibited at decision-making points in a building could be a result of glare or inadequate illumination on signage. Stopping and moving slowly down steps might indicate the need for illumination on stairways. Generally, unnatural movement through a space indicates a problem with the interior, which may be corrected by improving the lighting environment.

Unnatural movements associated with tasks and the subsequent adjustments are important to observe in commercial interiors. For example, the unnatural movement of having to shield one's eyes to read a sign or see objects could be the result of glare from a light source. When people are engaged in a task, there are a variety of activities to observe and record. For example, in watching someone work at a computer, specific activities to observe include any modifications made to body positions or the environment that are the result of poor lighting, such as glare, veiling reflections, exposed lamps, or inappropriate illumination levels. Frequently, poor lighting forces people performing a task to sit in unnatural positions in a chair. For example, while sitting in a chair, an individual might have to lean toward a light source in order to have adequate illumination on a book. To avoid glare on a VDT screen, people working at a computer might lean uncomfortably forward or backward. In addition to sitting in uncomfortable positions, poor lighting can cause people to adjust elements in their environment, such as the location of a desk, table, or chair. People moving their chairs in a restaurant could be the result of feelings that the downlights are casting horrific shadows on their faces.

In addition to observing unnatural movements, it is also important to observe undesirable actions. For example, in observing a retail store, poor lighting might be the reason why people ignore merchandise in a department. In an educational setting, children might not use resources in the corner of the classroom because the area is dark and gloomy. A gallery in a museum might not be well attended because the corridors leading to the space might be poorly lit or the paintings are difficult to observe because of glare or low levels of illumination. Behavior that is not consistent with the purpose of the space is very important to note. Based upon all data collected in the programming process, how lighting can improve the interaction of people and their environment may then be determined.

Assessment of Lighting Systems and Research Initiatives

Comprehensive programming involves an assessment of the lighting system and the physical attributes of an interior that might affect the quality of illumination. This involves visiting the site and creating an inventory of luminaires, lamps, controls, electrical outlets, daylight integration, architectural features, room configurations, furniture, colors, and material finishes. Photographs of the interior should be taken to assist with the schematic and design development phases of the lighting design process. In addition, sketches should be developed of the floor plan, wall elevations, reflected ceiling plan, and perhaps light distribution patterns. Sketches should be drawn quickly. At this stage of the lighting design process, approximate dimensions are sufficient. For some projects, a floor plan and reflected ceiling plan might exist. (Exact dimensions of interiors are recorded during the design development phase.)

As illustrated in Figure 21.2, each sketch of a room should include dimensions and the approximate location of interior elements such as

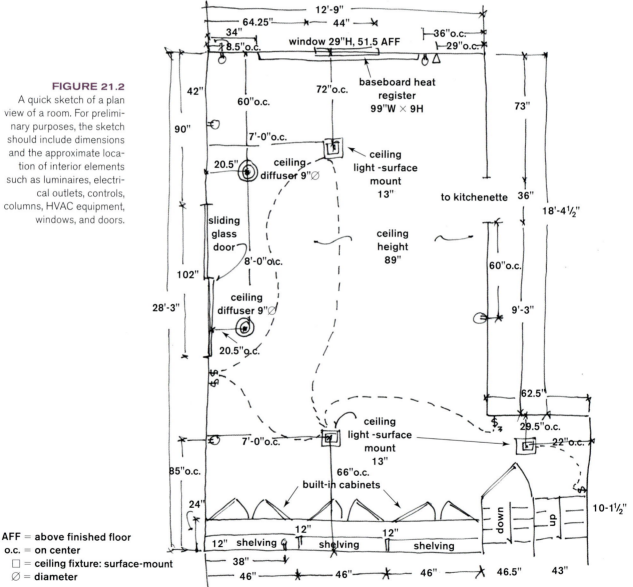

FIGURE 21.2
A quick sketch of a plan view of a room. For preliminary purposes, the sketch should include dimensions and the approximate location of interior elements such as luminaires, electrical outlets, controls, columns, HVAC equipment, windows, and doors.

AFF = above finished floor
o.c. = on center
☐ = ceiling fixture: surface-mount
∅ = diameter

luminaires, electrical outlets, controls, HVAC equipment, loudspeakers, sprinklers, smoke alarms, emergency fixtures, signage, windows, skylights, significant architectural details, structural members, cabinets, closets, and doors. For example, drawing a plan the approximate shape of the room created the floor plan in Figure 21.2. The overall room dimensions were recorded along with the approximate location of windows, electrical outlets, switching arrangements, wall-mounted luminaires, cabinets, and doors. Elevations should include the vertical dimensions of the location of windows, architectural elements, luminaires, switches, and electrical outlets (Figure 21.3). The reflected ceiling plan illustrates the location of columns, HVAC equipment, luminaires, ceiling tiles, and any other elements located on the ceiling (Figure 21.4). Figure 21.5 is a sketch of how light strikes a wall elevation with a fireplace. Illumination distribution sketches are useful to

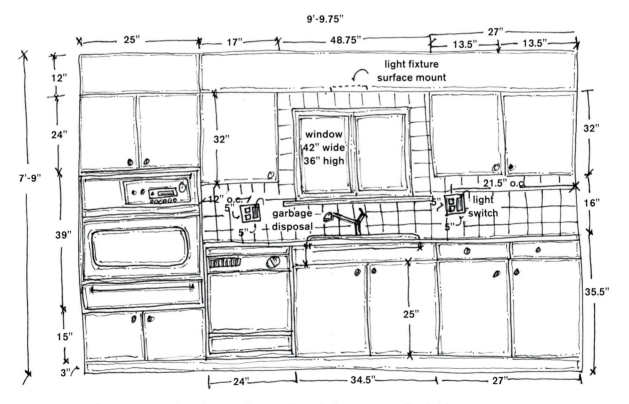

FIGURE 21.3 A quick sketch of an elevation of a room. For preliminary purposes, the sketch should include vertical dimensions of the location of windows, architectural elements, luminaires, switches, and electrical outlets.

FIGURE 21.4 A quick sketch of a reflected ceiling plan of a room. For preliminary purposes, the sketch should include the location of columns, HVAC equipment, luminaires, ceiling tiles, and any other elements located on the ceiling.

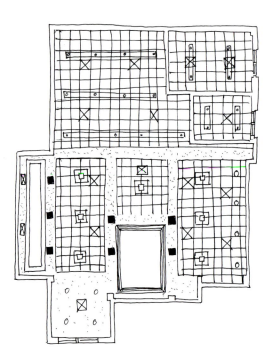

▣ = **Pendant-mounted fixture**
○ = **Recessed fixture**
⊠ = **HVAC Ceiling Diffuser**
■ = **Column**
▭ = **Pendant-mounted fixture**

FIGURE 21.5 A quick sketch of light striking a wall elevation with a fireplace. Note the shape of the light on the wall and the variations in intensity.

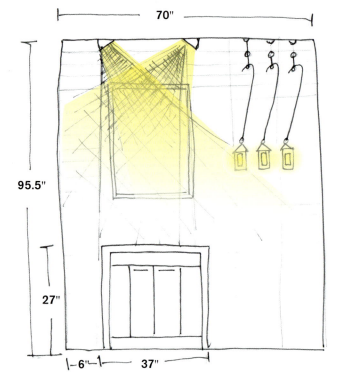

the interior designer in understanding the shapes of light and patterns of intensity of a light source. Therefore, sketches should include the shape of light beams and variations in intensity. An effective approach to drawing distribution patterns is to use dark-colored paper and various shades of white or yellow to represent variations in illumination intensities.

In addition to sketches of rooms, an interior inventory should include a description of elements included in a lighting system. Table 21.5 provides a guide that can be adapted for conducting an inventory of residential or commercial interiors. Some of the required information is germane to residential and commercial interiors; however, as demonstrated in the guide, supplemental data are needed to accommodate the purposes of the two major categories of interiors. Descriptions of luminaires should include the size, finish, material, style, installation method, condition, and type of light distribution, such as direct or indirect. Complete descriptions of lamps may be difficult to obtain because of remote locations, or the lamp's identification information, which was printed on the glass, is no longer readable.

TABLE 21.5
Interior Assessment

Client: **Location:**   **Date:**

Lighting Inventory

Room	Lighting Method[a]	Lighting Layer[b]	Luminaire Style/Color/ Finish	Light Distribution[c]	Location	Lamp	Wattage/ Code CRI CCT	Ballast/ Trans- former	Controls	Location of Windows/Other Apertures for Daylight	Problems/ Remarks

a Daylight, recessed, surface-mounted, suspended, track/cable, structural, furniture integrated, portable.
b General, task, accent, decorative.
c Indirect, direct, semidirect, semi-indirect, diffused.

(Continued)

TABLE 21.5 *(Continued)*
Interior Assessment

**Lighting Assessment
Room:**   **Lighting Method(s):**

Lighting	Yes	No	Details
General Lighting Concerns			
Appropriate level(s) of illumination			
Appropriate layers of lighting			
Appropriate amount of daylight			
Appropriate mood and atmosphere for activities			
Appropriate luminaire to promote the desirable image and value			
Appropriate balance of illumination between rooms			
Appropriate balance of illumination between zones			
Appropriate patterns of light, shade, and shadow			
Appropriate luminaires/lighting methods for the geometry of the space			
Appropriate flexibility of lighting in multifunctional spaces			
Appropriate lighting for special needs, such as video-conferencing, audio-visual presentations, medical procedures			
Appropriate illumination in transitional areas			
Problems with patterns of light			
Dark areas or corners			
Adequate perimeter lighting			
Appropriate consideration for axial planning			
Appropriate environment for light art			
Luminaires/Lamps			
Appropriate style/size of luminaires			
Problems with size/style of luminaire dominating the interior			
Problems with distribution of light on a task			
Appropriate relationship among the user, task light source, and furniture dimensions			
Appropriate localized lighting			
Appropriate lighting for visual art and special collections			
Problems with glare			
Problems with exposed lamps			
Problems with heat from lamps			
Problems with lamps/luminaire maintenance			
Problems with fading			

(Continued)

TABLE 21.5 *(Continued)*

Interior Assessment

Luminaires/ Lamps *(continued)*			
Problems with ceilings appearing dirty			
Problems with shade or shadows			
Undesirable striations or scallops on walls			
Potential ergonomic problems due to lighting			
Problems with veiling reflections			
Problems with flickering			
Problems with color accuracy			
Problems with the apparent color of a room			
Problems with the appearance of facial features of skin tones			
Lighting System Controls			
Problems with location of controls			
Problems with manipulating controls			
Problems with noise from controls			
Problems with how controls are calibrated			
Problems with the location of controls for detecting motion			
Convenient switching arrangement			
Safety, Security, Energy			
Adequate illumination for egress during an emergency			
Emergency lighting calibrated to allow enough time to leave a space and building during an emergency			
Emergency lighting mounted in a variety of locations			
Location of electrical outlets in compliance with ADA regulations			
Location of switches in compliance with ADA regulations			
Problems with luminaires interfering with people or architectural elements, such as door swings			
Location of luminaires in compliance with ADA regulations			
Problems with safety, including stairways, bathrooms, and kitchens			
Problems with faulty wiring, frayed cords, or overloaded circuits			
Lamp type and wattages comply with manufacturer's specifications			
Appropriate luminaires for wet conditions			
Luminaires interfere with viewing emergency fixtures and signage			

(Continued)

TABLE 21.5 *(Continued)*
Interior Assessment

Safety, Security, Energy *(continued)*			
Appropriate lighting for emergency personnel who are trying to help people exit a building during an emergency			
Adequate lighting at security checkpoints			
Appropriate transitional lighting in areas around elevators			
Problems with lighting systems swaying in a tall building			
Problems with seeing signage			
Problems with energy efficiency			
Additional comments			

Material/Finish Interior Assessment
Client:

Room	Period/Style	Wall Color(s)	Wall Texture/ Finish	Ceiling Color	Ceiling System	Floor Covering Type/Color(s)	Floor Finish	Window Treatment	Exterior Shading Devices	Special Collections

Interior Architecture Assessment
Client:

Room	Significant Architectural Elements	Lighting Enhance Architecture	Noteworthy Exterior Views	Security Concerns	Safety Concerns	Energy/ Environmental Concerns	Circulation Concerns	Luminaires Appropriate Style/Size	Universal Design Concerns

However, whenever possible, lamp information should include the manufacturer, type of source, wattage, codes, shape, and size. Ballast and control information should also be recorded. The lumen output of lamps should be measured in task areas. Any flickering occurring from a lamp or humming from auxiliary controls should be noted.

In analyzing the lighting system, the purpose of light sources should be noted, including general, task, accent, and decorative lighting. Brightness, glare, and veiling reflections should also be recorded, including the source(s) of the problem. Patterns of light, shade, and shadow should be described, including an assessment of the effectiveness of the variations. Lighting methods should also be examined to determine the effectiveness of the sources for purposes related to daylight integration, safety, security, energy conservation, wayfinding, creating the appropriate mood, and the illumination of architectural elements. The inventory of interior elements should include a description of furniture, window treatments, floor coverings, wall surfaces, ceilings, significant architectural details, views, visual art, special collections, and exterior shading devices.

The programming phase is an excellent time to research current local, state, and federal codes and regulations. Chapter 14 discusses important legislation, associated organizations and agencies, building codes, energy regulations, ADA, light pollution, and lamp disposal practices. Codes and regulations must also be identified for projects involving historic buildings. A review of current literature should be conducted to determine the most effective lighting systems and practices. Current information regarding a specific setting, such as an educational facility, should also be reviewed. To identify lighting products that have state-of-the-art technology, manufacturers' representatives should be contacted, and a thorough review of product literature should be conducted.

A thorough analysis of the data collected in the programming phase of the lighting design process provides the foundation for the project's lighting criteria. In general, lighting criteria should focus on the health, safety, and welfare of people and on protecting our environment. The needs and priorities of the client and end users and the characteristics of the environment determine specific lighting criteria. Considerations include accommodating the purpose of the space, lighting methods, structural constraints, budget, time line, and psychological and physiological factors. Lighting criteria should be developed in consultation with other team members of the project.

Lighting criteria identified at the end of the comprehensive programming phase should be reviewed and approved by the client before proceeding to the schematic design phase. The next two phases of the lighting design process—schematic design and design development—generate plans for the project. However, as one progresses through a project, it is common to return to activities associated with previous phases. For example, in the design development stage, it may be necessary to collect more information from end users. Flowing back and forth between the phases of the lighting design process can improve the outcome of the project. However, it is critical to get agreement from the client and all members of the team when changes are made to previously approved documents.

SUMMARY

- Successful management of an interior design business includes planning the details of a project. The planning process can help to identify most of the factors critical to the success of the project, including costs, code restrictions, installation requirements, maintenance factors, and professional expertise.
- The lighting design process may be divided into the following seven phases: (1) project planning, (2) comprehensive programming, (3) schematic design, (4) design development, (5) contract documentation, (6) contract administration, and (7) evaluation.
- The primary purposes of planning are to identify a profile of the project and to determine resources required to achieve the objectives.
- To develop the best possible lighting plan, a lighting designer should be involved at the planning stage of the entire project.
- The profile of the project, for planning purposes, should include a preliminary understanding of the needs of the owner and end users as well as elements of the property.
- Information gathered during initial discussions with the client and

from site visits is useful in identifying professionals who are needed to plan and implement the project.

■ A clear process for communication is especially important when changes occur in a project.

■ In consultation with the client, the project's team members should develop a comprehensive plan, which includes the list of activities, responsible individuals, time line, required resources, estimated costs, and billing dates.

■ Comprehensive programming is the phase for collecting data regarding the end users, physical characteristics of the space, and applicable codes, ordinances, and regulations.

■ To obtain information about end users and the interior, effective methodologies are interviews, surveys, and field observations.

■ Interview and survey questions should always ask about the present situation and anticipated needs in the future.

■ The primary purpose of field observations is to watch how people behave in a specific lighting environment.

■ In observing how people interact with lighting, the most important behavior to observe is when people seem to have difficulty moving and working in the space.

■ Behavior that is not consistent with the purpose of the space is important to note while conducting observations.

■ Comprehensive programming involves visiting the site and creating an inventory of luminaires, lamps, controls, electrical outlets, daylight integration, architectural features, room configurations, furniture, colors, and material finishes.

■ An analysis of an existing lighting system should include a description of the condition of the luminaires, lamps, ballasts, and controls.

■ Sketches should be developed of the floor plan, wall elevations, reflected ceiling plan, and perhaps light distribution patterns.

■ The programming phase is an excellent time to research current local, state, and federal codes and regulations. A review of current literature should be conducted to determine the most effective lighting systems and practices.

■ Data collected in the programming phase of the lighting design process provide the foundation for the project's lighting criteria.

Exercises

1. Develop a plan for a commercial project that includes factors critical to the success of the project. Use Table 21.1 as a guide for creating an outline of the plan. In a written report outline the plan for the project, and include a proposed time line including start/finish dates.

2. Identify a commercial client and the end users of a space. Use Table 21.3 as a guide for creating a list of questions for interviews and surveys. Questions should be specific to the end users. In a written report include the following information: (a) a list of the questions, (b) an outline of the plan for interviewing and surveying the end users, (c) the rationale for different questions, and (d) the rationale for who will be interviewed and surveyed.

3. Identify three different public spaces. Use Table 21.4 as a guide for creating an observation guide for each site. Visit each site as often as needed so that you will be able to present generalizations of how lighting affects behavior in a space. In a written report include the following information: (a) a summary of the observations and the lighting system, (b) a summary of the strengths and weaknesses of the lighting in each space, (c) recommendations for improving the lighting environment, and (d) a list of questions that would be useful to ask the end users of the space.

4. Identify a public space. Use Table 21.5 as a guide for conducting an inventory of the lighting system and attributes of the interior. In a written report include the following information: (a) a lighting inventory, (b) a lighting assessment, (c) material/finish interior assessment, and (d) interior architecture assessment. The report should also include sketches of the interior that are relevant to the current lighting system.

5. Based upon the data collected in Exercise 4, identify relevant information that should be researched and develop a list of the lighting criteria. In a written report include the following information: (a) a list of the research that should be conducted to complete the project, (b) a list of the lighting criteria, (c) the rationale for the lighting criteria, and (d) suggestions for implementing the schematic design phase.

REFERENCES

Alderman, R.L. (1997). *How to Prosper as an Interior Designer: A Business and Legal Guide.* New York: John Wiley & Sons.

Allen, P.S., Jones, L.M., and Stimpson, M.F. (2004). Beginnings of Interior Environments, 9th edition. Upper Saddle River, NJ: Pearson/Prentice Hall.

American Institute of Architects (2000). *Architectural Graphics Standards,* 10th edition. New York: John Wiley & Sons.

Benya, J., Heschong, L., McGowan, T., Miller, N., and Rubinstein, F. (2001). *Advanced Lighting Guidelines.* White Salmon, WA: New Buildings Institute.

Birnberg, H.G. (1999). *Project Management for Building Designers and Owners.* Boca Raton, FL: CRC Press.

Burstein, D., and Stasiowski, F. (1982). *Project Management for the Design Professional.* New York: Watson-Guptill.

Burde, E. (1992). *Design Presentation Techniques.* New York: McGraw-Hill.

Ching, F.D.K. (2003). *Architectural Graphics,* 4th edition. New York: John Wiley & Sons.

Coleman, C. (ed.) (2001). *Interior Design Handbook of Professional Practice.* New York: McGraw-Hill.

Doyle, M.E. (1999). *Color Drawing: Design Skills and Techniques for Architects, Landscape Architects, and Interior Designers,* 2nd edition. New York: John Wiley & Sons.

Farren, C.E. (1999). *Planning and Managing Interior Projects,* 2nd edition. Kingston, MA: R.S. Means.

Getz, L. (1986). *Business Management in the Smaller Design Firm.* Newton, MA: Practice Management Associates.

Gibbs, J. (1997). *A Handbook for Interior Designers.* London: Sterling Publications.

Illuminating Engineering Society of North America (IESNA) (2000). *Document DG-3-00: Application of Luminaire Symbols on Lighting Design Drawings.* New York: Illuminating Engineering Society of North America.

International Association of Lighting Designers (IALD) (2002). *Guidelines for Specification Integrity.* Chicago: International Association of Lighting Designers.

Kilmer, R., and Kilmer, W.O. (1992). *Designing Interiors.* New York: Harcourt Brace.

Kliment, S.A. (1998). *Writing for Design Professionals.* New York: W. W. Norton.

Knackstedt, M.V. (2002). *The Interior Design Business Handbook.* New York: John Wiley & Sons.

Koenig, P.A. (2000). *Design Graphics: Drawing Techniques for Design Professionals.* Upper Saddle River, NJ: Pearson Education/Prentice Hall.

Koomen-Harmon, S., and Kennon, K. (2001). *The Codes Guidebook for Interiors,* 2nd edition. New York: John Wiley & Sons.

Kriebel, T.M., Birdsong, C., and Sherman, D.J. (1991). Defining interior design programming. *Journal of Interior Design Education and Research, 17(1),* 29–36.

Liebing, R.W. (1999). *Architectural Working Drawings,* 4th edition. New York: John Wiley & Sons, Inc.

Mitton, M. (1999). *Interior Design Visual Presentations: A Guide to Graphics, Models, and Presentation Techniques.* New York: John Wiley & Sons.

Nissen, L., Faulkner, R., and Faulkner, S. (1994). *Inside Today's Home,* 6th edition. New York: Harcourt Brace.

O'Leary, A.F. (1992). *Construction Administration in Architectural Practice.* New York: McGraw-Hill.

Pile, J.F. (1988). *Interior Design.* New York: Harry N. Abrams.

Pile, J.F. (1995). *Interior Design,* 2nd edition. New York: Harry N. Abrams.

Pile, J.F. (2003). *Interior Design,* 3rd edition. New York: Harry N. Abrams.

Piotrowski, C.M. (1992). *Interior Design Management: A Handbook for Owners and Managers.* New York: John Wiley & Sons.

Piotrowski, C.M. (2002). *Professional Practice for Interior Designers,* 3rd edition. New York: John Wiley & Sons.

Ramsey, C.G., and Sleeper, H. R. (2000). *Architectural Graphic Standards,* 10th edition. New York: John Wiley & Sons.

Reznikoff, S.C. (1989). *Specifications for Commercial Interiors: Professional Liabilities, Regulations, and Performance Criteria.* New York: Whitney Library of Design.

Reznikoff, S.C. (1986). *Interior Graphic and Design Standards.* New York: Whitney Library of Design.

Siegel, H., and Siegel, A. (1982). *A Guide to Business Principles and Practices for Interior Designers.* New York: Whitney Library of Design.

Smith, W.D., and Smith, L.H. (2001). *McGraw-Hill On-Site Guide to Building Codes 2000: Commercial and Residential Interiors.* New York: McGraw-Hill.

Stasiowski, F., and Burnstein, D. (1982). *Project Management for the Design Professional.* New York: Whitney Library of Design/Watson-Guptill Publications.

Steffy, G.R. (2002). *Architectural Lighting Design,* 2nd edition. New York: Van Nostrand Reinhold.

Thompson, J.A. (ed.) (1992). *ASID Professional Practice Manual.* New York: Whitney Library of Design.

Veitch, R.M., Jackman, D.R., and Dixon, M.K. (1990). *Professional Practice: A Handbook for Interior Designers.* Winnipeg, Canada: Peguis Publishers.

Wakita, O.A., and Linde, R.M. (2003). *The Professional Practice of Architectural Working Drawings,* 3rd edition. New York: John Wiley & Sons.

Williams, D.J. (1996). *Preparing for Project Management.* New York: American Society of Civil Engineers.

CHAPTER 22

Lighting Design Process: Design Phases

OBJECTIVES

- Understand how to analyze and synthesize the data collected in the comprehensive programming phase.

- Describe the brainstorming process, including sketching techniques, that can assist with the conceptualization of the lighting design.

- Identify the purposes of the design development phase.

- Apply an understanding of the design development phase to a lighting project.

- Understand and describe the most salient factors in conducting oral presentations.

PHASES of the lighting design process—project planning and comprehensive programming—are discussed in Chapter 21. This chapter continues these discussions with a focus on schematic design and design development. The primary purpose of these two phases is to develop detailed plans for the lighting design. (The lighting design process is advanced and concluded in Chapter 23.) Throughout all the phases, a lighting designer should be constantly communicating with the client and other professionals involved in the project. In particular, it is important to be aware of the location of ductwork and sprinkler heads, because these elements can affect the location of lighting systems.

An important element in the success of the lighting design process is obtaining client approval at the conclusion of each phase and before proceeding to the next stage. This approval process is important to ensure that the client is in full agreement with the lighting design, costs, and schedule. If a lighting designer proceeds to the next phase before receiving client approval, valuable time and resources may be wasted. A client may be reluctant to pay for services without having approved them. And a lack of communication can seriously affect the working relationship. An unhappy client will not use the designer again and may make negative comments to potential clients. This is a serious problem because a great deal of business in the field of interior design is generated by repeat business and word-of-mouth.

Schematic Design

The schematic design phase is composed of analyzing the results obtained during the comprehensive programming stage and then developing initial design concepts for the interior illumination.

Program Analysis and Synthesis

Data gathered in the programming phase include information about the client, end users, physical characteristics of the space, and applicable codes, ordinances, and regulations. For each category, a synopsis should be written that reflects information most germane to the project. Identifying salient facts requires a thorough analysis, synthesis, and evaluation of the data.

Data collected through interviews, surveys, and field observations may be summarized by: (1) thorough analysis of the data by reading the content numerous times, (2) creating a detailed description of the results, (3) developing a prioritized list of lighting requirements, and (4) determining potential problems. The results of the analysis should be in written and sketch form. Responses from numerous interviews and surveys must be analyzed by identifying recurring themes or patterns. For example, in interviews of 50 people, only 2 might indicate the need for higher illumination in a corridor. This low response rate suggests that the illumination level might be appropriate and that perhaps the two people who mentioned the light in the corridor have different perceptions of brightness than most people do. Thus, new lighting for the corridor might not be included in the new lighting design. In contrast, if most of the people interviewed or surveyed identify a lighting problem in the corridor, then solutions should be developed.

The detailed results of the interviews or surveys should include health concerns, visual impairments, and anthropometric measurements. In addition, a summary of information collected from commercial clients should include business and property data. A synopsis of the activities includes a room-by-room description of the actions that occur in specific locations within the space. The purpose of each luminaire should also be noted. The summary should prioritize activities and include mention of special lighting needs, technology, furniture, and existing luminaires. Sketches can be useful in identifying the location of luminaires, windows, technology, and furniture. Positive and negative perceptions of the lighting methods used in each room should be included. The synopsis of the interviews should conclude with a list of the anticipated changes to the lighting design.

The results of field observations should be a synthesis of all the visits. Multiple observations should be analyzed in the same way that responses from numerous interviews and surveys are analyzed. Therefore, the summary report should identify only items that occur on a regular basis. The synopsis of people in the space should include a description of individuals, activities, unnatural movements, and modifications or adjustments to the environment that might be the result of poor lighting. A summary of how people are using the space involves the role of lighting in conducting activities, adherence to the principles of universal design, preferred areas, and unoccupied spaces. Many of the results related to specific locations within a building can be depicted in freehand sketches.

A summary of the interior inventory should be in written and sketch form. Table 21.5 and sketches may be used to summarize an inventory of the lighting. As illustrated in Figure 22.1, in addition to indicating the location of luminaires, controls, electrical outlets, and windows, a sketch may demonstrate the distribution and illumination intensity of light sources. The sketch in Figure 22.1 is keyed to identify general, task, accent, and decorative light sources. The data collected in the lighting assessment may also be presented in words and schematics. For example, in responding to the item "Appropriate balance of illumination between zones," a written explanation might include that lighting is not balanced in the space because the individual is writing at a desk using a portable luminaire with very high wattage, and the surrounding area is very dark because of the reflectance color of the walls. A sketch of the situation would indicate the location of the desk, luminaire, and walls. In addition, as shown in Figure 22.2, a sketch can illustrate changes in the three major illumination zones. The sketch can help a lighting designer to visualize the lighting problems and provide a way of examining possible locations for new lighting systems.

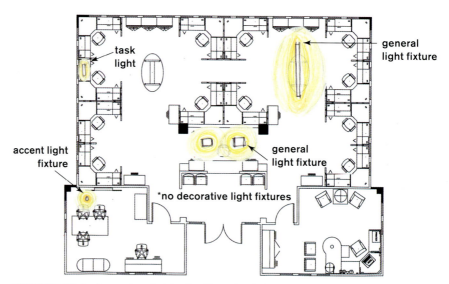

FIGURE 22.1 An overlay sketch of a floor plan indicating the distribution and illumination intensity of light sources. The sketch is keyed to identify general, task, and accent light sources.

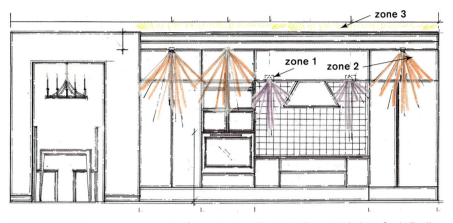

FIGURE 22.2 An overlay sketch of an elevation demonstrating a technique for indicating changes in the three major illumination zones: (a) the first zone is represented by the purple color, (b) the second zone is shown by using the orange color, and (c) the third zone is represented by the yellow color.

The various categories listed in the lighting assessment guide, including general lighting concerns, luminaires/lamps, lighting system controls, and safety/security/energy, may all be summarized in written reports and sketches. These summaries are different from the results of an inventory of the lighting and interior. Inventory reports are an objective listing of the lighting elements. In contrast, the assessment process is a means of subjectively reviewing the lighting plan. Thus, the analysis focuses on problems, constraints, positive attributes, and perceptions of the lighting environment. The summary should include an analysis of the adequacy of power, complexities with access, and structural constraints.

In addition to the written summaries, sketches can be developed using creative coding schemes that depict and reinforce the strengths and weaknesses of a lighting plan. For example, Figure 22.3 shows a floor plan with a coding scheme that delineates safety, energy, glare, and shadow concerns. Notes on the sketch provide additional information related to problems, such as cave-like areas, difficulties with reading signage, and ornamental details. A sketch of an interor might also show illumination zonal patterns of light sources (Figure 22.4). Sketches of elevations should indicate how light sources affect a

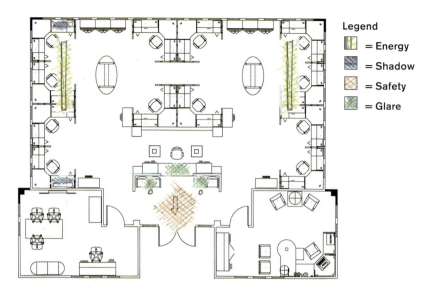

FIGURE 22.3 An overlay sketch of a floor plan illustrating a coding scheme method for indicating safety, energy, glare, and shadow concerns.

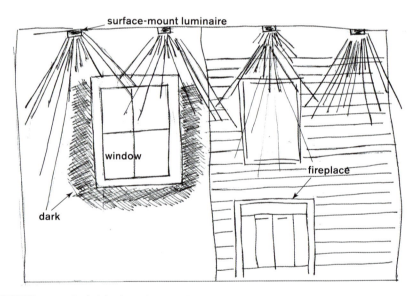

FIGURE 22.4 A sketch of an elevation demonstrating a technique for indicating illumination zonal patterns of light sources. Light rays indicate where artificial and natural light sources are falling and intensity patterns.

vertical plane, such as dark surfaces surrounding windows, striations, or undesirable scallops.

An analysis of the material and finish interior should examine the relationship between the quality of illumination emitted from each luminaire and the characteristics of a surface, fabric, or texture. For example, a note should be recorded that discomfort glare occurs when the spotlights, recessed in the ceiling, strike the east wall, which is painted with a high gloss-paint. A summary should include any concerns about reflectance, textures, glare, or constraints with ceiling systems.

The analysis of the interior architecture should focus on the positive and negative attributes of the space. Within the context of the light sources, the analysis should review significant architectural details, geometry of the space, exterior views, and appropriateness of the size and style of luminaires. For example, the interior assessment might indicate that a space with very tall ceilings seems dehumanizing to the end users. In examining the lighting in the space, observations reveal that the track lighting system is highlighting the ceiling, while illumination at human scale is sparse. Thus, the analysis of the interior should indicate the relationship between the uncomfortable space and how the lighting contributes to negative reactions.

The analysis should cover the characteristics of the interior architecture and the results derived from interviews, surveys, and observations. For example, interview results might indicate that end users have reported problems with finding departments in a retail store, and observations further support this. By examining these results and the physical characteristics of the interior, it may become evident that people have difficulty with circulation because the directional signage is dark and its location is too high on the wall. The programming results should be analyzed within the context of the behavioral elements of the interior architecture, including safety, security, circulation, and universal design.

The final analysis of the results of programming should be a synopsis of current research related to light sources, human behavior, safety, energy, and environmental conservation. The report should also include a summary of new products and state-of-the-art technologies employed in lamps, luminaires, and controls. The analysis of current codes should involve identifying existing violations that must be corrected and a list of regulations that are relevant to specifying a new lighting system.

Conceptualization

The results of the analysis serve as the basis for the conceptualization process of the schematic design phase. In this stage, a lighting designer and other professionals involved in the project engage in a comprehensive brainstorming process. There are a variety of methods to brainstorming, and every team of professionals may have a preferred method. Some of the most important factors associated with achieving effective results include allowing everyone to participate, an initial acceptance of all ideas, and exploring all possibilities to solve problems. In addition, effective brainstorming is dependent upon a topical inquiry that is clearly understood by all members of the team. The topical inquiry is essentially the issue that will be explored during the brainstorming session. An example of a topical inquiry for a lighting project might be: "What are the concerns involved in providing task lighting for the staff working on the third floor of the ABC building?" The inquiry needs to be concise and understood by the participants because brainstorming ideas that are irrelevant for a project can waste a great deal of time. This can be discouraging to people, and they might be reluctant to be involved in future sessions.

The team of participants should determine the topical order for brainstorming lighting solutions. For example, for a large office project, the sessions might be organized according to space, activities, or end users. The order may be predicated on the size of the project. Large, complex projects require a great deal more organization than do small structures. Thus, for large projects, the team members involved in brainstorming sessions will have to consider the complex interaction between spaces and activities. Regardless of the organizational structure of the sessions, discussions should always reflect the data and the lighting criteria that were developed during the comprehensive programming phase. Each space in the project will have to be reviewed with respect to the architect's vision, characteristics of the end users, business attributes of commercial clients, activities, behavior, perceptions, anticipated changes, current research, safety, and building codes. In addition, lighting approaches for each space should be based upon the positive and negative attributes of the existing lighting system, materials, finishes, and interior architecture.

Brainstorming sessions can be an intensely creative process and should include written comments and sketches. Brainstorming sessions should explore all possible solutions for a lighting problem. For example, when exploring the options available for an existing lighting system, the team might consider whether the luminaires should be retrofitted, replaced, refurbished, renovated, rewired, or reconfigured. Options for improving lamps could be higher output, longer life, enhanced color, upgraded ballasts, relamping, or improved optics. Various methods should also be explored, such as recessed, surface-mounted, track systems, or pendants. Discussions should also focus on options that address the lighting criteria. For example, one of the lighting criteria for a project might indicate that the mood for a restaurant be romantic during dinner hours. Therefore, brainstorming could explore which lighting method, luminaire, lamp, and level of illumination would create a romantic feeling within the specific attributes of the restaurant's environment.

A variety of sketching techniques can be used in brainstorming sessions about lighting. During the brainstorming sessions it is common to review past drawings, so sketches should be saved, and a clean sheet should be used at the beginning of each new concept. A preliminary drawing of a floor plan with furniture arrangements can serve as the basis for planning lighting. In brainstorming for lighting options, suggestions may arise related to improving the relationship among illumination, furniture arrangements, and architectural elements. Thus, by simultaneously considering all the elements that affect lighting during the brainstorming sessions, the final plan for the interior is likely to result in a quality environment. An effective method for brainstorming lighting is to use tracing paper as an overlay for floor plans and elevations of the space. An overlay enables the team members to visualize the integration of lighting with the interior architecture, furniture, windows, doorways, and special features.

Each overlay should depict a different aspect of the lighting design. Overlays may be created to demonstrate lighting systems, distribution patterns of illumination, zoning considerations, locations of layered lighting, sequencing hierarchies, viewing angles, spill light, and throw distances (Figures 22.5 a and b). Overlays on elevations help team

Sequencing Hierarchies

1. **Mission Statement**
2. **Artist's Sculpture**
3. **Plaques/Awards–Community**
4. **Wayfinding–Restrooms**
5. **Conferencing/Discussion Areas**

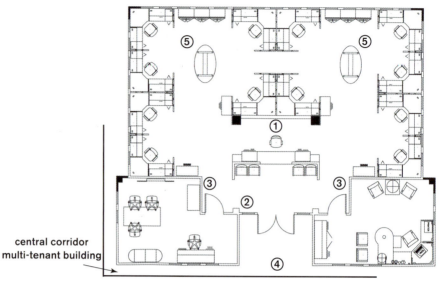

central corridor
multi-tenant building

FIGURE 22.5 a An overlay sketch of a floor plan demonstrating zoning considerations and sequencing hierarchies.

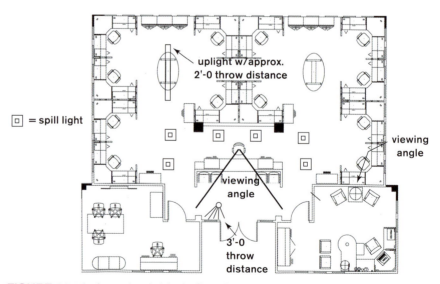

FIGURE 22.5 b An overlay sketch of a floor plan demonstrating viewing angles, spill light, and throw distances.

members to visualize how lighting may affect vertical planes and partitions. Sketches should also be developed that illustrate the dimensional requirements of task lighting (Figure 22.6).

Sketches developed during brainstorming sessions should be compared to the schematics created during the analysis of the programming results. For example, Figure 22.3 demonstrates a sketch of a floor plan with a coding scheme that delineates safety, energy, glare, and shadow concerns. In this example, it would be essential to make sure that the conceptual schematics address items related to safety, energy, glare, and shadows. In addition, whenever possible, sketches should be created of anticipated changes concerning end users and the interior. A drawing of anticipated growth areas should be a separate overlay (Figure 22.7). A series of overlays might be created to illustrate lighting changes with preset scene arrangements (Figure 22.8). Sketches of architectural details and schematics of custom-designed luminaires should also be developed during the conceptualization process (Figure 22.9).

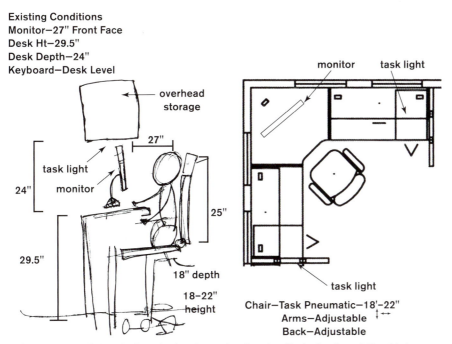

FIGURE 22.6 A sketch of a side elevation and a plan view illustrating the relationship between the anthropometric data of an end-user, furniture, and lighting.

FIGURE 22.7
An overlay sketch of a floor plan illustrating anticipated growth areas and potential lighting needs.

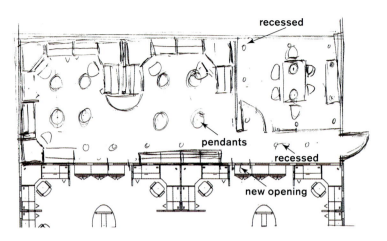

FIGURE 22.8
An overlay sketch of a floor plan illustrating preset lighting scene arrangements.

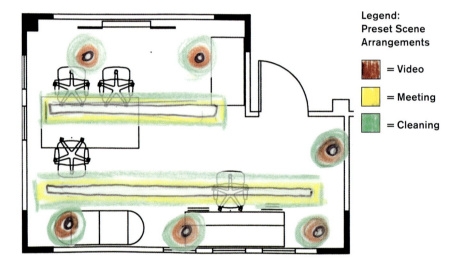

FIGURE 22.9
A sketch of architectural details and illumination patterns.

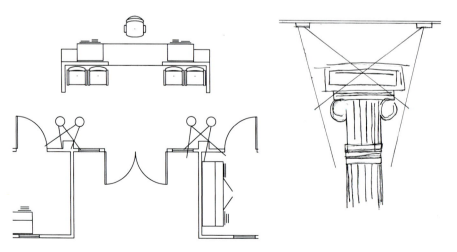

During the brainstorming sessions, the team often must identify several lighting plans. One reason to develop multiple designs is to have alternatives to present to a client. The schematic design phase is the best time to make sure the client is pleased with the lighting design, because at this stage everything can easily be changed. Once a project proceeds beyond the schematic and design development phases, changes to the design can be expensive or even impossible. Alternatives presented to a client may take a variety of themes, such as different lighting methods, styles of luminaires, price ranges, and approaches that require different time lines.

Multiple lighting solutions may also be necessary to accommodate current unknowns related to the project, such as reflectance values of surfaces, dimensions of new furniture, location of partitions, or special architectural features. For example, the lighting criteria might require accent lighting for a central display unit in a retail store. Many of the characteristics of the interior architecture would have to be known in order for the designer to identify the specific lighting for this type of precision application. Therefore, lighting options may have to be developed that would accommodate various structural scenarios.

In reviewing the most promising lighting plans, a matrix can be a valuable tool. As shown in Table 22.1, the lighting criteria could be listed in the rows of the matrix, and the various lighting options in the columns. In examining the matrix, each option can be evaluated to determine how well the option addresses each of the lighting criteria. A variety of variables could be inserted in a matrix. For example, lighting methods, luminaires, or controls could be evaluated by the lighting criteria. Every team member should evaluate the items in a matrix, and a summation of the results provides a perspective based on a consensus.

At the conclusion of the schematic design phase, the team of professionals has recommendations to present to the client. These may include a concept statement, freehand sketches, photographs of luminaires, a list of lighting equipment, preliminary costs, and projected time lines. The professionals performing installations are responsible for preparing preliminary costs for this work. The concept statement is a summary of the main ideas and lighting plans. The concept should demonstrate a clear understanding of the project and an

TABLE 22.1

Matrix of Lighting Criteria and Proposed Solutions*

	Illumination Option Portable Luminaire A	Illumination Option Portable Luminaire B	Illumination Option Portable Luminaire C	Illumination Option Portable Luminaire D
Lighting Criteria Ergonomic features				
Lighting Criteria Glare is avoided from a variety of positions				
Lighting Criteria Appropriate dimensions for the size of the desk				
Lighting Criteria Appropriate price range for the project's budget				
Total +				
Total −				

Notes*

1. Identify lighting criteria and several illumination options. You may list as many as you wish.
2. Every member on a team should evaluate how well each illumination option accommodates the lighting criteria. Provide a rating using the following scale:

   + + +   Strong relationship   −   Weak nonrelationship

   + +   Moderate relationship   − −   Moderate nonrelationship

   +   Weak relationship   − − −   Strong nonrelationship

3. Total the number of +'s and −'s for all team members.
4. The best illumination options will have the greatest number of +'s.

indication of how the lighting design addresses its needs. In reviewing the schematic design, it is important that the client understand and agree with the analysis of the situation and support the lighting plan. The discussion should be interactive, and, when necessary, the lighting designer might have to develop new options until the client is satisfied with the design. Approval of the schematic design should be accompanied by a signed agreement.

Design Development

The design development phase provides an opportunity to formulate the creative ideas. The purposes of the design development phase are to work through the details of the conceptual lighting design and produce presentation mediums and specifications for the client's approval.

Presentation Mediums and Specifications

The design development phase begins after the client approves the concepts presented in the schematic design phase. The tasks involved in this phase are especially critical to the success of the project because the results are used to form the contractual agreements with the client, contractor, manufacturers, and suppliers. Therefore, it is important to think through and research all the details related to the lighting systems. In addition, a lighting designer should make sure that the client fully understands and approves the lighting design, how the lighting will affect the environment, and appropriate operation and maintenance practices.

Working through the details of the project requires a thorough examination of the lighting system in every room. The variables to consider include lamps, luminaires, controls, daylight integration, power sources, installation methods, and maintenance procedures. A detailed analysis of each item necessitates contacting manufacturers, suppliers, and tradespeople associated with fabrication and installing the lighting system. Each source provides information the designer needs to develop the particulars of the project, including specifications, cut sheets, prices, availability, delivery dates, material lists, construction details, and installation requirements.

In addition to identifying specifications of the lighting system, it is also important to verify other elements of the project that may affect the quality of illumination. Changes naturally occur during the execution of a project. Any modifications to the parameters of the project may require changes to the lighting design. Items to confirm include final selection of furniture, finishes, textures, colors, styles, windows, daylight integration devices, and the geometry of the spaces. It is also important to keep abreast of changes to the project's budget and schedule. Alterations to the budget may reduce funds available for the lighting systems. Therefore, in working out the details of the lighting design, it is imperative that the design work with the other professionals and the consultants on the project and that the lighting designer be flexible in altering a design.

A comprehensive approach to gathering information from manufacturers, suppliers, and tradespeople requires obtaining exact costs of lighting systems, including materials and labor for fabricating structural units or custom-designed luminaires. Selecting the exact lamps required for the parameters of lighting methods should be the first items specified, because the characteristics of the light source dictate the resultant lighting effects. For example, specific lamps must be selected to accommodate a project's lighting criterion that stipulates a particular beam spread, throw distance, or energy savings. Once the lamps are selected, luminaires and controls appropriate to operate the lamps can be researched and specified.

Specification details for lighting methods that do not require a manufacturer's luminaire, such as cove lighting, daylight integration, or custom-designed fixtures, can be very complex. In addition to specifying the lamps, lamp holders, and controls, a lighting designer must work with craftspeople to determine costs and the feasibility of installing the system. For example, a cove lighting installation may require wood for the fascia board, paint for the interior of the unit, an exterior finish, lamp holders, lamps, and an installation method. This project would require material and labor costs from a craftsperson and an electrician. Only tradespeople have the expertise to determine costs and the feasibility of an installation. In examining details of the lighting design, a lighting designer can ensure that the location of a luminaire does not interfere with elements in the interior, such as door swings and architectural details.

Specifications and updates of the total project serve as the foundation for developing presentation mediums and requirements for the lighting design. The design team should determine the most appropriate presentation drawings and specifications. Common drawings include a floor plan with a lighting overlay, a reflected ceiling plan, elevations, lighting detail drawings, perspectives, and axonometric views. These drawings may be hard-line (drafted), freehand, or created using computer-aided design (CAD) or computer-aided design and drafting (CADD) technology. Lighting software programs can demonstrate virtual interiors and provide the flexibility to quickly change the lighting system or attributes of the interior (Figure 22.10). For example, the software allows a lighting designer to produce a virtual room of the project, with exact dimensions, architectural details of a space, surface colors, textures, and a proposed lighting system. The software illustrates how the lighting system affects the interior within the parameters determined by the characteristics of the space. When

FIGURE 22.10 A virtual interior developed by *AGI32* lighting software program.

presenting the virtual lighting design to the client, various solutions may be explored by immediately changing the type of lighting method, lamp, luminaire, point of installation, or characteristics of the interior. This tool is a tremendous help in enabling a client to visualize a lighting design. Furthermore, the ability to view multiple options assists a client in knowing which design is most appropriate for the project.

The medium used to present the lighting design may be determined by the style of a design firm or by the tool that best presents the specific details of a project. Presentation mediums for lighting designs must depict all aspects of a space that are affected by the plan, including luminaires, the location of light sources, beam spreads, and illumination intensities. An overlay over a floor plan can illustrate the location of fixtures in a room and the switching arrangements. A reflected ceiling plan can demonstrate how luminaires affect the design of the ceiling. Elevations, lighting detail drawings, perspectives, and axonometric views are excellent illustrations of the design of luminaires, vertical locations of fixtures, beam spreads, and illumination intensities. These drawings can also help people to visualize the relationship between luminaires and furniture, special collections, openings in walls, visual art, or architectural details. To demonstrate light distribution and variability of intensities, an effective technique is to create black-and-white drawings, with shades of yellow for illumination (Figure 22.11). For presentations, drawings can be mounted on boards or included in a job notebook.

FIGURE 22.11
Overlay of a sketch of a wall elevation demonstrating a graphic technique for indicating the relationship between luminaires, openings in walls, and architectural details. The black and white drawing, with shades of yellow for illumination, can be a very effective method for demonstrating the effects of illumination.

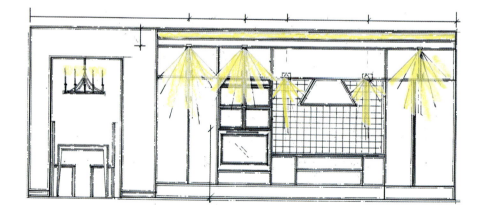

One of the challenges with presenting drawings of lighting designs to clients is in helping them to understand how two-dimensional drawings translate into three-dimensional space. Frequently, clients do not understand architectural drawings and details, especially of lighting plans. Therefore, to help a client visualize a space, models, mock-ups, and prototypes of luminaires may be built. Generally, these mediums are used for special situations because of their expensive production costs. They may be helpful in demonstrating a complex lighting design or illumination for a space with extraordinary features. To demonstrate the effect of illumination, light sources can be added to the units. Some firms build these mediums as working pieces for design development and never show the units to the client. Within this context, the mediums are easier and cheaper to construct, because the completed project does not need the time-consuming finishing touches that accompany formal presentation materials.

Drawings must be consistent with details provided in specifications. For example, luminaires on a lighting plan must be the same dimensions described in the specifications. The quantity and type of luminaires must also be identical. Notes on a drawing can be helpful in explaining complex specification details of a lighting system. Working out the details of the specifications includes researching expertise, which might be needed to help specify and install special lighting systems. Experts might not be available at the location of the project, thus, costs can be high to hire professionals from communities far from the site. This problem is common when specifying new technologies.

Developing details includes determining optimum dates for ordering lighting systems, billing, and phases of project construction and installations. To minimize costs, the progression from wiring, drywall installation, and mounting luminaires to final calibrations of controls must be carefully coordinated. For example, electricians may be scheduled to install luminaires on specific dates. If there is a delay in the delivery of luminaires, the next available time for the electricians to return to the site might be several weeks later. This may result in costly delays and budget overruns. Costs can increase because electricians might charge extra fees to return to the site, and a delayed opening for a profit-making business, such as a retail store, is lost revenue.

Extensive details must be identified for lighting systems that are integrated with furniture or built-in units, such as kitchen cabinets. A lighting designer must talk with the craftspeople responsible for constructing the unit to determine the feasibility of installing a specific lighting system in the cabinetry and to find out venting requirements, costs, and a time line. Top-notch cabinetmakers are very busy and may not be able to work on a piece within the project's time line, so another cabinetmaker who might be more expensive would need to be found, or the lighting method changed.

To organize the details of a project, a useful tool is a systematic project outline, which is developed in coordination with the contractor's schedule (Table 22.2). This outline may be shared with anyone responsible for implementing the project, including vendors, manufacturers, contractors, distributors, staff, and consultants. The outline should describe, room-by-room, lighting methods, lamps, luminaires, ballasts, transformers, mounting methods, and controls. The outline should also include dates and names of the individuals responsible for tasks, such as bidding, ordering, profile of installations, calibration of controls, billing, payment submissions, the moving schedule, and end-user training sessions. As changes in the project occur, the systematic project outline must be updated and shared with all relevant individuals, including the client. Constant communication with the client and other professionals helps to reduce disappointments with changes and reinforces an honest working relationship.

Presenting technical information to a client requires a format, such as a job or project notebook, that enables materials to be compiled in a professional manner. The notebook should be given to the client during the presentation. The job notebook may include a variety of documents, such as the concept statement, drawings, lighting specifications, manufacturers' cut sheets, sketches of custom-designed luminaires, samples of finishes, detailed budget estimates, revised consultation fees, bidding recommendations, maintenance guidelines, and projected time lines. Lighting specifications may be presented in a schedule and should include all the required information for bids and purchase orders (Table 22.3). Budget estimates may be presented in a format that includes additional costs related to shipping, taxes, deposit amounts, and discount details (Table 22.4).

TABLE 22.2
Systematic Project Outline

Project: **Room:**
Lighting Method: **Date:**

Activity/Item	Individual(s) Responsible	Start Date	End Date	Task Completed	Notes
Bidding lighting system					
Order lighting system					
Installation profile					
Framing					
Rough wiring					
Recessed luminaire installation/ transformers/relays					
Sheetrock installation					
Wall finish					
Luminaire installations/ controls/trim					
Calibration of controls					
Billing client					
Payment submission					
Move-in					
End-user training sessions					
Postoccupancy evaluation					

Oral Presentations

During the design phases of a project, a lighting designer may make numerous presentations to the client. Presentations can range from very informal and one-on-one with a client to elaborate addresses to a large committee. Generally, presentations are scheduled at major

TABLE 22.3

Lighting System Schedule

Luminaires

Mark	Manufacturer	Number/Name	Light Distribution	Dimensions	Shielding	Finish	Mounting Method
A	XYZ Company	2356-9	Bidirectional	1'X 4'	Flat-blade louver	White	Recessed

Voltage	Ballast	Factory Options	Accessories	Quantity	Notes
120 volt	Electronic instant-start	Emergency battery pack		1	

Lamps

Mark	Manufacturer	Ordering Code	Lamp Type	Watts	Diameter inches	Length	Base Type
A	ABC Company	F32T8/730	T8	32		48"	Bipin

CRI/CTT	Approx. No. of Hours	Approx. No. of Lumens	Finish	Quantity Per Fixture	Notes
75/3000K	20,000	2850	Warm white	2	

Controls

Mark	Manufacturer	Number/Name	Description	Faceplate Style	Faceplate Finish	Keypad and Button Style	Button Colors
A	ZZZ Company	Controlmatic	Passive infrared occupancy sensor	Modern	White	Touch	White

Mounting Method	Wireless/2-Wire	Voltage	Options	Quantity	Notes
Ceiling	2-wire	120 volt		1	

TABLE 22.4
Budget Estimate Form

Lighting System Budget Estimate
ABC Firm
1222 Madison Street
Madison, NY 23409

Client Name: **Project:**
Address:
Date:

Room	Item	Quantity	Description	Unit Price	Total Price
Subtotal					
Tax					
Shipping					
TOTAL					
Deposit					
Total Due upon Delivery					

decision-making stages in the project, such as schematic design and design development. In addition, when unexpected changes arise during the ordering or construction phases, a lighting designer must present the situation to the client and offer appropriate solutions. Presentations that focus on providing updates on the status of the project are excellent ways to consistently communicate with the client and demonstrate the lighting designer's commitment to the project.

Presentations and discussions with the client are opportune times to demonstrate a lighting designer's expertise, experience, and abilities. Rarely will a client commit to spending thousands of dollars without having confidence in the lighting designer. To commit to a project and the projected costs, a client must have faith in a lighting designer's abilities to know the best approaches to the project and the experience to execute the design. In addition to well-prepared presentations, photographs of past projects and referrals from previous clients can help demonstrate expertise.

Presentations focused on the lighting design can be especially challenging to prepare. Because many clients are not familiar with the technology, it can be difficult for them to visualize the aesthetic elements of illumination. In addition, when a lighting designer has been hired to only develop the lighting design, coordination must be orchestrated with other professionals who may be presenting other elements of the interior, such as space planning, architectural details, or material specifications. Therefore, the presentation format is dependent upon the professionals involved in the project, as well as the audience and location. A presentation format should be tailored to each client and project. When the presentation is to one person, the format generally is informal and might include several visuals. Presentations to many individuals will generally require mediums that allow everyone in the audience to see the lighting design. This can be especially challenging when illustrating small features of a lighting plan or unique attributes of a luminaire.

Presentation may be conducted at a variety of locations, including the lighting designer's studio, a client's office, a conference room, the site of the project, the site of a previous job to illustrate a specific technique or lighting system used, or a lighting showroom. Different locations require different presentation formats. Many locations will not have the technological support for computer-generated presentations. When preparing the presentation, it is important for the interior designer to know the conditions and facilities available. In addition, a backup plan should be created for when technology fails. Presentations at selected sites can be very helpful in demonstrating a lighting technique and how illumination affects an environment. This is especially useful for lighting presentations, because clients frequently need actual examples to fully understand the complexities of illumination. A presentation at the site of the project can demonstrate specific problems to a client, such as dark areas in the space, glare, or the condition of lamps and luminaires. Presenting at the site also provides the designer with the opportunity to help a client visualize a luminaire in the space by holding the fixture in the approximate mounting position.

Presentations made at the location of a previous project may be helpful in illustrating a lighting technique that is proposed for the new job. This location may also be effective for new construction projects. In discussing a previous project, it is important to assure the client that the existing lighting design is meant to illustrate only a technique or application. The explanation should also indicate that the proposed lighting design for the new site is created to accommodate the unique requirements of the end users, activities, and architectural elements. Duplicating a lighting design can indicate a lack of understanding of the project and stifle a client's desire to have ownership of the concepts.

Compromising the uniqueness of a lighting design is not a concern when conducting a presentation at a showroom. Lighting showrooms can be an excellent resource for showing a client a proposed luminaire and the illumination effects derived from distribution patterns, variations in intensity, beam spread, and preset scenes. In addition, some showrooms have mock-ups of various lighting methods and applications. For example, some spaces have various luminaires for accent lighting. Thus, during a presentation, the client can observe multiple approaches to accent lighting and decide which method is preferred. Some showrooms have multiple boxes containing different types of lamps and various CRI and CCT ratings (Figure 22.12). Each box may be viewed by clients so that they may learn how a specific lamp affects colors, materials, textures, and complexions. The exact materials and colors specified for a project can be placed in the boxes. The client can then visualize how specific lamps will affect the proposed materials. These demonstration units are especially useful when the boxes are located next to one another and identical materials are viewed

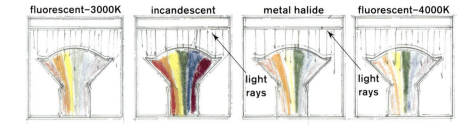

FIGURE 22.12
Each demonstration box has a different lamp to illustrate how qualities of a light source can affect colors and materials. These demonstration units are an excellent means to show a client the affect of lamp sources on colors, textures, materials, and complexions.

using different lamps. This enables the client to simultaneously compare and contrast the lighting effects on colors and materials.

A variety of mediums can be used to present a lighting design to a client. In addition to boards and drawings, a lighting designer may use PowerPoint slides or videos. PowerPoint is a convenient format for presenting text and illustrations of luminaires, lighting techniques, and photographs of previous projects. When presenting at a location different from the project site, a video may be included to demonstrate existing lighting problems or specific features of the interior that are affected by illumination. A video can also be useful in explaining a lighting design at another site. To produce a video, a lighting designer may hire a professional video production consultant.

In developing the content of the presentation, an important factor is how the lighting design will be presented within the context of the entire project. Any proposed elements of an interior that affect illumination should be presented prior to the lighting design. Examples of these elements are colors of surfaces, special architectural details, furniture, or a kitchen design. Presenting this information before the lighting design provides the context for the proposed illumination plans. During the presentation of interior elements, it is important for the interior designer to be attentive to the reactions of the client. When a client does not like a proposal, such as a particular color or furniture style, a lighting designer should make an attempt to acknowledge the concerns and present possible alternatives.

A typical presentation format includes an introduction, an analysis of the situation, descriptions of plans, and a conclusion. Throughout the presentation, an attempt should be made to involve the client in the discussion of the lighting design. A copy of the agenda should be given to everyone attending the presentation, and, at the appropriate time, the client should be given the job notebook. The introduction presents the overall concept of the lighting design. An analysis of the situation should focus on the results of the comprehensive programming phase. Data gathered during this phase should serve as an objective rationale for the lighting plans. In presenting the proposed lighting design, items should be prioritized according to the most salient needs of the client and end users. For example, when a client's priority is energy conservation, the presentation should demonstrate how the lighting design is energy-efficient. In describing the lighting design, an effective approach is to "walk" through each space and discuss plans. This room-by-room method is a convenient way to describe the layers of lighting in each space, illumination zones, and transitional lighting patterns.

In describing plans, it is important to define lighting terms. There are many terms a client will not understand, such as *voltage types, throw distances, luminaires,* or *lamps.* The word *lamp* is especially problematic because most people associate the term with the portable fixture. When clients do not understand a term, they frequently become distracted and lose interest in the design. Therefore, in developing the presentation script, the interior designer should assume that the client does not know lighting terminology and explain terminology.

In addition to educating a client about lighting terms, demonstrations of how to operate a system are informative and helpful. Generally, clients are reluctant to purchase a lighting system they don't understand how to operate or maintain. For example, preset scenes may be confusing to program. Demonstrating to clients how controls are programmed can help build confidence in their ability to operate the technology. Furthermore, clients will feel more comfortable with a lighting system if they are given a manual that describes operational functions, maintenance, and cleaning requirements. Since clients do not frequently purchase lighting systems, they may be astounded at the costs. An explanation for the costs should accompany the presentation. Part of the rationale may focus on the long-term ROI or on energy management and economics. Generally, costs should be discussed toward the end of the presentation because focusing on the numbers rather than the lighting design may distract a client. Costs can be summarized in the job notebook, which generally should be given to the client at the end of the presentation.

Depending upon the reactions of the client, revisions to the lighting design might have to be made. Once a client is in complete agreement with the lighting design, the contract documentation phase can begin. Upon approval by the client, a lighting designer develops recommendations for lighting specifications and submits the information to the registered professionals for review and final determination. Registered professionals, such as architects and engineers, begin the contract documentation phase by developing working drawings, specifications, sections, cut sheets, and purchase orders.

SUMMARY

- The schematic design phase is composed of analyzing the results obtained during the comprehensive programming stage and then developing initial design concepts for the interior illumination.
- Data collected through interviews, surveys, and field observations may be summarized in the following ways: (1) thorough analysis of the data by reading the content numerous times, (2) creating a detailed description of the results, (3) developing a prioritized list of lighting requirements, and (4) determining potential problems.
- Sketches may be developed with creative coding schemes that depict and reinforce strengths and weaknesses of a lighting plan.
- The results of the analysis serve as the basis for the conceptualization process of the schematic design phase. In this stage, a lighting designer and other professionals involved in the project engage in a comprehensive brainstorming process.
- Brainstorming sessions should include written comments and sketches, and they should explore all possible options for a lighting solution.
- At the conclusion of the schematic design phase, materials presented to the client may include a concept statement, freehand sketches, photographs of luminaires, a list of lighting equipment, preliminary costs, and projected time lines.

- The purposes of the design development phase are to work through the details of the conceptual lighting design and produce presentation mediums and specifications for the client's approval.
- Specifications and updates of the total project serve as the foundation for developing presentation mediums and as the requirements for the lighting design.
- The medium used to present the lighting design may be based upon the style of a design firm or determined by the tool that best enables the client to visualize the specific details of a particular project.
- To organize the details of a project, a useful tool is a systematic project outline, which is developed in coordination with the contractor's schedule.
- Presenting technical information to a client requires a format, such as a job or project notebook, that makes it possible for materials to be compiled in a professional manner.
- Generally, presentations to a client are scheduled at major decision-making stages of the project, such as schematic design and design development.
- A presentation may be conducted at a variety of locations, including the lighting designer's studio, a client's office, a conference room, the site of the project, a previous job, or a lighting showroom.
- A variety of mediums may be used to present a lighting design to a client. In addition to boards and drawings, a lighting designer may use PowerPoint slides or videos.
- A typical presentation format includes an introduction, an analysis of the situation, descriptions of the plans, and a conclusion.
- In describing plans to a client, it is important to define lighting terms and demonstrate how to operate a lighting system.

Exercises

1. Visit three buildings and conduct field observations. For each site, record how people are affected by the lighting design. Analyze and synthesize the observations. Make recommendations for improving the space. Summarize your results in a written report and include illustrations, photographs, or sketches.

2. Develop a schedule for a conceptualization brainstorming session. Include the format and topical inquiries for developing lighting plans. Engage in a brainstorming session with five or six students. Record comments and develop sketches, overlays, and a conclusive matrix. Summarize the process and results in a written report and include sketches, overlays, and the matrix.

3. Select five photographs of public interiors. For each space, identify the purpose of the space and provide a description of the lighting systems. Identify the information that should be gathered for detailed analysis of the space. Summarize your results in a written report and include the photographs.

4. Arrange interviews with electricians and cabinetmakers. Develop a questionnaire that focuses on costs and variables that affect lighting installations. Utilize the questionnaire to conduct the interviews and summarize the results in a written report. Include in the summary a reflective statement that addresses how you may be able to use the results when you are working as a professional.

5. Select a photograph of both a residential and a commercial interior. For each space, develop a presentation agenda and script and identify visuals that would be helpful in presenting the lighting design to a client. Summarize the results in a written report and include the photographs.

REFERENCES

Alderman, R.L. (1997). *How to Prosper as an Interior Designer: A Business and Legal Guide.* New York: John Wiley & Sons.

Allen, P.S., Jones, L.M., and Stimpson, M.F. (2004). *Beginnings of Interior Environments,* 9th edition. Upper Saddle River, NJ: Pearson/Prentice Hall.

American Institute of Architects (2000). *Architectural Graphics Standards,* 10th edition. New York: John Wiley & Sons.

Benya, J., Heschong, L., McGowan, T., Miller, N., and Rubinstein, F. (2001). *Advanced Lighting Guidelines.* White Salmon, WA: New Buildings Institute.

Birnberg, H.G. (1999). *Project Management for Building Designers and Owners.* Boca Raton, FL: CRC Press.

Burde, E. (1992). *Design Presentation Techniques.* New York: McGraw-Hill.

Burstein, D., and Stasiowski, F. (1982). *Project Management for the Design Professional.* New York: Watson-Guptill.

Ching, F.D.K. (2003). *Architectural Graphics,* 4th edition. New York: John Wiley & Sons.

Coleman, C. (ed.) (2001). *Interior Design Handbook of Professional Practice.* New York: McGraw-Hill.

Doyle, M.E. (1999). *Color Drawing: Design Skills and Techniques for Architects, Landscape Architects, and Interior Designers,* 2nd edition. New York: John Wiley & Sons.

Farren, C.E. (1999). *Planning and Managing Interior Projects,* 2nd edition. Kingston, MA: R.S. Means.

Getz, L. (1986). *Business Management in the Smaller Design Firm.* Newton, MA: Practice Management Associates.

Gibbs, J. (1997). *A Handbook for Interior Designers.* London: Sterling Publications.

Illuminating Engineering Society of North America (IESNA) (2000). *Document DG-3-00: Application of Luminaire Symbols on Lighting Design Drawings.* New York: Illuminating Engineering Society of North America.

International Association of Lighting Designers (IALD) (2002). *Guidelines for Specification Integrity.* Chicago: International Association of Lighting Designers.

Kilmer, R., and Kilmer, W.O. (1992). *Designing Interiors.* New York: Harcourt Brace.

Kliment, S.A. (1998). *Writing for Design Professionals.* New York: W.W. Norton.

Knackstedt, M.V. (2002). *The Interior Design Business Handbook.* New York: John Wiley & Sons.

Koenig, P.A. (2000). *Design Graphics: Drawing Techniques for Design Professionals.* Upper Saddle River, NJ: Pearson Education/ Prentice Hall.

Koomen-Harmon, S., and Kennon, K. (2001). *The Codes Guidebook for Interiors,* 2nd edition. New York: John Wiley & Sons.

Kriebel, T.M., Birdsong, C., and Sherman, D.J. (1991). Defining interior design programming. *Journal of Interior Design Education and Research, 17(1),* 29–36.

Liebing, R.W. (1999). *Architectural Working Drawings,* 4th edition. New York: John Wiley & Sons.

Mitton, M. (1999). *Interior Design Visual Presentations: A Guide to Graphics, Models, and Presentation Techniques.* New York: John Wiley & Sons.

Nissen, L., Faulkner, R., and Faulkner, S. (1994). *Inside Today's Home,* 6th edition. New York: Harcourt Brace.

O'Leary, A.F. (1992). *Construction Administration in Architectural Practice.* New York: McGraw-Hill.

Pile, J.F. (1988). *Interior Design.* New York: Harry N. Abrams.

Pile, J.F. (1995). *Interior Design,* 2nd edition. New York: Harry N. Abrams.

Pile, J.F. (2003). *Interior Design,* 3rd edition. New York: Harry N. Abrams.

Piotrowski, C.M. (1992). *Interior Design Management: A Handbook for Owners and Managers.* New York: John Wiley & Sons.

Piotrowski, C.M. (2002). *Professional Practice for Interior Designers,* 3rd edition. New York: John Wiley & Sons.

Ramsey, C.G., and Sleeper, H.R. (2000). *Architectural Graphic Standards,* 10th edition. New York: John Wiley & Sons.

Reznikoff, S.C. (1986). *Interior Graphic and Design Standards.* New York: Whitney Library of Design.

Reznikoff, S.C. (1989). *Specifications for Commercial Interiors: Professional Liabilities, Regulations, and Performance Criteria.* New York: Whitney Library of Design.

Siegel, H., and Siegel, A. (1982). *A Guide to Business Principles and Practices for Interior Designers.* New York: Whitney Library of Design.

Smith, W.D., and Smith, L.H. (2001). *McGraw-Hill On-Site Guide to Building Codes 2000: Commercial and Residential Interiors.* New York: McGraw-Hill.

Stasiowski, F., and Burnstein, D. (1982). *Project Management for the Design Professional.* New York: Whitney Library of Design/Watson-Guptill Publications.

Steffy, G.R. (2002). *Architectural Lighting Design,* 2nd edition. New York: Van Nostrand Reinhold.

Thompson, J.A. (ed.) (1992). *ASID Professional Practice Manual.* New York : Whitney Library of Design.

Veitch, R.M., Jackman, D.R., and Dixon, M.K. (1990). *Professional Practice: A Handbook for Interior Designers.* Winnipeg, Canada: Peguis Publishers.

Wakita, O.A., and Linde, R.M. (2003). *The Professional Practice of Architectural Working Drawings,* 3rd edition. New York: John Wiley & Sons.

Williams, D.J. (1996). *Preparing for Project Management.* New York: American Society of Civil Engineers.

CHAPTER 23

Lighting Design Process: Final Phases

OBJECTIVES

■ Identify working drawings used to illustrate a lighting design.

■ Describe details that should be included in lighting working drawings and specifications.

■ Describe contracts that are frequently used for a lighting design.

■ Identify the tasks associated with contract administration of a lighting project.

■ Understand the purpose of the postoccupancy evaluation and how to apply the process to a lighting design.

FINAL phases of the lighting design process consist of developing contract documents, contract administration, and evaluation. These phases are very exciting because the project becomes a reality. However, these phases can also be stressful because a lighting designer executes legally binding contracts with various businesses involved with the project, including the client, suppliers, contractors, and tradespeople. Changes to the original specifications can be costly and create delays. Furthermore, a variety of problems and conflicts may occur during construction and installation. Since these stages do not involve creative processes, frequently a lighting designer is not about fulfilling these responsibilities. The last phases are absolutely critical to the success of a lighting design. And since these are the last experiences a client remembers, it is essential to conclude with a positive impression. Therefore, sufficient time must be allocated to developing accurate documents, consistent communication, careful supervision, and effective problem solving.

In studying the content in this chapter, it is important to analyze the material within the context of generic lighting information. Generally, architectural, engineering, and interior design firms develop a preferred format for drawings, specifications, and contracts. Standardized requirements are reviewed by an attorney and then serve as a template for developing contract documents. Moreover, each firm may have staff members who are responsible for developing specific documents, such as specifications or purchase orders. Thus, the information presented in this chapter is intended to be a guide to the procedures and contractual requirements of engaging in the final phases of the lighting design process.

Contract Documents

Contractual documents include working drawings and written specifications.

Working Drawings

A graphic representation of a lighting system is depicted in working or construction drawings. Working drawings supplement specifications that are written descriptions of the parameters of the lighting system. Working drawings and specifications are the basis for ordering products, installing wiring, and determining the location of luminaires, outlets, and controls. In contrast to presentation illustrations, which are produced in the design development phase, working drawings represent a legal contract. Therefore, as contract documents, working drawings are accurately scaled, contain detailed illustrations, and must demonstrate that plans comply with local codes. Working drawings for a lighting design are developed in coordination with mechanical, plumbing, and structural systems. Laws mandate that registered professionals, such as architects and engineers, stamp working drawings and specifications. Therefore, a lighting designer develops drawings of a lighting design, which must then be submitted to registered professionals for review and further development. To help retain the original intent of the lighting design, a lighting designer should ask to review the working drawings prior to their being submitted to the local building department, contract closures, financial institutions, or a bidding process.

Commonly used working drawings are a plan of the lighting, electrical, lighting/electrical, and reflected ceiling. Drawings also may include elevations, sections, and details. Lighting schedules and general notes located on drawing sheets provide additional information regarding the lighting system. The production format, including dimensions, should be coordinated with other professionals working on the project. Drawings may be printed on sheets or presented in a job notebook. Generally, lighting plans generated by CAD software are developed in layers. This enables the designer to examine the relationships between lighting and other elements of a project. For example, a lighting plan can be viewed with the HVAC system to make sure components do not overlap. An assessment of the electrical plan and furniture arrangements can help to ensure access to power for portable luminaires. Cross-referencing of details on working drawings must also be performed with written specifications. (Specifications are discussed in the next section of this chapter.)

Symbol legends, located on working drawings, are essential for describing the type of luminaires, wiring configurations, switching systems, and outlets. Symbols and abbreviations are used to communicate complex details of a lighting design. To promote standardization throughout the building industry, an American Institute of Architects (AIA) task force developed symbols and abbreviations for architectural working drawings. Many of these symbols and conventions, such as door swings and mechanical systems, are used on working drawings for a lighting design. In addition, there are specific symbols for electrical plans, including convenience outlets, switch outlets, auxiliary units, general outlets, and switching arrangements (Figure 23.1).

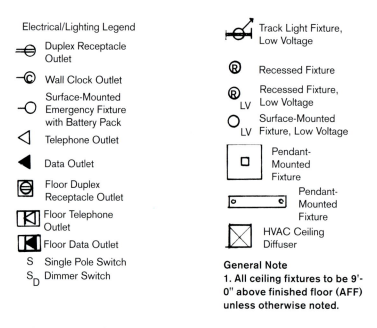

FIGURE 23.1 Symbols for electrical plans, including convenience outlets, switch outlets, auxiliary units, general outlets, and switching arrangements.

In 2000, the IESNA developed guidelines for standardized luminaire symbols on lighting drawings. The format is composed of a base luminaire symbol set and a series of modifiers. Combining base symbols with modifiers enables a lighting designer to indicate specific details regarding the attributes of a lighting system. For example, as shown in Figure 23.2, the base symbols are: (a) luminaires represented in four shapes, (b) strip luminaires, (c) linear sources, and (d) exit signs. These symbols form the foundation for representing a luminaire. As noted by the IESNA (2000), whenever possible, the symbols should be drawn in the approximate size (to scale), and shape of the luminaire. To provide more details regarding a luminaire, the IESNA developed primary modifiers, which are added to the base symbols. As illustrated in Figure 23.3, primary modifiers are categorized according to mounting technique, optic orientation, and lighting for emergency purposes. Any of the modifiers may be used with base luminaire symbols. Thus, a strip luminaire symbol could have an emergency modifier.

To provide additional details regarding a lighting system, the IESNA created another set of modifiers. As demonstrated in Figure 23.4, this subset includes information relating to mounting heights, subscripts,

OR
OR
OR
Luminaire:
(drawn to approximate shape and to scale or large enough for clarity)
Luminaire: Strip type
(length drawn to scale)
Linear source: e.g., Low voltage strip, neon, or fiber optic.
(length drawn to scale with cross mark at breaks and/or ends)
Exit sign: Mounting, number of faces (filled in), and arrow as shown

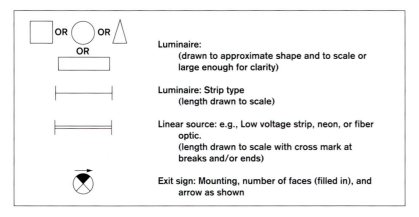

FIGURE 23.2 Base luminaire symbols including shapes, strip luminaires, linear sources, and exit signs. These symbols form the foundation for representing a luminaire.

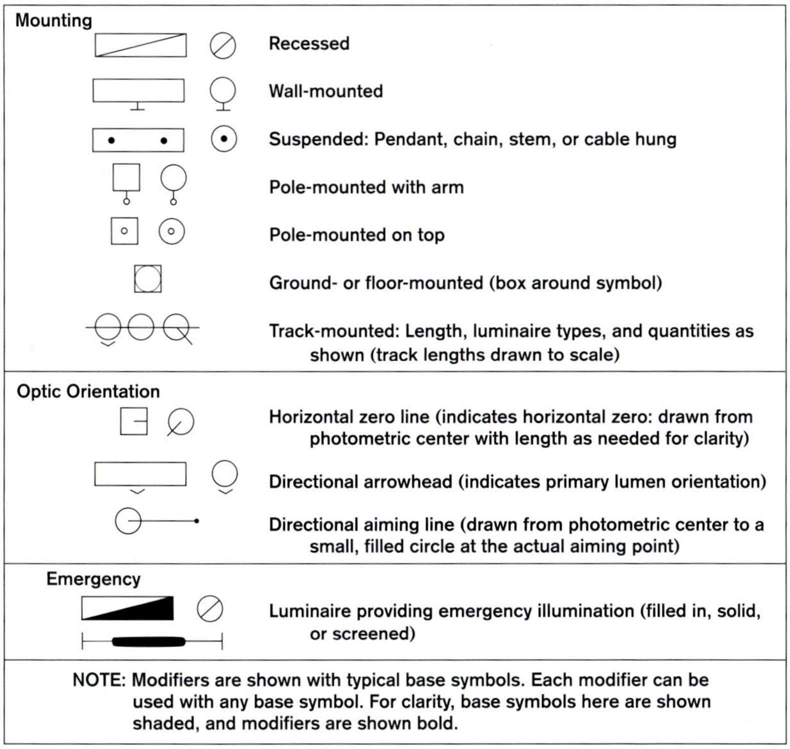

Mounting
Recessed
Wall-mounted
Suspended: Pendant, chain, stem, or cable hung
Pole-mounted with arm
Pole-mounted on top
Ground- or floor-mounted (box around symbol)
Track-mounted: Length, luminaire types, and quantities as shown (track lengths drawn to scale)
Optic Orientation
Horizontal zero line (indicates horizontal zero: drawn from photometric center with length as needed for clarity)
Directional arrowhead (indicates primary lumen orientation)
Directional aiming line (drawn from photometric center to a small, filled circle at the actual aiming point)
Emergency
Luminaire providing emergency illumination (filled in, solid, or screened)
NOTE: Modifiers are shown with typical base symbols. Each modifier can be used with any base symbol. For clarity, base symbols here are shown shaded, and modifiers are shown bold.

FIGURE 23.3 Primary luminaire modifiers categorized according to mounting technique, optic orientation, and lighting for emergency purposes. Any of the modifiers can be used with base luminaire symbols.

and luminaire identifiers. To illustrate how multiple modifiers may be added to the base luminaire symbols, the IESNA developed a chart with descriptions. The illustration in Figure 23.5 is only an example of how to incorporate base symbols and modifiers. In practice, numerous

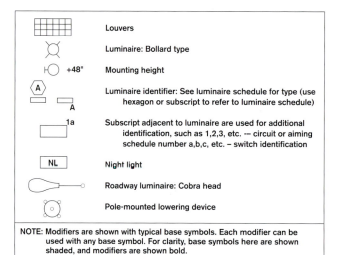

	Louvers
	Luminaire: Bollard type
+48"	Mounting height
A	Luminaire identifier: See luminaire schedule for type (use hexagon or subscript to refer to luminaire schedule)
1a	Subscript adjacent to luminaire are used for additional identification, such as 1,2,3, etc. -– circuit or aiming schedule number a,b,c, etc. – switch identification
NL	Night light
	Roadway luminaire: Cobra head
	Pole-mounted lowering device

NOTE: Modifiers are shown with typical base symbols. Each modifier can be used with any base symbol. For clarity, base symbols here are shown shaded, and modifiers are shown bold.

FIGURE 23.4 Subset of luminaire modifiers, including information relative to mounting heights, subscripts, and luminaire identifiers.

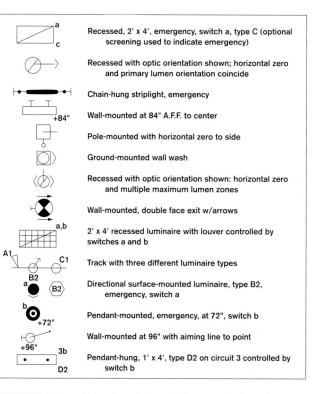

a / c	Recessed, 2' x 4', emergency, switch a, type C (optional screening used to indicate emergency)
	Recessed with optic orientation shown; horizontal zero and primary lumen orientation coincide
	Chain-hung striplight, emergency
+84"	Wall-mounted at 84" A.F.F. to center
	Pole-mounted with horizontal zero to side
	Ground-mounted wall wash
	Recessed with optic orientation shown: horizontal zero and multiple maximum lumen zones
	Wall-mounted, double face exit w/arrows
a,b	2' x 4' recessed luminaire with louver controlled by switches a and b
A1 C1 B2	Track with three different luminaire types
a B2 B2	Directional surface-mounted luminaire, type B2, emergency, switch a
b +72"	Pendant-mounted, emergency, at 72", switch b
+96"	Wall-mounted at 96" with aiming line to point
3b D2	Pendant-hung, 1' x 4', type D2 on circuit 3 controlled by switch b

FIGURE 23.5 Examples of how to incorporate base luminaire symbols and modifiers.

luminaire symbols might be created based upon the specifics of a lighting system and the mounting location. The IESNA guidelines for luminaire symbols are an excellent means of communicating many of the complexities associated with the technology of contemporary lighting systems. The IESNA symbols should be used on all lighting drawings and the descriptions must correspond to the specifications. Manufacturers' cut sheets are important documents to include with lighting specifications. Thus, a recommended practice is to draw the luminaire symbol on the manufacturers' cut sheets. This designation on the product literature helps to clarify exactly which luminaire is represented by a specific symbol. As the field of lighting progresses, it is anticipated that the IESNA will create additional symbols and modifiers.

Working drawings for lighting designs include a view of the lighting, electrical, and lighting/electrical plans. A lighting designer may prepare conceptual working drawings for the lighting and associated electrical needs. As mentioned earlier, registered professionals must stamp their approval on all working drawings. Complex structures require separate lighting and electrical plans. Frequently, drawings for residential and small commercial buildings have one plan, which illustrates lighting and electrical requirements. As illustrated in Figure 23.6, a lighting plan includes the location of luminaires, switches, and control loops. The luminaire should be scaled and represent a close approximation of the shape of the fixture. Complicated drawings might not have enough space to show scaled luminaires. For these situations, letters and subscripts may be used to identify specific luminaires. Either a circle or a hexagon surrounds the letters. The symbol and a brief description of the luminaire are listed in the legends.

Dimension lines and notes may be used to identify the exact size and location of luminaires. Measurements are from the center (o.c.) of a luminaire to a fixed architectural element, such as the face of an exterior wall, window mullions, or the center of partitions. Spacing between multiple luminaires that are located in the same room is indicated by measurements from an architectural element to the center of each fixture. A plan may also include mounting heights of fixtures that are located on vertical planes or that are suspended from the ceiling. The mounting height of luminaires located on a vertical plane, such as a wall or column, is from A.F.F. to the center of the fixture (o.c.). The distance for suspended fixtures is from A.F.F. to the bottom of the luminaire.

Switching arrangements are illustrated by the applicable switch symbol and control loops. As demonstrated in Figure 23.6, control loops are drawn from the switch(s) to the luminaire that is controlled by the switch(s). Control loops on a lighting plan are curved and straight lines represent wiring runs on electrical plans. Whenever possible, furniture arrangements should be included in a lighting plan. Drawing techniques for this purpose include overlays, layers, or by adding furniture to the plan. Combining the placement of furniture with the lighting plan can be very helpful in ensuring that the luminaire is accurately positioned for a specific task or that it fulfills the intended purpose. Identifying the exact location of a luminaire takes into consideration differences in furniture dimensions, the number of items in a room, and how a space is arranged. For example, to ensure that a chandelier will be centered over a dining table, all the furniture

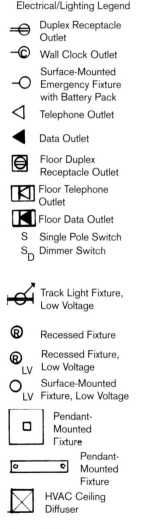

Electrical/Lighting Legend

⊖ Duplex Receptacle Outlet

©̶ Wall Clock Outlet

−O Surface-Mounted Emergency Fixture with Battery Pack

◁ Telephone Outlet

◀ Data Outlet

⊜ Floor Duplex Receptacle Outlet

⊠ Floor Telephone Outlet

◼ Floor Data Outlet

S Single Pole Switch

S_D Dimmer Switch

Track Light Fixture, Low Voltage

Ⓡ Recessed Fixture

Ⓡ_LV Recessed Fixture, Low Voltage

O_LV Surface-Mounted Fixture, Low Voltage

Pendant-Mounted Fixture

Pendant-Mounted Fixture

HVAC Ceiling Diffuser

General Note

1. All ceiling fixtures to be 9'-0" above finished floor (AFF) unless otherwise noted.

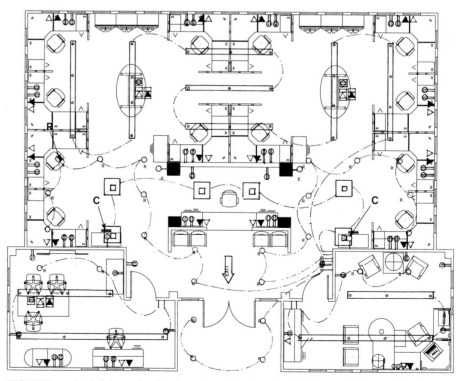

FIGURE 23.6 A lighting plan that indicates the location of luminaires, switches, control loops, dimension lines, and notes.

should be positioned on the plan, and then the location of the luminaire may be determined. Furniture dimensions, and placement in a room, also affect the location of luminaires intended for unique purposes, such as highlighting artwork.

Electrical plans can be extremely complicated and technical. As with all working drawings, registered professionals must officially approve the documents. Generally, a lighting designer will be asked to describe only the lighting design, and then engineers determine power requirements. Detailed electrical plans illustrate wiring runs from electrical panels to all equipment in a building, including lighting systems. Elements related to lighting systems in an electrical plan include luminaires, switches, outlets, junction boxes, and auxiliary units (Figure 23.7). Straight lines indicate wiring runs on electrical plans. Small commercial buildings and residences often have one plan that combines electrical and lighting specifications. A lighting/electrical plan includes the location of luminaires, switches, outlets, auxiliary units, junction boxes, and control loops (Figure 23.8).

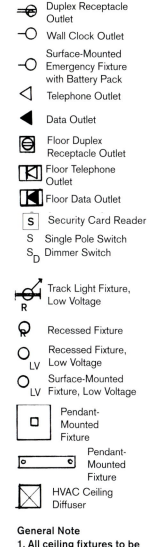

Electrical/Lighting Legend

⊖ Duplex Receptacle Outlet

○ Wall Clock Outlet

○ Surface-Mounted Emergency Fixture with Battery Pack

◁ Telephone Outlet

◀ Data Outlet

⊖ Floor Duplex Receptacle Outlet

◤ Floor Telephone Outlet

◤ Floor Data Outlet

S Security Card Reader

S Single Pole Switch

S_D Dimmer Switch

Track Light Fixture, Low Voltage

○ Recessed Fixture

○ Recessed Fixture, Low Voltage LV

○ Surface-Mounted Fixture, Low Voltage LV

□ Pendant-Mounted Fixture

Pendant-Mounted Fixture

⊠ HVAC Ceiling Diffuser

General Note
1. All ceiling fixtures to be 9'-0" above finished floor (AFF) unless otherwise noted.

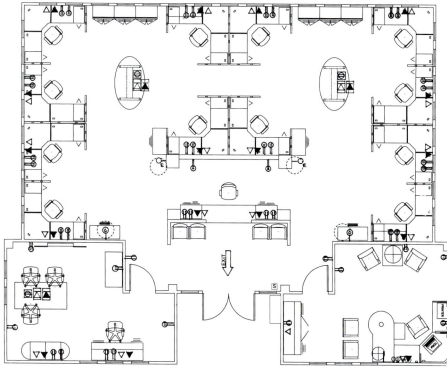

FIGURE 23.7 An electrical plan including outlets, junction boxes, auxiliary units, furniture, and telephone/data outlets.

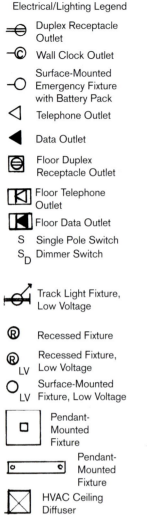

Electrical/Lighting Legend

⊖ Duplex Receptacle Outlet

©ᶜ Wall Clock Outlet

○ Surface-Mounted Emergency Fixture with Battery Pack

◁ Telephone Outlet

◀ Data Outlet

⊖ Floor Duplex Receptacle Outlet

▣ Floor Telephone Outlet

◀ Floor Data Outlet

S Single Pole Switch

S_D Dimmer Switch

Track Light Fixture, Low Voltage

Ⓡ Recessed Fixture

Ⓡ_LV Recessed Fixture, Low Voltage

○_LV Surface-Mounted Fixture, Low Voltage

▢ Pendant-Mounted Fixture

▭ Pendant-Mounted Fixture

⊠ HVAC Ceiling Diffuser

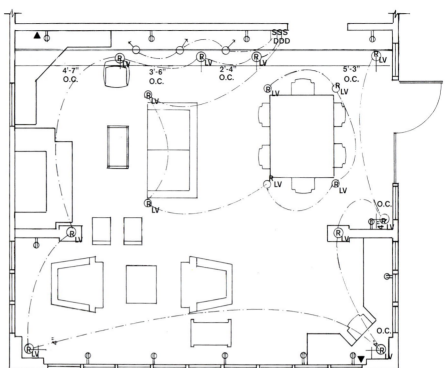

FIGURE 23.8 A lighting/electrical plan indicating the location of luminaires, switches, outlets, control loops, and furniture.

In addition to recommending lighting systems, a lighting designer should provide suggestions for the location of switches and outlets. The location of these elements can significantly affect how well people function in a space. As discussed in Chapter 13, switches and outlets should be located in a position that reflects the principles of universal design. The location of switches and outlets should always coincide with how people function in a space. Switches should be located on the lock side of a door and at various other convenient locations within a room or space. Outlets should be convenient to reach from a variety of positions. Outlets are inexpensive to install during the construction phase. Thus, the number of outlets should be determined by power needs, not a standardized layout. Sufficient outlets should be installed to provide electricity to all portable luminaires without the need of extension cords, outlet adapters, or extending the fixture's cord for a long distance.

The location of outlets should also be dependent upon the space configuration of vertical planes and furniture arrangements. For example, the location of outlets should be coordinated with a fireplace, built-in cabinets, or artwork. Generally, outlets should not be centered on a wall, because electrical cords connected to the outlet may become a focal point. In addition, reaching an outlet can be very difficult when a large piece of furniture, such as a breakfront in a dining room, is placed in front of the outlet. The location of outlets should support furniture arrangements. This can be especially challenging in rooms that have furniture positioned away from walls. A frequent solution to this problem is installing floor outlets. On an electrical plan, dimension lines extending from the outlet to fixed architectural elements indicate the location of floor outlets. Outlets and switches are elements of the interior. Thus, they should harmonize with the style, colors, and furnishings of the environment. Specifications for switches and outlets should include recommendations for products that enhance the design concept.

A **reflected ceiling plan** is frequently included in working drawings. The plan is the image one would see when looking in a mirror located on the floor. Therefore, the plan illustrates the design of the ceiling, including the location of luminaires, architectural elements, and any HVAC equipment. A reflected ceiling plan is helpful for analyzing the functional and aesthetic components of the horizontal plane. Functionally, the plan is useful in determining whether the location of luminaires accommodates activities in the room and does not interfere with other structural elements on the ceiling plane. The appearance of the ceiling affects the design of the interior space, especially in rooms with tall ceilings. In addition, a reflected ceiling plan helps the interior designer visualize how well the arrangement addresses the elements and principles of design.

A working drawing of a reflected ceiling plan includes the location of luminaires, switches, control loops, ceiling tiles, and any other element that intersects with the ceiling (Figure 23.9). These items can include partitions, heating air ducts, diffusers, exposed beams, columns, speakers, skylights, cornices, coves, soffits, sprinkler heads, emergency lights, and signage. Some plans include specific luminaire details, such as lamp aiming directions. Ceiling materials and changes in ceiling

> *Reflected ceiling plan*
> *A contract working drawing that illustrates the design of the ceiling, including the location of luminaires, architectural elements, and any HVAC equipment.*

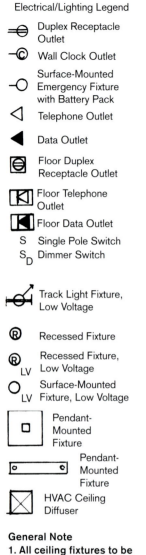

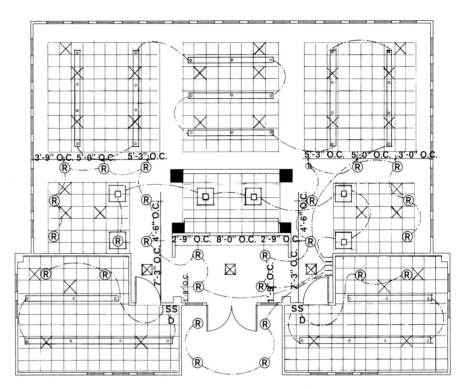

FIGURE 23.9 A reflected ceiling plan including the location of luminaires, switches, control loops, ceiling tiles, and other elements intersecting with the ceiling.

heights should also be noted on the plan. The location of luminaires should be dimensioned following the same method used in a lighting plan. However, when a luminaire is located in the center of a ceiling tile, dimension lines do not have to be drawn. The arrangement of ceiling tiles should enhance the shape and size of the ceiling. When necessary, partial tiles are located along the perimeter of the room.

Sections and elevations are useful working drawings for illustrating the location of wall luminaires, switches, outlets, windows, and doors. Sections can demonstrate the effects of illumination on each floor in multistory structures. For example, sectional views can be very helpful to designers for analyzing light distribution patterns emitted from skylights in an atrium. Sections may also reveal the location of floor-mounted luminaires and mechanical or electrical elements in ceiling cavities. Elevation measurements provide a view of the arrangement of luminaires and other elements that can affect the composition of a wall, including furniture, objects, windows, or architectural features

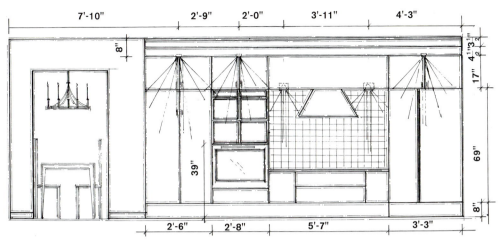

FIGURE 23.10 An elevation of a wall that indicates the arrangement of luminaires and other elements that can affect the composition of a wall.

(Figure 23.10). Elevations are especially effective in demonstrating the location of wall-mounted luminaires, valances, coves, or soffits.

Working drawings of integrated lighting systems, such as bookcases, soffits, or kitchen cabinets, require detailed illustrations. Detailed working drawings must communicate precise information to a fabricator and an installer. As scaled drawings, details indicate the exact size and location of all elements contained in an integrated system, including lamps, lamp holders, ballasts, transformers, structural elements, return air slots, baffles, reflectors, glass, access grilles, cables, brackets, wiring, projectors, and mechanical support (Figure 23.11). Notes on detail drawings may include dimensions, material specifications,

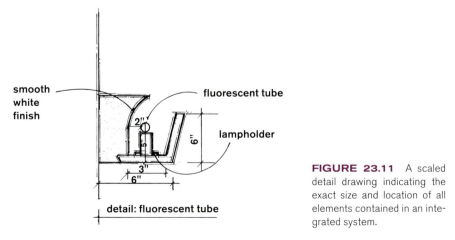

FIGURE 23.11 A scaled detail drawing indicating the exact size and location of all elements contained in an integrated system.

finishes, paint colors, and construction methods. In designing an integrated lighting system, it is important to include how heat generated by lamps will be dissipated and the means of access to lamps for replacement purposes.

Specifications

Supplementary to working drawings are lighting specifications, which are important contract documents. Generally, information provided in specifications will override cross-referenced details illustrated in working drawings. Therefore, specifications must be accurate, comprehensive, and written in a clear and concise manner. Lighting specifications can be included in the furniture, furnishings, and equipment (FF&E) document. To assist in the development of accurate details, the International Association of Lighting Designers (IALD) published a manual entitled Guidelines for Specification Integrity (2002). Topics include: (1) building a foundation for specifying, (2) processes in the design, construction document, bidding, and construction phases, and (3) specification approaches and languages (IALD, 2002). In writing lighting specifications, these guidelines should serve as a resource.

In addition to the IALD manual, another important specification document is *Masterformat*™, 2004 Edition, produced by the Construction Specification Institute (CSI). Available at www.csinet.org, *Masterformat*™ serves as a specification guide for the construction industry. The electrical division covers interior lighting. Within the electrical division, CSI has the following major headings: (a) "26 00 00–Electrical," (b) "26 10 00–Medium-Voltage Electrical Distribution," (c) "26 20 00–Low-Voltage Electrical Transmission," (d) "26 30 00–Facility Electrical Power Generating and Storing Equipment," (e) "26 40 00—Electrical and Cathodic Protection," and (f) "26 50 00—Lighting." Each heading has subheadings, which further refine a topic. For example, the "26 50 00—Lighting" category includes "26 51 00 Interior Lighting." Thus, when using *Masterformat*™ for specification purposes, the designer should refer to this section.

Many specifications are written to address the three specific areas of "general," "products," and "execution." The general section provides overall requirements of lighting specifications, such as complying with codes, laws and reference standards. The most commonly cited codes and laws include ASHRAE/IESNA 90.1-2001; MEC-95; IECC-03; NFPA 5000; ANSI; NEC; ADA; OSHA; BOCA; and California Title 24. Reference standards cited in specifications include UL listing; IESNA photometric measurement and testing procedures; National Electrical Manufacturers Association (NEMA) and American Society for Testing and Materials (ASTM). Some products may not have performance criteria. In this situation, some professionals will not accept the product or will request the appropriate organization to test it.

The product section describes characteristics of lighting systems for a project. This section includes a detailed description of the elements of a lighting system. For designers to understand how to accurately specify products, they should talk with manufacturers' representatives, read product literature, and visit manufacturing facilities. Walking through a factory and discussing products with the individuals responsible for making components of lighting systems can provide invaluable insight and details regarding specifications. Written lighting specifications contain numerous details, including quality standards, performance criteria, materials, dimensions, methods of construction, and installation requirements. Specifications for custom luminaires should also include intellectual property clauses. Some of the items that could be included in lighting specifications are listed in Table 23.1. The list is not intended to be inclusive, but should serve as a guide.

As a supplement to the written specifications, manufacturers' cut sheets should be included with contract documents. Cut sheets provide the detailed information that is required to price, order, and install a product (Figure 23.12). In addition, the process for product delivery can be complex and the timing must be precise. Therefore, to maintain control of the process, specifications should include instructions for storage and delivery, as well as bidding regulations. The document should also specify who is responsible for paying freight, storage, and delivery charges.

A lighting designer can dedicate an enormous amount of time and energy to specifying the ideal lighting system for a project. All these efforts may be lost when recommendations are altered or ignored during

TABLE 23.1

Lighting System Considerations for Specification Documents

General Considerations	Lamps	Luminaires	Controls	Installation
Quality requirements	Lamps/ballasts (IES	Material	Sensitivity settings	Mounting method
Performance criteria	testing and	Finishes	Time settings	Mounting height
Photometric distributions	measurements standards	Dimensions	Manual override policies	Length of pendants
Illumination levels	and procedures)	Aperture size	Compatibility with lamps	Operational orientation
Method(s) for calculating	Lamping configuration	Distribution	and ballasts	Mounting hardware
illumination levels	Number of lamps	Housing size	Infrared or ultrasonic	Full instructions for
Dimensions	Wattages	Accessories	technologies	installation and main-
Materials	Total wattage for	Factory options	Coverage patterns	tenance
Voltages	luminaires with multiple	Emergency battery pack	Built-in light level sensing	Light leaks policies
Visual comfort probability	lamps	Aiming/rotational	Automatic control policies	Plumb requirements
(VCP)	CRI and CCT	hardware	Energy management	Aiming adjustments
Transformers	requirements	Locking devices	system integration	procedures
Ceiling, wall, and floor	Filament design	Type of lenses	Finishes	Installation according to
reflectance	Diameter in inches	Type of louvers	Faceplate style/color	industry standards,
Sound rating requirements	Length	Type of baffles	Keypad and button	local codes, and
Dry, damp, or wet locations	Base type	Photometric calculations	style/color	manufacturer's
Standards and testing	Initial lumen	Quality issues: cracking,	Wireless or two-wire	instructions
procedures	requirements	discoloration	Control with A/V	Security mount
Highest quality	Average life/start hours	Minimum coefficient of	presentations	
Highest efficacy	Beam spread	utilization (CU)	Thermostat integration	
Warranties	Dimming ballast	Vandal-resistant	Noise requirements	
Luminaires supplied with	No PCBs or other	requirements	Motorized window	
appropriate lamps	hazardous materials	Theft-resistant features	treatments	
Easy access of lamps for	Disposal requirements	Relamping attachments	Installed in existing fixture	
cleaning and relamping	Multiple lamps—parallel	and locking mechanisms	Preinstalled	
	or series	Cord length requirements	Dimming ballast	
	Minimum ballast efficacy	for pendants	Number of controllers per	
	factor (BEF)	Adjustable cable length	lighting zone	
	Maintain a light output at	requirements	Wall box, tabletop,	
	XX%	Qualifications for custom	security mount	
	Flicker restrictions	luminaires		
	Lamp shielding			
	requirements			
	Replacement policies for			
	defective lamps			
	Lamp lumen loss			
	requirements			
	Dirt depreciation			
	requirements			
	Relamping and cleaning			
	requirements			
	Consistency with quality			
	of lamps			

FOCAL POINT

SOFTLITE II ^{2x2}

FS2 22B

2'x2' low profile recessed indirect with matte satin white reflector and perforated lamp shield

1, 2 & 3 Lamp T8

1 & 2 Lamp Biax

2 & 3 Lamp T5 & T5HO

Row Mount **RLP**

Features

- Softlite adds dimension to a space and provides a quality of light similar to suspended indirect luminaires.
- Two-piece endcaps provide row-mount capability for all configurations of Softlite II.
- Basket assembly retained by self-aligning torsion springs pulls down for easy relamping.
- Lamps are shielded by a perforated basket to provide soft downlight component.
- Ballast is accessible from both top and bottom side of unit.
- See Linear and Sconce sections for companion luminaires.

Construction
One piece die-formed 20 Ga. C.R.S., 2'x2' recessed reflector/housing. Detachable perforated basket lamp shield is CNC formed 22 Ga. C.R.S., with white acrylic lens insert. Die cast aluminum end caps complete shield assembly. Optional C.R.S. radial blade louver constructed of .75" high 20 Ga. blades on 1" frequency.

Weight: 17 lbs

Optic
Integrally welded one piece 20 Ga. C.R.S. reflector, finished in matte satin white powder coat. Lamp shield is detachable, perforated basket assembly of CNC formed 22 Ga. C.R.S. and white acrylic insert.

Electrical
Luminaires are pre-wired for specified circuits, with thermally protected Class "P" electronic ballasts.

Biax: Electronic instant start 270mA, <20% THD or optional electronic program start 270mA, <10% THD

T8 Lamps: Electronic instant start 265mA, <20% THD or optional electronic program start 265mA, <10% THD

T5 Lamps: Electronic program start 170mA, <10% THD

T5HO Lamps: Electronic program start 300mA, <10% THD

Optional DALI and other dimming ballasts available. Consult factory

for specifications and availability. UL and cUL Listed.

Emergency
Emergency battery packs provide 90 minutes of illumination. Initial lumen output for lamp types are as follows:

T8 Lamps: Up to 550 lumens
Biax Lamps: Up to 700 lumens

Battery pack requires unswitched hot from same branch circuit as AC ballast.

Finish
Luminaire housing, reflector and all steel components are finished in polyester powder coat applied over a 5-stage pretreatment. Standard finish for housing and all steel components: matte satin white (min. 94% reflectance).

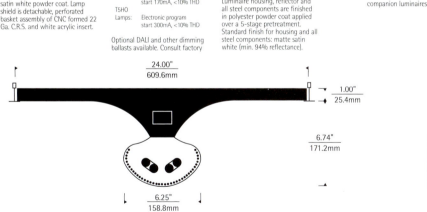

24.00"
609.6mm

1.00"
25.4mm

6.74"
171.2mm

6.25"
158.8mm

THE
ART OF
LIGHT™

FIGURE 23.12 A cutsheet from a luminaire manufacturer. A recommended practice is to draw the luminaire symbol on the manufacturers' cutsheets.

(Continued)

FIGURE 23.12 *Continued*

Fixture Type: _____

Project Name: _____

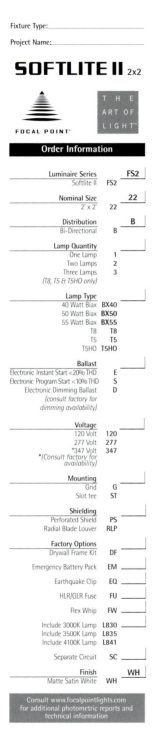

SOFTLITE II 2x2

FOCAL POINT®

THE ART OF LIGHT™

Order Information

Luminaire Series	**FS2**
Softlite II	FS2

Nominal Size	**22**
2' x 2'	22

Distribution	**B**
Bi-Directional	B

Lamp Quantity
One Lamp	1
Two Lamps	2
Three Lamps	3
(T8, T5 & T5HO only)	

Lamp Type
40 Watt Biax	BX40
50 Watt Biax	BX50
55 Watt Biax	BX55
T8	T8
T5	T5
T5HO	T5HO

Ballast
Electronic Instant Start <20% THD	E
Electronic Program Start <10% THD	S
Electronic Dimming Ballast	D
(consult factory for dimming availability)	

Voltage
120 Volt	120
277 Volt	277
*347 Volt	347
(Consult factory for availability)	

Mounting
Grid	G
Slot tee	ST

Shielding
Perforated Shield	PS
Radial Blade Louver	RLP

Factory Options
Drywall Frame Kit	DF
Emergency Battery Pack	EM
Earthquake Clip	EQ
HLR/GLR Fuse	FU
Flex Whip	FW
Include 3000K Lamp	L830
Include 3500K Lamp	L835
Include 4100K Lamp	L841
Separate Circuit	SC

Finish	**WH**
Matte Satin White	WH

Consult www.focalpointlights.com for additional photometric reports and technical information

 TWO LAMP BIAX SOFTLITE

Luminaire:	2x2' two lamp biax recessed luminaire with matte white reflector and perforated lamp shield.
Filename:	FS2222PS.BX
Catalog #:	FS2-22-B-2-BX40-E-120-G-PS-WH
Efficiency:	64%
Independent testing laboratory report no. 12003.0	

Candlepower Distribution

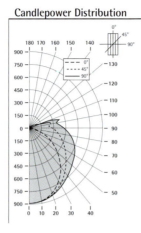

Vertical angle	Horizontal angle					Zonal lumens
	0°	22.5°	45°	67.5°	90°	
0°	915	915	915	915	915	
5°	917	917	915	908	907	87
15°	878	879	886	885	882	250
25°	798	807	827	836	842	381
35°	684	704	742	770	782	463
45°	547	582	651	705	730	499
55°	389	443	557	648	678	489
65°	235	327	479	600	638	457
75°	117	225	411	531	567	399
85°	33	156	329	448	486	325
90°	6	134	289	402	436	
95°	14	134	247	352	382	254
105°	50	165	263	376	388	271
115°	55	116	109	50	48	81
125°	46	76	66	0	0	37
135°	31	50	40	0	0	20
145°	19	0	0	0	0	2
155°	0	0	0	0	0	0
165°	0	0	0	0	0	0
175°	0	0	0	0	0	0
180°	0	0	0	0	0	

Lumen Summary

	Zone	Lumens	% Lamp	% Fixt
	0°-30°	718	11.4	17.9
	0°-60°	2169	34.4	54.0
	0°-90°	3351	53.2	83.5
Total	90°-180°	664	10.5	16.5
Luminaire:	0°-180°	4015	64	100.0

Luminance Data CD/M²

Vertical Angle	0	45	90
45	2178	2019	2264
55	1910	1945	2367
65	1566	1983	2641
75	1273	2170	2993
85	1066	2502	3696

Spacing	1.2 ‖
Criterion:	1.3 ⊥

Co-Efficients of Utilization

Floor								20								
Ceiling		80				70			50		30		10		00	
Wall	70	50	30	10	70	50	10	50	10	50	10	50	10	00		
RCR 0	73	73	73	73	70	70	70	65	65	60	60	55	55	53		
1	65	62	58	55	62	59	53	55	50	50	46	46	43	41		
2	59	53	48	44	56	51	42	47	40	43	37	40	35	33		
3	53	46	41	36	51	44	35	41	33	38	31	35	29	28		
4	49	41	35	30	46	39	30	36	28	33	26	31	25	23		
5	44	36	30	25	42	34	25	32	23	29	22	27	21	19		
6	41	32	26	22	39	31	21	29	20	26	19	24	18	17		
7	38	29	23	19	36	28	18	26	18	24	17	22	16	14		
8	35	26	20	16	33	25	16	23	15	21	14	20	14	12		
9	32	23	18	14	30	22	14	21	13	19	12	18	12	11		
10	30	21	16	12	28	20	12	19	12	18	11	16	10	09		

Numbers indicate percentage values of reflectivity.

Installation Details

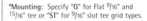

*Mounting: Specify "G" for Flat 9/16" and 15/16" tee or "ST" for 9/16" slot tee grid types.

**Drywall Frame Kit: Specify "DF" Drywall Frame Kit for drywall ceiling conditions. Use tie-wire or screws to secure frame kit.

Cut out dimensions: Min. 24.125" / Max. 24.563"

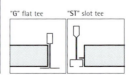

"G" flat tee   "ST" slot tee

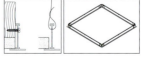

Sept 2003 Focal Point LLC. reserves the right to change specifications for product improvement without notification.

the contract document phase. Therefore, specifications must be clearly written with respect to substitution policies. The ability to permit, limit, or prohibit substitutions in specifications can be determined by the client. For example, state and government organizations are required by law to purchase products or services through a bidding process. Frequently, the law requires a minimum of three bids for any purchases over a specified amount of money. Generally, in these situations, specifications do not indicate a specific manufacturer but focus on descriptive requirements. These **open specifications** often indicate that product substitutions must be equal to the product described in the document. These specifications are difficult to write because in order to ensure the desired outcome, every detail must be included and accurate. Specifications without proper details may result in a product being substituted with an inexpensive knockoff. **Closed specifications** are specific regarding a product and manufacturer. These documents include the provision that substitutes are not allowed without the approval of the lighting designer. Under circumstances in which several products are acceptable, the specifications should still be very specific regarding product attributes, including performance criteria.

The execution section in specification documents describes installation methods, testing procedures, and maintenance provisions. Some of the installation considerations are identified in Table 23.1. Some lighting systems are installed very early in the building process and are used to provide illumination for the duration of construction. For extensive projects, this time period and dirt accumulation can affect lumen output. Thus, specifications may include a clause that indicates new lamps must be installed prior to the users' moving in. Testing a newly installed lighting system is important to ensure that lamps are properly aimed and that objects are in clear focus. Controls must be calibrated to the appropriate sensitivity level and properly timed for automatic shut-offs. To address varying lighting conditions, lighting systems should be tested during the day and evening. Some systems may have to be reviewed during different climatic conditions. On some occasions, field-testing may reveal that a specific lamp does not fulfill

Open specifications
Contract documents that do not indicate a specific manufacturer and that do not focus on descriptive requirements.

Closed specifications
Contract documents that are specific about a product, manufacturer, and requirements.

the intent of the lighting design. The beam spread might be too wide, or the color rendering may not be appropriate. Whenever possible, ineffective lamps should be replaced. Generally, the contractor is responsible for handling the adjustments. Thus, a lighting designer should consult with the contractor when the lighting system is fine-tuned.

Contract Administration

Contracts are used to initiate the construction phase of a project.

Contracts and Implementation

A lighting designer prepares contracts with various individuals and businesses, including clients, manufacturers, suppliers, fabricators, vendors, independent contractors, and craftspeople. However, some lighting projects may require that bidding and contracts be processed through the contractor, architect, or electrical contractor. Contracts may be customized, or preprinted documents may be provided by various professional organizations. Any contract used by a lighting designer should be reviewed and approved by an attorney. A letter of agreement is frequently used as a contract between a lighting designer and another party when the designer is bidding a project, requesting services, or purchasing products. For example, a lighting designer can use a letter of agreement to request a cabinetmaker to build a bookcase with an integrated lighting system. The agreement should specify the materials supplied by the cabinetmaker and the responsibilities of the lighting designer. For example, the cabinetmaker might supply all the materials to fabricate the bookcase, except for the lighting system. Thus, the agreement could also indicate that the lighting designer must supply the lighting system to the cabinetmaker by a specific date.

Letters of agreement may also specify design fees, unit pricing, delivery charges, shipping instructions, time lines, and any other terms or applicable conditions. Some other common business forms used by a lighting designer are purchase orders, billing statements, and change orders. Purchase orders are used to request materials or products, such as luminaires, from a supplier. Billing statements indicate the amount owed to a lighting designer and terms of payment. A change order business form details alterations to the original specifications. A change order may be necessary when a product is discontinued, a mistake was made in the specifications, or a client decides to change the previously approved lighting design. The form must specifically indicate the parameters of the change and contain signatures of all individuals affected by the modification, such as the client, lighting designer, fabricator, or contractor.

A lighting designer may be involved in several activities associated with the construction phase, including reviewing documents, purchasing products, project management, monitoring costs, and site supervision. The construction phase is a critical stage of the lighting design process, because the work performed affects the quality and integrity of the design. Therefore, it is important for a lighting designer to be actively involved during this stage. The results of construction should reflect the design concept, working drawings, and specifications. Generally, monitoring a construction project requires a focus on service and management. Dedicating quality time to construction administration demonstrates to a client a commitment to the project and a high level of professionalism. These positive impressions create loyal clients.

Another important element in providing good service is consistent and informative communication. A lighting designer must regularly communicate with the client and all parties involved in the lighting design, including the contractor, electricians, electrical distributors, manufacturers, and craftspeople. Regularly scheduled communication times are an excellent way of keeping a client apprised of construction updates. In addition, regular visits to the construction site should be scheduled. Throughout the contract administration phase, questions arise that need a prompt response from the lighting designer. Slow response times can delay a project and could prompt an undesirable change in the lighting design. Throughout the construction administration phase, time should be dedicated to considerable paperwork. All activities related to the project should be recorded for billing purposes, or the details can be used to determine fees for future projects. Time dedicated to a project may be considerable when the site is at a remote location or a long distance from the lighting designer's firm. Charges for travel time and related expenses must be negotiated with the client. In addition, when supervising a project in an unfamiliar community, the lighting designer must dedicate time to identifying quality tradespeople and resources.

A recurring task during the construction administration phase is reviewing documents. This involves examining documents related to the lighting design, such as working drawings, specifications, shop drawings for fabricating custom luminaires, or details of cabinetry with integrated lighting systems. To ensure that project specifications are being followed, business forms such as bids, contracts, purchase orders, acknowledgments from manufacturers, and invoices should be reviewed for accuracy. In reviewing or writing purchase orders, manufacturers' representatives can be helpful resources. Prior to submitting a purchase order, it is advisable to ask the representative to review the document. These individuals are knowledgeable about their products, their company's coding systems, and any changes that have recently occurred or that will be occurring in the near future. In reviewing a purchase order, a manufacturer's representative should notice when a number recorded is not accurate or when there is an order for a finish that is not available in a specific luminaire. Representatives can be helpful when they know a product will soon be discontinued. In such a situation, a new product might be selected, because a discontinued luminaire could be difficult to maintain. In addition, accessories that may be needed in the future might be impossible to purchase. Whenever possible, prior to purchasing a luminaire, ask the representative to demonstrate the product.

Once products and materials have been ordered, time must be dedicated to monitoring delivery dates and time sequencing with the other construction activities. The ideal situation is having a product delivered at the precise time it is to be installed. Unfortunately, this rarely occurs, but the goal is to synchronize the process as much as possible. Storage of luminaires can be costly and damage can easily occur. Delays in delivery can significantly affect the construction schedule and can be very costly. All products and materials should be carefully inspected when they arrive from the manufacturer. For custom luminaires, it is important to monitor the prototypes, as they are produced throughout the manufacturing process. Items should be scrutinized to ensure that the delivered product meets the description recorded in the purchase order and that nothing is damaged. Examining the product includes checking for the inclusion of all items ordered, such as accessories, mounting hardware, replacement lamps, or transformers. Reviewing for damage involves identifying broken parts, defects, scratches, irregular finishes, or problems with the packing materials. Examining packaging materials is important, because damage to a product might be the result of the carrier and not the manufacturer. The manufacturer must be notified immediately of any irregularities.

An important element of project management is coordinating deliveries and installations. Tracking shipping dates from a manufacturer is helpful in preparing for the eventual installation of the lighting system. For example, prior to installation the site must be ready for the lighting system, delivery arrangements to the location must be confirmed, and tradespeople responsible for installing the system must be ready to perform the job. In planning installation dates, it is important to make sure that conflicts will not arise between people who are scheduled to work at the site at the same time period. Heavy and large luminaires require special considerations for delivery and installation. As identified in construction specifications, substantial structural support must be built for these luminaires. In addition, special arrangements must be made to ensure that the people assigned to deliver and install the luminaire are qualified to do so.

Site supervision during construction and installation must be conducted in accordance with local laws and regulations. By monitoring work performed at a construction site, a lighting designer can reinforce the importance of a quality installation. The quality of the installation is determined by a variety of factors, including proper handling of luminaires, accurate opening sizes, fixtures being plumb and level, and the lack of light leaks. Furthermore, care must be taken to protect finishes of surfaces surrounding a fixture, such as drywall, wall coverings, paneling, wood trim, or paint finishes. Installers should be given handling instructions for luminaires and lamps. Finishes and surfaces can be ruined by oil from hands, dirt, or grease. Site supervision during installations can help enormously in ensuring quality results.

The installation process includes aiming, focusing, and calibrating controls. As mentioned earlier in this chapter, a lighting designer should work with the contractor to perform these actions. The initial lighting of the system, or **commissioning**, should also be done with the contractor. In reviewing the illuminated system, a lighting designer can comment only on those issues allowable by local codes and regulations. Generally, comments may focus on the accuracy of product specifications, damage to luminaires, effects of lighting, and the appropriateness of the relationships between end users, tasks, and the interior environment. During the walk-through, a lighting designer should make a punch list of items that are missing or that must be repaired or replaced. Concerns and problems should be submitted in writing to the appropriate registered professionals, such as contractors, subcontractors, or the architect.

Upon satisfactory completion of the lighting system, a lighting designer may assist with scheduling the move-in and on-site supervision. Being present during the move-in can be very valuable in making sure furniture, artwork, and other objects are positioned correctly for specific tasks or a desired lighting effect. Once move-in is complete, a variety of documents should be given to the client, including product warranties, operational recommendations, maintenance manuals, and recommendations for changes in the future. Operational recommendations should include any information relevant to using a lighting system, such as programming controls, adjusting luminaires to accommodate different users, maximum wattages, and instructions for aiming and focusing. The maintenance manual should include relamping recommendations, replacement instructions, and materials and methods for cleaning lenses, finishes, and lamps. Many of the instructions provided in the maintenance manual should be provided directly from manufacturers. It is advisable to create a system for labeling which lamp(s) should be installed in a specific fixture, because, during relamping, the wrong lamp can be installed in a luminaire. Recommendations for future changes should include suggestions for modify-

Commissioning
The initial lighting of a system.

ing a lighting system to accommodate changes in tasks or the interior environment. These can include modifications to partitions, additional employees, or changes in a display in a retail environment.

Postoccupancy Evaluation

The purposes of postoccupancy evaluation (POE) are to assess the effectiveness of the lighting design, make modifications whenever possible, and acquire information that may be used to improve future projects. Evaluations should be conducted at various intervals after move-in. A good approach is to visit the site within the first three months after move-in, six months later, and then at least one year later. A follow-up after two years demonstrates a commitment to the integrity of the design and can lead to new work because frequently discussions may be on upgrades or new lighting systems. Post-move-in visits are also a good opportunity to make sure new end users are acquainted with the proper operation of the lighting system and that luminaires are accurately adjusted.

The primary focus of the evaluation should be to determine how well the lighting design accommodates the goals of the project. Thus, in determining an approach to the evaluation, a useful starting point is to reexamine data collected in the programming phase of the lighting design process. Questions used in surveys and interviews can serve as the foundation for determining the level of satisfaction with the lighting design. POE may be informal discussions with the client and end users or a formalized process involving considerable analysis of the data. Field observations also may be helpful in evaluating how well people interact with the lighting system. Many factors will determine the appropriate method, including the number of end users, the complexity of the project, and the uniqueness of the lighting design.

In determining the appropriate methodology, input should be derived from the client and other professionals involved with the project. A client can provide valuable insight into what is appropriate for the end users and the working conditions of the environment. In circumstances in which the lighting design is one component of an entire project, another professional, such as the architect or a contractor, could initiate POE. Frequently, to determine the level of satisfaction with an entire project, a survey may be conducted that contains general questions. For example, a question might be: "How satisfied are you with the quality of lighting?" A response to this question will provide information regarding a satisfaction level; however, it does not reveal which elements of the lighting design are the most satisfactory or whether there are any illumination problems. Whenever possible, items on a survey or an interview guide should be written in a manner that elicits specific information and details regarding the lighting design. The cyclic nature of the lighting design process continues by using the results obtained during the POE phase to inform future projects. Combining this information with technological advances in lighting systems is invaluable to the success of designing a quality lighting environment.

SUMMARY

- A graphic representation of a lighting system is depicted in working or construction drawings. Working drawings and specifications are used to order products, install wiring, and determine the location of luminaires, outlets, and controls.
- Commonly used working drawings are a plan view of the lighting, electrical, lighting/electrical, and reflected ceiling. Drawings also may include elevations, sections, and details. Lighting schedules and general notes located on drawing sheets provide additional information regarding the lighting system.
- In 2000, the IESNA developed guidelines for standardized luminaire symbols on lighting drawings. The format is composed of a base luminaire symbol set and a series of modifiers.
- A lighting plan indicates the location of luminaires, switches, and control loops.
- Detailed electrical plans illustrate wiring runs from electrical panels to all equipment in a building, including lighting systems. Elements related to lighting systems on an electrical plan include luminaires,

switches, outlets, junction boxes, auxiliary units, and wiring for controls.

■ A reflected ceiling plan includes the location of luminaires, architectural elements, and any HVAC equipment.

■ Sections and elevations are useful working drawings for illustrating the location of wall luminaires, switches, outlets, windows, and doors.

■ Detail working drawings must be drawn to communicate precise information to a fabricator or an installer.

■ Supplementary to working drawings, lighting specifications are extremely important contract documents. To assist in the development of accurate details, the International Association of Lighting Designers (IALD) published a manual entitled Guidelines for Specification Integrity (2002). In addition, another important specification document is Masterformat™, produced by the Construction Specification Institute (CSI).

■ Contracts are used to initiate the construction phase of a project. A lighting designer prepares contracts with various individuals and businesses, including clients, manufacturers, suppliers, fabricators, vendors, independent contractors, and craftspeople.

■ A lighting designer must regularly communicate with the client and all parties involved in the lighting design, including the contractor, electricians, electrical distributors, manufacturers, and craftspeople.

■ A recurring task during the contract administration phase is reviewing documents.

■ Once products and materials have been ordered, time must be dedicated to monitoring delivery dates and time sequencing with other construction activities.

■ Site supervision during construction and installations must be conducted in accordance with local laws and regulations.

■ The installation process includes aiming, focusing, and calibrating controls.

■ The purposes of a postoccupancy evaluation (POE) are to assess the effectiveness of the lighting design, to conduct modifications whenever possible, and to acquire information that can be used to improve future projects.

Key Terms

closed specifications   open specifications

commissioning   reflected ceiling plan

Exercises

1. Review a set of working drawings and specifications prepared by an architectural firm. Analyze the lighting and electrical specifications. In a written report address the following items: (a) a lighting inventory, (b) an electrical inventory, and (c) symbols and descriptions provided in the legends.

2. Identify a floor plan for a residential or commercial building. Develop a set of lighting working drawings for the structure, including a plan view of the lighting, electrical, and reflected ceiling. Follow IESNA (2000) guidelines for the lighting symbols.

3. Identify a floor plan for a residential or commercial building. Develop a set of lighting working drawings for the structure, including a section, elevations, and details. Follow the IESNA (2002) guidelines for the lighting symbols.

4. Develop lighting specifications for the project identified in exercises 1 or 2. Content presented in Table 23.1 and the IALD's manual entitled Guidelines for Specification Integrity (2002) may be used as a guide for writing the specifications.

5. Identify a commercial client and the end users of the space. For the purpose of conducting a POE, develop a list of questions for interviews and surveys. Questions should be specific to the end users of the space. In a written report include the following information: (a) a list of the questions, (b) an outline of the plan for interviewing and surveying the end users, (c) the rationale for different questions, (d) the rationale for who will be interviewed and surveyed, and (e) identify how the results will be used for future projects.

REFERENCES

Alderman, R.L. (1997). *How to Prosper as an Interior Designer: A Business and Legal Guide*. New York: John Wiley & Sons.

Allen, P.S., Jones, L.M., and Stimpson, M.F. (2004). *Beginnings of Interior Environments*, 9th edition. Upper Saddle River, NJ: Pearson/Prentice Hall.

American Institute of Architects. (2000). *Architectural Graphics Standards*, 10th edition. New York: John Wiley & Sons.

Benya, J., Heschong, L., McGowan, T., Miller, N., and Rubinstein, F. (2001). *Advanced Lighting Guidelines*. White Salmon, WA: New Buildings Institute.

Binggeli, C. (2002). *Building Systems for Interior Designers*. New York: John Wiley & Sons.

Birnberg, H.G. (1999). *Project Management for Building Designers and Owners*. Boca Raton, FL: CRC Press.

Browning, H.C. (1996). *The Principles of Architectural Drafting*. New York: Whitney Library of Design.

Burstein, D., and Stasiowski, F. (1982). *Project Management for the Design Professional*. New York: Watson-Guptill.

Burde, E. (1992). *Design Presentation Techniques*. New York: McGraw-Hill.

Ching, F.D.K. (2003). *Architectural Graphics*, 4th edition. New York: John Wiley & Sons.

Ching, F.D.K. (2002). *Building Construction illustrated*, 3rd edition. New York: John Wiley & Sons.

Clough, R.H. (1986). *Construction Contracting*, 5th edition. New York: John Wiley & Sons.

Coleman, C. (ed.) (2001). *Interior Design Handbook of Professional Practice*. New York: McGraw-Hill.

Crawford, T., and Bruck, E.D. (2001). *Business and Legal Forms for Interior Designers*. New York: Allworth Press.

Doyle, M.E. (1999). *Color Drawing: Design Skills and Techniques for Architects, Landscape Architects, and Interior Designers*, 2nd edition. New York: John Wiley & Sons.

Farren, C.E. (1999). *Planning and Managing Interior Projects*, 2nd edition. Kingston, MA: R. S. Means.

Fielder, W.J., and Frederick, H.J. (2001). *The Lit Interior*. Boston: Architectural Press.

Getz, L. (1986). *Business Management in the Smaller Design Firm*. Newton, MA: Practice Management Associates.

Gibbs, J. (1997). *A Handbook for Interior Designers*. London: Sterling Publications.

Gorman, J. (1995). *Detailing Light: Integrated Lighting Solutions for Residential and Contract Design*. New York: Whitney Library of Design.

Illuminating Engineering Society of North America (IESNA) (2000). *Document DG-3-00: Application of Luminaire Symbols on Lighting Design Drawings*. New York: Illuminating Engineering Society of North America.

International Association of Lighting Designers (IALD) (2002). *Guidelines for specification integrity*. Chicago: International Association of Lighting Designers.

International Interior Design Association (1999). *Forms and Documents Manual*. Chicago: International Interior Design Association.

Kilmer, R., and Kilmer, W.O. (1992). *Designing Interiors*. New York: Harcourt Brace.

Kliment, S.A. (1998). *Writing for Design Professionals*. New York: W. W. Norton.

Knackstedt, M.V. (2002). *The Interior Design Business Handbook*. New York: John Wiley & Sons.

Koenig, P.A. (2000). *Design Graphics: Drawing Techniques for Design Professionals*. Upper Saddle River, NJ: Pearson Education/ Prentice Hall.

Koomen-Harmon, S., and Kennon, K. (2001). *The Codes Guidebook for Interiors*, 2nd edition. New York: John Wiley & Sons.

Kriebel, T.M., Birdsong, C., and Sherman, D.J. (1991). *Defining interior design programming*. Journal of Interior Design Education and Research, 17(1), 29-36.

Lamit, L.G. (1994). *Technical Drawing and Design*. Minneapolis/St. Paul: West Publishing Company.

Laseau, P. (2001). *Graphic Thinking for Architects & Designers*, 3rd edition. New York: John Wiley & Sons.

Liebing, R.W. (1999). *Architectural Working Drawings*, 4th edition. New York: John Wiley & Sons, Inc.

Lohmann, W.T. (1992). *Construction Specifications: Managing the Review Process*. Boston: Butterworth Architecture.

McGowan, M., and Kruse, K. (2003). *Interior Graphic Standards*. New York: John Wiley & Sons.

Mitton, M. (1999). *Interior Design Visual Presentations: A Guide to Graphics, Models, and Presentation Techniques*. New York: John Wiley & Sons.

Nissen, L., Faulkner, R., & Faulkner, S. (1994). *Inside Today's Home*, 6th edition. New York: Harcourt Brace.

O'Leary, A.F. (1992). *Construction Administration in Architectural Practice*. New York: McGraw-Hill.

Pile, J.F. (1988). *Interior Design*. New York: Harry N. Abrams Inc.

Pile, J.F. (1995). *Interior Design*, 2nd edition. New York: Harry N. Abrams Inc.

Pile, J.F. (2003). *Interior Design*, 3rd edition. New York: Harry N. Abrams Inc.

Piotrowski, C.M. (1992). *Interior Design Management: A Handbook for Owners and Managers*. New York: John Wiley & Sons.

Piotrowski, C.M. (2002). *Professional Practice for Interior Designers*, 3rd edition. New York: John Wiley & Sons.

Preiser, W., Rabinowitz, H., and White, E. (1988). *Post-Occupancy Evaluation*. New York: Van Nostrand Reinhold.

Ramsey, C.G., and Sleeper, H.R. (2000). *Architectural Graphic Standards*, 10th edition. New York: John Wiley & Sons.

Reznikoff, S.C. (1986). *Interior Graphic and Design Standards*. New York: Whitney Library of Design.

Reznikoff, S.C. (1989). *Specifications for Commercial Interiors: Professional Liabilities, Regulations, and Performance Criteria*. New York: Whitney Library of Design.

Siegel, H., and Siegel, A. (1982). *A Guide to Business Principles and Practices for Interior Designers*. New York: Whitney Library of Design.

Smith, F.K., and Bertolone, F.J. (1986). *The Principles and Practices of Lighting Design: Bringing Interiors to Light*. New York: Whitney Library of Design.

Smith, W.D., and Smith, L.H. (2001). McGraw-Hill On-Site Guide to Building Codes 2000: Commercial and Residential Interiors. New York: McGraw-Hill.

Stasiowski, F., and Burnstein, D. (1982). *Project Management for the Design Professional*. New York: Whitney Library of Design/Watson-Guptill Publications.

Steffy, G.R. (2002). *Architectural Lighting Design*, 2nd edition. New York: Van Nostrand Reinhold.

Thompson, J.A. (ed.) (1992). *ASID Professional Practice Manual.* New York: Whitney Library of Design.

Travisono, J. (ed.) (1997). *E Source Technology Atlas Series: Lighting.* Boulder, CO: E Source.

Veitch, R.M., Jackman, D.R., and Dixon, M.K. (1990). *Professional Practice: A Handbook for Interior Designers.* Winnipeg, Canada: Peguis Publishers.

Wakita, O.A., and Linde, R.M. (2003). *The Professional Practice of Architectural Working Drawings*, 3rd edition. New York: John Wiley & Sons.

Wang, C. (1979). *Plan & Section Drawing.* New York: Van Nostrand Reinhold.

Williams, D.J. (1996). *Preparing for Project Management.* New York: American Society of Civil Engineers.

GLOSSARY

accent lighting Illumination designed to highlight an object or area in a space.

accommodation A function of the eye that enables one to see objects at varying distances.

adaptation A function of the eye that alters itself to the amount of brightness entering the pupil.

ambient lighting Overall illumination in a space, including lighting that allows people to walk safely through a room and that sets the mood or character of the interior. Also referred to as *general lighting*.

apertures Openings in walls and ceilings, such as windows and skylights.

arc fault circuit interrupter (AFCI) A device used to stop an electrical current when sparks occur from defective electrical equipment or wiring.

arc lamp A light source created by using a battery of 2000 cells to heat sticks of charcoal. The flame produced is in the shape of an arc.

amps (A) A measure of the quantity of electrical particle flow in a circuit.

angle of incident The rays of light emitted from a light source before they strike an object or surface.

backlighting Illumination that is directly behind an object. Also referred to as *silhouetting*.

baffle A linear-shaped or round unit of a luminaire designed to shield light from view.

ballast A control device used with an electric-discharge lamp that starts a lamp and controls the electrical current during operation.

barn doors Extensions mounted on the head of a luminaire for the purpose of controlling a beam of light.

bayonet base A typical base used with the arbitrary shape incandescent lamp.

beam spread The distribution of a light source ranging from narrow to wide.

bipin base A base with two pins, commonly used on fluorescent tubes and halogen lamps.

brightness An effect from a light source at a high illuminance level that can be perceived as either positive or distracting.

bulb A rounded glass element that surrounds the electrical components of a lamp.

candela (cd) The SI unit of measurement of luminous intensity. One candela represents the luminous intensity from a source focused in a specific direction on a solid angle called the *steradian.*

candelabra A term for a pair of candelabrum.

candelabrum A unit that has more than one holder for candles.

candlepower The measurement for the intensity of a light source in candelas.

candlepower distribution curves Graphs that illustrate the direction, pattern, and intensity of light emitted from luminaires.

candlestick A unit that holds a single candle and are the most commonly designed holder for candles.

cave-like Referring to undesirable dark areas, caused by improper distribution of illumination.

central control system An electronic device that uses a microprocessor to monitor, adjust, and regulate lighting in many areas or zones within a building.

chandelier Unit that is suspended from the ceiling and that has multiple holders for light sources.

chromaticity The degree of warmness or coolness of a light source; measured by kelvins (K). Also referred to as *color temperature.*

circadian rhythm A biological function that coordinates sleep and awake times through hormonal and metabolic processes.

circuit breaker A safety device designed to protect wires and electrical fixtures from excessive electrical loads.

clavilux A console instrument used to create lumia.

closed specifications Contract documents that are specific about a product, manufacturer, and project requirements.

coefficient of utilization (CU) The ratio of initial lamp lumens to the lumens on a work surface.

cold-cathode lamp A discharge light source similar to a neon lamp.

color constancy Expectations people have about the color of common objects.

color rendering index (CRI) Measurement of how good a light source makes objects appear. The index range is from 0–100. The higher the CRI number, the better the color-rendering ability of the source.

color temperature The degree of warmness or coolness of a light source; measured by kelvins (K). Also referred to as *chromaticity.*

color wheel Circular arrangement of colors in a fixed order.

commissioning The initial lighting of a system.

compact fluorescent lamp (CFL) A lamp that is made with one or two small, linear fluorescent lamps with a screw base. The ballast is a separate control gear or is built into the unit as an integral part of the system.

complement The color directly opposite a color on the color wheel.

cool colors Colors in the blue, green, and violet end of the color spectrum.

cornice lighting Illumination technique that may be mounted on a wall or above a window; the light is directed down.

correlated color temperature (CCT) A color temperature, in kelvins, determined by the x and y location on a color diagram (developed by the International Commission on Illumination).

cove lighting Illumination technique that is mounted on a wall or ceiling; the light is directed up toward the ceiling.

cowl A component at the end of a track light designed to shield light from view.

cross-lighting Light directed from the right and left of a task or object.

crown-silvered lamp A lamp with a silver coating on the top of the bulb.

daylight (skylight) Desirable natural light in a space.

daylight factor (DF) The ratio between the amount of daylight in specific areas in a room and the light outdoors.

dappled lighting An effect that creates multiple, irregular spots of light and shadow on objects and in a space. An example is when light filters through leaves and branches of trees.

decorative lighting Luminaires that provide illumination and are also artistic pieces.

diffused light Distribution of light in all directions.

diffused reflectance The phenomenon that occurs when a material in a matte finish causes incident light to scatter in a variety of directions.

diffuser Cover on a luminaire that scatters light in many directions; made from white plastic or etched glass.

dimmer An electrical device designed to decrease light output by reducing power to a lamp.

direct glare A distracting high illuminance level that is frequently caused by viewing a bare light source.

direct light Distribution of light when at least 90 percent of the illumination is downward.

disability glare A distracting high illuminance level that prevents one from seeing.

discharge lamp An electrical light source that produces illumination without filaments and operates on low or high pressure. An electric current passes through a vapor or gas.

discomfort glare A distracting high illuminance level that makes it difficult to see.

dispersion The area of illumination emitted by a light source.

downlight luminaire Recessed ceiling-mounted luminaire. Also referred to as high-hat luminaire.

efficacy A rating based on the lumens per watt consumed; reflects the energy efficiency of a lamp.

electric-discharge lamp An electrical light source that produces illumination without filaments and operates on low or high pressure. An electric current passes through a vapor or gas.

electrical circuit Circuit composed of a voltage source and a load, connected in a complete loop of circuit using electrical conductors, such as wires.

electrical standard An early term for a luminaire.

electrodeless lamp An electrical light source that uses an electromagnetic (EM) field to excite gases within a tube. The EM field is produced by a microwave or induction discharge.

electroluminescent lamp An electrical light source that operates through an interaction between an electrical field and a phosphor.

end-emitting fiber optic lighting system Light illuminates through the cylindrical optical fibers and is visible at the end of the fibers.

equivalent sphere index (ESI) A metric measurement demonstrating a comparison between an ideal illumination condition within a sphere and the results of a specific lighting system.

eye's field of vision The central and peripheral areas that are visible to the eye.

fiber optic lighting system A lighting system that utilizes a remote source for illumination. Light is transmitted through a bundle of optical fibers.

fill light Direct and/or indirect light that helps to reduce the intensity of dark areas.

filter A device, usually made from glass or plastic, used to alter the characteristics of a light beam.

flame-shaped lamps Decorative small lamp in the shape of a flame. The bulb is clear or frosted glass.

flood (FL) A wide beam spread.

fluorescent lamp An electric-discharge light source that generally uses electrodes, phosphors, low-pressure mercury, and other gases for illumination.

footcandle (fc) Amount of light that falls on a surface in a 1-foot radius of the source.

fresnel refractor Lens of a luminaire composed of concentric circles with a flat or domed surface.

furniture-integrated luminaire Unit that has lamps mounted in the cabinet; generally hidden from view. The most common furniture pieces with integrated lighting are office systems, curio cabinets, breakfronts, and bookcases.

fuse A safety device, generally found in older structures, designed to protect wires and electrical fixtures from excessive electrical loads.

gas lamp A luminaire consisting of a metal pipe and an open flame fueled by gas.

gaselier A suspended unit that has several arms to distribute gas to a burner; often has etched glass shades.

gaselier-electrolier A suspended unit that has arms directed toward the ceiling and the floor. The unit directed toward the ceiling accommodates gas and the unit aimed at the floor contains incandescent lamps.

general lighting Overall illumination in a space, including lighting that allows people to walk safely through a room and that sets the mood or character of the interior. Also referred to as *ambient lighting.*

glare A distracting high illuminance level that can cause discomfort or be disabling.

glare-shielding wall An exterior wall that absorbs most of the glare and heat from the sun, while reflecting light into the interior space.

grazing A lighting technique whereby the light source is placed close to a surface or object in order to highlight interesting textures and produce dramatic shadows.

ground fault circuit interrupter (GFCI) A device that shuts off power to an appliance when there is an interruption in the electrical current.

halogen (tungsten-halogen) lamp An incandescent lamp that uses a tungsten filament and halogen gas.

halogen regenerative cycle The operational process in which evaporated tungsten is redeposited on a halogen lamp's filament.

harvesting daylight Capturing daylight for the purpose of illuminating interiors.

HID high-bay A cone-shaped fixture designed to accommodate the shape of HID light sources.

high-hat luminaire Recessed ceiling-mounted luminaire. Also referred to as *downlight.*

high-intensity discharge (HID) lamp Electric-discharge lamp that includes mercury, metal halide, and high-pressure sodium.

high-pressure sodium (HPS) lamp A high-intensity discharge electrical light source that uses sodium vapor for illumination.

hologram A photographic plate that records an image in holography. The word *hologram* has Greek origins that translate into "whole thing" or "whole image."

holography A method of photography that records an image, or hologram, without an image-forming lens .

hue The name of a color.

illuminance The total amount of light on a surface; measured in lux (lx) or footcandle (fc).

illumination zone An imaginary division of space that includes three areas: the immediate task, the area surrounding the task, and the background.

illuminator The box that contains the light source for a fiber optic lighting system. The fiber optics originate from the illuminator.

incandescence Light produced by having an electric current heat the tungsten filament of an incandescent lamp.

incandescent carbon-filament lamp A light source that uses an electrical current to heat the conductive material until incandescence is produced.

indirect glare A distracting high illuminance level that is caused by a light source reflecting off a surface or object.

indirect light Distribution of light with at least 90 percent of the light directed toward the ceiling.

indirect natural light Illumination derived from reflections from clouds, the moon, and stars.

intensity The strength or purity of a color.

interreflection Result of light bouncing back and forth within an enclosed space or structure.

key window A window shape that allows light to enter a room at all levels; however, to reduce glare, the greatest amount of light is emitted in the area above where people sit or stand.

lamp The electrical light source unit. Common vernacular is *bulb*.

lamp life The operational time of a lamp expressed in hours.

lamp lumen depreciation (LLD) A metric measurement that examines the loss of lumens resulting from the design of a lamp.

lantern Unit that holds a candle(s) and is either a suspended or a portable fixture.

laser A light amplification caused by an emission radiation device that stimulates emission radiation in order to amplify coherent light.

layered lighting An illumination plan that includes natural light and multiple electrical light sources.

leadership in energy and environmental design system (LEED) Created by the U.S. Green Building Council. The program is a voluntary, national standard for developing high-performance sustainable buildings.

light A form of energy that is part of the electromagnetic spectrum.

light art A medium that utilizes illumination as the artwork. Light art can sculpt an object, space, or environment. A combination of light, sound, and movement, which often is integral to light art, may prompt a range of sensory reactions in a viewer.

light attic The area above the visible component of a display case that can be used to conceal light sources.

light-emitting diodes (LEDs) Semiconductor devices that have a chemical chip embedded in a plastic capsule. The light is focused or scattered by the use of lenses or diffusers.

light loss factor (LLF) The amount of illuminant lost because of the type of lamp, ambient temperature of the space, time, input voltage, ballast, lamp position, interior conditions, or burnouts.

light output The amount of illumination produced by a lamp; measured in lumens.

light pollution The excessive glow of light in the evening sky.

light-shielding wall A wall that exists on the outside of a building and absorbs most of the glare and heat from the sun while reflecting light into the interior space.

light trespass The result of excess lighting and light sources aimed in inappropriate directions.

lighting designer A professional who plans, specifies, and oversees the implementation of the natural and electrical illumination for residential and commercial interiors.

line voltage An electrical application that operates at 120 volts, but some large-scale commercial lighting applications may operate at 277 volts.

localized lighting A technique that allows a user to position light sources where they are needed and at the appropriate illumination level.

louver A grid-shaped unit of a luminaire designed to shield light from view.

low-pressure sodium (LPS) lamp An electrical discharge light source that uses sodium vapor at partial pressure.

low-voltage lighting An electrical application that usually operates at 12 volts.

lumen (lm) A measurement of the light output of a lamp.

lumens per watt (lpW) A rating that describes the amount of electricity consumed for a given amount of illumination.

lumia A form of light art that blends light, color, and movement.

lumidyne A device used to create lumia by projecting a light source through a moving rotor.

luminaire An element of a lighting system that includes the light source, housing elements, ballasts, transformers, controls, a mounting mechanism, and a connection to electrical power.

luminaire dirt depreciation (LDD) The loss of light that results from dirt and dust accumulation.

luminaire efficacy ratio (LER) A ratio of the number of watts consumed per the entire luminaire system.

luminance A unit of measurement that determines the amount of light in the eyes of users of a space after reflection or transmission from a surface.

luminous ceiling Lighting method on a ceiling that utilizes rows of fluorescent lamps behind diffused lenses.

luminous exitance The unit of measurement that indicates the total quantity of light reflected and emitted in all directions from a surface or material.

luminous flux The unit of measurement that indicates the total amount of illumination emitted by a source; measured in lumens (lm).

luminous intensity The unit of measurement from a source in a specific direction, on a solid angle called the *steradian*.

lux (lx) The international system of units (SI), unit of illuminance.

mercury lamp A high-intensity discharge electrical light source that uses radiation from mercury vapor for illumination.

metal-halide (MH) lamp A high-intensity discharge lamp that utilizes uses chemical compounds of metal halides and possibly metallic vapors such as mercury.

metamerism A phenomenon in which two samples appear to be the same color under one light source but do not match under another light source.

mirror-reflecting (MR) lamp Small halogen lamps that use mirrors to reflect light. The most common versions are MR-11 and MR-16s.

mock-up A full-sized model of a proposed lighting system and its structural elements.

modeling An emphasis on the three-dimensions of a piece of surface through light, shade, and shadows.

Munsell color system A method for classifying colors using a letter and number designation that identifies a particular hue with a given value and intensity.

nadir Zero on a polar candlepower distribution curve.

natural light Illumination from sunlight, the moon, and stars.

neon lamp A special application of cold-cathode lamps produced by a craftsperson who bends the heated glass into the various shapes of the design. A transformer with a high-voltage source is directed to the electrodes.

nocturne An artistic genre that involves painting or drawing in darkness.

occupancy sensor A device designed to turn lights on or off depending on whether people are present in a room.

oculus An opening in a dome of an architectural structure.

ohms (R) A measure of a circuit's ability to resist or impede the flow of electrical current.

oil lamps Luminaires that use an oil substance and a wick to produce light.

open specifications Contract documents that do not indicate a specific manufacturer and that do not focus on descriptive requirements.

parabolic aluminized reflector (PAR lamp) A reflector lamp with a very thick glass; can be used outdoors.

parallel circuit Lamps that operate independently of one another and are not load-sensitive.

persistent, bioaccumulation, toxic (PBT) A classification that indicates a material is toxic, remains in water or land indefinitely, and accrues in the world's ecosystem.

photobiology The science that examines the interaction of light and living organisms.

photometry The units of measurement for light, including the effects of vision.

photosensor Device that detects the amount of illumination in the space, and then sends signals to control electrical light sources.

polychlorinated biphenyls (PCBs) A toxic material used in ballasts produced prior to 1978.

portable luminaires Table and floor fixtures; generally plugged into a wall socket.

presbyopia A decrease in the eye's ability to change the shape of the lens. This affects an individual's ability to focus on near or distant objects.

prototype A model of a new product or a new version of an existing lighting system.

quality lighting A layered illumination plan that reduces energy costs, conserves natural resources, allows users of the space to function comfortably, feel safe, and appreciate the aesthetic components of the environment.

radiometry A scientific area that focuses on measuring the quantity of radiant energy.

radiosity A type of radiative-transfer calculation utilized in lighting software.

recessed luminaire Fixture that is installed above a sheetrock or suspended-grid ceiling.

recessed spots Luminaires mounted in a ceiling or furniture piece and that have a lamp that distributes the light in a concentrated area.

reflected ceiling plan A contract working drawing that illustrates the design of the ceiling, including the location of luminaires, architectural elements, and any HVAC equipment.

reflectance The ratio of incident light to the light reflected from a surface or material.

reflector contour The unit of a luminaire designed to reflect light.

reflectors Devices in luminaires that are shaped to redirect light by reflection.

refraction Deflecting a light ray from moving in a straight path.

refractors Devices designed to redirect light through the scientific principal of refraction

relamping Replacing lamps that have burned out or are operating at less than an acceptable performance level.

relative visual performance (RVP) A metric measurement indicating how well a task can be performed with a specific luminaire in a fixed horizontal location.

restrike Result of a lamp having to start again because of a power interruption or reduction in voltage.

room cavity ratio (RCR) A formula designed to accommodate the proportions of a space and the distance from the luminaires to a work surface.

rotating heads Equipment that controls a light beam through panning and tilting the housing unit

rushlights Luminaires made from a tall grasslike plant that utilize melted fat to create illumination.

scanner Equipment that reflects light off a moving mirror to create movement.

seasonal affective disorder (SAD) A condition seemingly associated with an individual's inadequate exposure to sunlight.

semi-direct lighting Distribution of light with most of the illumination directed downward and some of the light directed upward.

semi-indirect lighting Distribution of light with most of the illumination directed upward and some of the light directed downward.

semi-recessed luminaire Fixture that has some of the housing above and some below the ceiling.

semi-specular reflectance The phenomenon that occurs when a partially shiny material causes incident light to scatter primarily in one direction.

series circuit Lamps that operate together as one system.

shade A device either opaque or translucent that shields a bare lamp from view.

short circuit Practically no resistance to electrical flow; typically the result of a wiring error or a malfunction in an electrical component.

side-emitting fiber optic lighting system Light illuminates through the cylindrical optical fibers and is visible along the sides of the fibers.

simultaneous contrast A phenomenon that occurs when a color appears to change as a result of surrounding colors.

soffit lighting Illumination technique that is a built-in wall element close or next to the ceiling; generally directs the light down on a task.

solar geometry The movement of the earth around the sun.

spot (SP) A narrow beam spread.

spotlight projector A device that allows a designer to select a very precise area to be illuminated.

snuffer Originally an individual who maintained burning candles by cutting off the burnt piece of the wick. Subsequently, the term has come to be used for the tool that is used to extinguish candle flames.

specular reflectance The phenomenon that occurs when a shiny material causes incident light to scatter in one direction.

spill light Wasted light that is emitted from an opening in a luminaire.

steradian A solid angle used to measure luminous intensity from a source in a specific direction.

structural luminaire Illumination technique that is an element of the architectural interior.

sunlight Light from the sun that enters a space directly.

surface-mounted luminaire Fixture that is installed on a ceiling or wall or under a shelf or cabinet.

suspended luminaire Fixture that is installed on a ceiling and extends into the room by a cord, chain, pole, or wires.

sustainable design A concept that focuses on products and processes that protect the environment and conserve energy for future generations.

switch A device that controls a luminaire by regulating the flow of electricity. A circuit is closed when a light is on, and is open when the light is off.

task lighting Illumination that is specific to each task that is performed in a space.

throw distance The space between a lamp and the farthest point the light beam strikes.

timer A device designed to control lighting systems by turning lights on and off at designated times.

toxicity characteristic leaching procedure (TCLP) A test developed by the Environmental Protection Agency (EPA) to test the mercury content of lamps. To pass the TCLP test, the range of mercury content must be between 4 and 6 milligrams without additives.

track luminaire Fixture that has multiple heads mounted on an electrical raceway.

transformer An electrical device that converts voltages in a system.

transmission The passing of light rays through a material.

tungsten-halogen lamp An incandescent lamp that contains halogen.

universal design An approach to the physical environment that is focused on accommodating the needs of all people, whenever possible, without modifications.

uplight Luminaire that directs the light up; generally a portable luminaire.

valance lighting Illumination technique that is mounted above a window; the light is directed up and down.

value The lightness or darkness of a color.

veiling reflections Reduction in light contrast on a task as a result of reflected images on a surface.

visual acuity The ability of the eye to see details.

visual comfort probability (VCP) A rating that represents the percentage of people who might experience disability glare when they are seated in the least desirable location in a space.

volts (V) A measure of the amount of electrical "stimulus" that enables current to flow through a circuit.

wall bracket lighting Illumination technique that is mounted on a wall and in which the light is directed up and down.

wall-light Unit that is mounted on a wall with one or multiple holders for candles.

wallslot A structural lighting system that is integrated in the ceiling and distributes light down on vertical surfaces.

warm colors Colors in the yellow, orange, and red end of the color spectrum.

watts (W) A measure of an electrical circuit's ability to do work, such as produce light and waste heat.

Anthropometric Data

	Static Eye Level Standing		Static Eye Level Seated		Static Reach		Dynamic Reach	
Population	**Male**	**Female**	**Male**	**Female**	**Male**	**Female**	**Male**	**Female**
British adults (aged 19-65 years)								
inches	64	59	31	29	26	24	31	28
mm	1630	1505	790	740	665	600	780	705
US adults								
inches	67	60	32	30	26	24	31	28
mm	1710	1525	800	750	670	610	785	710
French adults								
inches	61	59	31	30	28	24	30	28
mm	1560	1500	795	750	655	600	770	700
German adults								
inches	64	60	32	29	26	24	31	28
mm	1635	1530	800	740	665	610	780	715
Japanese adults								
inches	61	56	31	29	24	22	27	24
mm	1540	1425	785	735	610	550	690	620
Hong Kong Chinese adults								
inches	61	56	31	28	24	22	28	25
mm	1555	1425	780	720	620	560	705	635
Indian adults								
inches	60	56	29	27	25	22	29	26
mm	1535	1420	740	690	625	565	735	660
Elderly (aged >65 years)								
inches	60	56	29	27	25	22	29	26
mm	1535	1420	740	685	625	565	735	660
Child (10 years)								
inches	50	50	24	24	20	19	23	23
mm	1275	1275	600	615	515	495	580	585
Wheelchair				Forward	Forward	Sideways	Sideways	
inches			48	48	18	16	25	23
mm			1220	1160	455	410	645	580

* Data are for populations in the 50th percentile.

Source of data: Pheasant, S. (1986). *Bodyspace: Anthropometry, Ergonomics and Design.* London and Philadelphia: Taylor & Francis.

Base Types and Bulb Shapes

INCANDESCENT LAMPS
Filament Designations, Base Types, Bulb Shapes

Filament Designations (Not Actual Sizes)

Filament designations consist of a letter or letters to indicate how the wire is coiled and an arbitrary number sometimes followed by a letter to indicate the arrangement of the filament on the supports. Prefix letters include C (coil) — wire is wound into a helical coil or it may be deeply fluted; CC (coiled coil) — wire is wound into a helical coil and this coiled wire again wound into a helical coil. Some of the more commonly used types of filament arrangements are illustrated.

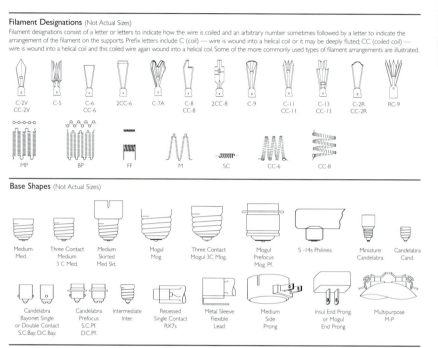

C-2V / CC-2V | C-5 | C-6 / CC-6 | 2CC-6 | C-7A | C-8 / CC-8 | 2CC-8 | C-9 | C-11 / CC-11 | C-13 / CC-13 | C-2R / CC-2R | RC-9

MP | BP | FF | M | SC | CC-6 | CC-8

Base Shapes (Not Actual Sizes)

Medium Med. | Three Contact Medium 3 C Med. | Medium Skirted Med Skt. | Mogul Mog. | Three Contact Mogul 3C Mog. | Mogul Prefocus Mog. Pf. | S -14s Philinea | Miniature Candelabra | Candelabra Cand.

Candelabra Bayonet Single or Double Contact S.C.Bay. D.C.Bay. | Candelabra Prefocus S.C.Pf. D.C.Pf. | Intermediate Inter. | Recessed Single Contact RX7s | Metal Sleeve Flexible Lead | Medium Side Prong | Insul End Prong. or Mogul End Prong | Multipurpose M-P

Bulb Shapes (Not Actual Sizes)

The size and shape of a bulb is designated by a letter or letters followed by a number. The letter indicates the shape of the bulb while the number indicates the diameter of the bulb in eighths of an inch. For example, "T-10" indicates a tubular shaped bulb having a diameter of ⁵⁄₈ or 1¼ inches. The following illustrations show some of the more popular bulb shapes and sizes.

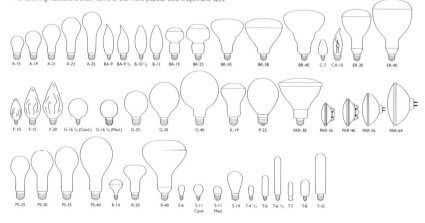

A-15 | A-19 | A-21 | A-23 | A-25 | BA-9 | BA-9½ | B-10½ | B-13 | BR-19 | BR-25 | BR-30 | BR-38 | BR-40 | C-7 | CA-10 | ER-30 | ER-40

F-10 | F-15 | F-20 | G-16½ (Cand.) | G-16½ (Med.) | G-25 | G-30 | G-40 | K-19 | P-25 | PAR-38 | PAR-36 | PAR-46 | PAR-56 | PAR-64

PS-25 | PS-30 | PS-35 | PS-40 | R-14 | R-20 | R-40 | S-6 | S-11 Cand. | S-11 Med. | S-14 | T-4½ | T-6 | T-6½ | T-7 | T-8 | T-10

COMPACT FLUORESCENT LAMPS
Base Types and Bulb Shapes

Base Types (Not Actual Sizes)

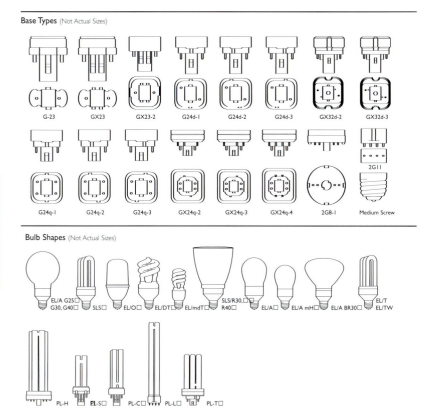

G-23 GX23 GX23-2 G24d-1 G24d-2 G24d-3 GX32d-2 GX32d-3

G24q-1 G24q-2 G24q-3 GX24q-2 GX24q-3 GX24q-4 2G8-1 2G11 Medium Screw

Bulb Shapes (Not Actual Sizes)

EL/A G25□ G30, G40□ SLS□ EL/O□ EL/DT□ EL/mdT□ SLS/R30,□ R40□ EL/A□ EL/A mH□ EL/A BR30□ EL/T EL/TW

PL-H PL-S□ PL-C□ PL-L□ PL-T□

Base Types and Bulb Shapes (Continued)

FLUORESCENT LAMPS
Fluorescent Base Types and Bulb Shapes

Base Types (Not Actual Sizes)

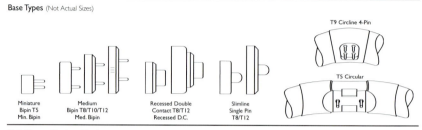

Miniature Bipin T5 / Min. Bipin

Medium Bipin T8/T10/T12 / Med. Bipin

Recessed Double Contact T8/T12 / Recessed D.C.

Slimline Single Pin T8/T12

T9 Circline 4-Pin

T5 Circular

Bulb Shapes (Not Actual Sizes)

The size and shape of a bulb is designated by a letter or letters followed by a number. The letter indicates the shape of the bulb while the number indicates the diameter of the bulb in eighths of an inch. For example, "T12" indicates a tubular shaped bulb having a diameter of ¹²⁄₈ or 1½ inches. The following illustrations show some of the more popular bulb shapes and sizes.

T5 Miniature Bipin

T8 Medium Bipin

T10 Medium Bipin

T12 Medium Bipin

T8 Recessed Double Contact

T12 Recessed Double Contact

T12 Recessed Double Contact (Jacketed)

T8 Single Pin Slimline

T12 Single Pin Slimline

T12 Medium Bipin U-Bent Lamp (6")

T12 Medium Bipin U-Bent Lamp (3")

T8 Medium Bipin U-Bent Lamp

T5 Circular

T9 Circline 4-Pin

FLUORESCENT

HIGH INTENSITY DISCHARGE LAMPS

HID Bulb Shapes and Base Types; HID Warnings, Cautions and Operating Instructions

Base Types (Not Actual Sizes)

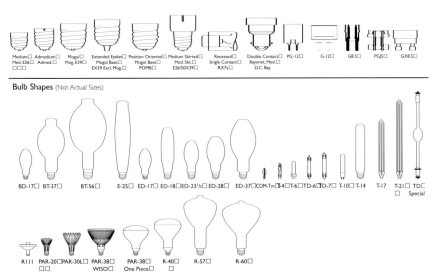

Medium□ Admedium□ Mogul□ Extended Eyelet□ Position Oriented□ Medium Skirted□ Recessed□ Double Contact□ PG-12□ G-12□ G8.5□ PGJ5□ GX8.5□
Med. E26□ Admed.□ Mog. E39□ Mogul Base□ Mogul Base□ Med. Skt.□ Single Contact□ Bayonet, Med.□
□□□ EX39 Excl. Mog.□ POMB□ E26/50X39□ RX7s□ D.C. Bay

Bulb Shapes (Not Actual Sizes)

BD-17□ BT-37□ BT-56□ E-25□ ED-17□ ED-18□ED-23½□ ED-28□ ED-37□CDM-Tm□T-4□T-6□TD-6□TD-7□ T-10□ T-14 T-17 T-21□ TD□ Special

R111 PAR-20□PAR-30L□ PAR-38□ PAR-38□ R-40□ R-57□ R-60□
□□ WISO□ One Piece□

WARNINGS, CAUTIONS AND OPERATING INSTRUCTIONS for MasterColor® Ceramic Metal Halide Lamps: Single Ended CDM-T G12, CDM-TC G8.5 and CDM-Tm PGJ5 (Universal); Double-Ended CDM-TD RX7 (Horizontal ± 45°, Enclosed Fixtures Only)

Warnings, Cautions and Operating Instructions

R "**WARNING:** These lamps can cause serious skin burn and eye inflammation from short wave ultraviolet radiation if outer envelope of the lamp is broken or punctured. Do not use where people will remain for more than a few minutes unless adequate shielding or other safety precautions are used. Certain lamps that will automatically extinguish when the outer envelope is broken or punctured are commercially available." This lamp complies with FDA radiation performance standard 21 CFR subchapter J. (USA:21CFR 1040.30 Canada:SOR/DORS/80-381)

If the outer bulb is broken or punctured, turn off at once and replace the lamp to avoid possible injury from hazardous short wave ultraviolet radiation. Do not scratch the outer bulb or subject it to pressure as this could cause the outer bulb to crack or shatter. A partial vacuum in the outer bulb may cause glass to fly if the envelope is struck.

WARNING: The arc-tube of metal halide lamps are designed to operate under high pressure and at temperatures up to 1000° C and can unexpectedly rupture due to internal or external factors such as a ballast failure or misapplication If the arc-tube ruptures for any reason, the outer bulb may break and pieces of extremely hot glass might be discharged into the surrounding environment. If such a rupture were to happen, **THERE IS A RISK OF PERSONAL INJURY, PROPERTY DAMAGE, BURNS AND FIRE.**

Certain lamps that will retain all the glass particles should inner arc-tube rupture occur are commercially available from Philips Lighting Company.

RELAMP FIXTURES AT OR BEFORE THE END OF RATED LIFE. Allowing lamps to operate until they fail is not advised and may increase the possibility of inner arc tube rupture.

This lamp contains an arc tube with a filling gas containing Kr-85 and is distributed by Philips Lighting Company, a division of Philips Electronics North America Corporation, Somerset, New Jersey, 08875.

CAUTION: TO REDUCE THE RISK OF PERSONAL INJURY, PROPERTY DAMAGE, BURNS AND FIRE RESULTING FROM AN ARC-TUBE RUPTURE THE FOLLOWING **LAMP OPERATING INSTRUCTIONS** MUST BE FOLLOWED:

LAMP OPERATING INSTRUCTIONS:

1. RELAMP FIXTURES AT OR BEFORE THE END OF RATED LIFE. Allowing lamps to operate until they fail is not advised and may increase the possibility of inner arc tube rupture.

2. Use only in fully enclosed fixtures capable of withstanding particles of glass having temperatures up to 1000°C. Lens/diffuser material must be heat resistant. Consult fixture manufacturer regarding the suitability of the fixture for this lamp.

3. Do not operate a fixture with a missing or broken lens/diffuser. At high lighting levels or when illuminating light-sensitive materials the use of an extra UV filter is recommended.

4. Operate lamp only within specified limits of operating position.

5. Before lamp installation/replacement, shut power off and allow lamp and fixture to cool to avoid electrical shock and potential burn hazards. When inserting a new CDM-Tm lamp, twist the lamp 45° clock-wise in the holder to ensure proper electrical and mechanical connection.

6. Use only auxiliary equipment meeting Philips and/or ANSI standards. Use within voltage limits recommended by ballast manufacturer.
   A. Operate lamp only within specified limits of operation.
   B. For total supply load refer to ballast manufacturers electrical data.
   C. Operate CDM-T (G12 base), CDM-TC (G8.5 base) and CDM-Tm (PGJ5 base) lamps only on thermally protected ballasts.
   D. Operate CDM-TC lamps (G8.5 base) and CDM-Tm (PGJ5 base) only on electronic ballasts.

7. Periodically inspect the outer envelope. Replace any lamps that show scratches, cracks or damage.

8. If a lamp bulb support is used, be sure to insulate the support electrically to avoid possible decomposition of the bulb glass.

9. Protect lamp base, socket and wiring against moisture, corrosive atmospheres and excessive heat.

10. Time should be allowed for lamps to stabilize in color when turned on for the first time. This may require several hours of operation, with more than one start. Lamp color is also subject to change under conditions of excess vibration or shock and color appearance may vary between individual lamps.

11. Lamps may require 4 to 8 minutes (10-15 minutes for CDM-Tm) to re-light if there is a power interruption.

12. Take care in handling and disposing of lamps. If an arc tube is broken, avoid skin contact with any of the contents or fragments.

HID

Spectral Power Distribution Curves

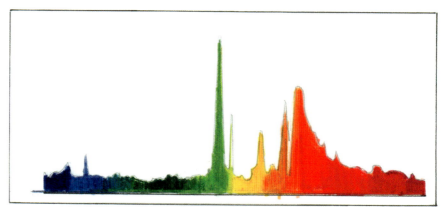

CERAMIC METAL HALIDE

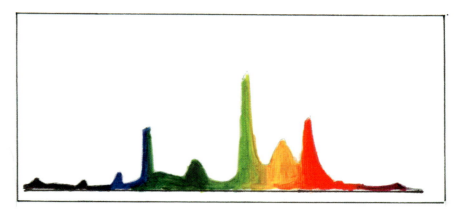

FLUORESCENT 4100 K

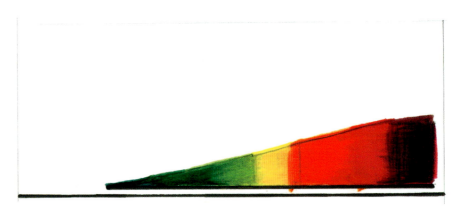

INCANDESCENT

FOCAL POINT

1x4
LUNA

FLU 14B

1'x4' recessed indirect with electronic ballast and optional radial blade louver.

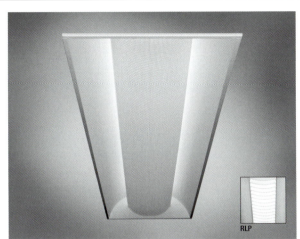

U.S. Patent No. DES. 397,819

RLP

2 Lamp T8

2 Lamp T5 & T5HO

3 Lamp T8

3 Lamp T5 & T5HO

Construction
One piece CNC formed 20 Ga. C.R.S. 1'x4' recessed lay-in reflector/housing 5" in depth. 20 Ga. C.R.S. ends form finished housing. Top access 20 Ga. C.R.S. ballast compartment. Lamps are shielded by detachable CNC formed 22 Ga. C.R.S. perforated lamp shields with acrylic lens insert. Optional C.R.S. radial blade louver constructed of .75" high 20 Ga. blades on 1" frequency.

Weight: 16 lbs

Optic
CNC formed 20 Ga. C.R.S. reflector, finished in matte satin white powder coat (94% min. reflectance).

Electrical
Luminaires are pre-wired for specified circuits. Ballasts are thermally protected and have a Class "P" rating.

T8 Lamps: Electronic instant start 265mA, <20% THD or optional electronic program start 265mA, <10% THD

T5 Lamps: Electronic program start 160mA, <10% THD

T5HO Lamps: Electronic program start 160mA, <10% THD

Optional DALI and other dimming ballasts available. Consult factory for specifications and availability. UL and cUL listed.

Emergency
Emergency battery packs provide 90 minutes of illumination. Initial lumen output for lamp types are as follows:

T8 Lamps: Up to 550 lumens
T5 Lamps: Up to 550 lumens
T5HO Lamps: Up to 825 lumens

Battery pack requires unswitched hot from same branch circuit as AC ballast.

Finish
Luminaire housing, reflector and all steel components are finished in polyester powder coat applied over a 5-stage pretreatment. Standard finish for housing and all steel components: matte satin white (min. 94% reflectance).

Features

- Optional radial blade louver offers a distinct look that highlights interior architecture (see inset).
- One piece luminaire housing provides easy installation.
- All luminaire combinations may be continuously row mounted. Ballast is accessible from above via adjacent ceiling tile.
- Perforated shields easily snap out for simple relamping.
- High angle uniform distribution of light on vertical surfaces.

March 2004

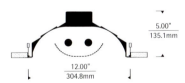

5.00"
135.1mm

12.00"
304.8mm

THE ART OF LIGHT

Fixture Type: _____

Project Name: _____

LUNA 1x4

FOCAL POINT®

THE ART OF LIGHT

Order Information		
Luminaire Series		**FLU**
Luna	FLU	
Nominal Size		**14**
1' x 4'	14	
Distribution		**B**
Bi-Directional	B	
Lamp Quantity		
Two Lamps	2	
Three Lamps	3	
Lamp Type		
T8	T8	
T5	T5	
T5HO	T5HO	
Ballast		
Electronic Instant Start <20% THD	E	
(T8 only)		
Electronic Program Start <10% THD	S	
Electronic Dimming Ballast	D	
(consult factory for dimming availability)		
Voltage		
120 Volt	120	
277 Volt	277	
*347 Volt	347	
*(Consult factory for availability)		
***Mounting**		
Grid	G	
Slot tee	ST	
Shielding		
Perforated Shield	PS	
Radial Blade Louver	RLP	
Factory Options		
Air Return	AR	
Dust Cover	DC	
Drywall Frame Kit	DF	
Emergency Battery Pack	EM	
Earthquake Clip	EQ	
HLR/GLR Fuse	FU	
Flex Whip	FW	
Include 3000K Lamp	L830	
Include 3500K Lamp	L835	
Include 4100K Lamp	L841	
Separate Circuit	SC	
Finish		**WH**
Matte Satin White	WH	

TWO LAMP T8 LUNA

Luminaire:	1'x4' two lamp T8 recessed indirect troffer with white reflector and perforated lamp shield.
Filename:	FLU2T4P5T8
Catalog #:	FLU-14-B-2-T8-E-120-G-PS-WH
Efficiency:	59%
Independent testing laboratory report no. 98800	

Candlepower Distribution

Vertical angle	Horizontal angle 0°	22.5°	45°	67.5°	90°	Zonal lumens
0°	1305	1305	1305	1305	1305	
5°	1288	1286	1286	1286	1286	123
15°	1272	1272	1277	1282	1285	362
25°	1133	1134	1147	1159	1164	531
35°	982	989	1009	1031	1039	634
45°	835	849	877	893	895	674
55°	620	636	652	633	600	568
65°	402	412	360	374	379	381
75°	200	158	173	180	178	185
85°	34	34	37	36	39	39
90°	0	0	0	0	0	0
95°	0	0	0	0	0	0
105°	0	0	0	0	0	0
115°	0	0	0	0	0	0
125°	0	0	0	0	0	0
135°	0	0	0	0	0	0
145°	0	0	0	0	0	0
155°	0	0	0	0	0	0
165°	0	0	0	0	0	0
175°	0	0	0	0	0	0
180°	0	0	0	0	0	

Lumen Summary

Zone	Lumens	% Lamp	% Fixt
0°-30°	1016	17.2	29.0
0°-40°	1650	28.0	47.2
0°-60°	2892	49.0	82.7
0°-90°	3498	59.3	100.0
Total Luminaire: 0°-180°	3498	59.3	100.0

Luminance Data CD/M²

Vertical Angle	0	45	90
45	3513	3690	3766
55	3216	3382	3112
65	2830	2534	2668
75	2299	1989	2046
85	1161	1263	1331

Spacing   1.2
Criterion   1.3

Co-Efficients of Utilization

Floor								20						
Ceiling	80				70			50		30		10		00
Wall	70	50	30	10	70	50	10	50	10	50	10	50	10	00
RCR 0	71	71	71	71	69	69	69	66	66	63	63	60	60	59
1	65	63	61	59	64	62	58	59	56	57	54	55	53	51
2	60	56	52	49	59	55	48	53	47	51	46	49	45	44
3	55	50	45	42	54	49	41	47	41	45	40	44	39	38
4	51	44	39	36	49	43	35	42	35	41	34	39	34	33
5	46	39	34	30	45	39	30	37	30	36	30	35	29	28
6	43	35	30	26	42	35	26	33	26	33	26	32	26	24
7	39	32	26	23	38	31	23	30	23	29	23	28	22	21
8	36	28	23	20	35	28	20	27	20	26	20	26	19	18
9	33	25	20	17	32	25	17	24	17	24	17	23	17	16
10	31	23	18	15	30	23	15	22	15	21	15	21	15	14

Numbers indicate percentage values of reflectivity.

Installation Details

***Mounting:** Specify "G" for Flat 9/16" and 15/16" tee or "ST" for 9/16" slot tee grid types.

"G" Flat tee   "ST" slot tee

****Drywall Frame Kit:** Specify "DF" Drywall Frame Kit for drywall ceiling conditions. Use tie-wire or screws to secure frame kit.

Cut out dimensions: Min. 12.125" / Max. 12.563"
Min. 48.125" / Max. 48.563"

March 2004 Focal Point LLC reserves the right to change specifications for product improvement without notification.

FOCAL POINT LLC. 4201 South Pulaski Rd, Chicago, Illinois 60632 USA T 1.773.247.9494 F 1.773.247.8484 E-MAIL info@focalpointlights.com WEBSITE www.focalpointlights.com

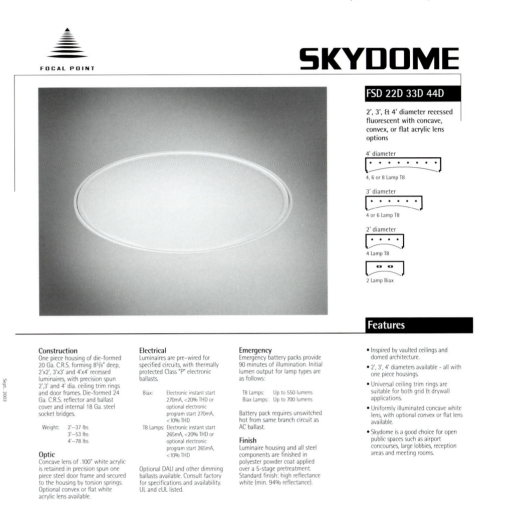

FOCAL POINT

SKYDOME

FSD 22D 33D 44D

2', 3', & 4' diameter recessed fluorescent with concave, convex, or flat acrylic lens options

4' diameter

4, 6 or 8 Lamp T8

3' diameter

4 or 6 Lamp T8

2' diameter

4 Lamp T8

2 Lamp Biax

Features

Sept. 2003

Construction
One piece housing of die-formed 20 Ga. C.R.S. forming 8⁵/₈" deep, 2'x2', 3'x3' and 4'x4' recessed luminaires, with precision spun 2',3' and 4' dia. ceiling trim rings and door frames. Die-formed 24 Ga. C.R.S. reflector and ballast cover and internal 18 Ga. steel socket bridges.

Weight:	2'—37 lbs
	3'—53 lbs
	4'—78 lbs

Optic
Concave lens of .100" white acrylic is retained in precision spun one piece steel door frame and secured to the housing by torsion springs. Optional convex or flat white acrylic lens available.

Electrical
Luminaires are pre-wired for specified circuits, with thermally protected Class "P" electronic ballasts.

| Biax: | Electronic instant start 270mA, <20% THD or optional electronic program start 270mA, <10% THD |
| T8 Lamps: | Electronic instant start 265mA, <20% THD or optional electronic program start 265mA, <10% THD |

Optional DALI and other dimming ballasts available. Consult factory for specifications and availability. UL and cUL listed.

Emergency
Emergency battery packs provide 90 minutes of illumination. Initial lumen output for lamp types are as follows:

| T8 Lamps: | Up to 550 lumens |
| Biax Lamps: | Up to 700 lumens |

Battery pack requires unswitched hot from same branch circuit as AC ballast.

Finish
Luminaire housing and all steel components are finished in polyester powder coat applied over a 5-stage pretreatment. Standard finish: high reflectance white (min. 94% reflectance).

- Inspired by vaulted ceilings and domed architecture.
- 2', 3', 4' diameters available - all with one piece housings.
- Universal ceiling trim rings are suitable for both grid & drywall applications.
- Uniformly illuminated concave white lens, with optional convex or flat lens available.
- Skydome is a good choice for open public spaces such as airport concourses, large lobbies, reception areas and meeting rooms.

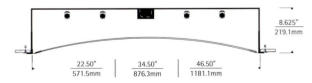

8.625"
219.1mm

| 22.50" | 34.50" | 46.50" |
| 571.5mm | 876.3mm | 1181.1mm |

THE
ART OF
LIGHT

Fixture Type:_____

Project Name:_____

SKYDOME

FOCAL POINT®

THE ART OF LIGHT

Order Information

Luminaire Series	**FSD**
Skydome	FSD
Nominal Size	
2' Diameter	22
3' Diameter	33
4' Diameter	44
Distribution	**D**
Direct Symmetrical	D
Lamp Quantity	
Two Lamps	2
(2' Diameter Only)	
Four Lamps	4
Six Lamps	6
Eight Lamps	8
Lamp Type	
40 Watt Biax	BX40
(2' Diameter Only)	
T8	T8
Ballast	
Electronic Instant Start <20% THD	E
Electronic Program Start <10% THD	S
Electronic Dimming Ballast	D
(consult factory for dimming availability)	
Voltage	
120 Volt	120
277 Volt	277
*347 Volt	347
*(Consult factory for availability)	
Mounting	**U**
Universal	U
Shielding	
Concave	CR
Flat	FL
Convex	CX
Factory Options	
Emergency Battery Pack	EM
HLR/GLR Fuse	FU
Include 3000K Lamp	L830
Include 3500K Lamp	L835
Include 4100K Lamp	L841
Separate Circuit	SC
Finish	**HW**
High Reflectance White	HW

Consult www.focalpointlights.com for additional photometric reports and technical information

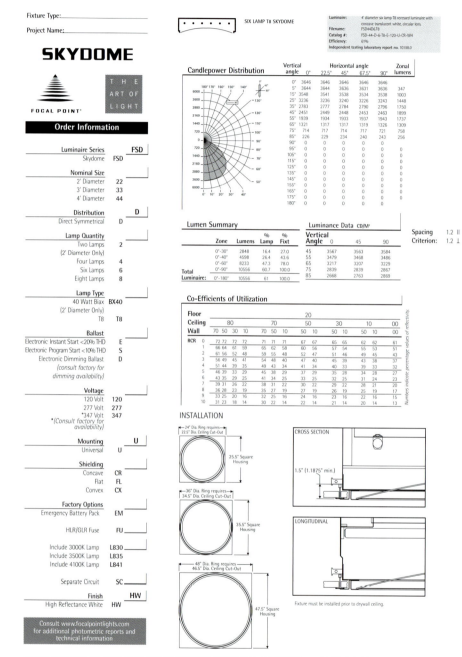

SIX LAMP T8 SKYDOME

Luminaire:	4' diameter six lamp T8 recessed luminaire with concave translucent white, circular lens.
Filename:	FSD44D6.T8
Catalog #:	FSD-44-D-6-T8-E-120-U-CR-WH
Efficiency:	61%
Independent testing laboratory report no. 10198.0	

Candlepower Distribution

Vertical angle	0°	Horizontal angle 22.5°	45°	67.5°	90°	Zonal lumens
0°	3646	3646	3646	3646	3646	
5°	3644	3644	3636	3631	3636	347
15°	3548	3541	3538	3534	3538	1003
25°	3236	3236	3240	3226	3243	1448
35°	2783	2777	2784	2790	2796	1750
45°	2451	2449	2448	2453	2463	1899
55°	1939	1934	1933	1937	1943	1737
65°	1321	1317	1317	1319	1326	1309
75°	714	717	714	717	721	758
85°	226	229	234	240	243	256
90°	0	0	0	0	0	
95°	0	0	0	0	0	
105°	0	0	0	0	0	
115°	0	0	0	0	0	
125°	0	0	0	0	0	
135°	0	0	0	0	0	
145°	0	0	0	0	0	
155°	0	0	0	0	0	
165°	0	0	0	0	0	
175°	0	0	0	0	0	
180°	0	0	0	0	0	

Lumen Summary

	Zone	Lumens	% Lamp	% Fixt
	0°-30°	2848	16.4	27.0
	0°-40°	4598	26.4	43.6
	0°-60°	8233	47.3	78.0
Total	0°-90°	10556	60.7	100.0
Luminaire:	0°-180°	10556	61	100.0

Luminance Data CD/M²

Vertical Angle	0	45	90
45	3567	3563	3584
55	3479	3468	3486
65	3217	3207	3229
75	2839	2839	2867
85	2668	2763	2869

Spacing: 1.2 ‖
Criterion: 1.2 ⊥

Co-Efficients of Utilization

Floor						20						
Ceiling	80			70			50		30		10	00
Wall	70	50	30	10	70	50	10	50	10	50	10	50	10	00
RCR 0	72	72	72	72	71	71	71	67	67	65	65	62	62	61
1	66	64	61	59	65	62	58	60	56	57	54	55	53	51
2	61	56	52	48	59	55	48	52	47	51	46	49	45	43
3	56	49	45	41	54	48	40	47	40	45	39	43	38	37
4	51	44	39	35	49	43	34	41	34	40	33	38	33	32
5	46	39	33	29	45	38	29	37	29	35	28	34	28	27
6	43	35	29	25	41	34	25	33	25	32	25	31	24	23
7	39	31	26	22	38	31	22	30	22	29	22	28	21	20
8	36	28	23	19	35	27	19	27	19	26	19	25	19	17
9	33	25	20	16	32	25	16	24	16	23	16	22	16	15
10	31	23	18	14	30	22	14	22	14	21	14	20	14	13

INSTALLATION

←24" Dia. Ring requires→
22.5" Dia. Ceiling Cut-Out

25.5" Square Housing

←36" Dia. Ring requires→
34.5" Dia. Ceiling Cut-Out

35.5" Square Housing

←48" Dia. Ring requires→
46.5" Dia. Ceiling Cut-Out

47.5" Square Housing

CROSS SECTION

1.5" (1.1875" min.)

LONGITUDINAL

Fixture must be installed prior to drywall ceiling.

Sept. 2003 Focal Point LLC. reserves the right to change specifications for product improvement without notification.

Numbers indicate percentage values of reflectivity.

FOCAL POINT LLC. 4201 South Pulaski Rd, Chicago, Illinois 60632 USA T 1.773.247.9494 F 1.773.247.8484 E-MAIL info@focalpointlights.com WEBSITE www.focalpointlights.com

FOCAL POINT

SOFTLITE II ¹ˣ⁴

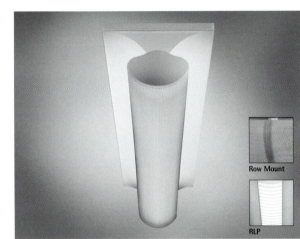

Row Mount

RLP

FS2 14B

1'x4' low profile recessed indirect with matte satin white reflector and perforated lamp shield

1, 2 & 3 Lamp T8

1, 2 & 3 Lamp T5 & T5HO

Features

Construction
One piece die-formed 20 Ga. C.R.S., 1'x4' recessed reflector/housing. Detachable perforated basket lamp shield is CNC formed 22 Ga. C.R.S. with white acrylic lens insert. Die cast aluminum end caps complete shield assembly. Optional C.R.S. radial blade louver constructed of .75" high 20 Ga. blades on 1" frequency.

Weight: 19 lbs

Optic
Integrally welded one piece 20 Ga. C.R.S. reflector, finished in matte satin white powder coat. Lamp shield is detachable, perforated basket assembly of CNC formed 22 Ga. C.R.S. and white acrylic insert.

Electrical
Luminaires are pre-wired for specified circuits, with thermally protected Class "P" electronic ballasts.

T8 Lamps: Electronic instant start 265mA, <20% THD or optional electronic program start 265mA, <10% THD
T5 Lamps: Electronic program start 160mA, <10% THD
T5HO Lamps: Electronic program start 160mA, <10% THD

Optional DALI and other dimming ballasts available. Consult factory for specifications and availability. UL and cUL Listed.

Emergency
Emergency battery packs provide 90 minutes of illumination. Initial lumen output for lamp types are as follows:

T8 Lamps: Up to 550 lumens
T5 Lamps: Up to 550 lumens
T5HO Lamps: Up to 825 lumens

Battery pack requires unswitched hot from same branch circuit as AC ballast.

Finish
Luminaire housing, reflector and all steel components are finished in polyester powder coat applied over a 5-stage pretreatment. Standard finish for housing and all steel components: matte satin white (min. 94% reflectance).

- Softlite adds dimension to a space and provides a quality of light similar to suspended indirect luminaires.
- Two-piece endcaps provide row-mount capability for all configurations of Softlite II.
- Basket assembly retained by self-aligning torsion springs pulls down for easy relamping.
- Lamps are shielded by a perforated basket to provide soft downlight component.
- Excellent solution for shallow plenum spaces. Softlite II extends 1" into ceiling.
- Ballast is accessible from both top and bottom side of unit.
- See Linear and Sconce sections for companion luminaires.

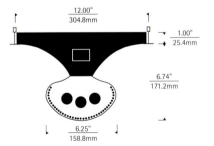

12.00" / 304.8mm

1.00" / 25.4mm

6.74" / 171.2mm

6.25" / 158.8mm

THE ART OF LIGHT™

Fixture Type: _____

Project Name: _____

SOFTLITE II 1x4

FOCAL POINT®

THE ART OF LIGHT™

Order Information

Luminaire Series		FS2
Softlite II	FS2	

Nominal Size		14
1' x 4'	14	

Distribution		B
Bi-Directional	B	

Lamp Quantity	
One Lamp	1
Two Lamps	2
Three Lamps	3

Lamp Type	
T8	T8
T5	T5
T5HO	T5HO

Ballast	
Electronic Instant Start <20% THD (T8 only)	E
Electronic Program Start <10% THD	S
Electronic Dimming Ballast (consult factory for dimming availability)	D

Voltage	
120 Volt	120
277 Volt	277
*347 Volt	347
*(Consult factory for availability)	

Mounting	
Grid	G
Slot tee	ST

Shielding	
Perforated Shield	PS
Radial Blade Louver	RLP

Factory Options	
Drywall Frame Kit	DF
Emergency Battery Pack	EM
Earthquake Clip	EQ
HLR/GLR Fuse	FU
Flex Whip	FW
Include 3000K Lamp	L830
Include 3500K Lamp	L835
Include 4100K Lamp	L841
Separate Circuit	SC

Finish		WH
Matte Satin White	WH	

Consult www.focalpointlights.com for additional photometric reports and technical information

TWO LAMP T8 SOFTLITE

Luminaire:	1x4' two lamp T8 recessed luminaire with matte white reflector and perforated lamp shield.
Filename:	FS2214P5.T8
Catalog #:	FS2-14-B-2-T8-E-120-G-PS-WH
Efficiency:	79%
Independent testing laboratory report no. 12000.0.

Candlepower Distribution

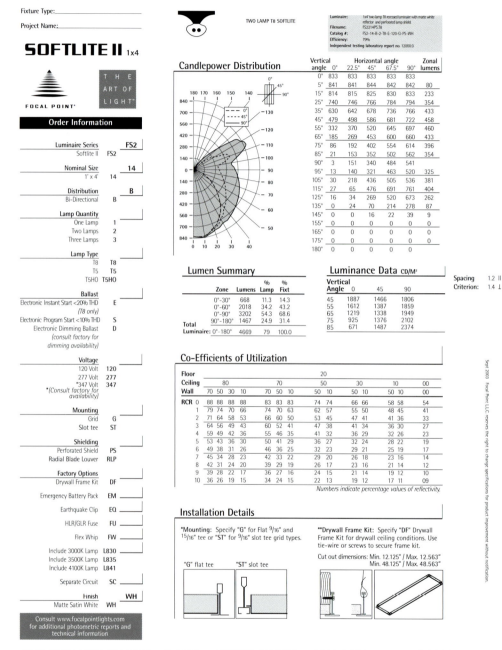

Vertical angle	0°	22.5°	45°	67.5°	90°	Zonal lumens
0°	833	833	833	833	833	
5°	841	841	844	842	842	80
15°	814	815	825	830	833	233
25°	740	746	766	784	794	354
35°	630	642	678	736	766	433
45°	479	498	586	681	722	458
55°	332	370	520	645	697	460
65°	185	269	453	600	660	433
75°	86	192	402	554	614	396
85°	21	153	352	502	562	354
90°	3	151	340	484	541	
95°	13	140	321	463	520	325
105°	30	218	436	505	536	381
115°	27	65	476	691	761	404
125°	16	34	269	520	673	262
135°	0	24	70	214	278	87
145°	0	0	16	22	39	9
155°	0	0	0	0	0	0
165°	0	0	0	0	0	0
175°	0	0	0	0	0	0
180°	0	0	0	0	0	

Lumen Summary

	Zone	Lumens	% Lamp	% Fixt
	0°-30°	668	11.3	14.3
	0°-60°	2018	34.2	43.2
	0°-90°	3202	54.3	68.6
	90°-180°	1467	24.9	31.4
Total Luminaire:	0°-180°	4669	79	100.0

Luminance Data CD/M²

Vertical Angle	0	45	90
45	1887	1466	1806
55	1612	1387	1859
65	1219	1338	1949
75	925	1376	2102
85	671	1487	2374

Spacing 1.2 ‖
Criterion: 1.4 ⊥

Co-Efficients of Utilization

Floor								20							
Ceiling		80				70			50			30		10	00
Wall	70	50	30	10	70	50	10	50	10	50	10	50	10	00
RCR 0	88	88	88	88	83	83	83	74	74	66	66	58	58	54
1	79	74	70	66	74	70	63	62	57	55	50	48	45	41
2	71	64	58	53	66	60	50	53	45	47	41	41	36	33
3	64	56	49	43	60	52	41	47	38	41	34	36	30	27
4	59	49	42	36	55	46	35	41	32	36	29	32	26	23
5	53	43	36	30	50	41	29	36	27	32	24	28	22	19
6	49	38	31	26	46	36	25	32	23	29	21	25	19	17
7	45	34	28	23	42	33	22	29	20	26	18	23	16	14
8	42	31	24	20	39	29	19	26	17	23	16	21	14	12
9	39	28	22	17	36	27	16	24	15	21	14	19	12	10
10	36	26	19	15	34	24	15	22	13	19	12	17	11	09

Numbers indicate percentage values of reflectivity.

Installation Details

*Mounting: Specify "G" for Flat 9/16" and 15/16" tee or "ST" for 9/16" slot tee grid types.

**Drywall Frame Kit: Specify "DF" Drywall Frame Kit for drywall ceiling conditions. Use tie-wire or screws to secure frame kit.

Cut out dimensions: Min. 12.125" / Max. 12.563"
Min. 48.125" / Max. 48.563"

"G" flat tee   "ST" slot tee

Sept 2003 Focal Point LLC. reserves the right to change specifications for product improvement without notification.

FOCAL POINT L.L.C. 4201 South Pulaski Rd, Chicago, Illinois 60632 USA T 1.773.247.9494 F 1.773.247.8484 E-MAIL info@focalpointlights.com WEBSITE www.focalpointlights.com

FOCAL POINT

GROOVE

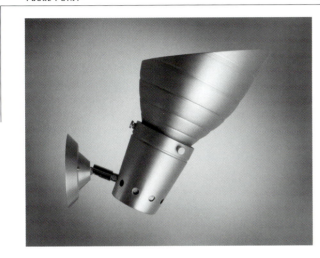

Adjustable, Wall-Mount Compact Fluorescent or Incandescent Luminaire.

1 Lamp 18w. & 26w. Triple Tube Compact Fluorescent

A15, A19, and A21, 100w. max

Features

Construction
Housing, reflector and canopy are each one-piece precision-spun 14Ga., 3002-0 aluminum, (.063" min. thickness). Housing: 4.64"H x 3.68"Dia. Reflector: 60°angle cut reflector, 6.97"Dia. aperture with grooved cylindrical pattern. Canopy: 1.32"H x 4.52"Dia. stepped design with (2), #8 screws for mounting canopy to junction box bracket. Junction box bracket provided for use with 3" octagonal junction box. 340° horizontal adjustment and 90° vertical tilt swivel arm finished in polished chrome .

Weight: 4 lbs

Optic
14Ga., 3002-0 anodized aluminum reflector with diffuse satin matte surface for lamp image reduction.

Electrical
Luminaires are pre-wired for single circuit with thermally protected Class "P" electronic ballast.

Incandescent: Medium base porcelain socket. For lamp types A15, A19 and A21,100w. max.

Fluorescent Lamp: Single lamp triple tube compact fluorescent, 4-pin, 18w.-(GX24q-2) or 26w.-(GX24q-3).

UL and CUL listed.

Finish
Luminaire housing, reflector and canopy are clear anodized with polished satin finish. Reflector interior has matte diffuse finish.

- Housing, reflector and canopy are spun with high quality aluminum. Decorative grooves in reflector create interest and a strong design presence.

- Uniquely designed two-tone reflector features satin finished exterior and matte diffuse interior, which controls lamp imaging while maintaining high efficiency.

- Wall-Mount luminaire provides adjustable indirect light source.

- 340° swivel mounting arm and 90° tilt adjustment allows precise light adjustment.

- Ideally suited for retail, hospitality, lobbies, corridors, open ceiling areas and other specialty applications.

- See pendant section for companion luminaires.

THE
ART OF
LIGHT

6.97"
177.0mm

60°

11.97"
304.0mm

Fixture Type: _____

Project Name: _____

GROOVE

THE ART OF LIGHT™

FOCAL POINT®

Order Information

Luminaire Series	**FGR**
Groove	FGR
Profile	**A**
Profile	A
Lamp Quantity	**1**
One Lamp	1
Lamp Type	
18W Triple Tube, GX24q-2	18TT
26W Triple Tube, GX24q-3	26TT
120V Only, 60W Max., A15-Med	A15
120V Only, 100W Max., A19-Med	A19
120V Only, 100W Max., A21-Med	A21
Ballast	**E**
Electronic <15% THD	E
Voltage	
120 Volt	120
277 Volt	277
*347 Volt	347
*(Consult factory for availability)	
Mounting	**WM**
Wall Mount	WM
Factory Options	
Include 3000K Lamp	L830
Include 3500K Lamp	L835
Include 4100K Lamp	L841
(fluorescent lamps only)	
Finish	**NA**
Natural Anodized	NA

Consult www.focalpointlights.com for additional photometric reports and technical information

Photometric Report:

FGR-A-1-18TT-E-XXX-WM-NA

Luminaire: One lamp triple tube, compact fluorescent wall-mount Indirect with electronic ballast

File name: FGR-A118.IES ⊞ **IES FORMAT**

Lamp:
GE:	F18TBX/*/A/4P
Osram/Sylvania:	CF18DT/E/*
Phillips:	PL-T18W/*/4P

* Manufacturer's color temperature designation

Efficiency: 74.7%

Lumen Summary

Zone	Lumens	% Lamp	% Fixt
90°-120°	145.6	12.1	16.2
90°-130°	289.0	24.1	32.2
90°-150°	651.6	54.3	72.7
90°-180°	896.3	74.7	100.0
Total Luminaire: 0°-180°	896.3	74.7	100.0

Candlepower Distribution

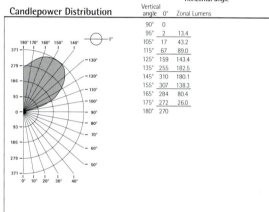

Vertical angle	Horizontal angle 0°	Zonal Lumens
90°	0	
95°	2	13.4
105°	17	43.2
115°	67	89.0
125°	159	143.4
135°	255	182.5
145°	310	180.1
155°	307	138.3
165°	284	80.4
175°	272	26.0
180°	270	

Co-Efficients of Utilization

Floor													20	
Ceiling		80				70			50		30		10	00
Wall	70	50	30	10	70	50	10	50	10	50	10	50	10	00
RCR 0	71	71	71	71	61	61	61	41	41	24	24	8	8	0
1	65	62	59	57	55	53	49	36	34	21	20	7	6	0
2	59	54	50	46	50	46	40	32	28	18	16	6	5	0
3	54	47	42	38	46	40	33	28	23	16	14	5	4	0
4	49	42	36	32	42	36	28	25	20	14	12	5	4	0
5	45	37	31	27	38	32	24	22	17	13	10	4	3	0
6	41	33	27	23	35	28	20	19	14	11	9	4	3	0
7	38	29	24	20	32	25	18	17	12	10	7	3	2	0
8	35	26	21	17	30	23	15	16	11	9	6	3	2	0
9	32	24	19	15	27	21	13	14	9	8	6	3	2	0
10	30	22	17	13	25	19	12	13	8	8	5	2	2	0

Numbers indicate percentage values of reflectivity.

Feb. 2004 Focal Point LLC reserves the right to change specifications for product improvement without notification.

FOCAL POINT L.L.C. 4201 South Pulaski Rd, Chicago, Illinois 60632 USA T 1.773.247.9494 F 1.773.247.8484 E-MAIL info@focalpointlights.com WEBSITE www.focalpointlights.com

FOCAL POINT

COVELIGHT 26

FCV 26

Low-profile cove mounted
2" x 6" luminaire with indirect
asymmetric distribution.

1 Lamp T8

1 Lamp T5 & T5HO

2 Lamp T5 & T5HO

Features

Construction
One piece housing of die-formed
22 Ga. C.R.S. forming 2"H x 6"W
rectangular profile. Socket bridge
and 20 Ga. Galvanized end caps
are mechanically fastened.

Weight: 4' unit—7 lbs
8' unit—14 lbs

Optic
Die-formed 20 Ga. steel reflector
with aluminum insert, finished in
high reflectance white paint
(90% reflectance).

Electrical
Luminaires are pre-wired with
factory installed branch circuit
wiring with over-molded quick
connects. All ballasts are thermally
protected and have a Class "P"
rating.

*Consult Ballast Ordering Guide on
following page for ballast
specifications*

Optional DALI and other dimming
ballasts available. Consult factory
for specifications and availability.
UL and cUL listed.

Emergency
Emergency battery packs provide
90 minutes of one lamp
illumination. Initial lumen output
for lamp types are as follows:

T8 Lamp: Up to 550 lumens
T5 Lamp: Up to 550 lumens
T5HO Lamp: Up to 825 lumens

Battery pack requires unswitched
hot from same branch circuit as
AC ballast.

Finish
Luminaire housing and reflector
are finished in high reflectance
white paint (90% reflectance).

- High performance indirect luminaire
  designed for concealed cove
  applications.
- Covelight provides pleasing and
  even illumination that highlights
  architectural details.
- Continuous row installations may be
  configured with 2', 3', 4', 5', 6', 7' and
  8' luminaires.
- Shorter housing design for T5 lamps
  minimizes socket shadows.
- Enhanced ease of installation: simple
  plug connection eliminates need to
  access electrical components in luminaire housing.

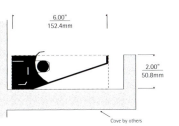

6.00"
152.4mm

2.00"
50.8mm

Cove by others

THE
ART OF
LIGHT

January 2005

Fixture Type:_____

Project Name:_____

COVELIGHT 26

FOCAL POINT®

THE ART OF LIGHT

Order Information

Luminaire Series		FCV
Covelight	FCV	

Profile		26
2" x 6"	26	

Lamping	
1 Lamp T8	1T8
*1 Lamp T5	1T5
*1 Lamp T5HO	1T5HO
*2 Lamp T5	2T5
*2 Lamp T5HO	2T5HO

*(T5 units supplied
to match lamp length
See **Luminaire Lengths** chart
for more information)

Circuit	
Single Circuit	1C
Dual Circuit	2C

(note: Dual circuit available on
two lamps only)

Voltage	
120 Volt	120
277 Volt	277
*347 Volt	347

*(Consult factory for
availability)

Ballast	
Electronic Instant Start <20% THD	E
(T8 Only)	
Electronic Program Start <10% THD	S
Electronic Dimming Ballast	D

(consult factory for
dimming availability)

Mounting		CV
Cove	CV	

Factory Options	
Emergency Circuit	EC

(consult factory for details)

Emergency Battery Pack	EM
HLR/GLR Fuse	FU
Include 3000K Lamp	L830
Include 3500K Lamp	L835
Include 4100K Lamp	L841

Finish		HW
High Reflectance White	HW	

Luminaire Length		XX'
*Designate run length in feet		

Nominal lengths: 2',3',4',5',6',7',8'
*(T5 units supplied
to match lamp length
See **Luminaire Lengths** chart
for more information)

Corner Flex Whip		
18" Flexible conduit with Plug	CFW	

Supplied for every corner condition. Specify
run and pattern details when ordering.

Luminaire Lengths

	T8 Lengths	T5 Lengths
2'	24"	22.4"
3'	36"	34.3"
4'	48"	46.1"
5'	60"	57.9"
6'	72"	68.5"
7'	84"	80.3"
8'	96"	92.1"

Continuous run lengths may be configured with combinations of 2', 3', 4', 5', 6', 7' and 8' nominal luminaire lengths.

Ballast Ordering Guide

Code	Lamping	Specifications
E	T8	Electronic instant start 265mA, <20% THD
S	T8	Electronic program start 265mA, <10% THD
S	T5	Electronic program start 160mA, <10% THD
S	T5HO	Electronic program start 160mA, <10% THD
D	T8	Standard dimming range from 100% to 10% lumen output. Consult factory for further specifications.
D	T5HO	Standard dimming range from 100% to 1% lumen output. 4' lamps only. Consult factory for further specifications.
D	T5	Standard dimming range from 100% to 10% lumen output. 4' lamps only. Consult factory for further specifications.

Continuous Run Installation Detail

Branch circuit thru-wire harness with plug allows for easy continuous run installation without accessing luminaire interior.

Corner Installation Detail

18" long flexible conduit with plug simplifies corner installation. For even corner illumination, a maximum 3" distance from end of cove to end of luminaire is recommended.

January 2005 Focal Point L.L.C. reserves the right to change specifications for product improvement without notification.

FOCAL POINT L.L.C. 4201 South Pulaski Rd, Chicago, Illinois 60632 USA T 1.773.247.9494 F 1.773.247.8484 E-MAIL info@focalpointlights.com WEBSITE www.focalpointlights.com

Candlepower Distribution Graphs for Selected Luminaires
(Continued)

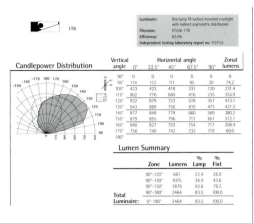

1T8

Luminaire:	One lamp T8 surface mounted covelight with indirect asymmetric distribution.
Filename:	FCV26-1.T8
Efficiency:	83.5%
Independent testing laboratory report no. 11277.0	

Candlepower Distribution

Vertical angle	0°	22.5°	45°	67.5°	90°	Zonal lumens
90°	0	0	0	0	0	0
95°	114	112	111	95	20	74.2
105°	423	423	418	331	120	231.4
115°	802	776	660	416	235	355.9
125°	932	879	723	519	357	413.1
135°	943	889	756	610	473	421.3
145°	877	849	779	660	569	380.2
155°	879	855	796	713	651	312.1
165°	840	827	793	754	717	206.4
175°	756	749	742	732	719	69.0
180°						

Lumen Summary

	Zone	Lumens	% Lamp	% Fixt
	90°-120°	661	22.4	26.9
	90°-130°	1075	36.4	43.6
	90°-150°	1876	63.6	76.2
Total	90°-180°	2464	83.5	100.0
Luminaire:	0°-180°	2464	83.5	100.0

2T5HO

Luminaire:	Two lamp T5HO surface mounted covelight with indirect asymmetric distribution.
Filename:	FCV26-2.T5H
Efficiency:	79.5%
Independent testing laboratory report no. 11073.0	

Candlepower Distribution

Vertical angle	0°	22.5°	45°	67.5°	90°	Zonal lumens
90°	0	0	0	0	0	0
95°	219	238	268	320	88	231.0
105°	1012	988	914	1008	442	700.1
115°	1820	1862	1897	1554	859	1139.8
125°	2706	2631	2401	1876	1242	1399.1
135°	3157	3042	2652	2251	1614	1437.4
145°	2862	2752	2622	2306	1790	1199.4
155°	2986	2946	2792	2496	2073	990.4
165°	2879	2839	2717	2507	2244	637.7
175°	2562	2533	2475	2381	2293	219.0
180°						

Lumen Summary

	Zone	Lumens	% Lamp	% Fixt
	90°-120°	2071	20.7	26.0
	90°-130°	3470	34.7	43.6
	90°-150°	6107	61.1	76.8
Total	90°-180°	7954	79.5	100.0
Luminaire:	0°-180°	7954	79.5	100.0

Light Levels (maintained footcandles)

10" MD

ceiling height	Floor Reading Interval						
	2'	4'	6'	8'	10'	12'	14'
10' 6"	12	13	12	10	9	7	5
9' 6"	15	15	13	11	9	7	5
8' 6"	16	16	14	12	9	6	5
7' 6"	18	18	15	11	8	6	5

15" MD

ceiling height	Floor Reading Interval						
	2'	4'	6'	8'	10'	12'	14'
10' 6"	13	13	13	11	9	7	5
9' 6"	15	15	14	11	9	7	5
8' 6"	17	17	15	12	9	7	5
7' 6"	17	18	14	11	8	6	4

Light Levels (maintained footcandles)

15" MD

ceiling height	Floor Reading Interval						
	2'	4'	6'	8'	10'	12'	14'
10' 6"	45	47	45	38	31	24	19
9' 6"	53	55	50	41	32	25	19
8' 6"	60	62	53	42	32	24	19
7' 6"	61	62	50	37	27	20	15

24" MD

ceiling height	Floor Reading Interval						
	2'	4'	6'	8'	10'	12'	14'
10' 6"	48	52	48	41	34	28	22
9' 6"	55	59	51	42	34	27	21
8' 6"	54	55	48	39	30	22	17
7' 6"	72	72	60	46	34	25	19

January 2005. Focal Point LLC reserves the right to change specifications for product improvement without notification.

Luminaire: One lamp T5HO surface mounted covelight with indirect asymmetric distribution
Filename: RCV26-1T5H
Efficiency: 82.5%
Independent testing laboratory report no. 11072.0

1T5HO

Candlepower Distribution

Vertical angle	0°	22.5°	45°	67.5°	90°	112.5	135.0	157.5	180.0	Zonal lumens
90°	0	0	0	0	0	0	0	0	0	0
95°	212	216	235	273	37	58	72	70	70	168.3
105°	1043	1045	1006	665	202	90	102	124	131	508.9
115°	1741	1626	1301	686	395	231	153	155	158	669.5
125°	1813	1662	1226	743	580	425	295	230	224	686.3
135°	1576	1429	1117	867	761	634	493	408	384	646.3
145°	1236	1176	1061	923	878	817	694	614	593	554.4
155°	1207	1178	1104	1024	1016	1009	908	848	824	469.7
165°	1158	1142	1117	1101	1105	1109	1099	1061	1044	312.7
175°	1121	1117	1115	1120	1122	1129	1129	1131	1131	107.3
180°										

Lumen Summary

	Zone	Lumens	% Lamp	% Fixt
	90°-120°	1347	26.9	32.7
	90°-130°	2033	40.7	49.3
	90°-150°	3234	64.7	78.4
	90°-180°	4123	82.5	100.0
Total Luminaire:	0°-180°	4123	82.5	100.0

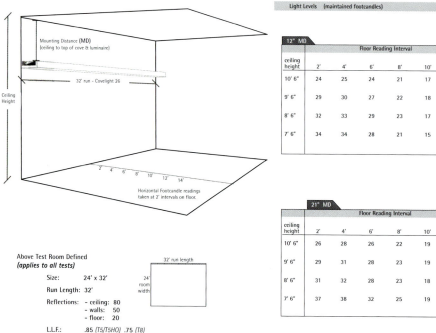

Ceiling Height

Mounting Distance (MD)
(ceiling to top of cove & luminaire)

32' run - Covelight 26

2' 4' 6' 8' 10' 12' 14'

Horizontal Footcandle readings taken at 2' intervals on floor.

Above Test Room Defined
(applies to all tests)

Size: 24' x 32'
Run Length: 32'
Reflections: – ceiling: 80
– walls: 50
– floor: 20
L.L.F.: .85 *(T5/T5HO)* .75 *(T8)*

Table values are maintained footcandles.

32' run length

24' room width

Light Levels (maintained footcandles)

12" MD

ceiling height	Floor Reading Interval						
	2'	4'	6'	8'	10'	12'	14'
10' 6"	24	25	24	21	17	13	11
9' 6"	29	30	27	22	18	14	11
8' 6"	32	33	29	23	17	13	10
7' 6"	34	34	28	21	15	11	8

21" MD

ceiling height	Floor Reading Interval						
	2'	4'	6'	8'	10'	12'	14'
10' 6"	26	28	26	22	19	15	12
9' 6"	29	31	28	23	19	15	12
8' 6"	31	32	28	23	18	14	11
7' 6"	37	38	32	25	19	14	11

January 2005 Focal Point LLC reserves the right to change specifications for product improvement without notification.

FOCAL POINT LLC. 4201 South Pulaski Rd, Chicago, Illinois 60632 USA T 1.773.247.9494 F 1.773.247.8484 E-MAIL info@focalpointlights.com WEBSITE www.focalpointlights.com

726 | APPENDIX A

FEATURES

HOUSING

High quality metal housing.

Available in white (standard) or black finish. A variety of finishes also available.

Matte black baffle standard.

STEM

Extruded aluminum stem conceals fixture wiring and allows rotation up to 330°.

Pivot mechanism allows adjustment up to 90° from vertical.

ADAPTOR

Low-profile, injection-molded track mounting adaptor for easy attachment to Lithonia 1 or 2 circuit track. Snap lock secures adaptor to track.

ELECTRICAL SYSTEM

Medium-base porcelain socket.

LISTING

Fixtures are UL 1574 listed.

Listed and labeled to comply with Canadian Standards.

ACCESSORIES

Accepts a variety of lens, barn doors, filters and louvers. Shipped separately. See options and accessories tab for more information.

Catalog Number		
Notes		Type

Incandescent Line Voltage

LTC

Roundback

PAR16, 20, 30, 38 Lamps

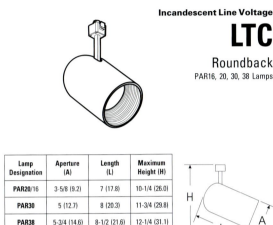

Lamp Designation	Aperture (A)	Length (L)	Maximum Height (H)
PAR20/16	3-5/8 (9.2)	7 (17.8)	10-1/4 (26.0)
PAR30	5 (12.7)	8 (20.3)	11-3/4 (29.8)
PAR38	5-3/4 (14.6)	8-1/2 (21.6)	12-1/4 (31.1)

All dimensions are in inches (centimeters).

ORDERING INFORMATION

Example: **LTC RNDB PAR20 MB WH**

Choose the boldface catalog nomenclature that best suits your needs and write it on the appropriate line. Order accessories as separate catalog numbers (shipped separately).

LTC	RNDB			
Series	**Head Style**	**Lamp Designation**[1]	**Trim Type**	**Finish**[3]
LTC	RNDB Roundback cylinder	PAR20 PAR20 and PAR16 compatible (75W maximum)	MB Matte black baffle (standard)	**Architectural Colors** (powder finish)[4]
		PAR30 PAR30 long-neck compatible (75W maximum)[2]	WB White baffle	**Standard Colors**
				WH White (standard)
		PAR38 PAR38 compatible (Q250W maximum)		DBL Black
				DWHG Matte white, textured
				DBLB Matte black, textured

Classic Colors

DMB Medium bronze
DNA Natural aluminum
DSS Sandstone
DGC Charcoal gray
DTG Tennis green
DBR Bright red
DSB Steel blue

Plated Finishes

AB Antique brass
PB Polished brass
PCHR Polished chrome

Accessories

Order as separate catalog numbers.

LTFH500	Filter holder for PAR20 and PAR16. Specify white (WH) or black (DBL).
LTFH700	Filter holder for PAR30. Specify white (WH) or black (DBL).
LTFH800	Filter holder for PAR38. Specify white (WH) or black (DBL).
F500[5,6]	Lens for use with 500 series filter holders and barn doors.
F700[5,6]	Lens for use with 700 series filter holders and barn doors.
F800[5,6]	Lens for use with 800 series filter holders and barn doors.
L500[6]	Eggcrate louver for use with 500 series filter holders.
L700[6]	Eggcrate louver for use with 700 series filter holders.
L800[6]	Eggcrate louver for use with 800 series filter holders.
LTBD500	Barn door for PAR20 and PAR16. Specify white (WH) or black (DBL).
LTBD700	Barn door for PAR30. Specify white (WH) or black (DBL).
LTBD800	Barn door for PAR38. Specify white (WH) or black (DBL).

NOTES

1 For lamp ordering information, refer to options and accessories tab.

2 When utilizing short-neck lamps, socket extender is required. Order separately. TP30 SE.

3 White stem mounted fixtures have white stems and adaptors. All other stem-mounted fixtures have black stems and adaptors. For alternate stem/adaptor color add AWH (white) or ABL (black) after finish color. Example: DMB AWH

4 Additional architectural colors and custom color matches available; please see brochure 794.3.

5 For lens type (color selection information) refer to options and accessories tab.

6 A filter holder or barn door is required when ordering a louver or lens.

Downlighting & Track

Sheet #: 105-LINE-RNDB LINE-200

LTC Roundback

LAMP PERFORMANCE DATA

The lighting performance data charts shown provide lighting levels (footcandles), beam pattern (in feet), rated lamp life.

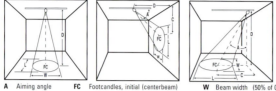

A Aiming angle	**FC** Footcandles, initial (centerbeam)	**W** Beam width (50% of CB candle power)
D Distance (feet)	**L** Beam length (50% of CB candle power)	**C** Distance to beam center (feet)

Lamp	Rated Life	Beam Spread	0° Aiming Angle					30° Aiming Angle					45° Aiming Angle					60° Aiming Angle				
			D	FC	W	L	C	D	FC	W	L	C	D	FC	W	L	C	D	FC	W	L	C
60PAR16/HAL/NSP	2000	10°	4	313	0.7	0.7	N/A	4	203	0.8	0.9	2.3	3	196	0.7	1.1	3.0	2	156	0.7	1.4	3.5
			6	139	1.1	1.1	N/A	6	90	1.2	1.4	3.5	4	110	1.0	1.4	4.0	3	69	1.1	2.2	5.2
			8	78	1.4	1.4	N/A	8	51	1.6	1.9	4.6	5	71	1.2	1.8	5.0	4	39	1.4	2.9	6.9
60PAR16/HAL/NFL	2000	30°	2	325	1.1	1.1	N/A	2	211	1.2	1.5	1.2	2	115	1.5	2.3	2.0	2	41	2.1	5.5	3.5
			4	81	2.1	2.1	N/A	3	94	1.9	2.2	1.7	3	51	2.3	3.5	3.0	3	18	3.2	8.2	5.2
			6	36	3.2	3.2	N/A	4	53	2.5	2.9	2.3	4	29	3.0	4.6	4.0	4	10	4.3	10.9	6.9
50PAR20/H/SP10	2500	10°	4	375	0.7	0.7	N/A	4	244	0.8	0.9	2.3	4	236	0.7	1.1	3.0	2	188	0.7	1.4	3.5
			6	167	1.1	1.1	N/A	5	156	1.0	1.2	2.9	4	133	1.0	1.4	4.0	3	83	1.1	2.2	5.2
			8	94	1.4	1.4	N/A	6	108	1.2	1.4	3.5	5	85	1.2	1.8	4.6	4	47	1.4	2.9	6.9
50PAR20/H/FL25	2500	25°	3	167	1.3	1.3	N/A	2	244	1.0	1.2	1.2	2	133	1.3	1.9	2.0	2	47	1.8	4.2	3.5
			4	94	1.8	1.8	N/A	3	108	1.5	1.8	1.7	3	59	1.9	2.8	3.0	3	21	2.7	6.2	5.2
			5	60	2.2	2.2	N/A	4	61	2.1	2.4	2.3	4	33	2.5	3.7	4.0	4	12	3.6	8.3	6.9
75PAR30/CAP/NSP	2500	9°	8	219	1.3	1.3	N/A	8	142	1.5	1.7	4.6	6	137	1.3	1.9	6.0	4	109	1.3	2.6	6.9
			10	140	1.6	1.6	N/A	10	91	1.8	2.1	5.8	8	77	1.8	2.5	8.0	6	49	1.9	3.9	10.4
			12	97	1.9	1.9	N/A	12	63	2.2	2.5	6.9	10	50	2.2	3.2	10.0	8	27	2.5	5.1	13.9
75PAR30/CAP/NFL	2500	30°	4	200	2.1	2.1	N/A	4	130	2.5	2.9	2.3	2	283	1.5	2.3	2.0	2	100	2.1	5.5	3.5
			6	89	3.2	3.2	N/A	6	58	3.7	4.4	3.5	4	71	3.0	4.6	4.0	3	44	3.2	8.2	5.2
			8	50	4.3	4.3	N/A	8	32	5.0	5.9	4.6	6	31	4.6	6.9	6.0	4	25	4.3	10.9	6.9
75PAR30/CAP/FL	2500	40°	4	125	2.9	2.9	N/A	3	144	2.5	3.1	1.7	3	79	3.1	5.0	3.0	2	63	2.9	9.7	3.5
			6	56	4.4	4.4	N/A	4	81	3.4	4.1	2.3	4	44	4.1	6.7	4.0	3	28	4.4	14.5	5.2
			8	31	5.8	5.8	N/A	5	52	4.2	5.1	2.9	5	28	5.2	8.4	5.0	4	16	5.8	19.3	6.9
120PAR/CAP/SPL/SP	3000	9°	10	250	1.6	1.6	N/A	10	162	1.8	2.1	5.8	6	246	1.3	1.9	6.0	4	195	1.3	2.66	6.9
			12	174	1.9	1.9	N/A	12	113	2.2	2.5	6.9	8	138	1.8	2.5	8.0	6	98	1.9	3.9	10.4
			14	128	2.2	2.2	N/A	14	83	2.5	2.9	8.1	10	88	2.2	3.2	10.0	8	49	2.5	5.1	13.9
120PAR/CAP/SPL/FL	3000	30°	4	313	2.1	2.1	N/A	4	203	2.5	2.9	2.3	4	110	3.0	4.6	4.0	2	156	2.1	5.5	3.5
			6	139	3.2	3.2	N/A	6	90	3.7	4.4	3.5	6	49	4.6	6.9	6.0	3	69	3.2	8.2	5.2
			8	78	4.3	4.3	N/A	8	51	5.0	5.9	4.6	8	28	6.1	9.2	8.0	4	39	4.3	10.9	6.9
120PAR/CAP/WFL	3000	50°	4	125	3.7	3.7	N/A	4	81	4.3	5.4	2.2	2	177	2.6	4.8	2.0	2	63	3.7	21.5	3.5
			6	56	5.6	5.6	N/A	6	36	6.5	8.0	3.5	4	44	5.3	9.5	4.0	3	28	5.6	32.2	5.2
			8	31	7.5	7.5	N/A	8	20	8.6	10.7	4.6	6	20	7.9	14.3	6.0	4	16	7.5	42.9	6.9
150PAR/SP	2000	12°	8	215	1.7	1.7	N/A	8	139	1.9	2.3	4.6	6	135	1.8	2.6	6.0	4	107	1.7	3.5	6.9
			12	95	2.5	2.5	N/A	12	62	2.9	3.4	6.9	8	76	2.4	3.4	8.0	6	48	2.5	5.2	10.4
			16	54	3.4	3.4	N/A	16	35	3.9	4.5	9.2	10	49	3.0	4.3	10.0	8	27	3.4	7.0	13.9
150PAR/FL	2000	30°	4	215	2.1	2.1	N/A	4	139	2.5	2.9	2.3	4	76	3.0	4.6	4.0	2	107	2.1	5.5	3.5
			8	54	4.3	4.3	N/A	6	62	3.7	4.4	3.5	6	34	4.6	6.9	6.0	3	47	4.3	10.9	6.9
			12	24	6.4	6.4	N/A	8	35	5.0	5.9	4.6	8	19	6.1	9.2	8.0	4	12	6.4	16.4	10.4
Q250PAR/SP10°	4200	10°	10	400	1.8	1.8	N/A	10	260	2.0	2.3	5.8	8	221	2.0	2.8	6.0	4	313	1.4	2.9	6.9
			15	178	2.6	2.6	N/A	14	133	2.8	3.3	8.1	10	141	2.5	3.5	10.0	6	139	2.1	4.3	10.4
			20	100	3.5	3.5	N/A	18	80	3.6	4.2	10.4	12	98	3.0	4.2	12.0	8	78	2.8	5.7	13.9
Q250PAR/FL30°	4200	30°	8	141	4.3	4.3	N/A	6	162	3.7	4.4	3.5	4	199	3.0	4.6	4.0	3	125	3.2	8.2	5.2
			12	63	6.4	6.4	N/A	8	91	5.0	5.9	4.6	6	88	4.6	6.9	6.0	4	70	4.3	10.9	6.9
			16	35	8.6	8.6	N/A	10	58	6.2	7.3	5.8	8	50	6.1	9.2	8.0	5	45	5.4	13.7	8.7

All data was calculated from each lamp manufacturer's published data and is subject to normal lamp variations. Maximum footcandle is usually at the aiming point, but not always on wider spread lamps. Lamp data supplied by manufacturers is approximate and individual lamp performance may vary.

LITHONIA LIGHTING®

An AcuityBrands Company

Sheet #: **105-LINE-RNDB**   ©1999 Acuity Lighting Group, Inc. 10/99   105-LINE-RNDB.p65

Lithonia Lighting
Acuity Lighting Group, Inc.
Recessed Downlighting
One Lithonia Way, Conyers, GA 30012
Phone: 800-315-4935 Fax: 770-860-3106
In Canada: 1100 50th Ave., Lachine, Quebec H8T 2V3
www.lithonia.com

LITHONIA LIGHTING®

Catalog Number	
Notes	Type

Incandescent Line Voltage

LTC
Soft Square
PAR16, 20, 30 Lamps

FEATURES

HOUSING
High quality metal housing.
Available in white (standard) or black finish. A variety of finishes also available.
Matte black baffle standard.

STEM
Extruded aluminum stem conceals fixture wiring and allows rotation up to 330°.
Pivot mechanism allows adjustment up to 90° from vertical.

ADAPTOR
Low-profile, injection-molded track mounting adaptor for easy attachment to Lithonia 1 or 2 circuit track. Snap lock secures adaptor to track.

ELECTRICAL SYSTEM
Medium-base porcelain socket.

LISTING
Fixtures are UL 1574 listed.
Listed and labeled to comply with Canadian Standards.

Lamp Designation	Aperture (A)	Length (L)	Maximum Height (H)
PAR20/16	3-3/4 (9.5)	7 (17.8)	10-3/4 (27.3)
PAR30	5 (12.7)	7-7/8 (20.0)	11-7/8 (30.2)

All dimensions are in inches (centimeters).

ORDERING INFORMATION

Example: **LTC SFTS PAR20 MB WH**

Choose the boldface catalog nomenclature that best suits your needs and write it on the appropriate line. Order accessories as separate catalog numbers (shipped separately).

LTC	SFTS	Lamp Designation[1]	Trim Type	Finish[2]
Series	**Head Style**			**Architectural Colors** (powder finish)[3]
LTC	SFTS Soft square	**PAR20** PAR20 and PAR16 compatible (75W maximum)	**MB** Matte black baffle (standard)	**Standard Colors**
			WB White baffle	**WH** White (standard)
		PAR30 PAR30 compatible (75W maximum). Short-neck and long-neck compatible.		**DBL** Black
				DWHG Matte white, textured
				DBLB Matte black, textured
				Classic Colors
				DMB Medium bronze
				DNA Natural aluminum
				DSS Sandstone
				DGC Charcoal gray
				DTG Tennis green
				DBR Bright red
				DSB Steel blue

NOTES
1 For lamp ordering information, refer to options and accessories tab.
2 White stem mounted fixtures have white stems and adaptors. All other stem mounted fixtures have black stem and adaptors. For alternate stem/adaptor color add AWH (white) or ABL (black) after finish color. Example: DMB AWH
3 Additional architectural colors and custom color matches available; please see brochure 794.3.

Downlighting and Track

Sheet#: **185-LINE-SFTS**   LINE-210

LTC Soft Square

LAMP PERFORMANCE DATA

The lighting performance data charts shown provide lighting levels (footcandles), beam pattern (in feet), rated lamp life.

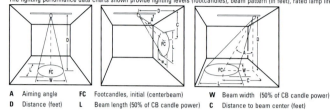

A Aiming angle	**FC** Footcandles, initial (centerbeam)	**W** Beam width (50% of CB candle power)
D Distance (feet)	**L** Beam length (50% of CB candle power)	**C** Distance to beam center (feet)

Lamp	Rated Life	Beam Spread	0° Aiming Angle					30° Aiming Angle					45° Aiming Angle					60° Aiming Angle				
			D	FC	W	L	C	D	FC	W	L	C	D	FC	W	L	C	D	FC	W	L	C
60PAR16/HAL/NSP	2000	10°	4	313	0.7	0.7	N/A	4	203	0.8	0.9	2.3	3	196	0.7	1.1	3.0	2	156	0.7	1.1	3.5
			6	139	1.1	1.1	N/A	6	90	1.2	1.4	3.5	4	110	1.0	1.4	4.0	3	69	1.1	2.2	5.2
			8	78	1.4	1.4	N/A	8	51	1.6	1.9	4.6	5	71	1.2	1.8	5.0	4	39	1.4	2.9	6.9
60PAR16/HAL/NFL	2000	30°	2	325	1.1	1.1	N/A	2	211	1.2	1.5	1.2	2	115	1.5	2.3	2.0	2	41	2.1	5.5	3.5
			4	81	2.1	2.1	N/A	3	94	1.9	2.2	1.7	3	51	2.3	3.5	3.0	3	18	3.2	8.2	5.2
			6	36	3.2	3.2	N/A	4	53	2.5	2.9	2.3	4	29	3.0	4.6	4.0	4	10	4.3	10.9	6.9
50PAR20/H/SP10	2500	10°	4	375	0.7	0.7	N/A	4	244	0.8	0.9	2.3	3	236	0.7	1.1	3.0	2	188	0.7	1.4	3.5
			6	167	1.1	1.1	N/A	5	156	1.0	1.2	2.9	4	133	1.0	1.4	4.0	3	83	1.1	2.2	5.2
			8	94	1.4	1.4	N/A	6	108	1.2	1.4	3.5	5	85	1.2	1.8	5.0	4	47	1.4	2.9	6.9
50PAR20/H/FL25	2500	25°	3	167	1.3	1.3	N/A	2	244	1.0	1.2	1.2	2	133	1.3	1.9	2.0	2	47	1.8	4.2	3.5
			4	94	1.8	1.8	N/A	3	108	1.5	1.8	1.7	3	59	1.9	2.8	3.0	3	21	2.7	6.2	5.2
			5	60	2.2	2.2	N/A	4	61	2.1	2.4	2.3	4	33	2.5	3.7	4.0	4	12	3.6	8.3	6.9
75PAR30/CAP/NSP	2500	9°	8	219	1.3	1.3	N/A	8	142	1.5	1.7	4.6	6	138	1.3	1.9	6.0	4	109	1.3	2.6	6.9
			10	140	1.6	1.6	N/A	10	91	1.8	2.1	5.8	8	77	1.8	2.5	8.0	6	49	1.9	3.9	10.4
			12	97	1.9	1.9	N/A	12	63	2.2	2.5	6.9	10	50	2.2	3.2	10.0	8	27	2.5	5.1	13.9
75PAR30/CAP/NFL	2500	30°	4	200	2.1	2.1	N/A	4	130	2.5	2.9	2.3	2	283	1.5	2.3	2.0	2	100	2.1	5.5	3.5
			6	89	3.2	3.2	N/A	6	58	3.7	4.4	3.5	4	71	3.0	4.6	4.0	3	44	3.2	8.2	5.2
			8	50	4.3	4.3	N/A	8	32	5.0	5.9	4.6	6	31	4.6	6.9	6.0	4	25	4.3	10.9	6.9
75PAR30/CAP/FL	2500	40°	4	125	2.9	2.9	N/A	3	144	2.5	3.1	1.7	3	79	3.1	5.0	3.0	2	63	2.9	9.7	3.5
			6	56	4.4	4.4	N/A	4	81	3.4	4.1	2.3	4	44	4.1	6.7	4.0	3	28	4.4	14.5	5.2
			8	31	5.8	5.8	N/A	5	52	4.2	5.1	2.9	5	28	5.2	8.4	5.0	4	16	5.8	19.3	6.9

All data was calculated from each lamp manufacturer's published data and is subject to normal lamp variations. Maximum footcandle is usually at the aiming point, but not always on wider spread lamps. Lamp data supplied by manufacturers is approximate and individual lamp performance may vary.

LITHONIA LIGHTING®

An *Acuity*Brands Company

Sheet#: 185-LINE-SFTS   ©1999 Acuity Lighting Group, Inc. 10/99   185-LINE-SFTS.p65

Lithonia Lighting
Acuity Lighting Group, Inc.
Recessed Downlighting
One Lithonia Way, Conyers, GA 30012
Phone: 800-315-4935 Fax: 770-860-3106
In Canada: 1100 50th Ave., Lachine, Quebec H8T 2V3
www.lithonia.com

Lighting Manufacturers, Distributors, and Suppliers

Control And Equipment Manufacturers

Advance Transformer
http://www.advancetransformer.com

BRK Electronics
http://www.brkelectronics.com

Bryant Electric
http://www.bryant-electric.com

Dexin International
http://www.dexin.com

Douglas Lighting Controls
http://www.douglaslightingcontrol.com

Fulham Company
http://www.fulham.com

Honeywell
http://www.honeywell.com

Intelligent Lighting Controls
http://www.ilc-usa.com

Labsphere
http://www.labsphere.com

Leviton Manufacturing
http://www.leviton.com

Litecontrol
http://www.litecontrol.com

Litetouch
http://www.litetouch.com

MagneTek
http://www.magnetek.com

Novitas
http://www.novitas.com

Pace Technologies
http://www.pacetech.com

Pass & Seymour Legrand
http://www.passandseymour.com

RAB Electric Manufacturing
http://www.rabweb.com

Sensor Switch
http://www.sensorswitch.com

TORK
http://www.tork.com

The Watt Stopper
http://www.wattstopper.com

Lamp Manufacturers

Broada
http://www.broada.com

Bulbtronics
http://www.bulbtronics.com

Duralamp USA
http://www.duralamp.com

Eiko
http://www.eiko-ltd.com

GE Lighting
http://www.gelighting.com

Halco Lighting Corporation
http://www.halcolighting.com

Ledtronics
http://www.ledtronics.com

Lights of America
http://www.lightsofamerica.com

Lumenyte International Corporation
http://www.lumenyte.com

Osram Sylvania
http://www.sylvania.com

Panasonic Lighting
http://www.panasonic.com

Philips Lighting
http://www.lighting.philips.com

Satco Products
http://www.satco.com

Schott-Fostec, LLC
http://www.schott-fostec.com

Westinghouse Light Bulbs
http://www.westinghouselightbulbs.com

Luminaires

AAMSCO Manufacturing
http://www.aamsco.com

Access Lighting
http://www.accesslighting.com

ALKCO
http://www.alkco.com

The American Glass Light Company
http://www.americanglasslight.com

American Lighting
http://www.americanlighting.net

Arroyo Craftsman Lighting
http://www.arroyo-craftsman.com

Artemide
http://www.artemide.com

ATYS
http://www.atys-inc.com

Banci
http://www.banci.it

Bayworld Industries
http://www.bayworld.com

Bega/US
http://www.bega.com

Belfer Lighting Group
http://www.belfer.com

Beta-Calco
http://www.betacalco.com

Beth Weissman
http://www.bweissmanart.com

B-K Lighting
http://www.bklighting.com

Boyd Lighting Company
http://www.boydlighting.com

Bruck Lighting Systems
http://www.brucklighting.com

Capri
http://www.caprilighting.com

Casella
http://www.casellalighting.com/

Chimera
http://www.chimeralighting.com

City Lights Antique Lighting
http://www.citylights.nu

Citybarn Antiques
http://www.citybarnantiques.com

Color Kinetics
http://www.colorkinetics.com

Columbia Lighting
http://www.columbia-ltg.com

Cooper Lighting
http://www.cooperlighting.com

Dabmar
http://www.dabmar.com

Design Centro Italia
http://www.italydesign.com

Designplan Lighting
http://www.designplan.com

Dynalite Selection
http://www.dynalite.com

Ela Company
http://www.ela-lighting.com

Elco Lighting
http://www.elcolighting.com

Elite Lighting
http://www.elitelighting.com

Engineered Lighting Products
http://www.elplighting.com

Eye Lighting International
http://www.eyelighting.com

Fiberstars
http://www.fiberstars.com

Fibre Light U.S.
http://www.fibrelightus.com

Flos
http://www.flos.net

Fontana Arte
http://www.louielighting.com

Halo
http://www.cooperlighting.com

Hampstead Lighting
http://www.hampsteadlighting.com

Hans Duus Blacksmith, Inc
http://www.inlightenstudios.com

HEWilliams
http://www.hew.com

Historical Arts & Casting
http://www.historicalarts.com

House of Troy
http://www.houseoftroylighting.com

Hubbardton Forge & Wood
http://www.hubbardtonforge.net

Ivalo Lighting
http://www.ivalolighting.com

Johnson Art Studio
http://www.johnsonartstudio.com

Juno Lighting
http://www.junolighting.com

Justice Design Group
http://www.jdg.com

Kartell
http://www.kartell.com

Kim Lighting
http://www.kimlighting.com

Koch and Lowy
http://www.kochlowy.com

LaMar Lighting
http://www.lamarlighting.com

Lampa
http://www.lampa.com

Latigo Lights
http://www.latigolights.com

LBL Lighting
http://www.lbllighting.com

LED Effects
http://www.ledeffects.com

Lee's Studio
http://www.leesstudio.com

Leucos Lighting
http://www.leucos.com

Lighting by Gregory
http://www.lightingbygregory.com

Lightolier
http://www.lightolier.com

Lightron
http://www.lsilightron.com

Lightway Industries
http://www.lightwayind.com

Lightworks
http://www.lightworks.com

Limn Company
http://www.limn.com

Lite Energy/Horizon
http://www.liteenergy.com

Lithonia Lighting
http://www.lithonia.com/

Los Angeles Lighting
http://www.lalighting.com

Luceplan
http://www.luceplan.com

Lucifer Lighting
http://www.luciferlighting.com

Lumileds
http://www.lumileds.com

Luminaire
http://www.luminaire.com

Lumux Lighting
http://www.lumux.net

Lutron Electronics
http://www.lutron.com

Luxam
http://www.lumax.com

Luxo Corporation
http://www.luxous.com

Lyn Hovey Studio
http://www.lynhoveystudio.com

Mark Lighting
http://www.marklighting.com

Maxlite
http://www.maxlite.com

MP Lighting
http://www.mplighting.com

Murano Due
http://www.muranodue.com

Museum of Modern Art
http://www.moma.org

National Specialty Lighting
http://www.nsl-ltg.com

Natural Lighting
http://www.daylighting.com

Nessen Lamps
http://www.nessenlighting.com

Newstamp Lighting
http://www.newstamplighting.com

Nora Lighting
http://www.noralighting.com

Norbert Belfer Lighting
http://www.belfer.com

Norlux Corporation
http://www.norluxcorp.com

O'Luce
http://www.oluce.com

Pathway the Lighting Source
http://www.pathwaylighting.com

Peerless Lighting
http://www.peerless-lighting.com

Poulsen
http://www.louispoulsen.com

Prescolite
http://www.prescolite.com

Prisma Lighting
http://www.prismalighting.com

Prisma NA
http://www.prisma-na.com

Progress Lighting
http://www.progresslightingoutlet.com

Promolux Lighting International
http://www.promolux.com

RSA Lighting
http://www.rsalighting.com

SLD lighting
http://www.sldlighting.com

SNS Technology, LLC
http://www.snstechnologyllc.com

Spectrum Lighting
http://www.spectrumlighting.com

SPJ Lighting
http://www.spjlighting.com

Steel Partners Inc.
http://www.steelpartnersinc.com

Sternberg Vintage Lighting
http://www.sternberglighting.com

Sunled Corporation
http://www.sunled.com

Sunrise Lighting
http://www.sunriselighting.com

Tech Lighting
http://www.techlighting.com

Times Square Lighting
http://www.tslight.com

Translite Sonoma
http://www.translite.com

Turn of the Century Lighting
http://www.turnofthecenturylighting.com

Vision 3 Lighting
http://www.vision3lighting.com

WAC Lighting
http://www.waclighting.com

Xenon Light
http://www.xenonlight.com

Yankee Craftsman
http://www.yankeecraftsman.com

Zaneen
http://www.zaneen.com

Zelco
http://www.zelco.com

Recycling Corporations

Advanced Environmental Recycling Corporation
http://www.aerc-mti.com

Bethlehem Apparatus Company
http://www.bethlehemapparatus.com

Chemical Waste Management
http://www.stanford.edu/dept/EHS/prod/enviro/waste/

DYNEX Industries
http://www.dynex.com

Earth Protection Service
http://www.earthpro.com

Full Circle Recyclers
http://www.fcrecyclers.com

Lamp Recyclers of Louisiana
http://www.i-55.com/lamprecyler/

Lighting Resources
http://www.lightingresourcesinc.com

Mercury Recovery Services
http://www.dtsc.ca.gov/HazardousWaste/Mercury_Recovery/

U.S. Ecology
http://www.americanecology.com

USA Lights
http://www.usalight.com

Zumtobel Staff
http://www.zumtobelstaff.com

Professional Organizations, Government Agencies, and Trade Associations

ADA Guide
http://www.access-board.gov/adaag/html/adaag.htm

Adaptive Environments
http://www.adaptiveenvironments.org/about/index.php

American Council for an Energy-Efficient Economy
http://www.aceee.org

American Hospital Association
http://www.hospitalconnect.com/DesktopServlet

American Hotel and Motel Association
http://www.ahma.com/

American Institute of Graphic Designers
http://www.aiga.org

American Lighting Association
http://www.americanlightingassoc.com

American National Standards Institute
http://www.ansi.org

American Optometric Association
http://www.aoanet.org

American Institute of Architects
http://www.aia.org

American Society of Civil Engineers
http://www.asce.org

American Society of Furniture Designers
http://www.asfd.com

American Society of Heating, Refrigeration and Air Conditioning
http://www.ashrae.org/

American Society of Interior Designers
http://www.asid.org

American Society of Landscape Architects
http://asla.org

American Solar Energy Society
http://www.ases.org

Architectural Lighting
http://www.archlighting.com

Architectural Record
http://www.architecturalrecord.com

ARCOM Master Systems
http://www.arcomnet.com

Arthritis Foundation
http://www.arthritis.org/resources/HomeLife/design.asp

Association for Energy Engineers
http://www.aee.org

Association of Energy Service Professionals
http://www.aesp.org

Association of General Contractors of America
http://www.agc.org

Association of Registered Interior Designers of Ontario
http://www.arido.on.ca

British Contract Furnishing Association
http://www.bcfa.org.uk

Building Official Code Administration
http://www.bocai.org

Building Operating Management
http://www.tradespress.com

Building Owners & Managers Association
http://www.boma.org

Buildings Magazine
http://www.buildings.com

Business and Institutional Furniture Manufacturers Association
http://www.bifma.com

Center for Health Design
http://www.healthdesign.org

Certified Ballast Manufacturers
http://www.cerbal.org

Chartered Institution of Building Services Engineers
http://www.cibse.org

Color Association of the United States
http://www.colorassociation.com/splash.html

Color Marketing Group
http://www.colormarketing.org

Construction Specifications Institute
http://www.csinet.org

Construction Symbols and Terminology
http://www.constructionworknews.com

Consulting-Specifying Engineer Magazine
http://www.csemag.com

Contract Lighting Magazine
http://www.contractlighting.net

Contract Magazine
http://www.contractmagazine.com

Cost Estimating Resources
http://www.jsc.nasa.gov/bu2/resources.html

EC & M Publications
http://www.ecmweb.com

Electric Power Research Institute (EPRI) Lighting Office
http://www.epri.com

Electrical News
http://www.electricalnews.com

Energy Efficient Building Association
http://www.eeba.org

Energy and Environmental Building Association
http://www.eeba.org/default.htm

Energy User News
http://www.energyusernews.com

Eyetronics
http://www.eyetronics.com

Fabric Educational Resources
http://www.fabriclink.com

Florida Solar Energy Center
http://www.fsec.ucf.edu

Foundation for Interior Design Education Research
http://www.fider.org

Foundations for Design Integrity
http://www.ffdi.org

Frame Magazine
http://www.framemag.com

Green Building Guide
http://www.energybuilder.com/greenbld.htm

Green Lights Program
http://www.epa.gov/greenlights.html

Home Furnishings International Association
http://www.hfia.com

Human Factors Science
http://www.ergogero.com/pages/HFLinks.html

Human Systems Information Analysis Center
http://iac.dtic.mil/hsiac/

Illuminating Engineers Society of North America
http://iesna.org

Industrial Designers Society of America
http://www.idsa.org

Institute of Store Planners
http://www.ispo.org/

Interior Design Society
http://www.interiordesignsociety.org

Interior Designers of Canada
http://www.interiordesignerscanada.org

International Association of Lighting Designers
http://iald.org/index.htm

International Code Council
http://www.intlcode.org

International Conference of Building Officials
http://www.icbo.org

International Colour Authority
http://www.internationalcolourauthority.com

International Commission on Illumination
http://www.cie-usnc.org

International Council of Graphic Designers
http://www.icograda.org/web/home/index.html

International Council of Qualifications for Lighting Professions
http://ncqlp.org

International Dark Sky Society
http://www.darksky.org

International Facility Management Association
http://www.ifma.org

International Furnishings and Design Association
http://www.ifda.com

International Interior Design Association
http://www.iida.org

Intertek Testing Services
http://www.etlsemko.com

Lambda Research Corporation
http://www.lambdares.com

LD+A Magazine
http://www.iesna.org

Light Forum
http://lightforum.com

Lighting (Resources)
http://www.lighting.com

Lighting Analysts
http://www.lightinganalysts.com

Lighting Dimensions Magazine
http://www.lightingdimensions.com

Lighting Research Center–Rensselaer Polytechnic Institute
http://www.lrc.rpi.edu

Lightsearch
http://www.lightsearch.com

Maintenance Solutions
http://www.facilitiesnet.com

Metropolis Magazine
http://www.metropolismag.com

Mondo*Arc Magazine
http://www.mondiale.co.uk/

National Association of Homebuilders Research Center
http://www.nahbrc.org

National Association of Women in Construction
http://www.nawic.org/

National Council for Interior Design Qualifications
http://www.ncidq.org

National Council on the Qualification of Lighting Professionals
http://ncqlp.org

National Fire Protection Association
http://www.nfpa.org/Home/index.asp

National Institute of Occupational Safety and Health
http://www.cdc.gov/niosh/homepage.html

National Kitchen & Bath Association
http://www.nkba.org

National Lighting Bureau
http://www.nlb.org

National Research Council
http://www.nationalacademies.org/nrc

National Technical Information Service
http://www.ntis.gov

National Trust for Historic Preservation
http://www.nationaltrust.org

Neocon Trade Shows
http://www.merchandisemart.com

NIST Child Anthropometric Data
http://www.itl.nist.gov/iaui/ovrt/projects/anthrokids/ncontent.htm

Occupational Safety & Health Administration
http://www.osha.gov

Pacific Energy Center
http://www.pge.com

PeopleSize 2000
http://www.openerg.com/psz.htm

Quebec Furniture Manufacturers Association
http://www.qfma.com

Residential Lighting
http://www.vancepublishing.com

Retail Construction Magazine
http://www.retailconstructionmag.com

Safework
http://www.safework.com

SearchSpec.com
http://www.SearchSpec.com

Southern Building Code Congress International
http://www.sbcci.org

Underwriter's Laboratories
http://www.ul.com

U.S. Census Bureau
http://www.census.gov/mcd

Universal and Barrier-Free Design
http://www.dezignare.com

Windows and Daylighting Group
http://windows.llbl.gov

INDEX

CREDITS

Chapter 6

Figure 6.3 – Photograph © Corbis/Image Source

Figure 6.11a – Photograph © Getty Images/Andersen Ross

Figure 6.11b – Photograph © Getty Images/Ira Montgomery

Chapter 7

Figure 7.2 – Adapted from Prudential Lighting

Figure 7.4 – Reprinted from the *IESNA Lighting Handbook* (9th ed) with permission from the Illuminating Engineering Society of North America.

Figure 7.5 – Adapted from Philips Lighting.

Figure 7.9 – Photograph © Reto Guntli/zapaimages

Chapter 8

Figure 8.4a – Photograph © Leslie Garland Picture Library/Alamy

Figure 8.4b – Photograph © Corbis/Jose Luis Pelaez

Figure 8.4c – Photograph © Leslie Garland Picture Library/Alamy

Chapter 9

Figure 9.1 – Photograph © Corbis/David Reed

Figure 9.2 – Photograph © Corbis/Thomas A. Heinz

Figure 9.4, 9.5 a-e, and 9.6 – Courtesy, Acuity Brands Lighting

Figure 9.7 – Courtesy, WAC Lighting © 2004

Chapter 10

Figure 10.3 – Photograph © Corbis/John Madere

Chapter 11

Figure 11.3 – Photograph © Massimo Listri/Corbis

Figure 11.6 – Photograph © Réunion des Musées Nationaux/Art Resource, NY

Figure 11.8 – Photograph © Corbis/Francis G. Mayer

Figure 11.12 – Photograph © Réunion des Musées Nationaux/Art Resource, NY

Figure 11.20 – Fabrication and installation by Galen Winchip. Photo courtesy, author's collection.

Chapter 12

Figure 12.1 – Courtesy, Energy Information Administration (EIA) of the U.S. Department of Energy, Office of Integrated Analysis and Forecasting.

Figure 12.2 – Adapted from: Energy Information Administration (EIA), *International Energy Annual 2001*, DOE/EIA-0219(2001) (Washington, DC, February 2003), web site www.eia.doe.gov/iea/.
Projections: EIA, System for the Analysis of Global Energy Markets (2004).

Figure 12.3 – Adapted from: Energy Information Administration (EIA), *International Energy Annual 1999*, DOE/EIA-0219(99) (Washington, DC, February 2001). Projections: EIA, World Energy Projection System (2002).

Figure 12.4 – Information reprinted from the *IESNA Lighting Handbook* (9th ed) with permission from the Illuminating Engineering Society of North America.

Figure 12.5 – Adapted from: History: Energy Information Administration (EIA), Office of Energy Markets and End Use, International Statistics Database and *International Energy Annual 1999*,

DOE/EIA-0219(99) (Washington, DC, February 2001). Projections: EIA, World Energy Projection System (2002).

Figure 12.6 – Reproduction from www.epa.gov/dfe.

Figure 12.8 – Courtesy, International Dark Sky Association.

Chapter 13

Figures 13.1 and 13.2 – Reprinted with permission of the USHMM and Edward Owen. Published source: Winberg, Jeshajahu and Elieli, Rina. The Holocaust Museum in Washington. Rizzoli, 1995, p. 115.

Figure 13.3 – Photograph © Beateworks Inc./Alamy/Daniel Linnet

Figure 13.4 – Photograph © Red Cover/Ken Hayden

Figure 13.5 – Courtesy, Anglepoise Ltd., lamp designed by George Carwardine.

Chapter 14

Figure 14.1 – Adapted from: research from Dresden University of Technology (Rust & Munoz, 2003).

Figure 14.2 – Photograph © Jason Turner/Associated Press

Figure 14.5 – Photograph © Alamy/Oote Boe

Figure 14.6 – Courtesy, Color Kinetics Incorporated.

Chapter 15

Figure 15.1 – Reprinted with permission of Richard Prince and Gladstone Gallery, New York. Installation View: Gladstone Gallery, April - June 2005. Photographer: David Regen. All rights reserved.

Figures 15.7a-d – Photographs © Lightolier

Chapter 16

Figure 16.1 – Photograph © Erich Lessing/Art Resource, NY

Figure 16.2 – Reprinted with permission of The Charles Hosmer Morse Museum of American Art, Winter Park, FL, © The Charles Hosmer Morse Foundation, Inc.

Figure 16.4 – Photograph © The Museum of Modern Art/Licensed by SCALA/Art Resource, NY

Figure 16.5 – Photograph © Corbis/Diego Lezama Orezzoli. Designer: Oscar Niemeyer

Figure 16.7 – Photograph © National Gallery of Australia and the Artists Rights Society

Figure 16.8 – Photograph © National Gallery of Australia

Figure 16.9 – Reprinted with permission of Dale Chihuly and James Carpenter. All rights reserved.

Figure 16.10 – Reprinted with permission of Critz Campbell

Figure 16.11 – Reprinted with permission of © Tatsuo Miyajima and SCAI, Tokyo. Photographer: Michael Tropea

Figure 16.12 – Courtesy, Cork Marcheschi

Figure 16.13 – Courtesy, Helen Nugent for Haelo Design

Figure 16.14 – Reprinted with permission of the Solomon R. Guggenheim Foundation. Photograph by David Heald © The Solomon R. Guggenheim Foundation, New York.

Figure 16.15 – Courtesy, Robert Irwin, installation at Dia Center for the Arts, New York City, 1998. Photographer: Thibault Jeanson. Courtesy, Dia Center for the Arts.

Figure 16.16 – Reprinted with permission of Phototèque des musèes de la ville de Paris (ou PMVP)/Cliché: Ladet/Degraces. All rights reserved.

Figure 16.17 – Reprinted with permission of Dale Chihuly. Photographer: Terry Rishel

Figure 16.18 – Thomas Wifred, "Untitled", Opus 161, 1965-1966. From the collection of Carol and Eugene Epstein. Image courtesy of the Clavilux Restoration Project (www.wilfred-lumia.org).

Figure 16.19 – Courtesy, Paul Friedlander, paul@paulfriedlander.com

Figure 16.20 – Courtesy, Brad Koerner

Figure 16.21 – Reprinted with permission of the Cincinnati Art Museum/Michael J. Campbell.

Figure 16.23 – Courtesy, Margaret Benyon

Chapter 17

Figure 17.1 – Photograph © Corbis/ Jose Fuste Raga

Figure 17.2 – Photograph © Corbis/Lawrence Manning

Figure 17.5 – Reprinted with permission of Osamu Murai.

Figure 17.6 – Photograph © Corbis/Karen Tweedy-Hlmes

Figure 17.7 – Photograph © Richard Bryant/arcaid.co.uk

Figure 17.9 – Photograph © Corbis/G.E. Kidder Smith

Figure 17.10a – Photograph © Corbis/Archivo Iconografico, S.A./CORBIS

Figure 17.10b – Photograph © Jacques Mussot

Figure 17.11 – Photograph © Corbis/John Heseltine

Figure 17.12 – Photograph © Corbis/Massimo Listri

Figure 17.13 – Photograph © Corbis/Roger Wood

Figure 17.14 – Photograph © Corbis/Mimmo Jodice

Figure 17.16 – Photograph © Corbis/ Arthur Thévenart

Figure 17.19 – Photograph © Corbis/Francis G. Mayer

Figure 17.20 – Courtesy, Edifice/Corbis

Figure 17.21 – Photograph © Tim Griffith/Esto

Figure 17.22 – Courtesy, Silvestrin Archive

Figure 17.23a – Photograph © Corbis/Hans George Roth

Figure 17.23b – Photograph © Corbis/Adam Woolfitt

Figure 17.24 – Photograph © Corbis/Adam Woolfitt

Figure 17.25 – Photograph © 2005 Barragan Foundation, Switzerland/ProLitteris, Zürich, Switzerland.

Figure 17.26 – Photograph © Alene Stickles/www.greatbuildings.com

Figure 17.27 – Photograph © Corbis/Dennis Marsico

Figure 17.28 – Photograph © Corbis/Farrell Grehan

Figure 17.29 – Photograph © Roberto Schezen/Esto. All rights reserved.

Figure 17.30 – Photograph © Corbis/Peter Aprahamian

Figure 17.31 – Photograph © Biliothèque nationale de France. All rights reserved.

Figure 17.32 – Photograph © Corbis/Warren and Wetmore

Figure 17.33a – Photograph © Corbis/Richard Cummins

Figure 17.33b – Photograph © Corbis/Jim Zuckerman

Figure 17.34 – Photograph © Thomas Dix/Esto. All Rights Reserved.

Figure 16.35 – Photograph © Wolfgang Hoyt/Esto. All rights reserved.

Chapter 18

Figure 18.1 – Photograph © Erich Lessing/Art Resource, NY

Figure 18.2 – Photograph © Photofest. *The Spiritualist* is an Eagle Lion Production.

Figure 18.3 – Reprinted with permission of the North Carolina Museum of Art.

Figure 18.4 – Photograph © Scala/Art Resource, NY

Figure 18.5a – Photograph © The Corcoran Gallery of Art/Corbis; creator: Charles Bird King

Figure 18.5b – Reprinted with permission of Staatliche Kunstsammllungen Dresden Gemaldegalerie Alte Meister/Klut.

Figure 18.6 – Photograph © Magnum/Lu-Nan

Figure 18.7 – Photographs © Photofest. *T-Men* is an Eagle Lion Production

Figure 18.8a – Photograph © National Gallery Collection by kind permission of the Trustees of the National Gallery, London/Corbis

Figure 18.8b – Photograph © Francis G. Mayer/Corbis

Figure 18.9a – Reprinted with permission of the National Gallery of Art.

Figure 18.9b – Photograph © Bildarchiv Preussischer Kulturbesitz / Art Resource, NY

Figure 18.10a – Photograph © Scala/Art Resource, NY

Figure 18.10b – Reprinted with permission of Statens Konstmuseer, Stockholm.

Figure 18.11a – Reprinted with permission of Maastricht Noortman.

Figure 18.11b – Photograph © The Art Institute of Chicago

Figure 18.12 – Photograph © The Kobal Collection/RKO

Figure 18.13 – Photograph © Raymond Depardon/Magnum Photos

Figure 18.14 – Photograph © Scala / Art Resource, NY

Figure 18.15 – Photgraph © Fine Art Photographic Library, London/Art Resource, NY

Figure 18.16 – Photograph © Frank & Helen Schreider/National Geographic Image Collection

Figure 18.17 – Photograph © Réunion des Musées Nationaux /Art Resource, NY

Figure 18.18 – Reprinted with permission of the Museo Thyssen-Bornemisza. Copyright Carmen Thyssen-Bornemisza.

Figure 18.19 – Photograph © Alison Wright/Corbis

Figure 18.20 – Photograph © The Kobal Collection/MGM/Clarence Sinclair Bull

Figure 18.21 – Photograph © The Kobal Collection

Figure 18.22 – Photograph © Erich Lessing/Art Resource, NY

Figure 18.23 – Photograph © Photofest

Figure 18.24a – Photograph © Ferdinando Scianna/Magnum Photos

Figure 18.24b – Photograph © Sergio Larrain/Magnum Photos

Chapter 20

Figure 20.1 – Photograph © Arcaid/Alamy

Figure 20.2 – Photograph © Craig Lee/San Francisco Chronicle/Corbis

Figure 20.3 – Photograph © Beateworks Inc./Alamy

Figure 20.5 – Photograph © JG Photography/Alamy

Figure 20.6 – Photograph © Corbis

Figure 20.7 – Photograph © Royalty-Free/Corbis

Figure 20.8 – Photograph © Plainpicture/Alamy

Figure 20.9 – Photograph © Beateworks/Getty Images

Figure 20.11 – Photograph © Arcaid/Alamy

Figure 20.12 – Photograph © Stone/Getty Images

Figure 20.13 – Photograph © Chuck Pefley/Alamy

Chapter 22

Figure 22.10 – The Emmanuel Celler Courthouse located in Brooklyn, New York, was designed by C. Brooke Carter and Sasaluk Seangsukh. Courtesy, Domingo Gonzalez Associates.

Chapter 23

Figure 23.2 – 23.5 – Information adapted from: *IESNA Lighting Handbook (9th ed)* with permission from the Illuminating Engineering Society of North America.